Actors' & Performers'

YEARBOOK

2026

Actors' & Performers' YEARBOOK 2026

Foreword by Aileen Gonsalves

methuen | drama
LONDON · NEW YORK · OXFORD · NEW DELHI · SYDNEY

METHUEN DRAMA
Bloomsbury Publishing Plc, 50 Bedford Square, London, WC1B 3DP, UK
Bloomsbury Publishing Inc, 1359 Broadway, New York, NY 10018, USA
Bloomsbury Publishing Ireland, 29 Earlsfort Terrace, Dublin 2, D02 AY28, Ireland

BLOOMSBURY, METHUEN DRAMA and the Methuen Drama logo are trademarks of Bloomsbury Publishing Plc

Twenty-second edition published in Great Britain 2026

Copyright © Bloomsbury Publishing Plc, 2026

Foreword copyright © Aileen Gonsalves, 2026

All rights reserved. No part of this publication may be: i) reproduced or transmitted in any form, electronic or mechanical, including photocopying, recording or by means of any information storage or retrieval system without prior permission in writing from the publishers; or ii) used or reproduced in any way for the training, development or operation of artificial intelligence (AI) technologies, including generative AI technologies. The rights holders expressly reserve this publication from the text and data mining exception as per Article 4(3) of the Digital Single Market Directive (EU) 2019/790.

Bloomsbury Publishing Plc does not have any control over, or responsibility for, any third-party websites referred to or in this book. All internet addresses given in this book were correct at the time of going to press. The author and publisher regret any inconvenience caused if addresses have changed or sites have ceased to exist, but can accept no responsibility for any such changes.

A catalogue record for this book is available from the British Library.

A catalog record for this book is available from the Library of Congress.

ISBN: PB: 978-1-3505-6484-8
ePDF: 978-1-3505-6485-5
ePub: 978-1-3505-6486-2

Printed and bound in Great Britain

For product safety related questions contact productsafety@bloomsbury.com.

To find out more about our authors and books visit www.bloomsbury.com and sign up for our newsletters.

Publisher's note

Welcome to the 2026 edition of the *Actors' and Performers' Yearbook*! This *Yearbook* originally began life as the *Actors' Yearbook* back in 2004 under the stewardship of the late, great Simon Dunmore, who I had the immense privilege of working with until his death in 2014. It was originally published by A&C Black, who were bought by Bloomsbury in 2002.

Inspired by A&C Black's *Writers' & Artists' Yearbook*, the *Actors' Yearbook's* original intention, as set out by Simon Dunmore in his 2004 introduction, was to "make some more detailed sense of the ever-diversifying world of professional acting, from training to the wide range of companies offering work in all media, via the brokers (agents and casting directors) of much of that work".

Over the 21 years, the aim of the *Yearbook* hasn't changed very much at all, while the landscape that actors are working in has, of course, changed immensely. The *Yearbook* has, therefore, broadened its scope to include 'performers'as well as just actors; to offer a survey of the wide range of work available to actors today, with many working across multiple mediums in their career; and to reflect the many ways in which actors can now navigate this world and give their work exposure.

In more recent years, we have invited an industry figure to introduce each edition and interview some of their key collaborators and contacts about their experience in the industry and what advice they would give others on that journey. You'll find all of those interviews in this *Yearbook* you have today.

Lastly, as the industry and society more widely finally move to prioritize diversity, equity and inclusion, we have been keen to ensure our *Yearbook* reflects – and even helps drive – that change, including developing our section on resources for Disabled actors and inviting contributors to the *Yearbook* that represent a diversity of perspectives, backgrounds and heritages.

We hope that you continue to enjoy the *Yearbook* and its future editions. We take on board the comments and thoughts from our readers to enhance each new edition.

Anna Brewer
Senior Publisher

Acknowledgements

With thanks to Aileen Gonsalves for agreeing to write the foreword to this year's edition and for carrying out the four new interviews in it; to James Grieve for his suggestions on the listings and editorial input on the section introductions; to contributors past and present who together offer so much helpful advice to anyone navigating the industry; to Richard Gresham for securing the advertising; and to Alysoun Owen, Eden Phillips Harrington and their team, especially Alice Rose and Zara Relphman, for wrestling all the content into this book.

Contents

Publisher's note	v
Acknowledgments	vi
Foreword – Aileen Gonsalves	xi
Praise for the *Yearbook*	xiv

Training

Introduction	1
Training for the under-18s	3
Arts Emergency – Julie Hesmondhalgh	6
Interview: David Mumeni; *Levelling the playing field: actors from working- and benefit-class backgrounds*	9
Drama schools	12
Taking charge of your creative journey – Kalungi Ssebandeke	23
What are drama schools looking for? – Geoffrey Colman	27
Reframing the future of actor training – Pamela Jikiemi	31
The Mentor & The Void – Mark Weinman	37
Interview: Paul Harvard; *Opening doors: inclusivity, innovation and the collective acting studio*	41
It's warm up north – Adelle Hulsmeier	45
Short-term and part-time courses	49
Private tutors and coaches	57
An actor's journey into directing (and back again) – Harry Burton	62

Agents and casting directors

Introduction	69
Agents	70
Interview: Michael Wiggs; *Nurturing talent: an agent's frame of mind*	99
CPMA: the Co-operative Personal Management Association	103
Voice-over agents	105
Presenters' agents	108
Casting directors	110
Interview: Gemma McAvoy; *Self-tapes: an agent's perspective*	124
Showcases – Richard Evans CDG	127
Interview: Gemma Hancock & John Cannon; *Auditioning for stage and television*	131
Casting for musical theatre – David Grindrod	134
A strategy for acting success – Ken Rea	136
Woman in a brown skirt – Sophie Stanton	140

Theatre

Introduction	143
Interview: Lee Hall; *Theatre as community: overcoming barriers for participation*	144
Interview: Pooja Ghai; *Rooted in story: a journey from actor to changemaker*	148
Interview: Cherrelle Skeete; *Active listening in a community of nomads*	151
Interview: Naomi Ackie; *An actor's advice: navigating your way through the industry*	154
Interview: Paterson Joseph; *Success and not getting sacked*	157
Producing theatres	160
Interview: Tom Ross-Williams; *Inclusivity and allyship for the future of the industry*	178
Effective audition speeches – Simon Dunmore	181
Understudying – Andrew Piper	190
Independent managements/theatre producers	194
Interview: Hazel Holder; *Voicing kindness*	200

Ignition, inspiration and the imposter
  – Scott Graham ... 203
Middle- and smaller-scale companies ... 207
Starting your own theatre company
  – Pilar Ortí ... 233
Interview: Brian Hook & Kate McStraw; *Jack of all trades – and then some* ... 237
Finding funding for projects
  – Sinead Mac Manus ... 240
Actors and writers: an imperfect creative marriage – Lucian Msamati ... 244
Interview: Tuyèn Đỗ; *Acting, writing and making work* ... 248
Get seen as an actor/comedy writer/performer – Chris Head ... 251
Interview: Paapa Essiedu; *An actor's values: establishing principles for success* ... 254
Interview: Geoff Whiting; *Routes to stand-up comedy* ... 258
Pantomime ... 261
English-language European theatre companies ... 267
Fringe theatres ... 269
Interview: Ned Bennett; *The direction of collaboration* ... 279
Edinburgh or bust: is it worth it?
  – Shane Dempsey ... 282
Open Book: fairer finances for fringe theatre – Piers Beckley ... 285
Children's, young people's and theatre in education – Paul Harman ... 288
Children's, young people's and theatre-in-education companies ... 290
Festivals ... 301
Role-play companies ... 305

Media

Introduction ... 309
Auditioning for camera – Nancy Bishop ... 310
Interview: Zates Atour; *Owning the frame: grit, growth and giving back* ... 313
Independent film, video and TV production companies ... 316
Film schools ... 324
Actors and video games – Mark Estdale ... 326
Radio and audiobook companies ... 329
Media festivals ... 332

Disabled actors

Introduction ... 335
Opportunities for disabled actors and practitioners ... 336
Support for disabled actors and practitioners ... 345
Rights, advice and support ... 348
Opportunities for disabled actors
  – Jamie Beddard ... 350
First steps (as it were) as a disabled actor – Zak Ford-Williams ... 353

Resources

Introduction ... 357
Equity ... 358
Beyond #metoo – Kelly Burke ... 359
Spotlight, casting directories and information services ... 363
'Point me in the right direction': navigating the casting services
  – Isabelle Farah ... 365
Be prepared for publicity
  – Jayne Trotman ... 368
Photographers ... 371
Getting the most from your photographs – Angus Deuchar ... 378
The changing face of voice overs
  – Simon Cryer & Marina Caldarone ... 381
Showreel, voicereel and website services ... 386
Showreels: creation and maintenance
  – Anthony Holmes ... 389
Digital wellbeing for actors
  – Sinead Mac Manus ... 393
Interview: Daniel Heale; *Building your personal brand on social media* ... 397
Accountants ... 400

Tax and National Insurance for actors
 – Philippe Carden 404
Equity Pension Scheme
 – Andrew Barker 408
Physical and mental fitness for actors
 – Alex Caan 411
Interview: Claire Cordeaux; *Mental health in the performing arts* 415

Funding bodies 418
Publications, libraries, references and booksellers 422
Organisations, associations, societies and contacts 427
Bibliography 435
Webography 445
Index 447

Foreword

When people ask me to describe myself, I usually say: I was born in Kenya, my heritage is Goan, and I came to Britain when I was three years old – as a refugee. My name, Aileen Gonsalves, is a blend of stories. I was named after an Irish nun in Kenya. My surname is Portuguese because Goa remained under Portuguese rule until 1961. That unique cultural tapestry – Kenyan, Goan, British – has never just been background noise; it's been the foundation of who I am and how I move through the world.

This convergence of histories gave me something invaluable: an outsider's eye, but also permission. Permission to explore, to shift, to reinvent. To embrace complexity, to refuse categorisation. To be many things at once, unapologetically. I learned early on that identity is not fixed – it's expansive, dynamic and creative. That sense of freedom has guided my career in theatre.

If I'd had a resource like the *Actors' & Performers' Yearbook* when I was starting out, I would have read it cover to cover. This book gathers the information, contacts, advice, and inspiration you need to navigate the creative industry. And when you're trying to figure out how to be an artist in the world, that kind of guide is priceless.

When people ask me now what I do, I say I'm a theatre practitioner – a deliberately broad term that includes actor, director, writer, dramaturg, singer, teacher, acting coach, leadership coach and, yes, even inventor of a new acting method. It may sound like a long list, but it feels completely natural to me. These roles don't conflict – they coexist. They feed each other. They're all driven by the same curiosity, the same deep need to connect.

I trained as an actor at the Royal Central School of Speech and Drama more than thirty years ago. It was a formative time, full of excitement and discovery. But the journey hasn't always been easy or affirming. In the early stages of my career, being versatile wasn't always welcomed. 'Jack of all trades' was often said like an accusation. "You're doing too much," people would say. "Just pick one thing. Be an actor. Commit." On tough days, when the phone didn't ring and self-doubt crept in, I'd wonder if they were right.

But then the work would come. And the roles I played, on and off stage, in the creative teams around me would demand flexibility. Someone needed to write the next scene: I'd write. A director dropped out: I'd step in. A teacher was ill: I'd take the class. I wasn't flitting around. I was responding to the moment.

That's why I resonate deeply with the full version of that phrase: 'Jack of all trades, is a master of none ... but oftentimes better than a master of one.'

One of the pivotal turning points in my artistic journey happened entirely by chance. I was temping in an office and a computer programmer handed me a copy of *True and False* by David Mamet. I devoured it during my lunch break, then went out and bought five more copies to post to friends. "I'll be talking about this book for the rest of my life,' I told them. And I wasn't wrong.

That book led me to the work of Sanford Meisner and one phrase of his in particular: 'You can't say ouch until you've been pinched.' It struck something in me. I watched a Meisner repetition class soon after and was electrified. I saw actors alive, present, reacting moment to moment, unguarded and truthful. I couldn't look away. And I couldn't go back to how I worked before. I had fallen in love with truthful, heart-opening acting. The alchemy that happens between actor and the text, actor and actor, actor and audience, when something real is taking place.

That started me on a new path. I developed what has become the Gonsalves Method, my own approach to acting – rooted in Meisner, but evolved for today's actor. It focuses on five conditions that help actors remain fully outward-focused, connected to their scene partner, while also responding truthfully within the character's given circumstances.

I knew actors needed a method that was efficient, reliable and consistently led to authentic performance – not only in rehearsals, but under pressure, on stage or screen. I tested and refined my method while running the MA Acting course at ArtsEd, where I constantly encouraged students to create their own work – which they did: forming companies, hiring each other. They had a shared language, a shared understanding, and they were empowered by it. I encourage every actor I teach to make their own work.

I've now used this method across hundreds of performances – Shakespeare, new writing, musicals – and I've trained actors, directors, educators, choreographers and even politicians. It's been used to form ensemble companies, build productions, shape curricula. Today, 25 accredited teachers deliver it in institutions across Europe, as it gradually gains traction as a standardised approach to actor training.

Saying, "I've created a new acting method" doesn't always go down well. Some responses were outright hostile: *"Who do you think you are?"* But I couldn't stop. I'd seen what was possible when actors truly connected. I couldn't unsee it. And I couldn't keep it to myself.

At the heart of my work is one essential question I ask every artist: "When was the last time you felt something in a theatre?" Most people pause. Some struggle to answer. But the answer should be simple: *"The last time I was in a theatre."* That should be the norm.

That's our job as actors and performers. To make people feel. If the actor is present, attuned and responding truthfully, the audience will feel what they feel. That's what it means to be 'living truthfully under imaginary circumstances.' That's the power actors have. Find collaborators, teachers, books, classes, practices that help you do that.

This work has also led me back to the Royal Shakespeare Company, where I've acted, directed and educated for over 25 years. I first got there through a twist of fate. I was once cast in a leading role in a BBC adaptation of *Midnight's Children*, which was later cancelled. I was heartbroken. But then I ended up assisting on the RSC stage version of that same story; we created something far richer and more meaningful than I could have imagined.

Some of you reading this may already know you want to act. I knew early on. Apparently, I used to march into kids' parties and ask, 'When is it my time to sing?' Later, in my teens, a drama teacher cast me in *Macbeth*, as Witch 2 and the Porter, in a production staged underground in the cave labyrinth of Kents Cavern, Torquay. I remember thinking: *One day, I'll come back here with my own company. And I'll be Lady Macbeth!* And I did.

In 2011, I founded Butterfly Theatre Company and we performed Shakespeare in extraordinary spaces – caves, castles, forests – across Europe. That early sense of ambition, of wild possibility, stayed with me. But with time, I also learned that 'discovery first' is a valid path too. You don't have to know exactly what you want. Some of my most meaningful creative chapters began in uncertainty, with a single, shaky step into the unknown.

Bring your doubts. Bring your energy. Bring your whole unique self. Some of my happiest memories involve self-made theatre. There's joy in creating with your peers, in laughing, messing about, discovering together. That, to me, is success.

In a time of enormous cultural, political, and technological change, the role of the artist is more important than ever. You are not just observers – you are creators of meaning. You are the ones who help us feel, understand, transform.

To me, theatre and performance is a kind of life simulator. Just as flight simulators help pilots land safely, theatre helps us navigate life – with compassion, with empathy, with honesty.

The *Actors' & Performers' Yearbook* is like a flight manual for artists. It equips you with what you need to take off, to explore, to soar.

So to every actor, performer, artist, and creative soul reading this: know your power. Don't limit yourself. You are creative equals. Be the artist only *you* can be.

And I leave you with a quote from Hamlet that's held me through many chapters: '*There is nothing either good or bad, but thinking makes it so.*'

Read this *Yearbook*. Let it empower you. Let it challenge and inspire you. And whatever you do enjoy the moments.

Aileen Gonsalves is a theatre director, actor, writer and creator of the Gonsalves Method – a pioneering approach to actor training taught in drama schools and universities in many countries. With over 28 years in theatre, film, television and radio, she has worked extensively with the Royal Shakespeare Company as an actor and director and is an Associate Director of Kali Theatre Company. She is the founder of Butterfly Theatre Company, known for immersive Shakespeare productions in extraordinary locations across Europe. She ran the MA in Acting at ArtsEd and was Head of Acting at Drama Studio London. She is author of *Shakespeare and Meisner* (Arden Shakespeare 2021) and a forthcoming book on the Gonsalves Method (Methuen Drama 2026), both with Dr Tracy Irish.

Praise for the *Yearbook*

'The wide range of information and contacts should be
a huge help to those undertaking their new journey.'

**Dame Judi Dench,
Actor**

'Wherever you are from and whatever your background, this book has the
resources and tools that can help you navigate your way. There is a wealth of
information from industry contact details to articles and interviews.'

**Sam Stevenson,
Casting director**

'A brilliant resource to have on your journey. No matter where
you find yourself in your career, it can give you a new direction,
tactics or focus when you feel a bit lost.'

**Syrus Lowe,
Actor**

'The *Actors' & Performers' Yearbook* is the industry's best kept secret
in my view. A one-stop shop for insight and vital information.
I cannot recommend it highly enough.'

**Lucas Msamati,
Actor and writer**

'This book is brilliant. I've been in the biz for over 30 years and
I would have loved to have this when I was starting out, but
I'm really glad it exists now. Bravo to all contributors.'

**Paterson Joseph,
Actor**

'If I'd had a resource like the *Actors' & Performers' Yearbook* when I was starting out,
I would have read it cover to cover. This book gathers the information, contacts, advice
and inspiration you need to navigate the creative industry. And when you're trying to
figure out how to be an artist in the world, that kind of guide is priceless ... the *Actors'
& Performers' Yearbook* is like a flight manual for artists. It equips you with what
you need to take off, to explore, to soar ... Read this *Yearbook*. Let it empower you.
Let it challenge and inspire you. And whatever you do enjoy the moments.'

**Aileen Gonsalves,
Theatre Director, Actor, Writer and Creator of the Gonsalves Method**

Training

Introduction

Not all professional actors have had formal training but for the vast majority their training is the foundation of their craft. Brilliant actors make acting seem effortless but like a graceful Swan gliding across water, there is a lot of hard paddling beneath the surface. High quality, comprehensive training can be the difference between sink or swim.

For all aspiring actors, the decision to train will involve major life, time and financial commitments and sacrifices. It is a huge undertaking and not something that can or should be taken lightly. But if you are passionate about being an actor and are committed to your profession then it is likely an investment worth making and one that will stand you in good stead for the rest of your working life. Your training will give you grounding in the essential basics of voice and movement technique; helping you to develop your voice as an instrument that can cope with the rigours of eight shows a week and training your body for the physical exertion of performance. You will be instructed by specialists in stage combat so you can wield a spear like a Roman Centurion, dialect so you can pass for a Californian native and jazz so your pas de bourrée is en pointe. You will be exposed to a wide-range of theories, techniques, exercises, games and improvisations to broaden your horizons and exercise your imagination. You will perform Shakespeare, Greek tragedy, Restoration comedy and new writing. You will be inducted into the exigencies of the industry to build your resilience and prepare you for professional life. In a highly competitive industry there are few opportunities to learn on the job so training ensures you are ready for anything thrown at you on stage or on set.

Sometimes overlooked, but perhaps most important, training means time spent with a group of your peers who will learn with you, inspire and galvanise you and may become lifelong friends. Many people rate their drama school years amongst the best of their life.

If you are committing to training it is important to sign up to a professionally recognised course, ideally at an established drama school. There are some wonderful acting related university degree courses and many part-time, short-term or foundation courses which will give you some grounding in acting craft but for true professional credentials a full-time drama school course of at least a year is essential for most people.

For those who have already trained, there are many opportunities to learn new skills and refine those already acquired. As in any high performance arena, staying at the top of your game demands constant practise. Short courses and workshops can keep you sharp, keep you connected and add useful ballast to the 'skills' section of your CV to enhance your chances of finding work.

This section is largely devoted to those who are 18 and over. Whilst there is wide-ranging, valuable training for those under that age, the confines of this book limit listings to only the major organisations.

Note: Under all headings in this section, it is especially important to **check for the latest information on the relevant websites**. *Actors' & Performers' Yearbook* makes every effort

2 Training

to ensure that such information is correct and up-to-date, but some information is liable to ongoing amendment.

Listings in this section:
- Training for the under-18s, page 3
- Drama schools, page 12
- Short-term and part-time courses, page 49
- Private tutors and coaches, page 57

Training for the under-18s

Very few children who enjoy performing will go on to be professional actors in adulthood but the benefits of engagement in drama as a child can last a lifetime.

Youth theatre groups, drama clubs and workshops exist in almost every town and city in the UK and can provide a fertile environment for young people to learn and grow. Theatre helps children explore the parameters of their imaginations. In singing, dancing and acting, children have an outlet to express themselves and learn more about themselves. Playing characters helps cultivate knowledge, understanding and empathy for others. By necessity, theatre involves teamwork and performing can help breed confidence and sociability. Many children have come out of their shell and found acceptance and friendship at their local youth theatre.

Opportunities for children to perform can be found online or on social media, and many are members of the National Association of Youth Theatres – see below. Some may offer public productions for proud parents and grandparents. Some will be allied to agencies to promote their members for professional work. But this should never be the primary objective. The most important thing is to have fun. If a child then finds a passion that becomes a career that's just an added bonus.

Boden Studios
Unit 713, 275 New North Road, Islington, London N1 7AA
tel 020-8447 0909, *mobile* 07545 696835
email info@bodens.co.uk
website www.bodens.co.uk
Facebook /bodensperformingarts
Principal Adam Boden

Established in 1973. A part-time performing arts school for children and young adults aged 3–19. Offers classes 7 days a week, covering acting for stage, screen acting, singing and dancing.

Bodens College of Creative Arts is a free entry, full-time sixth form offering diplomas (equivalent to 3 A Levels). See **https://bodenscollege.co.uk** for more information. Courses include:
• Level 3 Extended Diploma Acting (2 years)
• Level 3 Extended Diploma Musical Theatre (2 years)
• Level 3 Extended Diploma Theatre Production (2 years)

British Youth Music Theatre
Head office: Yorkshire Dance, 3 St. Peter's Square, Leeds LS9 8 AH
London office: Mountview, 120 Peckham Hill Street, London SE15 5JT
tel 0113 320 1018
email mail@bymt.org
website https://britishyouthmusictheatre.org
Facebook /britymt
X @britymt
Instagram @britymt
Creative Director Emily Gray

British Youth Music Theatre (previously Youth Music Theatre UK) is the UK's national company providing musical theatre activities for young people aged 11–21 across the UK. It is one of the seven National Youth Music Organisations (NYMOs) supported by Arts Council England; its core programme links young people from local/regional productions into formal training at drama school – so successful auditionees will be talented, with many going on into the creative industries. BYMT has a strong relationship with the teaching union, NASUWT, who are its principal sponsors, and with Trinity College London, who formally assess the activities.

Auditions for young performers take place around the UK in January and February, and successful applicants join the companies of 6 fully staged productions at venues and festivals around the country in the summer holidays.

BYMT's programme includes workshops, courses, training schemes and projects that help young people develop their skills and abilities in the performing arts. This includes the opportunity to work with artistic teams to create new music theatre. BYMT also creates similar pathways for young writers, composers and musicians as well as those interested in technical theatre. BYMT offer a wide range of outreach opportunities with schools, youth services and cross-cultural groups.

Training opportunities for graduate directors, assistant directors, assistant MDs, designers and choreographers working alongside its professional staff are also available.

4 Training

National Association of Youth Theatres (NAYT)
c/o Friargate Theatre, Lower Friargate, York YO1 9SL
tel 0330 229 0820
email info@nayt.org.uk
website www.nayt.org.uk

Founded in 1982, this educational charity for youth theatre practice in England. The organisation supports the development of youth theatre activity through training, advocacy, participation programmes, and information services. Registration is open to any group or individual using theatre techniques in their work with young people, outside formal education.

NAYT responds to enquiries from young people, teachers, parents, carers, youth workers and social services looking for information and advice about youth theatre provision or career or educational opportunities. This free service puts young people in direct contact with youth theatres.

National Youth Arts Wales (NYAW)
Office 202, 2nd Floor, Trafalgar House,
5 Fitzalan Place, Cardiff CF24 0ED
tel 029-2280 7420
email nyaw@nyaw.org.uk
website www.nyaw.org.uk
Facebook /nationalyouthartswales

Formed in 2017 to represent the National Youth Brass Band of Wales, National Youth Wind Orchestra of Wales, National Youth Choir of Wales, National Youth Dance Wales, National Youth Orchestra of Wales, and National Youth Theatre of Wales (NYTW).

The National Youth Theatre of Wales was founded in 1976 and has since provided opportunities for hundreds of young people, many of whom are now actively involved with the theatre as professional actors, directors, writers, designers and stage managers. The NYTW is aimed at young people aged 16–22 (either born in, or living in Wales) who are drawn from all over the country. With guidance from its Creative Activist, the youth theatre prepares and rehearses during the summer of each year for a series of high-profile public performances. Membership awarded following a successful audition process and bursaries are available.

In addition, the NYTW spearheads a development programme of workshops and education activities, designed to increase interest and participation in youth theatre.

National Youth Music Theatre (NYMT)
39 Third Avenue, Frinton-on-Sea, Essex CO13 9EF
email enquiries@nymt.org.uk
website www.nymt.org.uk
Artistic Director Chris Cuming

Offers exceptional opportunities in pre-professional, musical theatre training for talented young people of all backgrounds aged 10–23 years through skill workshops, masterclasses and residential courses led by industry professsionals, through commissioning and presentation of exciting new work, and – in collaboration with some of the UK's leading creative minds – producing bold, new realisations of major works of the core repertoire.

These opportunities exist for stage performers, musicians, technicians, musical directors, choreographers and designers.

Represents the very best in work with young people through musical theatre, enabling thousands of youngsters across the UK to develop both their creative and personal potential, leading Andrew Lloyd-Webber to dub it "the best youth music theatre in the world".

National Youth Theatre of Great Britain (NYT)
443–45 Holloway Road, London N7 6LW
tel 020-3696 7066
email info@nyt.org.uk
website www.nyt.org.uk
X @NYTofGB
Instagram @nationalyouththeatre
Artistic Director Paul Roseby

Founded in 1956 as the world's first youth theatre. The world-leading youth arts organisation. Delivering free performance opportunities, courses and masterclasses, with a range of funded places, bursaries and fee-waivers, it nurtures and showcases exceptional performers and theatre technicians from Great Britain and Northern Ireland.

Every year the NYT visits over 70 arts venues and schools across the UK in the search for young people aged between 14–25 to join their company. The NYT also offers a range of digital activities for young people to take part in from home. Once successfully auditioned, members can be involved with ambitious productions both on stage and backstage, as well as developing skills in facilitation and creative leadership. The NYT also runs a social inclusion programme featuring long-term engagement with non-mainstream schools, and accredited courses for those not in education or training, as well as many open access projects and community productions.

The NYT's world renowned alumni include: Helen Mirren, Daniel Craig, Colin Firth, Rosamund Pike, Daniel Day Lewis, Zawe Ashton, Chiwetel Ejiofor, Orlando Bloom, Catherine Tate, Ben Kingsley, Ashley Jensen, Derek Jacobi, Timothy Dalton, David Walliams, Matt Lucas, Hugh Bonneville, Matt Smith, Adeel Aktar, David Harewood, Regé-Jean Page, Ed Sheeran and Florence Pugh. Backstage NYT graduates have gone on to work in key roles at the world's biggest theatres and events including Olympic ceremonies, award-winning large-scale theatre productions and global tours of the world's biggest music artists. Cultural leaders who started their careers with NYT include Lynette Linton (Artistic Director, Bush Theatre), Bryony Shanahan (Artistic Director, Royal Exchange Theatre), Gbolahan Obisesan (former Artistic Director, Brixton House), Michelle Terry (Artistic Director, Shakespeare's Globe), Matthew Warchus (Artistic Director, Old Vic Theatre) and many more.

Scottish Youth Theatre

email enquiries@scottishyouththeatre.org
website www.scottishyouththeatre.org
Facebook /scottishyouththeatre
Instagram @scottish_youth_theatre

Scottish Youth Theatre is a national young artists' development organisation for aspiring, emerging and early-career aged 14–25 years-old who are based in Scotland. The company creates opportunities that are inspired and shaped by young people, based on their needs and aspirations as creatives and their diverse and unique perspectives. The company's purpose is to collaborate with young theatre artists to create experiences and events that reverberate in their lives, their communities and their country.

The company runs on a project-to-project basis, providing space, care and creative stimulus to explore theatre. With Scottish Youth Theatre, young artists can develop and refine their practice through learning new skills, exploring new perspectives, making and touring new work, learning about the professional industry and connecting with like-minded individuals and professional artists. The company cultivates an environment where participants are at the helm of their own creative journey and the work they make is their opportunity to interrogate, question and reflect on things that matter to them.

Scottish Youth Theatre is a non-membership-based organisation.

Youth Theatre Ireland

7 North Great George's Street, Dublin 1, Republic of Ireland
tel +353 (0)1 878 1301
email info@youththeatre.ie
website www.youththeatre.ie
Facebook /YouthTheatreIreland
X @YouthTheatreIrl
Instagram @youththeatreireland

A national development organisation for youth theatre founded in 1980. It supports a network of youth theatres which deliver year-round programmes of drama workshops and performance opportunities to young people aged 12–21 from cities, towns and villages across Ireland.

Advocates the inherent value and the unique relationship between young people and theatre as an artform, and is committed to extending and enhancing young people's understanding of theatre and to raising the artistic standards of youth theatre across the country. The organisation supports youth drama in practice through an annual programme that includes the National Youth Theatre, The Young Critics, Empower Youth Theatre Encounter, National Festival of Youth Theatres and The Youth Theatre Practice Symposium. It commissions new writing, publications, resources as well as research and policy development. It provides drama facilitator training and other services.

With a membership of over 50 youth theatres throughout the country, Youth Theatre Ireland supports the sustained development of youth theatres in partnership with local authorities, youth services, theatres and arts centres.

Arts Emergency

Julie Hesmondhalgh
The crisis in arts education: how working-class artists are being squeezed out of the industry

I had an unexpectedly lovely train journey pre-pandemic. Lucky enough to have managed to reserve a seat at a table in a typically over-crowded carriage, I was planning to shove my earphones in, bury my head in a book and disengage from my fellow passengers. So, when the strangers at my table started to chat to one another – and to me – my heart sank a bit. But it ended up being one of the most interesting and engaging journeys I've ever had.

My cross-country companions were Alan, a middle-aged gay actor; Kate, a young maths teacher at a struggling comprehensive school in West London; and Henry, a Ghanaian-born scientist working in Washington DC. We covered so much in that two hours between London and Manchester: childhood, sexuality, racism, Trump and perhaps inevitably – there being a teacher amongst us – education. Kate talked with sadness about how the new GCSEs were taking their toll on teachers and pupils alike at her school and how she'd been working every evening and weekend to try to get her Year 11s through them. She said that the school was already feeling the effects of the cuts in arts subjects; that although she was a maths teacher, the erosion of subjects that had enhanced her students' creativity and awakened their minds to the wider world was already taking its toll on the mental health of the young people. Henry talked passionately about how, although he was a scientist by trade, it was the arts that gave him joy, that refreshed him and rebooted him after long days at the lab. Music venues, theatres, cinemas: these were his hang-outs of choice. Alan and I both talked about the opportunities that we had taken for granted as we started out in the performing arts – opportunities that no longer exist for young people growing up in towns like ours; from families like ours.

> **Arts Emergency**
> Unit W3, 8 Woodberry Down, London N4 2TG
> email info@arts-emergency.org
> website www.arts-emergency.org

I, along with a dozen of my mates, left my hometown of Accrington at the age of 18 to go to drama school in London, after a brilliant theatre studies teacher at our local Further Education college inspired us all to make a go of it and audition. There were five of us from that course at LAMDA at the same time at the end of the 1980s, all on *full grants* from our Local Education Authority. That FE performing arts course, I found out this week, no longer exists. Neither does the full local authority grant, of course. And nor, I'd venture, does the philosophy that an education in the arts, or a desire to have a career in the arts, is a worthwhile pursuit for people from backgrounds like mine.

There has been an insidious mindset creeping into our national psyche, no doubt massively exacerbated by the prohibitive costs of higher education tuition fees, that somehow a career in the arts is pie-in-the-sky and unrealistic, and that an arts or humanities degree or drama/art school training is not worth the investment. God forbid that anyone should be enthusiastic about learning for learning's sake and want to study philosophy or classics, never mind acting or dance because of a personal passion for the subject, without wondering and worrying about how to make that choice economically viable in the long term. As Nicky Morgan, the then Conservative Education Minister famously said in 2014,

'Arts subjects limit career choices', warning young people that studying arts at higher education could 'hold them back for the rest of their lives'.

The majority of educationalists, of course – even those working in science and maths subjects like my travelling companion Kate – would disagree. The study of the arts, and in particular the performing arts, are partly encouraged in top public schools, I'm sure, because of the confidence, social skills and interpretative thinking that develop as a result. The wealthy have never been discouraged from indulging their passion for music, film, painting, theatre and dance. A government report in November 2017 recorded that the creative industries were indeed thriving with the '£92bn sector growing at twice the rate of the economy' (**www.gov.uk** *Creative industries' record contribution to UK economy*, 29 November 2017).

But it appears that a huge swathe of the population, namely the state educated, the less well-off, the working class, for whom the decision to saddle oneself with over £27,000 debt at the start of their adult life is a major consideration, are being massively disincentivized to engage with the arts and humanities, from school onwards. It starts with funding cuts and continues as arts subjects are moved into a more theoretical and less practical curriculum framework at GCSE level. The controversial English Baccalaureate and its exclusion of arts is seen by many as the nail in the coffin of any meaningful creative education. Drama, art, dance and music at school have often been the only access young people have had to learning those skills.

There are, luckily, amazing organisations picking up the pieces and attempting to fill the gaps that current government policy is leaving. There is hope. Groups of people are crowdfunding to create bursaries to allow students from less privileged backgrounds to access arts and performance degrees. Theatres and art spaces are investing in outreach work to pull hard-to-reach communities into their buildings through youth theatre and specialised groups. Teachers and directors are setting up free training programmes, and watching their talented students overcome sometimes unbelievably challenging personal circumstances to thrive and succeed in an arts industry that they have been told is not for them: organisations like Alt, Nottingham-based Talent First and the mighty Arts Emergency.

Set up in 2011 by comedian Josie Long and campaigner Neil Griffiths, the Arts Emergency philosophy and aim are simple and effective: to create an 'Alternative Old Boys' Network'; to open up the same opportunities naturally afforded to those privileged few, who grow up with those school and family connections firmly in place, to everyone. They have pulled together an enormous number of experts and practitioners from a vast array of specialised areas and connected them with young people from backgrounds that have meant they have little access to the arts. Free talks and events are regularly made available, and when the scheme spread to the North a couple of years ago I became involved as a supporter and speaker in schools and colleges.

There is an incredibly successful mentoring scheme that I have witnessed first-hand as my husband, the writer Ian Kershaw, has been a mentor for over a year now. His first mentee, a sparky seventeen-year-old aspiring writer and the first in her family to access higher education, won't mind me saying that she thrived under the programme. Together, they saw theatre, attended talks by leading writers, met people in the industry and visited studios and rehearsal rooms. She grabbed the opportunity she was offered to write for a local theatre-in-education tour and did work experience at CBBC. She is now at university studying English with a creative writing pathway as part of her BA.

Maisie (not her real name) was clear about what she wanted to do from the off and Arts Emergency enabled her, creating networks that simply don't ordinarily exist for people like her. But sometimes the work they do is about opening up unknown worlds to their participants. Another young person might, for example, be passionate about, and fascinated by, films and filmmaking, but have no access to the world of the studio floor or editing suite or post-production house. He or she might be a fantastic and naturally gifted vision mixer or a sound recordist, but unless they're given the opportunity to experiment in these roles, they'll never know. As Arts Emergency say: 'You can't be what you can't see.'

The working-class artists who were encouraged and supported by the state from the 1950s through to my generation growing up in the 1980s and early 1990s, who are now part of the cultural landscape of the UK as writers, actors, directors, dancers, visual artists, musicians, directors, etc. are the last of their kind. Or could be, if we don't act to change the current climate of exclusion. A culture without diversity is a sick one. If our future artists only come from a narrow stratum of society (the most well-off and privately educated) then who will be left to tell the stories of the rest of us? Who will hold a mirror to our world and ask the important questions about how we live now? Because art exists not only to entertain, but to reflect and inform and inspire. At its best, it can be transcendent and transformative and completely democratic; in that it is, or should be, available to us all, regardless of where we're from and who we are. The more diverse our culture, the wider the world of the stories we experience, the richer we all are for it. Perhaps most importantly, it creates, as I experienced on that Pendolino train a few weeks back, a point of connection in an increasingly isolating and fractured world.

Julie Hesmondhalgh was born and grew up in Accrington, Lancashire. She trained at LAMDA and set up Arts Threshold Theatre in the early 90s. She co-runs Take Back Theatre Collective in Manchester. Her *Working Diary* was published in 2019. She is best known for playing Hayley in Coronation Street from 1998–2014. She has worked extensively in theatre, TV and radio.

Levelling the playing field: actors from working- and benefit-class backgrounds

David Mumeni, actor and founder of Open Door
Interview by Rob Ostlere

David Mumeni is a performer, writer and acting teacher, and the artistic director and founder of Open Door, a charity supporting young people who want to apply for drama school but face financial barriers. Open Door offers an eight-month part-time intensive course, with successful acting and production arts applicants receiving free auditions and financial support for interviews, as well as mentoring and a range of other help. David trained as an actor at Drama Centre and has gone on to work extensively at the highest levels of the industry. Here he talks about the need for organisations like Open Door, makes the case for drama school training and shares advice for students and those in the first few years of their careers.

What were you seeing in the industry that led you to create Open Door?
It was about addressing inequality by making sure that everyone who wanted to go to drama school got their fair go. Part of that was making the audition process affordable for young people from working- and benefit-class backgrounds, and also finding talent from places outside London.

As well as finding these young people, mentoring them and supporting them financially with applications, you've also been working directly with the schools to make changes.
Yes, for example getting a wider intake of people by pushing the drama schools to do more auditions across the country. Or pushing to change the audition panels, making sure they're diverse in all the different ways, be it class or race or gender. We also looked at the way the panels sometimes behaved. It's not about having to be super, super nice but if you don't create a space that allows someone to be comfortable they're just not going to do their best work. I've also been talking to the schools which don't redirect actors in the first round. What we've seen with some of our young people we mentor – who maybe haven't had access to youth theatres or good drama departments at school – is that they can transform and be amazing simply by asking them the right questions: "What's this speech about for you? How do you relate to it? What do you want? Who are you speaking to?" You're expecting all these young people to all come in at the same level and they're not. You have to give redirection in the first round.

And the drama schools have taken all this on?
Not as urgently as we'd like. There's a lot of work that still needs to be done but some have been really responsive. The auditions have changed. The schools are looking at the curriculums and the classes they teach.

You've previously made the case brilliantly for drama schools

Well, you do learn there! Acting is a skill, and you get the chance to practice doing that every day. Whereas if you go straight into the industry, you're not necessarily going to do that much acting, especially to start with. Even if you did a couple of plays and a week on a TV series that's only sixteen or seventeen weeks' acting. And that's in a good year!

And you've done a lot of myth-busting. One idea that comes up is that the schools are too expensive, but you've managed to get all these great students in from lower income backgrounds.

With the schools we work with there is no such thing as too expensive because the big ones all have student finance. Affordability is only a problem with schools that don't have that; although the privately-run drama schools do offer bursaries and DaDAs (Dance and Drama Awards), it can still be a struggle. With the loans – it is a debt, of course it is – but you're only going to pay that back if you earn enough. Also, with most of these big schools there's massive bursary funding to assist with living costs. And we've highlighted the issue at schools where they might need more.

And students get a lot for their money, relatively.

People are paying nine grand a year to go to an amazing university but they're doing three or four hours a week contact-time in a lecture hall full of people. Drama school, you get triple that in a day with some of the best teachers in the country in a room of sixteen to twenty people. And then you get a showcase at the end!

With Open Door you've given advice to students about changes in the industry, especially casting and how that impacts choosing material for their showcases.

With showcases, I say to the students worrying about typecasting that agents are going to assume you can do different stuff and are going to try to put you up for as much as possible. So just show *you*, rather than worrying about, "What do I need to present to be signed?" Present good acting. Rather than trying to fit yourself into some archetype, pick pieces that might be challenging when you're working on them, but which, when you perform them, you can do so with ease. That sort of thinking applies throughout your third year. Your main focus has to be on acting to the best of your ability, being a nice person when you chat to people, and hopefully things will happen for you.

What about auditioning advice?

It's the same thing we tell the Open Door young people when they audition; you've got no control over what this panel thinks. One panel might like you, one panel might not. Your job is to go, "This character is connecting with this character, I'm playing this objective. I'll do my interview, show you what I'm actually like and then leave. If you don't like it, you don't like it". There's power in that. That's some of the work we do at Open Door. It takes eight months to get a young actor to a place of confidence where they realise they have no control over what people think. All you can say is, "I did the best job I could do in the circumstances that were given and in the time I had".

Talking about the industry more widely now, how do people balance having an awareness of inequalities without letting that preoccupy them and hold them back?

It's really hard to quantify why you are where you are in your career. If I think about my mixed-race background, perhaps it's got me this far because I'm a little bit different to other people but it might have limited me in all these other ways. The point is it's really hard to be sure of whether something doesn't happen for you because of your class, your race or your accent or whatever. Of course, that's not to deny that those barriers aren't there. But if you go around thinking everything you don't get is because of that, I don't think that's a healthy way to look at it. Wherever you can, separate the two: "Have I not got this because the industry is tough?" or "Have I not got it because of a barrier?" Sometimes it might be very clear, and I've felt that. But I've come up against these barriers and I've done OK so my thought is let me try and help others with solutions.

And actors can take positive steps themselves to address inequalities?

When I started Open Door people said to me, "You're creating these actors but there's no work for them". I feel like it's a little bit different now and I don't have that fear. Of course, there are still a lot of the same types of writers working but people are breaking through and people do want to hear original stories and original voices. But if that work isn't being made for you, you can create it. And that doesn't mean you have to write it. I've known lots of people who wanted to change agents for example, and put on a show to do that. They've not been able to write something but they've said I'm going to get my friend to write it, and I'm going to get my director-friend to direct it, and another actor in to play this part and develop it. And sometimes that play goes on further: to Edinburgh, another theatre, into TV development.

It's important to balance focusing on the problem and the solutions?

We have to find ways of using the passion and the anger, putting it into some sort of positive action that is effective. We need tangible solutions, schemes and work: be it writers' programmes, or things like Sabrina Mahfouz creating a scheme for ethnic minority theatre critics, or something like Open Door. Next, we need to start supporting new voices in producing; to see more diversity among the people in charge.

To find out more about Open Door and to apply, go to **www.opendoor.org.uk**. You can support the charity's work by following them on social media **@opendoorpeople** and donating at **www.opendoor.org.uk/donate**

Rob Ostlere is the author of *The Actor's Career Bible*, published by Bloomsbury, a practical guide to building an acting career based on in-depth interviews with over seventy-five industry experts. He trained at National Youth Theatre and RADA and has since worked widely across television, theatre and film. *The Actor's Career Bible* is available at **www.bloomsury.com**. You can also find out more **@actorscareerbible** on Instagram, at **www.actorscareerbible.com** and on the book's YouTube channel. Rob can be found via **@robostlere** on social media, where there is more information about his latest acting and writing work.

Drama schools

There is a core of established drama schools which belong to an organisation called the Federation of Drama Schools (**www.federationofdramaschools.co.uk**). The seventeen Federation members all run accredited courses offering practice-based, vocational training courses, quality assured by experienced professionals. There are also, of course, well-respected courses that are not part of the Federation of Drama Schools.

It is important to check the current funding arrangements for each course you intend to apply for. Don't rely on the arrangements in place last year as things change regularly. Almost all of the drama schools offer a three-year BA degree in acting – in spite of the fact that there is little or no written component to the courses, let alone formal, written exams. Historically, the schools took the 'degree' route to help students get funding on the same basis as those following conventional academic courses. Degree status actually means very little in the acting profession, and courses with degree status are not necessarily better than those without it. Funding for some accredited one and two-year courses is available, but not with the same frequency as for three-year courses.

It is worth spending time checking through all the courses listed below. Look at the online prospectuses for any school that you feel could be viable for you – and read each one thoroughly. Important considerations include whether you could be eligible for funding whether student loan, scholarship or DaDA award for your fees and maintenance. Central London comes with higher living costs than out of London. Above all, it's important to try to assess which schools and courses you feel would suit you best and to apply, via UCAS **www.ucas.ac.uk**, to as many as you can afford the audition fees and travel costs for. Some schools offer means-tested audition fee waivers. Don't forget to factor in the cost of overnight accommodation, if necessary.

The plain truth is that competition for places is so intense that you need to audition for as many places as you possibly can. Every time you do another audition you will learn more about the techniques of auditioning than any book or class can teach you. Don't be disheartened if it doesn't go your way. Many people take two or three years of auditioning, and sometimes more, before they get places. If you are determined to become a professional actor, you have to take rejection in your stride, learn from it and keep on trying until you succeed. Finally, carefully check the application deadlines, funding details and audition specifications of each school to which you intend to apply – there are some considerable variations. Many schools will have audition guidelines and advice for applicants on their website.

Notes:
- For general information on funding for fees and maintenance loans, see **www.gov.uk/browse/education/student-finance**.
- Places on some courses are currently funded through Dance and Drama Awards (DaDAs). These were introduced in the late 1990s, and provide funding for about two-thirds of successful applicants. For more details, check each relevant school's prospectus and website – also look at **www.gov.uk/dance-drama-awards**.

Drama schools

- For the latest details on member of the Federation of Drama Schools please see FDS website **www.federationofdramaschools.co.uk**.

*Member of the Federation of Drama Schools

ArtsEd*
14 Bath Road, Chiswick, London W4 1LY
tel 020-8987 6666
email info@artsed.co.uk
website https://artsed.co.uk
Facebook /artsedlondon
X @artsedlondon
Principal Louise Jackson

One of the UK's leading drama schools, offering outstanding conservatoire training on the BA (Hons) courses in Acting and Musical Theatre.

Degree courses are validated by City, University of London. Dance and Drama Awards are available, linked to the Level 6 approved Trinity College London diplomas and ArtsEd also awards bursaries from its own funds. Applications for courses and awards should be made direct to the school.

Acting courses:
- BA (Hons)/ Level 6 Diploma Acting in Acting (3 years). Applicants must be aged 18 or over.
- BA (Hons)/ Level 6 Diploma Musical Theatre in Musical Theatre (3 years). Applicants must be aged 18 or over.
- MA Acting (1 year postgraduate). Applicants must be aged 21 or over.
- Full-time Foundation Musical Theatre – Cert HE (1 year). Applicants must be aged 18 or over.
- Full-time Foundation Acting – Cert HE (1 year). Applicants must aged 18 or over.

The Bridge Theatre Training Company
Admin: The Bridge at Cecil Sharp House,
2 Regent's Park Road, London NW1 7AY,
Courses: Held in the Camden area
tel 020-7424 0860
email admin@thebridge-ttc.org
website www.thebridge-ttc.org
Joint Artistic Directors Mark Akrill, Judith Pollard

The Bridge is a non-profit organisation which provides intensive training for a professional acting career. Courses include comprehensive career guidance, and a graduating season of public productions in London theatres, with a West End showcase in front of agents, directors and casting directors.

Bridge students receive training in acting, singing, dance, improv, Shakespeare, combat and much more. Bridge students also study screen acting and will record a video showreel.

Full-time acting courses:
- Professional Acting Course (2 years). Applicants must be aged 18 or over.
- Professional Acting Course (one year postgraduate/ post-experience). Applicants must be aged 21 or over, with a university degree or relevant experience.

- 3-day and 5-day options are now available for both the one-year and 2-year courses.

Bristol Improv Theatre
50 St Paul's Road, Bristol BS8 1LP
mobile 07936 617158
email hello@improvtheatre.co.uk
website https://improvtheatre.co.uk
Facebook /BITheatre
Instagram @bristolimprovtheatre

The UK's first full-time dedicated improv theatre. They create, teach and perform spontaneous theatre that is ambitious and unapologetic. Work and training is based in long-form, narrative theatre, using an approach that has been built from training with improv practitioners from all over the world, and years of teaching and performing professionally.

They offer flexible pathways for learning improv at any level of experience or ability. This ranges from drop-in style classes to longer weekly courses and intensive weekend workshops. Also regularly host UK and internationally renowned improv instructors, who deliver worshops and courses at their theatre in Bristol.

There is currently no wheelchair access.

Bristol Old Vic Theatre School*
1–3 Downside Road, Clifton, Bristol BS8 2XF
tel 0117 973 3535
email enquiries@oldvic.ac.uk
website www.oldvic.ac.uk
Facebook /BOVTS
Instagram @bovtsbristol
Principal Fiona Francombe, Director of Drama Ali de Souza

All courses are entirely vocational and are validated by the University of the West of England.

Applications for all courses are made directly to the School via the website. All applicants are auditioned – please see our website for details of the relevant selection process.

- MA Screen Acting (1 year, 38 weeks).
- MFA in Professional Acting (1 year, 40 weeks, for international students).
- Summer Foundation Course in Acting (10 weeks).

For details of the range of short courses and masterclasses available, please see the School website.

City Lit
1–10 Keeley Street, Covent Garden,
London WC2B 4BA
tel 020-4582 0413
email drama@citylit.ac.uk
website www.citylit.ac.uk/courses/acting-diploma-level-3

14 Training

The Acting Diploma (Level 3) is an intensive year-long course that provides students with a thorough foundation in actor training.

Working with industry professionals and experienced teachers, candidates will develop skills in actor's voice, movement and physicality. Students will hone their craft across a range of specialisms, from classical training through to screen performance. Students will perform in a full-scale theatre production at the end of the course.

The course timetable is designed to fit around part-time employment.

Applicants for the course will ideally have completed a full Level 2 Foundation in Drama course or equivalent (at least one years' actor training).

Entry is by audition. Please prepare two 2-minute monologues (one classical, one contemporary) and be prepared to attend a 3-hour workshop. No audition fee. Auditions from April for September course start.

Students can apply for an Advanced Learner Loan from Student Finance England for up to £2,225 of the fees for this course. For more information contact the Drama department at **drama@citylit.ac.uk**.

Court Theatre Training Company
The Courtyard Theatre, Bowling Green Walk, 40 Pitfield Street, London N1 6EU
tel 020-7739 6868
email info@courttheatre.org.uk
website https://ourttheatre.org.uk
Instagram @courttheatretrainingcompany
Principal/Director Tim Gill

The Court Theatre Training Company site has wheelchair access and provides support for students with learning support needs.

Full-time acting courses:

• BA (Hons) Acting (2 years)

Taught on a 2-year accelerated program, this distinctive course is specially designed for the practical training of actors resident within the professional environment of a working theatre and is taught by working practitioners in the field. The course fee is £11,130 per academic year. Applicants must be aged 18+ and hold 80 UCAS entry points on entry. Mature students up to any age may be accepted with no UCAS point requirement if they show potential at audition/interview. Public funding is available via the Student Finance Company. Applications should be made directly via the website or via UCAS throughout the year.

Course is validated by Bucks New University.

The Dorset School of Acting
Lighthouse, 21 Kingland Road, Poole, Dorset BH15 1UG
tel (01202) 922675
email admin@dorsetschoolofacting.co.uk
website https://dorsetschoolofacting.co.uk
Co-founders & Principals James Bowden, Laura Roxburgh

The 1 year diploma course in Acting & Musical Theatre has a 100% success rate in placing students at reputable drama schools for further training or into professional work. It is designed to provide a real insight into the rigours of drama school training, giving classes in acting, dance, voice and singing, tutorial sessions, theatre visits and business advice. It does not expect applicants to be strong in all disciplines when they audition.

Acting courses offered:

• One Year Diploma in Acting & Musical Theatre (30 weeks) – the qualification gained is Trinity ATCL Level 4 in Drama & Speech. Applicants should be aged 16+. Applications should be made directly to the school by the middle of August.

• Fully funded 2-year vocational sixth form for students aged 16–19 (level 3) in Acting (60 weeks) – the qualification is an extended diploma equivalent to 3 A levels. The course is designed to give students a strong foundation in the fundamentals of the performing arts industry with an acting bias. Applications should be made directly to the school by the middle of August.

Drama Studio London (DSL)*
1 Grange Road, London W5 5QN
tel 020-8579 3897
email admin@dramastudiolondon.co.uk
website www.dramastudiolondon.co.uk
Facebook /dramastudiolondon
Instagram @dramastudiolondon
Director of DSL Emma Lucia Hands

Provides full time, professional acting training, for the profession by the profession, for adults with passion and talent. For more information and to apply, visit the website or contact **admissions@dramastudiolondon.co.uk**. Diploma students have the option of taking the Trinity College London National Certificate in Professional Acting, along with their DSL Diploma.

• One Year MA/PGDip in Professional Acting validated by University of West London (UWL)
• 2 Year MFA in Professional Acting with Independent Production, validated by UWL
• 3 Year BA (Hons) in Professional Acting, validated by UWL
• Foundation Diploma in Performance (Cert HE) (One year)

East 15 Acting School*
Loughton Campus: Hatfields, Rectory Lane, Loughton IG10 3RY
tel 020-8508 5983
email east15@essex.ac.uk
Southend campus: Elmer Approach, Southend-on Sea SS1 1LW

Drama schools

tel (01702) 328200
website www.east15.ac.uk
Facebook /east15actingschool
Instagram @east15actingschool

Full-time acting courses: All BA (Hons) courses are full-time, 3 years. There is no fixed deadline for application, but it is recommended to apply as early as possible as courses may close at any time.
• BA (Hons) Acting
• BA (Hons) Acting (International)
• BA (Hons) Acting & Community Engagement
• BA (Hons) Acting & Contemporary Theatre
• BA (Hons) Acting & Fight Performance
• BA (Hons) Acting & Physical Theatre
• BA (Hons) World Performance
• Certificate of Higher Education in Theatre Arts (one year)

All acting courses require a successful audition. For additional academic requirements see course details on the website.

Other full-time undergraduate courses:
• Certificate of Higher Education in Theatre Arts (one year)
• BA (Hons) Stage Management (with pathways) (3 years)
• BA (Hons) Creative Producing (Theatre & Short Film) (3 years)

Post-graduate courses:

Postgradutae courses are aimed at graduates or those with relevant work experience who are interested in a career in stage, TV, film, and radio, as an actor, filmmaker, or director. All courses require a successful audition or interview.
• MA Acting (one year)
• MA in Acting (International) (one year)
• MFA Acting (International) (2 years)
• MA Acting for Digital Media (one year)
• MFA Acting with Digital Media (2 years)
• MA/MFA Theatre Directing (one year)
• PhD Research Degrees

Please see the website for details of the above courses.

École Internationale de Théâtre Jacques Lecoq

116 Rue de la Carreterie, 84000 Avignon, France
tel +33 (0)4 88 61 93 13
email contact@ecole-jacqueslecoq.com
website www.ecole-jacqueslecoq.com
Facebook /ecole.jacqueslecoq
Instagram @ecolejacqueslecoq
Principal Mrs Anne Astolfe

Founded in Paris in 1956, with the aim of producing a young theatre of new work, generating performance languages which emphasise the physical playing of the actor. Focuses on art theatre, but with the view that theatre education is broader than the theatre itself: "It is a matter not only of training actors, but of educating theatre artists of all kinds." Provides as broad and durable a foundation as possible for every student. Also offers part-time courses. See also the company's entry under *Short-term and part-time courses* on page 51.

Full-time acting courses:
• Professional Course (Certificate; 2 years). Public funding: AFDAS, OCPO, France Travail (only for people living and working in France). Applications should be made direct to the school from November to June (generally after June there is a waiting list). Applicants must be aged 21+ with initial theatre training and stage experience.

Federation of Drama Schools

Liverpool Institute For Performing Arts, Mount Street, Liverpool L1 9HF
email info@federationofdramaschools.co.uk
website www.federationofdramaschools.co.uk
Instagram @federationofdramaschools

The Federation of Drama Schools (FDS) brings together established UK drama school training providers as a group to develop discussion, resources and projects which support and promote accessible, high-quality professional performers training, and to communicate to prospective students the range of training options available within the drama school contexts. FDS aims to provide current and relevant information to prospective performers, staff, parents and the industry, to ensure a pipeline of talent continues to emerge from drama schools to shape and inform the contemporary performance industries.

Fourth Monkey

97–101 Seven Sisters Rd, Finsbury Park, London N7 7QP
tel 020-7281 0360
email office@fourthmonkey.co.uk
website www.fourthmonkey.co.uk
Facebook /FourthMonkeyTC
X @FourthMonkeyTC
Instagram @fourthmonkey
Artistic Director Steven Green, Director of Training Charleen Qwaye

Established in 2010 to provide innovative and inclusive industry responsive training courses. Works to develop and empower the next generation of professional actors and creative theatre makers and challenge the status quo of traditional conservatoire training.

Accredited training courses:
• BA (Hons) Acting (2 year accelerated degree)
• BA (Hons) Acting (3 year, full-time)

Training

- CertHE Acting & Theatre Making (one year foundational course)

Courses are awarded by Falmouth University.

GSA, Guildford School of Acting*

University of Surrey, Stag Hill Campus, Guildford GU2 7XH
tel (01483) 684040
email gsaenquiries@gsa.surrey.ac.uk
website https://gsauk.org
Facebook /gsauk
X @the_gsa
Instagram @guildfordschoolofacting
Head of School Prof. Catherine McNamara

Founded in 1935 and is part of the University of Surrey. GSA is a vibrant community of performers, performance makers, creative practitioners and technicians graduating from a wide variety of programmes each year. From 1964 onwards has concentrated on the vocational training of actors and stage managers.

Full-time courses: Applications for undergraduate courses should be made via UCAS (applicants must be aged 18 or over, with 3 A levels). Applications for the BA (Hons) Theatre (conversion by distance learning) and for Foundation and Postgraduate courses (applicants must be aged 21 or over) should be made direct to the University of Surrey.

- Foundation (CertHe) Acting (1 year)
- Foundation (CertHe) Musical Theatre (1 year)
- BA (Hons) Acting (3 years)
- BA (Hons) Actor-Musician (3 years)
- BA (Hons) Applied and Contemporary Theatre (3 years)
- BA (Hons) Musical Theatre (3 years)
- BA (Hons) Theatre Production (3 years)
- BA (Hons) Theatre (1 year online learning conversion programme)
- MA Acting (1 year)
- MA Musical Theatre (1 year)
- MA Stage and Production Management (1 year)
- MA Theatre (Part time online learning) (2 years)
- MFA Acting (2 years)
- MFA Musical Theatre (2 years)
- MFA Theatre (Part time online learning) (2 years)
- PhD Theatre

Guildhall School of Music & Drama*

Silk Street, Barbican, London EC2Y 8DT
tel 020-7628 2571
email acting_applications@gsmd.ac.uk
website www.gsmd.ac.uk/drama
X @guildhallschool
Vice Principal & Director of Drama Orla O'Loughlin

Full-time acting courses:

- BA (Hons) Acting (3 years)

Innovative in structure and approach, our Acting programme is committed to the development of each student's unique and individual practice. We aim to develop actors who are tenacious and versatile, able to move with confidence between stage, screen, digital and audio platforms and classical, contemporary and experimental repertoire. Our programme is based in the heart of the City of London, with a generous staff-student ratio and a high number of teaching hours. When you begin your training with us, you should normally be at least 18 years old with a minimum of 2 A Level passes or equivalent.

Applications to the course are made directly to the School through our online application portal. Students from a wide range of ages and backgrounds are selected by audition and interview, with no previous acting experience required.

The International College of Musical Theatre (ICMT)

68 Wallis Road, Hackney Wick, London E9 5LH
tel 020-7253 3118
email info@theicmt.com
website www.theicmt.com
Principals/Directors Kenneth Avery-Clark, Christie Miller

Courses offered:

- Professional Development EU Musical Theatre Course (train in London and Hamburg; one- to 2-years)
- Level 4 Diploma in Musical Theatre Foundation Course (one year)
- Top-up Musical Theatre Course (3 months)
- Musical Theatre Course (6 months)
- Accelerated BA (Hons) Musical Theatre Performance (2 years)

Specific academic requirements apply for the BA (Hons) program. Entry is by audition only. Applicants must be skilled in at least 2 of the 3 disciplines: acting, singing and dance. Train for a week in New York (one-year course).

Welcomes candidates with disabilities and will consider each on a case-by-case basis, according to the strength of their audition.

International School of Screen Acting

Studio G101, 415 Wick Lane, London E3 2JG
tel 020-8709 8719
email enquiries@screenacting.co.uk
website www.screenacting.co.uk
Facebook /screenactingUK
Instagram @screenactinguk
Directors David B. Craik, Mark Normandy

Founded in 2002, ISSA is the leading specialist screen acting school in the UK. It runs as a full-time screen-acting school dedicated to preparing actors for today's TV and film industry.

Full-time acting courses:

- One-year Intensive Screen Acting. Fast, full-time intensive course focusing on equipping the student

actor with the means to encompass the challenges of a demanding industry. Audition requried.
• 2-year Screen Acting. In-depth screen actor training preparing actors for the intense demands of the industry. Audition required.

Italia Conti*

Italia Conti, 2 Henry Place, Victoria Way, Woking, Surrey GU21 6BU
email info@italiaconti.co.uk
website www.italiaconti.com
Vice Principal & Director of School of Acting Bradley Hawkins

Offers comprehensive acting courses for aspiring actor-artists in the performing arts industry. The practical training and professional development programmes equip students with the skills and knowledge to excel as versatile actors across stage, screen, and audio platforms. It is one of the country's leading institutions for vocational acting courses with an emphasis on professional development and employability.

Full-time acting courses:

Entry requirements: Age: 18+ by August 31st in the year of entry. GCSE Level 2 English and Maths (Grade 4 or above) or equivalent. 64 UCAS points or recognition of non-standard entry qualifications/experience.

• BA (Hons) Acting (3 years). In-depth training preparing students for professional acting. Enhances technical skills, artistic versatility, and personal growth.
• BA (Hons) Acting (Musical Theatre) (3 years). In-depth training preparing students for professional acting. Enhances technical skills, artistic versatility, and personal growth.
• CertHE Acting (Foundation) (one year). Lays foundation for full-time actor's training. Provides a comprehensive acting principles and prepare students for entry to BA Acting course.
• CertHE Acting (Musical Theatre) (Foundation) (one year).

Postgraduate courses:
• MA Creative Arts Practice (15 months full time, 30 months part time). Online.
• MA Creative Arts Leadership (15 months full time, 30 months part time). Online.
• MA Creative Arts Education (15 months full time, 30 months part time). Online.
• MA/MFA Teaching & Coaching Voice / Movement (13 months full time, 24 months part time).

Other courses offered:
• Musical Theatre (BA, FdA, Diploma, CertHE)
• Dance (BA, Diploma, CertHE)
• Online and Short courses

LAMDA (London Academy of Music & Dramatic Art)*

155 Talgarth Road, London W14 9DA
tel 020-8834 0500
email enquiries@lamda.ac.uk
website www.lamda.ac.uk

LAMDA is the oldest drama school in the UK and a pioneering conservatoire that provides exceptional vocational training through full-time and short courses. LAMDA prepares students for thriving careers in acting, directing, musical theatre, and production and technical arts. You can see their acting alumni on stage at the National Theatre, the RSC, Shakespeare's Globe, on London's West End, on Broadway and on the BBC, HBO, Netflix, Apple TV+ and the big screen.

LAMDA's award-winning redevelopment opened in 2017 in Barons Court, West London. The building has 3 theatres, 16 rehearsal spaces, 3 dance studios and an audio recording studio. In 2021 LAMDA was granted full degree awarding powers. In 2023 LAMDA opened new state-of-the-art facilities to train students in virtual production and motion capture after receiving £1.9 million in funding from the Office for Students. LAMDA has a range of scholarships and bursaries available to ensure that the most talented students can access training, regardless of their financial circumstances.

Full-time acting courses:
• BA (Hons) Professional Acting (3 years). Minimum entry age is 18. Admission is by audition and interview.
• BA (Hons) Production & Technical Arts: Stage & Screen (3 years). Minimum entry age is 18. Admission is by interview.
• Foundation in Stage and Screen (CertHe) (6 months). Minimum entry age is 18. Admission is by audition and/or interview.
• MFA Professional Acting (2 years). Minimum entry age is 18, but due to the experience necessary for this course, most students will be 21 and over and hold a first degree in a relevant subject. Admission is by audition and interview.
• MA Classical Acting for the Professional Theatre (one year). This course is for students with a BA or BFA degree or equivalent. Students without this qualification must demonstrate a comparable level of knowledge and experience. Admission is by audition and interview.
• MFA Classical Acting: Performance & Practice (18 months). Minimum entry age is 18, but due to the experience necessary for this course, most students will

be 21 and over and hold a first degree in a relevant subject. Admission is by audition and interview.
• MA Musical Theatre (one year). Minimum entry age of 21. This is an advanced-level course for those who have a Musical Theatre BA/BFA or professional experience. Admission is by audition and interview.
• MFA Musical Theatre (18 months). Minimum entry age of 21. This is an advanced-level course for those who have a Musical Theatre BA/BFA or professional experience. Admission is by audition and interview.
• MA Directing (one year). Minimum entry age of 18. Applicants must have an undergraduate degree or equivalent professional experience. Admission is by interview.

Please visit **www.lamda.ac.uk** for further details, application deadlines and fees, as well as information on all other LAMDA courses.

The Liverpool Institute for Performing Arts (LIPA)*

Mount Street, Liverpool L1 9HF
tel 0151 330 3000
email admissions@lipa.ac.uk
website www.lipa.ac.uk
Facebook /LIPALiverpool
X @LIPALiverpool
Instagram @lipaliverpool
Principal & Ceo Professor Sean McNamara

LIPA offers the following acting courses – Foundation Acting (Stage & Screen), Foundation Acting (Musical Theatre), BA (Hons) Acting, BA (Hons) Acting (Musicianship), BA (Hons) Acting (Musical Theatre), BA Hons Acting (Screen & Digital Media), MA Acting.

Full-time acting courses:

• Foundation Acting (Stage & Screen) and Foundation Acting (Musical Theatre) (one year). Aimed at people who are passionate about a career as an actor or in musical theatre but not quite ready for a conservatoire-level degree course. It's an opportunity to immerse yourself in rigorous training that will prepare you for auditions, accredited drama school and degree-level training.
• BA (Hons) Acting (3 years). This course focuses on the individual. You are not just an actor, but also an artist. At LIPA you can become an independent, inventive practitioner. You can be someone who harnesses what's unique to you and tackles diverse performance styles across different platforms.
• BA (Hons) Acting (Musicianship) (3 years). LIPA offers training that prepares actors with instrumental skills for rehearsal, performance, production, interdisciplinary creation, and industry engagement.
• BA (Hons) Acting (Musical Theatre) (3 years). This intensive and practical course aims to create highly skilled actors who are accomplished singers and dancers. These multi-faceted performers will be equipped to work in classic and contemporary musical theatre.
• BA (Hons) Acting (Screen & Digital Media) (3 years). Our intensive and practical course focuses on fundamental technical acting skills, while putting you at the cutting edge of acting for screen and digital platforms.
• BA (Hons) Acting (Contemporary Performance) (3 years). For actors interested in experimental and innovative approaches to storytelling. You will develop essential acting skills while working across media to develop unique multidisciplinary and non-conventional ways of engaging audiences.
• MA Acting (one year). This intensive and highly practical MA will enable you to develop and enhance your acting skills to a professional level. Guided by LIPA's world-class teaching team you will become part of a creative and collaborative community.

Liverpool Theatre School

35 Sefton Road, Liverpool L8 5SL
tel 0151 728 7800
email info@liverpooltheatreschool.co.uk
website www.liverpooltheatreschool.co.uk
Facebook /LiverpoolTheatreSchool
X @LTSchool
Instagram @liverpooltheatreschool

Performing arts centre based in the heart of Liverpool offering the highest standard of training from beginners' classes to full-time professional training. Aims to produce musical theatre performers, dancers and actors that have the skills, knowledge and attitude to be successful in an increasingly demanding profession. Application form can be downloaded online and sent to **auditions@liverpoolcentralstudios.com**. Courses for those 16 and above.

Courses offered:

• BTEC Level 3 Extended Diploma in Musical Theatre
• Diploma in Professional Musical Theatre (Level 6) (3 years)
• Diploma in Professional Dance – Contemporary Dance (Level 5) (2 years)
• Diploma in Professional Dance (Level 6) (3 years)

Level 6 courses are accredited by Trinity College, London.

London School of Dramatic Art

4 Bute Street, London SW7 3EX
tel 020-7581 6100
email enquiries@lsda-acting.com
website www.lsda-acting.com
Facebook /LSDA.Acting
X @LSDA_Acting
Instagram @lsda_acting
Principal Jake Taylor, *Administrator* Hana Kovacs

Offers a range of comprehensive courses designed to develop individual creative talents, and to provide a thorough grounding in all aspects of performance as part of a student's preparation for a working life as an actor. There is currently no wheelchair access to the

Drama schools

main building or training rooms: if this affects applicants who would like to know when these spaces become accessible, please let the school know. All auditions are free and no international student fees are charged. No formal qualifications are required as the training is vocational: "We look more at potential and at levels of creativity."

Full-time courses:
- Advanced Diploma in Acting (1 year). No public funding available. Applications should be made to the school by the end of September. Applicants must be aged 18 or over.
- Foundation Diploma in Acting (1 year). No public funding available. Applications should be made direct to the school by the end of September. Applicants must be aged 18 or over.

London School of Musical Theatre
83 Borough Road, London SE1 1DN
tel 020-7407 4455
email info@lsmt.co.uk
email auditions@lsmt.co.uk
website www.lsmt.co.uk
Facebook /LondonSchoolMusicalTheatre
X @TheLSMT
Instagram @thelsmt
Principal & Course Producer Adrian Jeckells

Full-time courses:
- Musical Theatre Diploma Course (1 year). Age range for entry is 18–35.

London Studio Centre (LSC)
artsdepot, 5 Nether Street, Tally Ho Corner, North Finchley, London N12 0GA
tel 020-7837 7741
email info@londonstudiocentre.ac.uk
website www.londonstudiocentre.org
Facebook /LdnStudioCentre
Instagram @ldnstudiocentre
Director Nic Espinosa, *Dean of Studies* Robert Penman

London Studio Centre is a professional dance and musical theatre conservatoire accredited by the Council for Dance, Drama and Musical Theatre (CDMT).

Courses include:
- BA (Hons) Professional Dance Performance
- FdA Dance Performance
- CertHE Dance and Musical Theatre
- BA (Hons) Professional Performance (top up)
- MA Dance Performance
- MA Dance Producing and Management
- MA Dance Education/PG Cert Teaching Professional Theatre Dance
- London Studio Centre Associate Programme

Courses validated by Middlesex University. LSC's facilities include state-of-the-art dance and drama studios and access to fully equipped theatres. LSC graduates are regularly seen performing on stage in London's West End and in international dance companies.

Manchester School of Theatre at MMU*
Cavendish Street, Manchester M15 6BG
website www.theatre.mmu.ac.uk

Full-time acting courses:
- BA (Hons) Acting (3 years full-time). Applicants must be aged 18 or over with 3 A levels or equivalent. Applications should be made through UCAS by January.
- BA (Hons) Drama and Contemporary Performance (3 years, full-time; 6 years, part-time). Applicants must be 18 or over with 3 A levels or equivalent. Applications should be made through UCAS.
- MA/MFA Performance. Applicants must be aged 21 or over with a degree in a related subject. (1 year/18 months).

Mountview*
120 Peckham Hill Street, London SE15 5JT
tel 020-8881 2201
email enquiries@mountview.org.uk
website www.mountview.org.uk
Facebook /mountviewldn
X @mountviewLDN
Instagram @mountviewldn
Principal Sally Ann Gritton

Full-time acting and musical theatre courses:
Applications for the courses listed below should be made direct to the school.

BAs validated by the University of East Anglia and Trinity College London. Applicants must be aged 18 or over at the start of the course. Entry is based on performance at audition, previous formal academic qualifications are not essential. Dance and Drama Awards are available for a significant number of students.
- BA (Hons) Performance – Acting (3 years)
- BA (Hons) Performance – Actor Musicianship (3 years)
- BA (Hons) Performance – Musical Theatre (3 years)
- BMus (Hons) Piano for Theatre (3 years)

MAs validated by the University of East Anglia. Applicants must be aged 21 years or over at the start of the course. Students who do not hold an undergraduate degree will need to undertake an access assignment to establish suitability for undertaking the MA.
- MA/MFA Creative Practice - Producing (MA one year/MFA 2 years)
- MA/MFA Creative Practice - Directing (MA one year/MFA 2 years)
- MA/MFA Creative Practice - Dramatic Writing (MA one year/MFA 2 years)
- MA/MFA Music Direction (MA one year/MFA 2 years)

- MA Performance - Acting (one year)
- MA Performance - Musical Theatre (one year)
- MA Theatre for Community and Education (2 years part-time)
- MA Site-Specific Theatre Practice (one year)
- MA Theatre Directing (one year)
- MFA Intimacy Practice (2 years)

Oxford School of Drama*
Sansomes Farm Studios, Woodstock,
Oxford OX20 1ER
tel (01993) 812883
email info@oxforddrama.ac.uk
website www.oxforddrama.ac.uk
Facebook /TheOxfordSchoolofDrama
Instagram @oxford_drama
Principal Edward Hicks

The smallest of the drama schools, it has a 94% employment rate and an 'Outstanding' Ofsted rating. Provides a significant number of Dance and Drama Awards and Advanced Learner Loans for its One and 3 Year courses.

The 3 Year and One Year courses are recognised by industries around the world, boasting successful alumni including writers, directors, filmmakers and actors, Claire Foy (*The Crown*), Freddie Dennis (*Queen Charlotte: A Bridgerton Story*) and Dipo Ola (*Ludwig*) are 3 recent examples. Graduates of the 6-month Foundation Courses in Acting and Acting with Musical Theatre include Aimee Lou Wood (*White Lotus*) and Nicola Coughlan (*Bridgerton*), with onward destinations including RADA, LAMDA, Bristol Old Vic Theatre School, and their own 3 and One Year Courses. Entry for all courses is by audition only, and there are audition fee waivers available. Visit **www.oxforddrama.ac.uk/apply** to find out more.

Full-time acting courses: Applications for the courses listed below should be made direct to the school.

- 3 Year Acting Course. Applicants must be aged 18 or over.
- One Year Acting Course. Applicants must be aged 21 or over.

Courses validated by Trinity College London and Equity membership is award to all who complete the course.

Royal Academy of Dramatic Art (RADA)*
62–64 Gower Street, London WC1E 6ED
tel 020-7636 7076
email enquiries@rada.ac.uk
website www.rada.ac.uk
Facebook /RoyalAcademyofDramaticArt
Instagram @royalacademyofdramaticart
Principal Niamh Dowling

RADA offers vocational training for actors, stage managers, designers and technical stage craft specialists.

Full-time undergraduate and postgraduate courses:
- Foundation Course in Acting (non-HE)
- Foundation Degree (FdA) in Technical Theatre and Stage Management
- BA (Hons) in Acting
- BA (Hons) in Technical Theatre and Stage Management (progression year)
- MA Theatre Lab
- MA Theatre Costume
- MA Playwriting
- MA Performance Lighting Design
- MA Stage Management

RADA makes it possible for students to become courageous artists through practical, intensive and rigorous training, offered at the highest level of teaching with unparalleled links to the industry. Its impressive track record of graduates are award-winners and leaders in their field across theatre, film, television and audio. Graduates are employed as actors, directors, writers, producers; lighting, sound, costume and prop designers, scenic artists; stage managers and production managers.

RADA also creates opportunities for the wider community to engage with training through short courses and widening participation projects.

Rose Bruford College*
Lamorbey Park, Burnt Oak Lane, Sidcup DA15 9DF
tel 020-8308 2600
email hello@bruford.ac.uk
website www.bruford.ac.uk
X @rosebruford
Instagram @rosebruford
Principal & Ceo Prof. Randall Whittaker

Full-time acting courses: Applicants for the BA degree courses listed below must be over the age of 18 with the equivalent of a minimum of 2 A levels at grade C or above. BA Applications should be made through UCAS. Applicants for MA courses should be aged 21 or over and apply through the college website.

- Foundation Course in Dance and Musical Theatre (Cert HE) (one year)
- BA (Hons) Acting for Screen and Devised Performance (3 years)
- BA (Hons) Acting (3 years)
- BA (Hons) Actor Musicianship (3 years)
- BA (Hons) American Theatre Arts (3 years)
- BA (Hons) Contemporary and Popular Performance (3 years)
- BA (Hons) European Theatre Arts (3 years)
- MA/MFA Actor and Performer Training (one to 2 years)
- MA/MFA Actor Musicianship (one to 2 years)
- MFA Advanced Devising practice (2 years)
- MA/MFA Collaborative Theatre Making (one to 2 years)
- MA Devised Theatre and Performance (one year)
- MA/MFA Queer Performance (one to 2 years)
- MA/MFA Theatre for Children and Young People (one to 2 years)

Royal Academy of Music
Musical Theatre Department, Marylebone Road,
London NW1 5HT
tel 020-7873 7373
website www.ram.ac.uk/study/departments/musical-theatre
Gatsby Chair of Musical Theatre Daniel Bowling MMUS

Students are enrolled at the Royal Academy of Music, an institution of world renown, training students for more than 190 years. Students study for University of London degrees. Fellow students include instrumentalists, composers, jazz and commercial musicians, pianists and opera singers.

Full-time acting courses:
- MA Musical Theatre performance (one year)
- Musical Theatre performance (PGCert) (one year)

Aimed at graduates, mature students and experienced performers wishing to undertake a career in musical theatre. The course provides an intensive training in singing, acting, movement and voice to students of postgraduate (or equivalent) level. Includes extensive one-to-one tuition with expert tutors and industry showcase, projects for invited industry guests and public performances.

Royal Birmingham Conservatoire*
200 Jennens Road, Birmingham B4 7XG
tel 0121 331 5000
email conservatoire@bcu.ac.uk
website www.bcu.ac.uk/conservatoire/acting
Facebook /RoyalBirmCons
X @BirmCons
Instagram @mybcu
Principal Stephen Maddock, *Vice Principal (Acting)* Stephen Simms

Full-time acting courses:
- BA Applied Theatre
- BA Stage Management
- BA Acting
- MA/MFA/PgDip Acting

The Royal Central School of Speech and Drama*

ROYAL CENTRAL
SCHOOL OF SPEECH & DRAMA

UNIVERSITY OF LONDON

University of London, Eton Avenue,
London NW3 3HY
tel 020-7722 8183
email openevents@cssd.ac.uk
website www.cssd.ac.uk
Principal Josette Bushell Mingo OBE

Scholarships/Bursaries Central has a range of scholarships and bursaries available for students on undergraduate and postgraduate programmes. Visit the website for further details.

Undergraduate courses:

Performance
- BA (Hons) Acting: Classical and Contemporary
- BA (Hons) Acting: Contemporary and Devised
- BA (Hons) Acting: Musical Theatre

Practice
- BA (Hons) Drama and Applied Theatre
- BA (Hons) Performance and Contempoary Arts
- BA (Hons) Writing for Performance

Producing
- BA (Hons) Costume Production
- BA (Hons) Performance Design
- BA (Hons) Production Arts: Props, Painting and Set
- BA (Hons) Production Technologies and Stage Management

All applications to be made via UCAS by 14 January 2026.

Postgraduate courses:

Central offers a range of specialist MA course for those holding an undergraduate degree or with relevant experience. 2-year MFAs are also available in some course areas. All postgraduate applications should be made direct through Central's website.
- Acting Classical
- Acting Contemporary
- Acting for Screen
- Actor Training and Coaching
- Advanced Theatre Practice
- Applied Theatre
- Creative Producing
- Drama and Movement Therapy
- Movement: Directing and Teaching
- Musical Theatre: Acting and Performance
- Scenography
- Voice Studies: Teaching and Coaching
- Writing for Theatre, Film, Radio and Television

Royal Conservatoire of Scotland*
100 Renfrew Street, Glasgow G2 3DB
tel 0141 332 4101
email hello@rcs.ac.uk
website www.rcs.ac.uk
Facebook /rcsofficial
Instagram @rcsofficial
Principal Jeffrey Sharkey, *Director of the School of Stage & Screen* Marc Silberschatz

Founded in 1847, Scotland's national conservatoire is a global leader in performing arts education, consistently ranked in the top 10 of the QS World University Rankings. Specialist tuition across music, drama, dance, production, film and education under one roof creates an environment where artists move between disciplines, immersed in a culture of creativity and collaboration that sparks bold new work and ways of thinking.

Full-time acting programmes: Applications for the undergraduate courses listed below should be made via **www.ucas.com/ucas/conservatoires** by 14 January 2026. Applications for postgraduate courses listed below should also be made via UCAS by 31 March 2026. Please email **hello@rcs.ac.uk** for more information.

Courses available:
- BA Acting (full-time, 3 years)
- BA Performance for Deaf and Hard of Hearing Actors (full-time, 3 years)
- BA Musical Theatre (full-time, 3 years)
- Professional Graduate Diploma in Musical Directing (full-time, one year)
- MA Musical Theatre - Musical Directing (full-time, one year)
- MA Classical and Contemporary Text - Acting/Directing (full-time, one year)
- MFA Classical and Contemporary Text - Acting/Directing (full-time, 16 months)

Royal Welsh College of Music & Drama*

Castle Grounds, Cathays Park, Cardiff CF10 3ER
tel 029-2039 1361
email admissions@rwcmd.ac.uk
website www.rwcmd.ac.uk/study/acting, www.rwcmd.ac.uk/study/musical-theatre
Principal Helena Gaunt, *Director of Performance* Jonathan Mumby, *Head of Drama Performance* Ali de Souza, *Head of Musical Theatre* Vivien Care

Full-time acting courses:
Applications should be made through UCAS Conservatoires and not directly to the college.

- BA (Hons) Acting (3 years, full time). In this intensive practical and performance-based training course, you'll gain the skills and experience you need to sustain a career in theatre, screen and digital media. There is a range of support in place to help cover the cost of tuition, the details of which will depend on where the student normally lives.
- BA (Hons) Musical Theatre (3 years, full time). Explore a diverse range of singing, spoken voice, dance and acting methods in our course with numerous performance projects and at fully staged productions. There is a range of support in place to help cover the cost of tuition, the details of which will depend on where the student normally lives.
- MA Acting for Stage, Screen and Recorded Media (13 months, full time). Launch your acting career with intensive expert-led tuition and practical studio and rehearsal-based training in a professional working environment. Applicants should normally be at least 21 years old by the time of enrolment.
- MA Musical Theatre (10 months, full time). Meet the demands of today's industry with our course that blends acting and dance classes with one-to-one singing lessons and roles in two public performances. Applicants should normally be at least 21 years old by the time of enrolment.

Taking charge of your creative journey

Kalungi Ssebandeke

How do you as an actor take charge of your creative journey? Especially when your profession is heavily reliant on waiting for others in order for you to do your job. What do I mean by that? As a professional actor, arguably you need an agent who will put you forward for work. You then hopefully will be seen for auditions, courtesy of a casting director who will present you to a director or the producing team who then decide whether to hire you. The waiting during these processes can feel interminable.

Now, if you're Denzel Washington or Angela Bassett, admittedly you skip a lot of these steps, but even they have to do some waiting. The difference is that they have reached a stage in their career where they control what they wish to do. They have even gone as far as creating production companies to generate projects that they can produce or star in. The question then is: why don't you try to do the same? I can almost hear you scream in response, *because I'm not Denzel or Angela!* Well, here's my response to that, no, you're not, but you can take inspiration from them and take control of your creative journey to a great extent.

I'm hoping by the end of this article you will feel inspired to pursue this and feel more in the driving seat of your career.

Step One: Training

In order to improve your craft as an actor, you obviously need to sharpen your skills. You can do this via acting work like I did for close to ten years before I then went to drama school. There are advantages to this route: you follow gut instinct, draw on natural talent, take big risks due to lack of self-awareness or even not knowing how things are "meant" to be done. You can be electric, raw! But eventually the fuel may run out of the tank. You may come to a roadblock where there are only so many roles you feel you can successfully play, or be "allowed" to play, without a better understanding of the craft.

Now, I'm not suggesting that only when you train at a drama school do you get to have a flourishing career. There are plenty of actors who didn't train. But, as I found in this situation, there are likely to be roles you would like to do that feel to be out of your reach, both career wise and skill set-wise, if you haven't had this dedicated time in training.

In the past, the repertory model (where actors rehearse and perform multiple plays simultaneously) offered actors training through work and this was an invaluable and compelling alternative to training in an institutional setting. However, there aren't as many repertory companies these days so opportunities there are limited. Screen work is now prioritised over theatre and theatre itself is fast becoming exclusive to big name screen actors or a victim of a dearth in funding, so taking risks on untrained actors is becoming less likely.

To some people drama school can hold little appeal or just not feel to be a feasible option. I mean, why should I spend three years learning to do something I can do for free at my local theatre? Why pay all that money to be out of the industry and potentially miss out on being cast in that Netflix series? What if I simply can't afford the fees and everything attached to them? These are all valid questions. My response is this, however: if it's your first degree you're eligible for a student loan (though I appreciate you may not want to have a debt upon graduating); if you've got a degree already, there are scholarships available if you ask the prospective school and some drama schools have gone as far as waiving audition fees in order to make their doors as open as possible. A financial barrier should not limit your access to actor training, which is something many drama schools agree with. To remedy this, they ensure that all students offered a place get access to financial support, but they do encourage you to be proactive and do further research. For example, LAMDA offers scholarship support for 28% of their students. The Guildhall School of Music and Drama awards £2m worth of scholarships annually to eligible students, "awarded on the basis of talent, potential and individual financial need." So, do not let lack of access to tuition fees block you from pursuing acting training because as highlighted above there is support available.

As for the duration of the degree, firstly, it can be as short as one year. Secondly, even three years will seem brief in the grand scheme of things, assuming you go on to pursue a long and productive acting career. After nine years of professional acting, I then set aside three years to finally train at the Guildhall School of Music and Drama. I was told by some of my peers that I didn't need to train as I was working already. But for me it wasn't just about working, it was about the quality of work. Granted, prior to drama school I did a plethora of great jobs for TV and stage. But I felt in my gut that I could do more and three years' training was what I felt I needed to do in order to get the skills required to take on the roles I was hankering after.

Fortunately for me that worked out. I immediately was cast in a production of *Blood Knot*, a two-hander written by Athol Fugard and directed by Matthew Xia at the Orange Tree Theatre, a role for which I was nominated for Best Male Performance at the 2019 Offies. Three years later, I was cast as Othello in a production directed by Paul Hart and Anjali Mehra at the Watermill Theatre. Would I have played these roles had I not trained? Some may say yes; I say no. I wouldn't know where to start with even feeling confident enough to fathom taking on the role of Othello. But having spent three years honing my voice, movement and acting technique in a conservatoire setting, I felt ready and capable to take on these challenging roles and more.

That's what good training at drama school does for you as an actor. It exposes you to the very foundations of your voice and your body as an instrument. It gives you access to a technique that makes you a well-rounded actor who can tackle anything so that you can confidently demand with authority more challenging roles. And when you do get them, you are in good stead to take them on and not feel completely out of your depth like I did during my short stint at the RSC as an untrained actor. We all get overwhelmed, but an untrained actor can lack resilience to the point where a role becomes too much. Drama school strengthens that resilience and hopefully gives you the stamina, as well as a toolkit, to combat any doubts or problems that may arise.

Step Two: The Industry

What does it mean to be a working actor in the industry? What does that look like? Is it going constantly from job to job? Is it eight auditions a month? Is it award ceremonies? It can be all of those things. But it can also look like auditioning once every three months and sometimes even less. It can look like working on a school tour of a play no one else will ever see. It can look like doing 10 short films or it can look like having one line in a *Star Wars* film. The industry is that varied. But you can find ways to make it work for you.

If you have an agent, it doesn't mean you can rest on your laurels. Many agents are on a salary; they work for whatever parent company owns their agency or whoever their boss is. They may have hundreds of clients, so realistically you're not on their minds as much as they are on yours. As sad as it is, the industry isn't waiting for you. It was there before you and it will be there after you. So, don't think it owes you anything.

I would suggest that whatever job you take on, make sure it progresses your career. If it's a school tour of a new play, use that as a chance to try out a new accent or work on a skill that you feel is lacking. If it's one line in a *Star Wars* movie, then get that footage and put it at the start of your showreel. If you don't feel to be hearing enough from your current agent, contact a new agent and lead with the fact that you're in an upcoming *Star Wars* film and are looking for new representation to help you leverage this strong credit. If you are auditioning only once every three months, seek out some feedback from casting directors or from your agent. In those three months, take up a martial art or a new physical skill. This is key because it will not only help with discipline, but it will give you a new skill that will make you more attractive as an actor. And if martial arts are not your thing, then prepare your body and your mind, as well sharpening your voice, accent and acting techniques, through classes.

Don't let too much time go by without any creative fulfillment. The industry can seem like an impenetrable fortress and in some ways it is. There are so many barriers to entry, but there are ways in which you can kick those barriers down on your own terms without the frustration of waiting for others to do it for you. There is no shame in having a part-time job to pay rent plus other expenses. In fact, I would actively encourage you to get a job that can alleviate the financial stress you may feel when not working as an actor. I have done every kind of job, from being a drama teacher and stacking shelves in ASDA to working as a night porter in a hotel. And, as frustrating as it was to not be doing what I loved at the time, that brought me satisfaction knowing that I would have money to pay my rent, to travel, to go out on dates and to make my short films, but also to save and contribute to my pension. This is the reality of life as an actor. You need to think about these things. It may seem awkward to say that you stack shelves at ASDA, but how else will you pay your bills? It may be embarrassing to say you still live at home with your parents, but why? Why not stay there, save your money and move out once you have enough for a deposit and have a job that allows you to pay your mortgage? Do not allow any outside noise of what an actor's life "should" be like to influence how you live your life.

Many actors end up also being writers or directors. I am one of those actors. Michaela Coel is one of those actors. Phoebe Waller-Bridge is one of those actors. I understand the insistence for many of you to only focus on acting. After all, that's what you trained in. But, at the same time, the goal is to work as an actor. And if it means writing yourself a role in your play or directing a film in which you cast yourself then why not? Crucially, it also gives you a well-rounded idea of the creative process. And, most importantly, it gives you creative autonomy. You can rest assured that you don't need to take every acting job that comes your way because you've written yourself a scorcher of a role.

To really take charge of your creative journey you should set goals: Specific, Relevant Achievable, Measurable and Time-Based. If you want to be performing at the National Theatre in five years' time then you need to look into how to work towards that. It may mean training for three years at a drama school, shooting a monologue to add to your showreel, or inviting a National Theatre casting director to your showcase or to the first play out of drama school. At the end of the year, you should review your goals and see how close you are to achieving them and what you need to do to make them a reality. Don't stress if you don't get there; you may need to re-adjust.

Taking charge of your creative journey can seem like a taxing task, filled with seemingly insurmountable obstacles, but I personally feel that the creative rewards that you gradually accumulate in the form of self-actualisation, improved skillsets and a more proactive mind-set will make you a more creatively fulfilled and liberated actor.

Kalungi Ssebandeke is an award-winning actor/writer/director. Trained at the Guildhall School of Music and Drama, his acting credits include the titular role of Othello at The Watermill and *Blood Knot* by Athol Fugard at the Orange Tree. As a writer his debut play, *Assata Taught Me*, was staged at the Gate Theatre starring Adjoa Andoh. He was the recipient of the Roland Rees Bursary in 2020. In 2023 he won the JMK Directing Award for his production of *Meetings* by Mustapha Matura at the Orange Tree. He is the founder of directoyourfirstplay.com and regularly works as a project director at LAMDA.

What are drama schools looking for?
Geoffrey Colman

A lifelong contract

Many drama school applicants underestimate the fact that becoming an actor is about signing a sort of lifelong and extraordinary contract that contains the most incredible clause – one that requires the artist to metaphorically go to places both dark and light, to represent, live and die for us. Seven times a week or in fourteen takes. To successfully navigate such challenges one must possess a licence, for to 'go there' is not something that everybody can or wants to do. Not everybody has the talent. Not everybody is prepared to dedicate the years of preparation required to become an actor. Alas, many also underestimate the phenomenal personal responsibility of such an undertaking and delude themselves that it can be achieved by just wanting it very much – like a child wants ice-cream. I have not found this to be the case.

With the ongoing accusations of institutional racism and cultural elitism that the wider cultural sector continue to address, the drama school has also had to confront its now historic idea of training, and think again, very seriously, about how it can be something more than just a place for a few hand-picked individuals. As the enormity of the 2020 global pandemic became desperately apparent, the operational challenges faced by many drama schools in the UK – how to train its talented students online, remotely, far away from their world-famous studios; were superseded by longer-held, ethical questions about what tradition, in the light of 'Black Lives Matter' and 'Me Too', even meant – and certainly what it looked like. Whilst classes and rehearsals temporarily moved onto zoom, the sector set about reimagining its curriculum in the longer term. A post-pandemic return, never again legitimising discourses that had historically reproduced particular forms of classed, 'raced' and gendered exclusion. The conservatoire always, famously, aspired to the idea of industry 'nearness' but its historic enactment of this was formed by a profession awash with poor practices, received normative paradigms, prejudices and general professional 'truths' handed down as performance rules or lineage. The training sector has responded with urgent forcible change, and whilst their historic studios may remain the same, the environment in which professional training now happens is both alert to its past failings and hugely ambitious of real long-lasting positive change.

The professional or conservatoire sector comprises schools that subscribe to, and are measured by, a set of overarching industry-approved principles held by the Federation of Drama Schools (FDS) www.federationofdramaschools.co.uk. The core principles state that the selection process is by audition, and that training will be professionally aligned, intensive, and delivering at least 900 hours of practical contact teaching a year. Many thousands apply to the FDS schools each year, for a precious few places. Of course, conservatoire training is not for everyone. There are many university drama departments where the courses, whilst not offering 30+ professional contact hours per week, do offer a vast range of performance-related academic disciplines that can be studied both theoretically and practically. Such programmes, though perhaps less specialist, do offer the student excellent opportunities to act, write, and direct whilst developing their own individual performance interests and skills.

28 Training

Recent years have seen emerge a vast catalogue of non-professional diploma and degree-awarding courses offering performance-related study and preparation. Often curated by established conservatoires, such courses give the less experienced performer invaluable insight into the ways of the conservatoire system, and are particularly useful when considering whether professional actor training is a viable option.

What are you looking for? Do your research

Despite the existence of excellent regulating bodies such as the Quality Assurance Agency – which sets important benchmarks for the delivery of training, published student surveys and the names of famous alumni – across the conservatoire drama schools there is significant variation in terms of funding (including tuition top-up fees), quality of training, award outcomes (certificate, diploma, degree), and most certainly graduate employment prospects, which differ from school to school. So never mind the question about what are drama schools looking for – what are *you* looking for? Most candidates have such a limited, almost passive, expectation about what drama schools want at audition, and of the actual training itself. The first task is, therefore, not to perfect some extraordinarily well-honed accent or radical audition monologue interpretation, but rather, many months prior to this process, to undertake a sleeves-rolled-up systematic approach to a lot of very necessary research into the sector itself. If you are going to commit three years of your life to something, you really should find out what that something is!

All drama schools and university drama departments publish their entry requirements in either a glossy prospectus or more typically on a website, but, these only really describe required entry criteria, a brief course outline and, in the case of some drama schools, a list of suggested classical audition speeches. Drama schools require potential students to audition, whilst it is not unusual for the university sector to offer some, but not all, candidates an interview and workshop. Entry requirements and selection criteria vary from institution to institution, but in general terms, the university sector is looking for well-qualified students with excellent A-level or equivalent qualifications. The conservatoire sector, on the other hand, bases its selection much more on audition success than exam grades and is looking for 'evidence of ongoing commitment to acting' (such as having played featured roles in youth theatre production companies), 'evidence of a trainable voice and body', 'evidence of intellectual, emotional and physical skills', and so on. These competencies are all there waiting on the audition panellist's check list. There is not a section that refers to 'tingle factor' or 'star quality' because this is only found on the fame TV panellist's laminated sheet. Equally, there isn't an additional sub-criteria requirement listing particular body types to balance future casting designs not yet discussed.

The choice of audition speech preoccupies many candidates who unearth an astounding range of two-minute extracts – often inappropriately sourced from internet material that disallows any creative placement of their own heart and mind. Don't obsess about contrasting this or the other. Just select an extract from a play that is simple, clear, unfussy and – most important of all – one that allows for you to enter its world without a fight (and most certainly without the need to show that you are entering it). People do bring much worked-upon accents, props, shouts, peculiar moves, glances and screams, as though volume alone will do the trick. This should be avoided. Remember, too, that audition panellists experience the gamut of human suffering in two-minute chunks. But emotion in itself is not the gold medal if it is false, inappropriate or showy (especially without real context). The audition day is not merely there to equip the candidate with a jolly site tour or a space within which to recite a contrasting classical and contemporary speech. It might even, just possibly, offer some sort of snatched insight into how the course might be taught. To enter the world of drama school depends upon something far more fundamental than a set of well-worn, clichéd, seen-it-in-the-movies assumptions.

Both the conservatoire and university sector see the value of Open Day events – and so should you. The real answers required are sometimes just a little bit more abstract. Open Days afford a terrific and all-important onsite 'experience' of the building, its community of staff and students, and general but –nevertheless important – 'feel' of the place. Training institutions have rightly been questioned about how they construct their communities and, in particular, what they are doing to increase diversity. A recent parliamentary enquiry into access and diversity in the performing arts concluded that, despite many positive initiatives, drama schools needed to reform. One long-held perception that is difficult to dispel is that the whole audition process is very expensive. Whereas university drama departments accept applications via a centralised UCAS system, drama schools also ask for an additional fee. Many of the conservatoires within the Federation of Drama Schools now offer audition-fee waivers – offering free or heavily subsidized auditions to those facing the greatest barriers to attending.

If possible, attend a few plays or musicals performed by final-year students from different schools or departments as this can be extremely useful in that it demonstrates a very public slice of the quality of teaching and professional guidance offered. Once started, this level of cultural forensic work will certainly enable you to identify at least where you would like to study. But why do you want to become an actor? This is the real question that you must ask. Not so that you can decorate your application form or personal statement with incredible, but quite useless, prose (as often audition candidates do), but rather, align all future coordinates to it. You will need to refer to this answer for the rest of your life.

Audition actively, with clarity and commitment

It was the jaded theatre producer Emmanuel Azenberg who pessimistically described how successful entry into the ranks of the professional Broadway musical chorus required an alarming, but necessary, process of becoming a kind of *fabulous invalid* – a gradual giving up of self and becoming unable to do or cope with anything other than being in the chorus itself – never really knowing who deals the cards – and, in fact, never really knowing what the game is in the first place! Having been involved with drama school auditions for many years, I would suggest that his observation might just as well apply as a cautionary tale to those many thousands of audition candidates that approach the day with all-too-little consideration for the task and commitment ahead.

The craft of acting is not limited to a single method or approach; it is joyfully promiscuous. But for every actor we witness on our screens or in the theatre itself we also encounter a different sort of promiscuity. Some actors are famously trained and some are just famous, possessing a peculiar, but much desired, cultural tag. The 'celebrity' is often 'untrained', but connected to the performance industry by events that afford measurable charisma, enigma or sensation. As such celebrities may not in the short term need a drama school training, but rather, a constant stream of tabloid stories showing hasty late-night retreats from exclusive bars and restaurants. Such activities can (and occasionally do) open doors and give entry into the industry – but the hinges that hold them are tissue-thin – and the doors will not always remain permanently open!

Look diligently before you leap

Training is not casual, but quite conservative and very ordered indeed. One class follows another and then another. How do you fit into this delightful regime? It can be repetitive and exhausting. The panel will look for signs of someone who can cope with this or not. A professional training is a physical, emotional, muscular assimilation of many processes. Learning lines is not the issue – but learning the difficult routine and discipline of acting can be. The audition is as much about assessing this point as to whether a given Juliet or Hamlet is believable.

Like many momentous occasions in life the drama school audition can be so very memorable. Like the first day of the school summer holidays or the first page of a new novel or even your first kiss. For there to be a first day at drama school is an achievement in itself. And yet to audition is to be part of an occasion mixed with both excitement and fear. Excitement in that all the waiting and preparation is over – but also fear regarding what happens if a place is not offered. To be an acting student at a conservatoire drama school is not to be part of something that is either casual or meaningless. But success in the current climate is now also measured by other indictors. Most students juggle outside work commitments with a very heavy workload of study and somehow exist on far less money than is possible. Drama school training is impacting – it marks all those who experience it. Yes every move, every gesture and vocal shift is catalogued for later dissection. But this is why to be trained is not to take an unfathomable leap in the dark. Sacrifices will have to be made and we must ensure that in the new funding climate becoming an artist will not render a fearful voiceless future to all but a privileged few.

What drama schools want is to restore the helplessness of our own lives through the long productive and meaningful careers of future artists like you. Don't take an unfathomable leap. Only if you're utterly convinced should you sign the training contract – but prepare for this moment with diligence, care and humility. Good luck!

Geoffrey Colman works as a professional acting coach in theatre, film and TV, having been Professor/Head of Acting at The Royal Central School of Speech and Drama for many years. See more at **www.geoffcolman.com**.

Reframing the future of actor training

Pamela Jikiemi

For much of the 20th century, the entertainment industry was dominated by theatre. Highly regarded venues in the heartland of theatre in London's prestigious West End and renowned companies like the Royal Shakespeare Company (RSC) and what is now the Royal National Theatre (NT) set the standard for theatrical excellence.

Conservatoire drama schools teaching actor training extensively over 36+ contact hours a week, at a minimum of five to six days a week, over three years, offered the gold standard of vocational, intensive, rigorous, classical actor training. This conservatoire model focused purely on the development of craft, training the actor's imagination, voice, body and physicality, exploring stagecraft and presence. It provided the actor the ability to not only feel a lot, but to feel it on demand, to live truthfully in imaginary circumstances and to perform in front of a live audience.

This classical training, with its emphasis on Shakespeare, Ancient Greek, Restoration and Jacobean drama, had been taught from the viewpoint of differing practitioners, most of which sprung from Constantin Stanislavski and his codified approach. The vocal delivery was required to come from the base of the speech system predicated around Received Pronunciation (RP). The repertory theatre (rep) circuit, where an actor could build on their training by switching roles two or three times a week, had been the main point of entry for aspiring actors trained as well as the untrained. However, provincial audiences were increasingly unwilling to pay to see a cast of unknowns continue their practical education on the rep circuit. Television and the development of continuing drama increasingly provided that 'learning on the job' function.

The rep circuit was, therefore, on the wane by the time I was offered a place at drama school and yet repertory theatre had been my main reason for applying. My plan had been to train at drama school and then join a repertory company to embed the training, which to me seemed straightforward. But being the only Black and Global Majority student at the drama school I attended at that time, I soon came to realise that British Black and Global Majority actors had long struggled to gain acceptance into the profession. This was due to a few reasons but mainly as highlighted by the activist Naseem Khan in 1975.

Naseem Khan's (1975) survey, 'The Arts that Britain Ignores', was seminal in its breadth exploring the contribution to the arts landscape from diasporic communities. Khan was the first to highlight 'the proportion of Black students at drama schools' in Britain. It was the first publication of its kind to actively explore the nature and numbers of Black and Global Majority acting students enrolled at Britain's leading drama conservatoire schools in the mid-1970s. Khan investigated the relationship between actor training, stage management, the actor's union and the performing arts industry. She documented what she identified as informal practices,[1] which appeared to be excluding 'ethnic minorities' from taking part and being visible across the creative sector. The discriminatory practices that

---

[1.] Naseem Khan's results found that of the fifteen Black students of an intake of 675 in the nation's top twenty drama schools, five were international students.

Kahn outlined in her report were further highlighted by the *Guardian*. In 1975, the national newspaper reported that:

> ...for years at least one institution, the Central School of Speech and Drama, has been taking on its few Afro-Asian protégés on the understanding that they'll only stay for a term in their third year – the showcase year when students get their chance to shine – because frankly there just aren't enough Black parts to go around. (29 April 1975 n.a.n.p. BTMF).

The Central School of Speech and Drama was not the only drama conservatoire that practised this policy; however, it was the only one to go on record at the time confirming its institutional use. I experienced this being 'let go' in the second year of my drama school training in the late 1980s. It was the intervention by my parents and the suggestion of legal action which stayed their hand. Nonetheless, the subsequent casting in my third year was virtually non-existent. I was cast as a Kit Kat Girl in *Cabaret* but was cut in the second half with the proviso that 'no Blacks would have survived in Germany at that time'. Goodbye to Berlin for me indeed it was. Khan's report set out the inequities experienced by Black and Global Majority actors in the training sector, the industry and the actor's union Equity.[2] Actors' Equity union, at that time, operated as a closed shop: non-completion of the full training meant actors were ineligible for the union Equity card and which meant subsequently they had no access to paid professional employment opportunities. No card, no work. This was problematic due the fact that British theatre was the primary platform for actors to build their careers and reputations. Theatre at that time enjoyed high cultural prestige and status, attracting international critical acclaim, financial investment and significant public interest.

Fast-forward some 45 years and, in June 2020, acting conservatoires clamoured to publish Black Lives Matter statements in the wake of George Floyd's murder and worldwide anti-racism protests. The backlash from students to the premise of these statements was seismic. Acting conservatoires across the UK faced serious allegations from students for failing to address systemic and institutional racism, regionalism, inappropriate behaviour and the lack of safeguarding. Students were publicly questioning their training experience and what seemed to be an ongoing intransigence within conservatoires towards addressing real, meaningful, representational change. In light of all the allegations, an independent inquiry, conducted on behalf of one of the schools led by a then Queen's Council legal team, commented that the issues raised in their report around discriminatory practices were not limited to any institution but widespread across United Kingdom drama schools.

Somethings needed to change. That change came and it was precipitated by the global pandemic and the subsequent global lockdown.

The global lockdown accelerated a couple of areas that were significant points of tension within actor training. The first was the exploration of reframing representation in the pedagogy and the second was modernisation with the integration of digital innovation within traditional classical actor training and technical theatre and stage management training.

While the world was in lockdown, actors were able to build an online rapport and generate an audience by creating, performing and marketing their own work through the

---

[2] British Actor's Equity Association, known as Equity, operated as a 'closed shop' union until the 1980s when closed shop unions became illegal in the UK.

fast-growing arena of social media. This created a new dynamic for all actors, which has continued to build, but particularly regarding visibility and presence for actors who had previously been marginalised, who were now able to gain exposure far beyond the confines of a physical UK stage.

Streaming platforms want to capture the minds, disposable income, hearts and eyeballs of a global audience. This has created a new dynamic around the type of stories and subject matter being explored, whether they are narratives based on true life events or commissioned fictional drama. Many more creatives are now able to take their representational stories and explore the space to negotiate creating or reimagining them from stage to screen and increasingly from screen to stage. Conservatoire actor training in the UK needs to embrace the benefits of the rise of the streamed multi-platform content and the multi-faceted opportunities it presents, especially regarding representation, equality and inclusion. The impact of these changes offers the conservatoire and their graduates the potential to have a global reach, as screened content can be viewed worldwide, on demand increasing visibility and accessibility.

Streaming services and platforms that had been steadily rising in subscription take-up have exploded since the pandemic. Netflix, one of the biggest streaming platforms in the world and still growing, placed representation full screen, showcasing Shonda Rhimes's *Bridgerton*, a seminal period drama set in Regency England during the time of King George III's reign. It has been seen as a disruptor to the British ideological tradition of British actor training and on-screen portrayals of period history, race and class. The images and myths that have been taken for granted in the traditional British screen portrayal of period drama as part of the world of entertainment more often than not have deep historical roots and perpetuate evocative powerful, persuasive, ideological traditions. However, if *Bridgerton* subverted the period drama genre by creating an explosion of real debate around British history, representation, race, class and the white male/female gaze, then Rapman's 2024 *Supacell* (also a Netflix commission) has taken the debate around the entire drama genre quite literally into another much more powerfully persuasive representational multi-universe.

Streaming platforms have revolutionized the entertainment industry, significantly affecting theatre, film and the UK's terrestrial television channels. They are increasingly entering into multi-year first-look development, financing and production deals with multi-hyphenate management agencies for feature films. For actors, understanding this shift is critical. For acting conservatoires recognising and reframing the training is crucial.

British graduating actors now compete with a much broader international pool of talent, including those with significant screen credits, who may not have pursued the conservatoire route. This has seen a talent drain whereby actors have left the UK to build a career in America. This is due to the perception that opportunities, particularly for Black and Global majority actors, are much more readily available there compared to the UK and there is a much more open mindset towards who can play what and why.

There is a new symbiosis between theatre and screen that did not previously exist. Now, having significant screen credits enhances an actor's chances of being considered for prominent theatre roles. There may be several reasons for this. Actors who have screen credits often have a following from their film and screen work. They are, therefore, often much more recognisable and so able to draw in a wider range of audiences. As a result of the positive impact on ticket sales, theatrical producers are increasingly recognising the value of creating an ensemble on stage and backstage with heightened profiles and the built-in audience that they all bring.

Alongside the role of social media and its impact, there is also the changing digital landscape that actors are increasingly being asked to connect with. Conservatoires are starting to explore the need provide their students with professional exposure to the most advanced technologies that the craft of acting and an actor's body is increasingly required to synthesise with. They have taken significant steps towards integrating the digital landscape with the training to prepare its graduates in a way that reflects what the screen and theatre industry now demands. Theatre is now becoming increasingly mediatised. Digital video; live broadcast; moment-to-moment video projection; live feeds from hand-held mobile devices; immersive interaction; and vast, more enriched soundscapes and lighting of these different mediums boosts the offer of actor training and requires a modernisation of technical stage management training also.

The ubiquity of emergent technologies in the film, screen, audio and gaming sector, such as 3D Scanning Photogrammetry, Volumetric Video Capture, Motion and Performance Capture, are becoming increasingly prevalent aspects of the environment that actors are required to inhabit and experience. Whether it is wearing a motion capture suit to create the physicality and embodiment of a yet to be built 3D rendered character to working with other actors with an LED Volume Wall for the set, this latest technology creates a virtual set which means the surroundings of a sound stage are limited only by the background content.

The requirements for screen and audio acting require an outstanding level of skill, craft and trained imagination. Once on set, in the volume or audio booth, the process requires solid training techniques to support what is highly creative, disciplined, imaginative and physically demanding work. This process of connecting forward-facing actor training with emergent and advanced world-building technology is at the forefront of what it means to be a professional actor prepared for the future.

RADA, as part of its BA (Hons) Acting training and as part of my role as Head of Film, Television and Audio, produces six short films every year from professionally commissioned scripts and with a diverse professional crew. These multi award-winning films are internationally recognised for excellence and employ a range of digitally innovative scenarios that mirror the environment that actors may encounter on graduation when working on a professional production. I liaise with audio professionals to produce Commercial Voice-Over Demo Reels for inclusion in their graduate student profiles. This is an area often overlooked by conservatoires. It is through this work for the BBC that I was able to gain my equity card, despite being told at drama school in the 1980s that I 'had a good face for radio'. I have also introduced the provision of a residential 'Digital Futures' immersive training experience, working in collaboration with the Centre for Creative and Immersive eXtended Realities, University of Portsmouth, to ensure the RADA students gain a solid introduction and immersion in the use of digital technology and how they may be required to connect and interact with it in various scenarios.

The Royal Central School of Speech and Drama, LAMDA, Rose Bruford, East15 and Guildhall School of Music and Drama are now all starting to invest, develop and research into emergent technologies and their application, particularly in the areas of motion capture, digital innovation and performance and its inclusion as part of their undergraduate and post graduate actor-training offer.

With the importance of self-taping and its now accepted universal use for initial casting rounds and remote auditions, technical proficiency has become a critical skill for actors. Knowing how to set up a professional-looking self-tape space, including lighting, sound, background and framing can make a significant difference towards the casting outcomes.

Modern actors must be adept at transitioning between theatre, film, television, and audio. Each medium requires a different dynamic and clear understanding of that dynamic and what is required in terms of craft by the actor. This underscores the importance of a trained imagination, transferable skills, versatility, energy and adaptability as key parts of an actor's skill set.

In 2023 actors in America went on strike for (among several things) the right to have control over their own digital image. This is a very real concern as technology and Artificial Intelligence (AI) becomes increasingly advanced. There has been an exponential explosion in environments where everyone can distribute material digitally with maximum efficiency to everyone else worldwide. Conservatoire training needs to address the implications of this to fundamentally raise awareness around actors being their own brand and how to develop and protect it.

Today an actor might well focus solely on screen work for part of their career – the streaming platforms require a certain exclusive/loyalty not unlike the big Hollywood studio system of a previous era and the rights to one's image and its usage are increasingly nebulous. But in-between screen projects they might try to squeeze in a theatrical stage play project, be commodified as the face of a major brand extolling the virtues of perfume, aftershave or high fashion. They might be facilitating presentational skills for businesses, doing motion/performance capture/voicing characters for gaming brands and/or visual effects work, narrating an audiobook or producing a podcast.

There is a much bigger and recognised diversification of craft and young actors need to have a much more heightened sense of the range of an actor's working life and how much they can do for themselves to access it. Some of the most talented young actors today never trained at drama school yet are consistently in work moving fluidly between screen and stage. Training may not have been an option for any number of reasons, but these actors are in demand, and they are focused, disciplined, open, agile and learning on the job.

Can conservatoires in the UK consider meaningful change for the better and explore the progressivism needed to reframe the term 'classical' acting and technical training to create artists for the future? Conservatoire actor training requires focus, talent, determination, resilience and a willingness to make mistakes and to want to learn from them and move forward. Conservatoire actor training provides a set of skills that ensure your longevity and adaptability yet enable you to remain open and continue to learn throughout your life. Conservatoire actor training is not to be taken lightly – you must want to commit to learning about yourself, the world around you, and the idiosyncrasies of human behaviour and thinking. You need to develop analytical skills with your mind, which you then communicate through your body.

When exploring and deciding which school to apply to don't confuse celebrity with craft. Celebrity and fame for their own sake do not offer you anything. Investing in the craft of acting can give you a lifelong opportunity to learn, grow, develop and give back.

Then ask yourself does this school have an identity that sets it apart from the others? Does it have a sense of history and a reputation for staying ahead of the game?

Is it representational beyond the box-ticking variety? Who are the actors whose approach to craft I admire? Did they train? If so, where and how did they feel about their training experience? What does the teaching body look like? Is it representational? Is there anyone there that looks like you? Who teaches on the course you are applying for? Does its prospectus clearly set out the range of courses available? Has care been taken in the way the material in the prospectus has been set out? Have reasonable adjustments been taken for neurodivergent applicants so there is an equality of access to application information? Do the research.

There is a saying that it is our choices that really show us who we are and not our abilities. So if, after your audition experience, you are reviewing your choices around which drama school offer to accept and you can answer all the above questions, then you will truly recognise instinctively through your body which drama school will provide you with the form of training that will enable you to grow into the actor you know you were born to be.

No art form can survive unless it relates to its own age and fully embraces its challenges.

Pamela Jikiemi is Head of Film, Television and Audio at the Royal Academy of Dramatic Art (RADA), UK. She is classically trained (ALRA), holds an MA, PGCE AP, and is a Fellow of the Higher Education Academy (FHEA) and an award-winning filmmaker. She has commissioned and produced over 25 short films and directed four, winning the IRIS Prize for Education for a short film in 2023. She is currently a PhD candidate at University of the Arts, Chelsea. She continues to work creatively and extensively as an award-winning actor and voice actor, appearing most recently in Netflix series *Supacell*, Apple TV's *Ted Lasso*, and in BAFTA's Best Game of the Year award-winner *Baldur's Gate III*. Giving back to community is a priority for her and she is the editor of the book *Out of the Black Box: Conversations with Actors and Artists* (Methuen Drama, 2025).

The Mentor & The Void

Mark Weinman

I went charging across what I call 'the void' straight from university, where I had accumulated what I thought was a pretty impressive list of credits with the drama society. In my first year, I had won a MIFTA.[1] I didn't even audition for roles in my second year – I was getting straight offers from the big director dons in the department. By the third year, I was turning down parts. "This acting game is easy," I thought. "This is it. People are recognising my talents. People are telling me I'm good. I'm going to be an actor. Get me back to London … this will be a doddle."

When you begin to make this transition from education or training into the industry, then can begin the whispers of doubt: Are you ready for this? Do you have everything you need? Do you fully understand what you're about to get into? There are so many routes into the industry and if, like me, you didn't go to drama school, you may worry that you're not on the right one.

Some people try to polevault across the void without too much forethought, buoyed by a false sense of security, excitement and sometimes cockiness, focusing on the glamour of the industry and the fruits it will inevitably bear – your name in lights, your own trailer, your face on screen! Others may bottle it altogether and give up before really giving things a chance, daunted by the uncertainty that lies ahead.

A year passed after I left uni and in that time I'd had no professional acting work. I'd had as many auditions as I have fingers… on one hand. As many rejections from those as I have fingers … on the other hand. Hundreds of email submissions to casting directors and agents had gone unanswered. A debt-inducing 'headshot session' made me look as if I was modelling for the WHSmith Back-to-School catalogue. I was working full time at a pizza restaurant on low wages. People told me I needed to 'network', whatever that meant. They told me I wasn't being creative, I was out of practice. My confidence was crushed, my self-belief was in tatters. What had changed? Why didn't anyone want me in their plays? I was a MIFTA winner!

On reflection, it was the crossing of this void when I felt in most need of professional support and informed guidance – something beyond ad hoc and untested theories from the most well-meaning of people – and certainly something to offer some reassurance in those early, lonely days.

***

For the past three years, I have enjoyed working as a mentor for actors. Used as a title, 'mentor' can sound quite grand – it seems to imply a level of authority and status that perhaps contradicts the role as we see it today. The modern-day mentor is most commonly a volunteer, offering an act of service without financial gain. There need be no sense of status. Where a mentor remains purely an advisor, coach or guide, the engagement between mentor and mentee is a very human one, rooted in trust.

What I have learnt to be key to a successful mentor-mentee relationship is that the mentor is never 'better' – simply further along their career path – than the mentee. The

---

[1]. A delightful highlight of the university of Manchester theatrical calendar and the name given to the awards presented as part of their 'in-fringe' festival. A bit Like an Oscar – but also absolutely nothing like an Oscar.

decision to offer advice must always be in the interests of the recipient, though chances are it will also be an enriching experience for the mentor, as I have discovered.

Before officially becoming a mentor, I'd worked as a facilitator with young actors for over 10 years across youth theatres, social inclusion courses, community projects, drama schools and universities and I'm grateful to those employers that have allowed me space to develop in this role. During this time, one young person told me how a previous mentor she had been assigned for her course had failed even to respond to her numerous requests for contact. Others challenged the quality of mentorship available across aforesaid training programmes or expressed disappointment at the lack of mentorship opportunities. Expectations had been left unmet, and there was a feeling that some mentors had assumed the role primarily as an ego-boosting exercise, leaving the mentee feeling further behind the curve than before. These dispiriting conversations with young people highlighted the void that I felt existed between education/training/youth theatre and the professional industry.

The area is currently being supported through the excellent and determined work of several individual organisations and charities who are embracing the benefits of mentorship. The National Youth Theatre's creative pathway opportunities provide free training to those members who wish to explore them. Its brilliant REP company offers one-to-one mentorship opportunities for all successful course participants. Numerous drama schools have introduced mentors to students, during and after their time studying. Arts Emergency is making an incredible difference in supporting change in this area and certainly one worth supporting if you feel mentorship might be for you. Similarly, Jerwood Arts also boasts some impressive artist development programmes and bursaries, supported by mentors tailored to the artists needs. I nod joyfully to David Mumeni's incredible Open Door programme, which offers a 'buddy-up' scheme to help support young talented people who may not have the financial support or resources to pursue drama school. These are just a few examples, but yet proof, that mentorship really does work and that it could exist on a larger scale.

Good mentorship should be used by the mentee as a tool to scout out the industry. It encourages you to be inquisitive, to ask questions and to self-manage expectations. To learn how to make contacts and correspond. The crossing of the void, with a mentor by your side, should be gentle and paced, allowing time to prepare for the reality when stepping off on the other side.

As a football fan, I look at the gruelling club academy regimes. Of young players at top academy level, fewer than 1% will end up playing in the Premier League. Clubs face criticism for the lack of aftercare for these aspirants – the 99% who fall by the wayside – some of whom have been at the clubs since they were as young as five. They are effectively being dumped in the final stages of their football education, without alternative qualifications, any form of career back-up plan and sometimes with hardly surprising mental-health problems.

Is our industry so different? A pre-pandemic study by Queen Mary University of London indicated that only 2% of actors make a living from the profession, with 90% out of work at any one time. I wonder how different my run-up to the void might have looked had I considered such realities – certainly a little less Greg Rutherford thinking he was Marlon Brando. If the least people need to understand is what awaits beyond the void, whose responsibility is it to inform them? Can the industry be more transparent? And how far can mentorship go?

***

In 2020 I founded The Ten, a free mentorship programme for ten young people aged 18–25 all looking to cross the void. I selected mentees, with a focus in particular on working with young actors from under-represented backgrounds, who I believed had the potential to work as professional actors, not only in terms of talent, but also drive, with or without a drama school training.

"Why not start with one person and see how you get on?" my partner quite reasonably asked me – a number of times. It was June 2020, in the thick of Covid, nothing was going on workwise and it seemed like good timing. It was a time when those hoping to enter the industry might simply turn away from it, which would have been a great shame.

Being a mentor provided insights into the sorts of struggles I experienced starting out, but also new ones – notably the practice, demands and expectations of self-taping for today's young actors. I knew how difficult it can be, but I now see it from the perspective of those new to it.

I watched a few of my mentees struggle with the reality of the work involved when tapes are coming at you thick and fast: the expectation to learn all that material, make strong creative choices, find someone to read in with you, and find time to actually tape, edit and upload. And then have to accept that you might hear nothing back. Although it is worth referencing the free Yes/No tool that has since been rolled out by industry platform Tagmin, in collaboration with casting directors Anna Dawson and Amy Blair, which offers an option for actors to ensure they are always told when a role did not go their way. This feels to be an important step forwards in clarity and communication.

The anticipated workload, lack of acknowledgment and rejections were enough of a shock for one mentee to decide that acting was not for them. Although devastating for me to hear, considering their potential, how positive it was that they had come to their own decision at this point before a heavier toll might have been suffered. That mentee seemed totally at peace arriving at this conclusion – and with a clearer idea of what they wanted to pursue instead.

Being a mentor is not about suggesting that you've somehow made it (god knows, I haven't) or that you have all the answers (I really don't). It's about, firstly, listening and ensuring that the mentorship is driven by the mentee's needs. Secondly, it's about sharing – your thoughts, experience and ideas – in the hope that your insights might align with the other person's situation. Thirdly, it's about managing expectations. Social media might highlight the few stars who instantly landed a lead role with a major streaming service, but that doesn't make it the norm. The norm for an actor is an unrelated part-time job and working out how to do your tax return and going without work for months on end. For myself, another norm was becoming very well acquainted with daytime TV – a particular favourite being *Cash in the Attic*: a show that I imagine sends many an actor straight to investigate any unbeknownst loft space.

I found it important to be candid that I would offer practical and honest answers to questions, but that the answer wouldn't necessarily be right. We also discussed being able to challenge one another without taking offence. Good communication became key when it came to respecting each other's external personal commitments. There might be times when we would have to work around each other's schedules and this should never be taken to mean giving up or losing interest.

What I have enjoyed most is "sharing the wealth" in terms of experience, but also at times throwing open the contacts book: 'Write to this person, invite that person, email those people'. Those contacts might blame me for all those mentees clogging up their inboxes, but it feels like the right thing to do.

You might argue that it's counter-intuitive for actors to help actors when it's such a competitive field, but why should it be? And I'd like to take it further: imagine if, once you had worked professionally for ten years as an actor, it was made compulsory to mentor an actor at the beginning of their journey. You would take an interest in their work, make introductions, find time to see their work and offer feedback. You could commit to an hour a fortnight for a year, whether in person, on the phone or on Zoom.

And what if this 'act-of-service' was subsidised by our government, so that you were paid for your time? Where would the money come from? I don't know, but I point to France, where some 250,000 artists, performers and creatives receive state stipends to help cover costs between jobs, provided they work at least 507 hours per year. We would then have a full-circle mentorship programme, which would feed our rich arts and culture sector from which our country profits in so many ways.

It's my privilege still to be acting today. I've managed it for 15 years now and I'm grateful, though I would be lying if I said I hadn't come close at times to giving it all up. It remains an industry fraught with problems and, when you consider these alongside the competition for acting jobs, one might wonder quite what the attraction is. However, it's the community that all my mentees love and of which they want to be part. It's certainly the thing I still love the most. Mentoring has given me confidence that we can strengthen our industry and our circumstances from the inside. In very few professions do we encounter as many people as we do in ours. If we're open to sharing and helping each other out and treat that as an enriching experience, maybe we'll all find ourselves that bit further along.

Mark Weinman is an actor/writer working across stage and screen. His credits include *Ant Man and The Wasp: Quantumania*, *I May Destroy You*, *After Life* and *Captain Amazing*. He is an associate of the National Youth Theatre of Great Britain working as a director, facilitator and writer. He is also founder of The Ten, a not-for-profit mentorship programme which also offers affordable acting coaching and opportunities to the wider community. See more at **www.thetentalent.co.uk**.

Opening doors: inclusivity, innovation and the collective acting studio

Paul Harvard, founder, Collective Acting Studio
Interview by Aileen Gonsalves

Paul Harvard began his career as actor-musician working on award-winning productions for the National Theatre, in the West End and for regional theatres. He has led courses and trained actors for eighteen years, at a dozen of the leading conservatoires and universities in the UK – including Royal Central School of Speech and Drama, Drama Centre, MetFilm, Identity, GSA, Mountview, Rose Bruford, Webber Douglas, LCM and the Urdang Academy. His first play GHBoy, was produced in 2020 by his own production company at the Charing Cross Theatre. The play was conceived during a writers' course at the National Theatre and developed following grants from the Arts Council. He is the author of three books published by Nick Hern and his approaches to the teaching of acting through song are internationally recognised. Paul founded Collective Acting Studio in 2022 to make our society and industry a fairer place – by providing access to the highest-quality training for actors from underrepresented groups. See more on their website collectiveactingstudio.co.uk *and Instagram @collectiveactingstudio.*

So, Paul – I've known you for a number of years now, but always with you wearing different hats, actually. And that's something I've become fascinated with recently – the idea of multiplicity in creative identities. Would you describe your own career as being that of a 'jack of all trades'?
I would definitely say that my career has involved doing a number of different things. My original training and background was as an actor-musician – I trained at Rose Bruford College, which really set the tone for the way I've approached the rest of my career. At the time, that meant undertaking a rigorous classical actor training, while also studying composition and musical direction.

So I wasn't just being trained to interpret Shakespeare or Chekhov, but to write, arrange, and direct the music for the productions I was in. From the very beginning of my career, I wasn't confined to one role – I was performing in musicals where I played instruments, directing music for productions, composing professionally. And then, later on, I found myself writing plays, and eventually training actors too.

So if being a 'jack of all trades' means being someone who wears multiple hats – yes, I'd say I've embraced that. Though I think the phrase doesn't always do justice to what it really means to be a multidisciplinary artist.

Right, exactly. That phrase – 'jack of all trades, master of none' – is so often used dismissively, but people forget the full version: 'A jack of all trades is a master of none, but oftentimes better than a master of one.' So how has that multidisciplinary approach informed your work, particularly when it comes to training actors?
It's had a profound impact, actually. When I'm designing actor training or working with young artists, I often draw from across disciplines. I've never seen these skills – acting,

writing, composing, directing – as separate compartments. They feed into each other in fascinating ways. Recently in class, we were watching some of Steve McQueen's work. You can see his background as a visual artist in every shot he frames. Similarly, I often mention the story of Steve Jobs studying calligraphy – it seems so niche, so specific, but that aesthetic sensitivity ultimately shaped Apple's entire design philosophy.

In my own work, directing a play is never just about the blocking or dialogue. There's always a rhythm, a musicality – something intangible that I know comes from my musical background. It's like each skill has deepened the others.

Founding Collective Acting Studio must have been a defining moment in your career – a culmination of all those threads. What led you to take that step?

It really was a turning point. After spending a long time working in the traditional drama school sector, I reached a point where I felt that something needed to change. There was a gap between the kind of training being offered and the kind of industry artists were entering.

With Collective, we had the rare opportunity to start from a completely blank page and ask ourselves: *If we could design actor training from scratch, what should it look like?* That question became our blueprint.

Inclusivity was a core value from day one. Today, over 60% of our students come from the global majority, and we've made it a priority to integrate students with complex disabilities into our mainstream training programs. We didn't want separate pathways. We wanted a shared, diverse space that reflects the reality of the industry.

And how does Collective differ from more traditional actor training institutions?

The standard three-year BA just doesn't work for everyone, especially now. Many of our students are already working actors who want to sharpen their skills. Others are career-changers – people who had always dreamed of acting but didn't follow that path early on.

So we created alternative models. Our part-time drama school, for instance, runs two evenings a week in an apprenticeship-style format. If a student books a professional job, we refund their fees for the time they're away. They get to learn on *set* and then come back to the studio stronger. It's a model rooted in the reality of the industry and the economic pressures people face.

It's about flexibility, sustainability, and relevance. Training has to evolve with the times.

Absolutely. And it sounds like ongoing training is central to your philosophy as well. Why do you think that's so important?

There's this analogy I often use – if you trained for the Olympics, you wouldn't stop training the moment you qualified. And yet, actors often do just that. They train intensely at drama school, graduate, get an agent – and then stop developing.

That's why we've built Collective as a studio, not just a school. It's a place where artists can keep growing, whether they're just starting out or ten years into their careers.

The idea that creative development is lifelong – it's something I think we're finally starting to embrace more widely here in the UK.

So what do you do to support Collective's graduates once they leave the training environment?

Supporting graduates is essential. I remember finishing drama school and feeling like I'd fallen off a cliff.

At Collective, we've tried to build an infrastructure that helps our graduates create, produce, and showcase their work. We've got two theatre spaces, a recording studio, film equipment – it's all professional grade. And our training supports that infrastructure. It's cyclical.

This year we launched our first Fringe Festival. We produced four shows, and I'm thrilled to say one is transferring to a London theatre, another is heading to Edinburgh with funding from Phoebe Waller-Bridge's foundation, and two more were picked up by the Bush Theatre's new writers program.

We even offered a 70/30 box office split, so artists walked away with real income – sometimes over £2,500 for a three-night solo show. We're creating those paid opportunities so people aren't just gaining experience, but earning as they do it.

And we're doing the same with our film festival. Twelve short films made at Collective are going to be screened at the Prince Charles Cinema in Leicester Square. It's about real-world, meaningful next steps.

You've built something that truly addresses the challenges actors are facing right now. Speaking of which – what do you think are the biggest hurdles for actors entering the industry today?

Financial sustainability is, without doubt, one of the biggest challenges. And that's true across many sectors, not just the arts. But for actors, the early-career phase is particularly precarious. If we don't address this, we risk returning to a time when only the privileged can afford to pursue a career in the arts.

So how can the industry do better? What changes need to happen?

Training institutions need to rethink how they serve their communities. At Collective, we've designed a model where the training sustains a larger infrastructure. We use that infrastructure to create opportunities – performance spaces, film festivals, commissions. That cycle keeps the community alive.

There's no denying we're in a funding crisis, both in education and the arts. But we have to get creative. If we use what we have wisely, we can still make a real difference.

Let me ask something more personal. I've been exploring the idea of 'jack of all trades' as a phrase that sometimes limits people. Have you ever experienced that pushback? People questioning your identity, or what you do?

Yes, definitely. Especially early in my career, I encountered people who couldn't reconcile the idea of someone who could conduct an orchestra and perform Shakespeare. It was as if being good at one thing invalidated your seriousness about another.

But that just doesn't match what I see in the real world. I know so many artists who bring the same passion and commitment to multiple disciplines.

And yet, yes – there were times I felt boxed in, told to 'stay in my lane'. It's an incredibly limiting mindset, and I think it holds people back. Thankfully, things are changing.

Do you think the industry has moved on from that?

I do. There's a growing recognition of the value of multidisciplinary practice. Artists today are directing, writing, producing their own content. The old boundaries have blurred, and that's a good thing.

It's not about being unfocused – it's about being enriched. The skills transfer, the creativity expands. The industry is catching up to that reality now, and it's exciting to be part of that shift.

It's been absolutely wonderful talking to you, Paul. What you've built with Collective is more than just a school – it's a movement. Thank you for your time, and for sharing such thoughtful insights.

Thank you, Aileen. It's been a joy. And I'm hopeful. There's so much talent out there – we just need to keep opening doors.

Aileen Gonsalves is a theatre director, actor, writer, and creator of the Gonsalves Method – a pioneering approach to actor training taught in drama schools and universities in many countries.

It's warm up north
Adelle Hulsmeier

Overcoming the stigma that suggests the North East of England offers limited opportunities to actors, both trained and untrained, is difficult. At a time when travel and movement is significantly restricted, this article is timely in putting some of the more progressive opportunities offered in the North East of England on the map. It offers an overview of some of the exciting opportunities that are currently offered in this region, particularly Newcastle and Sunderland, hopefully helpful to today's aspirant actors when thinking about the extent of opportunities that may exist 'closer to home' or that may be worth re-locating for.

Sunderland Culture, Sunderland

Sunderland Culture, of which the Music, Arts and Culture (MAC) Trust, the University of Sunderland and Sunderland City Council are the founding partners, is a new organisation which was created to bring together Sunderland's most important cultural assets and activities.

This cultural initiative enjoys the benefits of the National Glass Centre, the Northern Gallery of Contemporary Art, Sunderland Museum and Winter Gardens, the Sunderland Empire, a 400-seat venue the Auditorium at the Fire Station, and music venue The Peacock.

The new and exciting Auditorium at the Fire Station which sits in Sunderland's Music, Arts and Cultural quarter, is the city's newest cultural venue. It offers dance classes, theatre workshops and a heritage centre. Live Theatre's Live Tales and DanceCity also operate from the venue. The Fire Station Auditorium is a versatile performance space which offers a year-round programme of live music, theatre, dance and comedy in a spectacular new state-of-the-art 550 seated or 800 standing capacity space. The auditorium provides a fantastic opportunity to bring artists, shows and performances to the city that have not been able to visit Sunderland before.

Live Theatre, Newcastle

Live Theatre has an international reputation as a new writing theatre. As well as producing and presenting new plays, there are extensive artistic opportunities for anyone looking to develop their acting skills from ages 11+.

The Elevator Programme supports the early career development of independent artists in the North East and across the UK. It incorporates writing courses and script developmental opportunities, bursaries and space for companies to develop new work.

Elevator is an annual festival which allows artists to present new theatre in Live Theatre's venue. Since 2014 Elevator has launched 25 brand new plays, worked with 17 associate artists and awarded 16 bursaries.

Every year, Live Theatre select emerging theatre artists/companies to be their associate artists, benefiting from exclusive opportunities and support such as mentoring and development time and space.

For young people Live Theatre offers the largest free youth theatre in the region, open to ages 11–25. Over 3 terms you can develop skills in stage craft, develop a new play to perform and explore scripts that have been produced and performed at Live Theatre. Young people aged 11–25 can also join the Wordplay group to explore the world of spoken word.

Arts Award is a national accredited qualification designed to grow young people as artists and arts leaders. Live Theatre often works in partnership with organisations such as The Prince's Trust as well as its own Youth Theatre members, and Live Theatre's plays, post-show talks and workshops can support young people to achieve Arts Award. Students taking Arts Award at Live Theatre have a 100% pass rate.

Creative Careers Week offers work experience for ages 14–18. 10 students are offered experience placements where they are introduced to the creative production, development, and finance and marketing departments within Live Theatre. Students can also work as a collective to creatively devise a 10–15 minute performance throughout the week.

Volunteer roles at Live Theatre are varied and available in Live Tales (a children and young people's writing centre) and in other areas of Live Theatre's work. They include supporting and encouraging children and young people to write, illustrating their stories or leading tours of the buildings. All volunteers receive ongoing training and support, a programme of social events and some discounts at Live Theatre. There are volunteering opportunities at Live Theatre, Newcastle, and The Fire Station, Sunderland.

Project A, Newcastle Theatre Royal, Newcastle

Project A is a one-year actor training programme, delivered from within Newcastle's Theatre Royal. Delivery takes place over 3 terms and 18 students are accepted on the programme each year. They have access to the main house auditorium, visiting professionals, studio theatre, rehearsal room and dedicated training space.

Over 90% of Project A's graduates are working professionally or gaining agent representation within six months of graduation.

The course is full time and students are expected to attend between 25–45 hours a week. In the first term you develop performance skills in relation to character creation and vocal and physical development. Term two is delivered by associate specialists and covers areas such as business, Shakespeare, Meisner and screen. The final term is the production term which takes students into an intensive rehearsal process, culminating in a showcase performance at the Theatre Royal.

Alphabetti Theatre, Newcastle

Alphabetti is a fringe venue in Newcastle that creates, produces, and programmes original work from emerging artists in music, theatre, comedy and poetry.

While they predominantly programme original work across the performing arts, if you've got an idea that doesn't quite sit in that section, they advise you still get in touch.

Northern Stage, Newcastle

Northern Stage is the largest producing theatre company in the North East of England. Northern Stage Filmmakers is a course for 16–25 year olds in partnership with My Life Productions, Woodhorn Museum and The Heritage Lottery Fund. During the course you can learn all aspects of filmmaking, including acting, directing, writing, producing, camera, sound and editing. The group produce a 30-minute documentary and a 15-minute fictional film (based on the true stories of the documentary) premiered at Northern Stage and Alnwick Playhouse.

Specialist Work Placements are open to Further Education and Higher Education Students, as well as bespoke professional placements for people already in the industry or seeking to learn more. The placements are open for 6 weeks a year and are tailored to meet the needs of the applicant.

NORTH training programme supports the development of North-East based performers and theatre companies. It comprises of actor training, small-scale touring and company development. Applicants must be 20+ at the time the course begins.

For younger creatives there are opportunities in their young company (open to 16–21 year olds covering three different programmes; the collective, the ensemble and the team) and open stages courses (weekly drama sessions for ages 5–7, 8–11 and 12–15).

A play in 10 weeks tops up knowledge and skills of the rehearsal process. The workshops cover working with script, character development, devising and performing.

North East-based theatre companies and individual theatre-makers can also apply to NORTH to support company development. Successful applicants could receive one week R&D (research and development) time in the Byker rehearsal space, one day with the associate director of Northern Stage, six essential skills workshops and four hours with a member of the Northern stage staff who can support ideas.

Each year Northern Stage will produce a small-scale touring production, featuring emerging North East actors.

Curious Monkey, Newcastle

Curious Monkey is an international award winning theatre company based in Newcastle and founded by artistic director Amy Golding. They offer volunteer placements for students or graduates looking for experience working within a professional theatre company, and from time to time they run bespoke internships for people who are interested in working in theatre.

Troupe is open to 14–21 year olds with a care background or living in supported accommodation. It offers a unique opportunity to get involved in theatre by seeing shows and shadowing professionals. The programme offers monthly theatre trips to one of Newcastle's cultural venues, accompanied by short workshop on the performances viewed, a Q&A before the performance, a backstage tour, and a chance to meet the artists involved in making the show. This programme offers opportunities to undertake master classes and workshops with professional artists that explore different theatre skills, ranging from stand-up comedy to lighting, set design or sound recording. There is also the opportunity to shadow artists on theatre projects and work alongside Curious Monkey's creative teams, gaining experience of different roles within theatre.

Curious Monkey welcome people seeking sanctuary in the UK through the Arriving project. The Arriving project is a place where people seeking sanctuary in the North East of England can be creative, can have new experiences and feel welcome. It's a place to meet up with friends and make new friends, through monthly trips to the theatre, and involvement with events and projects that are led by Curious Monkey's creative team – from yoga to salsa to creating theatre to writing a book. Curious Monkey also support Arriving group members who want to develop their skills in the performing arts to work one on one with artists in areas they show a particular interest in. The group are also involved in volunteering at events and projects to gain experience in different public facing roles, put their many varied skills to good use, practise English in different settings and be part of the Curious Monkey team.

Care about Care offers a creative conversation for those who work in, make decisions about or have experience of the care system through involvement with performance festivals in the North East which feature immersive theatre, spoken word, rap, dance, performances, virtual reality films, an interactive podcast, storytelling, workshops, open space discussion and debate.

Final thoughts

There is a plethora of opportunities for emerging and training artists to engage with. It will always be important to ensure that you are honing and updating your skills, and the aforementioned opportunities offer a broad range of exciting things to get involved with. They come with networking opportunities, access to industry professionals and chances to work in exciting theatre venues. Establish how proactive you want to be and pursue the opportunities that are available to you – weekends, evenings, holidays – there are opportunities available all year round, and experiences available that are diverse and exciting, which you may wish to pursue. Remember: this is not limited to London, it's warm up North too!

Important links

Sunderland Culture: **https://sunderlandculture.org.uk**
Live Theatre: **www.live.org.uk**
Project A: **www.theatreroyal.co.uk/taking-part/project-a**
Alphabetti Theatre: **www.alphabettitheatre.co.uk**
Northern Stage: **www.northernstage.co.uk**
Curious Monkey: **https://curiousmonkeytheatre.com**

Adelle Hulsmeier is a Senior Lecturer and Programme Leader at the University of Sunderland. Her career trajectory is characterised by her conviction to embed the notion of social change as an integral part of teaching and learning. Adelle has managed the Faculty of Arts and Creative Industries' collaborative relationship with Northumbria Police; a successful project that runs annually and as an embedded element within the Screen, Media and Performance programmes. In tandem with this, she also strategically leads an academic partnership with Live Theatre, Newcastle *(Live)*; which allows students to experience teaching and learning in an operational and professional theatre venue, extending the reach of HE beyond the parameters of a classroom environment.

Short-term and part-time courses

This section lists both taster opportunities for drama school aspirants and further training for professional actors.

Pre-drama-school courses

Competition for drama school places is intense. You may enhance your chances if you go on a pre-drama-school course. You might have done A-level Drama but school studies tend to be geared more towards the exam-passing and university entrance than auditioning for drama school. A more vocational course may give you an edge in drama school auditions, or be a productive next step if your first foray into drama school auditioning is unsuccessful. Whatever your acting background, a taster course – even if for just a week – can give you a good idea of what further help/training you might need in preparation for drama school auditions.

Additional skills

As well as the organisations listed below, there are lots of one-off workshops hosted around the country. Find them online, on social media or in newsletters like Artsadmin Anchor (www.artsadmin.co.uk/for-artists/anchor). Organisations like Equity and The Actors Guild host workshops for their members. Actors Centres are great places to sharpen up your existing skills and develop new ones, and great meeting places for actors to exchange ideas and information.

*Member of the Federation of Drama Schools

Academy of Creative Training
8–10 Rock Place, Brighton, East Sussex BN1 1PF
tel (01273) 818166
email info@actbrighton.org
website www.actbrighton.org
Principal Janette Eddisford

All classes are in the evenings and at weekends to allow students to undertake actor training whilst maintaining their domestic and financial commitments. Monthly payment options are available by arrangement. Entry onto long courses is via audition or attendance on an intensive workshop of 8 evenings held monthly throughout the year and designed as an introduction to actor training. Students embarking on the Diploma in Acting are eligible to audition for a bursary. Range of short courses and Summer Schools. The school operates an equal opportunities policy that includes disabled students, but there is limited access to the dance studio and washroom facilities.

Courses offered:
- ATCL Diploma in Acting (2 years). For students aged 18+.
- Intensive Foundation Course (1 year, 10 hours per week). For students aged 16+.
- Creative Playground (10 weeks of 3 hour Masterclasses, runs each term)
- Introduction to Playwriting (2 terms)

Academy of Performance Combat (APC)
email info@theapc.org.uk
website www.theapc.org.uk
Facebook /stagecombat
X @APCombat

Dedicated to bringing combat in any form, in any media into the 21st century. "We are absolutely committed to safer, more exacting techniques than any other organisation." Please see the website for more details of courses and qualifications offered.

ActUpNorth
tel (08448) 111740
email info@actupnorth.com
website https://actupnorth.com
Facebook /ActUpNorthTV
X @actupnorth
Instagram @actupnorth
Founder Peter Hunt, *Creative Director* David Crowley

ActUpNorth is a Spotlight-accredited, independent training programme for actors in the North of England. Classes take place in Leeds, Liverpool, Manchester and online. Their training programme has been designed to address the contemporary industry and covers a range of mediums and techniques. Terms last for 12–16 weeks and are divided into three modules, each of which lasts for approximately four weeks. Students attend one 2-hour class each week. Applicants must be aged 18 years or older and should apply online.

ArtsEd*
14 Bath Road, Chiswick, London W4 1LY
tel 020-8987 6666
email info@artsed.co.uk
website https://artsed.co.uk
Facebook /artsedlondon
X @artsedlondon
Principal Louise Jackson

Courses offered:
• Part-time Foundation Musical Theatre (2 terms). Applicants must be aged 18 or over.
• Part-time Foundation Acting (2 terms). Applicants must be over 18 or over.
• Saturday courses for young people aged 5 to 16+ years covering dance, drama and musical theatre.
• Holiday courses for young people aged 4 to 17+ years.
• Various courses in acting and musical theatre disciplines, including stage, screen, voice, dance and audition technique, are offered for varying skill levels throughout the year.

For full details on all courses offered at ArtsEd, please visit **www.artsed.co.uk**.

The Bloomsbury Alexander Centre
Bristol House, 80A Southampton Row,
London WC1B 4BB
tel 020-7404 5348 , *mobile* 078840 15954
email info@bloomsburyalexandertechnique.com
website www.bloomsburyalexandertechnique.com
Director Natacha Osorio

The centre specialises in teaching the Alexander Technique. Teachers are available for private lessons, with discounts available for students and actors. There are ongoing introductory workshops and courses, as well as vocal work for actors with experience of the AT. The introductory course runs for 4 weeks (1.5 hours a week) and costs £120. Also home to the Bloomsbury Voice Centre, offering the varied expertise of several voice coaches. *Note for disabled actors*: "Our premises are on the ground floor with 3 steps in the hall leading to our door."

British Academy of Dramatic Combat
email info@badc.org.uk
website www.badc.co.uk
Facebook /BritishAcademyOfDramaticCombat
X @BADC_UK
Instagram @badc_uk

The BADC is the longest established dramatic combat organisation in the UK. BADC teachers offer courses across the UK for performers to train in dramatic combat for all forms of performance media.
Upcoming courses and workshops are listed on our website, for all levels of experience, covering a variety of armed and unarmed weapon systems.

The British Academy of Stage & Screen Combat

6 Appleton Square, Mitcham, Surrey CR4 3SF
email info@bassc.org
email workshops@bassc.org
website www.bassc.org
Facebook /TheBASSC
X @TheBASSC
Instagram @TheBASSC

Founded in 1993 with the aim of improving the standards of safety, quality and training of stage combat, and promoting a unified code of practice for the training, teaching and assessing of stage combat within the United Kingdom.

All BASSC teachers have undergone a rigorous training programme and the examining members of the BASSC are highly qualified, experienced professionals with a tradition of working in theatre throughout the UK, including the National Theatre, RSC, Royal Opera House, The Royal Court, Donmar Warehouse, Liverpool Everyman, Theatre Royal York and Newcastle, and Shakespeare's Globe; as well as on television and film productions such as: *Vikings* (Seasons 1–6), *Vikings: Valhalla, American Patriot, Anna Karenina, Ironclad, The Eagle, Hammer of the Gods, Troy, Stardust, The Last Legion, Sherlock Holmes, Sherlock Holmes: A Game of Shadows* and *Lockwood & Co.*

BASSC teachers train students in stage combat at numerous drama schools, universities and colleges including: RADA, the Royal Central School of Speech and Drama, the Royal Birmingham Conservatoire, Drama Studio London, Young Actors Theatre Islington, ArtsEd and Acting Coach Scotland.

They also teach students outside of drama courses at independently run classes and workshops including the annual British National Stage Combat Workshop. Teachers run classes and workshops in the USA, Germany, Spain and Ukraine.

Since its formation the BASSC has established a reputation as the invigorating driving force behind stage combat in the United Kingdom, and is respected, both nationally and internationally, as the leading provider of professional-level stage combat training.

As a result of this, British Equity, in 1997, recognised the BASSC's Advanced Certificate as a valid qualification for entry onto the Equity Fight Directors' Training Scheme.

City Lit
Keeley Street, Covent Garden, London WC2B 4BA
tel 020-4582 0413
email drama@citylit.ac.uk
website www.citylit.ac.uk

The college offers an eclectic mix of disciplines such as acting, movement, voice, teaching, directing, technical theatre and stage management, mime, clowning, stage combat, comedy, dance, self-presentation, accents, voice overs, storytelling, TV presenting, radio, etc., which develop vocational, social and personal skills.

There are various small grants that might cover some of the course fee, travel, books or child-care. Visit the Performing Arts website at **www.citylit.ac.uk/courses/performing-arts/**.

The Comedy School
15 Gloucester Gate, London NW1 4HG
tel 020-7486 1844
website www.thecomedyschool.com
Facebook /keithpalmerthecomedyschool
X @comedyschooluk
Founder Keith Palmer

Founded in 1998. The only arts organisation of its kind in the UK which works with comedy in many different settings. Based in Camden, London. Offers workshops, masterclasses and intensive 6-week courses on improv, clowning, mime, comedy acting for TV, compère hosting, stand-up, puppetry and much more. Bookings taken on their website.

The Dorset School of Acting
Lighthouse, 21 Kingland Road, Poole,
Dorset BH15 1UG
tel (01202) 922675
email admin@dorsetschoolofacting.co.uk
website www.dorsetschoolofacting.co.uk
Co-founders & Principals James Bowden, Laura Roxburgh

Established in 2007, based in the Bournemouth and Poole area. Courses led by an experienced team of professionals.

Courses offered:
• Vocational Sixth Form in Performing Arts with Acting: Runs Monday to Wednesday. Equivalent to an extended BTEC Level 3 or A-Level qualification. Applicants should be aged 16–19.
• Online adult acting course (8 weeks): Suitable for all levels, from beginners to professionals.

Drama Studio London (DSL)*
1 Grange Road, London W5 5QN
tel 020-8579 3897
email admin@dramastudiolondon.co.uk
website www.dramastudiolondon.co.uk
Facebook /dramastudiolondon
X @Drama_Studio
Instagram @dramastudiolondon
Director Emma Lucia Hands

Courses offered:
• Adult Acting Summer School
• Young Actors Summer School
• Adult Evening Intensive Acting Course (10 weeks)
• Michael Billington Theatre Club

École Internationale de Théâtre Jacques Lecoq
116 Rue de la Carreterie, 84000 Avignon, France
tel +33 (0)4 88 61 93 13
email contact@ecole-jacqueslecoq.com
website www.ecole-jacqueslecoq.com
Principal Mrs Anne Astolfe

Founded in Paris in 1956, with the aim of producing a young theatre of new work, generating performance languages which emphasise the physical playing of the actor. Focuses on art theatre, but with the view that theatre education is broader than the theatre itself: "It is a matter not only of training actors, but of educating theatre artists of all kinds." Provides as broad and durable a foundation as possible for every student. As well as the part-time courses listed below, offers a 2-year full-time Professional Course. See also the company's entry under *Drama schools* on page 15. As a movement school, all classes require a great degree of physical movement, so applicants must be physically fit.

Courses offered:
• Introductory Course (one season, October–June). 5 hours per week.
• One-week workshops in March, July and September.

Entry to courses by application that includes a CV, cover letter and 2 recent photos (a portrait and a full-length photo).

Fourth Monkey
97–101 Seven Sisters Rd, Finsbury Park,
London N7 7QT
tel 020-7281 0360
email office@fourthmonkey.co.uk
website www.fourthmonkey.co.uk

A training provider with a difference, offering full- or part-time ensemble-based contemporary rep training and professional performance opportunities. See page 15 for details on full-time courses.

Courses offered: see website for current offering.

Accepts applications from all areas of society; the only factor impacting suitability on any training programme is the presence of talent, a desire to learn, enthusiasm to develop and a willingness to work as an ensemble company member.

Training

The Free Association, London
113 Southgate Road, London N1 3JS
email hello@thefreeassociation.co.uk
The Comedy Room, 51 Camden Park Road, London NW1 9BH
website https://thefreeassociation.co.uk
Instagram @FAImprov

The Free Association is London's premiere improv comedy theatre. Courses teach the fundamentals of long-form improv through to in-depth comedy performance and writing theory, and advanced improv forms and approaches. The courses work in a structured path, allowing actors to work their way up, adding to their skill-set at each stage. Week-long intensives and multi-week classes are offered.

The Giles Foreman Centre for Acting
Studio Soho, 2A Royalty Mews, Dean Street, London W1D 3AR
tel 020-7437 3175
email info@gilesforeman.com
website www.gilesforeman.com
Facebook /gilesforeman.centre
Instagram @gilesforeman
Director Giles Foreman, *Deputy Director* Lindsay Richardson

A professional acting studio – offering exciting courses and coaching by a range of experienced professional coaches in screen- and theatre-acting, movement, voice, improvisation, on-camera, Meisner technique, movement psychology and character analysis, directing and text analysis. Also, visiting specialist coaches from US and across Europe. The centre comprises 2 easy-access, large, bright, air-conditioned studios plus changing room, chill-out area and kitchen. Wheelchair-accessible, stair-lift and step-free studio facilities. Offers the opportunity for Alumni/graduates, aspiring and professional actors to further develop their skills through acting classes and workshops in both film and stage. Specialised intensive short courses offered by internationally renowned practitioners from all over the world.

Due to its location at the heart of the UK film, TV and theatre industry, GFCA also offers opportunities to meet casting directors, directors, producers through industry events. Professional coaches are available to prepare actors 1-1 for auditions and self-tapes and to develop characters for projects. ASIC-accredited institution. Registered centre for Trinity College London. For all ages 18+, courses are taught in small groups, for maximum focus.

Short courses offered (many start dates throughout the year)

- Complete Beginners/Introduction to Acting (Saturdays, 1 or 2 terms). Open entry
- Intermediate Acting (weekly sessions: 3 hours per session)
- Advanced / Pro actors: 4x weekly 3.5 hour evening sessions
- Workshops: specialised subjects and guest coaches (2-day, 5-day etc) - advertised on website and Instagram
- 4-week International intensive, taught by Giles Foreman and team every August and April (designed for advanced actors).
- **Long courses**
- Advanced Intensive Diplomas (Actor and Actor/Director modes – 20-month / 5-term). Subsidised scholarship available.
- Summation term each April-July, for graduates. Members of our Advanced diploma courses in Paris and London particularly welcome.

Online registration form for all short courses: https://forms.gle/iebrW7te7ak6wReA9 and for long courses: https://forms.gle/tF9hLNvztxuFfHYL7

GSA, Guildford School of Acting*
Stag Hill Campus, Guildford GU2 7XH
tel (01483) 684040
email gsashortcourses@gsa.surrey.ac.uk
website www.gsauk.org/short-course
X @the_gsa
Instagram @guildfordschoolofacting
Head of GSA Prof. Catherine McNamara

Courses offered:

- Pre-audition short courses. 2 pathways: Musical Theatre audition technique and Acting audition technique (2-day intensive). For students aged 17+.
- Evening dance classes.
- Diploma in Dance Education, awarded by the Imperial Society of Teachers of Dancing (ISTD).
- Summer and Junior Conservatoire for 14–18 year olds.

Guildhall School of Music & Drama*
Silk Street, Barbican, London EC2Y 8DT
tel 020-7628 2571
email shortcourses@gsmd.ac.uk
website www.gsmd.ac.uk/study-with-guildhall/short-courses-summer-schools

Guildhall School of Music & Drama is a vibrant, interntaional community of musicians, actors and production artists in the heart of London. Offers Short Courses and Summer Schools, online and in person, open to a wide range of ages and abilities in drama, music and production arts.

Courses offered:

- Acting in an Accent – General American (5 days)
- Acting Shakespeare (6 weeks)
- Acting Summer School for Ages 18+ (2 weeks)
- Acting through Song (6 weeks)
- Audition Technique: Acting (2 days)
- Improvisation (6 weeks)
- Introduction to Acting Practice (6 weeks)
- Introduction to Screen Acting (2 days)
- Monologues: Connecting to the Text (6 weeks)
- Shakespeare Masterclass (2 days)
- Singing for Beginners (8 weeks)
- Speaking Shakespeare: Classical Monologue (5 days)

Course spaces are limited and subject to change; early booking is encouraged. New courses and programme dates are added regularly. Check the website or contact via email for more information.

Hoopla, London
The Miller, 96 Snowsfields Road, London Bridge, London SE1 3SS
tel 020-7459 4395
email classes@hooplaimpro.com
website www.hooplaimpro.com
X @hooplaimpro
Director Steve Roe, Training Manager Jessie Rutland

Hoopla are the founders of the UK's first improv comedy club. Fun, friendly improv classes and shows at London's first improv theatre and biggest improv comedy school. Open to all and offers half-price or free places on improv classes to students, the unemployed or people on lower incomes. Works with a number of schools and charities to help make improv available to everyone. Various 6–8 week courses are available.

The Impulse Company
51 The Cut, London SE1 8LF
email erica@impulsecompany.org
website www.impulsecompany.org
Facebook /TheImpulseCompany
X @impulse_company
Instagram @impulsecompanyinternational
Director Scott Williams, Key contact Erica Chestnut

Established for over 20 years in the UK, Scott Williams' Impulse Company provides Meisner-rooted core training for the adult actor within a supportive and positive atmosphere. It also offers occasional short courses and workshops in the UK and New York.

Principal course offered:

• Modular Year course. 3 self-contained, 8-week terms. Entry is by interview, in October and January each year. 8+ hours per week.

International School of Screen Acting
Studio G101, 415 Wick Lane, London E3 2JG
tel 020-8709 8719
website www.screenacting.co.uk
Facebook /screenactingUK
Instagram @Screenactinguk
Directors David B. Craik, Mark Normandy

Founded in 2002, offers full-time training specifically in television and film acting, taking a holistic approach to creativity in relation to students' personal development.

Courses offered:

• 'Crash Course'. A week-long course offered at various times throughout the year. No audition required.
• Summer Course. A selection of 2-day and 5-day courses. Check the website for updates.

LAMDA (London Academy of Music & Dramatic Art)*

155 Talgarth Road, London W14 9DA
tel 020-8834 0500
email enquiries@lamda.ac.uk
website www.lamda.ac.uk/all-courses/short-courses

Training offered varies, from 14-week programmes to intensive day courses to upskill in a specific area. Short courses are available across disciplines, including classical acting, virtual production, and screen and audio, for both first-time students and professionals looking to expand their skillset.

Courses offered: Short-term courses are offered throughout the year in the following areas:

• Classical Acting Semester Programme (14 weeks). Students aged 18+.
• Shakespeare Summer School (8 weeks). Students aged 18+.
• Shakespeare Summer School (4 weeks). Students aged 18+.
• Introduction to Shakespeare (2 weeks). Students aged 16–18.
• Introduction to Actor Training (one week). Students aged 16+.
• Introduction to Screen Acting (2 weeks). Students aged 18+.
• Screen Acting Summer School (2 weeks). Students aged 16+.
• Screen Acting Fundamentals (2 weeks). Students aged 16+.
• Musical Theatre (one week). Students aged 16+.
• Acting in English as an Additional Language (2 weeks). Students aged 18 +.
• Youth Company (2 weeks). Students aged 16–17.
• Professional Self-Taping (course length varies). Students aged 18+.
• Acting Through Song (course length varies). Students aged 18+.
• Auditioning for Drama School (course length varies). Students aged 18+.
• Auditioning for Musical Theatre Programmes (course length varies). Students aged 16+.
• Introduction to Mocap (course length varies). Students aged 18+.
• Introduction to Virtual Production (course length varies). Students aged 18+.
• Introduction to Audio Performance (course length varies). Students aged 18+.
• Actor Refresh Classes (course length varies). Students aged 21+.

For more information on all LAMDA's courses, including fees and deadlines, please visit the website.

London School of Dramatic Art
4 Bute Street, London SW7 3EX
tel 020-7581 6100
email admin@lsda-acting.com
website www.lsda-acting.com
Facebook /LSDA.Acting
X @LSDA_Acting
Instagram @lsda_acting
Principal Jake Taylor, Administrator Hana Kovacs

Offers a range of comprehensive courses designed to develop individual creative talents, and to provide a thorough grounding in all aspects of performance as part of a student's preparation for a working life as an actor. There is currently no wheelchair access to the main building or training rooms: if this affects applicants who would like to know when these spaces become accessible, please let the school know. All auditions are free and no international student fees are charged. No formal qualifications are required, as the training is vocational: "We look more at potential and at levels of creativity".

Part-time 18+ acting courses:
- Diploma in Acting (2 years, 7.5 hours per week). Entry is by audition.
- Access to Acting (5 weeks, 4 hours per week)

Short-term 18+ acting courses:
- Introduction to Drama School (2 weeks in July)
- Introduction to Drama School (2 weeks in August)
- Screen Acting (one week in September)
- Audition Techniques (one week in September)

Manchester School of Acting
14–32 Hewitt Street, Manchester M15 4GB
tel 0161 238 8900
email info@manchesterschoolofacting.co.uk
website www.manchesterschoolofacting.co.uk
Key contact Mark Hudson

High-profile acting school offering part-time training for actors.

Method Acting London
32 Woodfield Road, London W9 2BE
tel 020-7622 9742, mobile 07764 680232
email main@methodacting.co.uk
website www.methodacting.co.uk
Principal & Director Sam Rumbelow

Within the specifically defined and well-established structure of the classes, a grounded, conscious understanding of the craft of acting is facilitated and the powerful creativity of thoughts, impulses and emotions are unlocked. Entry is after a detailed talk and discussion of the class and the applicant, conducted by phone.

Part-time/short-term 16+ acting courses:
- Main Method Studio Intensives
- Voice & Movement Classes
- Audition Technique Classes

Michael Chekhov Studio London
48 Vectis Road, London SW17 9RG
mobile 07968 691016
email info@michaelchekhovstudio.org.uk
website www.michaelchekhovstudio.org.uk
Facebook /MichaelChekhovStudioLondon
Director Graham Dixon

Founded in 2003, the MCSL provides actors (and directors) an opportunity to explore Michael Chekhov's unique approach to the art of acting. Many drama trainings are based upon 'closed systems' that look inside one's own psychology to create a character, but Chekhov created an 'open system' that permits actors to enter an objective creative world immediately using an increased ability to imagine and sense. Yearly programs of workshops and intensives on the basic techniques of Chekhov leading to more advanced work including ensemble initiatives and private coaching on the Chekhov approach to the art of acting and directing. Online training also available.

Morley College
North Kensington Centre: Wornington Road, London W10 5QQ; *Chelsea Centre*: Hortensia Road, London SW10 0QS; *Waterloo Centre*: 61 Westminster Bridge Road, London SE1 7HT
tel 020-7450 1889
website www.morleycollege.ac.uk/courses/subject-areas/dramatic-arts

Offers part-time acting classes from entry-level to advanced. Classes are led by specialist acting tutors with extensive professional experience. An Access Hardship Fund and concessionary fees are available to some students.

Courses offered: A range of evening and part-time acting skills courses are available. Some courses require tutor approval.

- Acting level 1, 2 and 3
- Acting: The Company
- Specialised courses: Acting for Camera, Audition Techniques for Drama School, Puppetry, Radio Drama
- Drama skills such as Confidence through Acting and Public Speaking, and including Acting Skills for Adults with Learning Disabilities

Mountview*
120 Peckham Hill Street, London SE15 5JT
tel 020-8881 2201
email enquiries@mountview.org.uk
website www.mountview.org.uk
Facebook /mountviewldn
X @mountviewLDN
Instagram @mountviewldn
Principal Sally Ann Gritton

Courses offered:
- Part-Time Musical Theatre – Vocational (1.5 terms), 7.5 hours of classes per week. Entry is by audition workshop or online interview.
- Part-Time Acting – Vocational (1.5 terms), 7.5 hours of classes per week. Entry is by audition workshop or online interview.

Short-term and part-time courses

• MA Theatre for Community and Education (2 years). Part-time, one day of in-person teaching each week, with one additional Friday and Saturday each term. Entry is by interview.

Oxford School of Drama*
Sansomes Farm Studios, Woodstock,
Oxford OX20 1ER
tel (01993) 812883
email info@oxforddrama.ac.uk
website www.oxforddrama.ac.uk
Facebook /TheOxfordSchoolOfDrama
Instagram @oxford_drama
Principal Edward Hicks

The Oxford School of Drama provides professional actor training in the form of 3-year, 1-year and 6-month Foundation courses. In addition to their full-time courses they offer a series of short courses. Their short courses cover subjects such as Screen Acting, Devising, and Audition Preperation. They also offer a series of professional development courses designed for the working actor to refresh and revisit their craft. Courses include Movement Craft Boost and Casting Craft Boost. Visit **https://oxforddrama.ac.uk/courses/short-acting-courses** to find out more.

Pineapple Dance Studios
7 Langley Street, London WC2H 9JA
tel 020-7836 4004
website www.pineapple.uk.com
X @pineappledance
Instagram @pineappledancestudios

Pineapple offers more classes than any other studio throughout Europe, and the widest variety of dance styles. The philosophy behind the creation of the Pineapple Dance Studios was to break down the elitist barriers surrounding dance, making it available to everyone – from the absolute beginner to the advanced and the professional dancer. Everybody is welcome: Pineapple offers classes for all levels and all ages. Approx. 400 classes per week (250 in studio and 150 streamed live), ranging across 40 styles from classical ballet to street jazz, hip hop to Salsa, Egyptian dance to Bollywood grooves.

The Questors Theatre Ealing
12 Mattock Lane, London W5 5BQ
tel 020-8567 0011
email studentgroup@questors.org.uk
website www.questors.org.uk
Course Director David Emmet

Provides part-time training for actors in the context of a working theatre. Financial support is available from a private trust fund for a limited number of students.

Courses offered:

• Acting: Foundation (one year). 6 hours of classes per week.
• Acting: Performance (one year). Only open to students who have completed the Foundation course.

Richmond Drama School
RACC, Parkshot, Richmond TW9 2RE
tel 020-8891 5907
email info@rhacc.ac.uk
website www.rhacc.ac.uk/courses/performing-arts-music

Courses offered:

Has an exceptional reputation for outstanding teaching and a strong history of placing students in top CDT drama schools; these include RADA, Central, Drama Studio, ALRA and Stella Addler (New York) amongst others. Many previous students, who have not desired an academic pathway, have been able to step straight into the professional industry.

Courses offered:

• Acting and Performing Skills for Budding Actors (12 weeks).
• Foundation Acting Techniques for Performance (10 weeks).
• Drama for Confidence (10 weeks).

Royal Academy of Dramatic Art (RADA)*
62–64 Gower Street, London WC1E 6ED
tel 020-7636 7076
email enquiries@rada.ac.uk
website www.rada.ac.uk/short-courses
Facebook /RoyalAcademyofDramaticArt
Instagram @royalacademyofdramaticart
Director Edward Kemp

RADA offers a range of in-person, online and blended courses.

Courses offered:

In-person:

• Acting for Camera
• Acting for Young Actors
• Acting Fundamentals
• Advanced Acting Fundamentals
• Advanced Scene Study for Actors
• Elements of RADA Workshops
• Fundamentals of Classical Acting (Manchester)
• Meisner
• Scene Study for Actors
• Short Course Saturdays
• Spoken English for Actors
• Stanislavski: Physical Action
• Telling Tales

Online:
• An Actor's Workout
• Elements of RADA Workshops
• Spoken English for Actors

Blended:
• Acting Fundamentals
• Advanced Acting Fundamentals
• Foundation Course in Acting (part-time)

Training

Other courses:
• The RADA Contemporary Drama Summer School (5 days). This course provides the opportunity to work on modern or contemporary texts. Students work in groups led by a director, with support from a voice and a movement instructor. Other playwrights talk about their work during special evening sessions, describing their experience of working with actors and what they expect from them, following presentations of excerpts from their plays by RADA graduates. Students present rehearsed material and receive feedback from the director and the voice and movement teachers on the last day of the course. Students below the age of 18 are not normally accepted; there is no upper age limit.
• Numerous other courses throughout the year. Please check the website.

The Royal Central School of Speech and Drama*

ROYAL CENTRAL
SCHOOL OF SPEECH & DRAMA
UNIVERSITY OF LONDON

64 Eton Avenue, London NW3 3HY
tel 020-7722 8183
email short.courses@cssd.ac.uk
website www.cssd.ac.uk/short-courses
Principal Josette Bushell Mingo OBE

Central offers a diverse range of part-time courses, both online and in person, run by industry professionals. Evening and Diploma courses include:
• Acting: An Introduction (evening, 8 weeks)
• Acting: Intermediate (evening, 8 weeks)
• Audition Technique for Drama School (evening, 8 weeks)
• Acting: The Play (evening, 8 weeks)
• Voice for Performance: An Introduction (evening, 8 weeks)
• Acting for Camera: An Introduction (evening, 8 weeks)
• Acting Diploma (part-time, one year)
• Gap Year Acting Diploma (part-time, one year)
• Performance Making Diploma for Learning Disabled and Autistic Adults (part-time, 2 years)

There are also Summer Short Courses, Continuing Professional Development and Artist Development Programmes available. Visit the website for full details.

Theatre Royal Haymarket Masterclass Trust

Theatre Royal Haymarket, London SW1Y 4HT
tel 020-7389 9660
email info@masterclass.org.uk
website www.masterclass.org.uk
X @Masterclasstrh

Patrons Dame Judi Dench, Sir David Hare, Dame Maureen Lipman, Elaine Page OBE, Jonathan Slinger

Masterclass is a theatre charity based at the Theatre Royal Haymarket that opens doors to young people from all backgrounds, aged 16–30, who are interested in the performance industry. The free programme provides workshops and talks with leading actors, directors, designers and writers working in theatre today, alongside unique performance experiences, apprenticeship opportunities and community projects.

Previous Masters have included Ryan Calais Cameron, Danny DeVito, Idris Elba, Tom Hiddleston, Anoushka Lucas, Lynette Linton and Phoebe Waller-Bridge. For details of forthcoming events, consult the website.

Theatre Workout Ltd

Kemsing Road, London SE10 0LL
tel 020-8144 2290
email enquiries@theatreworkout.com
website www.theatreworkout.com
Facebook /theatreworkout
X @theatreworkout
Director Adam Milford

Theatre Workout is a leading producer of theatre workshops in London's West End, Stratford-Upon-Avon and in schools across the UK.

Unseen Acting School

Spotlight Building, 16 Garrick Street, London WC2E 9BA
tel 020-3089 8536
email information@theunseen.co.uk
website https://theunseen.co.uk
Facebook /Theunseendrama
X @UNSEENDRAMA
Instagram @unseendrama

Founded in 2016. Nurtures new voices and diverse talent, encouraging students to discover what makes them unique as a performer. Courses are available for a range of levels, from beginners to advanced performers. Masterclasses are fully-directed sessions, teaching a range of techniques and incorporating scene work and feedback. Also holds monthly showcases attended by casting directors and agents.

Courses offered:

• Standard (6 weeks). 5 hours a week. Includes a certificate of completion.
• Professional (6 weeks). 5 hours a week. Includes a showcase submission with preliminary feedback, final internal feedback and external agency grading, and sharing of showcase piece to agents and casting directors.
• Professional plus (6 weeks). 5 hours a week. Includes a 30 minute one-on-one session with an agent, casting director or manager to discuss showcase feedback and develop a career strategy.

Private tutors and coaches

Acting Coach Scotland
Unit 34, 6 Harmony Row, Govan Workspace, Glasgow G51 3BA
tel 0141 440 1272
email hello@actingcoachscotland.co.uk
website www.actingcoachscotland.co.uk
Facebook /ActingCoachScotland
X @hello_acs
Instagram @Weareactingcoachscotland
Principal Nick J. Field

Established in 2008, with the aim of making high quality professional training available to all. Acting Coach Scotland offers 3 full-time courses: a unique drama school preparation HNC in acting; a unique professional HND in acting and performance, and a bespoke one-year full time diploma in stage and screen performance. Staff are working actors, producers, writers, directors and other specialists. No scholarships are currently available.

There are no specific academic requirements for entrance, acceptance is by audition and interview. Applicants should be 17 years or older. The average age of the students is 25. Application should be made directly to the school.

Intensive training in acting, improvisation, acting for camera, voice, accents and performance psychology. Students experience many public performances, and the PD/HND courses include a 3-week run at the Edinburgh Fringe, and considerable acting for camera training. Students who complete the PD/HND course are entitled to Graduate Membership of Spotlight.

Applications from applicants with disabilities are welcome. Successful candidates with disabilities will have a full needs assessment before the course begins.

Audition Doctor
Based in Borough, SE1
tel 020-7357 8237
email tilly.blackwood@gmail.com
website www.auditiondoctor.co.uk
X @auditiondoctors
Instagram @audition_doctor

Provides a bespoke service that gives invaluable support and insight into anything to do with finding your authentic, creative voice in the industry. Whether auditioning for drama school or in the profession at large, the sessions focus on finding your unique style that makes you stand out from the crowd. Initial consultations offered for £50. Teaches from home (wheelchair accessible). The nearest station is Borough on the Northern Line, around a 4-minute walk away. "I have been, and continue to be, a professional working actor for the last 30 years, and have been teaching for the last 10. I pride myself on my reputation for getting results, which I am pleased to say is evident in the many testimonials that you can find on my website". Audition Doctor has been listed in the top 10 Acting Coaches on the Acting in London website.

Ross Campbell
Private Studios, West London and Surrey
mobile 07956 465165
email rosscampbell@ntlworld.com
website https://rosscampbell.biz, www.dailysingingtips.com
Facebook /rosscampbelluk, / SingingAnExtensiveHandbook
X @rosscampbelluk

Specialises in singing and acting techniques, audition preparation, college entrance and related examinations and diplomas. Is happy to provide material for private students to use and to answer minor follow-up queries after a lesson.

Teaches in a private studio at home in Surrey and a private London studio. The nearest stations are West Brompton and Barons Court (a 7-minute walk). Has taught many actors, singers and triple threat performers for over 30 years, and has professionals in every West End show on a continuous basis. Ross is a professor at the Royal Academy of Music London; Fellow of The Royal Society of Arts; author of *Singing: An Extensive Handbook for all Singers and Their Teachers*; Director and Head of Singing and Musical Theatre at Musical Theatre UK (MTI); Consultant to Musical Theatre UK Ltd; Patron and Chief Advisor to the Ceo of International Performing Arts and Theatre Ltd; former Head of Music and Singing at Guildford School of Acting/University of Surrey (GSA); and a consultant to Musical Theatre Poland (MTP). He is also an award-winning author for the ABRSM.

Mel Churcher
mobile 07778 773019
email melchurcher@gmail.com
website www.melchurcher.com, www.actinganddrama.com

Teaches individuals one-to-one by Zoom and runs live workshops. See more details on her websites.

She has taught thousands of actors and aspiring actors over many decades. She has worked as an actor, voice and acting coach, and theatre director; taught at most major UK drama schools; coached on more than 75 films and TV series (see **www.imdb.me/melchurcher**); run national and international workshops; directed showreels; and authored 3 books: *Acting for Film: Truth 24 Times a*

Second (Virgin Books), *A Screen Acting Workshop* (Nick Hern Books) and *The Elemental Actor* (Nick Hern Books). Holds an MA in Performing Arts (Middlesex) and in Voice Studies (CSSD). "I am happy to help with most aspects of auditioning and working in theatre and film, including preparation for self-tapes, building confidence and overcoming nerves, and voice and breath work."

M.J. Coldiron
54 Millfields Road, London E5 0SB
mobile 07941 920498
email mcoldiron@mac.com

Offers audition coaching for professional and aspiring actors; advice about theatre and performance training in the US and the UK; and coaching in acting technique, public speaking and presentation skills. Charges £50 per hour, £130 for 3 sessions. Occasional group workshops. Can provide material for clients and is happy to receive minor follow-up queries. Teaches from home studio, with the nearest rail station being Hackney Central Overground. Has taught hundreds of successful actors over 30 years; please make contact for more details. Advises clients: "The theatrical profession is very demanding and is not to be sought for fame or fortune. It is also very competitive and you must work hard, but if you have talent, desire and discipline I can help you to improve your technique and gain in confidence."

The Confident Voice
School of Philosophy and Economic Science Building, 11–13 Mandeville Place, London W1V 3AJ
mobile 07976 805976
email neville@speakwell.co.uk
website www.speakwell.co.uk
Tutor Neville Wortman

At present online via Zoom. One-to-one hour tuition includes audition technique and voice. Services include coaching in elocution, communication techniques and self-awareness; also the establishment of confidence and natural performance. Neville specialises in dialogue, Shakespeare, musical comedy and lyrical interpretation. Fee details are available on application.

Bridget de Courcy
19 Muswell Road, London N10 2BJ
tel 020-8883 8397
email singinglessons@bridgetdecourcy.co.uk
website https://bridgetdecourcymusic.co.uk

Taught singing at the Actors Centre, Covent Garden for 19 years. Styles of singing taught include jazz, classical, opera, musical theatre, pop and contemporary. Initial lesson (including a consultation) is £85, with subsequent lessons for £75.

Antonia Doggett
Based in East London and Westcliff on Sea
email antoniadoggettcontact@gmail.com
website www.antoniadoggett.co.uk

Specialises in auditions, cold reading/sight reading, drama school audition, LAMDA exam preparation, communication and presentation, Speech and voice. Charges £40 per hour (£35 on Zoom) and prefers payment by PayPal or electronic transfer. Is happy to provide material for private students to use, and to answer minor follow-up queries after a lesson.

Teaches in East London, or happy to travel elsewhere in London or client's home for longer classes. Has been coaching for 18 years and previously trained with Teatr Piesn Kozla, Poland, assistant director for Stathis Livathinos, National Theatre of Greece.

Embodiment with Rebecca Reaney
Based in London (online and USA)
mobile 07398 617693
email rebeccareaneymovement@gmail.com
website www.rebeccareaneymovement.com
Instagram @rebeccareaney

Acting coach, intimacy coordinator and movement director. Supports actors in getting out of their 'thinking head' and instead connected to their mind and body working together, listening to instincts, impulses and trusting themselves and their choices. Specialises in supporting actors with embodiment, physicality, movement and intimacy. Suitable for auditions for drama school, castings (last minute if needed), bespoke ongoing actor training from beginners to professionals, embodied text analysis, character development, personal development, pre production/rehearsal period coaching and work as a creative.

Charges £75 per hour ($100 US dollars) with discounts if purchasing bundles of classes. For your investment you receive:

- Free consultation session before working together.
- One-to-one coaching session via zoom or in person (subject to availability).
- Pre-session planning based on the material or information sent beforehand to create a bespoke session tailored to your requirements and desired outcomes.
- Post-session follow up with notes from the session and any additional video or audio tracks to support your journey.
- Email contact for any ongoing queries.

"With extensive experience working as an actor in the industry both in the UK and USA, transitioning into coaching since 2018 has been fuelled with my continued passion for the industry and the importance of creating truth in storytelling that is connected to each individual embodying and breathing life into the characters they play. You are enough and I'll guide you to realise that."

Prue Gillett Actor Training
Based in Gloucestershire
email prue@pruegillett.com
website www.pruegillett.com

Specialises in Received Pronunciation and Accent Reduction, and Sanford Meisner's approach to acting. Charges £50 per hour for private sessions. Provides material for students' use, and will answer minor follow-up queries at no extra cost. Teaches one-to-one online and from home near Cirencester, Gloucestershire. Workshops at drama schools and other locations are arranged on request. Please see website for further details.

John Grayson
2 Jubilee Road, St Johns, Worcester WR2 4LY
mobile 07702 188031
email johngraysonvoiceartist@outlook.com
website www.johngraysonvoiceartist.com

Actor, singer and voice artist specialising in coaching audition speeches, voice over for actors, and public speaking and presentation for business people. Teaches via Zoom etc, or from home. Nearest station Worcester Foregate Street (good service from Birmingham), then a 10–15 minute walk. Can provide material if needed. Happy to receive follow up queries.

Martin Harris
17 Groveland Road, Wallasey, Merseyside CH45 8JX
mobile 07788 723570
email martin@auditioncoach.co.uk
website www.auditioncoach.co.uk

Specialises in one-to-one audition technique, including the selection and direction of audition pieces for aspiring and professional actors. Teaches sight reading and gives advice about the business. Charges £40 per hour. Accepts payment with cash or via Internet banking. Happy to provide material for private students to use, and will answer minor follow-up queries at no extra charge. Teaches online or at his home next to Wallasey Grove Road train station. Trained at Birmingham School of Acting, and has worked as an actor and director since 1992.

Jennifer Jane Hooker
Based in Central London
mobile 07725 977146
email jjanehooker@yahoo.com

Specialises in character work, scene breakdown, emotional and sensory work, and audition technique. Teaches both known actors and new students with emphasis on practical work – proven results in both drama school entry and auditions. Trained with Susan Batson of Susan Batson Studios, NYC, who sends her actors to JJ when they are in Europe. Certified practitioner of Core Competency Coaching, an effective technique to get rid of fears and judgements that stop us from reaching our true potential. Can provide material for use by private students.

Mark Hudson
MSA, 14–32 Hewitt Street, Manchester M15 4GB
tel 0161 238 8900
email mark@manchesterschoolofacting.co.uk
website www.manchesterschoolofacting.co.uk

International film-, television- and theatre-acting, dialogue and dialect coach.

Charlie Hughes-D'Aeth
Based in Greater London
email chdaeth@aol.com
website https://charliehughesdaeth.co.uk

Freelance text and voice coach. Currently voice coach at the Old Vic and previously consultant on RSC's *Matilda the Musical*. Offers coaching on practical voice technique for business and theatre/musical theatre. Also works with people living with Long Covid.

Martin McKellan
mobile 07425 204070
email leomckellan@yahoo.com
website www.martinmckellan.com

Specialises in auditions, acting classes and all aspects of voice work (accent and dialogue a particular area of expertise). Rates are negotiable and offers are available; please make contact for full details. Is happy to provide material for private students to use, and to answer minor follow-up queries at no extra charge. Will teach from home, from a client's home or at another location. Covent Garden is the nearest tube station, 3 minutes' walk away. Has taught thousands of actors and aspiring actors over the past 15 years, and has extensive experience as a freelance acting/voice coach working in the West End and in Regional Theatre and for both film and television.

Alison Mead
9 Victoria Road, Chislehurst BR7 6DE
tel 020-3601 7022, mobile 07770 672589
email alison@alisonmead.com
email alison.mead49@gmail.com
website www.alisonmead.com

Recently taught Meisner Techniques at Rose Bruford School of Performing Arts, Alison specialises in audition technique, accent work, sight reading, acting for camera and character building. Alison is a specialist in Meisner technique and Stanislavski in preparation for auditions and rehearsals. Charges are negotiable, but there is a basic rate of £40 per hour for private tuition (£70 for 2 hours). Sessions can be also be shared by 2 people for £60 per hour. Alison is happy to provide monologue and text material for private students to use, and to answer minor follow-up queries after a lesson.

Teaches at home, which is wheelchair-accessible or is happy to travel to student's home for a small extra charge. The nearest stations, Elmstead Woods and Mottingham, are 20 minutes from London Bridge. Trains to Bickley from Victoria run twice per hour and take 25 minutes. Alison will meet you from these stations with good notice. She also offers group workshops for schools and colleges designed specifically to meet the students' needs. Alison has taught Drama and Theatre Arts at degree level, A-Level and GCSE. She has adjudicated at 6 drama festivals for both adults and young people and runs her own theatre company, AMProductions. "Make sure this is the career for you and that it is what you want above all else."

Robin Miller
Based in London
email robinjenni@hotmail.com
website www.actorsandwriters.london/robin.miller/

Specialises in audition speeches, accents and dialects. Charges £25 per hour (special packages negotiable; preferred payment methods are cash or bank transfer), and is happy to answer minor follow-up queries at no extra charge. Teaches at home – no steps up to the house. Nearest station is St Margaret's, 12 minutes away, or Twickenham, 10 minutes away. Bus routes are H22, H37, 110 or 267. Also teaches at the client's home. Has 30 years' experience in the acting profession as an actress, writer, workshop leader, teacher and director; please see Spotlight and Mandy for further details. Advises actors that "choosing the right speech is incredibly important".

Mime the Gap
tel 07970 685982
email mimethegap@mac.com
website www.mimethegap.com
Contact Richard Knight

Richard Knight is a specialist in mime and movement who offers professional advice on movement, mime, mask, physical theatre, clown, Commedia dell'arte, slapstick comedy, physical comedy, and visual performances.

Frances Parkes
tel 020-8542 2777
email frances@maxyourvoice.com
website www.maxyourvoice.com

Group and one-to-one coaching online or face to face at Spotlight Studios, Old Diorama or Dragaon Hall in Central London.

Richard Ryder Dialect Coach
Based in London and Madrid
mobile 07967 352551
email richervoice@gmail.com
website www.richardrydervoice.com
website www.theaccentkit.com

Specialises in accents, voice and text coaching. Charges £95 per hour for actors paying themselves. Happy to provide material for private students to use, and to answer minor queries at no extra cost. Has more than 20 years' teaching and coaching experience, at the RSC, National Theatre, West End theatre, opera, TV and film. You can buy accent kits from the website and download The Accent Kit app.

Rebecca Semark
Based in Epping, Essex
tel 01992 574967 , mobile 07956 850330
email rebecca@semark.biz
website www.semark.biz

Specialises in audition technique, monologues and voice technique. Tuition for stage and drama school entrants includes singing and LAMDA exams. Also coaches public speaking for older students and adults. Teaches from home, online via Zoom or Skype. The closest station is Epping on the Central Line, which is a 5–10 minute walk. Has taught many performers, actors and aspiring actors for over 25 years. Has worked extensively in theatre and television as an actress and in many plays, musical theatre and television. Please call for an informal chat to discuss your needs.

Ros Simmons
120 Hillfield Avenue, Crouch End, London N8 7DN
tel 020-8347 8089
email ros@rossimmons.co.uk
website www.rossimmons.co.uk

One hour individual coaching session £85.00. There is a reduction to this rate for a commitment of 3 or more sessions.

Specialises in accents and dialects, voice and auditions, as well as Spoken English skills for those with English as a second language. Provides full accent breakdowns and is happy to answer minor follow-up queries.

Has taught around 1,000 actors and aspiring actors, in drama schools and privately, over a period of 20 years. Trained as an actor at the Polytechnic School of Theatre in Manchester, and has worked extensively in theatre, film, TV and radio.

The Society for the Teachers of the Alexander Technique
PO Box 78503, London N14 8GB
tel 020-8885 6524
email stat@alexandertechnique.co.uk
website https://alexandertechnique.co.uk
Facebook /alexander.technique.1
Instagram @alexandertechuk
LinkedIn @alexandertechniquesociety
Development Manager Esther Miltiadous, Committees Secretary Heather Penn

The Society for the Teachers of the Alexander Technique (STAT) provide the highest standards of teaching training and professional practice. They teach the Alexander Technique, a practical and demonstrable tool in training and honing performance skills. See the website for details of available teachers.

Sarah Valentine
email sarah@actorsaccentcoach.com
website www.actorsaccentcoach.com
Facebook /actorsaccentcoach

X @accentcoach1
Instagram @actorsaccentcoach

Accent coach for actors and voice actors with over 30 years of industry experience. Services offered include perfecting existing skills, learning new accents or reducing an accent. As well as one-to-one online coaching sessions, Sarah also offers DIY courses which can be downloaded from her website and a variety of free resources available on Youtube and TikTok.

Spoken States

Based in North London
email info@spokenstates.com
website www.spokenstates.com
Contact Anne Wittman

Specialises in coaching British and other non-US actors in a range of American dialects for audition and performance. Also works with accent correction for foreign speakers who would like to attain greater clarity of speech and to correct or soften their existing accent towards General American. Coaches RP for both native and foreign speakers; also coaches acting for audition and performance. Enjoys working with poets and other writers on presentation of their own material at readings.

Charges £60 for one hour, £85 for 90 mins and £110 for 2 hours. Happy to provide material for private students to use, and to answer minor follow-up queries at no extra cost. Teaches from home (wheelchair accessible), and is also connected with various institutions. Nearest tube stations are Finsbury Park or Highgate: the most direct route to the main teaching location is the W3 or W7 bus from Finsbury Park. Has taught at least 500 actors since 1994. Further details are available from the website.

An actor's journey into directing (and back again)

Harry Burton

Forty years ago I was a student at the Central School of Speech & Drama when an inspirational actor/director named Mark Wing-Davey directed a group of us in *The Winter's Tale* (Mark is currently Professor at NYU Graduate Acting after 15 years as Chair of Tisch NYU in New York, but back then famous for portraying the two-headed Galactic President Zaphod Beeblebrox in *The Hitchhiker's Guide to the Galaxy* on BBC TV). Mark had the cast playing the washboard and pretending to be deranged sheep – in fact he embodied the sort of deliciously unhinged sense of mischief and rather British anarchy that makes a mightily positive impression on young actors hungry to learn. From dreading Shakespeare, and feeling intimidated by the terrifying mysteries of verse-speaking, we were translated into an energised mob of gleeful enthusiasts undaunted by technical matters, freed up to delight in the wild, almost improvisatory excesses of sharing a knockout story.

The show only played to an audience of fellow students and college staff, but it was clearly (for this student at least) an unforgettable experience since I'm still excited now as I recall it. We were very lucky indeed at that time to be exposed to directors like Mark and others besides (Bardie Thomas, Tony Falkingham, David Terence, Penny Casdagli). They instilled in us a devotional love of storytelling, and a willingness to share with an audience in a spirit that was irreverent and nourishing.

Fast-forward a decade or so from that *Winter's Tale*. Mark was now Artistic Director of the Actors Centre in London's West End. He invited me to participate in a workshop probing the choreography of intimate yet workaday activities (chopping vegetables, ironing a shirt), to the accompaniment of fraught modernist chamber music. Asked "Why?", Mark would respond with an air of disarming innocence: "I just think it might be interesting." Which it was.

Wing-Davey's ethos at the Actors Centre, in other words, was to maintain a laboratory space, a place where research experiments exploring the creating of characters and the components of theatrical presence could be undertaken for their own sake. This was radical to me, but hardly revolutionary in the grand scheme of things. Most self-respecting theatre companies in the 60s and 70s had a church hall or a converted laundry dedicated to experimental work. Mark was simply carrying on the tradition he'd been brought up in, as well as being genuinely fascinated by.

It was a golden era for the Actors Centre. This much-needed institution is currently in deeply troubled times. I fervently pray it recovers swiftly and renews its original mission and identity. Back in the day under Mark's leadership practitioners of the calibre of the late, great Marcello Magni (of Complicité) were teaching there. We did an epic *Commedia* class with Magni in an abandoned warehouse in Whitechapel. An entire day was spent inching our grotesquely masked faces around a doorway only for maestro Marcello to stop us in our tracks: "Go back! For God's sake must you be so BORING? Come in again!"

Although the concept of continuous professional development was much more familiar to American actors than to young Brits, it nevertheless formed the basis of the Actors

Centre's sense of purpose. For me these classes were intoxicating experiences, stretching and challenging us to be more open and adventurous as performers and creative people. In this intensely playful atmosphere I could feel myself sprouting winglets of ambition. Before long I'd formed the grandiose notion of running a workshop of my own. Emboldened, I approached Mark and told him I was in the grip of an urgent urge to lead an experimental session. "What's it about?" Fair enough, I hadn't a clue. So I went away and pondered.

Until that moment in my youthful career (I was a pretty undeveloped thirty year-old – think of the Fool in the Tarot deck) I don't think I'd ever seriously considered leading anything, let alone directing. I suspected that directors with personal experience of acting were better equipped to guide actors into exciting performances through a savvy shorthand rather than extended exegeses. I knew I was flourishing under the easy authority Mark brought to his process, whether preparing a play or in an experimental class. His rehearsal room seemed free of hierarchy. Everything felt like a natural, collaborative, often joyous extension of focussed play. Mark's example showed us that a director must lead, but not dominate.

Working with more experienced actors, I picked up on a tendency to judge directors as either fantastic or useless. Harsh perhaps, but it's not hard for actors to become cynical. Actors after all are the ones who have to go out before an audience every night. Their workload can be doubled if the director is less than dynamic – individually actors have to honour their strand of the storytelling, while collectively doing their best to make an unbalanced production seem coherent.

It was my good fortune at this time to be cast and directed by Harold Pinter in a double bill of his plays at the Almeida – a very positive and undoubtedly formative experience. I witnessed and experienced intimately the supernatural patience with which he nurtured actors, instilling confidence and ownership.

I was still simply a performer in love with performing and the applause it brought, lost in the fantasy that I was a phone call away from being plucked from the pool tables of Portobello Road and plonked in the Hollywood Hills to fulfil my fate and become a star.

Working with Pinter was profoundly educational. We worked as a team, and he was its servant. As director he saw his work as fulfilling an obligation to lead us down a road of discovery, focussed at every step on realising the text. He claimed no absolute foreknowledge of how that text should be played merely because he happened to have written it. Indeed from time to time he would listen carefully to an actor's question before replying: "I'm afraid the author has no further information".

Pondering my overweening urge to lead a workshop, I considered that thus far in my career I'd quite often witnessed an actor turning to their leader for help – for leadership in fact – only for the director to mislead them, ignore them, or actually run away. If to lead is to serve, my three years at Central had taught me two potentially communicable skills that could conceivably be useful to others. One was that I could juggle. The other was seeded by a disastrous personal failure in a Restoration comedy. Paralysed in rehearsal by terror, I'd somehow neglected to create anything that could be passed off in performance as a 'character'. My tutors' stupefied reaction shook me badly. I discerned that, terrified or not, an actor has a contractual obligation failing all else to commit to playing *something*. My failure wasn't the director's fault exactly. On the other hand he'd been at a total loss as to how guide me towards success. The Sufi poet Rumi has some lines that encapsulate the dilemma. Writing about what he calls 'spiritual window-shopping', he nevertheless nails the risks and rewards of acting:

> Even if you don't know what you want,
> buy something, to be part of the exchanging flow.
> Start a huge, foolish project, like Noah.
> It makes absolutely no difference
> what people think of you.
> (Translated by Robert Bly)

So I figured I could at a push lead a (very basic) juggling workshop. More intriguingly, having died onstage in *She Stoops To Conquer* and lived to tell the tale, I had a growing intuition that I might potentially be helpful to performers who felt fearful, blocked, or all at sea.

Under Mark's gimlet eye, I began offering workshops focussed on guiding performers to find or re-connect to their full and uncensored relish of being on stage. All actors know at one time or another the absurd irony of longing desperately for work, only to find oneself too neurotic to enjoy it when it finally happens. Audiences would be stunned into disbelief were they privy even briefly to the hilariously toxic self-talk performers experience in their heads whilst attempting to act. Leaders of all types are the same: in a famous survey of CEOs, Death came second behind Public Speaking as the number one dread. Terror comes with the territory. Yet we all know how inspirational it is to watch an actor at the top of their game, or listen to a public speaker who is fully present, comfortable in their bodies, commanding in their use of voice and language.

After leading a few of these workshops without too many disasters (I'd furtively raid the percussion cupboard at my baby daughter's playgroup, my brave participants bashing away at the bongos, congas and castanets until I worked up enough courage to start the class), the implacable need to stretch my leadership wings and direct an actual play grew apace. This time Mark shook his head – understandably, given that my strategy largely consisted of the entitled conviction that yearning to direct a play would somehow prompt one to fling itself at me demanding to be directed.

Yet curiously this is not so far from what followed a while later. Some hopeful actors down at the Bridewell Theatre were working up a lunchtime production of *The Lover* by Harold Pinter. Their director had gone AWOL and my name had been put forward as someone who could possibly help. I didn't know that particular play, but – having myself been directed by Pinter – I had a certain (perhaps foolish) confidence that I could get the play on and with only a few days' rehearsal.

The actors were grateful and willing to work. I'd learned at the Almeida that rehearsing Pinter requires a process of patient investigation; a humble seeking out of clues. Most importantly I'd seen Harold nurture confidence and ownership in his cast. Having experienced his leadership close up it seemed the task of the director is to guide the rehearsal process with a firm hand, and encourage the actors to commit completely to the unfolding moment. Any actor with the courage to abandon safety and open themselves to the eternal present has an even chance of enjoying the experience of performing. It's precisely this performer's freedom and relish that audiences thrill to see in the theatre.

After a few rehearsals the play was definitely responding to the vigorous defibrillation we were applying to the existing shape of the production. An audience came and seemed to enjoy the performances. Perhaps the acting wasn't the best in town that season, but it was theatrical and passionate. We created something memorable in its own terms. Personally I couldn't deny the intense excitement of intimately interacting with a story, finding its life, excavating its rhythms, discovering its infinite detail, feeling the play move and surge, sensing that I'd found another side of myself, a side that naturally offered itself in service to the passionate sharing of a story.

Mark Wing-Davey moved on from the Actors Centre in 2002. His successor Matthew Lloyd was another intelligent leader and an excellent director – not least of numerous premieres by Philip Ridley. Matthew was ambitious to raise the organisation's profile. Perhaps he had this in mind when he encouraged me to do something seriously scary: invite Harold Pinter to be part of a workshop focussing on rehearsing scenes from his own plays. Pinter was on the mend from a very serious operation for oesophageal cancer. The celebrated director of dozens of plays throughout his career, he made a public statement to the effect that he no longer had the energy to direct. Obviously extreme stress isn't a great health strategy for a person recovering from a life-threatening illness. But I'd spent enough time with him to feel he was being over-cautious. He had plenty left in the tank and the idea of retirement was patently ridiculous. So I took my life in my hands and asked him.

"What's a workshop?", was his quizzical reply.

It turned out that in fifty years of professional activity no one had ever asked Harold Pinter to do a workshop. But his interest had sparked.

We did a workshop. He enjoyed it so much that afterwards he had to be dragged away from the bar. Mulling the event's success, I found myself questioning whether we'd missed a trick. More than once, with Harold's encouragement, an actor had found her courage and experienced a moment of breakthrough, the kind of electrifying leap in imagination and confidence that changes the course of a rehearsal. Such moments are charged with a sense of electric creative development. Everyone present bears witness to a flashpoint of theatrical discovery. Had a camera been recording, would it have picked up the galvanic currents underpinning the crucial phases of our work? Indeed can such things ever be captured in their essence? Or would it be like trying to film a ghost – an invisible energy sensed, but, when reviewed, nothing to see beyond the commonplace and mundane?

I'd always loved playing with cameras, so obviously the idea of somehow filming a rehearsal workshop with Pinter in the room was very exciting, if far-fetched.

I broached the subject with him. He listened with close attention, then asked my reason for wanting to film the session. I said we'd be creating a valuable archive, potentially of great interest to future generations of writers, actors and directors with an appetite to learn about Pinter's values and practices.

Coincidentally (though I'm not entirely sure I believe in coincidence), to further my dream of directing, I'd signed up to take the BBC TV Single Camera Directors Course. Pinter agreed to participate in the filmed session, at which point I turned to my tutors from the Directors Course at BBC Training & Development. They agreed to be my crew. The footage from the workshop became the basis of a documentary called *Working for Pinter*. Channel 4 paid for it, thanks to Pinter blessing the film with his full participation and various people vouching for me so as to reassure Channel 4.

All this activity created a strong impression – though I was slow to believe it – that I was becoming a director. This impression gathered substantial momentum when Ian

Rickson, then Artistic Director of the Royal Court, invited me out of the blue to direct rehearsed readings of Pinter's *The Room and The Dumb Waiter*. Initially flabbergasted, I soon worked out what had happened. Rickson had asked Pinter if he had a director in mind for these readings marking the Court's 50th birthday season. Knowing I had a burning desire to direct, and having observed me at work in our recent workshops, he answered by pointing the finger in my direction: "Him." Harold was a wonderful mentor: when he believed in you he believed in you unreservedly.

I think play readings are a fascinating theatrical form. They can generate tremendous potency. The accepted circumstances of a reading dictate that the actors have no rehearsal, minimal space for discussion or debate, and literally no time to work anything out or put a plan together. They're flying by the seat of their pants. But give them the right push at the right moment and they'll dive off the cliff with tremendous commitment and courage. Audiences won't analyse the difference between a rehearsed reading and a proper performance if they're not given time or space to. They simply respond to the guts of the actors, the vivid immediacy of the storytelling. If the cast rises instinctively to the challenge the whole enterprise has the potential to be charged with a powerful high-stakes energy, sometimes generating more heat and tension than a well-rehearsed show that's had ten previews and toured prior to opening in the West End. Those January 2006 rehearsed readings of *The Room and The Dumb Waiter* Upstairs at the Court went about as well as such things can. It's definitely risky, but a director who dares his or her actors to fly before they have any business knowing how to walk is sometimes richly rewarded.

Well, I certainly was. That night, unsuspected by me, the Guardian's theatre critic – also Pinter's official biographer – was in the audience. Michael Billington's notice was a beauty. There it was in black and white: I had become a director. One thing led to another. A few months later *The Dumb Waiter* opened at Trafalgar Studios, with Jason Isaacs and Lee Evans as Harold's hapless hitmen. Afterwards the playwright, still in his seat, gruffly informed us it was the greatest production of the play he'd ever seen. Lee and Jason blinked hard. I pinched myself. The producer wept. Ginger Spice photo-bombed Harold at the first-night party. Over dinner in a plush restaurant the producer asked me what I wanted to do next. "You hear that, my boy?" said Harold, grinning his wolfish grin. I nominated a play, and we began casting a few weeks later. A fortnight after that the producer dropped the project, and with it me. This, I came to understand, was not unusual in the world of directing. In my experience the fantasy of beginner's luck tends to be followed by a swift restoration of reality.

I'm still directing, still leading workshops, still happiest in a rehearsal room thrilling to those luminous moments of discovery when an actor finds the courage to step further into the unknown, further away from themselves, risking everything to strike theatrical gold. The essential willingness of actors to be vulnerable is a constant privilege to witness and nurture. The actors I admire always acknowledge that, while they may be key participants, the credit for our collective labour is always shared with something unseen and mysterious.

My word for that is 'mythological'. A mythic perspective on imagination gives us permission to magnify passion and pathos, to be truly theatrical yet maintain specificity and truthfulness. Audiences come to surrender to a story, to bear witness to the strange ordeal of being fully human. Their faith is that by the time they leave the theatre their molecules will have been rearranged. That's the challenge, and it's a noble one.

An actor's journey into directing (and back again)

Writers are my heroes, but I'm no good at directing plays that meander gently along existing pathways. The unpredictable, the mysterious, the incomprehensible, the life-and-death extremes we recognise from threshold moments in our own lives are the qualities that appeal to me in a play. Theatrical performance must reflect the true depths of the human situation for it to do its work. Most of the time, if we can just bring ourselves to look at life as it truly is, we have no idea how things will turn out, no idea who we are or who we're becoming. We feel most alive when conscious of a mythological sense that we're damned if we do and damned if we don't. The poet Theodore Roethke said it best: "The edge is all I have!"

Everything touched by myth comes full circle eventually, so I'm trying my hand at acting again, drawn back to the challenge of surrendering to imagination and play. Having taught acting for camera for a decade it's interesting, to say the least, to see whether the ideas I've advocated so passionately survive exposure to the real world. Returning after a break of fifteen years or so means being willing to begin afresh. No one remembers your work. Many of the industry people I knew twenty or thirty years ago have moved on. It's humbling and exciting to see what might happen.

Returning also means learning the joys of self-tapes, and of course re-acquainting myself with rejection – to say nothing of the possibility of success, however one defines it. "Success" is a charged word in our culture. The accepted definition has shrivelled to mean something merely material: an award, a cheque, a profile, a status. After forty years in this industry, my own notion of success has come a long way. I no longer glance anxiously sideways to compare my situation with what others are doing. Compare and despair, as the wise woman said. To be open to what comes, to be useful and of service – these are noble ambitions, sufficient unto the day. We all want to be chosen, to live our dreams and fulfil our potential. Often we're not best placed to see how far we've come. When the outcome is far from certain and doubt creeps in, I try to deploy Mark Rylance's gentle wisdom: "You are enough."

In other words these days I have a strong faith that if we keep ourselves honest, stay grounded and open to life on life's terms, the creative work that's ours somehow seeks us out. Who knows, it may even find us! The adventure is everything. If you're starting out, I wish you good luck on yours.

Harry Burton is an actor/director/coach, writer and filmmaker. Among many career highlights he especially relished singing Mozart's *Figaro* for BBC television, playing Professor Higgins in *My Fair Lady* at Drury Lane, several seasons of Shakespeare at the Open Air Theatre, Regent's Park, creating the role of Jimmy in Harold Pinter's *Party Time*, playing the lead in the world première of Noël Coward's *Post Mortem*, directing the première of *Barking in Essex* by Clive Exton in the West End, and the acclaimed Channel 4 documentary *Working with Pinter*. He also co-produced *A Thousand Years of Joy*, an Emmy award-winning documentary about the late American poet Robert Bly. Harry regularly directs and teaches at various drama schools. He tweets as @mataharifilms, which is also the handle of his You Tube channel. For more, see **www.WorkingWithPinter.com**.

Agents and casting directors
Introduction

Actors agents and casting directors are a relatively recent invention in the long and storied history of theatre but like all great innovations they made life easier and are now fundamental to the workings of the industry. In theory, agents absorb much of the administrative burden from actors who can then concentrate on the actual acting. Casting directors are a hive mind for theatres, producers and directors who no longer need to hold all the information about all the actors when they are hiring for roles. Actors dissatisfied with the institutional agent system formed the first co-operative agencies (see page 93) in the 1970s. This simple idea – with all members taking turns to 'man' the office – has since become established practise and a viable alternative to the traditional agencies. The best co-ops have as much professional credibility as their conventional agency counterparts. The majority of properly paid, professional acting work is brokered by agents and casting directors. The term 'casting agents' is used to describe walk-on agents who take the responsibility for casting walk-ons/extras in television and film. They have client bases comprising lots of different types and on request can supply a suitable crowd for any occasion. Thus they fulfil the roles of both agent and casting director for non-speaking parts that don't need to be auditioned.

Listings in this section:
- *Agents, page 70*
- *Co-operative agencies, page 93*
- *Voice-over agents, page 105*
- *Presenters' agents, page 108*
- *Casting directors, page 110*

Agents

A good agent understands contracts, knows the current rates in every field of work and most importantly – has plenty of professional contacts and access to far more casting information than most individuals can ever possess. Directors and casting directors rely on the agents they know and trust to help with the filtering process of whom to interview.

A good agent will work hard at promoting each of their clients; in return, they charge commission on every contract they negotiate – generally 10–20% (plus VAT, if appropriate). A good agent will only have as many clients as they can reasonably handle, and ensure they have a range of ages and types of actors to cover as many casting opportunities as possible.

Use the listings that follow to target your submission as accurately as possible by writing to specific people at agencies you have researched and chosen. Check for any details that could inform the content of your correspondence and whether each accepts any extras, like a showreel. Checking such details saves your time and theirs, and enhances your chances of receiving a positive response. Unless you have a good collection of professional credits, it is best to write to agents when they can see you performing.

If you are invited to meet an agent, remember you are the client. As much as you are auditioning for them, you should prepare questions that will help you ascertain if they are the right professional partner for you. Make sure you understand the scope of their role and rates of commission.

When seeking representation, you should only target agencies you think are the right fit for you. Look at their client list. Do they represent actors you admire and aspire to? Do they represent actors in your casting bracket? Do they have a track record of successfully promoting young actors, or actors from your background or speciality? Would you feel more comfortable as a small fish in the big pond of a large agency, or with more attention from a smaller agency?

When you've been taken on by an agent, it is important to establish how your working relationship will function. Be clear about areas of work you do – or don't – want to be suggested for, discuss your availability for auditions and interviews, agree how much promotion you should do for yourself, etc.

Do you need an agent? Technically, no. You can represent yourself. Spotlight will list you as 'Self-Represented' and provide your direct contact details to casting directors. Many actors are self-represented by choice or necessity, but for most an agent is a wise investment in professional credibility, industry access, wisdom and administrative support.

These listings only contain agents who represent adult actors.

†Member of the Personal Managers' Association

42†
Palladium House, 1–4 Argyll Street,
London W1F 7TA
tel 020-7292 0554
email info@42mp.com
website www.42mp.com
Partners Kate Buckley, Simon Beresford, *Managers* Ness Evans, Molly Cowan, Molly Wansell, Harrison Davies, Kelly Byrne, Ellie Martin-Sperry, Elle Cairns
Established 2013. Main areas of work are theatre, TV and film. Represents actors, directors, casting directors, writers and producers. Welcomes performance notices nationwide given a week's notice. Welcomes letters, CVs and photographs sent by email and showreels. Represents actors with disabilities.

A&J Artists
56 Park Avenue, Enfield EN1 2HW
tel 020-8004 3367

Agents 71

email info@ajartists.com
website www.ajartists.com
Managing Director Jo McLintock

Established in 1984. 2 agents represent actors. Areas of work include theatre, musicals, television, film and commercials.

Will consider attending performances with a minimum of 2 weeks' notice. Accepts submissions (with CVs and photographs) from actors previously unknown to the company if sent by email. Invitations to view individual actors' websites are also accepted.

Access Artiste Management Ltd

The Bloomsbury Building, 10 Bloomsbury Way, London WC1A 2SL
tel 020-3916 0270
email mail@access-uk.com
website www.access-uk.com
Manager Sarah Bryan

Established in 1999. Areas of work include theatre, musicals, television, film, commercials and corporate. Also represents directors, musical directors, choreographers, composers, playwrights and musical works.

Will consider attending performances in Greater London and elsewhere with one month's notice. Accepts submissions (with CVs and photographs) from professional actors previously unknown to the company. Showreels, voicereels and details of individual actors' websites should only be sent upon request. Welcomes enquiries from disabled actors.

Actors International Ltd

49 Greek Street, London W1D 4EG
tel 020-7118 2278
email mail@actorsinternational.co.uk
website www.actorsinternational.co.uk
Facebook /actorsintl
X @actorsintl
Agents Caroline Taylor, Lee Thomas

Established in 2000. 2 agents represent around 70 actors. Areas of work include theatre, musicals, television, film, commercials and corporate.

Will attend showcases/performances within Central London given as much notice as possible. Accepts email submissions only; no postal submissions will be considered.

The Agency | Dublin

25 Leeson Street Lower, Dublin D02 XD77, Republic of Ireland
tel +353 (0)1 661 8535
email office@theagency.ie
website www.theagency.ie
Instagram @theagency_dublin
Director Karl Hayden, *Agent* Claire Campbell, *Assistant* Ruby Furney

The Agency has been representing Ireland's foremost acting talent for stage and screen since its establishment over 30 years ago. In that time its multi-award-winning clients have appeared in numerous productions worldwide, and the company continues to set the standard for excellence in acting.

AHA Talent Ltd[†]

22–23 James Street, Covent Garden, London WC2E 8NS
tel 020-7250 1760
email mail@ahatalent.co.uk
website www.ahatalent.co.uk
X @AHActors
Agents Kirsten Wright, Mark Price, Darren Rugg, Kevin Brady, Chloe Brayfield, Amy Clarke, *Assistant* Eloise Mace

6 agents represent around 200 actors and creatives working in theatre, musicals, television, radio, film, commercials, computer games, corporate role-play and voice-overs. Creative clients include designers, directors, theatre makers, choreography, heads of departments and composers.

Will consider attending performances within Greater London given 2–3 weeks' notice. Welcomes submissions (with CVs, photographs, showreels, voicereels and sae) from actors previously unknown to the agency by post or email at **submissions@ahatalent.co.uk**. Does not accept email applications or invitations to view an actor's website. *Commission*: 10–15% depending on the medium.

All Talent Agency Ltd

4/1 161 West Street, Glasgow G5 8BN
tel 0141 418 1074, *mobile* 07971 337074
email info@alltentagency.co.uk
website www.alltalentagency.co.uk
Facebook /alltalentthesoniascottagency

Established in 2005. 2 agents represent approximately 150 actors. They provide opportunities in film, TV and fashion as well as training.

Will consider attending performances in Central London and Glasgow with at least 2–3 weeks' notice. Accepts submissions (with CVs and photographs) from actors previously unknown to the company. Invitations to view showreels or voicereels and individual actors' websites also accepted, and follow-up calls welcomed. Welcomes enquiries from disabled actors. *Commission*: Theatre from 10%; Film and TV 15%; Advertising 20%.

Anita Alraun Representation

Correspondence address: 1A Queensway, Blackpool, Lancashire FY4 2DG
tel (01253) 343784
Sole Proprietor & Agent Anita Alraun

One agent represents 20 actors. Areas of work include theatre, musicals, film, television, commercials, radio drama, corporate and some voice-overs.

72 Agents and casting directors

Accepts submissions (with CV, photograph and sae – essential for reply) by post only from trained/experienced actors previously unknown to the company. Emailed submissions will not be considered. Please do not send showreels or voicereels unless requested. *Commission*: Radio 10%; Theatre 12.5%; Film and TV 12.5%; Commercials 15%.

Amber Personal Management Ltd
Colony, 5 Piccadilly Place, Manchester M1 3BR
tel 0161 228 0236
email info@amberltd.co.uk
website www.amberltd.co.uk
Instagram @ambermgmt
Agents Sally Sheridan, Jasmine Parris, Estelle Jenkins

Works in theatre, musicals, television, film, commercials, corporate and voice-over. 3 agents represent 90–100 actors. Will consider attending performances in Manchester, Leeds, Liverpool and London if given a minimum of 2 weeks' notice.

Welcomes applications via email at apply@amberltd.co.uk. Encourages enquiries from actors with disabilities. Spotlight Link CVs preferred. *Commission*: Recorded Media (TV/Film/Commercial) 15%; Theatre, Musicals, Corporate 10%.

The American Agency
14 Bonny Street, London NW1 9PG
tel 020-7485 8883
email americanagency@btconnect.com
Instagram @theamericanagency
Agent Ed Cobb

Established in 2001. Areas of work include theatre, musicals, television, film, commercials, corporate and voice-overs.

Will consider attending performances within the Greater London area. Accepts submissions (with CVs and photographs) from actors previously unknown to the agency if sent by email. Invitations to view individual actors' websites, showreels and voicereels are also accepted. Welcomes enquiries from disabled actors. *Commission*: Theatre 10%; Other 15%.

Angel & Francis Ltd†
2–6 Boundary Row, London SE1 8HP
tel 020-7439 3086
email submissions@angelandfrancis.co.uk
website www.angelandfrancis.co.uk
X @AngelFrancisLtd
Director Kevin Francis, *Associate Agent* Sam Murphy

Established in 1976. 2 agents represent about 80 actors and leading TV/film casting directors and creatives. Areas of work include theatre, television, film and commercials. *Commission*: 10–12.5%.

Christopher Antony Associates
Building 3, 566 Chiswick High Road,
London W4 5YA
tel 020-8994 9952

email info@christopherantony.co.uk
website www.christopherantony.co.uk
Instagram @christopherantonyassociates
Agents Chris Sheils, Kerry Walker

Established in 2006. Offers a personal management service specialising in musical theatre. As theatre agents, represents a small and diverse list of artistes in the West End, UK tours and overseas.

APM Associates
Elstree Film Studios, Shenley Road,
Borehamwood WD6 1JG
tel 020-8953 7377
email apm@apmassociates.net
website www.apmassociates.net
X @apmassociates
Instagram @apmassociates
Managing Director Linda French, *Senior Agent* Allan Scott-Douglas

APM Associates represent UK and international performers and creatives in all genres of the entertainment industry.

APM Associates welcomes applications from experienced performers and creatives and graduates of accredited drama schools via email.

ARG (Artists Rights Group Ltd)†
4A Exmoor Street, London W10 6BD
tel 020-7436 6400
email argall@argtalent.com
website www.argtalent.com
Instagram @artists.rights.group
Managing Director Sue Latimer, *Agents* Katherine Darke, Sarah Spahovic, Claire O'Sullivan, *Assistants* Grace Evans, India Masih

Established in 2001. Represents approximately 60 actors, as well as presenters and production in the areas of theatre, musicals, film, TV and corporate.

Welcomes performance notices UK-wide, ideally with a week or more notice. Please send letters (with CV and photographers), showreels and photographs by email.

The Artists Partnership†
11-29 Smiths Court, Soho, London W1D 7DP
tel 020-7439 1456
email email@theartistspartnership.co.uk
website https://theartistspartnership.co.uk
X @TheAPartnership
Instagram @theartistspartnership
Ceo Roger Charteris, *Managing Director* Robert Taylor, *Agents* Alfred Califano, Alice Coles, Bhumi Ambasna, Christina Shepherd, Harley Morton-Grant, Harry Wilson, James Beresford, Jeanette Hunter, Kim Donovan, Laura Baker, Laura Stokes, Leigh Rodda, Luke Reilly, Miranda Heffernan (Commericals), Penni Killick, Rachel Briscoe, Sandra Chalmers, Saskia Mulder, Taylor Jefferson, Tom Shepherd, Zoe Stoker

Represents actors, directors, writers, experts and speakers for theatre, television, film, commercials, voice-overs, speaking and literary opportunities.

Jonathan Arun Group (JAG)†
37 Pearman Street, London SE1 7RB
tel 020-7840 0123
email info@jag-london.com
website www.jag-london.com
X @_jag_london
Instagram @_jag_london
Agents Jonathan Arun, Max Latimer, Rachel Chambers, Simon Grant Jones, Rob Hadden

Established in 2007. Main areas of work are theatre, film, television, musical theatre, commercials and American TV/film. Will consider attending performances if given at least 3 weeks' notice.

Please approach the agency by email only, with Spotlight link and showreel. Tries to respond to all, but if interested in taking further will always respond within 2 weeks.

Associated International Management (AIM)†
The John Maxwell Building, Elstree Studios, Shenley Road, Borehamwood WD6 1JG
tel 020-7831 9709
email info@aimagents.com
website www.aimagents.com
Key contacts Stephen Gittins, Alexander Clarkson, Jonathan Clarkson-Wild

Established in 1984. Agents represent around 60 actors. Areas of work include theatre, television, film and commercials.

Will consider attending performances within the Greater London area with at least 3 weeks' notice. Accepts submissions (with CVs and photographs) from actors previously unknown to the agency by email. *Commission*: 12.5%.

BAM Associates (UK) Ltd
Benets, Dolberrow, Churchill, Bristol BS25 5NT
tel (01934) 852762, *mobile* 07501 720047
email casting@ebam.tv
website www.ebam.tv

Represents 80 actors. Areas of work include television, film, commercials, theatre, musicals, corporate, radio and voice-overs.

Welcomes emailed submissions from actors seeking representation. *Commission*: Theatre 10%; Mechanical Media 15%.

Gavin Barker Associates Ltd†
2D Wimpole Street, London W1G 0EB
tel 020-7499 4177
email assistant@gavinbarkerassociates.co.uk
website www.gavinbarkerassociates.co.uk
Managing Director Gavin Barker, *Associate Director* Michelle Burke, *Agent* Chris Davis, *Agent/Assistant* Phil Mennell

Established in 1998. 4 agents represent 120 actors and a handful of creatives. Areas of work include theatre, musicals, television, film, commercials, corporate and voice-overs. Also represents directors and choreographers.

Will consider attending performances at venues in Greater London given at least 3 weeks' notice. Accepts submissions (with CVs and photographs) from actors previously unknown to the company if sent by email to **representation@gavinbarkerassociates.co.uk**. Follow-up calls are not welcome. Happy to receive showreels and voicereels. "We do not currently represent any disabled actors, but would consider each applicant on a case by case basis." *Commission*: 10–15%.

BBM†
7–10 Adam Street, London WC2N 6AA
tel 020-3773 9590
email info@bbm.agency
website www.bbm.agency
Managing Director Becky Barrett, *Agents* Danielle Crockford, Tracey Andrews

Established in 2014. Main areas of work are theatre, film, TV and commercials. BBM offers a personal management service with a strong focus on triple threat performers. The company represents 120 actors.

Welcomes applications from both experienced performers and new graduates from accredited schools. Please send submissions to **representation@bbm.agency** including your Spotlight link and showreel links. *Commission*: Theatre 12.5%; television commercials and all other entertainment activites 15%.

Belfield & Wards
26–28 Neal Street, London WC2H 9QQ
tel 020-3416 5290
email office@belfieldandaward.co.uk
website www.belfieldandaward.co.uk
X @BelfieldWard
Instagram @belfiedward
Co-founders and Agents Phil Belfield, Mark Ward, *Senior Agency Assistant* Shanika Stirling, *Agency Assistant* Rhiannon Taylor

Established in 2009. Areas of work include, but are no limited to, theatre, film, TV and radio.

Accepts submissions for representation via email; include a CV, headshot and cover letter. Considers all enquiries but are only able to respond to those they want to explore further.

Agents and casting directors

Olivia Bell Management†
Suite 102, 34–35 Berwick Street, London W1F 8RP
tel 020-7439 3270
email info@olivia-bell.com
website www.oliva-bell.co.uk
Managing Director Xania Segal, *Agents* Robin Hudson, Gavin Mills, Antony Read, Julie Gordon, Ellie Nelson, Sophia Evans

Established in 2001. Areas of work include theatre, musicals, television, film and commercials.

Will consider attending performances at venues within Greater London with a minimum of one week's notice. Accepts submissions (with CVs and photographs) from actors previously unknown to the company if sent by email. Invitations to view individual actors' websites and showreels or voicereels are also accepted. *Commission:* 12.5–20%.

Jorg Betts Associates†
The Barbon Buildings, 17 Red Lion Square, London WC1R 4QH
tel 020-3405 4546
email agents@jorgbetts.com

Established in 2001. Areas of work include theatre, musicals, television, film, commercials and corporates. Also represents directors, casting directors, choreographers and presenters.

Accepts submissions (with CVs and photographs) from actors previously unknown to the company.

Bloomfields Welch Management†
Working From Southwark, The Hoxton Hotel, Colombo Street, London SE1 8DP
tel 020-3176 8020
email submissions@bloomfieldswelch.com
website www.bloomfieldswelch.com
X @bwmgt
Director Emma Bloomfield, *Agents* Barnaby Welch, Clare Partridge, *Assistant* Cameron Sharp

Established in 2004. Areas of work include theatre, musicals, television, film, commercials and corporate. 3 agents.

Will consider attending performances anywhere, given at least 2 weeks' notice. Accepts submissions (with CVs and photographs) from actors previously unknown to the company via the website, but not by email or post. Invitations to view individual actors' websites, showreels and voicereels are also accepted. Welcomes enquiries from disabled actors.

Michelle Braidman Associates Ltd†
2 Futura House, 169 Grange Road, London SE1 3BN
tel 020-7237 3523
email info@braidman.com
website www.braidman.com
X @TeamBraidman
Instagram @michellebraidmanassociates
Directors Michelle Braidman, Alan Turner, *Agents* Nicola Whitworth, Rebecca Kirby, *Assistant* Sarah Hjort

Established in 1983. A leading international theatrical agency representing actors, directors and creative talent.

Submissions should be sent electronically to **representation@braidman.com**. Does not welcome phone calls.

Brill Talent Agency
5 Penta Court, Station Road, Borehamwood, Herts, WD6 1SL
03333 446566
email agency@brilltalent.co.uk
website www.brilltalent.co.uk
Facebook brilltalent
X @brilltalent
Bluesky @brilltalent.bsky.social
Instagram @brilltalent
Threads @brilltalent

Represents performers aged 4 to 99 from anywhere in the UK. The agency is fully inclusive, welcoming applicants of all backgrounds, abilities and identities. It is a boutique talent agency with a collaborative spirit and minimal internal competition. A member of the Association of Young Performers' Agencies (AYPA), committed to upholding industry standards and supporting emerging talent.

They are happy to attend performances across London and surrounding areas, reaching as far as Milton Keynes if they are available. For adult representation, Spotlight registration and UK residency are required.

Their books are always open because great talent can emerge at any time. All applications should be submitted via the website.

Commission varies based on the type of work

British Talent Agency®
website www.britishtalent.net

Established in 2009. Main areas of work include: film, TV, commercials, documentary, video games, all forms of theatre, musical theatre, dance cruises, resorts, voice over, presenting, modelling, events, corporate, webisodes, apps and new media. Represents professional actors, singers, dancers, sports professionals, writers, directors, presenters, comedians, models, recording artists and bands throughout the world including across the UK, USA, EU and Canada, and as far afield as the Middle East and Australia.

Welcomes contact by actors previously unknown to the agency, if made by website contact form with cover note and links to Spotlight and/or IMDb. No attachments. Please visit our website and read our contact policy before approaching. "Invitations to shows are always welcome."

BROOD†
49 Greek Street, London W1D 4EG
tel 020-7998 7861
website www.broodmanagement.com
X @broodlondon
Main Agent Brian Parsonage-Kelly

Represents 60 actors and personalities. Clients work throughout the industry from Hollywood to Fringe, corporates to cruises and soaps to commercials. Prospective clients please visit the website, apply by email only to **broodapplication@aol.com**.

The BWH Agency Ltd†
60 Margaret Street, London W1W 8TF
tel 020-7734 0657
email info@thebwhagency.co.uk
website www.thebwhagency.co.uk
Instagram @thebwhagency
Agents & Directors Joe Hutton, Bill Petrie, Lisa Willoughby, Andrew Braidford, *Agents* Holly Davidson, Nicole Robinson, Oliver Campbell, *Assistant* Louisa Foley

Established in 2004. Main areas of work are theatre, musicals, TV, film, commercials and radio. Welcomes submissions by email only, CVs, photographs and showreels. Are not currently taking on new clients.

CAM (Creative Artists Management)†
55–59 Shaftesbury Avenue, London W1D 6LD
tel 020-7292 0600
email reception@cam.co.uk
website www.cam.co.uk
Instagram @creativeartistsmanagement
Agents Dawn Green, Peter Brooks, Sam Boyd, Bex Elliff, Caitlin O'Farrell, Alexandra Scanlan, *Associates* Imogen Fuller, Lucinda Francis, *Agents Assistant* India Aujla, *General Assistant* Kyanne Smith

Founded in 1988. Main areas of work include film, television, theatre, musical theatre, commercials, corporate and voice over. Represents actors and casting directors. Accepts performance notices, mainly in London, but will consider travelling further afield depending on the show/venue/agent availability. Follow-up phone calls not necessary. *Commission:* Varies depending on contract.

Carey Dodd Associates†
Berkley Suite, 35 Berkley Square, Mayfair, London W1J 5BF
tel 020-7993 4992
email agents@careydoddassociates.com
email applications@careydoddassociates.com
website www.careydoddassociates.com
Agents Christ Carey, Samantha Dodd

Founded 2012. Represents actors and creatives across film, television and theatre. Offers consultancy in SFX/VFX, specialist movement, puppetry and performance capture.

Jessica Carney Associates†
4th Floor, 23 Golden Square, London W1F 9JP
tel 020-7434 4143
email assistant@jcarneyassociates.co.uk
website www.jessicacarneyassociates.co.uk
X @JessicaCarneyAs

Established in 1950. Areas of work include: theatre, television, films, commercials and musicals. Also represents technicians and craftspeople.

Cannot consider actors for representation unless they can be seen in performance (not showcase) within Greater London (requires 2–3 weeks' notice), or possess good mainstream TV credits. Only accepts submissions if sent by email to **representation@jcarneyassociates.co.uk**. Emails should contain a link to their Spotlight CV and showreel. *Commission:* TV/Film 12.5%; Theatre 10%; Commercials 15%.

CBL Management†
20 Hollingbury Rise, Brighton BN1 7HJ
mobile 07956 890307
email enquiries@cblmanagement.co.uk
website www.cblmanagement.co.uk
Facebook /cblmanagement
X @cblmanagement
Agents Claire Carpenter, Beth Eden, Linda Edwards

Established in 2007. 3 agents represent 90 artistes. Works in theatre, musicals, television, film, commercials, corporate and voice-over.

Welcomes CVs and photographs by email only.

CDA Ltd†
107 Walton Street, London SW3 2HP
tel 020-7937 2749
email cda@cdalondon.com
website www.cdalondon.com
Agents Belinda Wright, Laura Gibbons

Established 1980. 2 agents represent 75 actors.

Will consider attending performances at venues within Greater London with 3 weeks' notice. Accepts submissions (with CVs and photographs) from actors previously unknown to the company if sent by email to **representation@cdalondon.com**. Showreels, voicereels and invitations to view individual actors' websites are also accepted. *Commission:* Variable.

CDM Ltd†
5th Floor, 114 St Martin's Lane, London WC2N 4BE
email info@cdm-ltd.com
website www.cdm-ltd.com
Facebook /CDMLtdAgency
X @CDMLtdAgency
Instagram @cdmltdagency
Managing Director Michael Gattrell

Areas of work are theatre, musicals, TV, film, commercials and corporate. 3 agents represent 200 actors; directors, choreographers, designers and musical directors are also represented.

Will consider attending performances within Greater London and elsewhere, given as much notice as possible. Welcomes letters (with CVs and photographs) from actors previously unknown to the agency, sent by post or email. Does not welcome

76 Agents and casting directors

follow-up calls. Accepts showreels, voicereels and invitations to view individual actors' websites. Encourages applications from actors with disabilities.

Centre Stage Agency
7 Rutledge Terrace, South Circular Road, Dublin 8, Republic of Ireland
tel +353 (0)1 453 3599
email geraldine@centrestageagency.ie
website www.centerstageagency.com

Established in 1994, their work spans theatre, television, film, voice-over, commercials and web-based media.

Available to attend performances at Dublin venues with at least one week's notice. Accepts submissions (with CVs and photographs). Showreels are also welcome. Query via the form on the website. *Commission*: 10–15%.

Esta Charkham Associates Ltd
16 British Grove, Chiswick, London W4 2NL
tel 020-8741 2843
email office@charkham.net
website www.charkham.net

Established in 2010. Areas of work include theatre, film, TV, radio, commercials and comedy.

Will consider attending performances at venues in the Greater London area with at least 2 weeks' notice. Accepts submissions via email to **representation@charkham.net** with a covering letter. Does not accept follow-up calls.

City Actors Personal Management
email applications@cityactors.co.uk
website www.cityactors.co.uk
Agent Nikki Everson

Established in 2023. Represents actors working across all areas of Screen, Theatre and Musical theatre. Having previously worked for a leading Co-operative agency, Nikki maintains an ethos of collaboration, communication, supportive empowerment an development of actors' and creatives' careers within the industry.

Sharry Clark Artists
020-8349 9824; Welsh office (01792) 401112
email info@petercharlesworth.co.uk
email sharryclarkartists@gmail.com
website https://sharryclarkartists.wordpress.com
Facebook /SharryClarkArtists
X @SharryCArtists
Director Sharry Clark

Does not welcome unsolicited contact – including performance notices – from actors previously unknown to the company.

Clic Agency
Based in Bangor, Gwynedd
tel (01244) 324206, *mobile* 07979 713381
email clic@btinternet.com
website www.clicagency.co.uk
Facebook /p/Clic-Extras-100069791208505
X @clicagency
Proprietor Helen Pritchard

Established in 2008. Represents around 50 actors from all over the UK. Also carries out casting for productions being filmed in North Wales for principal and supporting artists.

Accepts submissions (with CVs and photographs) from actors previously unknown to the company, sent by email. Encourages enquiries from disabled actors and welcomes showreels, voicereels, follow-up calls and invitations to view individual actors' websites. *Commission*: Varies, but not more than 15%.

Cole Kitchenn Personal Management Ltd[†]
See the entry for InterTalent Rights Group on page 82.

Shane Collins Associates
Suite 112, Davina House, 137–149 Goswell Road, London EC1V 7ET
tel 020-7253 1010
email info@shanecollins.co.uk
website www.shanecollins.co.uk
Agents Shane Collins, Connor Dowd

Established in 1986. An independent and highly respected talent agency.

Accepts submissions from actors previously unknown to the company sent to **submissions@shanecollins.co.uk**. Include your CV, a photo, and a link to your showreel in the body of the message.

Conway Van Gelder Grant[†]
5th Floor, Strand Bridge House, 138–142 Strand, London WC2R 1HH
tel 020-7287 0077
email casting@conwayvg.co.uk
Agents John Grant (*Associate* Polly Dixon-Green, *Assistant* Phoebe Taylor), Alice Smith (*Assistant* Grace Devereux), Nicola van Gelder (*Assistant* Carlotta Cutrupi, *Associate* Clarissa Efthymiades), Rachael Swanston, Nicholas Gall (*Associate* James Evans), Kat Oliver, Georgie Davies (*Shared Assistant* Aodhán Griffin Barr), Greg Herst (*Associate* Emile Guignard-Rogers), David Lazenby (*Assistant* Olivia Olphin)

8 agents represent actors working in all areas of the industry.

Will consider attending performances within Greater London and occasionally elsewhere, given 3–4 weeks' notice. Accepts submissions by email from actors previously unknown to the agency, along with invitations to view an actor's website. Showreels and voicereels should only be sent if requested after initial contact has been made. Follow-up telephone calls and emails are not welcomed. *Commission*: Varies according to contract.

Cooper Searle Personal Management Ltd
3rd Floor, 207 Regent Street, London W1B 3HH
tel 020-7183 4851,
mobile 07538 561441, 07795 261662
email admin@coopersearle.com
website www.coopersearle.com
X @CooperSearle
Instagram @coopersearlepersonalmanagement
Theatrical Agency Director Emily Rose, *Agent* Paul Rose

Established in 2010. Represents around 60 clients. Main areas of work are theatre, musicals, television, film, commercials, corporate and stills.

Will try to attend performances if it is possible and welcomes approaches from actors. Will always see clients perform. Applications should be via email containing actor's Spotlight link and any other relevant material or links. The agency considers every application based on performance ability and marketability. *Commission*: 12.5–20%.

Lou Coulson Associates Ltd†
96 Webber Street, London SE1 0QN
tel 020-7734 9633
email info@loucoulson.co.uk
website www.loucoulson.co.uk
Agents Lou Coulson, Tom Reed, Megan Wheldon, Hannah Wilkinson, Amy Higgins, Victoria Davidson, Louise Bedford, *Assistants* Kim Wiles, Annabel Cotton, Georgie Sells

Represents actors working in all areas of the industry and has strong relationships with US agencies and managers.

Will consider attending performances within Greater London and occasionally elsewhere, given notice. Submissions made via website, follow-up telephone calls and emails not welcome. *Commission*: varies according to contracts.

Coulter Hamilton Rae (CHR)†
Glasgow office: The Pentagon Centre, Washington Street, Glasgow G3 8AZ
tel 0141 204 4058
email scotland@coulterhamiltonrae.com
London office: Suite 402B, Audley House 13 Palace Street, London SW1E 5HX
tel 020-7139 5027
email london@coulterhamiltonrae.com
website www.coulterhamiltonrae.com
Instagram @coulterhamiltonrae
Agents Julie Hamilton, George Rae, Gary Hamilton (Young Performers), Fran Bloomer (Commercial), *Junior Agents/Assistants* Shanna Logan, Rachel Spurrell

Coulter Hamilton Rae is one of the UK's leading talent agencies, focusing exclusively on performers and creatives in all media, with offices in London and Glasgow. Areas of work include theatre, television, film, commercials, corporate and voice-overs.

Accepts submissions (with CVs and photographs) from actors previously unknown to the company if sent by email. Showreels and voicereels are also accepted. *Commission*: 7.5–15% (sliding scale).

Creative Screen Management
1 Knightsbridge Green, London SW1X 7NE
mobile 07540 690676
email info@csmagt.com
website https://csmagt.com
Instagram @csm.agency
Chairwoman Camilla Storey, *Agent*s Nina Maki, Shannon Brassil

Areas of work include TV, film, theatre, commercials, corporate, musicals and pantomimes.

Accepts submissions via the contact form on their website (with CVs and Spotlight profile).

Curtis Brown Group Ltd†
Cunard House, 15 Regent Street, London SW1Y 4LR
tel 020-7393 4400
email actorsrepresentation@curtisbrown.co.uk
website www.curtisbrown.co.uk/section/actors/agents
Agents Tiffany Agbeko, Debi Allen, Martha Atack, Lara Beach, Emma Bennett, Jonty Brook, Dylan Browne, Josh Byrne, Thomas Caulton, Helen Clarkson, Grace Clissold, Camilla Cole, Jack Collins, Jacquie Drew, Oriana Elia, Mary Fitzgerald, Vanessa Fogarty, Richard Gibb, Jill Giffard, Emma Higginbottom, Meryl Hoffman, Sophie Holden, Alex Irwin, Jessica Jackson, Lucy Johnson, Cordelia Keaney, Alastair Lindsey-Renton, Adam Maskell, Sarah MacCormick, Charlene McManus, Abigail Millar, Grant Parsons, Joe Powell, Alex Sedgley, Josephine Shenkman, Sarah Spear, Kate Staddon, Frances Stevenson, Serena Sutherland, Isabelle Sweetland, Oliver Thomson, Sam Turnbull, Rosie Whitcombe, Olivia Woodward, *Associate Agents* Jessica Lax, Ruth Morrison, Thomas Caulton, Suze Azzopardi, Ashleigh Hall, Emma Power, Emily Hughes

One of Europe's oldest and largest independent literary and media agencies. Established over 100 years ago, there are now more than 20 agents within the Book, Media, Actors and Presenters Divisions, 5 of whom represent actors. Also represents writers, directors, playwrights and celebrities.

Submissions should be sent by post or email and addressed to 'Actors Agents'. They should include a covering letter with email address, CV, photograph, showreel (if actor has one) and sae for the return of the showreel. Tries to respond within 4–6 weeks. Does not meet potential clients before viewing their work. Does not accept emailed submissions. *Commission*: 12.5–15%.

78 Agents and casting directors

David Daly Associates
586 King's Road, London SW6 2DX
tel 020-7384 1036
email agent@daviddaly.co.uk
website www.daviddaly.co.uk
Partners & Agents Rosalind Bach, Leanne Batwell-Peters

Established in 1978. An actors' agency bringing over 45 years of experience to the entertainment industry.

Damn Good Talent
218 Chester House, 1-3 Brixton Road,
London SW0 6DE
07519 338657
email leanne@damngoodtalent.com
website www.damngoodtalent.com
Instagram @thedamngoodgroup

Damn Good Talent is a brand extension of the successful Damn Good Voices, set up in 2009. Their talent have graduated from some of the best drama schools throughout the world (some not so recently!). The list of artists (most of which they have been working with for a very long time), represents a broad range of artistic experience and can cover virtually any brief for Film, Theatre, TV or Commercials.

So, to find the face you're looking for either use the Search tool, browse at your leisure or call/email the office. Please refer to the website re the representation submission proceedure. Commission varies between 12.5% and 17.5% depending on the job type.

Denton Brierley†
12–18 Hoxton Street, London N1 6NG
tel 020-3866 5747
email info@dentonbrierley.com
Instagram @dentonbrierley
Agents Suzy Brierley, Gavin Denton-Jones, Sofe Goodwin, Katy Wale, Rosie Dibble

5 agents represent actors working in all areas of the industry. Will consider attending performances within Greater London, given 2 weeks' notice. Accepts email submissions (with Spotlight CVs, photographs and showreels) from actors previously unknown to the agency. *Commission*: varies according to contract.

Diamond Management†
PO Box 353, Hampton TW12 9EL
tel 020-7631 0400
email agents@diman.co.uk
website www.diamondmanagement.co.uk
Agents Lesley Duff, Jean Diamond

Established in 2003. Main areas of work are TV, theatre, commercials and film; also represents directors, MDs, writers and costume designers.

Welcomes letters (with CVs and photographs), follow-up phone calls, CVs and photographs sent by email, showreels and invitations to view actors' websites. Represents actors with disabilities. *Commission* 12.5%.

DQ Management
10 Argyll House, Marlborough Drive, Bushey, Herts. WD23 2PS
tel (01273) 721221, *mobile* 07713 984633
email dq.management1@gmail.com
website www.dqmanagement.com
Senior Partners Peter Davis, Kate Davis

Established in 2003. Areas of work include theatre, musicals, television, film, commercials and corporate. 2 agents represent 80 actors.

Will consider attending performances within the Greater London area and elsewhere with at least 2 weeks' notice. Accepts submissions (with CVs and photographs) from actors previously unknown to the company if sent by post. Invitations to view individuals' websites, showreels or voicereels are also accepted. Welcomes enquiries from disabled actors. *Commission*: Theatre 10%; West End 12.5%; TV/Film/Commercials 15%.

EBA
114 St Martin's Lane, London WC2N 4BE
tel 020-7734 9632
email info@eamonnbedford.com
email enquiries@eamonnbedford.com
website www.eamonnbedford.com
Agents Eamonn Bedford, Charlie Cox

Established in 2012. 2 agents represent 100 clients. Areas of work include theatre, film and TV.

Accepts CVs with photographs from those seeking representation, via email. *Commission*: TV and Film 12.5%, Theatre 10%.

Emptage Hallett†
Cardiff Office: 2nd Floor, 3–5 The Balcony, Castle Arcade, Cardiff CF10 1BU
029-2034 4205
email cardiff@emptagehallett.co.uk
London Office: 3rd Floor, 34–35 Eastcastle Street, London W1W 8DW
tel 020-7436 0425
email mail@emptagehallett.co.uk
website www.emptagehallettcardiff.co.uk, www.emptagehallett.co.uk
Instagram @emptagehallett, @emptagehallettcardiff
Directors Michael Emptage, Michael Hallett, Sarah Highland, *Associate Directors* Gemma McAv, Laura Nassim, *Senior Agent* Alexa Flynn, *Agents* Sam Harris, Jess Batty, *Voice-over Agent* Jody Salt, *Assistant Agents* Oriole Gunter, John-Webb Carter, *Office Administrator* Emily Lee

Cardiff Office: Founded in 1999, main area of work is theatre, TV, film, commercials, voice-over, videogames and corporate. Represents around 90 actors, and also directors, presenters, writers, intimacy co-ordinators and fight directors. Charges standard PMA rates. Will make every effort to attend performances in Cardiff, Bristol and surrounding areas. See website for representation applications.

London Office: Established in 1996, Emptage Hallett represents an exclusive list of actors, writers and casting directors working in film, television and theatre. See website for representation applications. Writers should email **writers@emptagehallett.co.uk**.

Committed to providing equal opportunities for all irrespective of sex, sexual orientation, gender reassignment, marital or civil partnership status, age, disability, colour, race, nationality, ethnic or national origin, religion or belief, political beliefs or membership or non-membership of a Trade Union.

Paola Farino
109 St George's Road, London SE1 6HY
tel 020-7207 0858
email info@paolafarino.co.uk
website www.paolafarino.co.uk

Established in 2007. Sole agent, works in theatre, TV, film, commercials, corporate and photography. Will consider attending performances within Greater London. Prefers to receive performance notices and all other approaches by email – include Spotlight PIN. "Check website first to see if there is anybody else represented with a similar MO."

Feast Management Ltd[†]
Oxford House, 49 Oxford Road, London N4 3EY
tel 020-7354 5216
email office@feastmanagement.co.uk
website www.feastmanagement.co.uk
X @FeastManagement
Director Sadie Feast, Helen Seagriff, Lisa Stark

3 agents represent actors. Areas of work include theatre, musicals, television, film, radio, commercials, corporate and voice-overs.

Will consider attending performances in the London area if plenty of notice is given. Accepts submissions, via the contact form on their website, from actors previously unknown to the company.

Fiorentini Mosson Talent Agency
(formerly Anna Fiorentini Agency)
tel 020-7682 3677, *mobile* 07904 962779
email rhiannon@afperformingarts.com
website www.afperformingarts.com/talent-agency
Agent Rhiannon Mosson

Established in 2008. Works in theatre, film, TV, commercials, corporate, musicals, music videos and promos. Represents actors with disabilities.

Kerry Foley Management Ltd
mobile 07747 864001
email kerry@kfmltd.com
website www.kfmltd.com
X @KFM_Agency
Director Kerry Foley

Established in 2011. Main areas of work are theatre, musicals, television, film, commercials and corporate. Also represents creatives, including directors, musical directors and choreographers. Will consider CVs and photographs sent by email. Agency is open to all actors on their merits.

James Foster Ltd
7 Bell Yard, London WC2A 2JR
tel 020-7434 0398
email info@jamesfosterltd.co.uk
website www.jamesfosterltd.co.uk
X @JamesFosterLTD
Managing Director/Senior Agent James Foster

Established in 1994. Previously Jean Clarke & Jeremy Brook Management. Areas of work include theatre, musicals, television, film, commercials, corporate and radio.

Will consider attending performances in Greater London with at least 3–4 weeks' notice. Accepts submissions from actors previously unknown to the agency by email (see website for further details). Showreels, voicereels and invitations to view an actor's website are also accepted, but follow-up calls and emails are not welcome.

Hilary Gagan Associates[†]
187 Drury Lane, London WC2B 5QD
tel 020-7404 8794
email hilary@hgassoc.co.uk
Agent Hilary Gagan

3 agents represent approximately 100 actors. Areas of work include theatre, musicals, television, film, commercials, corporate, voice-overs. Also represents directors and choreographers.

Will consider attending performances in Greater London with at least 2 weeks' notice. Accepts submissions (with CVs and photographs with name on back of photograph) from actors previously unknown to the agency (include sae). Invitations to view individual actors' websites, showreels and voicereels are also accepted. Follow-up calls are welcomed, as are enquiries from disabled actors. *Commission:* 7.5–15%.

Gardner Herrity[†]
24 Conway Street, London W1T 6BG
tel 020-7388 0088
email info@gardnerherrity.co.uk
website www.gardnerherrity.co.uk
Key contacts Andy Herrity, Nicky James

Areas of work include feature films, television, theatre, video games, voice overs and radio drama.

Will consider attending performances within the Greater London area with at least 3 weeks' notice. Accepts submissions if sent by email **representation@gardnerherrity.co.uk**. Welcomes enquiries from disabled actors. *Commission:* 10%.

Gilbert & Payne Personal Management
Room 403, 4th Floor, Linen Hall,
162–168 Regent Street, London W1B 5TB
tel 020-7734 7505
email ee@gilbertandpayne.com
website www.gilbertandpayne.com
X @GilbertandPayne
Instagram @gilbertandpayne
Director Elena Gilbert, *Key personnel* Elaine Payne

Established in 1996. Areas of work include theatre, musicals, television, film, commercials and corporate, with a particular emphasis on musical theatre. Also represents choreographers.

Will consider attending performances at venues in Greater London with a minimum of one week's notice. Accepts submissions for representation through the form on their website. Follow-up telephone calls are also accepted. *Commission*: Theatre 10%.

Global Artists†
6th Floor, 41–44 Great Queen Street,
London WC2B 5AD
tel 020-7839 4888
email info@globalartists.co.uk
website www.globalartists.co.uk
Facebook /GlobalArtists
Instagram @globalartistsuk

A personal management company representing professional actors. Areas of work include theatre, musical theatre, television, film, commercials and corporate. Also represents a limited number of theatre designers, choreographers, directors and musical directors.

Accepts submissions from actors previously unknown to the company, sent by email or by completing the form on their website. Does not welcome telephone enquiries or postal applications.

Gordon & French†
12–13 Poland Street, London W1F 8QB
tel 020-7734 4818
website www.gordonandfrench.co.uk
Agents Kate Bryden, Christina Cooke, Donna French

Established in 1972. Main areas of work are theatre, TV, film commercials and voice-over. Represents 70 performers.

Accepts requests for respresentation by post or email; the email address for submissions is **representation@gordonandfrench.co.uk**. If applying by post and would like material returned please enclose an sae. Every representation request is read but owing to the volume of material received the company is only able to respond to those submissions it would like to pursue. The company only caters for voice work for their existing clients and therefore are unable to accept these representation requests.

Grantham-Hazeldine Ltd†
Suite 427, The Linen Hall, 162–168 Regent Street,
London W1B 5TE
tel 020-7038 3737
email agents@granthamhazeldine.com
website www.granthamhazeldine.com
Instagram @ghagents
Agents Gina Rowland, Nicholas Errington, Romany Hoyland, *Associate Agent* Mark Light

Established in 1986. The agents represent actors and creatives. Areas of work include theatre, musicals, television, film, commercials, corporate and voice-overs. Also represents writers and stunt co-ordinators.

Accepts submissions (with CVs, photos and showreel) from actors previously unknown to the company if sent by email. *Commission*: Radio 10% plus VAT; Theatre 12.5% plus VAT; TV and Film 15% plus VAT.

Hamilton Hodell Ltd†
20 Golden Square, London W1F 9JL
tel 020-7636 1221
email info@hamiltonhodell.co.uk
website www.hamiltonhodell.co.uk
Instagram @hamiltonhodell
Agents Christian Hodell, Christopher Farrer, Alexander Cooke, Madeleine Dewhirst, India Harris-Sinclair, Sian Smyth, Joshua Woodford, Elizabeth Fieldhouse

The agency represents actors working in leading roles in film, television, theatre and radio productions.

HATCH Talent Ltd†
1 Bedford Row, London WC1R 4BU
tel 020-3950 6333
email info@hatchtalent.co.uk
website www.hatchtalent.co.uk
Instagram @hatch_talent
Agents Vic Murray, Michael Ford, Becky Williams, Mia Pavey *Mia PaveyAgent's Assistants* Nia Rees, Alice Coles, Sophie Cotton

Established in 2017. Currently representing over 150 clients. Areas of work include theatre, TV, film and radio; also represents presenters, comedians and writers. To be considered for representation, CVs, headshots, showreels and a short covering letter can be sent by email. Committed to a policy of equal opportunity. Electronic submissions only.

Jane Hollowood Associates Ltd
17/113 Newton Street, Manchester M1 1AE
tel 0161 237 9141
email info@janehollowood.co.uk
website www.janehollowood.co.uk
Agents Jane Hollowood, Cat Grose, Maz Cox

Established in 1998; 3 agents represent approx. 100 actors working in many areas of the industry.

Will consider attending performances across the country, depending on diary commitments and provided that 2–3 weeks' notice is given. Accepts email submissions (with CVs, Spotlight links and photographs) from actors previously unknown to the agency. Follow-up telephone calls are unwelcome. Commission: Theatre 10%; Radio, role-play and voice-overs 12%; television, film and commercials 15%.

Nancy Hudson Associates[†]
49 South Molton Street, London W1K 5LH
tel 020-7499 5548
email agents@nancyhudsonassociates.com
website www.nancyhudsonassociates.com
X @NHALtd
Director & Agent Nancy Hudson

Established in 1999. 2 agents represent 80 actors. Areas of work include theatre, television, film, commercials, radio, corporate and voice-overs.

Welcomes submissions by email with Spotlight link.

Hunwick Associates[†]
3F1, 44 Howe Street, Edinburgh EH3 6TH
tel 0131 225 3860
email office@hunwickassociates.com
website www.hunwickassociates.com
Agents Maryam Hunwick, Georgina Richardson

Personal management agency established in 2000. Represents actors in all media including several BAFTA and BIFA award-winning stage, screen and television artists.

Will consider attending performances at venues within Greater London and in Scotland given 4 weeks' notice. Accepts submissions (with CVs and photographs) from actors previously unknown to the company. Will also accept showreels. Commission: Theatre 10%; TV and Broadcast Media 12.5%; Commercials 15%.

Icon Actors Management
PHA/ICON Ltd., 1 The Downs, Altrincham, Chesire WA14 2QD
tel 0161 273 3344
email info@pha-agency.co.uk
website www.pha-agency.co.uk

Icon Actors Management is apart of the PHA group. Areas of representation include models, actors, presenters, creative professionals and voice-over artists. Apply for representation through the form on their website.

iD Agency Limited
6 Paramount Court, 41 University Street, London WC1E 6JP
mobile 07528 381833
email info@theidagency.co.uk
website www.theidagency.co.uk
Company Director Barbara Adie

Established in 2011. Works in theatre, musicals, TV, film, commercials, corporate and presenting. 2 agents represent 30 clients (actors and presenters).

Actors should send Spotlight link via email for consideration. Commission: 12.5%, 20% for commercial.

Identity Agency Group (IAG)[†]
20 Noel Street, London W1F 8GW
tel 020-3915 3980
email casting@iagtalent.com
website www.iagtalent.com
Agents Femi Oguns (Ceo), Ikki El-Amriti (Partner), Jonathan Hall (Partner), Julianna Bautista, Nina Malone

Established in 2006. Full representation with IAG is by invitation only. Does not accept submissions via email or post.

Imperial Personal Management Ltd
102 Kirkstall Road, Leeds LS3 1JA
tel 0113 244 3222, mobile 07961 513951
email info@ipmcasting.com
website www.ipmcasting.com
Facebook /IPMCasting
Instagram @ipmcasting
Managing Director Katie Ross

Established in 2007. 4 agents represent 30–50 actors working in television and film; also has a subsidiary company, IPM Crew. Recommends Imperial Photography.

Welcomes performance notices within the Greater London and Northern areas (within 50 miles of the company's postcode), and prefers one month's notice if possible. Welcomes CVs, headshots, Spotlight/IMDB link with a short covering letter from actors previously unknown to the agency, sent by email. Do not accept calls regarding representation and do not recommend sending a hard copy through the post. Encourages enquiries from actors with disabilities. Commission: 10–15%.

Inclusive Talent
Kinettles, Grange Road, Duxford, Cambs. CB22 4WF
mobile 07841 990611
email agent@inclusivetalent.co.uk
website www.inclusivetalent.co.uk
X @incTalentUK
Instagram @inclusivetalentuk
Founders Diane Janssen, Sarah Leigh

A talent agency that represents actors aged 18+ with at least 50% of clients, at any one time identifying as D/deaf, disabled and/or neurodivergent.

Independent Talent Group Ltd[†]
40 Whitfield Street, London W1T 2RH
tel 020-7636 6565
website www.independenttalent.com
Instagram @itg_ltd

Agents and casting directors

Areas of work include theatre, musicals, television, film, commercials, corporate and voice-overs. Also represents directors, writers, technicians and presenters.

Will consider attending performances at venues within Greater London. Please see the website for up-to-date submission policies. *Commission*: 12.5%.

International Actors London and Irish Actors London (IAL)
Penthouse 11, Bickenhall Mansions,
London W1U 6BR
tel 020-7125 0539
email ialagents@gmail.com
website www.ialagency.com
X @ialagency
Instagram @ialagency
Key contact Rachel O'Shea

Established in 2011. Works in theatre, TV, film, voice-over and commercials. 4 agents represent ethnically diverse and international actors based in the UK.

Will consider attending performances within the Greater London area, given 2–4 weeks' notice. Actors should apply by emailing their Spotlight link, which should have their showreel attached. Welcomes applications from actors with disabilities. *Commission*: Theatre 10%; Commercial Theatre 12.5%; TV, Film, Commercials and Voice-over 15%.

InterTalent[†]
(incorporating Cole Kitchenn Management Ltd)
33 Great Pulteney Street, Soho, London W1F 9NP
tel 020-7427 5681
email actors@intertalentgroup.com
website www.intertalentgroup.com
Company Directors & Senior Agents Brooke Kinsella, Ashley Vallance, Sam Day, Alexandra MacMillan, Caitlin Rae Boyle, Geri Spicer, Lucy Nooshin,
Associate Agents Bex Severn, Eve Crawford

For submission: go to the 'contact' section on the website. Cannot always guarantee a reply.

Jeffrey & White Management Ltd[†]
7 Paynes Park, Hitchin, Herts. SG5 1EH
tel (01462) 429769
email info@jeffreyandwhite.co.uk
website www.jeffreyandwhite.co.uk
Partners Gemma Towersey, Ellie Goodhew

Established in 1986. 2 agents represent approximately 70 actors. Areas of work include theatre, musicals, television, film, commercials and corporate.

Will consider attending performances given as much notice as possible. Accepts submissions (with CVs and photographs) from actors previously unknown to the company if sent by email. *Commission*: Theatre, Film and TV 12.5%; Commercials 15%.

Mark Jermin Management
Venue No. 1, 995A Carmarthen Road, Fforestfach, Swansea SA5 4AE
tel (01792) 45855
email info@markjermin.co.uk
website www.markjerminmanagement.co.uk
Agent Mark Jermin

Established in 2007. Areas of work include theatre, musicals, television, film, commercials, corporate and voice-overs.

Will consider attending performances at venues within London, Manchester and south and west Wales, given 2 weeks' notice. Accepts submissions by email (with CVs and photographs) for actors unknown to the agents. Also accepts unsolicited CVs (with photgraphs), via email. Happy to receive invitations to view actors' websites and to consider applications for representation from disabled actors. *Commission*: Negotiable.

JPA Management[†]
30 Daws Hill Lane, High Wycombe,
Bucks. HP11 1PW
tel (01494) 520978
email agent@jpaassociates.co.uk
website www.jpaassociates.co.uk
Agent Marylyn Phillips, Martin Hibbert

Established in 1995; part of JPA Associates. Main areas of work are theatre, TV, film and commercials. Represents over 40 actors. Welcomes CVs and photographs sent by email. Has a diverse and full-inclusive cast list. *Commission*: 10%–15%.

JWL (Jewell Wright Ltd)[†]
Soho Works, The Tea Building,
56 Shoreditch High Street, London E1 6JJ
tel 020-3865 0932
email agents@jwl-london.com
3rd Floor, 9000 Sunset Boulevard, West Hollywood, CA 90069, USA
website www.jwl-london.com, www.jwl-la.com
X @jwlartists
Instagram @jwlartists
Director Jimmy Jewell, *Agents* Sabrina Carter, Saskia Hooker

Established in 2005. Main areas of work are film, television, theatre, musicals, commercials and radio. 3 agents represent 90 actors.

Welcomes letters (with CVs and photographs, plus showreel) from individual actors previously unknown to the company if sent by email. Actively encourages enquiries from actors with disabilities. *Commission*: Theatre 15%; Television/Film 15%; Commercials 17.5%.

Keddie Scott Associates[†]
34 Bloomsbury Street, London WC1B 3QJ
tel 020-3490 1050

email info@keddiescott.com
website www.keddiescott.com
Facebook /KeddieScottAssociates
X @keddiescott
Senior Agents Fiona Keddie-Ord (London), Paul Harper (Scotland), Anthony Williams (North), *London Agents* Jonathan McHardy, Richard Vincent, Neil McNulty (Commercials), *Scotland Agent* Euan Nixon, *North Agent* Frankie Rogers

Established in 2005. Works in all areas of the performing arts industry, including TV, film, commercials, theatre, musical theatre (small-, mid- and large-scale) and corporate assignments of every nature. Please note that KSA operates on a Personal Exclusive Management basis.

Steve Kenis & Co[t]
Flat 8, 69 Drayton Gardens, London SW10 9QZ
tel 020-7434 9055
email sk@sknco.com
Agents Steve Kenis, Karen Holmes

Founded in 2000. 2 agents represent 14 actors, as well as writers, directors and technicians. *Commission:* 10%.

Kew Personal Management
PO Box 765, Redhill, Surrey RH1 9HB
mobile 07876 457402
email info@kewpersonalmanagement.com
website www.kewpersonalmanagement.com
Company Manager Kate Winn

Works in theatre, musicals, TV, film, commercials, corporate, voice-over and presenting.

Will consider attending performances in the Greater London area. Accepts emails from actors previously unknown to the company. Accepts showreels, voicereels and links to Spotlight pages. Also represents children. Happy to accept submissions from disabled actors.

Laine Management
tel 0161 789 7775
email info@lainemanagement.co.uk
website www.lainemanagement.co.uk
Facebook /LaineMgt
X @LaineManagement
Instagram @lainemgtltd
Company Director Samantha Rigby

Areas of work include theatre, television, film, commercials and corporate.

Will consider attending performances at venues in Manchester and the surrounding area with 2–4 weeks' notice. *Commission:* 15%.

Langford Associates Ltd
124 City Road, London EC1V 2NX
tel 020-7244 7805
email info@langfordassociates.com
website www.langfordassociates.com
Key personnel Barry Langford, Simon Hayes

Established in 1987. One agent represents 50–60 actors. Areas of work include theatre, television, film, commercials, corporate and voice-overs.

Will consider attending performances at mainstream venues within Greater London, given 2 weeks' notice. Accepts submissions (with CVs and photographs) by post or email. Email submissions should include no more than one small image (emails with multiple attachments will be deleted unread). 'Name' actors seeking representation may ring and speak to Barry Langford in complete confidence.

"Always happy to receive details by post and will regularly meet with new actors. Include a sae if actors wish details to be returned. Do not send unsolicited showreels. 10x8in photographs are preferable, and it is suggested that the photo is updated every 18 months, and that actors are listed on Spotlight."

Nina Lee Management[t]
tel 020-3842 2639
email nina@ninaleemanagement.com
website www.ninaleemanagement.com
Agent Nina Lee

Areas of work include theatre, TV, film, commercials, corporate and radio.

Welcomes performance notices, each one will be considered on its individual merits. Accepts submissions by email (with CVs and photographs).

Lime Actors Agency & Management Ltd
tel 0161 236 0827
email georgina@limemanagement.co.uk
website http://limemanagement.tv
X @LimeActors
Instagram @limeactors
Director Georgina Andrew

Established in 1997. One agent represents approximately 115 actors. Areas of work include theatre, musicals, television, film, commercials, corporate and voice-overs. Also represents musical directors.

Will consider attending performances at venues within Greater London and elsewhere given 4 weeks' notice. Accepts submissions (with CVs and photographs) from actors previously unknown to the company. Follow-up telephone calls, showreels, voicereels and invitations to view individual actors' websites are also accepted.

Eva Long
Norwood House, 9 Redwell Road,
Wellingborough NN8 5AZ
mobile 07736 700849
email evalongproductions@yahoo.co.uk
website website www.evalongproductions.co.uk
Key personnel Eva Long

Established in 2005. One agent represents 40 actors. Areas of work include theatre, musicals, television, film, commercials, corporate and voice-overs.

Will consider attending performances within the Greater London, Midlands and East Anglia areas, with at least one month's notice. Prefers to receive submissions (with CVs and headshots) by email, rather than by post. Showreels, voicereels and invitations to view individual actors' websites are also accepted. Welcomes enquiries from disabled actors. *Commission*: 15%.

Gina Long (Longrun Artistes)
55 Bellevue Road, Ramsgate CT11 8DN
tel (01843) 639747, *mobile* 07748 723228
email longrunartistes@icloud.com
website www.longrunagency.com
Founder/Director Gina Long

Established in 2005. Works in theatre, musicals, TV, film, commercials, corporate, voice-over and dance. 4 agents represent 120 clients. Will accept unsolicited applications from actors previously unknown to the agency, by post or email (with photographs).

Lovett Logan Associates[†]
London office: 151 Wardour Street, London WF1 8WE
tel 0131 478 7878
email casting@lovettlogan.com
Scottish office: 15 Carlton Road, Edinburgh EH8 8DI
tel 0131 478 7878
website www.lovettlogan.co.uk
X @LovettLogan
Instagram @_lovettlogan

Established in 1981. Areas of work include theatre, musicals, television, film, radio, commercials, corporate and voice-overs.

Will consider attending performances at venues in Greater London and Scotland (handled by Scottish office) with 2–3 weeks' notice. Accepts submissions (with CV, showreel link) from actors previously unknown to the company using form on their website.

MacFarlane Chard Associates[†]
Kings Cross Business Centre,
180–186 Kings Cross Road, London WC1X 9DE
tel 020-7636 7750
email enquiries@macfarlane-chard.co.uk
website www.macfarlane-chard.co.uk
X @MacFarlaneChard
Agent John Setrice

Founded in 1994. Works in all areas. Agents represent 120 actors, as well as directors, writers, producers, technicians and authors.

Will consider attending performances in London, given as much notice as possible. Welcomes emails from Spotlight registered actors previously unknown to the agency and encourages enquiries from actors with disabilities. Does not welcome follow-up calls. *Commission*: Varies.

MacFarlane Doyle Associates
tel 020-3600 3470
email office@macfarlanedoyle.com
website www.macfarlanedoyle.com
Agents Ross MacFarlane, Alys Drew

Established in 2009. Main areas of work are theatre, musicals, television, film, corporate, commercials and voice-overs. Each agent represents around 20 actors; directors and choreographers are also represented.

Welcomes performance notices and will travel to any area, given 3 weeks' notice. Prefers submissions by email which a Spotlight link. Represents actors with disabilities. *Commission*: Theatre, TV & Film 15%; Commercials 20%.

Management 2000
11 Well Street, Treuddyn, Flintshire CH7 4NH
tel (01352) 771231
email jackey@management-2000.co.uk
website www.management-2000.co.uk

Established in 2000. One agent represents 30 actors. Areas of work include theatre, musicals, television, film, commercials, corporate and voice-overs.

Accepts submissions (with CVs and photographs) from actors previously unknown to the company if sent by post. Follow-up telephone calls, showreels and voicereels are also accepted. *Commission*: 10–15%.

Marcus & McCrimmon[†]
tel 020-7323 0546
email info@marcusandmccrimmon.com
website www.marcusandmccrimmon.com
X @marcandmcc
Agents Sam James, Clive Marcus

Founded in 1999, an independent talent agency with a focus on creating and developing careers. Main areas of work are stage, musical theatre, TV, film and commercials.

Markham, Froggatt & Irwin[†]
Cunard House, 15 Regent St, London SW1Y 4LR
tel 020-7636 4412
email admin@markhamfroggattirwin.com
website www.markhamfroggattirwin.com
Instagram @markhamfroggattirwin
Agents: Film, TV and Theatre Alex Irwin, Jonty Brook, Anna Dudley, Richard Gibb, Tom Christensen, *Press and Publicity* Isabella Riggs

Works in theatre, musicals, television, film and commercials.

Scott Marshall Partners[†]
Holborn Studios, 49–50 Eagle Wharf Road, London N1 7ED
tel 020-7637 4623
email info@scottmarshall.co.uk
website www.scottmarshall.co.uk
Instagram @scott_marshall_partners
Agents Amanda Evans, Manon Palmer, Craig Sills, Adrianna Tsigara, Katie McCord, Tom Dale, Sarah Mowat, Lin Katelaite

Areas of work include theatre, musicals, television, film, commercials, corporate and voice-overs. Also represents directors (theatre and TV) and creatives.

Accepts submissions (with CVs and photographs) from actors previously unknown to the company if sent by email only to submissions@scottmarshall.co.uk. No postal submissions accepted.

McEwan & Penford†
Studio 11.B.1 The Leather Market, Weston Street, London SE1 3ER
tel 020-3735 8278
email hello@mcewanpenford.com
website www.mcewanpenford.com
Agents Aileen McEwan, James Penford, Leah Sheshadri

Established in 1988, the agency represents actors working in theatre, musicals, television, film and commercials. Actors will consider short film work if paid; submit a CV and script with enquiries.

Cannot accept postal submissions. Only attach one small image to emails. Please don't send showreels as files, prefers links to Spotlight, Vimeo, etc. Due to a high number of submissions the company will only respond if it wishes to take things further. Please give as much notice as possible for invitations to performances; unlikely to be able to travel outside of London.

McLean-Williams Ltd†
Unit F22B, Parkhall Business Centre,
40 Martell Road, Dulwich, London SE21 8EN
tel 020-3567 1090
email info@mclean-williams.com
website www.mclean-williams.com

Established in 2002. Represents clients working in theatre, musicals, television, film, commercials and corporate role-play.

Will consider attending performances within Greater London given 2 weeks' notice. Welcomes submissions (with CVs, photographs, showreels and voicereels) from actors previously unknown to the agency. Will also accept follow-up telephone calls, emails and invitations to view an actor's website.

McMahon Management
28 Cecil Road, London W3 0DB
tel 020-8752 0172
email mcmahonmanagement@hotmail.co.uk
website www.mcmahonmanagement.co.uk
X @McMahonMgmt

Established in 2009. Works in theatre, TV, commercials, corporate and film. Will consider attending performances within London and Greater London given 2 weeks' notice. Welcomes applications from trained actors from NCDT accredited drama schools or from actors with good experience and credits, through post or email. Happy to receive email requests with Spotlight link included. Does not welcome follow-up phone calls. *Commission*: Theatre 12.5%; TV, Film, Commercial and Corporate 15%.

Middleweek Newton Talent Management†
Cromer Studios, Holy Cross Church Crypt,
Cromer Street, London WC1H 8JU
tel 020-3394 0079
email agents@mntalent.co.uk
website www.mntalent.co.uk
Agents Lucy Middleweek, Ileana Cillario, Olivia Jaggers

Established in 2013. Areas of work include theatre, television, film and commercials.

Accepts submissions by email (with CVs and photographs). Also welcomes showreels and invitations to view individual actors' websites.

Milburn Browning Associates (MMB Creative)†
10 Bedford Square, London WC1B 3RA
tel 020-3582 9370
email talent@mmbcreative.com
website https://mmbcreative.com
Managing Director Michele Milburn, Agents Malcolm Browning, Tara Lynch

Milburn Browning Associates became part of the umbrella group MMB Creative in 2016. Manages a select client list providing a first-rate service and offers the clout and reputation that only comes with decades of experience and proven success.

Morello Cherry Ltd
tel 020-7993 5538
email apply@mcaa.co.uk
website www.mcaa.co.uk
Facebook /MorelloCherryPips
X @PipsCherry
Instagram @morellocherryaa

Established in 2007. Areas of work include film, television, SVOD, theatre and commercials. Morello Cherry Pips is their sister agency representing young actors and emerging talent.

Correspondence by email only. Accepts submissions via email only, with links to online CV, footage and images; requests no large file downloads. *Commission*: Standard Equity rates. Do not apply to both 'Morello' and 'Pips'.

Lee Morgan Management
St Vincent House, 30 Orange Street,
London WC2H 7HH
tel 020-3196 1740
email lee@leemorgan.biz
website www.leemorgan.biz
Instagram @leemorganmanagement

Established in 2005. Representing the finest talent working in the UK and internationally for stage, television, film and commercials.

MR Management†
67 Great Titchfield Street, London W1W 7PT
tel 020-7636 8737

Agents and casting directors

email info@mrmanagement.net
website www.mrmanagement.net
Agents Mark Pollard, Ross Dawes

Established in 2001. Main areas of work are theatre, musicals, TV, film and commercials. Also represents directors, presenters and writers. Welcomes CVs and photographs sent by email, showreels and voice tapes. Open to clients with disabilities but not currently representing any disabled actors. *Commission* 10–12.5% Theatre; 15% Film and TV.

Mrs Jordan Associates[†]
4 Old Park Lane, London W1K 1QW
tel 020-3151 0710
email apps@mrsjordan.co.uk
website www.mrsjordan.co.uk
Associates Seán D. Lynch, Guy Kean

Established in 2008. Areas of work include stage, television, film, commercials, corporate and voice-overs. Represents some regionally based actors. Does not represent walk-ons, extras, models or under-16s. 2 principal agents plus associates represent around 80 actors.

Will consider attending performances but would need to meet in advance. Unsolicited applications accepted by email only. Spotlight link imperative. Very happy to consider applications from actors with disabilities. Check website's New Applicants page for advice before you email us. *Commission:* 10–15%.

MSFT Management[†]
The Pink Studio, 1 Gilbert Street, Enfield EN3 6PD
tel 07917 157748
email agent@msftmanagement.com
website https://msftmanagement.com
Facebook /MSFTMANAGEMENT
Instagram @ msft_management
Founder Lennie Varvarides

Founded in 2011, this fast-growing personal management agency representing multi-skilled artists, dedicated to the progression of their clients. MSFT Management is specifically looking for mid-career actors to join the London-based agency.

Requirements: actors must be registered with Spotlight, have a showreel, professional headshots and ideally be a member of Equity to apply for representation. Make initial contact through social media, attending a Sunday Surgery workshop or by booking an consulation via the form on the website.

Elaine Murphy Associates
Suite 1, 50 High Street, London E11 2RJ
tel 020-8989 4122
email elaine@elainemurphy.co.uk
Director Elaine Murphy

Established in 1990. Employs 2 agents. Areas of work include film, TV, theatre, musicals, television, commercials, corporate and voice-overs.

Will consider attending performances within Greater London with plenty of notice. Accepts submissions (with Spotlight link) from actors previously unknown to the agency; showreels, voicereels and invitations to view individual actors' websites are also accepted.

Nelson Browne Management Ltd[†]
48 Warwick Street, London W1B 5AW
mobile 07796 891388
email enquiries@nelsonbrowne.com
website www.nelsonbrowne.com
Company Director Mary Elliott Nelson

Established in 2007. 2 agents represent 80–90 actors working in musicals, television, film, commercials, corporate and voice-over; also represents directors and actor/musicians.

Welcomes performance notices within the Greater London area, given 2 weeks' notice. Welcomes submissions from actors previously unknown to the agency by email with Spotlight link or links to showreels. Encourages enquiries from actors with disabilities. *Commission:* Theatre 10%; TV and Film 15%.

Northern Lights Management
Unit 20, Riverview, Rippondon HX6 4BL
tel (01422) 382203
email office@northernlightsmanagement.co.uk
website www.northernlightsmanagement.co.uk
Facebook /NLightsActorsM
X @NLightsActorsM
Instagram @northernlightsactorsm
Agents Maureen Magee, Angie Cowton

Established in 1996. Represents Northern and Northern-based actors. Areas of work include theatre, musicals, television, film, writers and corporate.

Accepts submissions (with CVs and photographs) from actors previously unknown to the company by email, but no large attachments. Links to showreels are also accepted. Telephone calls are not accepted.

Nyland Management
mobile 07902 246157
email casting@nylandmanagement.com
website www.nylandmanagement.com

2 agents represent 60 actors. Areas of work include theatre, musicals, TV, film, commercials, motion capture, corporate, role-play, promotions and voice-overs.

Accepts submissions from Spotlight members. Email only.

Paling and Jenkins
80–81 St Martin's Lane, London WC2N 4AA
tel 020-7043 2451
email contact@palingandjenkins.co.uk
website www.palingandjenkins.co.uk
Instagram @palingandjenkins
Agents Steven Paling, Debbie Jenkins, Dan Taylor, Steven Lewis, *Assistant* Millie Reynolds

Focuses on personal management with an emphasis on getting to know clients as individuals and helping develop careers. 4 agents represent approximtely 190 actors. Areas of work include theatre, musical theatre, film, television and commercials. Representation enquiries should be sent to: representation@palingandjenkins.co.uk with a Spotlight link and showreel.

Pemberton Associates Ltd
167–169 Great Portland Street, London W1W 5PF
mobile 07784 710923
email general@pembertonassociates.com
website www.pembertonassociates.com
Instagram @pembertonassociates

Established in 1989. Areas of work include theatre, musicals, television, film, commercials, corporate and voice-overs.

Will consider attending performances at venues with 2–3 weeks' notice, if looking for new clients. Accepts email submissions from actors.

Frances Phillips†
89 Robeson Way, Borehamwood, Herts. WD6 5RY
email frances@francesphillips.co.uk
website www.francesphillips.co.uk

Established in 1983 and representing 40 actors aged 16 and upwards. Areas of work include theatre, musicals, television, film, commercials, corporate and voice-overs. Submissions by email only considered if Spotlight View PIN number and date of birth details are included. CVs and photos will be requested at a later date if required.

Piccadilly Management
tel 07790 396418
email info@piccadillymanagement.com
website www.piccadillymanagement.com
Agent Amy Spencer

Established in 1985. Main areas of work include television, theatre, stage, commercials, corporate and voice-overs. Represents around 50 actors.

Welcomes approaches from actors previously unknown to the company, sent by post or email. Accepts invitations to view individual actors' websites and welcomes enquiries from actors with disabilities.

Janet Plater Management Ltd
Floor D, Milburn House, Dean Street, Newcastle upon Tyne NE1 1LF
tel 0191 221 2490
email admin@agentontyne.co.uk
website www.jpmactors.co.uk
X @JPMactors

Established in 1997. One agent represents approximately 65 actors. Areas of work include theatre, musicals, television, film, commercials, corporate and voice-overs.

Will consider attending performances with a few weeks' notice. Accepts submissions (with CVs and or photographs or Spotlight link) from actors previously unknown to the company if sent via email. Links to showreels welcome; if applying by email no large attachments. *Commission*: Maximum of 15%.

Morwenna Preston Management
tel 020-8835 8147
email info@morwennapreston.com
website https://morwennapreston.com
X @MorwennaPreston
Instagram @morwennaprestonmanagement
Agents Morwenna Preston, Emily Mason, Sara Hooppell

Three agents represent actors for theatre, radio, voice, television, film and commercials.

Welcomes performance notices 4 weeks in advance, and is prepared to travel within the Greater London area. Applications for representation should be done through the form on their website. Does not accept email submissions.

Price Gardner Management†
BM 3162, London WC1N 3XX
tel 020-7610 2111
email info@pricegardner.co.uk
website www.pricegardner.co.uk
X @pricegardnermgt
Contact Sarah Barnfield

Television, film, theatre, musical theatre, commercials, radio, voice-over and corporate. Submissions can be made via the website contact form or by post.

RBM Actors
3rd Floor, 1 Lower Grosvenor Place, London SW1W 0EJ
tel 020-7976 6021
email info@rbmactors.com
website www.rbmactors.com
Instagram @rbm_talent
Agent Richard Bucknall

Works mainly in theatre, television, film and commercials. 2 agents represent around 50 actors, and comedians/writers.

Will consider attending performances within Greater London, given 2–3 weeks notice. Welcomes applications through the form on their website, email or post (with CVs and photographs) from individual actors previously unknown to the company. Accepts showreels and voicereels, as well as invitations to view individual actors' websites. Encourages enquiries from actors with disabilities.

Redroofs Associates
26 Bath Road, Maidenhead, Berks. SL6 4JT
tel (01628) 674092, mobile 07825 598623
email info@redroofs.co.uk
website www.redroofs.co.uk/agency/agency-representation
Facebook /Redroofstheatreschool

88 Agents and casting directors

Established in 1947. The agency only represents Redroofs graduates and current students. It does not, therefore, welcome performance notices or representation enquiries from actors unknown to the school. Areas of work include theatre, musicals, television, film, commercials, corporate and voice-overs.

The Regan Talent Group
Aberdare House, Cardiff Bay, Cardiff CF10 5FJ
tel 029-2047 3993
email hello@reganmanagement.co.uk
website https://regantalentgroup.co.uk
Instagram @regantalentgroup
Agents Leigh-Ann Regan, Debi Maclean, Ffion Evans, Geraint Hardy, Oliver Williams, *Junior Agent* Emma Housley

Established in 2001. Represents actors, presenters, drag talents, creatives and content creators. Represents Welsh-language actors. Approach agency by email: **representation@reganmanagement.co.uk**; include a cover letter, showreel and Spotlight link.

Lisa Richards Agency†
Dublin office: 108 Upper Leeson Street, Dublin 4, D04 E3E7, Republic of Ireland
tel +353 (0)1 637 5000
email info@lisarichards.ie
London office: 6 Goodwins Court, St Martins Lane, London WC2N4LL
tel 020-7287 1441
email office@lisarichards.com
Nordic office: Merituliinkatu, 29 LI 21 00170, Helsinki, Finland
tel +358 (0)407 619 829
email raakel@lrnordic.com
website www.lisarichards.ie, www.lisarichards.co.uk, www.lrnordic.com
Managing Director Lisa Cook, *Agents* Lisa Cook, Richard Cook, Jonathan Shankey Rose Parkinson, Morris Epstein, Ami Cash, Rachel Byrne, Isabelle Dempsey, Raakel Huikuri (Actors Nordic), *Voice-over* Karen Hodge, *Literary* Faith O'Grady, *Comedy* Christina Dwyer, Fiona McCluskey, *Corporate* Eavan Kenny, *Creatives* Jasmine Daines Pilgrem, Siân Gordon, Laura Searle

Established in 1989, originally a theatrical agency but now provides representation for actors, comedians, voice-over artists, authors, playrights, directors and designers.

Welcomes performance notices if sent 3 weeks in advance, and is prepared to travel around Ireland and the UK. Welcomes submission (with CVs, photographs and showreels) from actors previously unknown to the company if sent by email, but not by post; does not welcome follow-up calls. Happy to receive showreels and invitations to view individual actors' websites. Welcomes enquiries from disabled actors. Submission guidelines on site for authors.

Rossmore Management†
Golden Cross House, 8 Duncannon Street, London WC2N 4JF
tel 020-7258 1953
email info@rossmoremanagement.com
website www.rossmoremanagement.com
Director Sarah Mitchell (Agent), Alison Lee, *Senior Assistant* Imogen Albert, *Assistants* Piolini-Castle, Catherine Tracey

Established in 1993. Areas of work include theatre, musicals, television, film, commercials, radio and voice-overs.

Will consider attending performances at venues within Greater London. Accepts submissions (with CVs, Spotlight link, covering letter and photographs) from actors previously unknown to the company by email or post. Please include sae. *Commission*: Theatre and Radio 10%; Film, TV and Commercials 15% plus VAT.

Royce Management
121 Merlin Grove, Beckenham BR3 3HS
tel 020-8650 1096
email office@roycemanagement.co.uk
website www.roycemanagement.co.uk

Established in 1980. 2 agents represent 50–60 actors. Areas of work include theatre, musicals, television, film, commercials, corporate and voice-overs.

Will consider attending performances at venues within Greater London with a minimum of one week's notice. Accepts submissions with a link to actors' Spotlight page by email. No attachments. *Commission*: Commercials 15%; All other work 10%.

Savages Personal Management Ltd
Lyric Hammersmith Theatre, Lyric Square, King Street, London W6 0QL
tel 020-7348 7875
email info@savagespm.co.uk
website www.savagespm.co.uk
Facebook /savagespm.co.uk
X @SAVAGESLondon
Instagram @savageslondon
Agents Justin Savage, Gemma Bowden, *Assistant* Georgina Lewis

Established in 2016. Areas of work are theatre, film, TV, musicals, commercials, corporate presenting and events. Represents approximately 95 actors, presenters, directors and writers. Will consider attending performances, given 3 weeks' notice. Welcomes enquiries from artists not previously known to the company by email with a link to a showreel and Spotlight page only. Cannot consider artists without a showreel or a Spotlight entry. Will try to respond to all applications. Represents actors with disabilities and from every sphere of life. *Commission*: theatre 12.5%, plus VAT; everything else 15% plus VAT.

Scream Management
Manchester Office: Tomorrow, MediaCity UK, Salford M50 2EQ
tel 0161 850 1996
London Office: 1st Floor, 11 Goodwins Court, Covent Garden, London WC2N 4LL
tel 020-7183 0181
email hello@screammanagement.com
website www.screammanagement.com
Facebook /ScreamManagement
X @screamtalent98
Instagram @scream_management

Established in 1998. Represents young actors for TV, film, commercials, voice-overs and stage. See website to book classes and attend workshops.

SDM (Simon Drake Management)
129 Ivor Court, Gloucester Place, London NW1 6BS
tel 020-7183 8995
email admin@simondrakemanagement.co.uk
website www.simondrakemanagement.co.uk
Agent Simon Drake

Established in 2007. Works in theatre, TV and film. No plans to expand their client list currently.

Dawn Sedgwick Management
3 Goodwins Court, London WC2N 4LL
tel 020-7240 0404
email dawn@dawnsedgwickmanagement.com
website www.dawnsedgwickmanagement.com
X @dawnsedgwickmgt
Instagram @dawnsedgwick
Key contact Dawn Sedgwick, Assistant Isabel White

Established in 1992. 3 agents represent 15 actors. Areas of work include theatre, television, film, commercials, corporate and voice-overs. Also represents presenters, comedians and writers.

Accepts submissions (with CVs and photographs) from actors previously unknown to the agency if sent by post, but not by email. Showreels, voicereels and invitations to view individual actors' websites are also accepted. Welcomes enquiries from disabled actors. *Commission*: 15%.

Select Management
PO Box 748, London NW4 1TT
mobile 07956 131494
email mail@selectmanagement.info
website www.selectmanagement.info
Agent Venetia Suchdev

Established in 2008. Areas of work include theatre, TV, film, commercial, voice over, print, modeling, corporate, dance and presenting.

All applications for representation to be made via the website registration process. All actors over the age of 17 considered. Spotlight registration is required. *Commission*: 20%; no commission on any work obtained by actors themselves.

Sharkey & Co. Ltd[†]
44 Lexington Street, London W1F 0LW
tel 020-7287 1923
email info@sharkeyandco.com
website www.sharkeyandco.com
website www.sharkeyvoices.com
Agent Simon Sharkey

Established in 2012, main areas of work are TV, film, theatre, musicals, cabaret and commercials, with a dedicated Voice Department for radio, voice-over, audio books, computer games and ADR. Represents 100 actors. Does not represent children.

Welcomes CVs and photographs sent by email with links to showreels and websites. Welcomes performance notices with a minimum of 2 weeks' notice, Greater London preferred. *Commission* Feature films and commercials 15%; TV and stage 12.5%; voice-over 10%.

Rebecca Singer Management
16 Albert Street, Banbury OX16 5DG
tel (01295) 261494, mobile 07801 259963
email office@rebeccasingermanagement.com
website www.rebeccasingermanagement.com
Facebook /singerstageschool
X @rsm_office
Instagram @singerstageschool
Agent Rebecca Singer

Established in 2016, after 23 years with the Richard Stone Partnership. Main areas of work are theatre, musicals, TV, film, commercials, corporate work, radio and audiobooks. Does not do commercial voice-overs. Represents over 50 actors and one fight director, and would be happy to represent actors if they move to directing.

Welcomes performance notices, preferably with a month's notice. Happy to travel within the London area if a theatre is accessible by public transport. Welcomes CVs and photographs sent by email, showreels and voice tapes. Would happily represent actors with disabilities. *Commission*: 12.5%.

Sandra Singer Associates
21 Cotswold Road, Westcliff-on-Sea, Essex SS0 8AA
tel (01702) 331616
email sandrasingeruk@aol.com
website www.sandrasinger.com
Key personnel Sandra Singer, Aimiee Singer

Main areas of work are with leads and featured artists for feature films, film, television, commercials and musical theatre. Specialises in artistes under 25 years of age, but is also a boutique agency of established artistes.

Accepts applications by email. No zip files, jpgs, or emails with large files unless requested. Showreels should only be sent on request.

Agents and casting directors

Smart Management
PO Box 64377, London EC1V 1ND
tel 020-7837 8822
email smartmanagement@btconnect.com
website www.smartmanagementactors.co.uk
Agent Mario Renzullo

Established in 2000. Areas of work include theatre, musicals, television, film, commercials, corporate and radio. Contact by post/email.

Will consider attending performances given one month's notice.

Stanton Davidson Associates[†]
St Martin's House, 59 St Martin's Lane, London WC2N 4JS
tel 020-7581 3388
email contact@stantondavidson.co.uk
website www.stantondavidson.co.uk
Bluesky @sdalondon.bsky.social
Instagram @sdalondon
Agents Geoff Stanton, Roger Davidson, Jamie Rowlands

Agency represents approximately 100 clients, actors, singers, producers, directors, designers, composers and musical directors. Areas of work include theatre, musical theatre, opera, film, television, radio, commercials, corporate and voice-overs.

Will consider attending performances both in and outside of Greater London, but request as much notice as possible. Accepts submissions from actors previously unknown to the company, preferably by email with a limited number of small attachments. If you can't resist the temptation to send a CV and photograph by post, please include an appropriately sized envelope for their return.

Harvey Stein Associates Ltd
tel 020-7175 7937
email info@harveystein.co.uk
website www.harveystein.co.uk
Managing Director Lois Harvey

Established in 2015, by senior agent and director Lois Harvey. Managing a small client list working throughout the industry. Happy to receive respresentation requests by email, but no large files, just links.

Stevenson Withers Associates[†]
tel 020-7720 3355
email talent@stevensonwithers.com
website www.stevensonwithers.com
X @SWATalent, @jenagent
Instagram @stevenson_withers
Agents Natasha Stevenson, Jennifer Withers

2 agents represent over 100 actors. Areas of work include theatre, musicals, television, film, commercials, corporate and voice-overs. Actors should approach the company by email only.

Stirling Management Actors Agency
490 Halliwell Road, Bolton, Lancashire BL1 8AN
07398 263181
email admin@stirlingmanagement.co.uk
website www.stirlingmanagement.co.uk
Facebook /stirlingactors
Instagram @stirling_actors

Established in 2008. Represent 70 actors and performers, including children. Areas of work include theatre, TV, film, commercials and corporate. Also represents cruise-ship singers and entertainers.

Will consider attending performances at venues in the north west given at least one weeks' notice, though preferably more. Accepts submissions by email (with CVs and photographs). Asks that Spotlight links and showreels be included if available. Commission: Theatre 10%, TV, film and commercials 15%, Voice-over and photoshoots 20%.

Katherine Stonehouse Management
Ealing Studios, Ealing Green, London W5 5EP
tel 020-8758 8452
email hello@katherinestonehouse.co.uk
website www.katherinestonehouse.co.uk
Agent Katherine Stonehouse

Established in 2009. Specialises in film, TV, theatre, musical theatre, commercials, voice-over, social influencer commercial partnerships and non-fiction writing.

The Talent Agency Ltd
Fairways, Deans Lane, Walton-on-the-Hill, Tadworth, Surrey KT20 7TS
mobile 07808 921286
email info@thetalentagencyltd.co.uk
website www.thetalentagencyltd.co.uk
Managing Director Mike Smith, Producer Daryl Smith, Consultant Sally James, Nick Smith

A management company established in 1974 and covering all aspects of clients' career and long-term development. Areas of work include television, film, commercials, corporate, music, publishing and social media. Also represents radio and TV presenters and sports stars.

Will consider attending performances at venues in Greater London and elsewhere, given 2–3 weeks' notice. Accepts submissions (with CVs and photographs) from actors previously unknown to the company, sent by post or email. Also accepts showreels and voicereels. Invitations to view individual actors' websites are only accepted if sent via email. Submitted CVs should be as complete as possible, and separate clearly professional experience from student productions. Applicants should always state if they have yet to acquire a professional role. Commission: 15–20% according to press, accountancy and PR agreements.

Tavistock Wood[†]
15 Regent Street, London SW1Y 4LR
tel 020-7494 4767

email info@tavistockwood.com
website www.tavistockwood.com
Agents Angharad Wood, Charles Collier, Bella Wingfield, Grace Cavanagh-Butler

Specialist boutique agency and management company representing around 190 clients across the fields of acting, writing and direction. The agency is now well known for an approach which places a strong focus on pan-European talent. Accepts submissions (with CVs and photographs) from actors previously unknown to the company by post only – these should be accompanied by a covering letter and a sae.

TCG Artist Management Ltd
3rd Floor, 207 Regent Street, London W1B 3HH
tel 020-7240 3600
email info@tcgam.co.uk
website www.tcgam.co.uk

TCG Ltd provides actors for work in all areas of the entertainment industry including feature films, TV, radio and theatre.

Katie Threlfall Associates[†]
13 Tolverne Road, London SW20 8RA
tel 020-8879 0493
email info@ktthrelfall.co.uk
website www.katiethrelfallassociates.com
X @KTThrelfall
Agent Katie Threlfall

Founded in 1996 as Hillman Threlfall; changed its name to Katie Threlfall Associates in 2006. One agent represents 90 actors in theatre, musicals, television, film, commercials and corporate.

Will attend performances at venues within Greater London if given one month's notice. Accepts submissions via email (with CVs and photographs) from actors previously unknown to the company. Welcomes showreels and invitations to view individual actors' websites. Address emails correctly to the agent. Only write in if you have a showreel, or with an invitation to a show: we do not take on or meet those whose work we do not know.
Commission: Commercials 15%, Television 12.5%, Theatre 10%.

Tildsley France[†]
tel 020-8521 1888
email office@tildsleyfrance.co.uk
website www.tildsleyfrance.co.uk
Agent & Company Director Alex France, *Junior Agent* Jess McShane, *Company Director* Kathryn Kirton

Established in 2003 as Janice Tildsley Associates and relaunched as Tildsley France in 2017. Areas of work include television, film, commercials and theatre.

Please check website for information before approaching for representation. *Commission*: 10–15%.

TMG London
Adam House, 7–10 Adam Street, The Strand, London WC2N 6AA
tel 020-7437 1383
Proprietor Tanya Greep

Established in 1981. Represent 70–80 actors. Areas of work include theatre, musicals, television, film, commercials, corporate and voice-overs.

Will consider attending performances at venues within Greater London with 2 weeks' notice if an actor is playing a substantial role. Accepts submissions by email. Showreels and voicereels should only be sent on request. *Commission*: 12.5%.

TTA (Top Talent Agency)
19–25 Salisbury Square, Hatfield, Herts. AL9 5BT
tel (01727) 855903
email admin@toptalentagency.co.uk
website www.toptalentagency.co.uk
Director & Head Agent Warren Bacci, *HR & Finance* Andy Musgrove, *Agents* Warren Bacci, Stanley Walton, Tilly Howes, Jude Greene, *Agent's Assistants* Simrita Khela, Louis Gaudencio, *PR and Social Media* Abi Giles

Established in 2008. 7 agents represent 300 actors (children and adults). Areas of work include theatre, musicals, television, film, commercials, corporate and voice-overs.

Will consider attending performances with one week's notice. To be considered for representation, please apply through the Top Talent website, **www.toptalentagency.co.uk**, and go to the 'join us' page. *Commission*: 15% for adults and 23% for child actors. Can represent disabled actors.

United Agents[†]
12–26 Lexington Street, London W1F 0LE
tel 020-3214 0800
email info@unitedagents.co.uk
website www.unitedagents.co.uk
Facebook /unitedagents
X @UnitedAgents
Instagram @unitedagents
Managing Director St John Donald, *Heads of Actors* Jess Alford, Sophie Austin, *Heads of Comedy* Maureen Vincent, Stephanie Moore, *Heads of Film, TV and Theatre* Giles Smart, Christian Ogunbanjo, *Head of Presenters* Matt Nicholls, *Head of Voices* Kate Davie

Established in 2007. The agency also represents writers, directors, producers, designers and other creatives.

Only accepts email submissions to one agent only with CV, headshot and showreel. Contact details can be found on the website on individual pages.

Urban Talent
Nemesis House, 1 Oxford Court, Bishopsgate, Manchester M2 3WQ
tel 0161 228 6866
email alex@urbantalentactors.co.uk
website https://urbantalent.tv

X @UrbanTalentMCR
Instagram @urbantalentactors
Agents Alex Daszewski, Lilli Griffith

Urban Talent represents 30–50 actors. Areas of work include theatre, television, film, commercials, corporate and voice-overs. Also represents presenters.

Accepts email submissions with Spotlight link and/or headshot, showreel and cover letter to **agents@urbantalentactors.co.uk** from actors previously unknown to the company.

Roxane Vacca Management[†]
61 Judd Street, London WC1H 9QT
tel 020-7383 5971
email info@roxanevacca.co.uk
website www.roxanevacca.co.uk
Instagram @roxanevaccamanagement
Agent Roxane Vacca, *Junior Agent* Jacob Knapper

Represent 60 actors. Does not welcome performance notice, but does accept representation enquiries through email. Also accepts showreels, voicereels and invitations to view individual actors' websites. *Commission:* Film & TV 12.5%; Theatre 10%; Commercials 15%.

VisABLE People Ltd
1 St. Mary's Street, Ross-on-Wye HR9 5HT
tel 020-3488 1998, *mobile* 07729 738317
email office@visablepeople.com
website www.visablepeople.com
Facebook /visablepeople
X @LouiseVisABLE
Instagram @visablepeople
Agents Louise Dyson MBE, Meg Bradley

Founded in 1994, VisABLE is the world's first agency representing only disabled people for professional engagements. It represents artistes with a wide range of impairments and in every age group, including children. 2 agents represent around 120 artistes in all areas of acting, including presenting.

Does not welcome performance notices. Happy to receive applications from disabled actors via VisABLE website only. Showreels should always be via a link sent by email. Also happy to receive invitations to view individual actors' websites. *Commission:* 10%–17.5% (commercials: 20% agency fee).

VSA Ltd[†]
187 Drury Lane, London WC2B 5QD
tel 020-7240 2927
email info@vsaltd.com
website www.vsaltd.com
Instagram @agencyvsa

Established in the 1950s by theatrical agent and impresario Vincent Shaw. Currently run by Agents Andy Charles and Tod Weller, with their Associate Agent Beccy Kilgariff. Their continued success depends on the relationships with their clients -

relationships they nurture and never take for granted. Represents 90 actors. Areas of work include theatre, film and television.

Suzann Wade MGMT
9 Wimpole Mews, London W1G 8PB
website www.suzannwade.com
Founder Suzann Wade

Areas of work include theatre, musicals, film, TV, commercials, corporate, animation, computer games and voice-over. Talent agency and personal management.

No direct emails or follow-up calls, representation interest via website contact form only. Encourages enquiries from disabled actors, American and Asian actors based in the UK, linguists and high-physicality actors.

Waring & McKenna Ltd[†]
1A Neal's Yard, London WC2H 9AW
tel 020-7836 9222
email info@waringandmckenna.com
website www.waringandmckenna.com
Instagram @WaringMcKenna
Agents Daphne Waring, John Summerfield, Richard Carey, Callum Pope

Established in 1993. 4 agents represent approximately 150 actors. Areas of work include film, TV, theatre, commercials, corporate and voice-overs both nationally and internationally.

Will consider attending performances at venues within Greater London and occasionally elsewhere, given at least one month's notice. Accepts submissions (with CVs and photographs) from actors previously unknown to the company, email preferable. Follow-up telephone calls are also accepted. Showreels and voicereels to be included in emails as links. *Commission:* Theatre and Radio 10%; TV and Low-Budget Films 12.5%; Commercials, Voice-overs and Feature Films over £4 million 15%.

WGM Atlantic Talent & Literary Group
4 Bloomsbury Square, London WC1A 2RP
tel 020-8044 1539
email hello@wgmatlanticgroup.com
website www.wgmtalent.com
Facebook /wgmtalent
X @WGMAtlantic
Instagram @wgmatlantictalent
Agents Madeleine Cotter, Guy Howe, Sophie Lucas, Hugo Midwinter, Nicky Lovick, Janet Hall

Established in 2015, the main areas of work are TV, film and theatre. Represents 70 actors, as well as writers and creatives.

Welcomes performance notices when given 2 weeks' notice. WGM Talent accepts letters (with CVs and photographs) sent by email, as well as voice tapes and invitations to view actors' websites from actors not previously known to the company. *Commission:* 12%.

Williamson & Holmes
5 Margaret Street, London W1W 8RG
tel 020-7240 0407
email info@whlondon.co.uk
website www.whlondon.co.uk
Instagram @williamsonholmes
Agents Jackie Williamson, Hugo Harold-Harrison, Carolyn Floyd, Charlotte Watts, *Assistant* Gemma Lovell

Established in 2005. Areas of work include theatre, musicals, television and film.

Accepts submissions from actors only with a link to Spotlight page. Unable to accept attachments, emails with attachments will not be read.

Winterson's†
59 St Martin's Lane, London WC2N 4JS
tel 020-7836 7849
email info@nikiwinterson.com
website www.nikiwinterson.com
Agents Niki Winterson, David O'Hanlon, Jess Jones, John Markham, Shauna Kiernan, Aleks Rusic, Rhianna Emily, Ebun Osobu, *Chief Operations Officer* Alasdair Cameron, *Assistants* Evie Walker, Dom Valentino, Molly Prendergast

Established in 2011. Main areas of work are theatre, TV, film, commercials and corporate. Represents over 250 actors. Also represents directors, writers and casting directors. Welcomes performance notices and will attend whenever possible within London. Welcomes letters, CVs via email with Spotlight links only. Please do not attach images or large files to emails.

Felix de Wolfe†
20 Old Compton Street, London W1D 4TW
tel 020-7242 5066
email info@felixdewolfe.com
website www.felixdewolfe.com
X @felixdewolfe
Instagram @felixdewolfe
Agents Caroline de Wolfe, Wendy Scozzaro, Rob Hughes, Dom Scozzaro

Areas of work include film, television, theatre, musicals, commercials, corporate and radio. Also represents directors, producers and writers.

Accepts submissions via the contact page on the website. *Commission:* Variable.

Edward Wyman Agency
23 White Acre Close, Thornhill, Cardiff CF14 9DG
tel wymancasting@yahoo.co.uk
website www.wymancasting.co.uk
Managing Director Judith Gay

Areas of work include television, film, commercials, corporate, photo shoots and voice-overs.

Accepts submissions from actors previously unknown to the company. Application forms can be downloaded from the website. Mobile phone number available on request. All submissions should include CVs and photographs and a valid DBS certificate. Welsh actors are particularly welcome. Most work South Wales-based. *Commission* 15%.

CO-OPERATIVE AGENCIES

An actors' co-op is a dedicated group of actors also working as agents as a not-for-profit enterprise. A co-op's ethos is democratic and its work includes finding work for the actors, negotiating contracts, terms and fees, offering career advice to clients, attending performances, and building relationships across the industry.

Before making an approach, it is important to understand what being a member of one of these entails, and to be clear about your reason(s) for wanting to join. Many co-ops have clear details for applicants on their websites.

21st Century Actors Management
tel 0870 039 2027
email info@21stcenturyactors.co.uk
website www.21stcenturyactors.co.uk

Co-operative management established in 1992. Areas of work include theatre, musicals, television, film, commercials and corporate. Members are expected to work 3 days in the office per month.

Will consider attending performances at venues in and around London. Accepts submissions (with Spotlight CVs) from actors previously unknown to the company if sent by email. Actors requesting representation should write stating why they wish to join a co-operative, and outlining their casting type and skills. *Commission:* Theatre, TV, commercials and film 10%.

1984 Personal Management Ltd
Suite 508, Davina House, 137 Goswell Road, London EC1V 7ET
tel 020-7251 8046
email info@1984pm.com
website www.1984pm.com
Instagram @1984personalmanagement

Co-operative management (CPMA member) representing 23 actors. Areas of work include theatre, musicals, television, film, commercials and corporate. Members are expected to work 4 days in the office per month unless paying commission.

Accepts emails (with CVs, photographs or link to Spotlight CV). Please see website Apply section for further details.

Actors Alliance
Unit 3.28, Chester House, Kennington Park, 1–3 Brixton Road, London SW9 6DE
tel 020-7407 6028
email actors@actorsalliance.co.uk
website www.actorsalliance.co.uk

Agents and casting directors

One of the longest running co-operatives, established in 1976. Managed by a membership of actors acting as agents for each other; members must be subscribed to Spotlight and Equity membership is encouraged. Areas of work include London/West End/touring regional theatre, musicals, TV, VOD, cinema-release features and independent films, commercials, corporates and voice-overs. Members are expected to work in the office at least one day a week and attend a monthly meeting unless acting professionally.

Applicants must be based in London and, given a minimum of 2 weeks' notice, agents will endeavour to attend an applicant's performance in Greater London. Welcomes applications via the form on the website. See www.actorsalliance.co.uk for more details.

Actors' Creative Team
7 Bell Yard, London WC2A 2JR
tel 020-8050 7462
email office@actorscreativeteam.co.uk
website www.actorscreativeteam.co.uk
X @ActorsCreativeT
Instagram @actorscreativeteam

Founded in 2001, this leading co-op agency is operated by its members who work as agents for each other as well as being clients. Clients regularly work in theatre, musicals, television, film, commercials and corporate projects. Members are expected to log in remotely to work 3 office days per month and to attend in-person, fortnightly meetings in Central London. The agency also runs in-house training to develop, explore and maintain performance skills. Welcomes performance notices for events, given at least 2 weeks' notice. Accepts emails from actors seeking representation, see the website for more details. Prospective clients need to include their reasons for choosing a co-operative agency in a covering email. *Commission*: Theatre up to 10%; Recorded media up to 12.5%.

The Actors File
Unit 5B, The Co-op Centre, 11 Mowll Street, London SW9 6BG
tel 020-7661 4033
email office@theactorsfile.co.uk
website www.theactorsfile.co.uk
Instagram @the_actors_file

Established in 1983. Co-operative management representing 25-30 actors. Areas of work include theatre, musicals, television, film, commercials, corporate and voice-overs. Members are expected to work approx. 3 days in the office per month and to attend business meetings.

Will attend performances at venues in Greater London and occasionally elsewhere. Accepts submissions via our website only.

The Actors' Group
tel 0161 834 4466
email enquiries@theactorsgroup.co.uk
website www.theactorsgroup.co.uk
Facebook /theactorsgroupmanchester
X @TAGmanchester
Instagram @tagmanchester

The Actors' Group (TAG) was established in Manchester in 1980 as the first co-operative agency outside London and has been representing talented actors based in the North ever since.

For over 40 years, TAG has been working with casting professionals in all areas of the industry. Our actors work throughout the UK and internationally. You can read about how the agency works, along with the latest information on applications at **www.theactorsgroup.co.uk/join-us**.

Actors Network Agency
55 Lambeth Walk, London SE11 6DX
tel 020-7735 0999
email info@ana-actors.co.uk
website www.ana-actors.co.uk
Instagram @anaactors

Established in 1985. Co-operative personal management representing 35-40 actors. Areas of work include theatre, musicals, television, film, commercials, corporate and role-play. Members are expected to work up to 4 days in the office per month.

Will consider attending performances at venues in Greater London and occasionally elsewhere, given as much notice as possible. Accepts submissions (link to Spotlight entry or CV and photograph together with any showreels) via email. *Commission* 10%; Commercials 12.5%.

Actorum Ltd
Unit 5, 11 Mowll Street, London SW9 6BG
tel 020-7636 6978
email info@actorum.com
website www.actorum.com

Co-operative management representing 25 actors. Operates on the principle of collective self-determination in the entertainment business with each actor working 4 days a month in the office when not working professionally.

Will consider attending performances at venues in Greater London and elsewhere, given 4 weeks' notice. All applications sent to **newapps@actorum.com**. Showreels, voicereels and invitations to view individual actors' websites accepted. *Commission*: Theatre 10%; TV, Commercials and Film 15%.

Alpha Actors
Unit 110, 3 Bradbury Street London N16 8JN
tel 020-7241 0077
email alpha@alphaactors.com
website www.alphaactors.com
Facebook /AlphaActors
X @AlphaActors
Instagram @alphaactors

Agents

A co-operative agency established in 1983, Alpha Actors currently represents 28 actors working in theatre, musicals, television, film, commercials and corporate work. Members are expected to work on average a total of 4 days in the office each month.

Welcomes submissions by email or by post with letter, CV and photograph, and will consider attending performances within Greater London, given as much notice as possible.

Arena Personal Management Ltd
Flat 4, 50 Carnwath Road, Fulham SW6 3DQ
tel 020-3488 1373
email info@arenapmltd.co.uk
website www.arenapmltd.co.uk

A hybrid co-operative of working and client members representing 20 London and southeast actors. Areas of work include theatre, television, film, commercials, corporate and voice-overs. Working members are expected to work one day in their home office per week and benefit from some preferred consideration for doing so.

Will consider attending showcases at venues in Greater London given 3–4 weeks' notice and if invited personally by an actor interested in a co-operative agency. Accepts submissions (with CVs and photographs) from actors previously unknown to the company by email only. Will also accept follow-up telephone calls, showreels, voicereels and invitations to view individual actors' websites. *Commission*: rates dependent on member status with both considered attractive.

AXM (Actors Exchange Management Ltd)
Unit 303, Jam Studios,
Biscuit Factory Business Complex,
100 Drummond Road, London SE16 4EQ
tel 020-7837 3304
email info@axmgt.com
website www.axmgt.com
X @AXMgt

Established in 1983. Co-operative management usually representing 20–25 actors. Areas of work include theatre, television, film, commercials, corporate, voice-overs and musicals. Members are expected to work 3–4 days in the office per month.

Will consider attending performances at venues in Greater London given sufficient notice. Accepts submissions (with CVs and photographs or Spotlight links) from actors previously unknown to the company if sent by email.

Bridges: The Actors' Agency Ltd
Studio S12, Out of the Blue Drill Hall,
36 Dalmeny Street, Edinburgh EH6 8RG
tel 0131 554 3073
email admin@bridgesactorsagency.com
website www.bridgesactorsagency.com

Facebook /bridgesactorsagency.com
X @bridgesactorsagency
Instagram @bridgesactorsagency

Established in 2008. At present the only co-operative agency active in Scotland. Areas of work include theatre, television, film, commercials, radio and corporate. Members are expected to contribute to the running of the office, and to attend meetings; therefore all prospective members must be based a commutable distance from Edinburgh or Glasgow.

Accepts submissions via emails: include a CV and headshot. Will also accept showreels, voicereels and invitations to view individual actors' websites. Welcomes invitations to attend performances and showcases.

Entry to the agency is via audition after a selection process. If successful, a stakeholder donation of £100 is required to join the agency which is refundable when membership is terminated. Prospective members must also be registered with Spotlight.

Castaway Actors Agency
13 Upper Baggot Street, 2nd Floor,
Dublin 4 D04 W7K5, Republic of Ireland
tel +353 (0)1 671 9264/9059
email castawayactors@gmail.com
website www.castawayactors.com

Established in 1988. A co-operative agency representing actors and providing top talent to the Irish and international entertainment industry for 30 years. Structured on a co-operative basis, members play an integral part in the running of all aspects of the agency and are expected to fulfil office duties throughout the year. Members are expected to fulfil office duties throughout the year. Areas of work include theatre, musicals, television, film, commercials, corporate and voice-overs. Accepts submissions with CVs, headshot and a cover letter from Dublin-based actors at **applicationsforcastaway@gmail.com**.

CCM Actors Agency Ltd
c/o 802 Garratt Lane, Tooting, London SW17 0LZ
tel 020-3697 1961
email casting@ccmactors.com
website www.ccmactors.com
Lead contact Lucy Aley-Parker, *Administrator* Mike Anfield

Established in 1993. Co-operative management representing up to 35 actors. Areas of work include theatre, film, television, musicals and commercials. Currently working from a virtual office.

Members will consider attending performances, with notice. The agency accepts applications via email (with photographs and link to Spotlight) from actors we feel can enhance the membership. Entry to the agency is via self tape followed by interview audition. Actors must be aware of how co-operatives work, and

96 Agents and casting directors

their role within them. Please see our website for application procedure. Information is available from Equity and Spotlight. Training fee of £100 (in 2 instalments) is charged on joining the agency. Prospective clients must also be registered in Spotlight.

Central Line
tel 0333 344 6244
email app@thecentralline.co.uk
website http://thecentralline.co.uk
Facebook /centralactors
X @centralactors

Co-operative management agency established in 1984. Areas of work include theatre, musicals, television, film, commercials, corporate and voice-overs. Also represents directors. Members are expected to work in the office as and when appropriate.

Will consider attending performances at venues in Greater London and elsewhere. Accepts submissions (with links to Spotlight) from actors previously unknown to the company, sent by email only. Will also accept follow-up telephone calls, showreels, voicereels and invitations to view individual actors' websites. *Commission*: 8–15%.

Circuit Personal Management Ltd
Suite 1.7, Universal Square, Devonshire Street, Manchester M12 6JH
tel 0330 995 0069
email circuitpm@outlook.com
email circuitrepresentation@gmail.com
website www.circuitpm.co.uk
X @CircuitPM
Instagram @Circuitinsta

Established in 1988; member of CPMA. Co-operative management primarily representing actors in the North West area. Areas of work include theatre, musicals, television, film, commercials, corporate and voice-overs. Members are expected to work approximately 4–5 days quarterly in our Manchester office and to attend monthly meetings.

Will consider attending performances at venues within the operating area, preferably with 3–4 weeks' notice. Accepts submissions from actors (with CVs and photographs) sent by post or email. Will also accept follow-up telephone calls. *Commission*: Theatre 10%; Radio and Voice over 10%; Film 14%.

Crescent Management
3rd Floor, 86–90 Paul Street, London EC2A 4NE
tel 020-8987 0191
email mail@crescentmanagement.co.uk
website www.crescentmanagement.co.uk

Established in 1991, the agency has 20–25 members working in theatre, musicals, television, film, commercials and corporate drama. Members are expected to work 2–3 days in the office each month.

Will consider attending performances within Greater London given 2 weeks' notice. Accepts submissions (Spotlight link and headshot) from actors previously unknown to the agency: please read the advice on how to apply given on the website. Will also accept follow-up telephone calls, showreels, voicereels and invitations to view an actor's website. *Commission*: Theatre 10%; Television 12.5%; Film 15%.

Denmark Street Management
tel 020-7459 4902
email mail@denmarkstreet.net
website www.denmarkstreet.net
X @DenmarkStMGMT

Established in 1985. Accepts submissions via the 'apply' link on the website only. Applicants must be members of Spotlight and Equity, and their profiles should contain recent professional headshots. Applicants should state why they would like to join a co-operative. A helpful guide is available on the website. Committed to diversity, equity and inclusion and is now completely remotely-based.

Direct Personal Management
Office 3.03, Wizu Workspace,
The Leeming Building, George Street, Leeds LS2 7HZ
tel 0113 266 4036
email office@directpm.co.uk
website www.directpm.co.uk
Facebook /DirectPersonalManagement
X @DPMActors
Instagram @DPMActors

Established in 1984 (formerly Direct Line Personal Management). Co-operative management normally representing 20 to 30 actors. Areas of work include theatre, musicals, television, film, commercials, corporate, role-play and voice-overs. Members are expected to work 2 days in the office each month.

Will consider attending performances with one month's notice. Accepts submissions (with CVs and photographs) from actors previously unknown to the company. Links to showreels, voicereels and invitations to view individual actors' websites are also accepted. "Please consult our website before applying. Every applicant's enquiry is read and replied to." *Commission*: 5–15%.

Frontline Actors' Agency
30–31 Wicklow Street, Dublin 2, Republic of Ireland
tel +353 (0)1 635 9882
email contact@frontlineactors.com
website www.frontlineactors.com
Facebook /FrontlineActorsAgency
X @FrontlineActors
Chair Tom Doonan

Established in 2000. Main areas of work are theatre, television, film, commercials, corporate and voice-overs. Co-operative agency with 28 actor members who are expected to work approximately one week per quarter in the office. Will attend performances in Ireland only, given 2 weeks' notice.

Welcomes letters (with CVs and photographs), showreels and invitations to view actors' websites. Encourages submissions from actors with disabilities.

IML

Estate Offices, Horseferry Road, London SW1P 2EH
tel 020-7587 1080
email info@iml.org.uk
website www.iml.org.uk

Founded in 1980, Independent Management is one of the oldest co-operative agencies representing professional actors. Has a consultant agent, and members work in the office one to 2 days a month.

Areas of work include theatre, musicals, television, film and commercials.

Apply via email with CV and showreels, also accepts invitations to see work. See website for more details.

Inspiration Management

tel 020-7012 1614
email mail@inspirationmanagement.org.uk
website www.inspirationmanagement.org.uk

Established in 1986, Inspiration is a co-operative actors' agency. Areas of work include theatre, television, film, commercials, corporate, audio and role-play. Members work 30 days for the co-op per year, when not engaged in professional acting work, and attend meetings once a month.

Actors can apply to join by email, with details of their shows where applicable, and are encouraged to consult the website prior to applying. Successful applicants will be invited to interview and audition. Commission: 10% across the board.

NorthOne Management

tel 020-7735 5061
email actors@northone.co.uk
website www.northone.co.uk
X @N1Management

Established in 1986. Co-operative management representing up to 25 actors. Areas of work include theatre, television, film, commercials and corporate. Members are expected to work 2–3 days in the office per month (hybrid working optional).

Will consider attending performances at venues within Greater London given at least one week's notice. Accepts submissions via their website application form (not by email or post). Applicants must explain why they wish to be representd by a co-operative agency. Will also accept follow-up telephone emails, showreels and voicereels. Prefers to hear from actors when currently performing. Administration and technical skills are advantageous. Applicants must be on Spotlight. Commission: 12%.

Oren Actors Management

Chapter, Market Road, Canton, Cardiff CF5 1QE
tel 029-2023 3321
email info@orenactorsmanagement.co.uk
website www.orenactorsmanagement.co.uk
Facebook /OrenActorsManagement
X @Oren_Actors
Instagram @oren_actors

Established in 1985, Oren Actors Management represents experienced and professionally trained actors for the industries of Theatre, Television, Film, Commercials, Radio, Voice over and Digital. All our clients are members of Equity and Spotlight. Members are expected to work 4 hours in the office per week when not in commissionable work.

Will consider attending performances at venues in Greater London, South Wales and South West England given 2 weeks' notice. Accepts submissions with CVs and headshots, showreels, voicereels and invitations to view actors' websites. Applicants are asked to state clearly why they have approached a co-operative. Commission: Coporate/Roleplay 5%; Theatre 8%; All other 10%.

Performance Actors Agency

137 Goswell Road, London EC1V 7ET
tel 020-7251 3974
email info@performanceactors.co.uk
website www.performanceactors.co.uk
X @PerformanceArts
Instagram @performanceactorsagency
Key personnel Lionel Guyett, Hilary Greatorex

Established in 1984. Co-operative management representing 30+ actors. Areas of work include theatre, musicals, television, film, commercials, corporate and voice-overs. Members are expected to work 3–4 days a month in the office.

Will consider attending performances at venues within Greater London and occasionally elsewhere. Accepts submissions by email from actors previously unknown to the company. Will also accept showreels and voicereels. New applicants must express specific interest in being part of a co-operative agency. See the website for current recruitment requirements. Commission: 10%.

RbA Management Ltd

Office A, 2nd Floor, Building 2, 360 Edge Lane, Liverpool L7 9NJ
tel 0151 708 7273
email info@rbamanagement.co.uk
website www.rbamanagement.co.uk

Established in 1995, RbA is a co-operative management representing up to 20 actors. Areas of work include theatre, musicals, television, film, radio, commercials, corporate and voice-overs. Members are expected to contribute4 working days in the office every 2–3 months.

Agents and casting directors

We will consider attending performances at venues in the North West (Manchester, Liverpool, North Wales) and nationally (digitally only). Applications should be made via the website at www.rbamanagement.co.uk/representation. *Commission*: Theatre 12.5%; everything else 15%.

Rogues & Vagabonds Management
Deptford Lounge, Giffin Street, London SE8 4RJ
tel 020-7254 8130
email rogues@vagabondsmanagement.com
website www.vagabondsmanagement.com
X @RandVManagement

Co-operative management representing 28–30 actors. Areas of work include theatre, television, film, commercials and corporate. Members are expected to work in the office 3 days per month.

Will consider attending performances anywhere, if given at least 3–4 weeks' notice. Accepts submissions (with CVs and photographs) from actors previously unknown to the company if sent by post or email to **joinrogues@gmail.com**. Showreels, voicereels and invitations to view individual actors' websites are also accepted. Welcomes applications from experienced, talented and driven actors from all backgrounds, experiences and all forms of diversity. *Commission*: Less than £300, no commission; Over £301, 10%; Over £600, 15%.

Rosebery Management Ltd
Oxford House, Derbyshire Street, London E2 6HG
tel 020-7684 0187
email admin@roseberymanagement.com
website www.roseberymanagement.com
X @roseberymgmt
Instagram @roseberymgmt

Established in 1984. Represents 40 actors in theatre, musicals, television, film, commercials, corporate work and voice-overs. Rosebery has a full-time Lead Agent. For applicantions email **roseberyapplications@gmail.com**.

Stage Centre Management Ltd
10 Chandos Avenue, London E17 4PB
tel 020-3978 0080
email info@stagecentre.org.uk
website www.stagecentre.org.uk

Established in 1982. London-based co-operative management agency. Areas of work include theatre, musicals, television, film, commercials and corporate. Members are expected to work from home on behalf of the agency, equivalent to 3 days per month, when not acting (there is no physical office); this commitment is flexible and can be discussed on application.

Will consider attending performances at venues within Greater London and elsewhere, given at least 2 weeks' notice. Accepts submissions from actors previously unknown to the company. Will also accept follow-up communications, showreels, voicereels and invitations to view individual actors' websites. Applicants should not apply if they are unable to provide visible evidence of their work (e.g. performance notice, showcase or showreel). *Commission*: 10–15% depending on job.

Tarquin Talent Agency Ltd
30 Wilton Road, Great Malvern, Worcs WR14 3RH
tel 020-3488 8071
email tarquin@tarquintalentagency.com
website www.tarquintalentagency.com
Facebook TarquinTalentAgency
X @tarquintalentagency
Bluesky @tarquintalentagency.bsky.social
Instagram @tarquintalentagency
Threads @tarquintalentagency
Young FEAA MD & Head Of Casting Tarquin Shaw

An International Agency that represents Adults and Children & Young Performers. Representing the country's leading actors and young performers in all areas of the industry. They have a reputation for finding the right actor for each job, specialising in young performers and adults through their Tarquin Talent Acting Agency or Tarquin Shaw's services as a Casting Director. Established in 1988, in 2025 they were a finalist in the 2025 TEAA Business awards for Best Agency of the Year. Member of The Entertainment Agents' Association (TEAA).

Nurturing talent: an agent's frame of mind

Michael Wiggs, founder of Creative Arts Management (CAM) and film producer
Interview by Maggie Norris

Michael Wiggs has worked in the industry for over three decades. He founded Creative Artists Management (CAM), building the company into one of the top boutique agencies in the UK, managing a raft of internationally successful actors and directors, as well as training and mentoring a generation of agents. He has also worked as a producer, collaborating with writers, directors and other creatives on a range of projects including short films, television series and independent films. Wiggs now runs Modern Collective, a bespoke management service, which he founded with Lucy Doyle.

I'm having lunch with the founder of Creative Arts Management (CAM), an acting agency which nurtured the careers of some of the UK's biggest industry names. This is quite a turnaround for a boy who left school at 15 with no qualifications and who by his own admission was at risk of getting into trouble.

I started from nothing. It's hard to explain to anybody how that time was because it was very elitist. We're talking about the 80s, you couldn't get a certain level of job if you didn't have a degree. The agents at the time were very, very posh.

You say you left home under a cloud. That must've made you determined to make a life for yourself in London?

Yes, I set it up on my own on what was called the Job Start. We're talking about the 80s: Maggie Thatcher and all that. If you had an idea for a business, Job Start gave you 35 quid a week. And so Creative Arts Management was born, in a business centre with a telephone and a shared fax downstairs. I was 24 at the time, but I'd been working since I was 15, so it didn't feel young even though people thought it was. And when I was coming up, it was my own company entirely and it was in a very good space. We moved to beautiful offices in Shaftesbury Avenue. The success continued for more than 35 years. Then I decided that I wanted to work in a different way. So, I set up a new agency, called Modern Collective, with Lucy Doyle, who I had worked with for 20 years.

So, no plans to ease into retirement as your 60th birthday approached? Did you feel you were at a crossroads? How was it – starting afresh?

It's just so liberating. It was a bit scary in a way. I had to detangle myself from a company that I'd literally been with for 35 years. I'd had the same email and phone number forever. I wanted to start again in a modern way; I didn't want to have an office, not even a WeWork or anything like that. I just wanted to work from wherever. So, we collaborated with people that designed an amazing website and Instagram. And my two major clients (from CAM) said, "Yeah, absolutely. Whatever you're doing, we're doing it with you".

Two major clients indeed. During 35 years of running CAM, you nurtured the careers of Martin Freeman and Ray Winstone. But despite having two giants of the industry on board, it's no longer seasoned professionals that you are looking to represent?

Well, I don't want to attract people that are already part-way or halfway through their career. It's at the very beginning that I like, that's what I'm interested in.

How do you nurture an actor, at the beginning of their career?

I'm strategic. I'm entrepreneurial naturally. I've always done it in a different way, punching way above my weight. Even as a young agent. As much as I love the casting process, I would also cultivate directors, writers and producers.

How did your relationship with Ray Winstone begin?

Ray had done the film *Scum* when he was 18. He had just been doing this, that and the other, but not much since. And so he came to me, he must have been about 32. I was two years in, working out of a business centre (with no clients of any note), but I was known for just going out and about. All of my people were in theatre and I was pounding on the door of the Royal Court because it was the real hot place at that time. Early 90s. It was when Stephen Daldry was there and Ian Rickson was running the studio and I got on very well with the casting director, Lisa Makin. I got all my clients in to do rehearsed readings for the new plays coming through the studios and those happened to be written by people like Joe Penhall and Jez Butterworth. So, my reputation as an agent was built through that.

And then I had a lot of actors work at the Royal Court. So, you just take casting directors, but also TV and film directors and producers, along all the time. Ray did Joe Penhall's first two plays at the Royal Court and then Patrick Marber's *Dealers' Choice* at the National and then in the West End. And the cream of the crop of the industry came along to see those, imagine all those press nights! They'd loved Ray in *Scum*, then suddenly to see him on stage – and of course he's so lovely and charming and all of that – that's what kick-started Ray's career. The collaboration has continued for 35 years. We've had so much fun. Been to a lot of film festivals with him. I didn't really know what Cannes Film Festival was to be honest. He had been there as a young guy and what he likes to do – he just likes to drive. So, we said we're going to drive down to Cannes! In a Jaguar, you know, in one of those old Jags. It took two and a half days. There's this amazing route in, where you go through the mountains down to Cannes and we sort of went in there and stayed in this terrible little cheap hotel. And we just had such a laugh. Then we kept going back to Cannes again and again and again. When Ray did *Indiana Jones* it was different – it's Spielberg – so you're on a yacht and being introduced to Goldie Hawn and all that kind of stuff. Obviously *Nil by Mouth* went there. That was the big one. That was 1997, so we drove down for that.

I was very lucky with Martin Freeman. He had already done lots of work. People had seen him come through drama school. He'd done lots of plays at the Royal Court, but he wasn't on my radar at all. And his agent, who he loved, was having a child and didn't want to come back to work. So, she was looking to place all of her clients with agents, and I think *Nil By Mouth* had just happened for Ray, which in our world was big. So, I was quite hot as an agent. He wanted to meet me. He came in with this big bag of VHSs and said, 'This is my work'. One of them was the pilot of *The Office*. They'd done it already and the BBC hadn't decided what to do with it. I watched it and said, "Yeah, this is absolutely fantastic". We got together and we stayed together and then that went to series and was an immediate hit.

In more recent years, you've started seeking out talent in different places. You recently took on a member from The Big House, Jake Walden. Jake played the leading role in *The Realness*, a musical about a young man leaving prison and the challenges he faces trying to get his life on track.

I said to Lucy [Doyle], this guy's fantastic. She was nervous. I hadn't looked after a young actor for a long time. I'd had 10 years where I was just sort of looking after Ray and Martin really and running the company and all that that entails. Lucy was like, "Slow down, slow down". So, I couldn't do anything. But he stayed in my mind. Five months went by, and I couldn't shake the feeling that I had missed an opportunity and, of course, you kept calling and gently encouraging me to take the next step. You had such faith in him. So, we arranged a meeting. Lucy and I met with him and, of course, he's lovely and charming and so professional. And we saw some tapes of a Netflix film he'd tested for in an audition workshop at The Big House and he translates so well to screen. He's just very, very charismatic. It's interesting because he's not been to drama school and he's faced some challenges in his life too, but he's learned so much at The Big House. So we took him on.

If you were to put yourself in a young actor's shoes now, what would you look for in an agent?

I would look at, say, a young casting director, like Isabella Odoffin, and look at her work, look at a film like *How to Have Sex*, look at all those young actors and see who represents them. It's all online now, thankfully. So, you can go on all the agents' websites and see if you like the work, if you like those actors. That's what I would do. And you can see how many clients they've got as well, which is quite important.

Why?

I never – even at my height – had any more than 35 to 40 clients. Whereas some people have 70 or 100. However, some agents work in a different way. They are at the bigger agencies where it is more of a numbers game for them. But if you get 100 clients and they do well, you might end up with two assistants or even three assistants. So, you have a first, second, and third. But if you're relying on them, and an actor gets scouted by the second or third assistant, who says to the named agent, "I've just seen this great person at The Big House, or this person from LAMDA" and the main agent says, "Yeah, yeah, I trust your taste. Take them on." You'll be under the umbrella of that named agent, but it will be the assistant that took you on. So, I think it's something to think through, as that assistant can move jobs and then suddenly you might be gone, as the main agent might not want to keep you as they didn't choose you. Personally, what I would do is try and find someone on the younger side, who is maybe already an associate agent (which is basically one step away) and who is building up their own list and raring to go.

And if you were interviewing a young actor and considering taking them on, what would deter you? What mistakes should a young actor avoid making in an interview?

If someone came in and they wanted to be a star, that would be a big problem. Jake Walden came in and said, "Look, I just want to build up my CV." He'd really thought about it. He was nervous, but he said – and this is what impressed Lucy and me – "Look, I'm fine. I work during the day. I can support myself. I just want to learn. I want to just build up my CV, but I only want to do quality stuff." If I had got a sense that it was all about red carpets for him, or anybody else, I would just get bored because I wouldn't be interested in that. You need to be interested in the quality of the creatives you work with. Success is too far away. Although, it can happen quickly, but usually when that happens, it's disastrous. Building a career slowly will make it sustainable.

Maggie Norris is the founder of The Big House **https://thebighouse.uk.com/**.

CPMA: the Co-operative Personal Management Association

Almost all actors' co-operative agencies belong to the Co-operative Personal Management Association (CPMA), which was created in 2002 to promote co-op agencies in the profession, encourage the highest professional standards, and represent the interests of co-op agencies to outside bodies, such as Equity and Government departments.

Actors represented by co-operative agencies run the agency themselves, through a democratic structure, and work as unpaid agents for each other. Some co-ops employ a co-ordinator or administrator (who is not an actor). Co-op agencies are non-profit-making, and any surplus funds are put back into the business. Co-op agencies began in the UK in 1970, since when many more have been established and thrive. Co-ops access the same casting information as conventional agents and suggest actors for jobs, negotiate contracts and fees, take commission on jobs, and recommend and promote their clients to casting directors (CDs) and others. There is often a fee to join a co-op, which is refunded when you leave. Other, non-refundable, fees may be charged, and there could also be a voluntary monthly levy to cover office costs, co-ordinator's fees, etc. Co-op members work in the office (typically two to four times a month), attend business meetings (usually monthly) to discuss aspects of running the agency, oversee the work of other co-op members (often with CDs), and consider the work of applicants.

Belonging to a co-op has many advantages: ·
• You quickly learn how the industry works, which can be very useful for newcomers and those returning to the profession.
• You are in contact with many industry professionals, which could help you get work.
• You are supported by other actors in the agency, some of who will have a lot of experience.
• You know which jobs you have been suggested for, and can monitor them.
• You have more influence over how you are represented, and can be more pro-active in your career.
• You can say which type of work you will or won't do, without fear of being asked to leave the agency.
• Usually, more than one person decides whom to suggest for a job. Many CDs acknowledge that co-ops often know their clients much better, and can sell them with honesty and confidence.
• Co-ops have smaller lists of clients, tend to avoid clashes, and commission rates are lower.

However, you should be aware that there can be drawbacks to being part of a co-op. As with conventional agents, standards vary; a co-op is only as good and professional as its members. Can you be sure that other members are working as hard for you, as you are for them? Continuity can also be a problem, with so many people involved. Although co-ops with a co-ordinator may have an advantage in this respect, measures such as detailed note-taking and not changing negotiators on a contract still need to be taken. And CDs tend to send breakdowns for major TV and film roles to the top agencies in the industry – although other parts will be sent to good co-ops.

To join a co-op you need to be a good agent (not just a good actor), committed, reliable and keen to support fellow actors. You must be prepared to get on the phone, talk to CDs, and sell your clients with knowledge and conviction, making intelligent and credible suggestions for roles. Consider, too, your personal commitments, such as doing non-acting jobs to earn money, and expenses, such as travel to and from the office, and joining/training fees.

If you are thinking of applying to a co-op, first ask if applications are being considered – and if so, how they should be submitted. Check CVs and photos on the agency's website to identify potential gaps. Co-ops usually want to see an applicant's work, so send a showreel or details of the show you're in (they tend not to go to drama school shows or showcases, unless someone has expressed interest).

To find out more about the agency, talk to current and former members. You might want to know when the agency was established; if any ex-members have returned; the extent of their contacts with CDs and with theatres; the range of casting information they receive; and whether they belong to the CPMA, which has a code of conduct (Equity particularly welcomed the creation of the CPMA for this reason). If the co-op is interested in your application, you will be interviewed by all available members. If offered a place, you will usually have a three- to six-month trial period. After discussion to see how both sides feel, you may then be offered full membership.

Please visit **www.cpma.coop** for further information.

Voice-over agents

This section lists agencies that specialise in voice-overs. Check the details of how each wishes to be approached, and refer to the 'Showreel, Voicereel and Website Services' section for more about getting a voicereel (or 'voice demo') made. Some of the larger conventional agencies have their own voice-over departments – generally for their existing clients only.

Ad Voice
40 Whitfield Street, London W1T 2RH
tel 020-7323 2345
email info@advoice.co.uk
website www.advoice.co.uk

Represent clients working in television and radio commercials, documentaries, corporate, animations and audiobook recordings. Submission via email.

Bespoke Voice Agency
5th Floor, Strand Bridge House, 138–142 Strand, London WC2R 1HH
tel 020-7287 1070
email voices@bespokeagency.co.uk
website www.bespokevoiceagency.co.uk
X @Bespoke_Voices
Instagram @bespoke_voices
Agents Kate Pulmpton, Hayley Ori, *Assistant* Grace Devereux

Areas of work include animated films, commercials, documentaries, audiobooks, video games and campaigns. *Commission*: 15%.

Calypso Voices
1–3 Old Compton Street, London W1D 5JB
tel 020-7734 6415
email calypso@calypsovoices.com
website www.calypsovoices.com
Director Jane Savage

2 agents represent 80 clients for voice-over work. Areas of work include television and radio commercials, documentaries, animation, corporate, audio books and on-air promotions.

Damn Good Voices
2:18 Chester House, 1–3 Brixton Road, London SW9 6DE
mobile 07702 228185, 07809 549887
email casting@damngoodvoices.com
website www.damngoodvoices.com
Instagram @thedamngoodgroup
Creative Director Simon Cryer, *Voice Agent* Georgia Hill, *Assistant* Alistair Spencer

Established in 2010. Damn Good Voices is a voice-over agency representing award-winning UK and US voice talent, working across all media including TV, film, radio, online, gaming, animation and corporate.

Represents over 300 actors and singers. Represenation requests should be made via the website only. Go to Representation in FAQs on the website. All submissions for representation are tracked and responded to personally. Submissions by email will not be accepted. *Commission*: 15%

hhush (Hamilton Hodell Universal Soundhouse)
20 Golden Square, London W1F 9JL
tel 020-7636 1221
email info@hhush.co.uk
website www.hhush.co.uk
Agents Hayley Ori, Carla Jones

Main areas of work: commercial voice over, animation and audiobooks. Welcomes emails (with CVs) from individual actors previously unknown to the agency. *Commission*: 15%.

Lip Service
8 Mayfield Gardens, London W7 3RH
tel 020-7734 3393
email bookings@lipservice.co.uk
website https://lipservice.co.uk

4 agents solely represent over 100 clients and a number of foreign clients. Areas of work include television, film, commercials and audio books.

Accepts submissions (with CVs and voicereels) from individual actors previously unknown to the company, sent by email or post. Please enclose an sae for their return.

Rhubarb Voices
1st Floor, 1A Devonshire Road, Chiswick, London W4 2EU
tel 020-8742 8683
email enquiries@rhubarbvoices.co.uk
website www.RhubarbVoices.co.uk
Key contact Johnny Garcia

Leading UK voice talent agency with experience casting voices into all platforms of the spoken word, including commercials, continuity and promos, corporate pieces, animation, games, ADR/lip-sync and more. Represents around 90 exclusive UK and North American artists, and more than 100 foreign-language artists.

Actors seeking representation should email their CV (including any voice-over work to date), a photo and an MP3 showreel. Please note that the agency prefers not to receive follow-up calls.

Shining Management Ltd
PO Box 1045, Chislehurst BR7 9AR
tel 020-7734 1981
email info@shiningvoices.com
website www.shiningvoices.com
X @ShiningVoices
Instagram @shiningmanagement
Agents & Co-directors Jennifer Taylor Cave, Clair Daintree

2 agents represent 80 clients. Areas of work include voice-overs for television, film, commercials, computer games, animation and audio books.

Accepts emailed submissions ONLY to shiningvoices@gmail.com. "Please do not ring with submission enquiries."

Sue Terry Voices Ltd
1st Floor, 35 Great Marlborough Street, London W1F 7JF
tel 020-7434 2040
email sue@sueterryvoices.com
website www.sueterryvoices.com
Founder Sue Terry, Director Vicky Hopewell

12 agents represent around 400 actors working in voice-overs only. Does not welcome unsolicited approaches by actors without performing agents. Commission: 15%.

Tongue & Groove
PO Box 173, Manchester M19 0AR
tel 0161 249 3666
email info@tongueandgroove.co.uk
website www.tongueandgroove.co.uk
Producers Bev Ashworth, John Basham

2 agents represent 50 clients. Areas of work include voice-overs for television, commercials and audio books.

Accepts submissions (with CVs and voicereels) from individual actors previously unknown to the company if sent by post. Also accepts voicereels and invitations to view individual actors' websites.

Vocal Point
Fin Studios, 22 Soho Square, London W1D 4NS
tel 020-7419 0700
email enquiries@vocalpoint.net
website www.vocalpoint.net
Agent Ben Romer-Lee

Areas of work include television, commercials and audio books. 2 agents represent approximately 110 clients.

Accepts submissions from actors previously unknown to the company. Invitations to view individual actors' websites are also accepted. Follow-up calls are not welcomed. Commission: 15%.

VoiceBank Ltd
45 Windsor Drive, Timperley WA14 5AN
tel 0161 973 8879
email elinors@voicebankltd.co.uk
website www.voicebankltd.co.uk
Director Elinor Stanton

Works in all areas: musicals, television, film, commercials, audio books and radio. Represents 42 clients.

Welcomes unsolicited voicereels and invitations to view individual actors' websites. Does not currently represent any actors with disabilities, but "this would not be a barrier to joining the company".

Voice Shop
1st Floor, 1A Devonshire Road, London W4 2EU
tel 020-8742 7077
email info@voice-shop.co.uk
website www.voice-shop.co.uk
Key contact Maxine Wiltshire

3 agents represent 42 clients working in television, film, commercials and audio-book recording.

Welcomes emails with MP3 audio samples from new actors, but prefers not to receive follow-up telephone calls or voicereels. All audio samples should contain appropriate material, and be professionally produced. Commission: 15%.

Voice Squad
76 Park Avenue North, London NW10 1JY
tel 020-8450 4451
email voices@voicesquad.com
website www.voicesquad.com
Director Neil Conrich

4 agents represent more than 1,300 clients. Areas of work include television, commercials and audio books.

Accepts submissions (with CVs and voicereels) from individual actors previously unknown to the company if sent by email.

Voicebank, The Irish Voice-Over Agency
39–40 Upper Mount Street, Dublin 2 D02 PR89, Republic of Ireland
tel +353 (0)1 235 1020
email voicebankvoices@voicebank.ie
website www.voicebank.ie
Company Directors & Owners Deborah Pearce, David Houlden

Voicebank are a voice-over agency only and represent actors, comedians and presenters for all aspects of voice work. Main areas of work include commercials, animations, games, audiobooks, corporate work, television, film and radio. A team of agents represent more than 300 artists.

Artist submissions accepted by email only: include CV, Spotlight link and demo reels of no longer than 2 minutes, as MP3 or wav files. Only likely to consider representing experienced voice-over talent and professionals in either acting, comedy or broadcasting. May also consider young newcomers to the industry who demonstrate a capability and confidence that is appropriate for the competitive nature of this industry. *Commission:* Varies

The Voiceover Gallery
1st Floor, 44 Berwick Street, London W1F 8SE
tel 020-7987 0951
110 Timber Wharf, 32 Worsley Street, Manchester M15 4NX
tel (01618) 818844
email info@thevoiceovergallery.co.uk
website www.thevoiceovergallery.co.uk
Directors Marylou Thistleton-Smith, Jason Thorpe

Areas of work include corporate, documentary, new media, television and radio advertising. Represents English voices and multiple foreign voices. *Commission:* 15%.

VSI (Voice & Script International)
128–134 Cleveland Street, London W1T 6AB
tel 020-7692 7700
email info@vsi.tv
website www.vsi.tv

1500 foreign-language and English-speaking voice-over clients. Areas of work include voice-overs for television, film, corporate and commercials.

Accepts submissions (with CVs) from individual actors and presenters previously unknown to the company, sent by post or email (**voices@vsi.tv**). Also accepts voicereels and invitations to view individual actors' websites. "We only use mother-tongue foreign-language speakers."

Yakety Yak All Mouth Ltd
27 Mortimer Street,
London W1T 3BL (postal address only)
tel 020-7430 2600
email hello@yaketyyak.co.uk
website www.yaketyyak.co.uk
Proprietor Jolie Williams

5 agents represent 200 clients. Areas of work include voice-overs for television, film, commercials, animation and audio books.

Books are currently closed, but submissions can be sent to **submissions@yaketyyak.co.uk** in MP3 format. *Commission:* 15%.

Presenters' agents

Becca Barr Management
tel 020-3137 2980
email info@beccabarrmanagement.co.uk
website www.beccabarrmanagement.co.uk
Instagram @beccabarrrmanagement

BBM represents an eclectic mix of talent ranging from presenters to experts, actors, social influencers and content creators.

Accepts submissions by email (with CVs and photographs). Showreels and voicereels are also welcome. Query via online form.

Bold Management Ltd
85 Bold Street, Liverpool L1 4HF
tel 0151-709 1791
email info@bold-management.com
website www.bold-management.com
Facebook /boldmanagement
X @boldmanagement
Instagram @boldmanagement
General Manager Joe Foster

Established in 2009, Bold Management is a talent management company representing TV personalities, influencers, singer/songwriters and sports people.

Celeb Agents
36 Soho Square, London W1D 3QY
tel 020-3198 2200
email sue@celebagents.co.uk
website https://celebagents.co.uk
Facebook /celebagentsuk
X @celebagents
Instagram @celebagents
Ceo David Hahn

Celeb Agents exclusively represents established celebrities. Their services include public relations, including managing interviews and social media accounts, and bookings for appearances and events. Clients include athletes, chefs, television personalities, comedians, presenters, musicians, actors, models and authors.

Jeremy Hicks Associates Ltd
26 Parkgate, London SE3 9XF
email info@jeremyhicks.com
website www.jeremyhicks.com
Agents Jeremy Hicks, Sarah Dalkin, Charlotte Leaper, Julie Dalkin

Represents presenters, writers and chefs.

Commission: 15% (10% for scriptwriters).

John Noel Management
Block B Imperial Works, Perren Street,
London NW5 3ED
tel 020-7428 8400
email jadeen@johnnoel.com
website www.johnnoel.com
X @JNManagement
Instagram @johnnoelmanagement
Director and Senior Agent Jadeen Singh

John Noel Management is a London-based talent agency representing presenters, comedians, experts and reality stars. They develop and nurture new talent and represent household names, working across television, radio, film, social, publishing and voice-over projects.

Knight Ayton Management
tel 020-3795 1806
email info@knightayton.co.uk
website https://knightayton.co.uk
X @KnightAyton

Represents leading broadcasters and presenters in factual television. Their clients include experts, authors and journalists, working in print, radio and podcasts across a wide variety of subjects.

M&C Saatchi Talent
36 Golden Square, London W1F 9EE
website www.mcsaatchitalent.com
X @mcsaatchigroup
Instagram @mcsaatchisocial
Founder Richard Thompson

Established in 2002, this talent management agency representing clients across the broadcast, commercial and publishing sectors. They champion inclusivity, represent diverse voices and promote meaningful change in the arts and entertainment industries.

Money Management UK
42A Berwick Street, London W1F 8RZ
tel 020-7287 7490
email info@moneymanagementuk.com
website https://moneymanagementuk.com
Instagram @moneysoho

Established in 2000, Money Management UK is a full-service talent management company. They manage every aspect of a client's career, including TV, radio, podcasts, live tours, and business and commercial opportunities. They also focus on the creation of intellectual property and content for their clients.

Perfect Match Presenters
email info@pmpagency.co.uk
website www.pmpagency.co.uk
Facebook /pmpagencyuk
X @pmpagencyuk
Instagram @pmpagencyuk

Perfect Match Presenters (PMP) maintains a database of experienced presenters who they place in a variety of presenting roles across the TV, radio, infomercials, live events, corporate events and products launches. Also runs workshops teaching essential presenting skills.

Rom Com Entertainment
email benji@romcomentertainment.com
website https://romcomentertainment.com/
Instagram @romcomentertainment
Founder Benji Rom

Talent management agency specialising in brand building for celebrity personalities working across broadcasting, entertainment and social media.

Sandra Singer Associates
21 Cotswold Road, Westcliff-on-Sea, Essex SS0 8AA
tel (01702) 331616
email sandrasingeruk@aol.com
website www.sandrasinger.com

2 agents represent approximately 40 main clients. "We are a specialist boutique agency representing some of the best talent in the UK for Acting and Musical Theatre." Also a leading Young Performers agency. Email requests in the first instance regarding representation. *Commission*: 10% Stage; 20% Screen.

Triple A Media
tel 020-7228 9007
email info@tripleamedia.com
website www.tripleamedia.com
Owner/Agent Andy Hipkiss

Established in 2007. Areas of work include television, radio and corporate. Also represents a number of other media professionals, including DJs, presenters and experts. Member of the Personal Managers Association (PMA).

Accepts submissions by email (with CVs and photographs) and welcomes showreels. Happy to represent actors with disabilities.

Jo Wander Management
111 Coppergate House, Whites Row, London E1 7NF
tel 020-7199 6324
email jo@jowandermanagement.com
website www.jowandermanagement.com
Managing Director Jo Wander

One agent represents 15–20 presenter clients.

Welcomes letters (with CVs and showreels) from individual presenters previously unknown to the agency, sent by post or email; will accept invitations to view individuals' websites.

Wendy Woolfson Talent and PR
email info@wwtalentandpr.com
website www.wwtalentandpr.com
Founder Wendy Woolfson

Wendy Woolfson Talent and PR is an agency specialising in talent management, actors, public relations, media and events. Their clients include celebrities, influencers, experts, broadcasters and brands.

Casting directors

Casting directors are human encyclopaedias of actors. They will see as a many productions as possible, watch actors on TV and in film, attend drama school productions and showcases. They build personal relationships with actors over time and keenly follow every step of their careers.

Theatres, producers and directors hire casting directors for that encyclopaedic knowledge and wisdom. Casting directors submit lists of potential actors for each part and then administer the process of casting by submitting offers to actors via agents, or inviting actors to audition.

Building relationships with casting directors can be more important to actors than building relationships with theatres and directors because it is often the casting director who suggests them for roles. If a casting director likes and trusts you, they will be quick to think of you for any production they are casting for any number of clients.

Remember casting directors are employed by someone else. Some may be employed on a full-time basis by a theatre or organisation but most work freelance and can be as concerned about where their next job is coming from as you are. If a casting director invites you to a meeting or audition, make sure you repay their faith in you; turn up on time, well prepared, and carefully absorb any brief they give you. You are auditioning as much for the casting director – who will soon be casting something else – as for the director or producer of this specific project.

You should approach casting directors in much the same way as you would agents but it's even more important to invite them to see you perform. They may be more project oriented than talent-oriented so whilst an agent is looking for talent to add to their client list, a casting director may be concentrating on specific talent for a specific project. Research what the casting director is currently casting, and target them accordingly. You can keep reasonably up to date with the activities of some casting directors by looking at the website of the Casting Directors Guild (CDG) (**www.thecdg.co.uk**).

*Member of the Casting Directors Guild

Pippa Ailion and Natalie Gallacher Casting*

Unit 61A, Eurolink Business Centre, 49 Effra Road, London SW2 1BZ
tel 020-3627 5664
email enquiries@pippaailioncasting.co.uk
Casting Directors Pippa Ailion CDG, Natalie Gallacher CDG, *Associate Casting Director*s Richard Johnston, Grace McInerny

Established in 1991, main areas of work are musical theatre and theatre. Pippa has cast over 200 productions internationally. She was awarded a special recognition Olivier Award in 2023. Natalie has worked with Pippa for 20 years. Together with Associates Richard Johnston and Grace McInerny, they have cast numerous productions for West End, The Old Vic, Almeida, Regents Park, Chichester Festival Theatre, The Young Vic, West Yorkshire Playhouse, Birmingham Rep, UK and International tours.

Current West End: *Hercules*; *MJ: The Musical*; *Moulin Rouge!*; *TINA: The Tina Turner Musical*; *The Book of Mormon* and *The Lion King*.

Current UK tours: *Moulin Rouge! World Tour*; *TINA: The Tina Turner Musical*; *The Book of Mormon*; *Dear Evan Hansen*.

Selected West End/UK tours: *Mean Girls*; *Natasha, Pierre and the Great Comet Of 1812*; *Come From Away*; *Coming to England*; *Hello Dolly*; *Ain't Too Proud*; *Get Up Stand Up*; *Beauty and The Beast*; *On Your Feet!*; *Dreamgirls*; *Funny Girl*; *Sunny Afternoon*; *Motown*; *Charlie and the Chocolate Factory*; *Wind in the Willows*; *Memphis*; *Bend It Like Beckham*; *Legally Blonde*; *Wicked*; *Billy Elliot*; *Top Hat*; *We Will Rock You*; *Here Lies Love*; *Fela!*; and *Spring Awakening*.

Film Dance Casting: *Rocketman*; *Wonka*; and Disney's *Snow White*.

Future Projects: *Top Hat* (Chichester Festival Theatre); *Grease - Secret Cinema*; *Sunny Afternoon* UK Tour; and *American Psycho* (Almeida).

Shaheen Baig Casting*
tel 020-7272 0522
email info@shaheenbaigcasting.com
website www.shaheenbaigcasting.com
X @sbaigcasting

Recent film work includes *Lady Macbeth*; *God's Own Country*; Carol Morley's *The Falling*; Ben Wheatley's *Free Fire*; Paddy Considine's *Journeyman* and the debut features of Stephen Merchant *Fighting with My Family* and Idris Elba *Yardie*. Shaheen has also worked on several acclaimed television projects including *Marvellous*, *Peaky Blinders*, *Black Mirror* (for Channel 4); *Guerrilla*, *National Treasure*, *Damilola: Our Loved Boy*; Philip K. Dick's *Electric Dreams* for Channel 4/Sony & Amazon and Shane Meadows' *The Virtues* for Channel 4.

BBC Studios Drama Productions Casting
London office: 3rd Floor, Television Centre, 101 Wood Lane, London W12 7FA
website www.bbcstudios.com
Casting Directors Rowland Beckley, John Cannon, Stephen Moore, Kevin Riddle, Rachelle Williams-Parker

Casting information: Casting Directors will accept letters and emails from actors (including CVs, headshots, showreels and performance notices). These should be addressed to the individual Casting Director (using **[name.surname]@bbc.com**) or one letter addressed to "The Casting Team" which will be seen by the whole department. However, actors are advised that the casting department is extremely busy and may not be able to reply. Please don't approach via social media such as X or WhatsApp.

Lesley Beastall Casting
tel 020-7727 6496
email assistant@lbcasting.co.uk
website www.lesleybeastallcasting.com
Casting Director Lesley Beastall

Works in commercials and film. Recent credits include: *Kids World* (Barclays), *The Pocket* (National Lottery) and *Mad About the Bread* (Warburtons).

Does not welcome performance notices or unsolicited submissions by actors previously unknown to the company, but will accept invitations to view individual actors' websites. Any such approach should be made by email only.

Rowland Beckley
See the entry for BBC Studios Casting above.

Leila Bertrand Casting CDG*
97 Edenham Way, London W10 5XA
tel 020-8964 0683, mobile 07976 187638
email leila@leilabcasting.com
website www.leilabertrand.com

Leila Bertrand has been a casting director for over 15 years. Casts across theatre, film, TV and commercials. Credits include, theatre: *Macbeth* at Arcola Theatre, Wilton's Music Hall and international tour; film: *Sea Monster* (dir. Mark Walker), BAFTA nominee.

Lucy Bevan CDG*
2 Burlington Gardens, London W3 6BA
tel 020-3968 4998
email assistant.lucybevan@mac.com

Main areas of work are film and television. Credits include: *The Batman* (2022), *Death on the Nile* (2022), *Venom: Let There Be Carnage* (2021), *Belfast* (2021) and *Cruella* (2021).

Hannah Birkett Casting
mobile 07957 114175
email hannah@hbcasting.com
Casting Director Hannah Birkett

Previously received awards British Arrows, D&AD, Ciclope and the CDA, as well as a Film Craft Cristal for best casting. Areas of work include television, film and commercials.

Will consider attending performances with one week's notice via email. Accepts CVs and photographs via email only.

Nicky Bligh CDG*
mobile 07968 788561
email nicky@nickyblighcasting.com
X @nickybligh

Covers TV and film, especially comedy. Has worked for numerous TV channels: BBC, SKY, Channel 4 and Comedy Central; and, production companies such as Tiger Aspect, Hat Trick and Universal Films. TV credits include *Bad Education*, *Psychobitches* and *Mrs Brown's Boys*.

Andy Brierley CDG*
email andy@andybrierley.com
website https://andybrierley.com
X @AndyBCasting

Andy has worked in casting for over a decade across a wide range of television, film and theatre projects such as *The Scandalous Lady W* and *Remember Me* (starring Michael Palin) for the BBC; *Top Boy* and *Run* (starring Olivia Colman) for Channel 4; and *Our Town* (Almeida Theatre). Recent credits include *Chemistry of Death* (2023), *Silent Witness* (2018–23) and *The Tunnel* (2017–18).

Agents and casting directors

Aisha Bywaters Casting
email info@aishabywaters.com
website https://aishabywaters.com
Will attend theatre in Greater London area with 4 weeks' notice. Accepts submissions from actors via email only.

Candid Casting*
email submissions@candidcasting.co.uk
website www.candidcasting.co.uk
Facebook /candidcasting
X @CandidCasting
Casting Director Amanda Tabak CDG

Main areas of work are television and film. See website for further details.

Cannon, Dudley & Associates
Dean Hill, Dean Street, East Farleigh ME15 0HT
tel (01622) 720740
email cdacasting@icloud.com
Facebook /cannon.dudley
Casting Director Carol Dudley CDG, CSA, Casting Associate Helena Palmer

Main areas of work are film, theatre and television. Recent credits include: *The Third Mother – Mother of Tears* (dir. Dario Argento); *Master Harold and the Boys* (dir. Lonny Price); and theatre productions for Hampstead, Edinburgh and the West End.

Will consider attending performances at venues in Greater London given as much notice as possible. Accepts submissions (with CVs and photographs) from actors previously unknown to the casting director if sent by post. Does not welcome email enquiries. CVs which are not submitted for specific projects or with reference to current shows or television performances cannot be kept for future reference. Telephone enquiries about current casting projects or progress of mailed submissions are not welcomed.

John Cannon CDG*
BBC Studios Drama Productions,
1 Television Centre, 101 Wood Lane,
London W12 7RA
tel 0303 080 1445 , mobile 07973 204550
email john.cannon@bbc.com

Currently Casting Director for *Casualty*.

Other recent television credits include: *Anfamol, Father Brown, The Sister Boniface Mysteries* and *Shakespeare & Hathaway*. Also *Holby City, Doctors, Silent Witness, Dalziel and Pasco, Mr Stink, Gangsta Granny, The Boy in the Dress, Grandpa's Great Escape, Big School, WPC 56, 32 Brinkburn Street, The Coroner* – all BBC. Previously Casting Director for the Royal Shakespeare Company.

Welcomes performance notices with at least 2 weeks' notice. Happy to receive emails from actors, as well as invitations to view individual actors' websites or online showreels. Please only contact via BBC email, not social media.

See also the entry for BBC Studios Casting on page 111.

Anji Carroll CDG*
mobile 07957 253769
email acarroll@newvictheatre.org.uk

At the end of 2023, after 40 years as a freelancer, Anji became the full-time Head of Casting at New Vic Theatre, Staffordshire. Shows include: *Marvellous* (which transferred and opened @sohoplace); *Tom, Dick and Harry* (transferring to Alexandra Palace); the award-winning *Snow Queen* and *Around the World in 80 Days* (plus Royal Exchange run, UK tour and transfer to New York and Miami); *The Jungle Book* (UK tour); *The Worst Witch* (UK tour and West End transfer); *Pippi Longstocking* (Royal and Derngate, Northampton); *The Beauty Queen of Leenane* (co-production with Queens Theatre Hornchurch); *Peter Pan* (Hull Truck Theatre); *Before the Party, Echos End, Aladdin* (Salisbury Playhouse); *The Ladykillers* (New Wolsey Theatre); and *The Lost Boy, Alice in Wonderland* (Theatre in the Quarter).

Television credits include: BBC2's comedy drama series *The Cup*; *The Bill* (over 50 episodes); *The Sarah Jane Adventures: Invasion of the Bane*; 2 series of *London's Burning* (32 episodes) and *The Knock* (4x90-minute episodes). Film credits include: *LUCY 2.0*; *Papadopoulos and Sons*; *West Is West*; *Mrs Ratcliffe's Revolution*; *Out of Depth* and *The Jolly Boys' Last Stand*. Also various drama-documentaries, including BBC 4's political drama series *Number Ten*.

Suzy Catliff CDG*
email soosecat@mac.com

Casting director, theatre director and dubbing director. Casts for television, film and theatre. Co-author of *The Casting Handbook* published by Routledge (2013). Recent casting credits include: Theatre Clwyd, Changeling Theatre and Hall for Cornwall. Television: UK Casting Associate for Shaftesbury Films in Toronto, work includes UK associate for *Murdoch Mysteries, Departure* and *Frankie Drake Mysteries* all for Shaftesbury Film, Toronto. Theatre directing includes Offie Award Winning La Maupin 2023. Dubbing projects include *The Glass Dome, Football Parents, Midsummer Night* and *Ehrengard*.

Urvashi Chand CDG*
Cinecraft, 69 Teignmouth Road, London NW2 4EA
tel 07980 213050
email urvashi@chandcasting.com
website https://cargocollective.com/chandcasting

Main area of work is film. Recent credits include: *Confession*; *Tomorrow*.

Will consider attending performances within the Greater London area and elsewhere with at least 2 weeks' notice. Accepts submissions (with CVs and

Casting directors 113

photographs) from actors previously unknown to the agency, by email. Showreels, voicereels and invitations to view individual actors' websites are also accepted.

Andrea Clark Casting
email andrea@aclarkcasting.com
website www.aclarkcasting.com
Bluesky @andcasting.bsky.social
Instagram @andcasting
Casting Director Andrea Clark

Works mainly in film, short films and commercials.

Accepts showreels links and invitations to view individual actors' websites or links to view Spotlight, Mandy, Backstage or IMDb pages. Emails with multiple or very large attachments can't be viewed. "When an actor has an agent, I prefer contact to be made via the agent."

Sam Claypole
email contact@samclaypolecasting.com
website www.samclaypolecasting.com
Casting Director Sam Claypole

Established in 2005. Works in film, TV, theatre, corporate and commercials. Recent credits include: *Comedy* for Hat Trick Productions, *Lagging* (Series 2 and 3) for BBC Studios.

Welcomes Spotlight, Casting Network, Mandy links to showreels, invitations to view actors' websites. Invitations to local North East or Yorkshire productions/tours and screenings welcome via email.

Ben Cogan
email beco.me@mail.com
website https://becocasting.com
X @Becomecast
Instagram @beco.me.boom
Casting Director Ben Cogan

Worked as a casting director in BBC Continuing Drama for 15 years before establishing BeCo.Me in 2015.

Recent film credits include: *One Night in Bath* (2025); *The Hunted* (2024); *Love Without Walls* (2023); *Evie* (2021); *Amaryllis* (2019); *Trendy* (2017); and *Just Charlie* (2017). Recent Shorts credits include: *The Outing* (2022); *Little Mary* (2022); *All That Glitters* (2021); and *The Man at the Bottom of the Garden* (2021).

Alastair Coomer*
See the entry for the National Theatre under *Producing theatres* on page 168.

Anna Cooper
Donmar Warehouse, 41 Earlham Street,
London WC2E 9NA
tel 020-7845 5812
email casting@donmarwarehouse.com
X WC2E 9NA

Currently Casting Director at the Donmar Warehouse. Anna was previously a freelance casting director. She started work at the Almeida Theatre in 2003 and then worked independently – largely in theatre.

Works include: Theatre *Macbeth*, *Constellations* (CDG Award for Best Theatre Casting), Film *Dunkirk*, *Mission: Impossible - Fallout*, Television *Doc Martin*, *Manhunt*.

Crampsie Linge Casting CDG*
email julia@crampsielinge.com
email wayne@crampsielinge.com
website https://crampsielinge.com
X @crampsielinge
Instagram @crampsielinge
Casting Directors Julia Crampsie, Wayne Linge

Established in 2023. Main area of work is television, theatre and film. Crampsie and Linge have collaborated on numerous projects at the BBC where Crampsie was Head of Casting for over 20 years. Work includes: *Our Girl* (BBC One); *We Hunt Together* (season two for Showtime/Alibi); *Father Brown* (BBC One); *Urban Myths: The Trial of Joan Collins* (King Bert/Sky); *Sister Boniface Mysteries* (BritBox North America / BBC Studios); *Five By Five* (Green Door Pictures / BBC Three); *Billionaire Boy, Gangsta Granny, Grandpa's Great Escape, The Boy In the Dress, The Moonstone* (King Bert/BBC One); *Shakespeare & Hathaway: Private Investigators* (BBC One) and *The Break* (BBC Three).

Kahleen Crawford Casting*
Film City Glasgow, Govan Town Hall,
401 Govan Road, Glasgow G51 2QJ
tel 0141 425 1725
email casting@kahleencrawford.com
website www.kahleencrawford.com
Casting Directors Kahleen Crawford, Danny Jackson, Caroline Stewart

Main areas of work include film and TV. Welcomes CVs and photographs from actors previously unknown to the casting director (of a reasonable file size), if sent by email. Happy to receive invitations to view productions in London, Glasgow and the surrounding areas, provided 1 week's notice is given. Also accepts links to online showreels. Only grants a general interview in special circumstances.

Crocodile Casting
9 Ashley Close, Hendon, London NW4 1PH
mobile 07900 148487, 07900 243458
email crocodilecasting@gmail.com
website www.crocodilecasting.com
Casting Directors Tracie Saban, Claire Toeman

Established in 1996 with the aim of constantly accessing new faces and fresh talent. The company casts for commercials, corporates and feature films. Sometimes holds general auditions to meet new actors and models. Also runs regular worshops.

Sarah Crowe Casting CDG*
92–96 De Beauvoir Road, London N1 4EN
tel 020-7286 5080
email info@sarahcrowecasting.co.uk
website www.sarahcrowecasting.co.uk
X @scrowecasting

Sarah has worked extensively in both TV and film specialising in comedy. Her credits include *The Death of Stalin* and *The Thick of It*, both directed by Amando Iannucci; and *Rev* (dir. Peter Cattaneo).

Gilly Poole CDG*
11 Goodwins Court, London WC2N 4LL
tel 020-7379 5965
email gilly@crowleypoole.co.uk
email suzanne@crowleypoole.co.uk

Casting Directors Suzanne Crowley, Gilly Poole

Known for: *Titanic* (1997), *A Knight's Tale* (2001).

Recent credits include, TV: *Extraordinary (2023)*; *Kate & Koji* (2020–22); *Killing Eve* (2018–22); West End: *Filthy Business* (2017)

Gary Davy CDG*
13 Islington High Street, Angel, Islington, London N1 9LQ
tel 020-7253 3633
email casting@garydavy.com
email office@garydavy.com

Casts for film and television. Casting credits include: *Small Axe* (BBC/Amazon); *The Tourist* (BBC/HBO); *The Man Who Fell to Earth* (Showtime/P+); *You Don't Know Me* (BBC); *Baptiste* (BBC); *Marcella* (ITV); *The Frankenstein Chronicles* (ITV); *The Enfield Haunting* (SKY); *Alex Rider* (Amazon/IMDBTV); and UK casting on *Band of Brothers* (HBO/BBC).

Film casting credits include: *Woman in Gold*, Steve McQueen's *Hunger*, *The Sweeney*, *Revenger's Tragedy*, *The Proposition*, *44 Inch Chest* and *Streetdance 3D*.

Kate Dowd Casting CDG*
Lyric Hammersmith, Lyric Square, King Street, London W6 0QL
tel 020-7828 8201
email kate@katedowdcasting.com

Credits include: film *Mad Max*, *The Bourne Identity*, *Eye in the Sky* and *The Hurricane Heist*; TV series *The Assets*, *Galavant* and *Still Star-Crossed*.

Carol Dudley CDG, CSA*
See entry for Cannon, Dudley & Associates.

Maureen Duff CDG*
PO Box 47340, London NW3 4TY
email info@maureenduffcasting.com
website https://maureenduffcasting.com

Main areas of work are film and television. Credits include: Film: *Closing The Ring*, *The Habit of Beauty*, *The Flying Scotsman*; TV: *Miss Scarlet & The Duke* S1–3, *Vera* S4–11, *The Fall* S1–3, *The History of Mr Polly*, *Tom Brown's Schooldays*, *Poirot* (several), *Marple* (several).

Jenny Duffy CDG*
email casting@jennyduffy.co.uk
website www.jennyduffycasting.co.uk

Main areas of work are film and television. Credits include: BAFTA winning *Murdered by my Boyfriend*, *Murdered by my Father*, *Murdered for being Different*, *Killed by my Debt*. Oscar and BAFTA nominated *Loving Vincent*.

Daniel Edwards CDG*
tel 020-7078 7451, 020-7096 0676
email office@danieledwardscasting.com
website www.danieledwardscasting.com
X @dedwardscasting

Daniel worked as an actor for over 25 years in film, TV and theatre (under the name Danny Edwards) before moving into casting in 2005. Casts independently as well as being Casting Associate to Kate Rhodes James. Recent TV credits include: *Blue Lights* (BBC), *A Town Called Malice* (Sky), *Grace* (ITV), *Showtrial* (BBC), *Malpractice* (ITV) and *This Town* (BBC).

He is RTS, CDG and Emmy award winning for his work on the Netflix global hit *Heartstopper*.

ET Casting Ltd.
Kemp House, 128 City Road, London EC1V 2NX
tel 020-3010 3030
email info@etcasting.com
website www.etcasting.com

Casting Directors Emily Tilelli, Zita Zutic Konak, Casting Associate Bex Reynolds

Established in 2011. Main areas of work are commercials, digital content, stills and feature films. Recent credits include: *Paul Dood's Deadly Lunch Break* (feature film) and *Tucked* (feature film). Will consider attending performances in the Greater London area, with a minimum of 3 weeks' notice.

Welcomes CVs and photographs sent by email, showreels and voice tapes, and invitations to view individual actors' websites.

Richard Evans CDG*
10 Shirley Road, London W4 1DD
tel 020-8994 6304
email richard@evanscasting.co.uk
website www.evanscasting.co.uk
website www.auditionsthecompleteguide.com

Main areas of work are theatre, musicals, television, film and commercials. Casting credits include: *The Rat Pack – Live From Las Vegas* (theatre).

Will consider attending performances at venues in Greater London and occasionally elsewhere, given sufficient notice. Requests 1–2 weeks before the opening night for theatre productions, and 2–3 days prior to transmission for television shows. Accepts follow-up telephone calls after a production has opened. Welcomes submissions (with CVs and photographs) from actors previously unknown to the casting director if sent by post, and email enquiries with links to Spotlight page, online showreel, etc. (but no large attachments).

Advises actors to: "Be specific, find out what people cast and their current projects, suggesting yourself for particular roles whenever possible. When inviting casting personnel to see your work, always ensure that the part you are playing is worth them coming to see, and offer complimentary tickets. Unless a part is very specific or hard to cast, we usually only invite artists in to audition whose work we have seen or have met, as this enables us to speak honestly and accurately about them to the creative teams with whom we are working. It is worth keeping in touch when you have something to say as your career progresses especially if you have met or know someone."

Rachel Freck CDG*

The Office, Flat 1, 28 Elmbourne Road,
London SW17 8JR
tel 020-8673 2455, *mobile* 07980 585017
email casting@rachelfreck.com

Credits include: *Ten Percent*, *Trying*, *Tin Star*, *Howards End*, *The Office* and *W1A*.

Martin Gibbons Casting

Based in Manchester and London
email info@martingibbons.com
website www.martingibbons.com
Casting Director Martin Gibbons CDG

Established in 2011. Main areas of work are film, television, commercials, theatre, music videos, corporate and voice-over. Will consider attending performances in Manchester and London.

Welcomes CVs and photographs sent by email, as well as showreels and voice tapes.

Tracey Gillham CDG*

tel 020-3778 0441
email tracey@traceygillhamcasting.co.uk
email michelle@traceygillhamcasting.co.uk
website www.traceygillhamcasting.co.uk
Associate Michelle Cavanagh

Main areas of work are film and television. For recent credits, please see Spotlight or the CDG website.

Nina Gold CDG*

Unit 20, 135 Salusbury Road, London NW6 6RJ
tel 020-8960 6099
email info@ninagold.co.uk

Main areas of work are film, television and commercials. Recent film credits: *Morbius* (2022); *Jurassic World: Dominion* (2022); *The Wonder* (2022); *Empire of Light* (2022); *Catherine Called Birdy* (2022); *Indiana Jones and the Dial of Destiny* (2023); *Firebrand* (2023). Recent TV credits: *Bad Sisters* (2022); *Andor* (2022); *Slow Horses* (2023); *Rain Dogs* (2023); *The Power* (2023). Other casting credits include: *Vera Drake*, directed by Mike Leigh (Thin Man Films); *The Life and Death of Peter Sellers*, directed by Stephen Hopkins; *The Jacket*, directed by John Maybury (Warner Bros); *Daniel Deronda*, directed by Tom Hooper (BBC TV); *Amazing Grace* and *Rome* both directed by Michael Apted; *Starter for Ten* directed by Tom Vaughan; *The Illusionist* directed by Neil Burger; and *Brothers of the Head* directed by Keith Fulton and Louis Pepe.

Jill Green CDG*

WAC Arts, 213 Haverstock Hill, London NW3 4QP
tel 020-3405 0222
email office@jillgreencasting.org
website www.jillgreencasting.org
Facebook /jillgreencasting
Instagram @jGreencasting
Casting Director Jill Green, *Casting Associates* Olivia Laydon, Tom Shiels

Casts for theatre and musicals, as well as workshops and readings. Casting credits include: Theatre: Becoming Nancy (Birmingham Rep); The Devil Wears Prada (Theatre Royal Plymouth/Dominion Theatre); War Horse (New London Theatre/Tours 2015–20/UK & Ireland tour 2024–25); The Little Big Things (@Soho Place); Crazy For You (Gillian Lynn Theatre/ Chichester Festival Theatre); *Dear Evan Hansen* (Noel Coward); *Jersey Boys* (Trafalgar Theatre/Prince Edward Theatre/Piccadilly Theatre/UK & Ireland tours); The Lion King Tour (UK and Ireland tour 2015–24/ International tour); Aladdin (Prince Edward Theatre/ UK tour 2023–24); *101 Dalmations* (Regents Park Open Air); *Bedknobs and Broomsticks* (UK tour). Film: dancers for *Paddington 2* and *Beyond the Sea*.

Will consider attending performances within Greater London and occasionally elsewhere, given a minimum of 4 weeks' notice. Accepts email submissions (with Spotlight links, footage/CVs and photographs attached) from actors who are currently appearing in a production or wish to submit for a specific role whilst the company is casting. Does not welcome blanket mailings, unsolicited emails or showreels (unless a sae is enclosed for their return).

David Grindrod CDG*

4th Floor, Palace Theatre, Shaftesbury Avenue,
London W1D 5AY
tel 020-7437 2506
email gbc@grindrodandburton.co.uk

Casts for musicals and films. Film credits: Dance casting *Nine*, Ensemble casting *Mamma Mia!* and *The Phantom of the Opera*. West End casting: *Chicago*, *Mamma Mia!*, *Ghost*, *Hairspray*, *Love Never Dies*, *Sister Act*.

116 Agents and casting directors

Will consider attending performances within Greater London and possibly elsewhere, given as much notice as possible. Does not welcome unsolicited submissions from actors. Casting breakdowns are released via Spotlight, therefore actors should only write in with reference to specific productions.

Louis Hammond CDG*
tel 020-7610 1579
email louis@louishammond.co.uk

Main areas of work are theatre, television and film. Casting credits include: *The Mountaintop* (Royal Lyceum Edinburgh); *The 14th Tale* (Fuel Tour); *A Dead Body in Taos* (Wilton's Music Hall/Tour); *The Strange Undoing of Prudencia Hart* (Royal Exchange, Manchester); *Barber Shop Chronicles* (Roundhouse/UK tour/BAM New York); *Beautiful Thing*, *Macbeth* (Bristol Tobacco Factory); *Kanye the First*, *Heroine* (High Tide); *The Sugar-Coated Bullets of the Bourgeoisie* (Arcola/High Tide); *The 5 Plays Project* (Young Vic); *Inkheart* (HOME Manchaester); *The Distance* (Sheffield Crucible/Orange Tree Richmond); *Romeo and Juliet* (Sheffield Crucible); *Creditors* (Young Vic); *Harrogate* (High Tide Festival); *The Fun Fair* (HOME Manchester); *Primtime*, *Creditors* (Young Vic); *Romeo and Juliet* (Sheffield Crucible); *The Funfair* (HOME Manchester); *Primtime*, *Violence and Son*, *Who Cares*, *Fireworks* (Casting Associate at the Royal Court); *Romeo and Juliet* (HOME, Manchester); *Amadeus* (Chichester Festival Theatre); *The History Boys* (Sheffield Crucible); *The Winter's Tale* (Open Air Theatre, Regents Park); *Driving Miss Daisy* (UK); *Rough Cuts/International Residencies* (Royal Court); *The Resistible Rise of Arturo Ui* (Liverpool/Nottingham); *Batman Live* (World Arena Tour). Film – *Mirrormask* and *Arsene Lupin*. TV – *The Bill* (Head of Casting).

Hammond Cox Casting
Soho Works Shoreditch, Unit 4.01 The Tea Building, 56 Shoreditch High Street, London E1 6JJ
tel 020-7734 3235
email office@hammondcoxcasting.com
website www.hammondcoxcasting.com
Casting Directors Michael Cox, Thom Hammond

Established in 2012. Works in film, commercials, music video and theatre. Recent credits include: Beady Eye (Music Video); Robinsons (Commercial) and *Flight of the Pompodour* (Short Film).

Gemma Hancock CDG*
Works in the casting department at BBC Studios, casting *Casualty*, *Father Brown* and *Sister Boniface Mysteries*. Previously her work as a freelancer encompassed film, theatre and TV.

See also the entry for BBC Studios Casting on page 111.

Harkin & Toth Casting*
Tramworks, 24-28 Hatherley Mews,
London E17 4QP
tel 020-7336 0433
email info@harkintoth.com
website www.harkintoth.com
Casting Directors Julie Harkin, Nathan Toth, Casting Associates Lucy Kate Smith, Oliver Scullion, Senior Casting Assistants Ollie Bazeley, Alisha Bappoo

Specialises in TV and film. Recent TV credits: *What It Feels Like For A Girl*, *Reunion*, *This City Is Ours*, *Dope Girls*, *The Sixth Commandment*; *Great Expectations*; *Industry* (seasons 1–4). Film credits: *Bring Them Down*, *Tuesday*, *The Toxic Avenger*, *Heart of Stone*; *Femme*; *My Policeman*; *Nocebo*; *Rogue Agent*.

Accepts links to view CVs, and online profiles or showreels via email. Welcomes performance notices via email, if given 2 weeks' notice.

Serena Hill
22A Whitehall Gardens, Acton W3 9RD
mobile 07425 710707
email serenahillcasting@gmail.com

Serena Hill joined Trafalgar Entertainment as the Casting Director in 2019. She began her Casting Director career at the Royal Court Theatre before moving to the National Theatre as Head of Casting under the successive artistic directorships of Richard Eyre, Trevor Nunn and Nicholas Hytner. She then took up the position of Casting Director at Sydney Theatre Company for artistic director Robyn Nevin, followed by co-artistic directors Cate Blanchett and Andrew Upton, and finally Kip Williams.

As a freelance casting director in the UK, Serena worked on BBC Television Film's *Heading Home*, written and directed by David Hare, and *Tumbledown* by Charles Wood, directed by Richard Eyre. Freelance casting in Australia includes productions of *War Horse* for the National Theatre/Global Creatures, *Les Misérables* for Cameron Mackintosh/Michael Cassel Group and the adult cast of *Matilda* for the Royal Shakespeare Company and Louise Withers Associates. Since returning to the UK she's cast *Macbeth* at Chichester Festival Theatre, *To Kill a Mockingbird* and *Juno and the Paycock* for for Sonia Friedman Productions, *Anything Goes*, *The King and I* UK tour, *A Strange Loop* and *Kiss Me Kate* for Trafalgar Productions, *The Brightening Air* for the Old Vic and *To Kill A Mockingbird* UK tour for Jonathan Church Theatre Productions.

Accepts links to view actors' CVs, on-line profiles, and showreels via email.

Lotte Hines CDG*
mobile 07793 966457
email lotte@lottehinescasting.com

Lotte was the Deputy Casting Director at the Royal Court between 2007 and 2014.

Recent credits include: TV: *Lady Chatterley's Lover*; *Lockwood & Co.*; West End: *As You Like It*; *The Wolves*; *Accidental Death of an Anarchist*.

Julia Horan CDG*
26 Falkland Road, London NW5 2PX
tel 020-7267 5261, *mobile* 07967 356869
email julia@horancasting.com

Julia has worked at the Young Vic, Royal Court, Almeida, Donmar and extensively in the West End and internationally.

Will consider attending performances within the Greater London area and elsewhere. Accepts submissions (with CVs and photographs) from actors previously unknown to the casting director, via email only.

Juliet Horsley CDG*
email juliethorsleycasting@gmail.com

Specialim includes theatre, films and television. She was a casting director at the National Theatre for almost 15 years.

Amy Hubbard CDG*
tel 020-3567 1210
email amy@amyhubbardcasting.com
Instagram @amyhubcast

Amy is an award-winning casting director with extensive experience on both blockbuster features (*Lord of the Rings*, *The Hobbit*) and TV series (*Homeland*). Recent credits include, film: *Good Luck to You, Leo Grande*; *The Honeymoons*; TV: *Hijack*, *Ludwig*.

Dan Hubbard CDG*
The Chandlery, 50 Westminster Bridge Road, London SE1 7QY
tel 020-3874 5270
email generalsubmissions@danhubbardcasting.com
website www.danhubbardcasting.com/index.html

Film credits include: *The Wrath of Man*; *Silent Night*; *Operation Fortune: Ruse de Guerre*; TV credits include: *Devils*; *Downtown Abbey*.

Accepts actor submissions by email only. Will accept invitations to performances in the London area, availability permitting.

Isabella Odoffin Casting*
email office@isabellaodoffin.com
X @isabellaodoffin
Instagram @isabellaodoffincasting

A London-based Casting Director working across film, television and theatre.

Janis Jaffa Casting
Based in London W12
email janis@janisjaffacasting.co.uk

Works mainly in TV, film and commercials.

Will consider attending performances within Greater London. Welcomes emails (with CVs and photographs attached) from individual actors previously unknown to the agency. Will accept showreels and invitations to view individual actors' websites by email.

Jina Jay CDG*
Facebook /JinaJayCasting
X @JinaJayCasting

Known for films and TV. Recent credits include: *Halo* (2019), *The First Lady* (2022), *Dune* (2021), *Enola Holmes* (2020), *Black Mirror* (2016–23) and *Wicked Little Letters* (2024).

Lucy Jenkins CDG (Jenkins McShane Casting)*
tel 020-8943 5328, *mobile* 07767 496826
email lucy@jmcasting.net
website www.jmcasting.net

Cast in partnership with Sooki McShane and works mainly for film, television, theatre and commercials. Casting credits include: *The Play that Goes Wrong* (Duchess Theatre); *Barbeque 67* (dir. Jonathan Banatvala for BBC Radio 4); *We Are The Best* (Live Theatre), *Dead Air* (Riverside Studios); *Runs in the Family* (Giant Films for Netflix); *Good Luck Studio* (Mischief).

Victor Jenkins Casting*
The Casting Office, 81 Rivington Street, London EC2A 3AY
tel 020 3457 0506
website http://victorjenkinscasting.com/index.html
X @verbalictor

Known for TV. Recent credits include: *Sherwood* (2022–24), *World on Fire* (2019–23), *The Bubble* (2022), *The Undeclared War* (2022), *Fleabag* (2016–19), *Unforgotten* (2015–19), *Humans* (2015–18) and *Broadchurch* (2013–17).

Sam Jones CDG*
mobile 07941 960998
email sam@samjonescasting.co.uk
website samjonescasting.co.uk

Previously Head of Casting for the RSC, the Almeida Theatre and, for the first 6 years of its life, National Theatre Wales. Currently a member of the Casting Directors' Guild and the International Casting Director Association, and is an Honorary Fellow of the Royal Welsh College of Music and Drama. During her career she has worked with both regional and international theatre producers and in the West End, including with Sir Peter Hall, Terry Hands, Steven Berkoff, Luc Bondy, Patrice Chereau, Emma Rice, Moira and Fiona Buffini, Polly Teale, Shared Experience, Told By An Idiot, Manchester International Festival (co-production with 59 Productions and Ballet Rambert), the Royal Court,

118 Agents and casting directors

Hampstead Theatre, Old Vic and Yong Vic. Recent TV and film work includes: *The English*, *Black Earth Rising*, *The Long Call*, *The Trick*, *Ridley Road*, *Wanderlust*, *Life*, *NW*, *Don't Forget the Driver*, *The Lost Honour of Christopher Jeffries*, *To Provide All People* and *The Hollow Crown*.

Kastwork*
Berth 9, Cumberland Basin, Prince Albert Road, London NW1 7SS
tel 020-7580 6101
email emma@kastwork.com
website https://kastwork.com
Director Emma Ashton

Areas of work include television, film and commercials. Recent credits include: *Brother* (commercial for Bacon, Copenhagen); *Galaxy* (commercial for RSA, London); *Hostel 1 & 2* (for International Production Co.).

Will consider attending performances in Greater London with at least one week's notice. Invitations to showcases are also welcomed. Accepts submissions (with CVs and photographs) from actors previously unknown to the company; invitations to view individual actors' websites are also accepted.

Kate and Lou Casting Ltd
mobile 07976 252531
website www.kateandloucasting.com
Facebook /kateandlou
X @kateandloucast

CDA award winner. Casts for film, drama, commercials, still photography, online content and short films. Recent credits include: National Lottery Advert – Michael Gracey, Argos Christmas Advert 2019 – Traktor, *This Time Away* – Magali Barbe.

Welcomes performance notices. Will accept emails (with CVs and photographs) from individual actors previously unknown to the company, and unsolicited CVs and photographs, sent via email. Does welcome showreels or invitations to view individual actors' websites.

Kennedy Casting
tel 020-8677 6710, mobile 07973 119369
email anna@kennedycasting.com
website www.annakennedycasting.com
Instagram @annakennedycasting

Welcomes performance notices, for productions within the Greater London area, with 2 weeks' notice. Will accept emails with CVs and photographs from individuals previously unknown to the casting director; also welcomes showreels and invitations to view actors' websites.

Beverley Keogh CDG*
218 Ashley Road, Hale, Altrincham WA15 9SR
tel 0161 273 4400
email [firstname]@beverleykeogh.tv
website www.beverleykeogh.tv
Casting Director Beverley Keogh, Michael Jackson

Main areas of work are television, film and commercials. Casting credits include: *The Feud*, *All Creatures Great and Small*, *Happy Valley*.

Accepts submissions (with CVs and photographs) from actors previously unknown to the casting director, sent by email.

Kharmel Cochrane Casting
Studio 111, 65 Alfred Road, London W2 5EU
tel 020-3735 9640
email office@kharmelcochrane.co.uk
website http://kharmelcochrane.com
X @KharmelCochrane

Kharmel first cut her cast teeth as a Casting Director on the acclaimed Daniel Wolfe music video *Time to Dance* starring Jake Gyllenhaal and Callum Turner. She followed up with award-winning films such as *Lilting* (2014) and the Bafta award-winning *Home* (2016). Recent credits include *Red Rose*; *The Northman*; *Mothering Sunday*. Main areas of work include film and TV, commercials, music videos, shorts. Get in touch via email.

Belinda King Creative Productions
Rua São João de Brito 122, 4100-452, Porto, Portugal
email casting@belindaking.com
website www.belindaking.com
X @belindakingprod
Instagram @belindakingprod

An award-winning global production company. Producers of the finest shows at sea and elite guest entertainers. Partnerships and projects include Seabourn, Sir Tim Rice, Color Line (Norway) and Princess Cruises. International auditions are held worldwide including London, New York, Los Angeles, Porto and Hamburg.

Casting: lead vocalists, commercial dancers, contemporary dancers, Latin/Ballroom dancers and cirque artists.

Suzy Korel CDG CDA*
mobile 07973 506793
email suzy@korel.org

Casting for TV commercials. Works in commercials, as well as films and theatre etc.

Karen Lindsay-Stewart CDG*
PO Box 2301, London W1A 1PT
tel 020-7439 0544
email asst@klscasting.co.uk
website www.klscasting.com

Known for *Harry Potter and the Philospher's Stone* (2001); *Penny Dreadful* (2014–16). Main areas of work are television and film. Recent films: *A Gaza Weekend* (2022); *Mummies* (2023). Other casting credits include: *Sylvia*, *Harry Potter and the Chamber of Secrets*, and *Cambridge Spies*.

Will consider attending performances at venues in Greater London with sufficient notice. Accepts submissions (with CVs and photographs) from actors previously unknown to the casting director. Do not send sae(s) for replies.

Carolyn McLeod Casting
3rd Floor, 28A Lower Marsh, London SE1 7RG
tel 020-7207 0188
email office@cmcasting.co.uk
website www.carolynmcleodcasting.com
Facebook /carolynmcleodcasting
X @CarolynMCasting
Instagram @carolynmcleodcasting

Main areas of work are film and television. Recent projects include: *Debriefing The President* for TNT; Independent features: *The Last Supper*, *Marked Men*, *Accused*, *After Everything*, *Boiling Point*, *Sweetheart* and *Villain*. Other projects include, for Netflix: *Irish Wish* with Lindsay Lohan, *Afterlife of the Party*, *The Princess Switch Trilogy* and *The Saint*. Along with productions for the BBC, ITV, Hallmark, SyFy Channel, Disney and Paramount Global including *Presence of Love* and *The Gray House*.

Given sufficient notice will consider attending performances at venues in and around Greater London and regionally. Will accept emailed broadcast or show notifications, also emailed submissions from actors previously unknown to the casting director. Showreels, voicereels and invitations to view individual actors' websites are also accepted, but receipt may not always be acknowledged due to the volume of submissions received.

Sooki McShane CDG (Jenkins McShane Casting)*
tel 020-8943 5328, mobile 07940 591612
email sooki@jmcasting.net
website www.jmcasting.net

Casts in partnership with Lucy Jenkins and works mainly in theatre, film and television. Casting credits include: *The Play that Goes Wrong* (Duchess Theatre); *Barbeque 67* (dir. Jonathan Banatvala for BBC Radio 4); *We Are The Best* (Live Theatre), *Dead Air* (Riverside Studios); *Runs in the Family* (Giant Films for Netflix); *Good Luck Studio* (Mischief).

Thea Meulenberg Casting
Keizersgracht 116 Amsterdam, The Netherlands
tel +31 (0)6 2905 7773, mobile +31 (0)6 5479 8109
email info@theameulenberg.com
website www.theameulenberg.com
Facebook /TheaMeulenbergCasting
Casting Directors Laurens Meulenberg, Sevina Stapert-Meulenberg

Established in 1980. Works in TV, film, commercials, corporate, print and photography. Provides casting solutions to the highest level of craftsmanship and creativity. Worldwide clients from USA, Dubai, India, the UK, Germany and the Netherlands.

Stephen Moore CDG*
email stephen@stephenmoorecasting.co.uk
website www.stephenmoorecasting.co.uk

Main areas of work TV and film. Recent credits include, for TV: *Father Brown* (BBC); *Sister Boniface Mysteries* (Britbox/BBC Studios); *Shakespeare & Hathaway: Private Investigators* (BBC); *Casualty* (BBC).

Will consider attending performances in Greater London with a few weeks' notice. Welcomes CVs, photographs and links to showreels sent by email.

National Theatre Casting Department
South Bank, London SE1 9PX
email casting@nationaltheatre.org.uk
website www.nationaltheatre.org.uk/about-us/skilled-makers/casting

See the entry for the National Theatre under *Producing Theatres*, page 168

Helena Palmer
mobile 07779 220394
email helenamppalmer@icloud.com

Freelance casting director working in theatre, film and TV. Casting work has spanned more than 20 years and has included working at the Royal Exchange Theatre, Manchester, the National Theatre and most recently the Royal Shakespeare Company. Has worked on a wide range of classical and contemporary plays and with directors including Maria Aberg, Michael Boyd and Philip Breen. Has also worked on a variety of UK, US and European film and TV productions. Recent projects include: *The Fever Syndrome* (Hampstead Theatre); *Cat on a Hot Tin Roof* (Royal Exchange Theatre); *Cymbeline* (The Royal Shakespeare Threatre); *No Pay? No Way!* (Royal Exchange Theatre); *untitled f*ck m*ss s**gon play* (Royal Exchnge Theatre).

Will attend theatre performance with a suitable amount of notice. Email submissions only.

Theo Park Casting
tel 020-7419 1159
email assistant@theoparkcasting.com
website www.theoparkcasting.com

Recent films include: *My Zoe* (2023); *The People We Hate at the Wedding* (2022); *Frankie* (2019). Recent TV includes *Ted Lasso* (2020–23); *The Lord of the Rings: The Rings of Power* (2022); *The Pentaverate* (2022); *Our Flag Means Death* (2022).

Susie Parriss Casting
email susieparrisscasting@gmail.com
website www.susieparrisscasting.com

Known for *Naked* (1993); *Secrets and Lies* (1996); *Hugo* (2011); and *Endeavour* (2012–19).

Recent TV includes: *Goodnight Sweetheart* (1993–2016); *Lewis* (2006–15); *Whitechapel* (2012); *Poldark* (2015–18); *Agatha Raisin* (2016–18) and *Victoria* (2016–19).

Agents and casting directors

Pereira Hind & Dawson Casting CDG*
Summerhall Place, Edinburgh EH9 1PL
tel 0131 290 2526
email simonepereirahind@gmail.com
website www.simonepereirahind.com

Works primarily in film, TV and theatre. Most recent credits include: *Gifted* (BBC), *An T'Eilean* (BBC), *The Primrose Railway Children* (BBC), *Restless Natives* (Perth Theatre), *Keli* (Lyceum), *Blood of My Blood* (Sony and Starz) and *Outlander* season 8 (Sony and Starz).

Able to attend performances in Edinburgh, Glasgow and sometimes London. Accepts CVs with photographs and showreels via email only. Happy to receive enquiries from actors previously unknown, particularly those based in Scotland. Not always able to respond though may keep details on file for future reference.

Kate Plantin CDG*
tel (01932) 782350
email kate@kateplantin.com
website www.kateplantin.com
Key Contact Kate Plantin

Established in 2000. Main areas of work include: theatre, film and television. Recent Castings include: Television: *Andy and the Band* (series 1–3) for CBBC. Theatre: *We'll Always Have Paris* and *Barefoot in the Park* (Mill at Sonning). Film: *Bolan's Shoes*, *Mercy Falls*, *97 Minutes*.

Will consider attending performances at venues outside of London given 3 weeks' notice and 2 weeks' notice if within Greater London. Accepts submissions by email (with CVs and photographs). Also welcomes showreels and invitations to view actors' websites.

Carl Proctor CDG*
15B Bury Place, London WC1A 2JB
mobile 07956 283340
email carlproctorcasting@gmail.com
website www.carlproctorcasting.com
Facebook /Carl-Proctor-Photography/100041555601798
X @ProctorCarl
Instagram @carlproctorphotography

Casts mainly for film and television. Casting credits include: *Dark Phone* (Channel 4), *Son of God* (dir. Christopher Spencer); *Blood Creek* (dir. Joel Schumacher); *Shadow of the Vampire* (dir. E. Elias Merhige); *The Wedding Date* (dir. Clare Kilner); *Mrs Palfrey at the Claremount* (dir. Dan Ireland); and *Twelfth Night* (dir. Trevor Nunn).

Asks that actors only contact by email. CVs and photographs are no longer kept on file as these details are available on Spotlight Interactive.

Andy Pryor CDG*
PO Box 77788, London SE5 5NE
tel 020-4541 4390
website www.andypryor.co.uk

Casts mainly for film and television. Casting credits include: *Doctor Who* (2005–25); *The Devil's Hour* (2022–24); *Mrs Harris Goes To Paris* (2022); *Gentleman Jack* (2019–22); *It's a Sin* (2021); and *The A Word* (2016–20).

Unsolicited submissions welcome but no guarantee of reply. Use contact form on website and include CV and photos. Accepts invitations to performances but will only be in touch if available.

Leigh-Ann Regan Casting (LARCA) Ltd
Aberdeen House, Mount Stuart Square,
Cardiff CF10 5LR
email leigh-ann@larca.co.uk
website https://leighannregancastingassociates.co.uk

Areas of work include television, film, commercials and theatre. Recent credits include: 21-part drama series for S4C/Fiction Factory (Ypris); 4 years casting *Caerdydd* for S4C/Fiction Factory.

Will consider attending performances in Greater London and elsewhere with at least one week's notice. Accepts submissions (with CVs and photographs) from actors previously unknown to the casting director.

Nadine Rennie CDG*
email nadinerenniecasting@gmail.com
X @JackPug72
Instagram @nadinerennie

Previously an in-house Casting Director at Soho Theatre, freelance since 2019. Specialises in new writing. A member of the CDG committe 2023–25.

Kate Rhodes-James CDG*
78 Kingston Road, Teddington TW11 9HY
tel 020-8943 3265
email office@krjcasting.com

Kate trained as an actress. After three years she decided it wasn't for her. She assisted the casting on *The Young Indiana Chronicles* and then assisted Debbie McWilliams on three Bond films. Her first solo project was *Cold Feet* (ITV) and then *The Lakes* (BBC). Recent credits include, film: *Napoleon* (2023); *House of Gucci* (2021); TV: *My Lady Jane* (2023); *Inside Man* (2022); *House of the Dragon* (2022).

Vicky Richardson CDG*
email vrichardson.casting@gmail.com

Previously Casting Associate at the Donmar Warehouse. Since becoming a freelance casting director, she has worked with the National Theatre, Regent's Park Open Air Theatre, Rose Theatre (Kingston), Royal Exchange (Manchester), Nuffield Theatre (Southampton), The Orange Tree and Cleanbreak.

Jessica Ronane*
See the entry for the Old Vic under *Producing theatres* on page 170.

Annie Rowe CDG*
98 St Albans Ave, London W4 5JR
mobile 07734 809597
email annie@annierowecasting.co.uk

Established in 2009. Main area of work: short and feature film, theatre.

Happy to receive performance notices, given 2 weeks' notification. Showreels and invitations to view actors' websites welcome by email only. Please submit via Spotlight link for a specific job, rather than unsolicited.

Neil Rutherford Casting
mobile 07960 891911
email neil@neilrutherford.com
website www.neilrutherford.com

A casting director since 2000, working mainly in theatre in the West End and internationally, having been Head of Casting at ATG until 2012 and now freelance.

Welcomes CVs and letters (with photographs) via email. Also happy to receive casting interview enquiries and production invites via the same method.

Nadira Seecoomar CDG*
tel 020-8892 8478
email nadira.seecoomar@gmail.com

Recent credits include, film: *The Festival* (2018); TV: *The Windsors* (2016–23), *The Toast of Tinseltown* (2022); *The First Team* (2020).

Select Casting Ltd
PO Box 748, London NW4 1TT
mobile 07956 131494
email info@selectcasting.co.uk
website www.selectcasting.co.uk
website http://pro.imdb.com/name/nm3052115/
X @selectcasting
Casting Venetia Suchdev

In 2004 Select Casting Ltd started up as an in-house extras agency for an already established production house. It gained independent status as a casting agency as well as an extras agency for actors and background supporting artistes in 2007. Select Management was established in 2008 to look after a handful of professional actors, dancers, presenters and models who are registered on Spotlight.

Initially specialising in the Bollywood market it quickly progressed to more regional film productions by film-makers from other regions in the Indian subcontinent. Also offers services to film-makers from the Middle East and Russia and a wider global market, allowing production companies to make one call and fulfil all their requirements for an international cast and crew globally.

Provides line production services and full accounting packages (including tax credits and day-to-day cash flow services etc).

Recent filmography: Bollywood films include: *Bhagam Bhag, Namastey London, Salaam-E-Ishq* and

Casting directors 121

Patiala House; Russian films include: *Platon*; Middle Eastern productions include: *El Malik Farourk (King Farouk)*; Hungarian-US productions include: *Magic Boys*; Chinese productions include: *Vanguard, Dual Crisis, Triumph in the Skies II, Passage of my Youth, Impman 4, Finding Mr Right 2, Flying Tiger 2*; British feature films include: *Keith Lemon - The Film* and *Kick, Robot Overlords*; Canadian TV series: *The Frankie Drake Mysteries*. Has also worked on several music videos, commercials, idents and promos etc.

Phil Shaw
Suite 476, 2 Old Brompton Road, South Kensington, London SW7 3DQ
tel 020-8715 8943
email philshawcasting@gmail.com

Main areas of work are theatre, television, film and commercials. Casting credits include: Originating Co-Exec Producer: *Wire in the Blood* (ITV pilot); *Deckies* (Channel 4 series pilot); *Days in the Trees* (BBC Radio); *The Bill* (Thames TV); *Body Story* (BBC TV doc/drama series); *Romans 12:20* (BAFTA nominated; Grand Jury Prize, ARPA, Los Angeles); *Winter Fiction* (NFTS); *The Killing of Sister George* (Oldham Coliseum); *The Turn of the Screw* (No. 1 tour); *Billy Liar*; *The Chalk Garden*; *People Are Living There* (King's Head Theatre); *Cock & Bull Story* (Old Red Lion); *Enjoy* (Watford Palace); *Angels in America* (Lyric, Hammersmith); *The Last Post* (BAFTA nominated; Grand Prize, Berlin Film Festival); *Italian Movies* (Indiana Productions, feature - UK casting). Currently in development: *Deadly* (UK/Canada TV drama series written/directed by Neil LaBute); *Cractchit* (West End stage play for Blue Orb Productions); and *How to Fight Loneliness* (TV adaptation of a stage play by Neil Labute).

Will consider attending performances at Central London venues, and also West End, NT and RSC understudy runs, given a minimum of 2 weeks' notice. Accepts postal submissions (with resume/photograph), emailed Showcards and performance notices, but does not welcome unsolicited showreels or email enquiries (unless a performance notice).

Michelle Smith Casting Ltd*
email enquiries@michellesmithcasting.co.uk
website www.michellesmithcasting.co.uk

Specialising in film, television and commercials. Recent TV casting credits include: *Reg* (BBC1), *Common* (BBC1), *Moving On* (BBC) and *The Teacher* (Channel 5). Recent film credits include: *The Messenger, Electricity, The Violators* and *Lies We Tell*.

Suzanne Smith CDG*
WAC Arts, 213 Haverstock Hill, Belsize Park, London NW3 4QP
email suzanne@Suzannesmithcasting.com

Works in film and television. Credits include: *Silo*; *Blood of My Blood*; *Outlander*; *Good Omens*; *Marie Antoinette*; *Insomnia*; *Franklin*.

122 Agents and casting directors

Emma Stafford
tel 0161 833 4263
email assistant@emmastafford.tv
website www.emmastafford.tv

Areas of work include television, film and commercials. Recent credits include: *200 Magazine*, Co-op Bank, Robinsons, *If I Were a Butterfly*.

Will consider attending performances within the North West area with at least 2 weeks' notice. Accepts letters (with CVs and photographs) from actors previously unknown to the agency; will also accept CVs and photographs sent by email, and view showreels.

Helen Stafford
14 Park Avenue, Enfield, London EN1 2HP
tel 020-8360 6329
email helenstaffordcasting@gmail.com

Casts in film and theatre, in both the UK and the USA. Recent credits include: Films: *The Phantom Warrior*, *The Bezonians*, *Righteous Villains Original Gangster*, *Smoking Guns* aka *A Punter's Prayer* and *Red Devil* (now *Red Rage*); Theatre: New York Broadway production transfers to London West End.

Will consider seeing actors perform in Central and Greater London, with 1 week's notice.

Robert Sterne CDG*
Arthive Studios, Unit 3, 29 Hindsley's Place, London SE23 2NF
tel 020-3793 5568
email robert@robertsterne.co.uk

Casting Director Robert Sterne

Main areas of work are film, television and stage. Recent film credits include: *Steve* (2025); *The Choral* (2025), *Paddington in Peru* (2024) and *Spaceman* (2024). Recent TV credits include: *Black Doves* (2024), *The Mirror and the Light* (2024), *Eric* (2024); *3 Body Problem* (2024); *The Crown* (2016–23); *The Responder* (2022); *The Serpent* (2021); *Chernobyl* (2019); and *Game of Thrones* (2011–19). Recent theatre credits include *Patriots* (Almeida, West End and Broadway) and various productions at The Bridge Theatre.

Gail Stevens & Rebecca Farhall Casting*
email office@gailstevenscasting.com
Instagram @gail_rebeccacasting

Main areas of work are television, film and commercials. Recent casting credits include: *28 Years Later* (2025), *Wolf King* (2025); *Pistol* (2022); *The House* (2022); *Yesterday* (2019); *Early Man* (2018); *T2: Trainspotting* (2017).

Sam Stevenson CDG*
email casting@samstevenson.net
website www.samstevenson.net

Works in theatre, television, and film.

Lucinda Syson Casting
5 Cavendish Road, London SW12 0BH
tel 020-7287 5327

Recent feature films and TV credits include: *Foundation* (2021–23); *The Diplomat* (2023); *The Sandman* (2022); Holmes & Watson: The Abandoned Case (2022); *Wonder Woman 1984* (2020); *The Alienist* (2018–20); *Terminator: Dark Fate*; and *Aladdin* (2019).

Amanda Tabak CDG*
See the entry for Candid Casting under *Casting directors* on page 112.

Tarquin Casting
30 Wilton Road, Great Malvern, Worcs WR14 3RH
tel 020-3488 8071
email tarquin@tarquintalentagency.com
website www.tarquintalentagency.com
Facebook tarquincasting
X @tarquincasting
Bluesky @tarquincasting.bsky.social
Threads @tarquincasting
Young FEAA Head of Casting Tarquin Shaw

Tarquin Shaw-Young FEAA has been a freelance Casting Agent for the last 25 years, casting mainly children and young performers in all areas of the industry. Awarded a fellowship in 2005 for services to Acting by the TEAA, he has cast performers from all ages and stages and is available as freelance casting director for your next production.

Tarquin is also a past president of the TEAA of great Britain and a member of the Variety and Light Entertainment Committee and National Councillor for the TEAA. Please contact Tarquin direct if you are looking to bring him in on your project as a casting director or consultant for your project.

Nicci Topping Casting
Huddersfield Media Centre,
7 Northumberland Street, Huddersfield HD1 1RL
tel (01484) 511988
2nd Floor, 49 Carnaby Street, London W1F 9PY
tel 020-7112 8156
email nicci@toppingcasting.co.uk
website https://casting.niccitopping.com
X @niccitopping

Works in television, film and commercials. Recent work includes: Films: *The Black Prince*; *Abducted*; TV: *The World According to Grandpa* (Channel 5); *Deep Fake Neighbour Wars* (ITV); *Peacemaker* (HBO Max); Commercials: *Strike*; *Pantene*; *Freemans*.

Welcomes performance notices within Greater London and elsewhere (Manchester, Leeds, Sheffield) if given 2 weeks' notice. Accepts letters (with CVs & photographs) from individual actors previously unknown to the agency, sent by post or email.

Casting directors

Jill Trevellick CDG*
92 Priory Road, London N8 7EY
tel 020-8340 2734
email jill@jilltrevellick.com

Main areas of work are film and television. Recent casting credits include: *Mr Bates Versus The Post Office*; *Downton Abbey*; *Save Me*; *Belgravia*; *Anne*; *The Midwich Cuckoos*; *Stonehouse*; *The Lazarus Project*.

Anne Vosser Casting
tel (01252) 404716, *mobile* 07968 868712
email anne@vosser-casting.co.uk

Main areas of work are theatre and musicals. Casting credits include: *We Will Rock You*, *Bat Out of Hell*, *9 To 5 The Musical* (West End and Touring).

Matt Western
mobile 07740 70207
email matt@mattwestern.co.uk
website www.mattwestern.co.uk

Main areas of work are film, television and commercials. Recent casting credits include: Film: *Soof 3* (2022); *Decrypted* (2021); *The Colour of Spring* (2020); TV: *Under the Vines* (2021–23); *Sukkwan Island* (2024).

Jeremy Zimmermann Casting
tel 020-7478 5161
email office@zimmermanncasting.com
Instagram @Zimmermanncasting

Main areas of work are film and television. Casting work includes: *Willow*, *Keeping Mum*, *Dog Soldiers* and *Hellboy*.

Will consider attending performances at venues in Greater London and elsewhere. Accepts email submissions (with CVs and photographs) from actors previously unknown to the casting director, but does not welcome postal submissions. Invitations to view individual actors' websites are also accepted.

Self-tapes: an agent's perspective

Gemma McAvoy, agent
Interview by Sam Stevenson

Gemma McAvoy runs the Cardiff Office of Emptage Hallett. She has worked in the industry for 25 years, both as a freelancer and for organisations including the Royal Shakespeare Company and the Welsh College of Music and Drama. She has been a member of BAFTA Cymru Management Committee and was an inaugural Board Member of National Theatre Wales. She has been an agent for the last 16 years. See www.emptagehallettcardiff.co.uk.

What has changed significantly in the last few years is a paradigm shift from in-person meetings to a self-tape culture. I'm interested to know what that change has meant for agents.

I used to say that I knew so much about my actors, but what I didn't know is what they did in the audition room. I would get details of the meeting, share it with my actor, talk to them about the project and the prep required, then they'd go off and do their thing. But with self-tapes actors require more assistance because they don't have a casting director or director giving them notes, a sense of the tone or an idea of what they're looking for. In the room you can ask questions. An actor can say, "I feel like this character is like this," and get feedback or a steer from the director and a sense of how that character fits into the world, which informs their choices. Now actors want that from me.

It wasn't always necessary for me to read the full script. I would read the scene that my client was being asked to prepare, but I probably wouldn't have the time to read every script that came in. Now I need to read everything with the same level of detail that the actors do because they may want guidance.

Sometimes an actor will ask if they can film a rough version to see if they are on the right track. Then I'm doing the job of a director because I'm giving notes ahead of them recording a more polished version. That takes time.

Different actors have different needs though. There are those who have made a choice about how they want to play the role, present us with a beautifully edited finished version and that's that - that's what I send to the casting director. But sometimes they send me three or four options for each scene, and they want to talk them through and be advised about which take to submit.

So much of your time is now dedicated to tasks that never used to be in your job description.

Exactly. There's also the technical aspect: editing and adding titles, making it polished because we want it to be the best it can possibly be. And there are myriad ways in which to submit the tapes. Some casting directors want idents, others don't; some want the ident at the end, others at the beginning; sometimes each take or scene is requested as a separate file, sometimes it needs to be edited together. There are also various ways in which a casting director wants the file uploaded. There's Tagmin, Dropbox, Vimeo, or the casting director's own platform. We have to follow a whole set of instructions and it's not the same process every time.

You have offices in London and Cardiff, and represent many actors who don't live in the London area. Has it been beneficial for them?
Absolutely. I think that more actors have been given opportunities to be considered for roles that they potentially wouldn't have been called in for. It spreads the net wider, but it does bring with it different challenges. Though self-taping cuts down on travel time and costs, actors will still have to fit it into their plans for the weekend or evening. Aside from prepping the material, they will be clearing the back bedroom to set everything up and looking for someone to read-in with them. And then there is taping for theatre, which brings different challenges.

Definitely. For me, self-tapes for theatre are only useful as an introduction to an actor and I consider them a precursor to meeting in-person.
The whole point of an audition is to see an actor's performance develop and come to life, to see how they respond to notes and direction. If you're making a decision about how to play a role in your bedroom, it's just so difficult. And for theatre, actors ask me all the time, "Do I do it like it's going to be on screen?" Because otherwise there's a danger of the performance being too big. They may feel that the scene would benefit from them standing up, but it can look huge on screen. You can find yourself submitting something you don't feel happy with because it isn't what you would do if you were in the room. It doesn't represent what you wanted to show them because it's halfway between a screen audition and a stage audition.

It is imperfect. I would suggest to an actor that the best thing to do in that situation is, yes, stand up and make sure you frame yourself properly. Stand up, but don't do a *stage audition*. However, your decisions around the text must be detailed. So, it's not about volume, either physically or vocally, but it is about really well-defined choices. It's still not ideal, but I think that's probably the way to approach it.
I think the most important thing, whatever the project is, is your performance. Your choices may not be those of the director's, but show that you understand the scene. Trust your instincts, imagination, and creativity, and focus on how you want to play the role. If the lighting is not perfect, there's nothing you can do about that. Offer the director what you would if you were in the room; go to the essence of that. When an actor embodies the role and they live that moment, you forget that there's washing in the background (actually, don't do that!). The strength of the performance is the main thing.

The choices you make are everything. I think it just goes to the heart of what it is to be an actor. And so even if the tape is technically imperfect, if you've done your work as an actor, that's really what we're looking for. I have seen laundry drying on a rack in the background and I do wonder how hard it would have been to just move it out of shot? Because, psychologically, I start to think, have you thought about this meeting? Are you thinking like an actor? I'm not looking for a very sophisticated setup, I don't expect that, but I do think that there are some basic choices in the way you present yourself that are important.
And I think there was a time when we thought self-tapes were a temporary fix and some actors treated the tape as, well, "I'll just do a rough read, but the casting director will know I can be better than this." And I've had to tell them that it is the same as going to an

audition. You must treat it like that. If you don't do a tape, it's the same as not turning up. And if you don't give it care and attention, it's the same as going to a meeting unprepared.

We used to meet fewer actors when the auditions were in-person, so you may not have had a high chance of being met, but if you made it into the room, the likelihood of getting the job was greater. Now there is a much higher probability of being considered, but the odds of getting the job are significantly diminished. I don't know which is better but it does mean that an actor probably has to be better prepared than before because the competition has swelled.

Self-tapes are here to stay; this is how it's going to be. So, get a space in your house, get a team of actors, friends that you will read-in for and they'll read-in for you. Get a little gang that you can call upon because a tape is so much better when the other person is acting. That's quite important. Get a tripod and, if you can, a light. And then I think trust your instincts in terms of performance. This is what you've been trained to do, this is your skill. Trust that you're right for the role and commit to it. Get organised with the technical aspect, then all you really have to do is think about your performance and telling the story. Trust yourself as you would in a room. This is the world we're in now, so let's find a way of doing it that's joyful. Feel proud of what you've sent off; try to think of it as you would if you left an audition and said, "Great to meet you," and then walked away.

Showcases
Richard Evans CDG

What is a showcase?
A showcase is an opportunity for performers or other creative artists to show their talents and work to potential employers, agents, casting directors, talent scouts and other influencers. This enables those people to see and evaluate that work and remember the performers taking part, which could lead to meetings, auditions, job offers, or representation by an agent, either at the time or at some point in the future.

Types of showcases
For performers, or students on performing arts courses, these usually take the format of a show, lasting around an hour, consisting of numerous short pieces, which can be acting (monologues, duologues or scenes), singing, dancing, or a combination of some or all of these. Performers also showcase their work by appearing in a play or musical, to which they can invite people, and when understudying. I love supporting covers when they get an opportunity to go on, as do many of my colleagues, so do please invite us to both organised understudy runs and when you're scheduled to appear with the main cast (no matter how little notice you have been given, in case somebody happens to be free to come).

Other types of showcases are arranged for stand-up comedians (which might take the form of new act competitions), singers and speciality acts, to enable them to be seen by casting professionals and bookers from comedy clubs, holiday parks and cruise lines. Some of these may be open to all, by audition, while others will be presented by agencies to promote the acts that they represent. On the other side of the creative spectrum, a showcase could be a rehearsed reading for playwrights or composers, an exhibition for artists or photographers, a book launch for authors or illustrators, or a gig or open mic night for musicians or songwriters. The list is endless, but as you're reading this *Yearbook*, we will concentrate on showcases for actors and performers, though the principles are easily adaptable.

Showcases for performers can be presented in several different formats. The most traditional of these is as a live show in front of an audience, for one or several performances. As well as receiving applause and reactions, there is also a chance that some of the guests will stay behind afterwards to meet and chat with the performers (we'll talk more about that later). This performance could also be livestreamed online, enabling a far wider audience to watch it from their offices or homes, without the need to travel to the venue. This livestream could also be recorded, so that invited guests can watch it at a time that suits them, or the showcase could be recorded without an audience, perhaps over several days and edited, like a TV drama, and a link and password to that recording then distributed. There were also showcases via Zoom during the Covid pandemic, but these should be avoided, as internet speeds between participants can vary radically.

What do agents and casting directors look for at a showcase?
As with everything in this industry, viewpoints are subjective and different people look for and like different things. The jobs and requirements of agents and casting directors also mean their needs will be different, but here is the general answer. An agent will look for someone that they believe they can sell, for whom they can build a long term career, has

the potential to get the job and will therefore make them money in commission. They will also look for useful types, someone who is perhaps different from everyone else they represent, who will be reliable and they will get on with. As a casting director, I look for potential and people that I would feel confident bringing in to meet a creative team, who will make me look good and are confident enough not to look out of place in an audition with far more experienced performers. This might be for a role that I am currently casting (giving someone their first audition and job out of college is the absolute best feeling) or keeping them in mind and bringing them in for a project in the future (sometimes many years after I have first seen them). Both agents and casting directors will not only look for talent but also people who have personality and will be employable again and again.

Preparing For a showcase

If you are on a training course, your showcase will be organised for you, and doubtless mentioned and discussed throughout your course, and especially in your graduating year. Sometimes, it may be built up as the most vital part of your course or the most important day of your career so far. While it is, indeed, an important day, it is not *the* most important, and being fed this information can put some people under immense pressure to succeed. Like any performance, it should be enjoyed, and the more prepared you can be, the more relaxed you will feel when the day arrives.

The first thing you should do, if you can, is to go and see a showcase, several if possible. If your course lasts for more than one year, chances are you and the rest of your cohort will get to see a rehearsal, if not the actual performance of the year(s) above you, to support those students taking part. If you are offered a place at a school or college, you could always be cheeky and ask if you could see their showcase before you start your course, or even while deciding, if the timing is right. If you have friends or siblings at other colleges, try to see their showcases too, which will enable you to compare and contrast.

Before rehearsals start for your showcase, start thinking about and looking at material that you could perform. Your tutors and director will doubtless advise you on this, but it's good to have your own ideas as well. Firstly, it is advisable to be original when choosing speeches or songs, which will be far more likely to grab the attention of audience members. When looking at the works of playwrights and composers, delve deeper than their better-known works, which will be performed frequently and heard regularly. Look online and see what else they have written, perhaps earlier in their careers. Wikipedia can be good for this, as can Doollee for playwrights. You can always try writing your own pieces, either on your own or in a group, but keep in mind that more light-hearted and comic pieces might get a more favourable reaction from the audience than those that are heavier or tragic.

Choose characters that fit your casting and type, that you could believably play now. Unless you have more than one native accent (for example, if one or both of your parents are from another country, or you were brought up in a different part of the world), avoid doing pieces using an accent which is not your own. While this may show off your skill, especially if you are competent in the accent concerned, doing this will give the audience a different first impression of you, which could be confusing. First impressions are important, and something that you never get a second chance to make, so it pays to think carefully, make the right choices and play you, or what you could be. If you have more than one piece to perform, you could use an alternative accent in a later piece. Your accent is less important when singing songs, especially if they're from American musicals, though it would be worth practising them in both American and your natural accent, so you can decide which works best for you.

When you and the showcases creatives have decided on what piece(s) you're going to perform, rehearse them thoroughly, getting the lines or lyrics into your head. In addition to scheduled rehearsals with the director, run the lines with a friend, or your scene partners whenever you have an opportunity. Think also about how the character(s) you're playing would be dressed and use costume to give an idea of this (though don't go over the top).

While your college or showcase organisers will doubtless invite the right people along to see it, don't be afraid to personally invite people you have met, who have expressed an interest in you, or those companies, directors or agents whose work you admire and feel is a good fit for your skills and talents. Several invitations can sometimes be more effective than just one, especially if sent at different times (nearer the date, perhaps). Let the organisers know that you are doing this and include the official contact details for RSVP on your invitation, as well as your own.

Before the programme goes to print (whether it is a booklet for a live show, or information on a website for recordings), double check that your professional name, the title of the play or musical from which the piece is taken, the name of the character, and that of the playwright or composers are all spelt correctly.

On the day

Your showcase will either be staged in a venue at your college, with which you'll be familiar, or an outside theatre, which may be totally new to you. When you get into the theatre, look around, work out if the staging of your pieces will need some adjustment, and take some time to run through your lines or lyrics with your scene partners. Also, work out how much sound you will need for your voice to be audible to everyone and reach the back wall of the auditorium. Even if you are equipped with a radio mic, these can sometimes fail, so be prepared to use your voice to compensate (adrenaline will play a big part in this), which will gain you sympathy and respect from the audience and make you look like a true professional, if this should happen. When it is your turn to go on stage, take a deep breath and go for it!

After the showcase

Now comes the part which many say is the most nerve-racking – networking, which means meeting those from the industry who have stayed to chat afterwards, usually over food and drink. When you come off stage, don't be tempted to change your clothes, as the longer you take, the more likely people are to leave. Go straight into the bar, wearing exactly what you wore on stage, which will increase the audience's recognition of you, smile and be prepared to chat. There's no guarantee that many people will stay, especially if your showcase is at lunchtime and they need to get back to work. Don't take this personally – those who are interested will get in touch with you via your college. Even if they don't, you can always contact them to thank them for coming and ask them to keep you in mind for the future, so ensure you are given a list of names and contact details of the industry folk who attended.

When approaching people, instead of asking if they enjoyed the show, or for feedback, a common tactic, which could invite a negative response, simply say "Thank you for coming!", which should then start a conversation. While conversations can't be forced, and you should ask the person subtly who they are and what they do, it doesn't have to be all about the industry. One memorable chat I had with a student turned from the usual acting topics to holidays and countries we had visited, which was refreshing and brought out her personality and enthusiasm. If nobody is talking to you, pick up a tray of food and offer it around, which might help, and avoid standing in large groups, which are harder for someone to approach, if they're only interested in talking to one person.

If the showcase is in London, or another major city, and your school or college is far away, it might be worth you staying nearby for a day or two afterwards (if your schedule and budget allow), in case anyone who attended wants to meet you for further discussions. While it's a gamble, doing this could not only save your time and money, having to travel back and forth, but also enable people to see you again while you're still fresh in their minds, rather than days or weeks later. If you are going to extend your stay, make people aware by including the information at the end of your programme biography and telling those who you chat with afterwards, making sure they have your contact details (having business cards to hand out is a great way of doing this).

Following up

You will have hopefully received a list of everyone who saw you on the day and will remember who you met and chatted with afterwards. Some might make contact with you, or have asked you to contact them, which you should do within a day or two, but if they haven't, send an email or card thanking them for coming and asking for a meeting or to be kept in mind in the future. In the case of agents, most good ones will only take on a very few graduates every year. There's nothing that says that everyone must be represented, so if you don't get offers immediately, don't be afraid to represent yourself, until you find the right agent for you.

Organising a showcase

Finally, here are some thoughts to help maximise success and attendance if you're ever organising a showcase in the future. Timing is an important factor, and busy people may be more likely to come if your showcase doesn't cut into their working day too much. Lunchtime, starting at 1:00 can be good, as can early evening, at around 6:30 or 7:00. Midweek might be better than Mondays or Fridays, but always check Spotlight's Graduate Performance Calendar for clashing dates before committing. Start a few minutes later than billed, and make sure there is access for latecomers, always keeping some seats empty for those who arrive at whatever time. Choose a venue that is centrally located and close to transport links. If you can negotiate a discount with the venue's bar and caterers, or even bring in your own food and drink, it will stretch your budget further. Email your invitations between 2 and 4 weeks before the date, follow up the invitation with a phone call (if numbers are in the public domain) and email a reminder on the morning of the showcase, to everyone you've invited, mentioning there are seats for them and that you hope to see them later.

Richard Evans CDG has been a casting director since 1989 and, prior to that, worked as an actor for ten years. During that time, he has cast productions in every media, written several books, devised and presented audition and career development workshops for students and performers, seen thousands of showcases, and has also mentored two groups of actors, who produced several successful showcases of their own. For tips, advice and resources on showcases, auditioning and performing, go to **www.auditionsthecompleteguide.com**.

Auditioning for stage and television
Gemma Hancock & John Cannon, casting professionals
Interview by Sam Stevenson

Gemma Hancock *currently works in the casting department at BBC Studios, casting* Casualty, Father Brown *and* Sister Boniface Mysteries. *Previously her work as a freelancer encompassed film, theatre and TV.*

John Cannon *has been working in casting for a little over 30 years. He joined the National Theatre casting department in 1989, moving to the Royal Shakespeare Company in 1993, where he became Head of Casting for five years. In addition, he has cast for many of the major theatre companies and worked in film and television. He is currently at BBC Studios casting* EastEnders, Father Brown *and* Sister Boniface Mysteries. *He is a member of the CDG.*

One of the questions that actors ask me the most is whether there are any significant differences in auditioning between screen and stage. We've worked together a great deal over the years in both mediums, so I'm interested to know your thoughts.

GH: For theatre, the audition is much more of a two-way experience between the actor and director, plus we're looking to create an ensemble, which we do in TV to a certain extent, but not nearly as much.

JC: *Television casting doesn't need to be so concerned with that because in most cases the actors are booked for a fraction of the time that they would be for theatre. And in a play the characters are likely to be serving a much bigger function, as opposed to playing a waiter for a day or a patient for an episode.*

GH: Even for a nice guest part, you're still fitting into someone else's story, especially if you're working on a continuing drama.

JC: *Plus, there is rarely any rehearsal in TV, so if you get the job the director wants you to do exactly what you did in the audition, where you are more or less expected to turn up having worked everything out for yourself. TV directors tend not to give the kind of notes that an actor might expect if they were meeting for a play and it is rare in a TV casting to have a detailed conversation about character etc.*

GH: Though there were a couple of theatre directors that we worked with together, Sam, who didn't necessarily want to chat or talk about character in detail.

Each director has their own process, don't they, regardless of the medium that they're working in. For an actor though, is the prep different for a theatre audition?

JC: *Attention to the entire script will probably take more time because you need to know how you fit into the plot, which might dictate your choices. For continuing drama you will only receive the sides you appear in.*

GH: And you might have to do a bit more background work on the writer and director, as well as the world of the play.

And in the room, do you think there are any differences? I'm thinking about size of performance, both vocally and physically.

GH: I think it's about vocal energy. Sometimes the vocal energy is too low, even for TV auditions, especially with theatre actors.

Because they under-compensate vocally in order to not be "theatrical"?

JC: *Perhaps. Though many directors don't want to see too much 'acting', it's still necessary to be audible.*

I think that vocal levels are even trickier to calibrate for a theatre audition. You might be auditioning for the Old Vic, but you are meeting in a standard sized room, so you can't be too loud because that would distort the performance. As soon as you step into the space, you need to assess how much vocal strength is required.

GH: It's also about focus. In a TV or film audition you need to know how to cheat your eyeline towards the camera while looking at the person you're reading with. The same goes for self-tapes because we need to see what's going on in your eyes. Theatre auditions are more physically freeing.

JC: *One thing to be aware of in all auditions is that the person who is reading-in is unlikely to be an actor and might not be very good, and you need to be ready not to let it put you off. TV dialogue is often speedier than for a play – directors always want you to think and speak at the speed of thought; and don't forget to listen and react when the other character in the scene is talking back at you.*

GH: Listening is the first thing that goes in an audition because of nerves.

JC: *That's why at the RSC Greg [Doran] might ask an actor if they had a monologue up their sleeve that they knew intimately, that they could confidently work on for directing purposes.*

GH: Peter [Hall] used to do that, didn't he? When actors were terrified about reading something unfamiliar, he'd say, "What else do you know? What else have you got?"

I've noticed that more actors are learning lines or attempting to. But 20 years ago, that wasn't so much the case. Have you seen a change in attitude?

GH: Definitely for self-tapes. Even pre-Covid, actors tended not to memorise the dialogue, but now everyone does – or they've just got very good at reading the sides and we can't tell! It's not a memory test though and trying to remember the lines can add to audition nerves.

JC: *And when it comes to memorising the material, either learn it properly or don't learn it. There's no halfway house, because the worst auditions are the ones when actors have half-learned the dialogue and fumble the read while trying to remember what they're going to say next.*

GH: Especially for in-person auditions; if you end up paraphrasing the dialogue, the person you're reading with won't be able to keep up with you. Some TV directors say, "Oh, it doesn't matter about the lines, just improvise", but that doesn't work for the person who is reading-in and has to give or receive cues.

JC: *Even seemingly simple dialogue will have a built-in rhythm, put there by the writer.*

GH: We always remember people who audition well and that's what matters.

JC: *Because it's all good for the future. It's the old adage, that the time you've got in the room is your time and that we want you to get the job.*

GH: The crucial thing to remember is that we've already decided that the actor is right for the part and that we're on their side; there also isn't a right way of auditioning or reading a scene. You can sometimes see the question in an actor's eyes – "is this what you want?". We're just looking for an actor to bring it to life in whatever way they choose. I think actors want it to be perfect and we're not looking for perfection; we're looking for something that we can work with.

It's up to us to be open, isn't it, about what the actor is bringing us. But they have to bring us something.
GH: It's like you say, Sam, the worst audition is when an actor does a general read, or if they're hedging their bets because they haven't quite decided how they want to do it. A director can't direct that.
JC: *Work it out before you come in, but try not to stress too much and remember that we want you to get the job.*

You've both worked at the BBC for several years now, is there anything that you miss about theatre casting?
JC: *Casting a new play is a really nice thing. With TV, if you're creating a new series or casting new regular characters that is closer to doing theatre because the process is so much more detailed – as opposed to fast and furious episodic casting.*
GH: I miss sitting and chatting to those directors that we've all worked with. It's just much more involved and creative, I guess, isn't it? It's like being an actor: you don't do theatre for the money, you do it for the gratification.
JC: *Yes, the work is the reward, isn't it?*
GH: We still see as much theatre as we can though and it's so satisfying when we hear a producer or director want to know where we found someone. It still gives me such a buzz when theatre actors who haven't done much telly absolutely smash a TV audition.

Watching an actor's stage work is so important; if you look at someone's show-reel, more often than not, they will have a lot of similar scenes because they've been cast in similar parts in TV. But they're likely to be cast differently in theatre which gives you an alternative perspective on their capabilities.
JC: *And, arguably, in TV we cast more to type. Actors are expected to act closer to their own personalities, whereas maybe a theatre role would take you into a somewhat different characterisation. That was one of the joys of the RSC, wasn't it? In a season of three plays that were cross-cast, you had a pretty good idea of what the actor playing Benvolio and Amiens in their first two plays was going to do with the roles. But later in the season, when they did the third play, there might be more of a gamble on how they were cast, and they'd come up with something so different from your expectations.*

It's wonderful when we can still be surprised by actors whose work we've followed for a long time.
JC: *Which is why we should never stop covering an actor's performances because as people age and change they develop new flavours to their work.*

Casting for musical theatre

David Grindrod

The process of producing/casting a musical can be a very long and costly affair. Everyone is looking for the next *Phantom of the Opera* or *Mamma Mia!*; years of work can go into the production you see on stage today. Workshops have now become a necessity in order to see if a show 'has legs', without spending too much money. In consultation with the producer and creative team, I will assemble a group of actors who may not be totally right for the roles but who work well in a workshop situation. If the green light is given after the workshop presentation, the casting process – in conjunction with everything else – begins.

A casting breakdown is drawn up: this consists of all the details required by agents and artists about the characters, vocal ranges, etc. plus the proposed dates of the production. Open calls are sometimes organised for specific roles, but normally the breakdown gets sent to agents via the Spotlight link, which reaches 500 agents/representatives at the touch of a button.

There is always a 'wish list' of actors whom producers would like in their production, but the bulk of submissions will come through agents, in the form of photos and CVs. Unsolicited mail is also received; sometimes it is difficult to keep all this on file due to sheer number of submissions. Either I or my associates will also attend college shows and presentations to look for specific talent.

When preparing your photos and CVs, always remember that these are the calling cards with which you promote yourself! A good photograph is not 'artistic' (i.e. showing a face half in shadow); rather, it should always present a good full face that really does look like you. Your CV should ideally be just one page stapled to the back of your photograph. It should include all relevant details (*not* forgetting contact details) to show your skills. Make this information clear and precise. If you feel that you are suitable for musical casting, be very accurate and truthful about your vocal range: don't make it complicated – basically, tenor or soprano, with the top of your range noted. We can normally tell your style by the shows you have appeared in.

The audition process normally begins with artists performing two contrasting songs that show range and personality. Make an effort to pick a song that is suitable for the show – not pop, for example, when you are up for Rogers & Hammerstein. Nerves will take over; therefore, don't sing the song you learnt yesterday, but perform something tried and tested (something you would be happy singing naked in Trafalgar Square!). When we ask, "Have you got something else?" we don't want the answer, "My agent said you only wanted two songs,"; have your book of audition pieces with you and give us the chance to choose an alternative. Actors often ask whether I have favourite songs that I like to hear – or songs that I don't: I only really mind when they come in with completely the wrong song for the production.

If an actor is successful, they will receive a call-back for a dance/movement call. This normally causes concerns, but actually it is not usually that specific; we only want to see whether a person is happy with his/her body. If the audition is for a major dance show, hopefully you will know your limitations, and either not audition at all, or be ready to throw yourself into the routine. Again, be honest: then you won't upset the creative team.

Further recalls take place with music and script from the show: the musical supervisor or associate director normally takes these calls. If you come in for the musical supervisor, come back with music prepared and your own song. *Always* bring your own song – it's a good reminder for the team. In addition to any script you are asked to read, you may get asked for a speech: have a couple of acting pieces prepared, and again, nerves will take over, so make sure you know them properly. Remember that these speeches are also to allow the director to assess how well you can respond to direction, and how readily you can take a note.

The culmination of the casting process – 'the finals' – is the most nerve-wracking experience, even for a highly experienced artist. Bring everything with you that you have been given. You may not get *asked* for everything, but have it just in case. You may have been asked to dress in a certain way; always put some thought into that, as directors can be blinkered at times ... I have known artists to arrive with a couple of outfits and ask me to pick one! The panel will consist of the whole creative team and the producers. At this stage I can't do any more for you – though hopefully I can keep the atmosphere in the room happy and 'up'. Stay calm, don't change anything that you have been told, and audition to the best of your abilities.

Now the wait to see if you have the role. Always remember that you have got this far in the process because you can sing and act far better than anyone else. In the end, the decision could come down to height, look, hair colour; funnily enough it may not have anything to do with your singing/acting skills at this point. And you may not get an instant answer; you may have to wait until other meetings have taken place. You may get put on 'hold': normally that means you are not first on the list, but if somebody above you declines the offer you may move up. If you are lucky, the phone call will come with a straight offer. How exciting is that ... Contractual details are then advised and, if all that is agreed, your date for first rehearsal is given. Always remember that you are a small part of the bigger picture – a small part of the jigsaw puzzle that goes together to form: The Musical.

David Grindrod founded David Grindrod Associates (DGA) with Stephen Crockett in January 1998, after 20 years' experience in the theatre in various roles ranging from assistant stage manager to general manager. Current West End casting includes *Chicago*, *Evita*, *The Lord of the Rings*, *Mamma Mia!* (worldwide), *Spamalot*, *The Sound of Music*. Films include *The Phantom of The Opera*. DGA are also casting consultants for *On The Town* and *Kismet* at the English National Opera, and belong to the Casting Directors Guild of Great Britain.

A strategy for acting success
Ken Rea

When you set out to be a doctor, a teacher or a hairdresser, you can usually expect a long and steady career. Not so with actors: the future can be one uncertainty after another. So what can you do to carve out a smoother career path that will give you more stability?

As Professor of Theatre at the Guildhall School of Music & Drama, I've trained actors from the very outset and have followed them through their careers. Many became hugely successful, but many also got stuck somewhere along the line, and others became dispirited then dropped out altogether. So my preoccupation has been: how much of this is within your power? What do you have to do to enjoy decades of fulfilling work on stage or screen, where you get better and better?

Most of the actors who now come to me for coaching and training have one common concern: "I'm getting good work," they tell me, "But I want to get bigger parts and work in better productions. How can I step up to that next level?"

At any stage of your career, this is a brilliant question to ask yourself because, if you're like most actors who want to be successful, then you are driven by growth – constantly trying to move forward rather than getting stuck. The point is: what does that next level look like to you and, in order to get there, what would you have to be doing differently that you're not doing now?

Based on my work with thousands of actors around the world, I'm going to show you a strategy for success. It won't guarantee you Oscars, though it will help smooth the way forward. But before we go any further, let me be clear about my view of 'success' – it's not about becoming a Hollywood star, it's doing work where you feel you're at your best, having a palpable, positive impact on your audience.

Getting the job

My strategy covers two main areas: getting the job and doing exciting work. Before you can dazzle them on the rehearsal room floor, you've got to deal with the hurdle of the audition. And even before that, how do you get yourself in front of the key people who can give you that dream job?

Taking a proactive approach to making yourself more visible in the industry can certainly help accelerate your success because more influential people get to know about you. So you need to be aware of your professional profile. Are you getting out and meeting fellow actors and directors? Are you emailing casting directors to let them know what you're doing? Are you perhaps creating work of your own, such as a short film or solo performance, that you can talk about?

Being sociable in the way you interact with other people is crucial. Some of the most successful actors I know have impeccable manners; they are polite, considerate and courteous in their behaviour, which draws people towards them and makes a positive lasting impression. Consequently, their network expands. How do you cultivate that kind of behaviour? A lot comes back to your values: showing genuine interest in others and being ready to help them is, in my experience, one of the most powerfully effective ways of building a social network.

A strategy for acting success

Then there is the thorny question of your online presence. When actors approach me for coaching, the first thing I look at is their showreel, then anything else they may have online, such as their Wikipedia or IMDb entry. These will tell me what level they are at and how I can help them. Although casting directors increasingly rely on self-tapes for auditions, your online entries are your electronic calling card; they establish your credibility. So make sure they look professional and well organised. Showreels, for example should have good production values in their lighting and sound quality. An IMDb entry, if you have one, can act like a website, storing any other photos or video clips you might have.

The problem with social media platforms such as TikTok, X or Instagram is that they can easily seem to take over your life, compelling you to keep up an unrealistic output of insanely optimistic visual material that shows you are living the high life beyond the dreams of ordinary mortals. Some of my actor friends have told me, "My mental health improved once I left social media." However, as a marketing tool it does have its uses, provided you maintain clear limits. Personally, I make it a rule to limit all my posts to theatre and acting, avoiding politics and family life. I use it mainly to promote my books or online acting courses. I also decided to put everything about my professional life in one website so that people could find me and I had control over the narrative. You must find your own way, but my advice is: set and keep to your boundaries.

Great acting jobs may be few and far between, and when you're out of work, it's scary how quickly your confidence can be eroded. So it's important that you maintain an upbeat attitude. Ask yourself: what am I doing each day that will advance my craft? This is a crucial initiative that keeps you in the present tense: '*I am* an actor'. It might be voice work, movement, reading plays or screenplays, line-learning, practising self-tapes or sight reading, but every day you're moving forward. The advice I give to actors is: commit to a realistic amount of time every day – even if it's ten minutes – and work on your skills. If you have a group of like-minded actor friends, you could also meet regularly and practise your improvisation skills together in a safe environment where you can make mistakes without professional pressures. One of my former students, Natasha Gordon, used to meet with friends once a week in the foyer of the National Theatre to read each other's play scripts and give feedback. She ended up with her play being put on, not only at the National but later transferring to the West End.

You also need to take care of your general fitness because the job of acting demands enormous energy, resilience and stamina. You've got to be match fit ready to go when the call comes. Everyone is different but it's helpful to have a physical routine that works for you. For me, it's a short *Qi gong* routine every day and also Pilates and swimming. For others it might be yoga or meditation.

Nearly half the actors I come across complain that their agent (if they're lucky enough to have one) is not doing enough for them. Some agents, seeing the long game, will nurture you like a benevolent aunt or uncle. But this is not a charity; it's a business relationship and it will have its limits. The agent can get you in front of the right people but what you do once you're in the room is up to you. The bottom line is that you're there to make money for each other. You should therefore be able to have candid discussions about what you can do to make the agent's job easier. And having both given it your best shot, if you find that after a year or two it's not really working, then be prepared to realise that it may be time to part company, not with bitter resentment, but being aware that you were not right for each other. However, it's always important to keep the door open, because one day you may want to come back.

In any audition there are certain things you will have no control over – you may not be the right physical fit or age for what the director has in mind. But once in the room you can enhance or sabotage a great first impression through the kind of energy you bring in. Of course it's not easy to look relaxed when you're trying to be impressive while dealing with the pressure. But one powerful solution is to adjust your mindset. For a start, spare a thought for the director, who wants you to be 'the one' and has maybe less than half an hour to predict the future: will this person bring the kind of energy I want in my cast, will they be easy to work with, how courageous are they, what will they be like under pressure?

Casting directors often say: "We want to see *you*." That's only possible if you can remove the veil of desperation to somehow take the pressure off. But how? It can be hugely liberating to considerer that this is a two-way transaction; in a sense you are auditioning the director as much as they are auditioning you. You've done your preparation, then you meet to explore whether you're right for each other and whether you like each other. You may be strapped for cash at the moment but you always have the power to say no. There's little point in signing up for weeks of rehearsal hell, which is unlikely to bring happiness or make you a better actor.

Doing exciting work

Once you've got the job, how can you work in such a way that the director will find you exciting and want to work with you again? A distinguished director once told me, "I hate auditions, so half the time I tend to employ my mates, whom I've worked with before." But what does exciting work look like? The way you work is the result of your preparation, your process and the values you bring to the job. Let's look at them one by one.

Meticulous preparation is your insurance policy. It reduces stress in the rehearsal room or on set. Faced with a major role, some of the best actors I know will start preparing months before rehearsals start. They'll do a forensic analysis of the text. A lot of this is about asking good questions to unlock the hidden clues: what is your character really trying to do underneath the words, why are they saying this, what do they most want and what strategies do they use to get that, what are they trying to conceal, why did they choose this word here and not that? Also, what options do you have in applying the character's tactics to get what they want?

When I'm helping an actor prepare for an audition I find these questions can be the most enjoyable and surprising part of the work. At first glance you might think, 'Well this is not much of a text.' And then, as you explore it, all sorts of possibilities start to come to life; your delivery is transformed from a bland reading to a compelling moment that gives you total ownership of what you are saying, where everything suddenly becomes crystal clear. The greatest writers offer endless choices; it's your job to explore them. Decades after performing in a Shakespeare or a Chekhov, for example, I sometimes still think: 'Yes, I could have said that line like this...' In western theatre, there's no such thing as a definitive performance. Use that fact to free yourself. Your excellence as an actor will depend on the brilliance of your creative choices in the service of the story.

That leads to your process. The actors you work with may have been trained in a very different methodology from yours, so you need to be flexible and open to them, yet also clear about what works for you in rehearsal that gets you to where you need to be. Ideally, you will be refining and reassessing that process throughout your working life, but you should always be open to new ideas and approaches. Acting technique should never be stuck in what people did 50 or 100 years ago; it's continually evolving. That also applies to working with directors. I know of numerous actors who came to grief because they resisted the director's process.

This takes us to your values. What really makes the difference between success and failure is how you apply your values as an actor in a way that will help make the production an exciting experience for everyone concerned. Some people light up the room and others sap the energy out of it. That's about your enthusiasm and it's a choice that is within your control. It's a habit you can choose to adopt. I've described the values and qualities that lead to success more fully in *The Outstanding Actor*, but here are a few factors that can make a difference.

Curiosity will motivate and energise you. Approach the production, whether on stage or screen with an optimistic attitude of, 'How can we bring this to life?' It's about looking for solutions and particularly in screen acting, bringing a range of choices to the director. To cultivate curiosity as a habit you need to be constantly alive to the world around you.

Most of the greatest actors have an innate sense of playfulness – they've not lost their inner child, which enables them to take risks. By risks I mean having the fearlessness to try out a solution that may not work in order to find a better, more exciting one. This can give you that sense of danger that thrills the audience when they don't know what is coming next. It's not about showing off, though; it's about daring to let your imagination fly, but always to serve the story.

Be generous with the people around you. Not everyone is easy to work with. A difficult actor who is making life hell for everyone may in truth be trying to mask a terrifying insecurity. And that goes for directors as well. Above all, make it a professional habit to bring positive energy into the room, day after day, which nurtures a feeling that, yes, this is going to work! Make it your default to say, "Yes, and.." rather than, "Yes, but…"

The secret of making qualities like these work for you as an actor is to get them into your everyday life. Only then will they become authentic. You can't suddenly fake enthusiasm in a rehearsal if you've never shown it in the street. A good question to ask yourself is: how often does a stranger instinctively smile at you as you pass by?

A final point about your success as an actor: remember that it doesn't all have to happen when you're still in your twenties or thirties. Unlike a ballet dancer or an athlete, as you get older, you simply move into different casting brackets and the greatest opportunities may come to you well into your seventies or eighties. There are many examples of this today. So the important thing is not to give up, but to keep going, fuelled by curiosity and enthusiasm, honing your skills to get better and better.

Ken Rea is a theatre director, acting teacher, and author of *The Outstanding Actor, Seven Keys to Success* (Bloomsbury). In addition to his online course, *Ken Rea Teaches Acting*, he runs masterclasses throughout the world and offers one-to-one coaching. As Professor of Theatre at the Guildhall School of Music & Drama, he has trained some of the UK's most prominent actors. His latest book is *Kicking Up a Storm, The Living Theatre Troupe in 1970s New Zealand* (Bloomsbury). See more at **www.kenrea.co.uk**.

Woman in a brown skirt

Sophie Stanton reflects on the Donmar Warehouse's pioneering commitment to providing more opportunities for female actors in its all-women Shakespeare Trilogy, which helped her to land her most significant roles to date: Falstaff in the Donmar's *Henry IV* and Mrs Rich in the RSC'S revival of *The Fantastic Follies of Mrs Rich* by Mary Pix.

I mourned my training when it ended. I consider myself fortunate that I did, but it was painful. Perhaps that's why for many years I compulsively enrolled on courses in whatever subject piqued my interest at the time.

On the cartoon course, perhaps a couple of years out of drama school, I titled one project, 'The Seven Stages of Wan'. It's a portrait of an actress as she journeys through her career from early childhood to old age, sans everything. I revisit it now with one question in mind – how prophetic was I in those early years?

The first three frames are self-explanatory: 'I wanna be Mary' depicts a child of nursery school age in the school nativity (I was always a shepherd in ours); 'I wanna be picked', aged fourteen she's auditioning for a production of Romeo and Juliet – we did *A Midsummer Night's Dream*. I was Puck. We also did The Mikado. I played Koko, the Lord High Executioner. A pattern was emerging. 'I wanna be unpicked' sees the young drama student suffering 'first-term fatigue syndrome' at the fictitious Deptford Academy of Dramatic Art, (DADA)... Whilst training, I played a wealth of older ladies – drunks, eccentrics, powerhouses of motherhood – and was all the better for it as a young mind at the very start of a career. Of course, there was no way I was going to get an agent from it, but I was truly stretched in most disciplines and, therefore, ironically, in my creative prime upon graduation.

The first couple of years were paltry. I played a mouse, Pimple, someone who'd been abused on *The Bill*. The worst corpse of my entire life occurred in a 'reminiscence show' we inflicted on older members of the community round various care homes, when one woman screamed, 'Oh, shut up! You are getting on my nerves' in the middle of my solo. Which rather hit the nail on the head and drove it into my heart. But it got me my Equity card.

'I wanna work' was the frame I saw myself in at the time of drawing the cartoon. Our female protagonist sits in a coffee shop with a male actor friend sharing a conversation she has had with her agent, desperate to get a job *of any description*. Both are smoking (how times have changed). She asks how his career is going. 'Well, great. But then, I'm a boy' is the response. (Or have they?) We fast-forward to the middle-aged actress outside a Winnebago. 'Love, I'm a bloody joke,' she says on the phone, 'I've got two sodding lines and some business with a rhino! It would be *nice* to play Lady M before it's too late, frankly!' In a letter to my former self I might comment that this insight into life for an actress of a certain age is uncanny. To which, my former self would undoubtedly reply, 'That's not me being insightful, it's the truth.' Which of course it is, unless you are exceptionally lucky. Or unless you get cast as a man. I wonder what I would have felt had I known then that I'd wait twenty-odd years to play a major role and that that major role would be an old fat bloke. I'm sure the old fat bloke bit of the equation wouldn't have been an issue having cornered the market in shepherds, traditionally male fairies, executioners and old ladies. But the wait?

And so to Falstaff in the Donmar Warehouse's all-female Shakespeare Trilogy (St Ann's Warehouse, New York, 2015; Donmar King's Cross, 2016). In one, rare twenty-four-hour period, I landed two smashing theatre jobs and was on a 'pencil' (they do fall through, don't ever trust a pencil) for a TV series that has so far run to three seasons and would no doubt have made a healthy dent in my mortgage. But it had been too long since I'd played a part I'd really had to work at. There is a rose called Falstaff. It is unmissable in a border – bold, broad, robust, its petals seem infinitesimal and it's almost the colour of electricity, at once mesmerising and repellent. Its lust for the world strikes me as so enormous that all that energy simply cannot last. Which is probably all I need to say about the role. It undoubtedly changed the landscape for me as an artist. You cannot turn that down. It just doesn't come around very often if you're a bird.

Don't get me wrong: many of the roles I have played have been absolute gems – in *Mercury Fur*, *England People Very Nice*, *Dying for It*, *Beautiful Thing*, *Ding Dong the Wicked*, *Nut*, *Ink*, *Made in Dagenham: The Musical* – in bastions of new writing: the Almeida, the Royal Court, the National, the Bush. Just too, too many to mention, providing exceptional material with which to carve out a notably varied career. But, still, a lot of them amount to cameos as they're in relief of the male protagonist, which is often all we can expect as 'character actresses'.

Falstaff gave me no choice but to step up as an artist. To stride out, to claim space and make noise unapologetically in a manner which is simply foreign to us as both women and as female actors. It was a language that I had barely spoken since childhood, in fact, when I had been permitted to play the noisy parts in school plays. I took inspiration from John Travolta strutting through the streets of NYC to the sound track of 'Staying Alive' – just feeling great about himself. I studied men who walk only in straight lines, taking for granted that the rest of us will step aside. I dropped my voice an octave and hit maximum volume. And, of course, I embraced the male spread. Falstaff gives it large.

Women, to this day, tend to be written small. Even the female juvenile lead is often written with a bias towards making the bloke-part look tender when he falls in love with her (which isn't a terribly progressive representation of men either, might I add, we must fight for both genders). Obviously, I get cast as the juve lead's mum or just that woman who's complaining in a shop. I call them the 'brown skirt parts'.

God forbid they should dress you in anything interesting; you might upstage the lead. Yesterday's conversation with a costume designer – 'I'm going to make you downbeat, muted. In contrast to, you know, *the politicians*.' The film is about the politicians, need I say, all male.

Unsurprisingly, Falstaff was the best possible preparation for the biggest female role I have played to date – Mrs Rich in *The Fantastic Follies of Mrs Rich*, an adaptation of Mary Pix's lost play *The Beau Defeated* of 1700 (RSC, Stratford, 2018). Mrs Rich is writ large, oh, yes she is. The delicious absurdity of her social pretension, the enormity of her wit, her kitsch, her pain and her glory, the cabaret, the vaudeville demanded by the writing – none of it could I draw on from having played the brown-skirt parts. All of my references were male. I spent a lot of time researching the work of drag queens. We just don't have permission to display as women. At best, it is not female tradition. At worst it is unsavoury. I had four soaring solos written by Grant Olding scored for four saxophones aspiring to be a string quartet (not since I was heckled by an old lady had I sung solo), I was gifted endless innuendos, ad libs, exquisite soliloquies and audience collusion. I learnt the harpsichord, how to vogue, wolf whistle, had costumes made which really should be behind glass at the Victoria and Albert museum and finally – finally — I got to perform my first professional sword fight. That part was Falstaffian.

God forbid this swathe of women in significant male roles should be relegated to a thing of the past because look at where it can lead. It would be nice not to have to play a man in order to fulfil an epic role of a lifetime, but those female roles are painfully rare. Women have to be represented bigger – not just more, but bigger. We cannot let this work fade. Do not go gentle into that good night. Thank you, Mr Dylan Thomas. I shall try very hard not to.

In the penultimate frame of my cartoon, our now older protagonist has indeed won the part of Lady M, but it's too late as her memory has gone and she suffers a mammoth dry in the 'dashed the brains out' speech. Two walk-on actors mutter bitchy comments behind her. It's bleak. And finally, we come to 'Dribble Hall; retirement home for dear old thesps'. We find the elderly woman at what is possibly her final Christmas, being entertained by Naff Theatre Company. Her face is full of loss, *wan*, but there's a soupçon of defiance left about the eyes. She says to herself, 'And so it came to pass'... This, the last frame, is again titled, 'I wanna be Mary'.

Perhaps this has answered my question. Perhaps I should've been delighted to know that I'd play an old bloke in twenty or so years because evidently in my mid-twenties I was already resigned to a life of artistic frustration simply because of my gender.

When the time comes, if I reach an age when I can expect to spend time somewhere like Dribble Hall, I do hope I have wits enough not to be saying, 'I wanna be Mary.' Mary's a dull part. Mary's basically there to give birth to one of the lead guys. Mary is Woman-in-a-Brown-Skirt. I hope, in my dotage, that I'm aiming higher than Mary. I wanna be saying, I dunno, 'I wanna be the Angel Gabriel.' Or I wanna be... !

God?

Now, God's a good part.

Sophie Stanton graduated from RADA in 1991 and has worked extensively in British theatre, television, film and radio ever since. She also sometimes writes and occasionally directs. Her first play *Cariad* was published in 2007. She is currently working on her second play with the generous support of the Arts Council England. Amongst other things.

Theatre
Introduction

Theatres and theatre companies/managements exist in many different forms and paid opportunities for live performance are available in multifarious contexts. The larger companies/managements often use casting directors (see page 110), who should usually be your first port of call, but building a personal relationship direct with venues, companies, producers and artistic directors can be hugely advantageous.

For all approaches, it is important to send your submissions to the person named – unless you have a personal contact.

Listings in this section:
- *Producing theatres, page 160*
- *Independent managements/theatre producers, page 194*
- *Middle- and small-scale companies, page 207*
- *Pantomine producers, page 261*
- *English-language European theatre companies, page 267*
- *Fringe theatres, page 269*
- *Children's, young people's and theatre-in-education companies, page 290*
- *Festivals, page 301*
- *Role-play companies, page 305*

Theatre as community: overcoming barriers for participation

Lee Hall, writer
Interview by Maggie Norris

Lee Hall is a writer who has written extensively for stage and screen. Born and raised in Newcastle upon Tyne, he attended Wallsend Young People's Theatre in his youth, igniting a passion for theatre and writing. Hall worked as a youth theatre fundraiser, before his playwriting career was launched with the broadcast of his writing on BBC Radio 4, including Spoonface Steinberg *(1997). Hall has written over a dozen published plays, including* The Pitmen Painters *(2007) and* Our Ladies of Perpetual Succour *(2015), which won the Laurence Olivier Award for Best New Comedy. He is widely known for having written the screenplay for* Billy Elliot *(2000), which he received an Academy Award nomination for, as well as writing the stage musical adaption of the film, which garnered him further acclaim and awards. Hall's other screenplays include* War Horse *(2011),* Victoria & Abdul *(2017) and* Rocketman *(2019).*

You have supported The Big House from the early days, why is our work of important to you?

I got into theatre because of the Youth Theatre movement, which was an important force in the 1970s and 80s. The idea was theatre and drama were a brilliant way of empowering people: the arts as a participatory thing, not just something you went to see 'experts' do. It was something anyone could take part in and get something out of. It enabled people like myself a) a forum for self-expression and b) a window into the world of the arts which might have otherwise seemed remote and 'not for me'. The Big House always seemed at one with the basic idea that participation in the arts could be transformative for those doing it and revelatory to those watching it because, on both sides of the 'curtain', people were given access to something that they would not have otherwise had.

Most young people at The Big House haven't been to the theatre before. How do we open up the space for wider, more diverse audiences? What needs to change? What are theatres getting wrong?

The politics surrounding representation have dominated the cultural conversation in theatre. Whilst it's obviously an important and perennial discussion, there is a danger that the wider question about the audience for all this gets neglected. The issue often occluded is about class. The predominant reason why theatre excludes the majority of people is that there's a perceived notion that theatre is concerned with middle-class perspectives. Thinking about your audience should be the primary concern of any theatre maker and should certainly be the primary view of the Arts Council. Too much arts policy and thinking is inward looking and we'd all do well to look into the auditorium. My way into theatre-going was by participation, so that's an important path to allowing people in. But I've always been a populist and have enjoyed working in popular forms like the musical which have much less of a problem getting non-theatre goers to attend. Theatres should be part of a community and should be serving that constituency. That's where I'd start.

What moves you to write?
To attempt to make something beautiful.

What's the best piece of advice you ever received about your career?
It's not a race.

Which part of the production process do you most enjoy, from research through to watching the finished work?
Each bit of the process is exquisite pain of one kind or another. The lovely thing is there are so many stages. But I love the rehearsal room because it's actually where you find out what your play is really about. It's so amazing having the thing you dreamt up in your bedroom becoming owned by other people.

The work at The Big House helps young people overcome barriers. This is a recurring theme in your work. What barriers did you have to overcome as a young person?
I had a very gilded childhood. I was blessed by meeting literally scores of people who were doing the kind of participatory work The Big House does. So I learned so much. There was always someone there to open a new door in my imagination. All the real barriers, of course, are internal ones: "Am I good enough?", "Do I know enough?", "Do I dare?". I believe these haunt everyone in one way or another. Obviously, it's harder to answer those questions if you can't see people making positive choices that look like you. But they still pertain wherever you are from. I learned to see all the things I thought were a disadvantage were actually assets. Coming from a northern working-class background, for instance, I foolishly thought was an impediment. It turned out to be my fortune. Use your 'weaknesses', they may be your superpower.

What makes you angry?
Injustice. A bully. Bad acting.

"Teach children the art of friendship" says Alexander McCall Smith (author). What do you wish you had learnt at school that would have helped you in life?
School seems to completely over-value individual attainment. I am an introvert so I find being self-contained relatively easy. But almost everything you do in life, and certainly everything you do in theatre, is about doing it with other people. Drama is about the only place in the school curriculum (off the sports field) where you can learn to make something collectively. To negotiate, support others, build a collective understanding, make something in common. It's what we all have to do every day. So my experience of making shows was vitally important, but I wish there was much more focus about how to argue, how to listen, how to come to consensus, how to make a point and take everyone with you, how to disagree constructively. How to be just. And how to be kind. Things, bizarrely, not yet taught to GCSE level.

Which part of the process of bringing a story to life do you most enjoy?
I think having a good idea is the best bit. The lightbulb moment when you know you've hit on something. It's brilliant and pure at that point. From then on it's always compromised

in one way or another. By your talent, your resources, by other people, by yourself. But there's an enormous pleasure in that moment of inspiration. Like many writers have reported before me, it does feel like it's nothing to do with you. It's like I've just been in the right spot to have 'received' the idea from some place else. The rest is hard work.

Which project has brought you most joy bringing to fruition?

I have been incredibly lucky to have made plays with my friends. Both *Billy Elliot* and my play *The Pitmen Painters* were conceived for, acted in and directed by people who were friends as well as collaborators. I think being amongst people who understood what I was trying to say was an incredible experience. I realise it's very, very unusual. I have loved making many many shows, but these two (which are companion pieces in many ways) were special because I was with people I'd known for years and with several people I'd known long before I actually became a writer. They were both on Broadway at the same time, bizarrely round the corner from each other. It seemed so unlikely that these plays about amateur working-class artists from the North East had made such a big journey. That was a pretty joyous moment.

When has an actor most surprised you in their interpretation of a part that you have written?

Actors constantly surprise me. They almost always find something you had no idea was in there. That's the wonderful thing about theatre – it's a shared enterprise. The meaning is created between people. It doesn't exist on its own. It is the collective act – finally completed by the audience that make it mean something. You don't really know what you've written and it's constantly changing. An actor lives and embodies this thing in a way you can never imagine as you write. They employ a completely different sort of intelligence to your words than you ever could. What's amazing in theatre is that what is obvious to one person is not at all obvious to another. That's why theatre, when it works, is so rich. The act of sharing these perspectives is fundamental to making and watching theatre. Increasingly, I realise theatre is a sort of Empathy Machine – certainly when it's done well.

Do actors make good writers?

Sometimes. Shakespeare. Pinter.

Have you had the career that you wished for?

No, thank God. I guess you set out on the journey with an adolescent perspective on the world, but writing has taken me to places I'd have never imagined when I was a gauche 18 year old. I certainly didn't set out to write screenplays or musicals, but they've given me and others a huge deal of pleasure. I've constantly had to rethink my prejudices about what I was doing. 80% of what I've written hasn't been produced. I've written several musicals, scores of screenplays, plays and other projects that will perhaps never see the light of day. It's a vast amount. So in some ways I have been incredibly unlucky. But, of course, I have written things that people have seen and enjoyed all over the world. I've made a good living and worked with some extraordinary people. A career is neither good nor bad. Many of my most favourite things are things never published in the author's lifetime. You just have to do it. Roll with the punches. Don't worry about the set backs. It's the good moments that matter.

We're in a cost-of-living crisis and for many a career in the creative arts may not seem feasible. What would your advice be?

Can we afford to neglect the arts in order to pay the gas and electric? Obviously marrying well, having an inheritance, or a win on the lottery might seem advantageous, but even a cursory look at the history of the arts will tell you that many of the best and most enduring pieces of writing were produced in penury. Of course, that does not account for the masterpieces that were stifled by circumstances, but the great thing about writing is, compared to almost every other artistic activity, it costs almost nothing to produce. You have to make a distinction in your mind whether you want writing to be how you make your money or whether you just want to do it anyway. There is no shame in being an 'amateur'. A poet who is able to make a living from writing poetry is clearly an exception in the entire history of poetry. Almost every writer has a compulsion to do so and generally they find a way to do it in spite of their circumstances. You're not owed a living just because you fancy calling yourself a writer. Obviously it's easier to find time to do it if your bills are covered, but you still have to have the discipline to do it. My main advice is: stop making excuses and write. Even if you are lucky enough to get something published or produced it's no guarantee that you'll make a living. It will certainly involve heartache, disappointment, self-doubt and possibly public opprobrium. So it's not for the fainthearted.

My best advice is: if you aren't sure you want to write this – don't bother. Otherwise, do it freely with all your imagination, wit, compassion, anger and joy. Stop worrying about the mechanics of life. This is the place you can escape from all that. That's when it will start to mean something to other people.

Maggie Norris is the founder of The Big House **https://thebighouse.uk.com/**.

Rooted in story: a journey from actor to changemaker

Pooja Ghai, Artistic Director, Tamasha
Interview by Aileen Gonsalves

Pooja Ghai is an award-winning director, dramaturg, actor and facilitator, leading transformative change in theatre by amplifying underrepresented voices and championing inclusive leadership. Her work is firmly rooted in anti-racism, social justice, and human rights, driving her commitment to dismantling oppressive structures and reshaping industry narratives.

As Co-Chair of Stage Directors UK and a trustee for Theatre Workshop, Pooja is dedicated to fostering equitable opportunities across the arts. She is also a 2021 Clore Fellow and an Associate Artist for Kali Theatre.

Currently, Pooja is the Artistic Director and Joint Ceo of Tamasha, a pioneering theatre company that challenges conventional narratives by celebrating voices from the Global Majority. Directing credits include: A Tupperware of Ashes *(National Theatre, Dorfman),* Great Expectations *(Royal Exchange Manchester/Tamasha),* The Empress *(RSC),* Lotus Beauty *(Hampstead Theatre/Tamasha),* Hakawatis *and* Lions and Tigers *(Shakespeare's Globe).*

So, Pooja, great to talk to you. While I don't know every detail of what you've been doing the last few years, I know you started out as an actor. I don't know if you still act, but you're now the artistic director of Tamasha Theatre company, and that journey – that evolution – is fascinating to me. I'm really interested in how you made that transition.

It's so interesting to think about that question now – especially now. I'm turning 50 this year, and when I look back, I realise I fell in love with storytelling when I was just 11. That's when I did my first play. I was in boarding school in Kenya. It was a musical – *Tom Sawyer* – and I played Aunt Polly. I've still got photos of it, which is probably why it's so lodged in my memory.

Being in Kenya, which was a British colony until 1963, meant there was this incredible mix of cultures – a huge expat and international community, a hybrid of lived experiences, social classes, and backgrounds all side by side. Underneath that was a strong, rooted, indigenous Kenyan culture – vibrant and beautiful. I'm deeply proud I was born there. Kenya shaped me – my values, imagination. The Kenyan philosophy is so much about collaboration, creativity, generosity, respect – values central to everything I do now as an artist and a leader.

I was born in Kenya too. It's lovely to hear you talk about it like that!

Ahhh! There really is something magical about that place – the landscape, the wildlife. In Kenya, nature dominates. You have to live with it. There's a humility that comes with that. I think that instinct – of coexistence, navigating layered realities – has fed my artistic instincts. I left Kenya at 14. But I knew even then that I wanted to keep telling stories. I didn't know you could make a career of it – not conventionally. I just knew it made me feel most alive.

How easy or difficult was it to get into performing in England?

My family didn't support the arts. They discouraged it. They weren't engaged either. They didn't understand it. So I had to find my way on my own. At school, I did LAMDA exams. Then I went to Oxford Brookes – not because I was passionate about psychology and sociology, but because it felt accessible. While there, I set up a drama society. We went to Edinburgh every year with student-led productions. I directed, produced, acted – everything. No rules, no mentorship. Just fire in the belly and a gang of students doing it. That was invaluable. It was scrappy and joyful and experimental – and taught me resilience. I didn't know it then, but I was already developing my directing voice.

When did the professional acting career begin?

Around 1999 or 2000. Tamasha had just been founded. Tara Arts was strong. *Goodness Gracious Me* was on TV. There was this flurry of "brownness" in the cultural landscape – they called it the "brown pound." Bollywood was exciting, and South Asian stories were just starting to be accepted – though often in reductive ways. I had an okay acting career. I worked consistently – but as a curvaceous brown woman, I was never the "leading lady." At 22, I was already cast as 65-year-old aunties. Very little room for complexity or range.

Right, yeah, I remember those days!

But I loved story. I loved rehearsal. I was always thinking about the bigger picture.

Like a director?

Exactly. I didn't realise it at first, but that was the director in me – making sense of the whole thing, not just my part. It clicked when I acted in Tanika Gupta's adaptation of *Great Expectations* in 2011. I realised I was more obsessed with the structure of the story than with my character. Tanika saw it and said, "For God's sake, would you just direct?" So I did. I gave it a try.

And what did that try look like? How did you step into that space?

I started directing readings. Exploring new writing. I was drawn to what was missing – in the work and in the sector. The lack of opportunity for many artists – I wanted to create space for the stories I wasn't seeing. I was deeply aware of systemic issues – the erasure, the gatekeeping. I realised we need real pathways. Enough confidence, bounce, artistic voice – a critical mass of artists – so when we enter spaces with our white peers, we normalise ourselves. People say it should all be about meritocracy. But that leads back to the same structures that excluded us. I need to change that – through the company I run and the artists I support.

You talk now about being a leader, and that evolution is huge – from actor to director to artistic director. That's where multidisciplinary people really matter. It's a new kind of leadership. And what you're doing – you're describing a new system. Black Lives Matter cracked something open. But now we need to build something better. And no one quite knows how.

I don't know either. But I know we have to try. That's what we're doing at Tamasha – that's our value system. Realigning our thinking to be so artist-centered that we get the best work and find the best business model to support it. And we have to stay rooted in integrity. I can't make art that doesn't feel truthful. I've never taken a job I couldn't connect to – and I won't start now. It's always been about the story.

Why do you love stories so much?
They're transformative. When a story is good – when it touches your heart – that catharsis can shift how you see something in your life. Stories have always existed. They've never left us. Even in the most devastated places – like Gaza, like Haiti – stories survive. They're resistance. They're life. For me – they're why I live. I don't want to do anything else.

It's been quite a journey so far.
I never knew I'd be a director or artistic director. Or that I'd have such a huge political passion for equality. But that's what I now realise. My leadership is about making art with integrity, in the space I can. I don't know how – its a challenge to fund that way of working because there's not much money. It's a challenge, but there's got to be a way.

How do you keep hope alive?
I don't know: I believe, I trust. It has never been as hard as it is right now. I think it's always been easier for me to hold onto hope – because I've always believed in the power of theatre. Despite the systemic racism of our sector, I always felt like it's something I wanted to do. Because stories still matter. Because artists still matter. Art and stories are political and I believe they can bring people together and make the world a better place. Now more than ever, that focus, intent and integrity is vital and stories should be part of the national debate reflecting our societies back at us for us to gain in depth understanding and critical thinking ...

You're doing new things at Tamasha, all the time, right?
Yes – we just piloted the Creative Wellbeing Lab. It's about giving artists – especially artists of colour – tools to integrate wellbeing into their work. We wanted something that reflected their nuanced experiences – shaped by trauma, migration, colonial legacies, identity.

We are developing Tamasha Tales, a co-creation project bringing artists with multidisciplinary skills together to respond to a brief around myths and folklore from the Global south. Theatre, spoken word, dance, music. Whatever form – we said: your story matters. We paid people and that mattered too. And like with SHIFT, it's a program all about decolonizing dramaturgy.

Right, that's really important.
The reason SHIFT came about was the Eurocentric lens in governance, programming and leadership. When artists get into commissioning, it's fine – until production. Then the characters get moulded, the story shifts. "Oh, it won't suit our audience." "Could you make it that?" You're not holding space for global perspectives. So the form gets lost – it's restructured into what we think will sell. SHIFT is a way for us to take a forensic look at our processes with artists to ensure we are creating the best environment for them to flourish.

It sounds like you're working every day with new ideas, new forms, and helping people discover how to tell their stories – even when they, or you, don't quite know what that looks like yet.
We're exploring how to foster bold imagination, radical thinking, and love – in a space where artists can tell the stories they want to tell.

Aileen Gonsalves is a theatre director, actor, writer, and creator of the Gonsalves Method – a pioneering approach to actor training taught in drama schools and universities in many countries.

Active listening in a community of nomads

Cherrelle Skeete, co-founder and Artistic Director of Blacktress UK
Interview by Joan Iyiola

Cherrelle Skeete is an actress, writer, cultural curator and consultant. She is co-founder and Artistic Director of Blacktress UK, a network and support group for Black womxn actors and creatives providing a platform to grow and connect through community. Cherrelle works across theatre, television and film and was on the 2019/2020 Soho Theatre Writers Lab. Cherrelle believes storytelling is a necessary tool to activate understanding, build bridges and heal ourselves so we can all move towards our own freedom.

How have you used community practices in your work as an artist?
I think community is the ultimate dialogue, a dialogue of active listening in the hope that no one gets left behind. I have to mention 'community' because no person is an island and I didn't just turn up here. It took a group of people to make various decisions and who said different things to support me and remind me who I am. To me, community is liberation, strength, a place to really learn. I've found a lot of solace in different communities. Your community is your chosen family, it's the place where you learnt your craft at different points. It might be the place where you learnt that you were actually good at something or where you felt seen for the first time when other parts of society weren't seeing you. It's a space that's about everybody who's responsible for taking care of it, a space that's cultivated, with a sense of community, similarities based on what that community is setting out to do. There'll be a certain demographic within that community, with similar cultural interests. I think it's something we as artists do. We're always looking for our tribe. When you're auditioning for something, you're looking for your tribe. Everyone involved is involved in a sense of community, it's everywhere.

Off the back of that, can you give us an overview about Blacktress, your reasons for setting it up and the work that you have created with this wonderful group?
Blacktress has been going for eight years. I'm a co-founder and I run it alongside my partner, Shiloh Coke. It's a network, support group, and we're curators. The work is Black women and femme-centered. We do Spark workshops, we ran a festival of Black women-led work early in its formation called the Blacktress Season. We've curated specific events, which again are Black-women-centred, but they're open to all. We have socials where we're celebrating women who may not necessarily be recognised within the mainstream and we'll see them first and celebrate them. This was a space cultivated out of many conversations I'd heard, women saying they felt alone, isolated, didn't feel seen or heard. So, we create a safe space which is often about healing. I believe those who've suffered most deserve the greatest victories and I think we're so victorious. Yes, I'm the founder but I'm not the sole custodian of that space. Every single person holds everybody's story, everybody's physical and spiritual being's space with a sense of care and thoughtfulness, consideration, compassion, curiosity and the ability to just listen.

What might you want to say to the graduating actors and performers of this year about the importance of this act of self-care?

Firstly, it's really important to spend some time on your own to get to know who you are – who you are without the noise, the industry stuff. Just strip back and learn so you can identify when you're feeling low and also identify what you need to get back to a place where you feel balance. Because the word self-care has been thrown around a lot, it's become this almost overused buzzword. I think what I'm going to start using is 'balance'. To get back to a place of balance. The first thing I say to graduates is find your tribe, you were put together with other people within your year group by circumstance. They may be your tribe, but you may also need to reconnect with yourself and find your people. Speak about your experiences, they're valid. Use the internet and reach out to people. We're all in it together, literally. There's no wrong way of doing it, they're all just experiences. Affirm your experiences for yourself by writing them out. I encourage everyone to journal, but if you don't like to write, maybe scrapbook. Do it for yourself first and then everything else will come from that in terms of connecting with people and you'll attract the right people who might be your future collaborators. That's the whole point: you want to be making art with people who respect you, respect the dignity of life, and you can be on the same page in terms of how you want to make art.

We're seeing a lot of anti-racism pledges from theatres and companies. What does leadership in this space look like to you?

If you look at your team of people who you work with and the building that you might work in and you see that there are opportunities being opened up, maybe think about what you would usually do and then challenge yourself to do something slightly different. Bring in someone who wouldn't necessarily be within that environment that you've created. If you're actively wanting change, as an artist, a venue, an organisation, then bring in people to do that. I think what we're asking for, is actually human kindness and it's not passive. It's a loving action. Create that space, even give up space. A lot of what we're doing is about the dismantling of the powers that be, speaking truth to power, which is not always easy.

In order for us to sit in this space where we can all sit together, it's 'I do something for you, you do something for me' and we're constantly going, making offerings of kindness in the space to find out what our collaborative power is.

The relationship is reciprocal. That's why I said community is for me the biggest dialogue, not one-sided. When you have community leaders, the pyramid is upside down and you as the leader are at the bottom. Because you're answering to people at the top and that's your community and it's actually about being of service. I want to create more spaces where we're doing more reimagining, talking about what we need, what are the active measures that we need to do. Do we need to ringfence tickets to make sure that we've got audience members? We can't be using the same tactics as before. We've got to up our game. If that wasn't working, let's try something else. We're very fortunate in the arts to lead on that because we are the people literally creating with our tools, our hands, our talent, the people that we come across. So, every kind of process that we're going into with our storytelling, you literally get to reset and restart again how you want this ship to run.

I think that's amazing. You know, in theatre you build this incredible relationship with people over the course of five months and then that's it! Then you start again with these nomadic people, but I think there's something so beautiful about that.

That's beautiful, our imagination is our superpower.

I think the most powerful thing that we have as a people, as Black people, as human beings, as creatives, whoever you are, is our imagination. In terms of culture, culture is a collection of concepts. There has to be a dialogue, we can't just have one concept all the time. The exchange has to be happening back and forth constantly and the concept grows, then we all agree and eventually that becomes a culture. There's a repetition of concepts that everybody agrees on. So, if we're saying that we want to keep reimagining, we've got to keep talking to each other, listening – actively listening – and, from that, take action.

You incorporate activism in your artistry. How would you encourage others to do the same?

Everyone is responsible for their own activism but, firstly, it's to be active. It's a movement of love, corny as that sounds. We're actually wanting to say, can we stop hurting each other, live peacefully, be kind, make space for those we're pushing out. When the theatres closed during the Covid lockdowns, obviously it was very sad, but we have to think about what happened to all of us, how these spaces function and if they're functioning in a way that's serving us as people. Let's re-evaluate our core values and what we need. Remember, those spaces belong to the people. Our taxes fund those buildings so we have to hold them accountable. Let's start with self, what do I need? What can I do to achieve the things I need to get me balanced? What spaces and environments for the people of certain communities they're meant to be serving are going to give them balance? Does the environment we're creating and cultivating support that? Re-evaluating and reconnecting, these are brilliant places to begin. This period has to be about us opening these spaces in a way that introduces different things, making these spaces more accessible for everybody. To serve the community, serve spaces where dialogues can be had and that requires everybody, everybody speaking and knowing what they need.

For more information about Blacktress go to www.blacktress.co.uk or follow them on Instagram @blacktress_uk. Follow Cherrelle directly at www.cherrelleskeete.com or @cherrelleskeete on Instagram.

An actor's advice: navigating your way through the industry

Naomi Ackie, actress and producer
Interview by Maggie Norris and Nkechi Simms

Naomi Ackie is an actor and producer. Born and raised in London, she trained at the Royal Central School of Speech and Drama. Ackie began her career acting for the stage, before a breakthrough film role in Lady Macbeth *(2016) brought her wider attention and acclaim, including the British Independent Film Award for Most Promising Newcomer. Her further work in film includes* Yardie *(2018),* Star Wars: The Rise of Skywalker *(2019), a widely praised portrayal of singer Whitney Houston in the biopic* I Wanna Dance with Somebody *(2022) and* Mickey 17 *(2025). Her television credits include* Small Axe *(2020),* Master of None *(2021) and* The End of the F***ing World *(2019), for which she received the British Academy Television Award for Best Supporting Actress.*

Nkechi Simms: What inspired you to pursue acting? And who or what resources did you look to at the start of your career?
I'm actually not quite sure what inspired me to start acting – it was really a gut feeling that I followed when I was a child. I loved making up stories and playing and I guess when I found out it was a job you could have, it seemed too good to be true! In terms of resources I'm lucky enough to be born in London surrounded by amazing theatre so that's where I started. I went to Saturday school, a place where you sang, acted and danced and then, as I grew up, I just kept seeking out places where I could play and keep practising.

NS: How have you built resilience on your journey? Particularly when dealing with rejection?
Rejection is always hard I guess; with this profession, you get exposure therapy as part of the deal. A big thing for me was learning, through talking to the wiser people in my life, that a rejection should not and does not affect my worth. I am worthy with or without this project or that job. That doesn't always ring true, but I think you get told "no" enough times and the world doesn't end, you begin to realise this is only a small part of a much bigger part of your life. We can't run away from rejection. Even if we weren't actors. So why not embrace it and learn from it and, sometimes, when they say "no" for a stupid reason, call them stupid in your head and keep moving forward.

NS: How do you keep yourself creative when not working?
Good question. Still working on this. I started writing during Covid and that was a thing that fuelled me for a long while. But now I'm trying to find creative outlets that have nothing to do with my job. I recently got out my mum's old sewing machines so I'm gonna have a go at upcycling ... Also need to book my pottery classes!

NS: Which skills have you had to develop in order to achieve success?
I've had to develop business skills. I didn't realise coming into this job that you are running a business and that business is your body and mind. Which means you have to switch

between looking after yourself (your energy, your mental health) and engaging in the fact that your talent is a commodity that can and should help you create the life for yourself that you want. It's sometimes hard to separate the two ... I find it difficult most of the time. The acting stuff comes with practice and confidence, but the business skills and learning when to say "yes", "no" or "not yet", is something you have to nurture.

NS: Is there anything that you wish you had known before coming in to the industry?
I wish I had known that there is nothing wrong with loosening up. Being slightly less strict with myself. I wish I had known the stakes aren't so high. I wish I had worried less. But maybe that's something we all do when we're young. The industry is fickle and can change on a dime. And existing as yourself within it can come at a cost. I wish I had known how to protect myself from that better. But, ah well, you live and you learn!

Maggie Norris: What influences your decision-making when considering taking on a role?
Hmmmm. I really don't know. I just wanna feel something. I wanna be able to visualize myself or a version of myself not yet thought up that can exist in that story. I wanna feel like I have something to offer. Also, something that scares me! That's always important.

MN: Your mum gave you very practical advice about a potential acting career and told you to learn your craft well. That is such great advice. Watching a documentary about Marilyn Monroe recently I was struck by how well she knew her craft and how she created her own opportunities within the industry. Have there been times when you have had to create your own opportunities? And is that something you want to do more of in the future?
Yeah, she was a very wise woman. I do. I definitely do. When I'm in a rest mode, I wait for inspiration to approach me. My mum also used to say you have to live life to inform your art so that's what I do. In the future, I hope I can find further opportunities for myself that add to the conversation!

MN: Having watched you be interviewed and having seen your work, you have a strong sense of playfulness. How do you retain that quality when you're working under pressure?
I think that's when you have to hold onto your sense of play more. I truly believe it's about relaxing into the atmosphere. Everything around us feeds into what we need in that moment. Yeah, it can be stressful sometimes, but my goodness when pressure is applied that's when diamonds are made. Lean in to it. Laugh with it. And get it done!

MN: Some people think that social media is crucial to success these days, but I gather that you are not active. How has that decision affected your career?
I actually have gone back on. Hahaha. I realized that it's important to share your work from your perspective. I'm still not great at it though. I'm not a great picture-taker day to day and, as my life is beautifully simple, sometimes I get self-conscious that the things I would share aren't that interesting!

MN: You have said that playing Whitney Houston in *I Wanna Dance With Somebody* involved a huge amount of preparation and was very much a team effort. The results were incredible. I am not going to ask you about that process, as that has already been well documented, but I would be interested to know if you would be prepared to go through that process again. And if so, who you would be interested to portray?

Oh, thank you so much. I think the further away I get from that project the more I think I would like to try it again. I'm not sure who for though! Time will tell, but I'm definitely open to finding real-life people to portray; the process was so enriching and taught me so much about myself. I would love to experience that again in a different mind space.

MN: You have achieved so much in your career in the first ten years. Do you have a sense of what you'd like to achieve over the next ten years?

Ah man, thank you. In the next ten? I have no idea! My goals have changed and I'm in a space of not knowing and being really cool with it. I know I want to keep acting.... maybe, finish these stories that have been in my head for years ... and ultimately, I would love to direct, but all in good time. I'm not in a rush like I was in my twenties.

Maggie Norris is the founder of The Big House https://thebighouse.uk.com/.

Nkechi Simms is an actor who trained with The Big House and has appeared on screen as a lead role in *PRU* (BBC), *Top Boy* (Netflix) and *Tell No Lies*.

Success and not getting sacked

Paterson Joseph, actor and writer
Interview by Sam Stevenson

Paterson Joseph is an actor and writer. He has performed extensively on British and American stages and has more recently been seen on television in Vigil, Noughts and Crosses, Peep Show, Timeless *and* The Leftovers. *He played Samuel Wells in the BBC thriller* Boat Story *and Arthur Slugworth in the* Wonka *movie. Writing includes* Sancho – An Act of Remembrance, Julius Caesar and Me: Exploring Shakespeare's African Play *and his debut novel,* The Secret Diaries of Charles Ignatius Sancho.

You've been a successful actor for more than 30 years and the breadth of your work is impressive: Inside No. 9, Vigil, **Horatio in** Hamlet, **to name just a few of the varied projects that you've been involved with. When you left drama school, was this the career that you planned or wished for, in as much as anyone can plan or wish for anything?**

Well, no, I didn't have any plans. I think if there was anything in my head, it was the purity of just trying to do good work with good people. That was it. That was my mantra. I wasn't interested in television or film. I was of that generation who, in the main, didn't think of themselves as anything other than theatre actors. And we'd be lucky to get that. We were quite a practical, grounded generation, I suppose. A sort of exchange between British and American actors has always existed, but Ralph Fiennes, for example, and that generation, seemed to me to really cement that bridge across the Atlantic.

Given the level of your success, I was surprised to read in a Guardian **Q&A in 2020 that you always fear you're about to be sacked. I can relate, by the way. And I wonder if many people working in show business feel the same. Because impostor syndrome and the fear of being found out seem to be rife.**

We all have it. Life's a confidence trick and even those who look confident, most of the time they're like us, they're not. You would think that being sacked is unlikely if you have a strong body of work behind you, but the feeling is still there. When I finish a job people ask, "Are you sad to finish?" No, I'm always happy to have got to the end without being sacked! Coming back from a radio recording once, I shared a taxi with the late, great Sir Antony Sher and he asked me where I was going. I told him that I was on my way to the National Theatre for the last performance of the show I was doing. "Are you sad to be leaving?" he asked. "No" I said, "I'm just happy I didn't get sacked. I know that probably sounds stupid to you?". And he said, "No, I know some very great actors who actually think exactly the same thing."

"Imposter syndrome" wasn't a phrase we would have used until recently but, yeah, that's exactly what it is. And, actually, I embrace the possibility: it keeps you sharp – I'm not sitting back on my laurels thinking that I'm amazing and that this is all going to be great. I always think, *I'd better get this right.*

Though, God, what an advantage not to have it! Sometimes when I leave an audition, I'm embarrassed by myself. Especially if it's for a job you really want to get, or a role you think you'd be good at, or maybe it has the potential to advance your career. It's frustrating when you rehearse the material at home and you know that you're doing good work and then you walk into the audition and something in you is too hungry. A tension starts to build that distracts you from the thing that you executed so well in your bedroom and now you're seeing the person behind the desk scratching their nose; they were smiling and now they're not, or they're looking away and somebody else is looking at their notebook. You just get thrown and you come out of yourself and into the room and your third eye activates and you're watching yourself and maybe you start perspiring a little. The worst thing is when a casting director very kindly says, *just take your time.* You think, *no, you've seen it, you've seen me!*

Once when that happened mid-audition, I made a decision to take a breath and go, *okay, you are being over-zealous and over-keen to get this job.* And I gave myself permission to come back to myself and I thought, *let me just give what I think is right. I'm offering this. If you don't like it, you don't like it, that's your taste, that's fine.* I got the role and it was one of the best jobs I've ever done, and I was the freest on camera that I've ever been.

Just offer up what you think is the right thing. Find yourself in that place. If they don't like it, there's nothing you can do about it. Bring your skill, bring your gift, bring what you created. And don't second-guess what the people in the room are thinking. Sometimes somebody's got indigestion or they're thinking about their mother who's just been taken into hospital. Sometimes they love you but have to consider whether you'll fit with the other actors that they've cast. You need to enter in a kind of cocoon of *I'm bringing you my art and I'm presenting it to you. Take it or leave it.* Not in any arrogant way, but just accepting who you are. And that would allow you, I think, to be malleable when they ask you to do it another way.

I subscribe to everything you just said because, for all of us, auditions are our job, and we all have to meet in the middle. Casting directors bring in the actors who they think are right for the part; the actor comes into the room with their offering; and the director is there, I hope, being open hearted and open minded.

It's helpful to be aware that directors and casting directors very much want the actor to succeed. If everybody came in knowing that we'd all be happy.

And then there are self-tapes, which don't give you the opportunity to meet face-to-face. How can a director tell whether they can work with somebody when they've only seen their tape? There's something about meeting in a room that enables a director to say, "I see what you've just done. Could you try this?" It's the immediacy of that way of working – I just think that there's nothing to beat it.

I worked on a gorgeous indie film last year, and every single part was cast either by self-tape or Zoom, which was a first for me. Tapes and Zooms have their uses, but I love my job when I'm in the room working with an actor and a director. Sitting at my desk, watching tapes is not the same thing. I heard one casting director express worry that this new culture of zooming and self-taping will make the casting director's job obsolete because anyone can ask for 100 self-tapes, watch thirty seconds of each and then bin them. But I think that we're needed now more than ever, because when the director says that they're not sure about actor x, it's our job to say, *I know that the tape wasn't perfect, but they were great in this production* or *I saw them at drama school and they're really promising – why don't we give them another go?*

I got a role in the pilot of a big American show that, in the end, didn't go to series. I had auditioned several times via self-tape and, over the course of the audition process, which went on for six months, they changed director four times. First, I played the role like it was a comedy because that's how it was written. Then they wanted something a bit more grounded, then with another change of director they wanted more darkness, but also with some wit. Eventually we had a chemistry read with a few other really lovely actors and being in the room with people worked in a way that can't be achieved when you're acting in isolation.

What do you think about memorising dialogue for an audition? I always feel that with theatre I don't want actors to be off-book, just familiar with the text. When I started casting, actors didn't have to memorise the dialogue, even for screen auditions. That's changed. I would rather an actor worked on the material than memorise the text and I think those are two very different things.
I'm really glad to hear you say that, but I'm wary because the director or producer may want it learned, and if I don't learn it, I'll be 'reading' it rather than acting with the reader.

That's a fair enough comment because, even though it's my preference, I may be working with producers and directors who wouldn't agree with that.
If I don't get a job after auditioning it can be for myriad reasons, but one of them is never going to be, well, *I didn't see his eyes* or *I couldn't read his interpretation because his gaze was down.* I'm never going to give you that out, do you know what I mean? So I will learn it out of sheer safety because otherwise I'm not confident about how it will be received.

When you left drama school, did you feel ready for the business?
I look at myself in 1988 when I graduated and my first audition probably would have for been for TV – it was for a children's serial called *Streetwise*, about bicycle couriers. And I remember thinking *why is the director getting a camera out?* I didn't know what to do. I didn't know anything about that machine and, when I got the job, I didn't know anything about standing on your spot. That felt weird to me. What do you mean, *don't stand there, that's not where your light is?* I didn't understand anything that was going on and, because I was so shy, I never asked, so I kind of learned it along the way. I was always very polite; just stood where people told me to and said what I had to say.

The cast were all quite young (Andy Serkis was in it) and I didn't know what I was conveying. I'm quite a smiler, but when a friend of my dad watched it and said, "But you're not smiling at all. Boy, that character, the man you play, you don't smile at all!" I realised that I'd been sort of crunching down because people tell you not to do too much on screen. There must have been a part of me that had just kind of peeled everything away; every bit of personality died.

And I still see that sometimes because the orthodoxy is that you don't have to do anything and it's such a lie. I mean, if you've got a face that can launch a thousand ships, then sure, maybe you can get away with being a blank canvas. But most of us need to have something going on.

What advice would you give to your younger self?
Be confident. You're good. Be confident. That's it really. And you wouldn't have got where you were if you weren't good at what you do. Just be confident in that. I was way too timid about my skills. I can write. So write! I can direct. So direct! Just do the things that you love doing. You're good at them. Be confident.

Producing theatres

Included in this section are the national and regional building-based companies that mount their own productions, co-produce with others, send shows out on tour and present touring productions. The majority are subsidised by the national Arts Councils in their respective countries but some operate independently or commercially. Most use standard Equity, UK Theatre, ITC (Independent Theatre Council) or SOLT (Society Of London Theatres) agreements and contracts.

In addition to these listings, check each theatre's website and social media for the latest news on their programming and activity. If you are approaching them, make sure you know the kind of work they produce and the core audience they cater for. They will all receive hundreds of generic 'please cast me' emails from actors so a bit of thought, care and specificity will make you stand out. Thoroughly check – and adhere – to each theatre's specific casting procedure.

Working in subsidised theatre will not make you rich but it can be exhilarating, rewarding and memorable. Theatres often have storied histories and incredible ties to their communities. Travelling to perform offers you an opportunity to live and work in a new place, amidst new colleagues, and play different stages and to different audiences. For many, working in subsidised theatre is the epitome of the acting profession.

Abbey Theatre Amharclann na Mainistreach
26–27 Lower Abbey Street, Dublin 1 DO1 K0F1, Republic of Ireland
tel +353 (0)1 887 2200
email info@abbeytheatre.ie
website www.abbeytheatre.ie
Facebook /abbeytheatredublin
X @AbbeyTheatre
Instagram @abbeytheatredublin
Artistic Director Caitriona McLaughlin, *Executive Director* Mark O'Brien, *Casting Director* Barry Coyle

Production details: The Abbey Theatre produces an ambitious annual prgramme of Irish and international theatre across its two stages and on tour in Ireland and internationally. The Abbey Theatre is committed to building the Irish theatre repertoire, through commissioning and producing new Irish writing, and re-imagining national and international classics in collaboration with leading contemporary talent.

Casting procedures: The Abbey Theatre is the only theatre in Ireland with a full time in-house casting department dedicated to seeking out new and emerging talent, as well as keeping abreast of the continued work and development of previously established actors from all over the country and abroad. The Abbey Theatre holds open auditions periodically throughout the year. The casting department attends performances throughout the year, nationally and internationally, as well as drama school showcases in Dublin and London.

Almeida Theatre
Almeida Street, London N1 1TA
tel 020-7359 4404
email info@almeida.co.uk
website https://almeida.co.uk
Outgoing Artistic Director Rupert Goold, *Incoming Artistic Director* Dominic Cooke

Production details: A small room with an international reputation. The Almeida makes brave new work that asks big questions of plays, of theatre and of the world around us. It brings together the most exciting artists to take risks; to provoke, inspire and surprise audiences; to interrogate the present, dig up the past and imagine the future. Stages approximately 6 productions each year.

Casting procedures: Productions are cast by external freelance casting directors on a project-by-project basis. Uses the UK Theatre/Equity Subsidised Rep contract and subscribes to the Equity Pension Scheme. Actively promotes the use of inclusive casting.

Alphabetti Theatre
St James Blvd, Newcastle-upon-Tyne NE1 4HP
tel 0191 261 9125
email admin@alphabettitheatre.co.uk
website www.alphabettitheatre.co.uk
Facebook /AlphabettiTheatre
Instagram @Alphabetti_theatre
Executive Director Ed Cole

Established in 2012, Alphabetti Theatre is based in Newcastle upon Tyne and incorporates two performance spaces, both of which seat 80 people. The first is a theatre space with raised audiences on three sides, and the second is a music and cabaret stage within a bar. They believe great art should be for everyone not just those who can afford it. They create, produce and programme new, original work from emerging artists across the performing arts, championing work in music, theatre, comedy and poetry. They create opportunities for both artists and audiences to experiment, evolve and discover; providing space for theatre companies, writers, directors, poets, comedians and musicians. Email for details.

Arcola Theatre
24 Ashwin Street, London E8 3DL
tel 020-7503 1645
email production@arcolatheatre.com
website www.arcolatheatre.com
Artistic Director Mehmet Ergen

Production details: Founded in 2000 by Mehmet Ergen and Leyla Nazli, Arcola Theatre is now one of the most respected arts venues in the UK. Housed in a converted factory in Hackney, Arcola produces daring, high-quality theatre in the heart of East London and beyond. They commission and premiere exciting, original works alongside rare gems of world drama and bold new productions of classics. Their socially engaged, international programme champions diversity, challenges the status quo, and attracts over 65,000 people to their building each year.

The theatre has 2 studio theatres and 4 other spaces suitable for rehearsals and other events. Every year it offer 26 weeks of free rehearsal space to culturally diverse and refugee artists; Grimeborn Festival opens up opera with contemporary stagings at affordable prices; and the Participation department creates over 13,500 creative opportunities for the people of Hackney and beyond. Their pioneering environmental initiatives are award-winning and aim to make Arcola the world's first carbon-neutral theatre.

Yvonne Arnaud Theatre
Millbrook, Guildford, Surrey GU1 3UX
tel (01483) 440000
website www.yvonne-arnaud.co.uk
Facebook /YvonneArnaudTheatre
Instagram @yvonnearnaud
Theatre Director and Chief Executive Joanna Read

Production details: The Yvonne Arnaud Theatre is a busy producing and presenting house, creating shows in Guildford and touring nationally. On both the main stage and in the Mill Studio an eclectic mix of classical and contemporary work by new, lesser-known and established writers is staged.

The Creative Learning department offers an exciting mix of activities for young people and adults all year round. The Yvonne Arnaud opened the 80-seat Mill Studio in 1993, to provide a venue for work that would not otherwise be seen in Guildford, championing unheard voices and diverse storytelling.

Barbican
Barbican Centre, Silk Street, London EC2Y 8DS
tel 020-7638 4141
email theatre@barbican.org.uk
website www.barbican.org.uk
Facebook /BarbicanCentre
X @BarbicanCentre
Instagram @BarbicanCentre

The Barbican showcases international theatre, dance, musicals and performance by leading companies, auteurs and emerging artists that challenge the idea of what theatre can be. It invests in the artists of today and tomorrow through the commissioning of new work, showcasing emerging talent and collaborating with their Artistic Associates, Boy Blue.

Belgrade Theatre
Belgrade Square, Coventry CV1 1GS
tel 024-7625 6431
email admin@belgrade.co.uk
website www.belgrade.co.uk
Facebook /BelgradeTheatreCoventry
X @BelgradeTheatre
Instagram @belgradetheatre
Ceo Laura Elliot, *Artistic Director* Corey Campbell

Production details: Produces a wide range of large and small scale productions.

Birmingham Repertory Theatre
6 Centenary Square, Birmingham B1 2EP
tel 0121 236 4455
website www.birmingham-rep.co.uk
Facebook /BirminghamRep
X @BirminghamRep
Instagram @TheRepBirmingham
Artistic Director Joe Murphy, *Deputy Artistic Director* Madeleine Kludje, *Associate Director* Iqbal Khan

Production details: Birmingham Rep is the only producing theatre in the UK's Second City and the oldest building-based theatre company in the UK. It has an unparalleled pioneering history and has been at the forefront of theatre in the UK for over 100 years. Its mission is to create artistically ambitious, popular history for, by and with the people of Birmingham and the wider world.

Over the last 15 years The Rep has produced more than 130 new plays as well as presenting over 60 productions on its three stages (the House, Studio and Door) every year; many of its productions have toured nationally and internationally. Its learning and outreach programme is one of the largest and most diverse in the UK and continues today with a youth theatre and the Rep Foundry programme.

Casting procedures: "The play's director, a casting director and sometimes a producer handle casting for all Main House and Studio productions. We currently make use of freelance casting directors, specific to each production, administered by the producers."

Birmingham Stage Company (BSC)
Suite 228, 162 Regent Street, London W1B 5TB
tel 020-7437 3391
email office@birminghamstage.com
website www.birminghamstage.com
Facebook /birminghamstage
X @birminghamstage
Actor & Manager Neal Foster

Production details: Founded in 1992, the BSC stages 5 shows each year, 4 of which tour nationally. Produces a range of plays with particular emphasis on its family shows, which visits 60 venues around the UK.

Casting procedures: Uses freelance casting directors and sometimes holds general auditions. Casting breakdowns are published on the website. "Do as much research as you can before submitting." Actively encourages applications from disabled actors.

Bridge Theatre
3 Potters Field Park, London SE1 2SG
tel 0333 320 0052
email info@bridgetheatre.co.uk
website https://bridgetheatre.co.uk
Facebook /bridgetheatrelondon
Instagram @_bridgetheatre
Artistic Directors Nicholas Hytner and Nick Starr

Production details: Founded by Nicholas Hytner and Nick Starr in 2017, the Bridge is the first theatre run by London Theatre Company. Commissions and produces new shows, as well as occasionally staging classics. Actors who have appeared on the stage include Maggie Smith, Ben Whishaw, Laura Linney, Ralph Fiennes and Jonathon Bailey. The 900-seat adaptable auditorium is designed to answer the needs of contemporary audiences and theatre-makers and respond to shows with different formats (end-stage, thrust stage and promenade). It is the first wholly new theatre of scale to be added to London's commercial sector in 80 years and draws local and international visitors.

Bristol Old Vic
King Street, Bristol BS1 4ED
tel 0117 949 3993
website https://bristololdvic.org.uk
Artistic Director Nancy Medina

Production details: Bristol Old Vic is a theatre company founded in 1946 and based in a complex which includes the unique Theatre Royal, opened in 1766 – the oldest theatre auditorium in the UK, which many think the most beautiful. Bristol Old Vic is also unique in its close working relationship with the Bristol Old Vic Theatre School. See website for more details on submission windows and related requirements.

Bush Theatre
7 Uxbridge Road, London W12 8LJ
tel 020-8743 3584
email info@bushtheatre.co.uk
website www.bushtheatre.co.uk
Facebook /bushtheatre
X @bushtheatre
Artistic Director Designate Taio Lawson, *Interim Executive Director* Angela Wachner

Production details: Founded in 1972, the Bush specialises in developing and producing new writing from the widest range of perspectives. Stages 10 productions a year, totalling around 289 performances. Also tours productions, although the bulk of performances are at the Bush itself. Up to 8 actors are employed on each production, and the company offers TMA/Equity approved contracts.

Casting procedures: Employs freelance casting directors and does not hold general meetings or issue public casting breakdowns. Welcomes letters and emails from actors previously unknown to the company. Does not welcome showreels or invitations to view actors' websites. Actively encourages applications from disabled actors and promotes the use of inclusive casting.

Chichester Festival Theatre
Oaklands Park, Chichester PO19 6AP
website www.cft.org.uk
Facebook /chichesterfestivaltheatre
Instagram @ChichesterFT
Artistic Director Justin Audibert, *Executive Director* Kathy Bourne

Production details: Chichester Festival Theatre is one of the UK's flagship theatres, renowned for the exceptionally high standard of its productions as well as its work with the community and young people. The Festival Theatre seats 1,300, the bold thrust stage design making it equally suited to epic drama and musicals; the Minerva Theatre seats 300 and is noted for premieres of new work alongside intimate revivals; and a new 110-seat venue, The Nest, is a vibrant space for dynamic work and the talent of tomorrow. The annual Festival season runs from April to October, during which productions originated at Chichester reach an audience of over 230,000 and frequently transfer to London as well as touring nationally and internationally. Year-round programming continues through the winter with high-class touring productions.

Casting procedures: Casting is done on a production-by-production basis.

Citizens Theatre
119 Gorbals, Glasgow G5 9DS
tel 0141 429 5561
email info@citz.co.uk
website www.citz.co.uk
Artistic Director Dominic Hill, *Executive Director* Kate Denby, *Participate Director* Dr Catrin Evans, *Production Administrator (Casting)* Jacqueline Muir

Production details: Internationally renowned, iconic Glasgow-based producing theatre. Creates ground-breaking theatre productions in-house and on tour, plus empowering participatory projects. In 2025, Citizens Theatre will welcome audiences new and old to they new home after a major redevelopment of our building. Offers UK Theatre/Equity approved contracts.

Casting procedures: Majority of casting is through agents. Do not have an in-house casting director. Works with a range of established casting directors or cast productions themselves. Casting queries should be directed to **jackie@citz.co.uk**.

Contact Theatre
Oxford Road, Manchester M15 6JA
email programming@contactmcr.com
website https://contactmcr.com
Executive Director Jack Dale-Dowd

Production details: Based in Manchester, Contact Theatre empowers young people through creativity and the arts to become leaders and agents of social change. They take a young-person centred approach to decision-making, and promote inclusion, access and understanding between communities. They inspire audiences with stories and experiences that reflect the diversity of their community, and nurture emerging artists, encouraging them to take creative risks, while also supporting their health and well-being. Contact Theatre is committed to anti-racism and environmental stewardship, actively working towards a carbon-neutral future.

Contact has striven to rewrite the rulebook on what 'theatre' can be and presents a range of artforms, including theatre, dance, live art, cabaret, spoken word, circus, comedy and music. The huge variety of participatory work with young people is integrated as closely as possible with the company's 'professional' programme which is comprised of in-house productions and touring theatre.

Casting procedures: Uses freelance casting directors and does not advertise casting breakdowns publicly. Welcomes letters (with CVs and photographs) from actors, but warns that it is unable to reply to unsolicited submissions. The theatre prefers not to receive showreels, emails and invitations to view actors' websites. Offers TMA/Equity approved contracts. Actively encourages applications from disabled actors and promotes the use of inclusive casting.

Curve
60 Rutland Street, Leicester LE1 1SB
tel 0116 242 3560
email contactus@curvetheatre.co.uk
website www.curveonline.co.uk
Facebook /CURVEtheatreLeicester
X @CurveLeicester
Instagram @curve_leicester
Chief Executive Chris Stafford, *Artistic Director* Nikolai Foster

Production details: A state-of-the-art theatre designed by world-renowned architect Rafael Vinoly. Has 2 auditoria, one with 750 seats and the other providing a 350-seat flexible smaller space. "A stunning glass façade encloses a magnificent foyer and mezzanine walkway, with views onto the café, bars, dressing rooms and workshop areas. The stage is placed at street level between the 2 auditoria."

Casting procedures: Uses both in-house and freelance casting directors. Holds general auditions; actors may write in for casting breakdowns as soon as productions are announced. Does not welcome unsolicited approaches by post or by email, showreels, or invitations to view individual actors' websites. Offers Equity-approved contracts as negotiated through TMA. Actively encourages applications from disabled actors and promotes the use of inclusive casting.

Derby Theatre
15 Theatre Walk, St Peter's Quarter, Derby DE1 2NF
tel (01332) 593939
website https://derbytheatre.co.uk
Facebook /DerbyTheatre
X @derbytheatre
Instagram @derbytheatre
Artistic Director Sarah Brigham

Production details: Derby Theatre has a long and rich history of delivering high-quality drama to audiences. Previously Derby Playhouse, Derby Theatre, which sits at the heart of the city, is now owned and run by the University of Derby. The theatre is rooted in the local community but international in its outlook, producing and presenting performances working with the best local, regional and national talent, as an Arts Council England National Portfolio Organisation.

Stages 4–6 productions annually in the Main House, and also works in youth theatre and TIE. Offers Equity-approved contracts as negotiated through UK Theatre, and subscribes to the Equity Pension Scheme.

Casting procedures: Uses freelance casting directors. Actors are invited to email enquiries to **casting@derbytheatre.co.uk**. Welcomes CV and headshots by email for general auditions. These are open to professional actors; those who are successful will be invited to audition. Applications from disabled actors are actively encouraged.

Donmar Warehouse
41 Earlham Street, London WC2H 9LX
tel 020-7240 4882
email office@donmarwarehouse.com
website www.donmarwarehouse.com
Facebook /DonmarWarehouse
Instagram @donmarwarehouse
Artistic Director Timothy Sheader, *Casting Director* Lotte Hines CDG

Production details: Independent producing house located in Covent Garden. The building originally served as a vat room and hop warehouse for the local brewery. In 1961 it was purchased by Donald Albery and converted into a rehearsal studio for the London Festival Ballet, which he formed with ballerina Margot Fonteyn. The theatre takes its name from them.

In the 1990s the Donmar was redesigned. The current theatre space retains the characteristics of the former warehouse while incorporating a new thrust stage.

Casting procedures: Does not hold open auditions but accepts invitations to see actors' onstage work. Welcomes emails with CV and headshots to casting@donmarwarehouse.com. Offers TMA/SOLT/Equity approved contracts.

The Dukes

Moor Lane, Lancaster LA1 1QE
tel (01524) 598500
email ask@dukeslancaster.org
website https://dukeslancaster.org
Facebook /dukeslancaster
X @TheDukesTheatre
Instagram @thedukeslancaster
Ceo Chris Lawson, *Programmer/Producer* Porl Cooper

Production details: A producing theatre with an independent cinema. Stages several home-produced shows each year in the main house (313 seats) and one in the studio (178 seats), with a focus on contemporary drama and outdoor, site-specific productions. Also runs a Youth Arts programme.

Casting procedures: Does not use freelance casting directors. Casting breakdowns are obtainable through the website, postal application (with sae) and Spotlight. Welcomes letters (with CVs and photographs) but not email submissions. Showreels and invitations to view individual actors' websites are also accepted. Offers TMA/Equity approved contracts. Actively encourages applications from disabled actors and promotes the use of inclusive casting.

Dundee Rep and Scottish Dance Theatre Limited

Tay Square, Dundee DD1 1PB
tel (01382) 227684
email info@dundeerep.co.uk
website www.dundeerep.co.uk
Facebook /DundeeRep and /ScottishDanceTheatre
Instagram @dundeerep and @scottishdancetheatre
Chief Executive Andrew Panton (Artistic Director)

Production details: Producing theatre housing Dundee Repertory Ensemble – Scotland's only permanent acting company. Stages various shows each year in the main house. Also offers a variety of classes and courses for all ages and runs a community engagement program.

East Riding Theatre

10 Lord Roberts Road, Beverley,
East Yorkshire HU17 9BE
tel (01482) 874050
email boxoffice@eastridingtheatre.co.uk
website www.eastridingtheatre.co.uk
Facebook /ertheatre
X @ertheatre
Instagram @ertheatre
Artistic Directors Michael Kinsey and Laura Peterson, *Creative Director* Vincent Regan, *Theatre Manager* Sasha Walker-Allen

Founded in 2014, ERT is a professional producing and receiving house. It is a registered charity and has a small paid staff. Many of the support functions are delivered by volunteers. ERT employs creative artists on a regular basis, building on its growing reputation as a high-quality performance venue. Minimum Equity rates apply.

The main house stages at least 2 in-house productions a year. Summer school attendees/ community casts appear in some in-house productions. ERT hosts the John Godber Company at least once a year

Additional skills required from actors include singing, the ability to play a musical instrument and to understake physical theatre. Other Lives productions are an associated company. They write and produce their own material, and tour to less accessible venues.

Gate Theatre

26 Crowndale Road, Camden, London NW1 1TT
tel 020-7229 5387
email info@gatetheatre.co.uk
website www.gatetheatre.co.uk
Facebook /gatetheatre
X @gatetheatre
Instagram @gatetheatre
Ceo & Executive Director Nicola Clements

Production details: Presents new writing and undiscovered classics from around the world in original and visually imaginative productions. Stages 5–6 shows each year. Also runs the *Gateways* programme which includes workshops, talks, commissions, artist opportunities and curated events.

Casting procedures: Does not accept unsolicited CVs/submissions. "Individual directors tend to cast from their own lists – contact with the director is the best way to ensure that your application is considered. The Gate Theatre Company is committed to promoting theatre as an activity for all." Accepts invitations to view work through the invitation form on their website.

Greenwich Theatre

Crooms Hill, Greenwich, London SE10 8ES
tel 020-8858 4447
email info@greenwichtheatre.org.uk
website https://greenwichtheatre.org.uk

Facebook /GreenwichTheatreLondon
X @GreenwichTheatr
Artistic Director James Haddrell

Production details: Programmes a mix of in-house and visiting productions. Received programming focuses on emerging companies, children's theatre and classic drama. Produces occasional showcases and semi-staged readings at different times of the year. Offers TMA/Equity approved contracts and subscribes to the Equity Pension Scheme.

Casting procedures: Generally uses freelance casting directors, but also post jobs on Spotlight or social media. "Please don't send unsolicited applications; do look at the vacancies section on the website, as we aim to provide advance information on our future productions, and answer standard questions."

Hampstead Theatre
Eton Avenue, London NW3 3EU
tel 020-7722 9301
email info@hampsteadtheatre.com
website www.hampsteadtheatre.com
Facebook /hampsteadtheatre
X @Hamps_Theatre
Instagram @hampstead_theatre
Producer & Chief Executive Greg Ripley-Duggan

Production details: Hampstead Theatre is a new-writing producing house, featuring new, mid-career and established writers. Plays are bold, original and entertaining. Presents at least 7 productions on the Main Stage each year, and 7 in the Downstairs studio.

Casting procedures: Main Stage casting director changes depending on the director of each production. Studio casting is led by the in-house producing team.

Harrogate Theatre
Oxford Street, Harrogate, North Yorks HG1 1QF
tel (01423) 502116
email info@harrogatetheatre.co.uk
website www.harrogatetheatre.co.uk
Facebook /harrogatetheatre
X @HGtheatre
Instagram @harrogatetheatre
Chief Executive David Bown

Production details: Stages award-winning pantomime productions in the main house and also works in Education (key contact, Hannah Draper). Its 2 performance spaces allow for producing and presenting theatre, dance, music and comedy. Also programmes the 2 major venues of The Royal Hall and Harrogate Convention Centre in the town centre on behalf of the lcoal authority.

Casting procedures: Uses freelance casting directors and sometimes holds general auditions. Offers Equity approved contracts as negotiated through TMA, and participates in the Equity Pension Scheme. Committed to inclusive and diverse casting.

Harrogate Theatre has no resident Artistic Director, and so unsolicited approaches are not welcome. Please check the website for any casting opportunities.

HOME
2 Tony Wilson Place, Manchester M15 4FN
tel 0161 200 1500
email info@homemcr.org
website https://homemcr.org
Ceo Karen O'Neill, *Senior Programme Producer* Remi Adefeyisan

Production details: HOME was formed by the merger in 2012 of the Library Theatre Company and Cornerhouse, HOME produces the best in contemporary theatre, visual art and film, learning and participation, creative industries and digital innovation. The company's venue, opened in spring 2015, comprises a 500-seat theatre, a 150-seat flexible studio space, a 500m^2, four metre-high gallery space, five cinema screens, education spaces, digital production and broadcast facilities, a café bar, restaurant and offices.

In 2025, HOME launched HOME Arches, a free, bespoke artist development hub designed to support artists across a variety of disciplines, providing free high-quality studio spaces, alongside an extensive programme of residencies, events and workshops. Spanning three railway arches situated between the main building and Whitworth Street West, HOME Arches offers 5,000 hours of free creating space annually, with 50% of studio space dedicated to artists from groups currently underrepresented in the industry, including members of the global majority, d/Deaf and disabled artists, and artists from lower socio-economic backgrounds.

HOME provides new opportunities for artists and audiences to create work in different ways together and serves as a social and cultural hub – in one building visitors can see original new work across the visual arts, theatre and film.

Offers TMA/Equity-approved contracts.

Casting procedures: HOME encourages applications from actors with disability, and promotes inclusive casting.

Hull Truck Theatre
50 Ferensway, Hull HU2 8LB
tel (01482) 224800
email admin@hulltruck.co.uk
email casting@hulltruck.co.uk
website www.hulltruck.co.uk
Executive Director Janthi Mills-Ward, *Artistic Director* Mark Babych

Hull Truck Theatre is a pioneering theatre with a unique Northern voice, locally rooted and global in outlook, inspiring artists, audiences and communities to reach their greatest potential.

It produces and presents inspiring theatre that relects the diversity of a modern Britain and provides the resources, space and support to grow people and ideas. It is an ambassador for Hull, a flagship for the region and a welcoming home for local communities.

Key Theatre

Embankment Road, Peterborough, Cambs. PE1 1EF
tel (01733) 852992
website https://keytheatre-peterborough.com/
Facebook /pborokeytheatre
Instagram @pborokeytheatre
Ceo & Creative Director Paul Jepson

Production details: Mainly a receiving house with occasional in-house productions including an annual pantomime. Stages dramas, musicals, comedians, variety shows and dance productions.

Kiln Theatre

(formerly Tricycle Theatre)
269 Kilburn High Road, London NW6 7JR
tel 020-7328 1000
email info@kilntheatre.com
website https://kilntheatre.com
Facebook /KilnTheatre
X @KilnTheatre
Instagram @kilntheatre
Artistic Director Amit Sharma, *Executive Director* Iain Goosey

Kiln Theatre sits in the heart of Kilburn in Brent, a unique and culturally diverse area of London where over 140 languages are spoken. A newly refurbished, welcoming and proudly local venue, with an internationally acclaimed programme of world and UK premieres. The work presents the world through a variety of lenses, amplifying unheard/ignored voices into the mainstream, exploring and examining the threads of human connection that cross race, culture and identity.

Education details: The ambitious Creative Engagement programme aims to champion the imagination, aspiration and potential of the Brent community young and old. It invests in creating meaningful relationships with young people to inspire and encourage their creativity, their confidence and self-esteem. Works with older people to create a thriving community around the theatre.

Casting details: Kiln Theatre encourages artists of all ages and backgrounds. Uses freelance casting directors for main house productions. For casting information contact the team at artistic@kilntheatre.com.

Leeds Playhouse

(formerly West Yorkshire Playhouse)
Playhouse Square, Quarry Hill, Leeds LS2 7UP
tel 0113 213 7800
website www.leedsplayhouse.org.uk
Chief Executive Shawab Iqbal, *Artistic Director* Tom Wright

Production details: Leeds Playhouse is a theatre that has existed in the heart of Yorkshire for over 50 years. As a registered charity (No. 255460) the Playhouse seeks out the best companies to create work which is pioneering and relevant. Leeds Playhouse recently underwent a £16m transformation which includes improved access to and around the theatre, a new city-facing entrance and the addition of a new studio theatre, the Bramall Rock Void.

A dedicated collaborator, Leeds Playhouse works with distinctive, original voices from across the UK. Its Artistic Development programme, Furnace, discovers, nurtures and supports new voices, while developing work with established practitioners. It provides a creative space for writers, directors, companies and individual theatre-makers to refine their practice at all stages of their careers.

The sector-leading Playhouse Connect team works with more than 12,000 people aged 4–95 every year connecting with refugee communities, young people, teachers and students, older people and people with learning disabilities, including working in specific areas of the city. The Playhouse pioneered Relaxed Performances ten years ago and more recently developed Dementia-Friendly performances both of which are becoming the norm across the industry. Leeds Playhouse is proud to be the first ever Theatre of Sanctuary for Refugees and People Seeking Asylum.

The Playhouse relies on support from many partners to make great things happen. The organisation is especially grateful for the continued support from funders including Arts Council England, Leeds City Council, The Liz and Terry Bramall Foundation, as well as many charitable trusts, business partners and individuals.

Offers TMA/Equity contracts and does not subscribe to the Equity Pension Scheme. Casting procedures: Currently Leeds Playhouse casts through agents' submissions and works with casting directors on productions on a show-by-show basis. Casting information is available on the website. Leeds Playhouse is an equal opportunities employer in relation to casting.

The Library Theatre

See the entry for HOME under *Producing theatres* on page 165.

Live Theatre

Broad Chare, Quayside,
Newcastle upon Tyne NE1 3DQ
tel 0191 261 2694
email info@live.org.uk
website www.live.org.uk
Facebook /livetheatre
X @LiveTheatre
Instagram @livetheatrenewcastle
Artistic Director Jack McNamara, *Executive Director* Jacqui Kell

Producing theatres 167

Production details: New writing theatre established in 1973. Produces 8–10 shows each year in the main house. Also runs TIE, Outreach and Community programmes.

Casting procedures: Does not use freelance casting directors. Welcomes submissions (with CVs and photographs), sent by post or email. Actors may write at any time. Holds annual Live Theatre Open Auditions. Showreels and invitations to view individual actors' websites are also accepted. Offers ITC/Equity approved contracts. Actively encourages applications from disabled actors and promotes the use of inclusive casting.

Liverpool Everyman & Playhouse Theatres

Everyman 5–11 Hope Street, Liverpool L1 9BH; *Playhouse* Williamson Square, Liverpool, L1 1EL
tel 0151 708 3700
email newworks@everymanplayhouse.com
website www.everymanplayhouse.com
Facebook /everymanplayhouse
X @LivEveryPlay
Instagram @liveveryplay
Creative Director Nathan Powell, *Chief Executive* Mark Da Vanzo

Two iconic theatres (one a state-of-the-art 400-seat thrust, the other a Grade II* listed 800-seat proscenium) with proud histories and national significance. The Playhouse, an integral part of the mid-scale touring network, has been entertaining audiences since 1866 and the Everyman has been renowned for its innovation and new writing since 1964. Between them, both theatres have welcomed millions of audience members and launched the careers of thousands of creative professionals.

They carry on a long, proud tradition of producing and presenting ground-breaking work for the widest audience across the region and beyond. "United by a passion for our art-form, a love of our region's culture and its people and a belief that theatre can transform lives, our mission is to use the power of theatre to inspire, entertain and nurture positive social change".

Lyric Hammersmith Theatre

Lyric Square, King Street, London W6 0QL
tel 020-8741 6822
email enquiries@lyric.co.uk
website https://lyric.co.uk
Facebook /LyricHammersmith
X @LyricHammer
Instagram @lyrichammersmith
Artistic Director Rachel O'Riordan

Production details: The Lyric Hammersmith Theatre produces bold world-class theatre.

"In our big, beautiful theatre, we tell stories that matter and work with exceptional talent to make ambitious, entertaining, inspiring shows for our audience in West London and beyond. We remove barriers to engagement and ensure young people have the opportunity to discover the power of their creativity, shaping the future of British theatre."

Casting procedures: Different directors cast their own productions, using freelance casting directors. Promotes recruitment of employees from diverse range of backgrounds.

Lyric Theatre

55 Ridgeway Street, Belfast BT9 5FB
email info@lyrictheatre.co.uk
website www.lyrictheatre.co.uk
Executive Producer Jimmy Fay, *Casting Director* Clare Gault, *Senior Producer* Morag Keating

Production details: Northern Ireland's leading full-time producing house for professional theatre. Presents a distinctive, challenging and entertaining programme of new writing as well as contemporary and classic plays by Irish, European and American writers.

Casting procedures: contact the Casting Director Clare Gault.

Does not normally use freelance casting directors. Welcomes submissions from all actors of any ethnicity, ability or nationality (Spotlight or online CVs preferred), sent by email. Actors may write in at any time. Advises actors to check the website for its future programme. Offers UK THEATRE/Equity approved contracts.

Manor Pavilion Theatre

Manor Road, Sidmouth, Devon EX10 8RP
tel (01395) 514413
(Box office), (01395) 576798 (Admin office)
email manorpavilion@eastdevon.gov.uk
website www.manorpavilion.com
Theatre Manager Graham Whitlock

Management of the summer season (12 plays in 12 weeks) is by Paul Taylor Mills Ltd. Performs all aspects of entertainment, including plays, musicals, comedies, concerts, variety shows, dance shows, professional ballet and pantomime.

Menier Chocolate Factory

4 O'Meara Street, London SE1 1TE
tel 020-7378 1713
email boxoffice@menierchocolatefactory.com
website www.menierchocolatefactory.com
Artistic Director David Babani

Production details: Opened in 2004. An award-winning 180-seat off-West End theatre which stages plays and musicals, live music and stand-up comedy.

Mercury Theatre
Balkerne Gate, Colchester, Essex CO1 1PT
tel (01206) 577006
email info@mercurytheatre.co.uk
website www.mercurytheatre.co.uk
Artistic Director Natasha Rickman

Production details: The Mercury is a regional theatre based in Colchester which creates, hosts, and tours performances nationally. Staging classic and contemporary drama, musical theatre, new writing, panto, dance, and comedy, the Mercury also supports new talent and runs a Community programme, connecting the diverse local communities.

Casting procedures: For all casting enquiries, email casting@mercurytheatre.co.uk.

The Mill at Sonning Theatre
Sonning Eye, Reading RG4 6TY
tel 0118 969 6039
website https://millatsonning.com
Facebook /MillAtSonning
X @MillAtSonning
Instagram @millatsonning
Managing & Artistic Director Sally Hughes

Production details: Popular 'dinner theatre' venue, producing a range of plays for audiences to watch while eating a meal.

Casting procedures: Forthcoming productions are listed on the website. Actors should send their details, along with specific casting suggestions, to the Artistic Director 2 months before each show.

National Theatre
South Bank, London SE1 9PX
email casting@nationaltheatre.org.uk
website www.nationaltheatre.org.uk/about-us/theatre-makers/casting
Artistic Director Indhu Rubasingham, Director of Casting Alastair Coomer CDG, Head of Casting Bryony Jarvis-Taylor CDG, Casting Associates Naomi Downham, Martin Poile CDG, Senior Casting Assistant Harry McDonald, Casting Assistant Kristen Coonjah

Production details: The National Theatre's mission is to make world class theatre that's entertaining, challenging and inspiring – and to make it for everyone. It aims to reach the widest possible audience and to be as inclusive, diverse and national as possible with a broad range of productions that play in London, on tour around the UK, on Broadway and across the globe. The National Theatre's extensive UK-wide learning and participation programme supports young people's creative education through performance and writing programmes like Connections, New Views and Let's Play. Its major new initiative Public Acts creates extraordinary acts of theatre and community; the first Public Acts production was 2018's Pericles. The National Theatre extends its reach through digital programmes including the free streaming service National Theatre Collection, and NT Live, which broadcasts some of the best of British theatre to over 2,500 venues in 65 countries. The National Theatre invests in the future of theatre by developing talent, creating bold new work and building audiences, partnering with a range of UK theatres and theatre companies.

Casting details: Actors known to the directors and writers working for the theatre may be approached directly, but casting is predominantly carried out through audition. The NT will first approach agents to check actors' availability, then audition a shortlist. New talent is actively sought out, and the casting team sees several performances a week within London and (less frequently) outside. The NT does consider actors who are currently unrepresented by an agent and encourages those actors to invite the department to see their work onstage. It also attends drama schools' showcases and will sometimes approach other casting directors known to the NT. The Casting Department champions diversity in all forms within casting decisions and is dedicated to creating a safe and supportive audition environment where actors are empowered to do their best work.

National Theatre of Scotland (NTS)
Rockvilla, 125 Craighall Road, Glasgow G4 9TL
tel 0141 221 0970
email info@nationaltheatrescotland.com
website www.nationaltheatrescotland.com
Facebook /NationalTheatreScotland
X @NTSonline
Bluesky @ntsonline.bsky.social
Instagram @ntsonline
Artistic Director Jackie Wylie, Director of Artistic Development Caroline Newall

Production details: The National Theatre of Scotland launched to the public in February 2006. It has no building, and instead takes theatre all over Scotland and beyond, working with new and existing venues and companies to create and tour theatre of the highest quality. This theatre takes place in the great buildings of Scotland, but also in site-specific locations, community halls and drill halls, car parks and forests. Rockvilla is The National Theatre of Scotland's first purpose-built facility and is a centre for creativity, production and talent development.

Scottish theatre has always been for the people, led by great performances, great stories and great playwrights. The National Theatre of Scotland exists to build a new generation of theatregoers, as well as reinvigorating the existing ones; to create theatre on a national and international scale that is contemporary, confident and forward-looking; to bring together brilliant artists, designers, composers, choreographers and playwrights; and to exceed expectations of what and where theatre can be.

Offers actors in-house ITC/Equity approved contracts and does not subscribe to the Equity Pension Scheme.

Casting procedures: Uses freelance casting directions who are brought on for each production. Has an in-house Casting Coordinator who manages the casting processes, including open calls and workshops, and who is the main point of contact within the National Theatre of Scotland for freelance Casting Directors and actors. The casting requirements of available roles on all productions are advertised on Spotlight. Breakdowns are sent to all UK agents and on occasion are distributed internationally. In the event that we are looking for more specialised or specific performers, breakdowns will be advertised on the Spotlight link board and other relevant channels including the casting page of the National Theatre of Scotland website.

The NTS Artistic team makes every effort to see every theatrical event produced in Scotland, maximising the number of actors that NTS sees. The team also responds to individual requests to see actors' work. All actors' CVs and headshots that NTS receives are acknowledged and kept on file in the NTS office. The NTS Casting Director reviews these files at regular intervals, and Directors are encouraged to go through these files before casting their productions. In addition, NTS holds at least one skills workshop a year at Rockvilla, for performers based in Scotland. Actively encourages applications from disabled actors and promotes the use of inclusive casting.

New Vic Theatre
Etruria Road, Newcastle-under-Lyme ST5 0JG
tel (01782) 717954
email admin@newvictheatre.org.uk
website www.newvictheatre.org.uk
Facebook /NewVicTheatreStaffordshire
X @NewVicTheatre
Artistic Director Theresa Heskins, *Head of Casting* Anji Carroll

Production details: Purpose-built theatre-in-the-round with a full programme of in-house drama, concerts and occasional touring productions. Stages 10 shows each year in the main house. Also very active with Outreach and Education programmes (contact Sue Moffat and Jill Rezzano respectively).

Casting procedures: Casting breakdowns are posted on Spotlight and in the casting section of the website. Submissions should be specific and reference a particular production and role.

The New Wolsey Theatre
Civic Drive, Ipswich IP1 2AS
tel (01473) 295900
email info@wolseytheatre.co.uk
website www.wolseytheatre.co.uk
Facebook /NewWolseyTheatre
Instagram @newwolsey
Chief Executive Douglas Rintoul

Production details: Mixed producing/receiving house, staging 4–5 produced or co-produced productions a year, often specialising actor-musician productions. Alongside these productions, there is talent development support for professionals in or from East Anglia, we have a vibrant Youth Theatre and we deliver creative projects with schools and communities; the contact for our Head of Creative Communities is Tony Casement.

Casting procedures: Casting procedures: open casting for East Anglian artists, we also use freelance casting directors. We welcome unsolicited approaches from local actors. Offers TMA/Equity-approved contracts. Actively looking for disabled actors, local actors and actor-musicians and promotes inclusive casting.

Northern Stage
Barras Bridge, Newcastle-upon-Tyne NE1 7RH
tel 0191 230 5151
email info@northernstage.co.uk
website https://northernstage.co.uk
Facebook /northernstage
Instagram @northern_stage
Artistic Director Natalie Ibu

Production details: Based in Newcastle, Northern Stage produces, co-produces and supports the production of great theatre for regional, national and international audiences in live and digital forms. As well as in-house productions, Northern Stage presents work from visiting companies throughout the year.

Casting procedures: Open auditions once a year, casting breakdowns through website, social channels and Spotlight. Young actors can apply to join the Young Company.

Nottingham Playhouse
Wellington Circus, Nottingham NG1 5AF
tel 0115 947 4361
email enquiry@nottinghamplayhouse.co.uk
website www.nottinghamplayhouse.co.uk
Facebook /nottmplayhouse
X @nottmplayhouse
Instagram @nottmplayhouse
Artistic Director Adam Penford, *Chief Executive* Stephanie Sirr

Production details: Nottingham Theatre Trust was founded in 1948 and moved to its current location in 1963. Produces around 10 shows each year in the 750 seater Theatre and the Neville Studio space. Also runs a Participation programme.

Casting procedures: Uses freelance casting directors. Casting breakdowns are available on Spotlight. Does not take unsolicited or general submissions. Artists living in or with a connection to the wider Midlands regions are invited to join 'Amplify' for networking and development opportunities and support.

Octagon Theatre
Howell Croft South, Bolton BL1 1SB
tel (01204) 520661
email casting@octagonbolton.co.uk
website https://octagonbolton.co.uk
Facebook /OctagonBolton

X @octagontheatre
Instagram @octagontheatre
Artistic Director Lotte Wakeham

Production details: The Octagon's new, more accessible theatre building opened in summer 2021. Stages several shows each year in the main auditorium, plus some work in the studio. Also runs Education, Outreach and Community programmes.

Casting procedures: Holds audition days in Bolton and London. Any professional actor can submit their details to the Octagon by email. The details will be kept on file for potential future auditions. Occasionally uses freelance casting directors.

Old Joint Stock Theatre

4 Temple Row W, Birmingham B2 5NY
tel 0121 200 1892
email ojstheatre@gmail.com
website https://www.oldjointstock.co.uk/
Facebook oldjointstock
X @Oldjointstock
Instagram @Oldjointstock
Threads @Oldjointstock
Artistic Director James Edge, *Associate Artistic Director* Emily Lloyd, *Marketing Manager* Liam Alexandru

Set up in 2006, they produce multiple in-house productions each year running for as long as 4-5 weeks and pay equity minimum. The theatre produces shows and provides opportunities for actors, writers, lighting and sound designers, set designers, directors and more.

The Old Vic

The Cut, London SE1 8NB
tel 0344 871 7628
email casting@oldvictheatre.com
website www.oldvictheatre.com
Facebook /OldVicTheatre
X @oldvictheatre
Instagram @oldvictheatre
Artistic Director (until September 2026) Matthew Warchus, *Artistic Director Designate* Rupert Goold, *Senior Casting Associate* Jessica Ronane, *Casting Coordinator* Saffeya Shebli

Production details: The Old Vic is London's independent not-for-profit theatre, a world leader in creativity and entertainment. The Old Vic is mercurial: it can be transformed into a theatre in the round, a space for live music and comedy, has played host to opera, dance, cinema, music hall, classical dramas, variety, big spectacles and novelty acts. It was the original home of the English National Opera, the Sadler's Wells dance company and the National Theatre. It's also been a tavern, a college, a coffee house, a lecture hall and a meeting place.

All of this is now in the bones of the building and is as important a part of its open-armed, inclusive, welcoming personality as its grand historic decor and the iconic performances and famous productions it has housed.

Open Air Theatre

Inner Circle, Regent's Park, London NW1 4NR
tel 0333 400 3561
website https://openairtheatre.com
Facebook /RegentsParkOpenAirTheatre
X @OpenAirTheatre
Instagram @RegentsParkOAT
Artistic Director Drew McOnie

Production details: Stages 4–6 shows each year in the main house, and a series of festival days throughout the summer season.

Casting procedures: Uses freelance casting directors, who send full casting breakdowns to agents as required for each production. "Unfortunately we are unable to consider unsolicited CVs."

Orange Tree Theatre

1 Clarence Street, Richmond TW9 2SA
tel 020-8940 0141
email admin@orangetreetheatre.co.uk
website www.orangetreetheatre.co.uk
Facebook /OrangeTreeTheatre
X @OrangeTreeThtr
Instagram @orangetreetheatre
Artistic Director Tom Littler

Production details: The Orange Tree produces and co-produces a mixture of new writing, re-discoveries, contemporary revivals in its uniquely intimate theatre in the round. Education and Participation work forms a major area of activity.

Casting procedures: Please email admin@orangetreetheatre.co.uk for casting enquiries. Actively encourages applications from disabled actors and promotes the use of inclusive casting.

Park Theatre

Clifton Terrace, Finsbury Park, London N4 3JP
tel 020-3697 4190
email info@parktheatre.co.uk
email submissions@parktheatre.co.uk
website www.parktheatre.co.uk
Facebook /ParkTheatreLondon
Instagram @parktheatrelondon
Artistic Director Jez Bond

Production details: Park Theatre programmes a balance of new writing and classics, plays and musicals across its two theatres - Park90 and Park200.

Looks for work that has a strong narrative and emotional drive and plays that can flourish within the intimacy of smaller theatres. Maintains a good gender balance of male and female roles on stage within a season as well as generally encouraging stories and casting from a range of ethnicities. Generally prefers productions with smaller casts and high production values.

Both produces and receives Equity-approved contracts and subscribes to Equity pension scheme, with UK Theatre agreement where applicable.

Producing theatres

Casting procedures: Uses freelance casting directors, but does not hold general auditions. Are open to invitations all year round, these should be emailed to **inviteus@parktheatre.co.uk** with details. Due to small staff, unsolicited CVs cannot be responded to.

Perth Theatre
Perth Theatre & Concert Hall, Mill Street, Perth PH1 5HZ
tel (01738) 472700
email info@perththeatreandconcerthall.com
website www.perththeatreandconcerthall.com
Chief Executive Christopher Glasgow

Production details: Perth Theatre, Horsecross Arts produces/coproduces 4 shows a year including a pantomime and programme work from independent touring companies and producing houses. Runs a broad Learning and Engagement programme, including the Youth Theatre, and are committed to providing innovative and relevant work for Scottish audiences.

The casting process aims to represent the breadth of Scotland's demographic and Perth Theatre welcomes approaches from local artists. See the casting page for further details **www.perththeatreandconcerthall.com/work-with-us**.

Pitlochry Festival Theatre
Port-Na-Craig, Pitlochry PH16 5DR
tel (01796) 484216
website https://pitlochryfestivaltheatre.com
Facebook /pitlochryfestivaltheatre
Instagram @pitlochryft
Artistic Director Alan Cumming, *Executive Director* Kris Bryce

Production details: Founded in 1951, Pitlochry Festival Theatre is a producing and presenting theatre located in Highland Perthshire. Comprises the main auditorium (capacity 544), Studio space for new writing and intimate performances (capacity 172), an extensive in-house workshop and production facility, and Explorers Garden, a predominantly woodland garden, containing open-air performance spaces, including an Amphitheatre seating 120. Presents a variety of performances throughout the year across all spaces. Visiting theatre, music, opera and other activities are also presented. Engagement programmes are run throughout the year.

Offers UK Theatre Equity contracts.

Queen's Theatre Hornchurch
Billet Lane, Hornchurch, Essex RM11 1QT
tel (01708) 443333
email info@queens-theatre.co.uk
website www.queens-theatre.co.uk
Facebook /QueensTheatreH
Instagram @queenstheatrehornchurch

Production details: Has been a producing theatre since it was first established in 1953. Stages a variety of shows each year in the main house, including revival plays, actor-musician musicals and new writing. Also runs TIE, Outreach and Community programmes. Runs a talent development programme for Essex and outer East London actors and theatremakers.

Casting procedures: Holds auditions per production 3–5 months in advance of rehearsals; actors should write to **casting@queens-theatre.co.uk** with a Spotlight link.

Rose Theatre Kingston
24–26 High Street, Kingston-upon-Thames, Surrey KT1 1HL
tel 020-8546 6983
email info@rosetheatre.org
website https://rosetheatre.org
Facebook /rosetheatrekingston
Instagram @rosetheatrekingston
Chief Executive Robert O'Dowd, *Artistic Director* Christopher Haydon

The Rose Theatre Kingston opened its doors to the public in January 2008 with English Touring Productions's production of *Uncle Vanya*, directed by Sir Peter Hall. The design of the theatre was inspired by the Elizabethan Rose on London's Bankside; Kingston's Rose has the same horse-shoe shaped auditorium and an open lozenge stage, creating a sense of intimacy between actors and audiences. The Rose auditorium has a capacity of up to 762 people across 4 tiers of seating. In addition to the main space there is a studio, capacity 120, and a gallery, capacity 60. These spaces host a variety of talks and workshops led by theatre writers and practitioners. The theatre also has a strong connection with Kingston University, where it facilitates the University's MA in Classical Drama.

The Rose presents a combination of home-produced drama and received work. Since opening, its home-grown productions have included *Love's Labour's Lost* and *A Midsummer Night's Dream*, directed by Sir Peter Hall; *The Winslow Boy* and *The Lady from the Sea*, directed by Stephen Unwin; and two rep seasons.

Royal & Derngate Theatres
19–21 Guildhall Road, Northampton NN1 1DP
tel (01604) 624811
website www.royalandderngate.co.uk
Facebook /RoyalandDerngate
X @RoyalDerngate
Instagram @royalderngate
Artistic Director Jesse Jones

Producing theatre; productions have toured the UK and transferred to the West End, Broadway, Shakespeare's Globe Theatre and the National Theatre. Visiting productions include musicals, dance, comedy and music.

A registered charity, the Get Involved programme engages the local community and foters new talent. Works with young people on site and in schools.

Royal Court Theatre
Sloane Square, London SW1W 8AS
tel 020-7565 5050
email info@royalcourttheatre.com
website www.royalcourttheatre.com
Facebook /royalcourttheatre
X @royalcourt
Artistic Director David Byrne, *Executive Director* Will Young

Production details: Since 1956 the English Stage Company at the Royal Court has focused on developing, funding and producing new writing. Productions frequently transfer to the West End and Broadway. Stages about 14 productions a year. Also presents an extensive play development programme incorporating workshops and rehearsed readings. Offers SOLT/TMA/UK Theatre/Equity-approved contracts and offers the Equity Pension Scheme.

Casting procedures: Welcomes submissions (with CVs and photographs) by post or email all year round. Please use **casting@royalcourttheatre.com**.

Royal Exchange Theatre
St Ann's Square, Manchester M2 7DH
tel 0161 833 9833
email box.office@royalexchange.co.uk
website www.royalexchange.co.uk
X @rxtheatre
Instagram @rxtheatre
Chief Executive Selina Cartmell, *Casting Director* Olivia Barr

Production details: Manchester's leading producing theatre company, comprising a main theatre and studio space. Presents 8–9 productions, on average, in the main theatre and 3–4 in the studio each year. The programme is a mixture of reimagined classics from the repertoire, musicals and an ambitious programme of new plays and contemporary theatre. Also runs Creative Learning and Community Engagement programmes involving schools, young people, community groups and theatre enthusiasts of all ages. Work is based around the theatre's repertoire and its unique building. Where possible, the department leads sessions in the theatre, and frequently works with other departments around the building to give participants an insight into how theatre, and particularly the Royal Exchange, work.

Casting procedures: Head of Casting works with a freelance associate who together coordinate casting for each show. Actors are recommended to keep their Spotlight profile up to date for the best chance of being considered for a role.

Will consider attending performances at venues in the North West and London with sufficient notice. Accepts submissions with a Spotlight link or CV to **casting@royalexchange.co.uk**. Regular open audition days are held throughout the year for actors in Greater Manchester. These auditions aren't for a particular production or opportunity, but to widen knowledge of local actors. Open audition dates can be found on the website.

Royal Lyceum Edinburgh
Grindlay Street, Edinburgh EH3 9AX
tel 0131 248 4800
email producingteam@lyceum.org.uk
website https://lyceum.org.uk
Facebook /lyceumedinburgh
X @lyceumedinburgh
Artistic Director & Joint CEO James Brining

Production details: The Royal Lyceum is one of Scotland's largest producing theatre companies with a season of in-house drama productions and co-productions. In addition, the theatre stages a Christmas show. Occasionally tours in Scotland and abroad, limited hosting of touring companies, and runs an ambitious and acclaimed Creative Learning Department.

Casting procedures: Casting managed by agencies or in-house. See **https://lyceum.org.uk/work-with-us/acting-and-writing** for up-to-date opportunities.

Royal Shakespeare Company
Royal Shakespeare Theatre, Waterside, Stratford-upon-Avon, Warks. CV37 6BB
tel 020-8016 5008
website www.rsc.org.uk
Co-Artistic Directors Daniel Evans, Tamara Harvey, *Executive Director* Andrew Leveson

Production details: The Royal Shakespeare Company creates Shakespeare for everyone, made in Stratford-upon-Avon and shared around the world. The Company performs plays by Shakespeare and his contemporaries, and commissions a wide range of original work from contemporary writers. Ensures Shakespeare and theatre are accessible to everyone through engaging live perfomances and learning and education work throughout the UK and across the world.

Casting procedures: Please send correspondence including invitations and submissions for specific productions to **charlie.metcalf@rsc.org.uk**, and preferably in relation to specific productions.

Shakespeare's Globe
21 New Globe Walk, Bankside, London SE1 9DT
tel 020-7902 1400
email info@shakespearesglobe.com
website www.shakespearesglobe.com
Facebook /ShakespearesGlobe
Instagram @the_globe
Artistic Director Michelle Terry

Production details: A reconstruction of Shakespeare's Globe, the theatre has a repertoire which includes the work of Shakespeare, his contemporaries and new writing. The season runs from April to October with up to 10 productions staged each year. Opened second theatre in 2014, The Sam Wanamaker Playhouse, a reconstruction of an indoor Jacobean theatre.

Casting procedures: Auditions take place throughout the year and are by invitation only. Welcomes emails with CVs and photographs or a link to your Spotlight profile: prefers invitations to see actors in performance. Actors should write to the Casting Department at **casting@shakespearesglobe.com**. Offers actors Equity-approved contracts through an in-house agreement. Actively encourages applications from disabled actors and promotes the use of inclusive casting. The website has more information about casting procedures.

Sheffield Theatres
55 Norfolk Street, Sheffield S1 1DA
tel 0114 249 5999
email customer.service@sheffieldtheatres.co.uk
website www.sheffieldtheatres.co.uk
Chief Executive Tom Bird, *Artistic Director* Elizabeth Newman

Production details: Comprises 4 theatres: the Crucible Theatre (thrust stage, 960 capacity), the Tanya Moiseiwitsch Playhouse (200–400 capacity), the Lyceum Theatre (pros. arch, 1,168 capacity) and the Montgomery Theatre (420 capacity). Stages 5–6 shows each year in the Crucible, 3–4 in the Playhouse and one to 2 in the Lyceum. Also runs learning programmes.

Casting procedures: Uses freelance casting directors. Welcomes letters (with CVs and photographs). Offers TMA/Equity approved contracts.

Sheringham Little Theatre
2 Station Road, Sheringham, Norfolk NR26 8RE
tel (01263) 822347
email boxoffice@sheringhamlittletheatre.com
website www.sheringhamlittletheatre.com
Facebook /sheringhamlittletheatre
X @SheringhamLT
Instagram @sheringhamlittletheatre
Theatre Director Debbie Thompson

Production details: A professional seaside repertory summer season which runs from August to September, compromising 3 plays.

Casting procedures: Holds general auditions. Actors should write between January and March, sending a CV and *recent* photograph. Email submissions not welcome. "As a small venue we are non-Equity, but we do work with Equity to pay a realistic wage; we also pay for accommodation and towards travel costs." Actively encourages applications from disabled actors and promotes the use of inclusive casting.

Sherman Theatre
Senghennydd Road, Cathays, Cardiff CF24 4YE
tel 029-2064 6900
website www.shermantheatre.co.uk
Facebook /ShermanTheatreCardiff
Instagram @shermantheatre
Artistic Director Designate Francesca Goodridge

Production details: Stages several shows each year and specialises in work for young audiences. Theatre comprises two spaces: the Main House which stages touring drama, comedy, dance and opera; and the Studio which stages touring drama, fringe theatre and stand-up comedy.

Casting procedures: Does not use freelance casting directors. Sometimes holds general auditions.

Soho Theatre
21 Dean Street, London W1D 3NE
tel 020-7287 5060
email info@sohotheatre.com
website www.sohotheatre.com
Facebook /sohotheatre
X @sohotheatre
Instagram @sohotheatre
Executive Director Mark Godfrey

Production details: Soho Theatre is London's most vibrant producer of new theatre, comedy and cabaret. Harnessing an artistic spirit that is based in new writing roots, the radical ethos of the fringe and the traditions of punk culture and queer performance, the company champions voices that challenge from outside of the mainstream, and sometimes from within it too. Soho Theatre is a registered charity and social enterprise and audiences are diverse in age, background and outlook.

Soho Theatre is mission driven: success is measured through the prodution, presentation and facilitation of new work; the artists and creative talent that are nurtured; and the diverse audiences that are engaged.

Soho Theatre houses a flexible 160-seat theatre, a studio space with 100-seat capacity and a 150-seat cabaret space in the basement, alongside the theatre bar, offices, rehearsal and meeting rooms. Soho hosts workshops, showcases, meetings and events; the company reaches an audience of 250,000 people a year at Dean Street, on tour, in Edinburgh and online. At Dean Street, all spaces are accessible and available for hire. For bookings and general information, please visit **www.sohotheatre.com**.

Casting procedures: Casting is carried out by freelance casting directors, engaged on a production basis.

Southwark Playhouse
Southwark Playhouse Borough,
77–85 Newington Causeway, London SE1 6BD
tel 020-7407 0234
email boxoffice@southwarkplayhouse.co.uk
Southwark Playhouse Elephant, 1 Dante Place,
London SE11 4RX
website https://southwarkplayhouse.co.uk
Artisitic Director (Ceo) Chris Smyrnios

Production details: Southwark Playhouse's central vision is to present work by the best new and emerging theatre practitioners based in, or visiting, the capital. In tandem with their theatre work, they run an extensive year-round participation programme, available completely free to participants. With 2 venues in Elephant & Castle (Southwark Playhouse Borough and Southwark Playhouse Elephant), everything the organisation does is driven by the belief that theatre exists to inspire, to empower, to challenge and to entertain.

Stephen Joseph Theatre
Westborough, Scarborough YO11 1JW
tel (01723) 370540
email enquiries@sjt.uk.com
website https://sjt.uk.com
Facebook /StephenJosephTheatre
Instagram @thesjt
Joint Chief Executives Paul Robinson (Artistic Director), Caroline Routh (Executive Director)

Production details: Produces 6 in-house shows per year, including co-productions with other venues. Has two performance spaces: a main space in the round and an end-on studio theatre. Focuses on new writing.

Casting procedures: Holds general auditions for local actors annually. Prioritise the casting of local and regional actors. Casting is done via their Casting Director, Sarah Hughes CDG. All casting enquiries should be directed to Sarah at **sarahhughescasting@gmail.com**.

Storyhouse
Hunter Street, Chester CH1 2AR
tel (01244) 409113
email info@storyhouse.com
website www.storyhouse.com
Facebook /storyhouselive
X @storyhouselive
Ceo Annabel Turpin

Founded in 2017, Storyhouse is an independent arts centre and creative hub in Chester which incorporates a library, mid-scale theatre, studio theatre and a cinema. It presents a year-round programme of theatre, comedy, dance and music events alongside a raft of creative festivals including Chester Literature Festival, Kalidescope and Childless.

They also run an open-air theatre every summer in the city's Grosvenor Park with 3 original productions plus a range of wraparound activity at the festival site. Equity approved contracts.

Theatr Clwyd
Raikes Lane, Mold, Flintshire CH7 1YA
tel (01352) 344101
email box.office@theatrclwyd.com
website www.theatrclwyd.com
Artistic Director Kate Wasserberg, *Executive Director* Liam Evans-Ford

Production details: The major drama-producing company in Wales. Although most work is presented in English, some pieces are performed in Welsh. Stages 5–6 shows in the main house, and 5–6 in the studio each year, with some mid- to large-scale productions touring Wales and England. Also runs TIE programmes.

Casting procedures: Theatr Clwyd employs freelance casting directors.

Theatre by the Lake
Lakeside, Keswick, Cumbria CA12 5DJ
tel (01768) 774411
email enquiries@theatrebythelake.com
website www.theatrebythelake.com
Facebook /tbtlake
X @tbtlake
Bluesky @tbtlake.bsky.social
Instagram @tbtlake
Artistic Director & Joint Ceo Liz Stevenson, *Head of Producing & Programming* Amy Clewes

Established in 1999, Theatre by the Lake is the only Arts Council funded producing theatre in Cumbria. Its purpose is to enrich the lives of local communities through theatre making. They create and share great theatre, develop and champion talent, and celebrate place and culture in the work they do across the county.

The theatre has 2 stages, a 400-seat Main House and 100-seat Studio and presents an annual programme of homemade shows throughout the year, as well as hosting a variety of festivals, visiting companies and community performances, playing to over 120,000 people per year.

Production details: Each year Theatre by the Lake produces 6–8 productions, often in partnership with other theatres and companies. They also host a wide variety of visiting companies, artists and community productions across our two spaces. Offers UK Theatre/Equity-approved contracts and subscribes to the Equity Pension Scheme.

Casting procedures: Works with a variety of freelance casting directors on our productions. When working in co-production, the lead producer tends to lead on the casting process. Holds annual open auditions for Cumbrian actors through our artist network 'Cumbrian Creatives'. Encourages Cumbrian actors and creatives to join the network in order to learn about opportunities at TBTL and beyond: **www.theatrebythelake.com/get-involved/artist-network**.

Theatre Royal Bath
Sawclose, Bath BA1 1ET
tel (01225) 448815
website www.theatreroyal.org.uk
Facebook www.facebook.com/TheatreRoyalBath
Director Danny Moar

One of the oldest theatres in Britain. Comprises three auditoria: the Main House, the Ustinov Studio Theatre and the Egg Theatre for children and young people. Founded 1805.

Theatre Royal, Bury St Edmunds
Westgate Street, Bury St Edmunds, Suffolk IP33 1QR
tel (01284) 769505
email artistic@theatreroyal.org
website www.theatreroyal.org
Artistic Director & CEO Owen Calvert-Lyons

Built in 1819, the theatre is the only surviving Regency theatre in the country. Produces an annual pantomime at Christmas and 2 other shows a year – a spring drama and a summer community production which includes professional actors working alongside local children and young people. Offers non-Equity contracts.

Casting procedures: Casting breakdowns are published via Spotlight only. Actors wishing to be considered for the pantomime should write to the theatre in April. (The spring and summer shows are cast in January/February and April/May respectively.) Only welcomes letters and emails (with CVs and photographs) from actors previously unknown to the company during these casting periods.

Theatre Royal Plymouth
Royal Parade, Plymouth PL1 2TR
tel (01752) 668282
email info@theatreroyal.com
website www.theatreroyal.com
Facebook www.facebook.com/theatreroyalplymouth
X @TRPlymouth
Instagram @theatreroyalplymouth
Chief Executive Officer & Executive Producer James Mackenzie-Blackman

Registered charity and the largest regional producing theatre in the UK housing three theatres – The Lyric, The Drum and The Lab. Delivers outreach work to engage young people and communities in Plymouth and beyond. Its production and learning centre, TR2, offers set, costume, prop-making and rehearsal facilities. Runs an Artist Development programme to support artists and creatives from the South West, helping individuals and companies to develop new work, connect and collaborate.

Theatre Royal Stratford East
Gerry Raffles Square, London E15 1BN
tel 020-8534 7374
email theatreroyal@stratfordeast.com
website www.stratfordeast.com
Facebook /theatreroyalstratfordeast
Instagram @statford_east
Artistic Director Lisa Spirling, *Executive Director* Hanna Streeter

Production details: Committed to new work which portrays the experiences of different social and ethnic communities, the theatre is constantly striving to present shows which resonate with its diverse local audiences. Stages 8 shows each year. Also runs Young People's, Outreach and Community programmes.

Casting procedures: Casting opportunities are advertised on the website. Welcomes submissions (with CVs and photographs) sent by post. Advises actors to research the theatre's work before writing, and to think carefully about their own suitability. Invitations to view individual actors' websites also accepted. Actively encourages applications from disabled actors and promotes the use of inclusive casting.

Theatre Royal Windsor
Thames Street, Windsor SL4 1PS
tel (01753) 863444
email info@theatreroyalwindsor.co.uk
website https://theatreroyalwindsor.co.uk
Facebook /TheatreWindsor
X @TheatreWindsor
Instagram @theatrewindsor
Theatre Director Anne-Marie Woodley

Production details: A long-standing, non-subsidised producing theatre. Shows run for 1–2 weeks. Stages new productions each year with some going on to tour.

Casting procedures: Does not use freelance casting directors. Welcomes letters (with CVs and photographs) but not email submissions. Offers TMA/Equity-approved contracts. Will consider applications from disabled actors to play characters with disabilities.

Tobacco Factory Theatres
1st Floor, Tobacco Factory, Raleigh Road, Southville, Bristol BS3 1TF
tel 0117 902 0345
email theatre@tobaccofactorytheatres.com
website https://tobaccofactorytheatres.com
Facebook /tobaccofactorytheatres
X @tftheatres
Instagram @tobaccofactorytheatres
Artistic Director Heidi Vaughan

Production details: Stages 6–8 productions a year in the theatre space and touring work, and also works with the local community. Does not always offer Equity-approved contracts. Offers contracts where possible.

Casting procedures: Casts in-house and holds open auditions. Casting breakdowns are available from the website and with instructions on how to apply via email. Welcomes emails from actors previously unknown to the company, but does not welcome showreels or invitations to view individual actors' websites. Actively encourages applications from disabled actors and promotes the use of inclusive casting.

Torch Theatre
St Peter's Road, Milford Haven SA73 2BU
tel (01646) 694192
email info@torchtheatre.co.uk
website www.torchtheatre.co.uk
Facebook /torchtheatre

Instagram @torchtheatrepembs
Artistic Director Chelsey Gillard

Production details: Stages several productions each year.

Casting procedures: Sometimes holds general auditions; see **www.torchtheatre.co.uk/torch-theatre-co/casting/** for current opportunities. Priority is given to those who have not met with the team before. Auditions are open to those who are currently based in West Wales. Actively encourages applications from disabled actors and promotes the use of inclusive casting.

Traverse Theatre
Cambridge Street, Edinburgh EH1 2ED
tel 0131 228 3223
email info@traverse.co.uk
website www.traverse.co.uk
Facebook /TraverseTheatre
X @traversetheatre
Instagram @traversetheatre
Artistic Director Gareth Nicholls

Production details: Scotland's premier new work theatre, telling new stories for a new era across a range of platforms. Presents a mixed programme of in-house productions, partner company work, live music and festivals, spanning its two in person theatre spaces, Traverse 3 digital platform, off-site and touring venues. Also runs extensive Engagement and Creative Development programmes generating new work; see website for more details.

Casting procedures: Casting calls and open auditions advertised on the website, social media and Spotlight. Show invitations are welcome via **casting@traverse.co.uk**. Particularly interested to hear from Scotland-based actors.

Tricycle Theatre
See the entry for Kiln Theatre under *Producing theatres* on page 166.

Tron Theatre
63 Trongate, Glasgow G1 5HB
tel 0141 552 3748
email box.office@tron.co.uk
website www.tron.co.uk
Artistic Director Jemima Levick, *Interim Executive Director* Neil Murray

Production details: The Tron Theatre has built a renowned reputation for producing and presenting ambitious, contemporary, and proudly subversive theatre, reflecting the world we live in and representing the people of Glasgow and Scotland. It has established itself as a vital, creative hub for the Scottish theatre sector as a powerhouse of home-grown, classic and contemporary Scottish work. (Seating capacity: main house 230, studio 50.)

Casting procedures: Casting is done by liaising with show director and Assistant Producer, and using details of actors on file. The Tron is an active participant in the Scottish Casting Network open audition initiative, working in collaboration with other building based theatres in Scotland. Actors can write at any time and their submissions will be kept on file. Accepts submissions (with CVs and photographs) from actors unknown to the company to **casting@trontheatre.co.uk**. Actors are employed under Equity-approved contracts, and the theatre participates in the Equity Pension Scheme. Encourages applications from global majority and disabled actors and promotes the use of inclusive casting.

Watermill Theatre
Bagnor, Newbury RG20 8AE
tel (01635) 45834
email admin@watermill.org.uk
website www.watermill.org.uk
Facebook /The Watermill Theatre
X @watermillTh
Instagram @TheWatermillTheatre
Artistic Director & Ceo Paul Hart, *Executive Director & Ceo* Claire Murray, *Casting & Producing Associate* Cydney Beech, *Outreach Director* Heidi Bird

Production details: A producing theatre, specialising in actor musicianship, where actors live onsite. Stages approximately 6 productions each year with runs of up to 12 weeks, including an annual youth theatre production. Recent productions have included: Shakespeare, Musical Theatre, New Writing and Classics.

Casting procedures: Regulary advertises roles using Spotlight and Open Hire. Welcomes emails (with CVs and photographs) with reference to specific castings only. Offers UK Theatre/Subsidised Theatre Agreement/Equity-approved contracts and subscribes to the Equity Pension Scheme. The Watermill Theatre is committed to equality of opportunity for all.

Watford Palace Theatre
20 Clarendon Road, Watford WD17 1JZ
tel (01923) 235455
website www.watfordpalacetheatre.co.uk
Facebook /watfordpalace
X @watfordpalace
Instagram @watfordpalace
Chief Executive and Director of Programming Steve Marmion

Production details: Producing theatre built in 1908 and refurbished in 2002–04. The theatre presents a varied programme including inventive, ambitious and inclusive drama, new plays, musicals, dance and family shows. All programme enquiries should be send to **programming@watfordpalacetheatre.co.uk**.

Casting procedures: Casts in-house and uses freelance casting directors. Unable to respond to individual CVs. Will consider applications from disabled actors to play disabled characters. Offers UK

Theatre/Equity agreements. Also involved in Education and Community theatre, for which enquiries should be sent to takepart@watfordpalacetheatre.co.uk.

Wiltshire Creative
Malthouse Lane, Salisbury SP2 7RA
tel (01722) 320117
email info@wiltshirecreative.co.uk
website www.wiltshirecreative.co.uk
Facebook /wiltscreative
X @wiltscreative
Instagram @wiltscreative
Artistic Director Gareth Machin, *Executive Director* Rosa Corbishley

Production details: Pan-arts organisation incorporating Salisbury Playhouse, Salisbury Arts Centre and Salisbury International Arts Festival. Produces a wide range of theatre and cross-artform work throughout the year, alongside an extensive Take Part programme and Theatre For Young People.

Casting procedures: Offers UK Theatre/Equity-approved contracts. Most productions are cast using freelance casting directors although occasionally in-house. Submissions for specific productions by email are welcome. Promotes inclusive casting, and actively encourages applications from disabled actors.

Worcester Repertory Company
The Swan Theatre, The Moors, Worcester WR1 3ED
tel (01905) 726969
email sarah-jane@worcestertheatres.co.uk
website www.worcestertheatres.co.uk
Facebook /worcstheatres
Instagram @worcstheatres
Artistic Director & CEO Sarah-Jane Morgan

Production details: Originally founded in 1968 and the breeding ground for directors such as David Wood OBE, John Doyle, Phyllida Lloyd CBE and Rufus Norris (Director of the National Theatre), the Worcester Rep. now stages productions all over the UK and internationally. With a refurbished main house and studio theatre, producing pantomimes, Shakespeare, new work and theatre-in-education tours. As with most companies, contracts are offered on a show-by-show basis but most actors work on more than one production with the company. The company is based at the Swan Theatre, Worcester.

Casting procedures: Casting is handled in-house. The comapny is happy to receive submissions from actors previously unknown to the company by email. Please addess all casting submissions to Sarah-Jane Morgan.

York Theatre Royal
St Leonard's Place, York YO1 7HD
tel (01904) 623568 (Box Office)
email admin@yorktheatreroyal.co.uk
website www.yorktheatreroyal.co.uk
Facebook /yorktheatreroyal
X @YorkTheatre
Instagram @yorktheatreroyal

Production details: One of the oldest theatres in the country; seats 750 in the Main House and 71 in the Studio. Productions include classics, new writing and the famous York pantomime every Christmas. Runs Outreach, Community programmes and Youth Theatre.

Casting procedures: Works with casting directors and agents to advertise professional opportunities. Do not contact the theatre directly, but recommends keeping CV and Spotlight up to date. Often posts announcements on their website and social media.

Young Vic
66 The Cut, Waterloo, London SE1 8LZ
tel 020-7922 2922
website www.youngvic.org
Facebook /youngvictheatre
X @youngvictheatre
Instagram @youngvictheatre
Artistic Director Nadia Fall

Production details: The Young Vic presents a wide variety of classics, new plays, forgotten works and music theatre. The theatre is especially concerned with the art of directing. The Creators Programme is the most comprehensive in the UK. This fusion makes the Young Vic one of the most exciting theatres in the world. "Our audience is famously the youngest and most diverse in London. We encourage those who don't think theatre is 'for them'".

Casting procedures: Uses freelance casting directors. Does not welcome direct submissions from actors. Offers TMA/Equity approved contracts. Actively encourages applications from disabled actors and promotes the use of inclusive casting. Use the form on their website to invite them to see your work.

Inclusivity and allyship for the future of the industry

Tom Ross-Williams, writer, director, filmmaker, community organiser and intimacy coordinator

Interview by Polly Bennett

Tom Ross-Williams is a writer, director, filmmaker, community organiser and intimacy coordinator. They were the Creative Director of The Advocacy Academy, a social justice organisation for young people from south London, and have worked as an actor at the RSC, Kneehigh, Soho Theatre and Bush Theatre. A major focus of their activism is LGBTQ+ rights and tackling Toxic Masculinity. They write and talk about these issues in various settings, including as a regular contributor to the Huffington Post, *a frequent panellist at WOW Festival and on BBC Radio4's* The Moral Maze.

What's your role as an educator of inclusivity issues?

Not everyone has equal access to bring their full selves as they come into a rehearsal room, so I explore how we create equitable spaces that acknowledge that. I ask: what does it feel like for the person who noone sits next to on the train because of how they look, to walk into that room. What does it mean for the person who is never asked to speak first to contribute versus those that are? Making change is like going to the source of the river; rather than taking people out of the river who are drowning, you need to find out who's chucking people in to begin with. I often teach a tool called 'Oops, Ouch', which allows people harmed by microaggressions to voice that ('ouch'), as well as the person who has exacted it and their likely good intentions ('oops'). We explore ways to communicate a metaphorical 'ouch' when harm's been done so it gets acknowledged, lessons are learnt, and we are able to move on. It's so much effort to make the person that's been harmed name it and that's why we need processes and systems that do that without all that emotional and cognitive labour. I provide new lenses to see the world and try making invisible privileges more visible.

Do you feel like it's working?

Young people are so on board with making rehearsal rooms, auditions and film sets safer and more inclusive, so it feels very hopeful. Unfortunately, I've done work in lots of places where it feels tokenistic, but elsewhere there are some exciting things happening. Pastoral care systems are in place and people are starting to introduce themselves with their pronouns. It's small but it's having a seismic effect on making people feel maybe not fully celebrated, but at least accepted.

Why is your role as an intimacy coordinator so important?

I'm really interested in consent practices and personal agency in performance. I don't feel like actors are encouraged to take agency very often and are too rarely asked to consider consent in the rehearsal process. I was mentored by Ita O'Brien and her guidelines have shifted this in the industry hugely. Seeing the gay sex scenes in *Sex Education* was the first time I've seen an uncomplicated loving gay sex scene between two teenagers on screen. That would have been profound for me as a young person. Intimacy coordination feels like a change that is going to be lasting and that's why I wanted to be a part of it. It feels like activism to me.

What is preventing change from happening throughout the industry?
People just aren't giving up their positions of power, basically. It's all very performative. Often when I explain privilege, I play a game where there are three rows of people and whoever throws a ball into the bin from their place wins a prize. The front row can get the ball in easily, a few in the second and back row, maybe one. And everyone cheers for the person in the back row. And that's what society does, point to the person in the back row and say, 'Well, if they got it in, you can too'. And in doing this, nobody in the front row gives up their seat.

There's been some controversies recently over funding which has got its money from a history of slavery, so there has been an influx of acknowledging sentiments but maybe they should just give the endowment away to people. Like, 'Oh my gosh, my big theatre that represents the whole of the UK that's been this historic place of systemic racism, what do I do?' You give up your seat, move on! It's very hard for people to do as it's been aligned to cancel culture. But we won't get anywhere by just cancelling people. It individualises a problem that is systemic. Harvey Weinstein did not create *all* sexual violence, but he was part of an industry that supported it. So we need to find more ways to have co-creative practices so that people are collectively responsible with more shared leadership and co-writers. It's not fair to put somebody in a very virtue-signalling way in a huge position of power and give them no support. That needs to shift.

What do you think about the conversations happening about queer parts being played by non-queer actors?
I often think about how Rikki Beadle-Blair cast me in the first film I ever did as a gay character before I'd even come to terms fully with my sexuality. There's a wonderful power of stepping into somebody else's shoes as an actor and I would hate for us to completely lose that by not allowing people to experiment, particularly as a young performer. But performing in an internal drama school situation is a very different situation than casting a big Hollywood film where another straight person is going to win an Oscar for playing gay. If you're doing a final production for a drama school and there are out queer performers and there's a really wonderful role that is all about queer identity and we give that to one of the actors who identify as straight, then that does become difficult. But there needs to be a bit more nuance around these conversations and more strategy.

OK, so let's say I'm the financier on an independent feature film. It's an amazing queer love story that will show people a version of queer intimacy that never been seen before, but I'm only going to get this financed if I get a famous lead actor. There currently aren't many 'big name' actors who are out and queer, so what do I do?
Ideally, you'd push for the few out queer 'big name' actors to be in your film. But, pragmatically, I want as many queer actors working as possible. So, if Keira Knightly said, 'I'll play this part but only if all of the supporting cast are queer, whether they're playing queer characters or not', that's interesting. The film gets financed and she gets to play an amazing role whilst giving lots of jobs to queer creatives, both on and off screen. After the Oscars, So White and #MeToo movements, lots of film actors signed inclusion riders to only work

on shows that have an equal gender split or a certain amount of people of colour working on it. Ending the conversation by saying a straight actor should never play a gay role does a disservice to some of the strategic choices that could be made to allow more queer actors to get their first screen role. Of course I want LGBTQ+ actors to play those roles and I would never condone a cis actor playing trans, so there is nuance there.

So really it's about allyship and changing the system that upholds itself.
I think the oppression of minority groups is upheld through diverting the attention to individuals and to small organisations, rather than looking at the systemic shifts. I guess that's why I'm quite keen on things like policy and LGBTQ+ education. There are so many worrying decisions this government is taking – they have bowed out of their Stonewall training. That decision alone is then going to feed into the decisions around LGBTQ+ education in schools and will obviously have an effect on our industry. Practices that really commit to focussing on liberation and anti-oppression take a lot more time and understandably we want quick fixes, but we need to think long term. I think a lot of these quick fixes mean diversity and inclusion policies are written, but then people aren't hired to make sure they're being enacted.

What I have been trying to do in the past few years is thinking about how I can remove the labour from people who've not been visible in the industry; give them an opportunity to really dream and to be artists and create those containers that support that creativity. This idea that we can't make work that's not about our own identity is difficult because it means that we don't have a world of allyship. I co-created a show with some young Latinx activists and I was ready for people to say that I shouldn't be the one to make that show because I'm not Latinx. I'm ready for criticism, but sometimes we need to be bold. I feel art should be able to do that: we're not reporters or journalists, we're artists.

To follow Tom's work visit www.tommyrosswilliams.com or follow them on social media @tomrosswilliams.

Effective audition speeches
Simon Dunmore

Audition speeches may be a fundamental part of the actor's 'toolkit', but a surprising number of otherwise good actors are not very good at doing them – and many make poor choices of material to use. It's true that most castings involve a reading, but sometimes audition speeches are asked for in advance, and occasionally you'll get, "We'd just like to see something else; what can you show us?" It would be very silly to be caught out because you haven't done an audition speech since drama school.

Essentially, audition speeches should be self-contained, well chosen, well researched, well staged and well gauged for the space you are in and for whoever is watching you – just like a good production of a play. In fact an audition speech should be a 'mini-production' (of a 'mini-play') in its own right.

Essential parameters
Length
An audition piece should be no more than two or two-and-a-half minutes long (that's roughly 300 words, depending on pace). Two minutes (or less) can be very effective provided that it contains all the parameters listed elsewhere in this article.

How many?
The important thing is to have a good range of audition material so that you've got a library to choose from to suit each given circumstance. I suggest at least half a dozen.

What types?
Your collection should consist of a good variety of characters you could credibly play. They should be within your 'playing range' and appropriate to your appearance: an audition speech is not an acting exercise; it's part of your marketing portfolio.

You should also aim to find material that rarely (if ever) appears elsewhere on the audition circuit. Judging acting is a highly subjective business, so it is generally better to find 'original' material to heighten your chances of not being compared to others. I suggest that you only use material that is popular if you feel sure you can perform it (them) extremely well – on a bad day ...

Accents
If you choose to do a speech written in a regional accent, make sure you can do that accent well enough to convince a native. (It is important to have at least one in your repertoire that features your own accent if it is a strong and 'characterful' one.) Some people choose to 'translate' a speech into an accent with which they are more comfortable, and this can work. However, watch that in doing this you are not sacrificing too much of the quality of the original language.

Sources of speeches
Don't just rely on plays that you know; you should be steadily expanding your knowledge of dramatic literature. Seeing, reading, sitting in libraries and bookshops (especially secondhand ones); even picking up an audition book to find inspiration for a playwright (previously unknown to you) whom you could explore further.

Look in novels, less well-known films, and good journalism (for instance) for material that could be made into good 'drama'. For example, Shakespeare copied (almost word-for-word) Queen Katherine's wonderful speech beginning 'Sir, I desire you do me right and justice ...' (*Henry VIII*, Act II, Scene 4) from the court record.

It's generally inadvisable to write your own speech(es). This rarely works, because very few actors are good playwrights. If you do decide to use a self-written piece, it can be a good idea to use a *nom de plume*; you're selling yourself as an actor, not as a playwright. You should also be prepared to talk about the whole play, even if you haven't written it yet.

Content
Too many people fail because they choose to do an indifferent speech. Even if they do it well, it somehow doesn't have much impact because of indifferent writing, lack of depth, and so on. Essentially you should go for pieces that have good 'journeys' – just like a good play.

It can be useful to find speeches that enable you to show your special skills (singing or juggling, for instance), but don't try to cram so much in that the sense is lost in a firework display of technical virtuosity. At the other extreme, avoid something that requires performance at one pace or on one note.

And, never set out to shock deliberately through content and/or crude language. That is not to say don't do 'shockers'; rather, don't set out with the specific idea of shocking your interviewer(s) as many people seem to intend. We've heard most of it before. I cannot describe how mind-numbingly tedious audition-days can become when peppered with such speeches.

Warning: There is now a lot of free audition material available online. Much of it is indifferently written; however, I have come across the occasional 'gem'.

Shape
Make sure that each of your pieces has a decent shape. In a sense it should be like a good play, with a beginning, middle and ending. Even if the character ends up back where he/she/they started, so long as he/she/they have travelled a 'journey' then that's fine.

Shakespeare and the classics
Traditionally you need to have at least one of these in your armoury. The fact is that most people perform them indifferently. Too many renditions seem as dead as their writers. The problem is that they are remote – in language and in content – from our direct experience, and therefore usually require much more research, thought and preparation than a modern speech.

Note: It's very tedious to see comedy Shakespeare speech done in a 'cod' West Country accent. If you can genuinely do one of the many variants of this accent, then that's fine, but his language works in every other regional accent in which I've heard it done.

'Trying on'
Try reading any speech that looks good to you (on the page) out loud, in front of someone else, before you start rehearsing it. If you do this, you'll get an even better idea of whether each speech really suits (and 'grabs') you. It's a bit like buying clothes: you see a pair of trousers (say) that look good on the hanger; sometimes you will feel completely different about them when you try them on. The opposite can also occur: you feel indifferent about a speech on the page; you read it out loud and it feels much, much better.

Effective audition speeches 183

Rehearsing your speeches
'What are you bringing on stage?'
You must bring your character's life history (gleaned from the play and supplemented by your imagination) into your performance. [As the character (i.e. in the first person), write notes of all the bits of information (big and small) that you find, in order to build his/her/their life.] Most of what you 'bring' won't be obvious to your auditioner(s). However, it will be immediately obvious if that 'life history' is not present. Just as 90% of an iceberg is underwater, a similar proportion of a good performance is also hidden ... but must be there, underneath, to support that performance.

It is particularly important to be clear about what actually provokes the character to start speaking – the 'ignition' that kicks your 'engine' into life. Try running a brief 'film' in your imagination, culminating in the event (for instance, a statement or a gesture from someone else) that is your cue.

Your invisible partner(s)
If you choose a speech addressing another character, then it is vital that that other person (and how they are reacting through the speech) is clear to you. It is generally better to imagine an adaptation of someone you know rather than to 'borrow' someone you've only seen on a flat screen. There can be a huge difference in how we perceive others between two and three dimensions.

It's not just them (and how they are reacting); it's also important to be clear about your relationship. As well as imagining what your character's lover looks like (for instance), you must also know the feel of their touch, their smell, and so forth – and many more personal aspects.

It is also important that any other people, places and events mentioned in the speech are similarly 'clear' in your imagination.

Your invisible circumstances
You should also bring the setting, clothes and practical items with you – in your imagination. (NB I could have written 'set, costumes and props', but I believe that it's important to think of everything being 'real' and not items constructed for a production.) I believe that actors neglecting these is the cause of a high proportion of failed and indifferent speeches. It's not just the visual images, it is also what the other senses give you: the 'brush' of a summer breeze across your face, for instance. Plays are not performed in 'real' rooms (there will be at least one wall missing) and every play has at least one non-appearing character mentioned. These absences are filled by the actors' imaginations. Do the same with these 'absences' in the audition circumstances.

It isn't just the major features that you should think about, but also the apparently minor details – for instance, the mark on a wall that suddenly catches your character's eye. It can be a good idea to draw a map (or groundplan) so that the whole 'geography' of your 'circumstances' is clear for you. Then fill out your imaginary location with as much detail as possible.

Interpretation
As you are creating a 'mini-production' of a 'mini-play' (the 'child' of its 'parent-play'), I believe that it's legitimate to make changes to the given circumstances of the speech when it occurs in the play, especially if such changes enhance your audition performance. (After

all, a 'child' can never lose the genetic code of its 'parents', but he/she/they will evolve their own personality, which will be different.) However, be prepared to justify it – and don't get defensive. There's usually no harm in honest disagreement.

That voyage of discovery
Be aware of the 'voyage of discovery' that shapes your speech. Don't anticipate the end at the beginning. This is a common fault in rehearsal, which is easily corrected – but a remarkable number of people fall into this trap when performing their audition speeches.

It can be very useful to write out a speech with each sentence (or even each phrase) on a separate line. It then appears less of a 'block' of words on the page and more a series of separate, but connected, thoughts and ideas. It is also a good idea to leave sufficient space between each line to write notes on what is the impulse to go on to say the next thing, and the next, and...

Beginnings
If you start your speech nebulously, your interviewer probably won't take in what you are doing for the first few seconds and may miss vital information that could make the rest of it a complete puzzle to them. You need to find a way of starting your speech that will grab their attention from the very beginning. This doesn't mean that the beginning has to be loud, simply that it should be positive and effective – almost as if the house lights were faded down and the curtain rising on... You!

Note: It can also be very useful to incorporate a simple movement to start a speech; a turn of the head, for instance.

Endings
It's also important to be clear as to why a character stops speaking after talking for two minutes. You need to be clear what your character's final thought is – crucially stopping his/her/their flow.

Finally
Ask yourself: "Are my speech and my presentation of it a good piece of 'Theatre?'"

Some practical considerations
Staging
Once you've done all the work set out in the previous paragraphs, you need to think carefully about how you stage each piece. Too many people seem inclined to put in extraneous moves either to compensate for the lack of the other character(s), or because they think the speech is boring if it doesn't contain enough movement. If you are properly 'connecting' to character and 'circumstances', the moves will follow naturally from each 'impulse'. However, much of the effect of your performance will be dissipated if your auditioners don't see enough of your face, and especially your eyes. In general (unless it is an address to the audience), they should be able to see three-quarters of your face for at least half the duration of the speech. To achieve this, orientate the other character(s) and 'circumstances' to suit the audition situation. For instance, place the imaginary person to whom you're talking at around 45 degrees to left or right in front of you. If your map (or groundplan) is clear in your mind, then it should be simple to angle it appropriately.

There is no point in placing a chair specifically to mark another character – or even the hat-stand which I once saw used as the object of some singular passions. If you do use such objects you'll usually find yourself concentrating on that object rather than your 'partner(s)'. They should be clearly lodged in your imagination so that the interviewer can 'see' them through you. Also, don't think that you have to stare at one place continually just to make it clear that he or she is there.

Chairs

A warning about chairs. There is a common variety of chair, as familiar as the bollard is to the motorway, that inhabits many popular audition venues. It can serve all kinds of functions as well as the simple one of being sat upon. However, don't rely on the well-known weight and balance of these plastic and steel functionaries for crucial elements of your well-prepared speech. You may suddenly find only chairs with arms or a room filled with wobbly ones. Be prepared to adapt to whatever form of seating is available.

Tip 1: Do a brief check on the mechanics of your audition-chair before you start your speech. For instance, you don't want to be thrown by the fact that the back is lower than that of the chair you rehearsed with…

Tip 2: If your audition-chair represents a different type of seat (a low, backless bench, for instance), sit on the chair as though you're sitting on that 'bench'.

Props

Avoid using props. As you haven't got a proper set, costume or lighting, too much of the visual emphasis goes on to the prop and consequently away from you. It is amazing how riveting even a small piece of paper produced for one of the numerous 'letter' speeches can become.

Props can be mimed: that mime doesn't need to be brilliant. And think how much easier it is to put down an imaginary glass on an imaginary table, without making a sound at the wrong moment. In using any imaginary prop, remember not just the shape as you 'hold' it in your hand but also its weight and its impact on your sense of touch.

The only exception to this can be a prop introduced briefly and then quickly discarded. Even then, make sure its impact doesn't take the focus from the rest of the speech.

Performing your speeches

Each presentation of a speech has to have the raw energy of a first performance. Unlike a first night, where the only new factor (in theory, at least) is the audience, you have to face numerous new and possibly unexpected factors when doing your audition speech. You need to be not only well rehearsed but also well prepared for how to cope with all the peripherals that are other people's responsibilities when you are actually doing a production. You are your own stage-management, wardrobe department, front-of-house manager, and so forth.

'Act in here?'

I don't think any audition-room is entirely satisfactory. They can be dirty and unkempt, too hot or too cold, too big or too small, have inconvenient echoes, have barely adequate waiting facilities and/or be hard to find down a maze of corridors. You'll be very fortunate if the whole session has only road traffic as a background noise. You have to be prepared to adjust the presentation of your speech(es) to each context – by fractionally slowing down and enhancing your diction slightly if there's an unavoidable echo, or scaling down your movement in a small room, for instance.

It's your space

You should regard the space in which you are doing your speech as your stage with which to do whatsoever you wish – as long as you have due reverence for the fabric of the building, for your interviewers and their goods and chattels. Move the chairs if you need to, take your shoes off if that's necessary, and so on ... but don't ask if it's 'all right' to do so. It can get very tedious for an interviewer if you keep on asking permission every time you want to change something. Providing it doesn't affect your audience directly, just get on with what is necessary for your performance.

Don't ask where to stand; your actor's instinct should tell you the optimum place for what you are about to do. Especially, don't ask permission to start, even if it's only with one of those pathetic little enquiring looks – another way of undermining yourself in your interviewer's eyes. Once you've been given your cue, it's all yours and in your own time.

Natural hazards

Be aware of natural hazards in the room: for example, a low afternoon sun pouring through the windows that blinds you as soon as you happen to turn into it. Don't, on the other hand, stand in the deepest shadow; nobody wants an actor who cannot find his or her light.

Your interviewer will probably be sympathetic if the unexpected suddenly interrupts you, but it really is your responsibility to spot this kind of thing beforehand and adjust accordingly. If it is something impossible to anticipate, then aim to recover as quickly as possible and get back into your speech. After all, if something goes wrong during a performance, you don't just stop until it's put right; you continue as best you can, and 99.9% of the time nobody in the audience will notice that anything went wrong.

Explanations

Minimise explanations about your speech. Ask yourself if you need them at all. In fact the best speeches are self-contained and don't need explanation beyond the character's name and possibly the title and the writer of the play. Whatever their individual faults, most directors do know a lot of plays, the characters within them and who wrote them. Be careful not to insult directors by telling them what they already probably know. (For example, "Hamlet from *Hamlet* by William Shakespeare.") On the other hand, make sure you know the title and writer of more obscure plays and be prepared to discuss them.

Sometimes, in the process of getting inside the character, actors forget to give these basic details. I don't think this matters (I enjoy trying to work them out for myself), but some directors have a nasty habit of interrupting actors' preparations with demands like "What are you doing, then?" If you do forget and are so interrupted, don't be so thrown that you rush into your speech.

Your interviewer as the other character

Some people try to use their interviewer as the other character for the purposes of their speech. This is not necessarily a good idea. It can work but is fraught with pitfalls.

First of all, do you need to ask permission beforehand? Politeness dictates that you should. After all, you are asking the auditioner to do the job of being in your play. He or she may say, "Yes, of course", but has probably been asked the same question in every other session of the day; it can get very tedious. Even if it is all right, the auditioner is probably not an actor, will become self-conscious in the process, not react in the way you anticipated, may well want to drop out of character to write notes and consequently won't be a consistent partner.

A pause for thought
Then, also do give yourself that moment of thought before starting a speech – a moment to immerse yourself within your character and circumstances. Almost everybody understands that it can be hard to change gear from chatting to acting. Don't think that you are wasting time; it'll only be a few seconds, and your interviewer will almost certainly have something else to write down before concentrating on you again. (For most actors a 'few seconds' feels much, much longer in these stressed circumstances.)

However, don't take too long to wind up into your speech with lots of heavy breathing or pacing about or even just standing quietly in a corner. That may be what you have to do before you go on stage, but most directors, however understanding, will begin to wonder what kind of lunatic you are and are you going to take up precious rehearsal-time with these warm-ups? Your 'pause for thought' should be as brief as you can make it without showing your inner turmoil. Properly done, this can be riveting to watch.

Starting
One of the hardest aspects of doing a speech is starting it from cold. If you are onstage at the beginning of a stage-production (especially on a first night), you'll experience an immense, and for some, terrifying, feeling of excitement and power as the audience goes quiet. You should aim to recreate this feeling just before you start your speech. It'll give you tingles up your spine and put a real 'kick' into your speech. This will 'communicate' to your auditioners and make them really look at you – even if they've had their heads down scribbling in the preceding seconds.

Tip: To help stimulate this process, get the smell of dust into your imagination – it's the pervading smell of any theatre.

Communication
You may well 'feel' your speech, but are you communicating it? Just because you are in a small room with only one person watching, don't mutter your speech at below conversation-level. How do I know you can fill a stage, however small, if you are not filling the room we're in? You have to make that room your stage, the interviewer(s) your audience. Think of them as being in the best seats in the stalls (the ones reserved for the critics on a first night) and aim just beyond the limits of the space. Only a lazy actor will give a smaller performance on stage just because there is a small audience.

Don't blast your interviewer out of his seat, either. Measure the acoustics: a lot of audition-rooms are part of church-hall complexes and tend to have high ceilings with the inevitable echo.

The 'need'
There is a 'need' that drives any speech; two minutes is a long time for someone to keep on talking. A long speech is a series of connected thoughts and ideas; underneath there has to be the 'need' to talk at such length. We all know people who 'go on' too much in everyday life – the odd person is able to sustain attention because of the energy and 'need' to communicate. The same is true on stage and in the audition.

Also, remember that your character hasn't usually planned to say so much. Essentially, the circumstances provoke the 'need' for them to add more, and more, and ...

Stopping
If you do need to stop during a piece – you've dried or it's started badly – do it positively and calmly, and do it without a grovelling apology. You may feel terrible but you have to

get yourself out of the mess without becoming embarrassing. You can even capitalise on having handled it well. A brief (and positive) "I'll start again" won't be held against you. If you dry or make a mistake significantly into a speech, just pause briefly and find your way back, just as you would in a public performance.

Bear in mind that most interviewers do not know how acting works. So if, say, your breathing starts going haywire, that's not a reason to stop unless it really is affecting the speech badly. You have left your teachers behind at drama school.

Finishing

When you finish you should keep the final thought in your mind and gently freeze for a moment, just as you would if you're left onstage at the end of a scene in a play. Then fade the imaginary stage-lighting (and close the curtains) at a suitable rate. (That 'moment' should last about a second. If you're unsure, say a multi-syllable word like 'Mississippi' in your head.) Then – without looking your interviewer(s) in the eye – relax back to your normal self, ready to move on to whatever your interviewer wants to do next. Many find the not 'looking your interviewer(s) in the eye' difficult, and a few even think that it might seem rude. However, if you do make eye contact at that crucial moment, you'll probably start to feel very vulnerable – and give out the 'vibe' that you're unconfident about your performance. Whatever you may really feel about that performance, there's nothing else that you can now do, except wait.

There may be a silence; your interviewer(s) may well want to write notes on what you've done. Just settle down and let them get on with it. Don't be thrown by that aching pause; you should quietly wait. The 'ball' is now very definitely in the interviewer's 'court' to restart the conversation.

'Thank you' (a)

There may be a vague "Thank you" or "Right", even "Mmmm" from the interviewer at the end of your speech. Don't read anything in to these vague expostulations. If you do you'll start to undermine yourself. We directors are usually thinking about what we're going to write down about your efforts. That thinking process is dominant and what comes out of our mouths is merely our acknowledgement that you've finished – an attempt at politeness that doesn't come out quite right. (I hear myself doing this constantly, but have never found a way round it.)

'Thank you' (b)

Some actors opt for a 'Thank you', or 'That's it', at the end. Sometimes this sounds pathetic; on others it comes across as sheer arrogance (watch the way some actors do curtain calls). If you've got a good enough 'ending', you've given the cue. The director may not respond to it immediately, but you should have clearly established that the 'ball' is now firmly in his, her or their 'court'. It's much better to say nothing.

Switching off

It is respected that it can take a few seconds to come back to reality, particularly if it's a very emotional speech. But it's fundamental to acting that just as you can 'switch on', you can 'switch off' with apparent ease. I will never forget a woman who did a wonderfully passionate speech from Arnold Wesker's *Four Seasons* and ended up in buckets of tears. She had done it extremely well but when it was over she simply could not stop crying and

Effective audition speeches 189

had to be taken from the room and given time to recover. What would have happened if she'd had to get similarly emotional on stage and then immediately go on to do a comic scene, as can occur? This is an extreme example which exemplifies the need to look very carefully at how you change back to reality.

'Why don't you try that again? This time standing on your head'
Don't get so stuck into a way of doing a speech that you cannot do it in any other way put to you. Some directors like to work on speeches. You should understand the insides of each speech so well that you could do it 'standing on your head'.

Advice
Some directors give constructive advice. In general, take that as a compliment, even if they are critical. Nobody will waste time and energy giving notes if they didn't at least like some aspect of you and your work. However, one director's constructive notes can become another's criticisms. In rehearsal an actor will take a note and try it out. Sometimes it doesn't work, and the moment has to be looked at again. Maybe it was only half-right. In an audition there is usually no time to rehearse that note to see if it works for you. So, when you do try it, and it perhaps doesn't quite work, you have no recourse to its originator for further amplification. Take such notes as suggestions to be utilised or discarded as suits you and your speech. That's how rehearsals should be anyway.

Final note
Working on audition speeches can be a wonderful way of keeping your 'acting juices' flowing through periods of unemployment.

Simon Dunmore directed productions for over 30 years – nearly 20 years as a resident director in regional theatres and, latterly, working freelance. In that time there were over 200 productions (of all styles, colours, shapes and sizes) – including several Drama School Showcases, Maugham's *Home and Beauty* and new plays about sex, WB Yeats' up-and-down relationship with Maud Gonne, one set inside a pyramid and another about Bismarck. Past favourites included: *The Promise* (Alexei Arbuzov), *Antigone* (Jean Anouilh), a seven-handed version of *Antony & Cleopatra* and too many others to mention. He also taught acting and worked in many drama schools and other training establishments around the country. He wrote several books: *An Actor's Guide to Getting Work* (fifth edition, 2012), the *Alternative Shakespeare Auditions* series, and was formerly the Consultant Editor for *Actors' Yearbook*.

Understudying
Andrew Piper

Some Frequently Asked Questions
Why would I want to do it?
What's not to like? Reasonable money, loads of free time, very few responsibilities, and the possibility of playing a meaty role alongside some of your theatrical heroes or belting out the solo of a show-stopper in a West End or major provincial theatre.

What are the 'down sides'?
If you're looking for a fast-track to stardom or are in this job for the glamour and glory, then this is not the job for you. There is no getting away from the fact that the understudies are the B-team. Understudying can be a thankless task – no one pays you much attention unless the actor you're covering is off (which may be never), there's very little to do, and most of the time you're essentially getting paid *not* to act – rather like a tuneless busker being given a tenner to go and play *somewhere else*!

Perhaps more so than almost any other acting job, this is very much 'a job'. If you can squeeze some art or advancement out of it too then that's great (in some cases miraculous), but this is definitely not a contract to go into with starry-eyed optimism.

How should I prepare?
Learn the lines! The amount of actual rehearsal time (as opposed to just watching the principal cast) may be fairly minimal. When you do get to rehearse there will be a lot to learn in a very short space of time, so the more solid you are on lines the more productive your rehearsal time will be, and the sooner you'll feel confident about being ready to go on. Do as much of the usual homework – character, historical research, cultural background, etc. – that you would do for any other part. You'll get less opportunity to discuss this in rehearsal (more on that later), but again it means you'll enjoy yourself more in the rehearsal room.

How much rehearsal will I get?
In short, not a lot – certainly not as much as the principal actors will have – but (depending how soon you're called to go on) enough to get you through. You probably won't start rehearsals at all until the main cast have been rehearsing for a while – at the very least the blocking needs to have been decided before you arrive – so the chances are you'll just get a few days (at best) before production week.

During production week itself, expect to be pretty much ignored completely by everyone: their focus is now purely on the principal cast and the technical running of the show. The job of the understudy during this period is to make notes on changes to his or her blocking, become familiar with lighting, sound and other stage effects, keep working on lines, stay available ... but generally just stay out of the way. Keep working on your part(s); you may only have had a few days' rehearsal by this point, but there have been enough instances of principal actors injuring themselves during a tech for you not to be complacent at this point!

Rehearsals are likely to be taken by the assistant director, or possibly even the company manager. If you're lucky, you'll have a little time for discussion about character and intentions (the more homework you've done before rehearsals, the more time you'll have), but an awful lot will be down to you to work out for yourself, simply by working on the script and watching the main cast at work.

Do I have to copy the principal actor's performance?
Understudy rehearsals differ from normal rehearsals in one important respect: all your moves (and many of your character choices) have already been decided and cannot be changed by you. In some ways this can be quite liberating – someone else has done all the hard work for you – but it can be challenging to take on these choices and make them your own. What you certainly don't want to do is produce a 'photocopy' of the principal actor's performance, which risks feeling like a hollow caricature; the challenge is to develop a performance which can slot in seamlessly to the main production, but which nevertheless feels like it's your creation. It can be disheartening to be so restricted in your choices, but trust that the principal actor's (and director's) instincts are good, and find a way to make it work for you.

Once the show is open, what are my responsibilities?
Most of your time will be spent either doing ensemble stuff on stage, or simply waiting in the dressing room. Apart from understudy rehearsals (one a week, perhaps, or possibly once a fortnight; if you're working for the RSC you may not have any understudy rehearsals at all once the show is up) your time is your own. If you're not needed for the curtain call, you may not be required to stay until the very end of the show. The rule of thumb is that you're free to go once the character you're covering has made his or her final entrance, but this can vary from production to production.

How often will I go on?
If you're working on a musical, the vocal demands of the piece will probably mean that principal performers will need to take occasional shows, or even just musical numbers, off to rest their voices, and so an understudy on a musical is pretty much guaranteed to be going on fairly frequently. In a straight play there is the distinct possibility that you will never go on at all, unless it's a long and demanding run. Even in the middle of a flu epidemic, the actor(s) you are covering may have a 'show must go on' mentality. They may be secretly hoping that the company manager will send them home, but will not voluntarily go off unless they are on the verge of being hospitalised.

It won't hurt to develop a good relationship with the actor you're covering, so that (a) they know that you actually want to go on (assuming you do; many understudies are quite happy not to) and (b) they may be more inclined to give you your moment in the sun when illness strikes and they're deciding whether or not they're fit enough to go on.

Incidentally, no company manager will allow a healthy principal to take a show off to give their understudy the chance to go on – that would be breach of contract – but I've heard stories of a few who may be wilfully credulous if the principal calls in sick for a matinee in the understudy's home town.

What's it like to go on?
When you get the call to go on, then just about everyone in the company – including the principal actors – will be focusing their energies on making sure that you have everything you need to give a good performance. Depending on how much notice you are given, you

may have an opportunity to run through bits of business on stage with the principals, and they may well offer you notes on how to play it. Some of these notes may be helpful, others won't be; take what you need and discard the rest. For the next few hours you are 'one of them', playing for the A-team, and you have to trust that your skill as an actor and all the preparation you've done will get you through. This isn't the time to try anything new; just do what you've rehearsed and everything will be fine.

Don't get star-struck about the people you're on stage with. These are your colleagues, your fellow artists, and whatever your relationship off stage might be, right now they are your equals, so don't be afraid to give a full-blooded performance. Some nerves are completely understandable, so if you know you tend to rush or be a bit quiet, say, when you're nervous, be aware of this and make a conscious effort to slow down or speak up, as appropriate.

Once the nerves have started to subside, allow yourself to enjoy it. Stay focused and in the moment, remembering all the things you've rehearsed, but now that you're playing with the A-team, take on the energy of the other actors and allow it to lift your own performance. Producers are generally happy if you can just get the lines out in the right order and hit your mark – as far as they're concerned you're just there to stop too many people asking for their money back – and if you can do that, then you've done your job, but if you've done your homework, then there's no reason why you can't take it further than that and give a bloody good performance.

Will I get an understudy matinee?

Depending on the agreement you have with the producers, there may be an opportunity for an understudy performance, especially if not all the understudies have had the chance to go on during the run of the show. It's not guaranteed, but if it is going to happen, it will usually be one afternoon when there's no public performance in the theatre (or a theatre on the tour that's reasonably close to London).

All the understudies will play their covered role (or sometimes roles), and may ask supporting members of the principal cast to come in and play the others. They are not obliged to say yes, since it's not in their contract to give up their afternoon off, and they're not getting paid for it; but if asked nicely, most actors are generally happy to help out if they can. If one of them isn't available for some reason, there may need to be some nifty doubling, or the company manager may go on with a book.

Who should I invite to see me?

The understudy matinee is your chance to invite all your friends, family, former colleagues, potential employers, casts from nearby theatres – just about anyone! – to come and see your performance. Tickets will usually be free, but there may be a limit on the number of tickets available to keep front-of-house staff costs down.

I mention inviting potential employers: this can be tricky, even if the show is in the West End. Excuses for casting directors' non-attendance may be along the lines of "Oh, it's so hard to get away from the office [50 yards from the theatre!] during the day," but in reality, producers' frequent indifference to the actual acting talent of the understudy – or, for that matter, the malaise that can set in in the understudy after years sitting in a dressing room doing crosswords – can result in some really quite uninspiring performances during these matinees, and the casting directors know it. (I'm talking about straight plays here; it's a rather different story in musical theatre, where understudies are usually working members of the ensemble and more regularly pressed into service in principal roles.) It's worth asking, nevertheless, although only if you're confident in giving them a show they'll be impressed with. Don't however think that this is your moment to get seen by every casting director in town – it won't be.

Should I do it again?

A good, reliable understudy is highly prized by producers, and may even be offered work on a new production before the principal actors are cast. But once known as an understudy (with the exception, perhaps, of the RSC), it can be hard to get them to see you as someone they might want to cast in a principal role. That may not be a problem for you – in the West End, at least, it gives you terrific freedom to do other things, especially if you have family commitments or are developing another career as a writer or voice-over, say – but a life of waiting in the wings is not for everyone. If you're coming to the end of one understudy job, you must think carefully (and discuss with your agent) about how much and what kind of understudy work you'd like to be put up for in the future. Regular understudying is not the occupation of the ambitious actor, so think carefully about what the benefits and pitfalls of taking a particular understudy job might be.

Andrew Piper trained at Bristol Old Vic Theatre School and edited *Actors' Yearbook* for the 2007 and 2008 editions. He understudied the role of Bernard Woolley in the original West End transfer of Chichester Festival Theatre's production of *Yes, Prime Minister*. Thanks are due to the more experienced understudies who offered their comments on early drafts of this article.

Independent managements/theatre producers

This section lists commercial organisations that mount West End and touring productions to mostly larger-scale venues – some of which originate in the subsidised sector. Some productions will be led by well-known actors but they will usually need supporting actors in the ensemble and to understudy those leads. In long-running productions, the understudies may get a chance to do their own performance – an Understudy run – which can be a useful showcase for agents and casting directors. Understudies will generally be required to attend rehearsals post-press night on one or two afternoons per week before the evening show, usually run by the associate, resident or staff director. Of course if you find yourself understudying, it pays to be as prepared as possible to go on at a moment's notice whether you have had rehearsal time or not. Theatre lore is full of stories of heroic understudies saving the day. It pays to be ready … tonight could be your night.

Touring can be demanding; long periods away from home, variable quality of accommodation, lots of travelling and adjusting to new cities and stages. But it can also be hugely rewarding and fun. When else do you get paid to explore a different place every week? Touring is incredible training; every time you play a new stage and new auditorium you have to adjust your performance, physicality and vocal quality. You will finish a tour with far greater experience and resilience than you had when you started. And hopefully a suitcase full of magical experiences and memories.

Ambassador Theatre Group (ATG)
39–41 Charing Cross Road, London WC2H 0AR
website www.atgentertainment.com
Ceo Ted Stimpson, *Chief Content Officer* Michael Lynas
Production details: ATG is the largest owner and operator of theatres in the UK, with a total of 58 venues across the world. It produces across the UK, Europe and the USA. Anywhere between 3 and 30 actors work on each production. Offers Equity approved contracts.
Casting procedures: Uses freelance casting directors. Welcomes letters (with CVs and photographs), but not email submissions. Actors may write at any time, but prefers contact to be made via an agent and preferably during pre-production. Advises actors against sending expensive photos 'on spec', especially if unaccompanied by a letter. Actively encourages applications from disabled actors and promotes the use of inclusive casting.

Contemporary Stage Company
9 Finchley Way, London N3 1AG
email contemp.stage@hotmail.co.uk
Artistic Director David Graham-Young
Production details: Founded in 1993, The Contemporary Stage Company's focus is on presenting plays and adaptations of novels, with an emphasis on work from cultures outside the English-speaking world.
Casting procedures: Occasionally uses freelance casting directors and holds general auditions. Welcomes CVs and letters from actors previously unknown to the company. Also welcomes invitations to view individual actors' websites and performance notices. Rarely has the opportunity to cast disabled actors.

Fiery Angel
3rd Floor, 26 Great Queen Street, London WC2B 5BL
email office@fiery-angel.com
website https://fiery-angel.com
Facebook /FieryAngelHQ
Directors Edward Snape, Marilyn Eardley

Fiery Angel is an independent production company producing drama, comedy, musicals and event theatre in London, on tour and internationally, for both adults and children.

Robert Fox Ltd
website www.robertfoxlimited.com
Director Robert Fox
Production details: Founded in 1980. Theatre and film production company specialising in large-scale theatre productions and musicals as well as feature

films. Performances are staged in the West End and on Broadway.

Casting procedures: Employs casting directors for specific projects and does not welcome unsolicited submissions from actors.

Sonia Friedman Productions
5th Floor, 65 Chandos Place, London WC2N 4HG
tel 020-7854 8750
email queries@soniafriedman.com
website www.soniafriedman.com
Facebook /SoniaFriedmanProductions
X @SFP_London
Instagram @sfpofficial
Producer Sonia Friedman, *Executive Director* Diane Benjamin, *Executive Producers* Pam Skinner (International), Ros Brooke-Taylor, *Associate Producers* Charlie Bath, Max Bittleston (International), David Nock, Aimee Hulme, Azera Jones

Production details: Sonia Friedman Productions is one of the West End's most prolific and significant theatre producers, responsible for some of the most successful theatre productions in London and on Broadway over the past two decades. Since 1990 SFP has produced more than 270 new productions and has won 67 Olivier Awards, 61 Tony Awards and 3 BAFTAs.

Productions include: the UK premiere of *The Book of Mormon* in London and on tour in the UK and Europe; *Harry Potter and the Cursed Child* in London, New York, Melbourne, San Francisco, Hamburg, Toronto and Tokyo; *Oklahoma!* at Wyndham's Theatre, London; *To Kill a Mockingbird* at the Gielgud Theatre, London; *Dreamgirls* on tour in the UK; *Funny Girl* in New York; *Leopoldstadt* in New York; *Merrily We Roll Along* in London and New York; *The Piano Lesson* in New York; *Mean Girls* at The Savoy Theatre, London and on tour in the US; and *The Shark Is Broken* at the Mirvish Theatre, Toronto.

David Graham Entertainment Ltd
3rd Floor, 14 Hanover Street, London W1S 1YH
mobile 07711 894826
email info@davidgrahamentertainment.com
website www.davidgrahamentertainment.com
Director David Graham

Production details: Theatre producer and concert promoter. Specialises in music ranging from leading West End singers, tribute bands and musicals. Stages around 4 productions in 80 theatres and concert halls on an annual basis, with more than 300 performances per year. Countries covered include Britain, Holland, Germany, Canada, Spain, Norway and Ireland. In general, 12 performers work on each production.

Casting procedures: Does not use freelance casting directors or hold general auditions. Casting breakdowns available via Script Breakdown, CastCall and other casting publications.

Michael Grandage Company (MGC)
4th Floor, Wyndham's Theatre, Charing Cross Road, London WC2H 0DA
tel 020-3582 7210
email info@michaelgrandagecompany.com
website www.michaelgrandagecompany.com
Facebook /michaelgrandagecompany
X @MichaelGrandage
Instagram @michaelgrandagecompany
Artistic Director Michael Grandage, *Executive Director* Stella McCabe, *Producer* Nick Frankfort

Production details: MGC is a London-based production company that produces stage and screen work across all media, nationally and internationally. Recent productions include *The Line of Beauty* (Almeida Theatre), *My Master Builder* (West End), *Backstairs Billy* (West End), *Orlando* (West End) and *Dawn French is a Huge Tw*t* (UK/international tours); and the film *My Policeman*. It also has a general management service and looks after a select group of creative practitioners.

Hartshorn-Hook Productions
Arts Theatre, 6–7 Great Newport Street, London WC2H 7JB
email executive.assistant@hartshornhook.com
website www.hartshornhook.com
Directors Louis Hartshorn, Brian Hook

Production details: Founded 2007. A commercial theatre company based in the West End. It provides general management services to theatre companies across the UK, whether professional productions or community projects. They have produced over 130 productions across 5 continents.

Casting procedures: Welcomes invitations to attend productions in Greater London.

Paul Holman Associates
Morritt House, 58 Station Approach, South Ruislip, Middlesex HA4 6SA
tel 020-8845 9408
email enquiries@paulholmanassociates.co.uk
website www.paulholmanassociates.co.uk/home
Facebook /PHApantos
Instagram @phapanto
Founder & Managing Director Paul Holman, *Creative & Casting Director* Nick George

Production details: Established in 1990. Produces pantomimes, summer shows and one-night attractions. See entry under *Pantomime producers* on page 262 for more details.

Colin Ingram Ltd
tel 020-8065 0427
email colin@coliningramltd.com
website www.coliningramltd.com
Director Colin Ingram

Production details: Theatrical producers and general managers. The company offers Equity-approved contracts and participates in the Equity Pension Scheme. "Please see the website for details of recent productions and venues."

Casting procedures: Uses freelance casting directors. Does not welcome unsolicited approaches from individual actors previously unknown to the company.

Gareth Johnson Ltd
Plas Hafren, Eglwyswrw, Crymych, Pembs. SA41 3UL
tel (01239) 89136 8
email gjltd@mac.com
website www.garethjohnsonltd.com

Production details: Founded in 2000, this general management company produces (for a client) up to 6 shows a year, West End, UK and overseas. Offers Equity contracts.

Casting procedures: Uses freelance casting directors and does not welcome unsolicited contact of any kind from actors. Policy on disabled actors as instructed by client.

Jonathan Church Theatre Productions
8th Floor, 55 The Strand, London WC2N 5LR
tel 020-7451 1732
email office@jctproduction.com
website https://jctproduction.com/
Director Jonathan Church, *Executive Producer* Becky Barber

Jonathan Church Theatre Productions is an award-winning London-based production company, producing high-quality theatre in the West End, nationally and internationally.

Current productions include: *The Seagull* (The Royal Lyceum Edinburgh, Chichester Festival Theatre), *Top Hat The Musical* (UK Tour), *A Chorus Line* (Japan Tour), *To Kill A Mockingbird* (UK Tour), *A Man For All Seasons* (Harold Pinter and UK Tour), *Singin' In The Rain* (China Tour) and *The Lion, The Witch, The Wardrobe* (Leeds Playhouse).

Offers Equity contracts and is a UK Theatre member and SOLT member.

Richard Jordan Productions Ltd
Mews Studios, 16 Vernon Yard, London W11 2DX
tel 020-7243 9001
email info@richardjordanproductions.com
Director Richard Jordan

Production details: Founded in 1998. Produces theatre in London and throughout the UK and internationally. Main area of work is new writing and revivals of plays; occasionally produces musicals. Company works as general managers and consultants for a wide range of producers and theatres in the UK and abroad. Stages around 10–20 productions annually with 300 performances during the course of the year. The company has produced and developed over 260 productions in the UK, as well as 28 other countries including 91 world premieres and 89 European, Australian or US premieres by both new and established writers. A new writing and musical theatre specialist, Richard has been at the forefront of developing and producing works by a diverse range of established and emerging writers and artists from around the world. He is the recipient of numerous major awards including the TONY, EMMY, and Olivier.

Casting procedures: Welcomes letters (with CVs and photographs) but not email submissions. Applications are particularly welcome if actors are currently in a production that the company can go and see. Advises that applicants should have an awareness of the type of work produced by the company before sending CVs.

Gavin Kalin Productions
tel 020-3151 0110
email info@gavinkalinproductions.com
website ww.gavinkalinproduction.com
Instagram @gavinkalinprods
Managing Director Gavin Kalin

Gavin Kalin Productions is an award-winning production company that specialise in producing theatrical content in the West End, on Broadway and internationally. Produces both original and adapted stories, working with up-and-coming and established talent.

Robert C. Kelly
PO Box 5597, Glasgow G77 9DH
tel 0141 533 5856
email robert@robertckelly.co.uk
website www.robertckelly.co.uk
Managing Director Robert Kelly

Production details: The company has 40 years' experience hosting productions across the UK, Ireland, Australia and New Zealand, with over 200 performances each year. Each year the company produces multiple pantomimes in the UK and Ireland. Offers Equity-approved contracts and subscribes to the Equity Pension Scheme.

Casting procedures: Uses freelance casting directors. Actively encourages applications from disabled actors and promotes the use of inclusive casting.

Bill Kenwright Ltd
BKL House, 1 Venice Walk, London W2 1RR
tel 020-7446 6200
email info@kenwright.com
website www.kenwright.com
X @BKL_Productions
Chief Executive David Gilbery, *Executive Producers* Julius Green, Jeremy Meadow

Award-winning prolific commercial theatre and film production company, presenting revivals and new works for the West End, international and regional theatres. Productions include *The Lightning Thief*, *Blood Brothers*, *Heathers*, and *Boys from the Black Stuff*.

Casting procedures: In-house and freelance casting directors. Enquiries (with CVs and photographs) to **info@kenwright.com**.

Independent managements/theatre producers

Lambert Jackson
website https://lambertjackson.co.uk
Facebook /lambertjacksonproductions
X @LJProds
Instagram @lambertjacksonproductions
Founders Jamie Lambert, Eliza Jackson

Established in 2018. Produces theatre, live events and concert tours, in the West End and across the UK. They produce original stories and work with well-known personalities including musicians, comedians and presenters.

Limelight Productions Ltd
57 Glenesk Road, London SE9 1AH
tel 020-8853 9470
email enquiries@thelg.co.uk
website www.thelimelightgroup.co.uk
Facebook /thelimelightgroup
X @Limelight_Group
Artistic Director Richard Lewis

Production details: Established in 1996. Stages 2–3 productions annually, touring the UK and internationally.

Productions include: *Peppa Pig Live, Teletubbies, LazyTown Live, Octonauts Live, Ben and Holly's Little Kingdom Live* and *Some Mothers Do 'Ave 'Em.* Offers Equity-approved contracts.

Eleanor Lloyd Productions
39–41 Charing Cross Road, 5th Floor,
London WC2H 0AR
website https://elproductions.co.uk
Associate Producer Cat Gray, Creative Producer Hart Fargo

London-based production company delivering work in the West End and on Broadway. Through their work, which has a contemporary focus, they support female and ethnically diverse creatives.

Cameron Mackintosh Ltd
1 Bedford Square, London WC1B 3RB
tel 020-7637 8866
website www.cameronmackintosh.com
Chairman Cameron Mackintosh, Head of Casting Paul Wooller, Casting Director Felicity French

Production details: Stages musical theatre productions worldwide.

Casting procedures: In-house casting. Does not hold general auditions. Welcomes letters (with CVs and photographs) as well as email submissions. Also accepts showreels and invitations to view individual actors' websites.

Middle Ground Theatre Co.
3 Gordon Terrace, Malvern Wells,
Malvern WR14 4ER
tel (01684) 577231
email middleground@middlegroundtheatre.co.uk
website www.middlegroundtheatre.co.uk
Instagram @middlegroundtheatrecompany
Artistic Director/Producer Michael Lunney

Production details: Established 1988. Theatre company producing drama to tour theatre venues and arts centres in the UK and Ireland. Stages 1 or 2 productions a year with 180 performances across around 25 venues. Covers the whole of Britain, Northern Ireland and Ireland. Size of cast varies from show to show. Offers actors non-Equity contracts and does not participate in the Equity Pension Scheme.

Casting procedures: Casts in-house. Casting breakdowns are not publicly available (Spotlight only). Welcomes submissions from actors (with CV and photograph) if sent by post or email. Also welcomes showreels and invitations to view individual actors' websites. Welcomes applications from disabled actors to play disabled characters and LGBTQ+ actors.

Mischief Theatre
3rd Floor, 62 Shaftesbury Avenue,
Londond W1D 6LT
website www.mischiefcomedy.com
Facebook /MischiefTheatre/
X @mischiefcomedy
Instagram @mischiefcomedy
Artistic Directors Henry Lewis, Creative Director Jonathan Sayer

Production details: Mischief was founded in 2008 by a group of acting graduates of LAMDA and began as an improvised comedy group. Mischief performs across the UK and internationally with original scripted and improvised work and also has a programme of workshops. The company is owned and controlled by its original members and is led by a creative group and its directors.

Francesca Moody Productions (FMP)
email hello@francescamoody.com
website https://francescamoody.com
Facebook /FMoodyProductions
X @FMP_Theatre
Instagram @francesca_moody_productions
Executive Producer Francesca Moody, Shedinburgh Producer Darcy Dobson, Production Coordinator Rory Thomas-Howes, Shedinburgh Assistant Producer Tom Chamberlain, Production Assistant Angel Mika Kemp, Creative Associate Jon Brittain, Production Associate Jack Boissieux

An Olivier Award-winning, Tony nominated production company whose work in theatre has originated 2 of the most globally successful television shows of the last decade: *Fleabag* and *Baby Reindeer*.

Makes original theatre, television, film and audio. Believes in finding the right home for the right story and growing it over time. From tiny fringe theatres to the West-End, to the next big Amazon television series and beyond.

Neal Street Productions
26–28 Neal Street, London WC2H 9QQ
tel 020-7240 8890
email post@nealstreetproductions.com
website www.nealstreetproductions.com
X @NealStProds
Instagram @nealstreetproductions
Company Director Nicholas Brown

Production details: Established in 2003, Neal Street Productions works across theatre, film and television. They run the Theatre Artists Fund to support theatre workers and freelancers in financial difficulty, as well as the The Screenwriter's Bursary Scheme and New Playwriting Commissioning Scheme to support new writers.

Casting procedures: They do not except any unsolicited scripts or treatments and will only accept material via an agent.

New Frame Productions
email hello@newframeproductions.com
website www.newframeproductions.com
Facebook /newframeprods
Executive Producers James Quaife, Robin Rayner

Established in 2020 in response to the Covid-19 pandemic, New Frame Productions is a live and digital production company that explores new ways of creating and sharing stories. They value inclusivity, artistic bravery, queerness, sustainability and bold storytelling, and work to remove barriers to access in the entertainment industry.

Norwell Lapley Productions Ltd
Unit 4, Brindley Close, Tollgate Industrial, Stafford ST16 3SU
tel (01785) 335736
email cdavis@nlp-ltd.com
website www.nlp-ltd.com
Non-Executive Chair Chris Davis, Managing Director Derrick Gask

Production details: Produces theatre in the West End and touring productions. Stages 4–5 productions annually and gives 250 performances during the course of the year at theatres nationwide.

Casting procedures: Uses freelance casting directors and does not deal directly with actors.

Playful Productions
39 Charing Cross Road, London WC2H 0AR
tel 020-7811 4600
email aboutus@playfuluk.com
website https://playfuluk.com/
Instagram @Playfulprods
Directors Matthew Byam Shaw, Nia Janis, Nick Salmon

Production details: Established in 2010. Produces plays and musicals for the West End, Broadway and on tour in the UK and internationally. Also provides general management and production accountancy services to other producers. 'Our team is driven by a love for the creative process and a passion for working with the hundreds of people we collaborate with to produce great theatre.'

Long-running productions: *Wicked* (Apollo Victoria) and *Moulin Rouge! The Musical* (Piccadilly Theatre). Touring productions: *Wicked*. Current productions: *MJ The Musical* (Prince Edward Theatre), *Born With Teeth* (Wyndham's Theatre), *Buena Vista Social Club* (Broadway), *All My Sons* (Wyndham's Theatre), *The Unbelievers* (Royal Court Theatre) and *Make It Happen* (Edinburgh International Festival and Dundee Rep Theatre).

PW Productions Ltd
114 St Martin's Lane, London WC2N 4BE
tel 020-7395 7580
email info@pwprods.co.uk
website www.pwprods.co.uk
X @PWProds
Chief Executive Iain Gillie

Production details: The company, which Peter Wilson founded in 1983, specialises in the production, general management and bookkeeping/accountancy for theatre presentations.

The Really Useful Group Ltd
6 Catherine St, London WC2B 5JY
website www.reallyuseful.com
Facebook /reallyusefulgroup
X @OfficialRUG

Production details: Founded in 1977 by Andrew Lloyd Webber. It is an international entertainment company actively involved in theatre ownership and management, theatrical production, film, television, video and concert productions, merchandising, records and music publishing.

ROYO
20 Denmark Street, London, WC2H 8NE
tel 020-3468 8584
email hello@royo.co.uk
website https://royo.co.uk
Facebook /RoomOnYourOwn
X @RoomOnYourOwn
Instagram @roomonyourown
Founders Tom de Keyser (Executive Director), Hamish Greer (Creative Director)

ROYO is a theatrical production studio dedicated to producing new commercial work, both original stories and in collaboration with existing brands. As well as their own productions, they also invest in, and work as producers and general managers on, productions across the UK.

Second Half Productions
email info@secondhalfproductions.co.uk
website www.secondhalfproductions.co.uk
Facebook /SecondHalfProds

Independent managements/theatre producers 199

Instagram @secondhalfprods
Directors Jeremy Herrin, Alan Stacey, Rob O'Rahilly

Specialise in original and adapted work that tackles the political landscapes of the past and present to engage audiences across the UK. They prioritise improving accessibility for those who are under-represented in theatre.

Stage Entertainment
De Boelelaan 30, 1083 HJ Amsterdam, Netherlands
tel +31 (0)20-305 2222
email info@stage-entertainment.com
website www.stage-entertainment.com
Facebook /StageEntertainmentInternational
Instagram @stageentertainmentcorporate
Ceo Arthur de Bok

Established in 1998, Stage Entertainment is a global theater production company, managing 16 theatres in Europe and licensing or touring work in the UK, US, Latin America, Australia and Japan. They specialise in musical theatre, working in collaboration to stage established classics and original work.

The Jamie Lloyd Company
email info@thejamielloydcompany.com
website https://thejamielloydcompany.com
Facebook /JamieLloydCo
X @JamieLloydCo
Instagram @jamielloydco
Founder Jamie Lloyd

Established in 2013, the Jamie Lloyd Company produces original and classic theatre in the West End and on Broadway. They specialise in working with well-known actors, including those making their theatre debut.

Trafalgar Entertainment
Head office: Export House, 5 Henry Plaza, Victoria Way, Woking GU21 6QX
tel (01483) 247400
website www.trafalgarentertainment.com
Facebook /trafalgarentertainment
X @TrafalgarEnt
Instagram @trafalgarent
Co-founders Howard Panter (Creative Director), Dame Rosemary Squire

Established in 2017. Produces original and classic plays, musicals and pantomimes for theatres in the West End, across the UK and around the world. Their work also incorporates performing arts education, theatre ticketing, the distribution of live-streaming content and the development of new and existing theatres.

UK Productions
Brook House, Mint Street, Godalming, Surrey GU7 1HE
tel (01483) 423600
email mail@ukproductions.co.uk
website www.ukproductions.co.uk

Managing Director/Producer Martin Dodd, *Artistic Producer* Damian Sandys

Production details: Established 1995. Produces pantomime, musicals and drama for No. 1 touring, nationally and internationally including West End and Broadway theatres. (See entry under *Pantomime producers* on page 262.) Offers non-Equity contracts ("roughly in line with Equity") and does not subscribe to the Equity Pension Scheme.

Casting procedures: Casting is done in-house. Does not hold general auditions. Casting breakdowns are distributed via Spotlight or direct to agents. Welcomes performance notices but not any other unsolicited form of correspondence. "Unsolicited CVs are generally a waste of time." Will consider applications from disabled actors to play characters with disabilities.

Wessex Grove
1st Floor, 39–41 Charing Cross Road, London WC2H 0AR
tel 020-3907 2544
email info@wessexgrove.com
website https://wessexgrove.com
Instagram @wessexgrove
Producers Benjamin Lowy, Emily Vaughan-Barratt

Established in 2020, Wessex Grove is a theatrical production company that produces and manages innovative and exciting work in the West End, on Broadway, and beyond.

West End International
The Old Brewhouse, Chesham Road, Wigginton, Herts. HP23 6EH
tel 07710 091245
email alison@westendinternational.com
website https://westendinternational.com/
Directors Martin Yates, Alison Price

Production details: Concert and theatre producers. Will accept casting enquiries and letters (with CVs and photographs) from actors previously unknown to the company, sent by post or email. Does not welcome unsolicited showreels.

Jamie Wilson Productions
1st & 5th Floor, 39-41 Charing Cross Road, London WC2H 0AR
tel 020-7240 0748
email info@jamiewilsonproductions.com
website https://jamiewilsonproductions.com
Producer Jamie Wilson, *Executive Director* Oliver Mackwood

Established in 2008, Jamie Wilson Productions is an independent production company specialising in original work and revivals. They have produced or co-produced over 90 productions in London and New York, and on tour throughout the UK and internationally.

Voicing kindness

Hazel Holder, dialect and voice coach
Interview by Joan Iyiola

Hazel Holder has been an actor, singer and theatre maker for over thirty years before retraining and receiving her MA in Voice Studies from the Royal Central School of Speech and Drama. Hazel has worked with pioneering companies such as Clod Ensemble, The Mono Box, Clean Break, Marginal Voices and Cast Women's Charity. She works across theatre, television and film.

How would you describe your role as a voice and dialect coach?
I think of myself as a bridge between the actor, the story and their performance. I think bridge is a helpful word because I believe the journey is just as important as the destination. I create imagery about where the actor is now, where they want to get to and how the work will enable them to reach their destination. When I started drama school at Mountview, I was dismissed after one term as the Head of Voice said I was 'untrainable as an actress' because I had a lisp. Thankfully, things have changed, and there are many actors now with speech impediments, but because my first encounter with a voice coach was incredibly negative, my own coaching comes from a place of deeper empathy. It's important that we don't demonise our differences in a creative space.

I want to touch on the fact that you were not always a voice coach. Tell us a bit about your pathway into the industry.
I started out in this industry as a precocious little child who loved to get up in front of everyone to sing and dance. I went to church and that gave me the confidence to sing in front of people. But I've also always relished the opportunity for growth, from working with Black Mime theatre company to singing in jazz bands and two acapella groups (Helen Chadwick Song Theatre and Orlando Gough's The Shout), to performing twice on Broadway with the National Theatre of Scotland and the Young Vic. It's been a really varied journey and I think, ultimately, the vibrations of all those different experiences are just living in my body. The variety of my work has kept me engaged and inquisitive because I know there are so many achievable choices out there.

So, what made you divert to coaching?
I've always been interested in using my voice as an instrument, not just as a thing of 'beauty.' I was performing in *Death and the King's Horsemen* at the National Theatre and a theme of the story was the clash of cultures between British colonialism and Yoruba traditions. This meant that I sang in Yoruba as well as a classical aria. During the run, Jeannette Nelson – Head of Voice at the National – said I think you should train to be a voice coach. I said no to her for a long time as I was scared about what that would entail. But thank goodness she persevered, and I eventually went to retrain in voice at Central. It turns out that as a mature student, my life/work experience was more valuable to the industry than my lack of a previous degree and I haven't looked back.

What are some of the best things that we can do as individuals to make sure our voice is looked after?
The first thing I would say, as we negotiate this extraordinary time, is to be joyful. To connect with the feeling of joy in your body, because when you have joy in your body,

it is reflected, manifested by a sense of ease in your voice. I encourage people to put music on and dance, sing along, put music on and lip-bubble to it to work the breath. I also encourage people to go out into open spaces and feel their voice energetically, play, laugh a lot as laughter opens the throat. Take this time to enjoy your body and voice as it will keep it prepared for work. When you're booked for a job, why not ask for vocal help, whether that is dialect or voice, as soon as the contract is signed, or make a gentle regime that you can incorporate into daily life. When you're brushing your teeth, stick your tongue out and give it a good brush! Leave your tongue hanging out and count so you're releasing the tongue root. Then when you're in bed remember to 'clean' your teeth with your tongue, as again, circling releases tongue root tension; to help you to get to sleep you can do breathing exercises, which will also gently work the muscles of expiration. You can release a long 'sss' or 'shhh' three times, breathing low into your belly and noticing your ribs widening.

I've seen that you've paved the way for many, particularly other ethnically diverse voice and dialect coaches. What is the motivation behind this?

Part of my motivation for changing things is purely selfish. I've felt very alone as a Black voice coach in this industry and, simply, I don't want to feel like that anymore. Voice work in the UK has traditionally been very white and very middle class and with the work that is produced and hopefully the work that is to come, we need to have all types of people in creative spaces. The industry needs to stop resisting diversity that isn't in front of the camera or onstage. Being a voice and dialect coach normally means that you're a department of one, but it doesn't have to be like that. I really want to be part of a community, to bounce ideas off each other and to literally have a voice and enable others to feel the same.

What are your hopes for the future of voice and dialect coaches?

I'm helping producers understand that they always need a voice department. The nature of voice work is such a delicate balance of personalities, technique, creativity and ability, and productions can receive so much from the variety of people and ideas in the space. Having Caribbean heritage and working in African theatre a lot I look at parts of the working models of British theatre and ask, 'Do they really serve us well?' By that I mean a short rehearsal schedule, not enough time for actors to embody the work, let alone makers to create, and so on. Everyone is working on empty and the fumes of adrenaline. We can learn a lot from observing how other cultures place value on the creative journey. I hope voice and dialect coaches can be part of the catalyst for change, by asking to shift parts of previous models to ones that better put the performers, the makers and the journey of making at the centre of the work.

We believe that your work is both technical and holistic. It focuses on who each actor is as an individual. Can you tell us about your technique and why you've honed it in this way?

When I was acting and singing, I knew I couldn't perform unless I was connected to my body, able to free my mind and let go of the voice that's telling me I can't do it. Now, as a coach, I look at the whole person to assess what they need and being a magpie for information I have a variety of approaches. I am neurodivergent, so I listen to a lot of audiobooks because reading takes me ages. I watch videos, take courses, observe life, talk a lot with everyone, talk a lot with myself, have therapy, so then, when I'm in the space working, I draw from all the things I've learnt and ask myself what this person needs, rather than what they expect me to offer them. I don't believe that there is a one-size-fits-all prescription for everyone or every voice: our life journeys are too rich and varied for that.

Anything else to add?

Be kind to people and kindness will come back to you. You can give truthful feedback kindly. I've been on the receiving end of anger and frustration as both an actor and a coach and it's uncreative and paralysing. When I've been on the receiving end of kindness my work is better. I want there to be playfulness and laughter in the rehearsal space so that people feel free and confident. I am reminded of Maya Angelou's words 'People will forget what you say, they will forget what you did, but they will never forget how you made them feel'. Never a truer word said.

To follow Hazel's work visit **www.hazelholder.com** or follow her on Instagram @hazel_holder.

Ignition, inspiration and the imposter

Scott Graham

I have been lucky enough to have been the artistic director of Frantic Assembly, the company I co-founded, since 1994. It frustrates and savages me from time to time, but that is all part of the relationship with a job that also sustains, educates and consistently surprises me. To be in a rehearsal room with a playwright and other fascinating humans is to engage in literary and historical analysis, sociology, philosophy, poetry, anthropology, politics, psychology, etc. Admittedly, we might not be talking as experts, but the breadth of that conversation, in pursuit of a better understanding of a character's predicament or the experience of an audience, is an invigorating privilege and often inspirational.

Having said that, my relationship with this career is complex.

Serendipity saw me being put forward for a play by a schoolteacher against my will and yet enjoying it immensely. Then I discovered a fascination for movement when I stepped in to help choreograph a physical scene between an Oberon, who did not turn up, and Titania, who was my first proper girlfriend. (It was not all good luck as Titania actually left me for Oberon!). When I plucked up the courage to join a drama society at university I was fortunate enough to meet people who would become some of my closest friends and allies, with whom we would have the audacity to form a company based on very little experience, a hell of a lot of energy and a sense of, well, why not?

Even back then, as soon as we learned something, we would try to teach it, to pass it on. I think this meant that we were always breaking processes down into their component parts to see how they really worked (my dad was a motor mechanic and this metaphor is as close I have got to following in his footsteps). As we had zero training, we did not have a short hand or vast technique to fall back on. If I was falling back on anything it was my years of playing sport. I could see the similarities. Sport and martial art gave me a good sense of my own balance and physicality and that awareness really helped, not only in making it more likely that I could achieve the movement, but also in puncturing some of the mystique around theatre and dance.

Sport has had a profound effect on how the company operates. We would do hundreds of workshops in schools and I would always attempt to make the students feel like they could be part of a games lesson or the best part of the playground. We were aiming for that euphoria of scoring a goal or winning as a team. I think I was trying to keep the people who might think this drama lark was not for them in the room in the hope that they, like me, would experience that revelation, see the similarities and apply their skills within the theatre studio.

When we created our free training programme, Ignition, it was with the purpose of attracting young men into our type of theatre. It was not created simply by feeling their absence, but by the strong belief that they were out there with all of their crossover skills, applying them elsewhere. They were never going to come to us because we were terrifying them. We had to look at the language we used and how we presented ourselves if we were to be an attractive proposition to these young men.

We trawled the country trying to get a diverse mix of young men who had little or no engagement in the arts and put them through an intense training programme where, in four days, they met for the first time and by the end had made and performed a show for a public audience. They were nurtured and supported by professionals at every step, but it was their bravery, generosity and commitment that got them through what can be a transformative week in their lives. Many graduates have gone on to work in theatre. Paapa Essiedu played Hamlet at the RSC in 2016. There might not be a more high-profile symbol of the success of this programme than this. Across the country, young men returned to their towns invigorated and empowered and I am immensely proud of that.

The success of Ignition has been extraordinary and in 2019 we launched our female version with a similar drive to bring new voices and energy into our theatre. Again, the focus is on the energy and ethics I have found in sport.

One of my most illuminating rehearsal periods was the creation of Frantic's boxing show, *Beautiful Burnout*. We had already researched the boxing world extensively and found intense, sensitive relationships at the heart of what might appear to be the coldest, loneliest and most brutal of sports. There is so much respect and care to be found inside these gyms. So much to learn and so much to be taught. There is something really beautiful to see how that boxer between rounds, sweating, gloves on, cannot drink or even pick up their bottle of water without a friend unscrewing it and holding it to their mouth.

We wanted to take some of that encouraging culture back into the rehearsal room for this show. In fact, we turned the room into a gym with weights, skipping ropes and punch bags set up. The effect on the performing company was startling. The room became so positive and energised. People would choose to train during their breaks. No one collapsed onto a sofa and bitched about agents. The focus was absolute.

All of this was born out of the intense circuit training and boxing warm ups. It had built a team and vast amounts of mutual respect. It was so successful that versions of it have been employed on most subsequent Frantic shows to build a culture of support, application and community. It builds the ensemble.

All of this validated my instinct about what sport could bring to theatre and how crossover skills were valuable. This was me bringing a world I felt comfortable with into the theatre experience.

My lack of training or what I might have considered a proper theatre background has, at times, made me feel like an imposter. I felt unsure, that I had no right to be right. I questioned my authority to write the *Frantic Assembly Book of Devising Theatre*[1] and needed some convincing. When I was invited to speak to academics as part of my role as Visiting Professor at Coventry University I initially felt a paralysing sense that I was a charlatan and had nothing to say.

But I have also found a lack of training has been liberating, allowing me to be inspired by a vast range of stimuli. I embraced my limitations and developed a way of working that suited me and those that might be like me. I have seen that method empower skilled actors and dancers too. I have seen how they break free from their training and technique and are refreshed.

Knowledge creeps up on you. It can take a long time to recognise that you have something to say and the authority to say it. I have seen plenty of people make all the right noises and present a veneer of authority. I have been intimidated by it but I have ultimately

---

[1]. *Frantic Assembly Book of Devising Theatre* by Scott Graham and Steven Hoggett, 2nd edition, Routledge, 2014.

seen through it. It comes from the same place as my imposter syndrome. It comes from our fear of the world looking at us and seeing that we might not know the answers. In theatre, what is so wrong about that? Just like my initial inexperience and limitations I have learnt to use this to my advantage. It is an exciting place to be.

When I was part of the creative team making *The Curious Incident of the Dog in the Night-Time*[2] I went through that initial fear of being found out, of being out of my depth, but what was so illuminating and empowering was seeing that same look on other people's faces. They were not trying to hide the fear that is an essential part of the creative process. We were all taking ourselves to places we were not sure about. We were taking risks, trying something new and encouraging each other to be brave. Seeing these respected and award-winning artists work in such an honest and relentless fashion was a formative creative experience that helped me deal with (accept rather than crush) my imposter syndrome and redefined my relationship with the rehearsal room.

It is now so clear to me that we enter a rehearsal room to find out what we don't yet know rather than enter to tell the world what we do know. I tell my MA students when they are setting up devising tasks, be the bad scientist, not the good scientist. The bad scientist mixes ingredients and blows their eyebrows off. As long as they remember that that concoction can do that then they have learnt something. They can use that again when the time is right. Don't be the good scientist who merely acts to prove their theory. They have not moved forward through the task. They have not discovered something new.

Training opportunities are the same. As we walk in through the door we should be asking, what can we take with us as we leave? Too often we enter with a mask and just pray it does not slip. I know I have.

This is why I love working with actors. Initially many hide behind that mask, but when you can help them to get to that place of truth you see how empowering that can be. I have seen the tiniest moment of physicality become the breakthrough for an actor to base a whole character on. Not a tic or an affectation. I mean a moment that links to the tension held within and makes sense of their interaction with the world around them. It feels seismic. It also comes from an understanding of the text. There is often a perception that physical work is not cerebral. This is a damaging miscalculation. We live the majority of our lives reading the world physically, displaying and reading nuance. I consider my movement direction to be 'direction through movement' and its ambition is to open up the text. I think it is so important that performers are open to the potential the physical approach can bring. Try not to hide what you think are your deficiencies, don't think of movement as something that you can or cannot do, it is what we *all* do! We tell and read stories physically all through our waking hours. Exploring this and embracing this nuance can only empower the actor.

This is why I love my job. I learn something every day. I learn about you, I learn about characters and I learn about me. When I get asked a question at a post-show discussion, I often think that the student believes they are asking me what I know without realising that the act of asking is helping me form those thoughts. Those thoughts can surprise me. I would not know that I thought that if they had not asked me that question.

[2.] As of July 2022, The National Theatre's Olivier and Tony Award-winning production of *The Curious Incident of the Dog in the Night-Time* (2012) has just finished its 10th Anniversary Tour across the UK and Ireland. Directed by Marianne Elliott and adapted by playwright Simon Stephens.

I think it is important to recognise that. We can crush ourselves under the expectation that we should know all the answers. This can close us off from meaningful collaboration and kill a rehearsal room or drama studio. Sometimes holding up your hands and saying, 'I don't know what to do here' is not an admission of defeat. It is the invitation to your collaborators to step up. It often takes that explicit moment of honesty.

Scott Graham is co-founder and artistic director of Frantic Assembly. Further information about Frantic Assembly and contact details can be found in their entry in our *Middle and smaller-scale companies* listings on page 214 of this *Yearbook*. The extensive Frantic Assembly website (**www.franticassembly.co.uk**) gives details and illustrations of their previous productions, and how to apply to take part in Ignition.

Middle- and smaller-scale companies

This section covers a huge range of companies from the prestigious and subsidised whose shows may play long tours in large theatres, to the small independents which survive with little or no public subsidy and perform wherever they can find an audience. The bigger companies operate much like the major building-based theatres and commercial producers. Smaller companies may not be able to afford casting directors and do everything themselves.

Small-scale touring theatre is often made on a shoestring budget with irrepressible reserves of passion, collaboration and tenacity. It can be hard work for actors who may need to spend long hours travelling between venues and helping to put up the set, but it is a right-of-passage for many subsequently successful performers, directors, playwrights and creatives who cut their teeth on the road. Working for small-companies to take shows to audiences who may never have the opportunity to visit a gilded West End proscenium arch can be infinitely rewarding and companies often form strong working relationships and even lifelong bonds.

As new companies spring up all the time, these listings only contain organisations that have been in existence for three years or more.

Note: Some of the companies listed are members of the Independent Theatre Council (ITC) – **www.itc-arts.org**.

20 Stories High
Toxteth TV, 37–45 Windsor Street, Liverpool L8 1XE
tel 0151 708 9728
email info@20storieshigh.org.uk
website www.20storieshigh.org.uk
Facebook /twentystorieshigh
Bluesky @20storieshigh.bsky.social
Instagram @20storieshigh
Artistic Director Keith Saha, *Executive Director* Leanne Jones

Production details: Established in 2006. Creates dynamic, challenging theatre which attracts new audiences, artists and participants. Produces theatre with working class and culturally diverse young people, emerging artists and world-class professionals. Arts Council NPO from April 2012. Generally stages one project annually, with around 40 performances in 20 theatres, schools and youth clubs in the North West and nationally. In general 2–5 actors are involved in each production. Offers Equity-approved contracts as negotiated through ITC.

Casting procedures: Holds general auditions. Casting breakdowns are available from the website and Equity Job Information Service. Welcomes letters (with CVs and photographs) from individual actors previously unknown to the company, sent by post or email, and is happy to consider invitations to view individual actors' websites. Actively encourages applications from artists of colour, disabled artists and others currently under-represented in the industry.

1623 Theatre Company
QUAD, Market Place, Cathedral Quarter, Derby DE1 3AS
tel (01332) 285434
email messages@1623theatre.co.uk
website www.1623theatre.co.uk
*Director*s Sam Beckett Jr (they/them), Jamie Brown (he/him), Ben Spiller (they/them)

Production details: Shaking, shaping and sharing creativity based on community experiences and Shakespeare's plays. This includes theatre performances, participatory activities, learning workshops and training sessions.

Casting procedures: Welcomes both CVs and letters from actors previously unknown to the company and unsolicited CVs and photographs. These should be sent via email. Also welcomes invitations to view individual actors' websites or productions. Happy to accept showreels. Actively encourages applications from artists who are deaf, disabled, emerging, female, global majority, LGBTQ+, neurodiverse and working class.

Access All Areas
Bradbury Studios, 138 Kingsland Road, London E2 8DY
tel 020-7613 6445
email hello@accessallareasproductions.org
website https://accessallareasproductions.org
Facebook /AccessAllAreasProductions

Bluesky @aaaprods.bsky.social
Instagram @accessallareasproductions
Artistic Director Nick Llewellyn

Makes award-winning, disruptive performance by learning disabled and autistic artists. Their productions create intimate moments of interaction between performers and public, occupying unexpected spaces in venues, on the streets, online, and in public buildings. As well as making shows, their company of Associate Artists works to make our culture more inclusive for learning disabled and autistic talent. They engage communities, train artists of the future, and work closely with TV, film, and theatre companies to make their work and workplaces more accessible.

They've developed a programme of work that challenges exclusion at every level of our culture. All their work, from productions, to consultancy, to creative workshops, is co-led by Access All Areas' learning disabled and autistic artists, ensuring lived experience drives everything they do. Their programme is split between Screen work, which includes all their collaborations with TV and film companies, and Theatre work, which includes their live shows, artist training, community engagement and sector change initiatives.

Accidental Theatre

12–13 Shaftesbury Square, Belfast BT2 7DB
tel 020-9032 5881
email info@accidentaltheatre.co.uk
website www.accidentaltheatre.co.uk
Facebook /AccidentalTheatre
Instagram @accidentaltheatre
Artistic Director Richard Lavery

Production Details: Established in 2012. Accidental's theatre is a collision of perspectives, art forms and unusual collaborations – curious stories told through vibrant, ambitious performances. Accidental works with playwrights, actors, filmmakers, DJs, choreographers, musicians, poets, painters, technicians and curators to craft plays for Ireland and the world stage. They are an in-person and online venue and media creation charity. Collective risk-taking is the inspiration that jolts their work into new theatrical territories and opens it up to new audiences. Accidental walks the tightrope between the unexpected and the impossible, exploring the intersection between British narrative and European aesthetic styles of theatre.

Casting Procedures: Uses in-house casting directors and hold general auditions. Welcomes enquiries, CVs and letters from actors previously unknown to the theatre. Also happy to receive unsolicited CVs, letters, showreels and invitations to view individual actors websites. Casting breakdowns are available from the theatre's website. Promotes inclusive casting, actively encourages applications from actors with disabilities to play characters with disabilities.

Actors of Dionysus (aod)

25 St Luke's Road, Brighton BN2 9ZD
mobile 07957 471949
email info@actorsofdionysus.com
website www.actorsofdionysus.com
Facebook /ActorsOfDionysus
X @aodtheatre
X @TamsinShasha
Instagram @actorsofdionysus, @lionhouse79
Artistic Director Tamsin Shasha, *Education Officer* Mark Katz, *Content Administrator* Izzy Grout, *Associate Directors* Katherine Sturt-Scobie

Production details: Award-winning national and international touring company founded in 1993. Executive Directors on the King's College London Greek Play. aod specialises in performing new adaptations of Ancient Greek drama and new writing inspired by myth, through a fusion of poetry, music and movement. "Our mission statement is to make magic from myth by reframing ancient Greek theatre for the 21st century, making it relevant, accessible and transformative through high-quality theatre that sparks debate and engagement with immediate global issues." Via its outreach arm, aod offers an established educational programme of workshops (digital and live), pre-show talks, publications, audio-CDs and DVDs and also offer workshops and performances in schools. Can tour throughout the year; venues include national and international touring venues, schools and arts centres. In general one to 5 actors work on each production.

Runs an award-winning and intimate urban venue called Lionhouse during Brighton Fringe, with a garden and interior space available to hire.

Casting procedures: Does not use freelance casting directors. Holds general workshop auditions; actors should write to request inclusion in early spring and summer. Casting breakdowns are available via the website and Spotlight. Does not welcome general submissions from actors but will accept invitations to view individual actors' Spotlight links and websites.

Actors Touring Company (ATC)

email atc@atctheatre.com
website www.atctheatre.com
Instagram @actorstouringcompanyatc
Artistic Director Matthew Xia, *Executive Director* Helen Jeffreys

Production details: Established in 1979, the Actors Touring Company are passionate about giving voice to the 'outsider within' and connecting global artistic voices to local communities. They work throughout the UK and internationally, from Scarborough to Hong Kong. At least 2 productions are staged annually, employing roughly 4–6 actors per production. Offers ITC/Equity-approved contracts.

Casting procedures: Works with specified casting directors on casting productions. Does not accept unsolicited CVs.

ARC Theatre Ensemble

Kingsley Hall, Parsloes Avenue, Dagenham, Essex RM9 5NB
tel 07483 342158
email info@arctheatre.com
website www.arctheatre.com
X @arctheatre
Instagram @arc_theatre_london_uk
Resident Writer and Co-Founder Clifford Oliver

Production details: Founded in 1984, Arc has built a strong core Management and Associate team bringing together an exceptional range of creative skills, educational experience and business and social expertise. The company is governed by an equally diverse and committed Board of Management. "We also benefit from a first-class pool of highly skilled, trained actors, storytellers, facilitators, workshop leaders, production managers and designers who are individually hand-picked to suit each programme or bespoke project." See the website for more details of its work.

Casting procedures: "To register your interest in working with Arc, please submit your details via info@arctheatre.com. We will keep your details on record and contact you when a suitable opportunity arises. Alternatively you can email your details to our General Manager, Nita Bocking: nita@arctheatre.com."

Attic Theatre Company

Mitcham Library, 157 London Road, Mitcham CR24 2YR
tel 020-8640 6800
email info@attictheatrecompany.com
website www.attictheatrecompany.com
Executive Director Victoria Hibbs, *Artistic Director* Tom Bellerby

Production details: Attic makes theatre for both traditional and non-traditional theatre spaces and audiences, and commissions new work as well as classic adaptations. Many of Attic's productions are staged within non-traditional and community spaces, employing both an urban and and rural touring model. Attic also runs an extensive community programme of work with older people and young people facing disadvantage, particularly refugees, asylum seekers, EAL students, young people with ASD/SEND and those with low emotional resilience. For recent and forthcoming poductions see the website.

Casting procedures: Uses freelance casting directors. Does not hold general auditions and does not accept casting enquiries or submissions from actors.

Badapple Theatre Company

PO Box 57, York YO26 8WQ
tel (01423) 331204
website www.badappletheatre.co.uk
Artistic Director & Writer Kate Bramley

Production details: Founded in 1998. Specialises in new comedy. Stages productions at a local rural touring level, national arts centre and small- to mid-scale theatre level.

Casting procedures: Uses direct mail castings to agencies. Actors with an interest in the company are free to contact the office at any time. Directors prefer to see actors in performance prior to castings, so welcomes updates of performances in the Yorkshire region that company directors would be able to attend.

Beyond Face

Knowle West Media Centre, Leinster Avenue, Bristol BS4 1NL
email opportunities@beyondface.co.uk
website www.beyondface.co.uk
Facebook /infobeyondface
Instagram @infobeyondface
Ceo/Artistic Director Alix Harris

Established in 2015. Provides opportunities for artists of the global majority to live, work and thrive in the South West theatre sector.

Big Telly Theatre Company

c/o Flowerfield Arts Centre, 185 Coleraine Road, Portstewart, Derry~Londonderry BT55 7HU
tel 028-7083 6473
email info@big-telly.com
website www.big-telly.com
Facebook /bigtellyni
X @BigTellyNI
Artistic Director Zoë Seaton

Production details: Big Telly Theatre Company is Northern Ireland's longest established professional, not-for-profit theatre company, formed in 1987 and based in Portstewart on the North Coast. The company brings world class theatre to small communities in Northern Ireland, and brings those voices to the world stage. It concentrates on hijacking familiar stories and spaces to make audiences feel both safe and brave. Making bold new stories that mix up traditions with and for the wider community.

Casting procedures: Casts on a project-by-project basis. Avoids the submissions of general CVs but welcomes invitations to see artists perform or a showreel of their work. All invitations should be sent to producer@big-telly.com. Has a strong commitment to diverse and inclusive casting.

Border Crossings

13 Bankside, Enfield EN2 8BN
tel 020-8366 5239
email info@bordercrossings.org.uk
website www.bordercrossings.org.uk
Artistic Director Michael Walling

Production details: Established in 1995. International company, working in theatre and combined arts, that creates dynamic performances by fusing many forms of world theatre, dance and music. Stages one or 2 productions per year touring to up to 15 venues including arts centres and theatres. Roughly 3–9 actors are used in each production. "We don't offer Equity contracts, although our own contracts are modelled on the ITC/Equity contract, and we usually pay above the minimum." Does not subscribe to the Equity Pension Scheme.

Casting procedures: Welcomes letters (with CVs and photographs) from actors previously unknown to the company. Invitations to view individual actors' websites and showreels are accepted. Actively encourages applications from disabled actors and promotes the use of inclusive casting.

Boundless Theatre
12 South Norwood Hill, London SE25 6AB
tel 020-7072 0140
email hello@boundlesstheatre.org.uk
website www.boundlesstheatre.org.uk

Production details: Established in 2001 (as Company of Angels). New and experimental work made with and for young audiences. Offers Equity approved contracts as negotiated through ITC.

Casting procedures: Actors may write at any time to request inclusion on the database for future reference. Performers previously unknown to the company should contact Boundless Theatre with their CV by email only. Boundless Theatre is an equal opportunities employer and actively encourages applications from BME and disabled actors in line with their policy on inclusive casting.

Bruiser Theatre Company
83 University Street, Belfast, BT7 1HP
tel 028 9024 3731, *mobile* 07540 477055
email info@bruisertheatrecompany.com
website www.bruisertheatrecompany.com
Facebook /BruiserNI
X @BruiserNI
Instagram @bruiserni
Artistic Director Lisa May

Production details: Founded in 1997, Bruiser focus on producing exciting and innovative theatre, presenting existing texts using physical theatre techniques. Each production consists of 2–14 actors and musicians and, on average, the company present 2 productions per year. This equates to a tour of around 45 performances at 16 venues.

Casting procedures: Uses in-house casting directors; casting breakdowns are available on the website. Actors will be required to submit a self-tape and successful applicants will be invited to audition.

Cahoots Theatre Company
St Martin's Theatre, West Street,
London WC2H 9NZ
email info@cahootstheatrecompany.com
website www.cahootstheatrecompany.com
Facebook /cahootstheatreco
Artistic Director Denise Silvey

Production details: Founded in 1999. Produces theatre, cabaret and CD recordings, as well as acting as a general management and press agent. Stages 3–5 productions a year, with 100 performances over 15 venues (arts centres, theatres and cabaret venues) in London, Edinburgh and New York. Productions may involve from one to 17 performers. Offers Equity approved and non-Equity contracts.

Casting procedures: Casting in in-house. Also publishes casting breakdowns on the Equity JIS. Welcomes emails (but not letters) with CVs and photographs from individuals previously unknown to the company. Does not welcome showreels, but is happy to receive invitations to view actors' websites. Will consider applications from disabled actors to play characters with disabilities.

Cambridge Shakespeare Festival
mobile 07955 218824
email mail@cambridgeshakespeare.com
website www.cambridgeshakespeare.com
Artistic Director Dr David Crilly, *Associate Directors* Dr Simon Bell, David Rowan

Production details: The Festival Company was established in Oxford in 1988 by Artistic Director Dr David Crilly. The main focus for the Company is the annual Cambridge Shakespeare Festival, which runs throughout July and August. Situated in the gardens of the Colleges of Cambridge University, its pastoral setting is one of the loveliest in the world.

Cardboard Citizens
Hoxton Works, London N1 6SH
tel 020-7377 8948
email mail@cardboardcitizens.org.uk
website www.cardboardcitizens.org.uk
Facebook /cardboardcitizens
X @cardboardcitz
Instagram @cardboardcitz
Artistic Director/Joint Ceo Chris Sonnex

Production details: Cardboard Citizens creates theatre and art with, for and about people with lived experience of homelessness, poverty, or inequity. Regular productions include national tour and community production.

Casting procedures: Hires actors through Casting Agents and their workshop programme. All actors must have some experience of homelessness, unless otherwise specified. More information can be found online at **cardboardcitizens.org.uk/work-with-us**.

The Castle Players
c/o Tilly Bailey & Irvine, 8 Newgate, Barnard Castle, Co. Durham DL12 8NG
mobile 07974 046802
email info@castleplayers.co.uk
website www.castleplayers.co.uk
Chair Sue Byrne

Middle- and smaller-scale companies 211

Production details: An amateur community theatre company limited by guarantee. Established in 1987. Undertakes major open-air summer productions in a specially constructed tiered-seat theatre. Also stages minimum of one touring production annually.

Casting procedures: Productions are cast from the local community at open auditions. Subscribe to the newsletter via the company website for regular updates. Uses in-house casting directors and holds general auditions; actors should write in January to request inclusion.

Chain Reaction Theatre Company

Millers House, Three Mill Lane, London E3 3DU
tel 020-8981 9527
email admin@chainreactiontheatre.co.uk
website www.chainreactiontheatre.co.uk
Facebook /ChainReactionTC
Instagram @chainreactiontheatre
Artistic Director Sarah Smit

Production details: Chain Reaction is an award-winning London-based charity that has been using theatre and media to ignite personal and social change since 1994. Chain Reaction works in partnership with schools, local councils, theatres and corporate organisations to produce high-quality, emotionally engaging theatre projects that transform the way people relate to themselves, their community and to wider society.

Chain Reaction works across both the public and private sector, ensuring that their work with vulnerable young people is at the heart of what they do. They currently have 12 educational shows in their repertoire, each designed for a specific age range from 5–16 years-old. Performances tackle sensitive and controversial topics including drug-awareness, sexual health, bullying, aspirations, emotional wellbeing, healthy eating and exercise. Using the power of creativity, Chain Reaction engages, educates and empowers people to reach their full potential in life. Whether delivering professional theatre performances or running youth theatres, creative media workshops, social action groups or interactive training programmes, their work increases people's skills, knowledge and understanding, whilst building resilience, self-esteem and confidence.

Casting procedures: General auditions when required. Casting in-house.

Cheek by Jowl

Stage Door, Barbican Theatre, Silk Street, London EC2Y 8DS
tel 020-7382 2391
email info@cheekbyjowl.com
website www.cheekbyjowl.com
Facebook /cheekbyjowl
Instagram @wearecheekbyjowl
Artistic Directors Declan Donnellan, Nick Ormerod

Production details: The company was founded in 1981 by Declan Donnellan and Nick Ormerod. The name conveys an intimacy between the actors, the audience and the text; the phrase 'cheek by jowl' is quoted from *A Midsummer Night's Dream* ("Follow! Nay, I'll go with thee cheek by jowl" (Act III, Sc II)).

Casting procedures: Casting Director for UK productions is Siobhan Bracke. It is asked that actors get their agents to contact Siobhan directly at **siobhan.bracke@gmail.com**. The casting process differs for non-UK shows from one production to the next. Does not accept unsolicited CV's. Opportunities are advertised on their website and social media.

Chickenshed Theatre

290 Chase Side, Southgate, London N14 4PE
tel 020-8292 9222
email info@chickenshed.org.uk
website www.chickenshed.org.uk
Managing Director Louise Perry, *Director of Education and Training* Paul Morrall

Founded in 1974, Chickenshed brings together people of all ages and from all backgrounds; it is a theatre for everyone. Through productions, performance training, education courses and our outreach projects, Chickenshed creates wonder out of chaos, and change out of challenge.

Using the power of performing arts Chickenshed helps people reach their full potential and feel accepted; and creates an inclusive environment where people don't stigmatise, label or disregard, but accept and welcome difference. Chickenshed's vision is a society that celebrates diversity and enables every individual to flourish.

Most Chickenshed show run from 3–6 weeks while the Christmas show runs for 7. Chickenshed has 4 performance spaces which are used during the Christmas show run but at other times performance spaces are available. The Rayne Theatre is an attractive and modern theatre space seating 300. The seating can be retracted to the rear wall creating a large, flat open space for performance or workshops. The Studio Theatre is 12m x 12m and is extremely versatile with seating for up to 140. Premises are accessible to disabled performers.

Casting procedures: Chickenshed generally produces in-house shows. Occasionally holds general auditions and uses website breaksown services. Please submit CVs throughout the year. Welcomes letters from individual actors previously unknown to the company and welcomes invitations to view individual actros' website and to visit other productions.

Actively promotes inclusive casting and believes that all of their actors should have access to all parts that are required. Usually casts from their own pool of actors but if there is a specific artistic casting requirement open calls may be considered.

Clean Break

2 Patshull Road, London NW5 2LB
tel 020-7482 8600
email general@cleanbreak.org.uk

website www.cleanbreak.org.uk
Facebook /cleanbreak
Bluesky @cleanbrk.bsky.social
Instagram @cleanbrk
LinkedIn /clean-break
Executive Director Natasha Bucknor (Interim), *Artistic Director* Anna Herrmann, *Producers* Dezh Zhelyazkova, Allison Birt (Maternity Cover)

Production details: Clean Break was founded in 1979 by 2 women serving sentences at HMP Askham Grange, who believed in the transformative power of theatre. The company's artistic mission is to create bold new plays by women playwrights, telling the often unheard stories of women and criminalisation, on stages across London, the UK and internationally. The company use theatre to transform the lives of women who have experienced the criminal justice system, or who are at risk of entering it. Their theatre workshops in prisons and in the community build women's confidence, resilience and wellbeing, alongside new creative skills. The average cast size is 3–5. Offers ITC/Equity-approved contracts and subscribes to the Equity Pension Scheme.

Casting procedures: Uses freelance casting directors. Does not issue breakdowns. Auditions are organised via actors' agents and personal management. Unable to accept unsolicited CVs or showreels from actors. "Clean Break employ only women to deliver our services in accordance with our exemption under the Equality Act 2010, Part 1 Schedule 9. We also actively seek to work with artists who have lived experience of the criminal justice system." Clean Break casting includes women auditioned via its Members Programme – a theatre making programme for women with experience of the criminal justice system or who are at risk. Actively encourages applications from disabled actors, actors from the global majority and promotes the use of inclusive casting.

Clod Ensemble

C2, 3 Cripps Yard, Soames Walk, Design District, Greenwich Peninsula SE10 0BQ
tel 020-7749 0555
email admin@clodensemble.com
website www.clodensemble.com
Artistic Directors Suzy Willson, Paul Clark

Production details: A small- to mid-scale company established in 1995. Creates original contemporary performance, primarily with dancers and musicians. Based in London, with some work touring the UK and internationally. Stages on average one production each year in the main house; also runs Learning and Talent Development workshops and courses.

Casting procedures: Holds general auditions and performers should write to request inclusion by email. Actively encourages applications from disabled performers and promotes the use of inclusive casting. Offers Equity-approved contracts as negotiated through ITC.

Complicité

Studio 15, Jolt Studios, 27 St. Aldate Street, Gloucester GL1 1RP
Unit 19, Artsadmin, Toynbee Studios, 28 Commercial St, London E1 6AB
tel 020-7485 7700
email email@complicite.org
website www.complicite.org
Facebook /TheatredeComplicite
Instagram @complicitetheatre
Artistic Director Simon McBurney

Production details: Award-winning theatre company founded in 1983. Constantly evolving its ensemble of performers and collaborators. Work ranges from entirely devised pieces to theatrical adaptations and revivals of classic texts.

Casting procedures: Invites performers to R&Ds. "We are always more inclined to meet actors previously unknown to us if they are familiar with our work (i.e. if they have seen a Complicité show or participated in an Open Workshop). Complicité's Creative Engagement Department programmes up to 2 Open Workshop seasons for actors each year."

Concordance

Finborough Theatre, 118 Finborough Road, London SW10 9ED
tel 020-7244 7439
email admin@finboroughtheatre.co.uk
website www.concordance.org.uk

Production details: A theatrical production company, founded by Neil McPherson in 1981, at the Finborough Theatre, London. The company presents new writing, revivals of neglected work and music theatre.

Creation Theatre Company

tel (01865) 766266
email boxoffice@creationtheatre.co.uk
website www.creationtheatre.co.uk
Facebook /CreationTheatre
X @creationtheatre
Instagram @creationtheatre
CEO & Artistic Director Dr Helen Eastman

Production details: Oxfordshire's largest producing theatre company. Specialises in classic texts in unusual locations. Performs in extraordinary spaces (e.g MINI car plant, The Bodleian Library, Oxford's historic Covered Market and The London Library). Since 2020, they broadcast live perfomances online to master the digital stage.

Casting procedures: Does less casting than they used to because of their full time Rep company. If you are within commuting distance of Oxford then actors or their agents are asked to email Michael Deacon (Deputy Producer) at **michaeldeacon@creationtheatre.co.uk**.

Cumbernauld Theatre at Lanternhouse
South Kildrum Ring Road, Cumbernauld,
Glasgow G67 2UF
tel (01236) 732887
email info@lanternhousearts.org
website https://lanternhousearts.org
CEO Sarah Price, *Operations Director* Amanda Young, *Creative Producer* Fraser Morrison

Production details: Established in 1978. A year-round producing theatre with a broad range of artist development and creative learning programmes. Produces a professional pantomime each year, together with other in-house plays, musicals and 'seasons'.

Casting procedures: Casting is done by the Creative Producer. Auditions are held all year round; actors can obtain casting breakdowns from the website or social media, plus Spotlight and Creative Scotland's website. Will consider invitations to visit other productions, but requests that no showreels be submitted. Actively encourages applications from disabled actors and promotes the use of inclusive casting. See **https://lanternhousearts.org/creative-opportunities/current-opportunities** for more.

Dark Horse
Lawrence Batley Theatre, Queen's Street,
Huddersfield HD1 2SP
tel (01484) 484441
email info@darkhorsetheatre.co.uk
website www.darkhorsetheatre.co.uk
Artistic Director Amy Cunningham

Production details: Established in 2000. Production company developing a range of live, recorded and digital projects led by trained actor/theatre-makers with moderate learning disabilities and promoting inclusive working practices. Typically one national touring production per year featuring 6–9 company actors as well as non-learning disabled actors.

Casting procedures: Occasionally uses freelance casting directors. Does not welcome unsolicited CVs. Actively encourages applications from disabled actors and promotes the use of inclusive casting. Offers Equity-approved contracts.

Eastern Angles Theatre Company
The Eastern Angles Centre, Gatacre Road,
Ipswich IP1 2LQ
tel (01473) 218202
email admin@easternangles.co.uk
website www.easternangles.co.uk
X @easternangles
Instagram @easternangles
Artistic Director Jake Smith

Production details: Founded in 1982 and based in East Anglia, Eastern Angles is a regionally focused theatre company with a broad world view in their approach to creating work. They seek to remove barriers that prevent people from participating in the shared experience of arts, heritage and culture. It tours theatre productions across East Anglia and also nationally on occasion. It stages 4–5 pieces each year, with an average annual total of 220 performances at 80 different venues. Performance venues include arts centres and theatres, educational and community venues, and site-specific locations. In general, 4 actors work on each production. EATC offers ITC/Equity Ethical Manager contracts as well as Equity pension contributions.

Casting procedures: Does not use freelance casting directors but does hold general auditions to find local talent. Casting breakdowns are on Spotlight and are not publicly available but may occasionally be posted on the website.

The Edge Theatre
Manchester Road, Chorlton, Manchester M21 9JG
tel 0161 2829 776
email bookings@edgetheatre.co.uk
website www.edgetheatre.co.uk
Facebook /theedgetheatre
X @theedgemcr
Instagram @edgemanchester
Artistic Director Janine Waters

Production details: The Edge is Manchester's award-winning theatre for participation and is a receiving and a producing house. Our beautiful venue has entertained, captivated and enthralled audiences with some of the best small scale touring theatre in the country, alongside our own productions made by our wonderful in-house creatives. They have worked with hundreds of actors and musicians; many are professional, some have learning disabilities, some have experience of homelessness and some are from the local community. As theatre makers they delight in creating shows which reflect the world that we live in, even if it's set them on the moon. They are honest, relevant and always full of hope. As a Manchester Cultural Partner, they play a vital role in the cultural offer of the city. As leaders in participation, they provide a range of opportunities for people to be creative.

Casting procedures: Uses in-house casting directors, but does not hold general auditions. Welcomes unsolicited CVs and photographs and showreels from actors who are strong singers only. Also happy to receive invitations to view productions in the north-west. Actively encourages applications from disabled actors and promotes the use of inclusive casting. Offers Equity/ITC-approved contracts.

ETT (English Touring Theatre)
25 Short Street, London SE1 8LJ
tel 020-7450 1990
email admin@ett.org.uk
website www.ett.org.uk
Facebook /weareETT
Instagram @englishtouringtheatre
Artistic Director Richard Twyman

Production details: ETT are a UK based international touring company. Creating theatre which is ambitious, imaginative, responsive and alive, ETT interrogates and celebrates contemporary England and reflects the diversity of the nation. It tours to mid-large scale venues nationwide, staging a balance of new and classic work, sparking dialogue and fostering connectivity. Each yeat ETT works with around 15 venue partners, touring to 25 towns and cities and reaching an average audience of 75,000 people.

Offers UK Theatre/Equity contracts and subscribes to the Equity Pension Scheme.

Casting procedures: Uses freelance casting directors and does not encourage unsolicited submissions from actors.

The Faction
17 Vanbrugh Park, London SE3 7AF
email info@thefaction.org.uk
website www.thefaction.org.uk
Facebook /TheFactionCo
X @_The_Faction
Artistic Director Mark Leipacher, *Associate Artist* Rachel Valentine Smith

Production details: Founded in 2008, an independent theatre company dedicated to innovative revivals of classical texts. Aims to generate and sustain an ensemble of actors who share and develop skills, and who can explore a 21st-century solution to the extinct repertory system. "We question what constitutes a 'classical text', and work to determine which authors' works complement and enhance our understanding and enjoyment of Shakespeare and his contemporaries and thus should be a permanent part of the repertoire."

Work takes the form of international projects, three-play repertory seasons, outdoor performances, staged readings and digital performances.

Casting procedures: Casts in-house. Casting breakdowns are available from the website, mailing list, email and Mandy. Welcomes letters (with CVs and photographs) from individual actors previously unknown to the company, sent by email. Also accepts showreels and invitations to view actors' websites and visit other productions. Encourages applications from disabled actors and promotes the use of inclusive casting.

Forced Entertainment
The Workstation, 15 Paternoster Row, Sheffield S1 2BX
tel 0114 279 8977
email fe@forcedentertainment.com
website www.forcedentertainment.com
Key personnel Tim Etchells (Artistic Director), Robin Arthur, Richard Lowden, Claire Marshall, Cathy Naden, Terry O'Connor

Production details: Since forming the company in 1984, the 6 core members of the group have sustained a unique artistic partnership, confirming their position as "trailblazers in contemporary theatre". The company's substantial canon of work reflects an interest in the mechanics of performance, the role of the audience, and the machinations of contemporary urban life. Its work, framed and focused by Artistic Director Tim Etchells, is distinctive and provocative, delighting in disrupting the conventions of theatre and the expectations of audiences. Forced Entertainment's trademark collaborative process – devising work as a group through improvisation, experimentation and debate – has made them pioneers of British avant-garde theatre, and touring all over the world has earned them an unparalleled international reputation. Visit the website for a full archive of work.

Forest Forge Theatre Co.
Pintail House, Duck Island lane, Ringwood, Hampshire BH24 3AA
tel (01425) 470188
email hello@forestforgetheatre.co.uk
website www.forestforgetheatre.co.uk
Facebook /ForestForgeTC
Instagram @forestforgetc
Co-Artistic Directors Lucy Phillips, Jo Billingham

Production details: Their work spans across touring productions, participation and artist development, with a focus on making and building connections between people. They use theatre to find the extraordinary in the ordinary.

Frantic Assembly
Brixton House Theatre, 385 Coldharbour Lane, London SW9 8GL
tel 020-3161 4031
email admin@franticassembly.co.uk
website www.franticassembly.co.uk
Facebook /franticassembly
Instagram @frantic_assembly
Artistic Director Scott Graham, *Executive Director* Kerry Whelan

Production details: Award-winning theatre company Frantic Assembly's method of devising theatre has been impacting theatrical practice and unlocking the creative potential of future theatre-makers for over 25 years. Frantic Assembly has toured extensively across Great Britian, and has worked in 40 countries internationally collaborating with some of today's most inspiring artists. Frantic Assembly are currently studied as leading contemporary theatre practitioners on 5 British and international academic syllabuses and introduce over 15,000 workshop participants to the company's process of creating theatre annually. With a history of commissioning writers such as Lemn Sissay, Anna Jordan, Simon Stephens, Abi Morgan and Bryony Lavery, the company has been accclaimed for its collaborative approach.

Frantic Theatre Company
32 Wood Lane, Falmouth TR11 4RF
tel 0870 165 7350
email bookings@frantictheatre.com
website www.frantictheatre.com

Production details: Founded in 1990. Stages 2 productions annually with around 900 performances in venues throughout the UK and Ireland every year. Venues include arts centres, village halls, theatres, outdoor venues, educational and community venues, private homes and hospitals. On average 2 actors work on each production.

Casting procedures: Holds general auditions. Actors should write in May and November to request inclusion. Casting breakdowns are available at Call Pro. Actors are advised not to telephone and to send their details only when they have researched the company's very specific work and are able to explain their suitability.

Graeae Theatre Company
Bradbury Studios, 138 Kingsland Road,
London E2 8DY
tel 020-7613 6900
email info@graeae.org
website www.graeae.org
Facebook /graeae
Bluesky @graeaetheatre.bsky.social
Instagram @graeaetheatrecompany
Joint Ceos Jenny Sealey (Artistic Director), Kevin Walsh (Executive Director)

Production details: Founded in 1980, Graeae boldly places D/deaf and disabled actors centre stage.

Graeae's signature aesthetic is the compelling creative integration of sign language, captioning and audio description, which engages with both disabled and non-disabled audiences. Championing accessibility and providing a platform for new generations of artists, Graeae leads the way in pioneering, trailblazing theatre. Graeae also run an extensive programme of creative learning opportunities throughout the year, training and developing the next generation of D/deaf and disabled artists. These programmes include Write to Play and Ensemble.s

Green Ginger
Unit 18, Albion Dockside Estate, Hanover Place,
Bristol BS1 6UT
mobile 07977 465850
email mail@greenginger.net
website www.greenginger.net
Facebook /greengingertheatre
Artistic Director Chris Pirie, *Patron* Terry Gilliam

Casting procedures: Does not hold open auditions. Does not accept unsolicited CVs. External casting directors are used to cast for productions.

Production details: Founded in 1978, Green Ginger creates and tours original theatre with complementary educational activities for all ages and all abilities. Green Ginger collaborates with major arts organisations, including Welsh National Opera and Aardman Animations. Its members teach at University of Bristol, École Supérieure Nationale de la Marionette (France) and the Royal Welsh College of Music and Drama.

Each production consists of 3–4 actors and, on average, the company presents 2 productions a year. The company tours extensively, having performed around the world for 40 years. Touring productions can be adapted to a variety of venues including schools, theatres, community spaces and outdoor and non-traditional theatre spaces. Offers Equity/ITC approved contracts at above minimum rates.

Casting procedures: Uses freelance casting directors and occasionally holds general auditions. Casting breakdowns are available online and on social media. Welcomes both CVs and letters from performers previously unknown to the company and unsolicited CVs and photographs. Also welcomes invitations to view individual actors' websites and showreels. The company welcomes the opportunity to cast performers with protected or under-represented characteristics.

Grid Iron Theatre Company
Suite 4/1, 2 Commercial Street, Edinburgh EH6 6JA
tel 0131 555 5455
email jude@gridiron.org.uk
email ben@gridiron.org.uk
website www.gridiron.org.uk
Facebook /gridirontheatre
Co-Artistic Directors Judith Doherty, Ben Harrison

Production details: Founded in 1995. Produces location- and site-specific theatre. Are an Edinburgh based new writing theatre company but their adventures have taken them to extraordinary places (e.g Edinburgh Zoo, Norwegian Fjords, General Security building in Beirut, Edinburgh airport, parks, housing estates, playgrounds and bars).

Casting procedures: Casting opportunities can be found on their website at **gridiron.org.uk/casting**.

Headlong Theatre
3rd Floor, 207 Waterloo Road, London SE1 8XD
tel 020-7633 2090
email info@headlongtheatre.co.uk
website www.headlong.co.uk
Facebook /HeadlongTheatre
Instagram @headlongtheatre
Artistic Director Holly Race Roughan, *Executive Director* Lisa Maguire

Production details: National touring theatre company dedicated to creating exhilarating contemporary theatre through a provocative mix of innovative new writing, reimagined classics and influential 20th century new plays.

Casting procedures: Offers TMA/Equity approved contracts. Casting not dealt with in-house. Independent casting directors used on a show-by-show basis; their names and information will be listed on the theatre website.

Highly Sprung Performance
Daimler Powerhouse, Sandy Lane Business Park, Sandy Lane, Coventry CV1 4DQ
tel 07780 626604
email team@highlysprungperformance.co.uk
website www.highlysprungperformance.co.uk
Facebook /highlysprungperformance
Instagram @highlysprung
Artistic Director Mark Worth, Executive Director Sarah Worth

Production details: Founded in 1999. Aims to create original and innovative performances exploring the relationship between dance, text and physical theatre. Also runs community and educational activities alongside productions. Tours extensively as a part of the UK's outdoor arts network. Visiting festivals and events, high streets and parks. They make bespoke performances for public spaces such as libraries, museums and community settings. Current productions include: Accelerate, CastAway, Grow in the Garden and Simile.

Casting procedures: Holds auditions in relation to specific projects. Actors should send CVs and photographs by email in response to casting callouts. Casting callouts advertised on website and social media.

Hijinx
Wales Millennium Centre, Bute Place, Cardiff CF10 5AL
tel 029-2030 0331
email info@hijinx.org.uk
website www.hijinx.org.uk
Facebook /hijinxtheatre
Instagram @hijinxtheatre
Artistic Director Ben Pettitt-Wade

Production details: An award-winning not-for-profit professional theatre company. Hijinx always casts actors with learning disabilities and Autism in their shows which tour the world.

Offers ITC/Equity-approved contracts and does not subscribe to the Equity Pension Scheme.

Casting procedures: Shows are cast by the Artistic Director. Welcomes letters, CVs and photographs from actors previously unknown to the company. Welcomes applications from disabled and non-disabled actors.

Historia Theatre Company
8 Cloudesley Square, London N1 0HT
tel 020-7837 8008, mobile 07811 892079
email historiatheatre@yahoo.co.uk
website https://historia25.wixsite.com/historicatheatre
Facebook /theatrecompanyhistoria
Artistic Director Catherine Price

Production details: Established in 1997, now a registered charity. "Historia presents plays that have their source or inspiration in history." One production annually, with 20–30 performances. Plays in small theatres in London mainly for short runs; touring productions visit theatres, arts venues, National Trust houses, museums, churches, schools and village halls both nationally and in London. Roughly 6–8 actors are used in each production.

Casting procedures: Does not use freelance casting directors or hold general auditions. Breakdowns are published via Equity's Job Information Service and Spotlight link. Unsolicited approaches from actors are discouraged. Will consider applications from disabled actors when casting for characters with disabilities.

Horse + Bamboo
679 Bacup Road, Waterfoot, Rossendale, Lancs. BB4 7HQ
tel (01706) 220241
email info@horseandbamboo.org
website www.horseandbamboo.org
Facebook /horseandbamboo
X @HorseandBamboo
Instagram @horseandbamboo
Creative Development Director Esther Ferry-Kennington, Executive Producer Jenn Camilleri

Production details: Established in 1978. A puppetry, mask and processional theatre. Houses a 90 seat theatre and bar, and a Creative Centre offering a rehearsal room and fully equipped making workshop for artists to collaborate, create and share their work. Also includes a unique archive of 4 decades of visual theatre, national and international touring, processional arts, puppetry, music and mask. Producers of Waterfoot Wakes annual summer festival. Offers Equity contracts. Members of ITC.

Casting procedures: Welcomes communication from touring theatre companies and socially engaged artists.

Icarus Theatre Collective
62 Gordon Road, High Wycombe, Bucks. HP13 6ER
tel 020-7998 1562
website www.icarustheatre.co.uk
Facebook /icarustheatre
X @icarustheatre
Instagram @icarustheatre
Artistic Director Max Lewendel

Production details: Icarus creates theatre that is kinetic, intellectual, and visceral: theatre that moves. We choose to relish what others shy away from, destroy boundaries when others would create rules. We explore harsh, brutal themes with a modern exploration of Theatre of the Absurd in classic and contemporary storytelling. We provide grants and mentoring to support productions which:

• Put female, LGBTQI+ and/or BAME artists in the central role of new productions

Middle- and smaller-scale companies

- Ensure disability and demographic are no barrier to making art
- Defy the stigmas surrounding mental health, proving it is a prevalent issue in our society and one that all our central characters live with.

Also work in Education, Outreach & Community, for which the key contact is **edu@icarustheatre.co.uk**.

Casting procedures: Uses in-house casting directors. Holds general auditions; actors should write in when advised to do so by the company's newsletter. Casting breakdowns are available from the website and are advertised in Spotlight. Welcomes letters (with CVs and photographs) sent by post or email but no attachments via email. Accepts showreels or invitations to view individual actors' websites or performances.

Jam Theatre Company

45A West Street, Marlow, Bucks. SL7 2LS
tel (01628) 483808
email office@jamtheatre.co.uk
website www.jamtheatre.co.uk
Facebook /JamTheatreCo
Instagram @jamtheatre
Artistic Director Jo Carter

Production details: Founded in 2005, Jam Theatre Company is a professional theatre company who produce professional shows as well as create their own. They work in every area of the creative and media arts, host workshops, master classes and also have a training school. Many of their shows are available for licensing to schools, performing arts colleges and professional theatre/production companies.

Casting procedures: Casting breakdowns are available through the website, Spotlight and Castweb. Welcomes CVs and letters from actors previously unknown to the company via email and online links to showreels. Also happy to receive production notices and invitations to view individual actors' websites. Will consider applications from disabled actors to play characters with disabilities.

Kabosh

Imperial Buildings, 72 High Street, Belfast BT1 2BE
tel 028 9024 3343
email paula@kabosh.net
website www.kabosh.net
Facebook /KaboshTheatre
X @KaboshTheatre
Instagram @kaboshtheatre
Artistic Director Paula McFetridge

Production details: Founded in 1994. Produces innovative and provocative socio-political work, with a focus on new writing, for national and international touring and site-specific work. Stages 2–5 productions annually. Tours to venues such as arts centres and theatres, and site-specific locations. In general 2–6 actors are involved in each production.

Countries covered include Northern Ireland, Republic of Ireland, England (including London), Scotland, Wales, parts of Europe and North America.

Casting procedures: Auditions are by invitation only. Actors should forward their CV via email to paula@kabosh.net. Does not host open auditions but tries to see as much local work as possible. Casts on a project by project basis.

Kali Theatre Company

The Albany, Douglas Way, Deptford, London SE8 4AG
tel 020-8694 6033
email info@kalitheatre.co.uk
website www.kalitheatre.co.uk

Production details: Founded in 1991 to develop and promote new writing by women of South Asian descent. One main production each year, usually commissioned from established playwrights and which usually tours. Nurtures emerging playwrights through a two level Writer Development Programme which culminates in an annual public reading of new plays. Has worked with writers such as Tanika Gupta, Rukhsana Ahmad, Nessah Muthy, Naylah Ahmed and Sonali Bhattacharyya among others.

Casting procedures: Welcomes CVs and photographs by email or Spotlight links from South Asian actors unknown to the company. Accepts links to showreels or individual actors' websites. Occassionally casts disabled actors. Advised to email to find out what and when we are casting before sending CVs and photos.

LipService

116 Longford Road, Chorlton, Manchester M21 9NP
mobile 07768 394609
email info@lip-service.net
website www.lipservicetheatre.co.uk
Facebook /LipServiceTheatre
X @LipServicetour
Instagram @lipserviceontour
Artistic Director Sue Ryding

Production details: Over the past 20 years, LipService has established itself as one of the leading comedy touring companies, producing shows for the theatre which have a strong base in popular culture.

LipService attracts audiences from a wide social mix and age range. Based in Manchester, the company has built up a solid touring circuit in the North of England and throughout the rest of Britain. Challenges its audience by setting up a recognisable form and subverting it. This is partly achieved by two women playing all the characters, but also by ingenious theatrical surprises.

Casting procedures: Uses casting directors of co-producing venue. Does not hold general auditions. Actors should write requesting inclusion when extra performers are needed for a new production. Casting breakdowns are available direct from the co-producingtheatre; details of co-producers are available via the website. Welcomes invitations from actors to view their work and from actors familiar with the company's work. Offers TMA/Equity-approved contracts.

London Bubble Theatre Co.
3–5 Elephant Lane, London SE16 4JD
tel 020-7237 4434
email admin@londonbubble.org.uk
website www.londonbubble.org.uk
Facebook /LondonBubble.Theatre
Instagram @bubbletheatre
Artistic Director Marie Vickers

Production details: The company cares about who gets to make theatre, see theatre and whose story gets told. They believe that everyone has a right for their stories to be seen and heard without limitations.

The company:
- Promotes equal access to arts and culturecultural reasons
- Embodies our core values of creativity, community and connection across all our work
- Believes everyone has stories to share and a right for those stories to be seen and heard
- Is a safe space for people from all backgrounds to express themselves creatively
- Values everybody's contribution and experience
- Designs projects with social and emotional wellbeing in mind
- Provides all activities free of charge to the people taking part so that finance isn't a barrier

Lurking Truth
Gwynfryn, Newtown Road, Machynlleth, Powys SY20 8EY
tel (01654) 702200
email davidianrabey@gmail.com
website www.theatre-wales.co.uk/companies/company_details.asp?ID=21
Artistic Director & Secretary David Ian Rabey

Production details: Founded in 1986, Lurking Truth present contemporary work and premieres by dramatists such as Howard Barker, David Ian Rabey, David Rudkin and Arnold Wesker. This is sometimes done in association with Aberystwyth University Department of Theatre, Film and Television Studies, and several alumni of the department have gone on to work with the company.

Casting procedures: Uses in-house casting directors. Welcomes unsolicited CVs (with photographs) sent by email. Also welcomes invitations to view individual actors' websites, but does not welcome showreels.

Magnetic North Theatre Productions
Summerhall, Summerhall Place, Ediburgh EH9 1PL
email mail@magneticnorth.org.uk
website www.magneticnorth.org.uk
Facebook /magnorththeatre
Artistic Director Nicholas Bone, Producer Anna Hodgart

Production details: Founded in 1999. Commissions and produces new plays, music-theatre, installations, online events and films. Also runs a cross art form Artist Development programme for early- and mid-career artists. Stages one to 2 productions annually and gives 20–40 performances during the course of a year. Tours on average to 12 venues annually. About 5 actors are involved in each production.

Casting procedures: Sometimes holds general auditions. Actors should write to request inclusion when productions are announced on the website. Casting breakdowns are publicly available through the website. Welcomes submissions (with CVs and photographs) sent by post or email. Also accepts invitations to view individual actors' websites. Advises that the company has a low turnover of productions and a small staff, and finds it difficult to respond to general enquiries about available work.

MANACTCO
(formerly Manchester Actors Company)
31 Leslie Street, Manchester M14 7NE
tel 0161 445 8477
email admin@manactco.org.uk
website www.manactco.org.uk
Artistic Director Stephen Boyes

Production details: Established in 1980 and now the North West's leading provider of theatre in schools. "We are emphatically *not* a TIE company." Reaches well over 60,000 young people each year with around 3–4 touring productions.

Casting procedures: Uses in-house casting directors and sometimes holds general auditions. Actors may write in June/July requesting inclusion. Casting breakdowns are available via Equity Job Information Service and specific casting websites, for example Mandy. Welcomes letters (with CVs and photographs) from individual actors previously unknown to the company, sent by post or email; also welcomes showreels and invitations to view individual actors' websites. Actively encourages applications from disabled actors and promotes the use of inclusive casting. "We give priority to formally trained actors who have completed recognised courses at drama school. We like actors who can face the rigours of touring with good humour!"

Meeting Ground Theatre Co.
4 Shirley Road, Nottingham NG3 5DA
tel 07730 384000
email info@meetinggroundtheatrecompany.co.uk
website www.meetinggroundtheatrecompany.co.uk
Artistic Directors Tanya Myers, Stephen Lowe

Production details: Since 1985, Meeting Ground has been celebrating the meeting of artists from different disciplines and cultures. Administered from its Nottingham base, the company draws together writers, actors, musicians, directors, puppeteers, designers and digital artists, and encourages community participation. Work is based on the belief that by creating artistic work, that crosses barriers, whether they be national, psychological, intellectual, cultural, spiritual or disciplinary, new sources of energy and creativity can be engendered. At the heart of the company's artistic policy and vision is the theatrical exploration of what we call the 'politics of the imagination'. Issues and questions that control the imagination and shape all our destinies. Currently focused on devising with elders and carers in the community.

Casting procedures: Offers ITC/Equity contracts and does not subscribe to the Equity Pension Scheme. Actively encourages applications from disabled actors and promotes the use of inclusive casting.

Middle Child
69 Humber Street, Hull HU1 1TU
website www.middlechildtheatre.co.uk
Facebook /middlechildhull
Bluesky @middlechildhull.bsky.social
Instagram @middlechildhull
Artistic Director Paul Smith

Production details: A Hull-based company creating gig theatre that brings people together for a good night out with big ideas. Tells untold stories which capture the electrifying moment when the beat drops, mixing original live music with bold new writing.

Casting procedures: Usually runs open auditions for productions and will share all details of these opportunities on the website, social media and artist development mailing list. Sign up to mailing list on the website to hear about opportunities. Occasionally casts directly, especially if there are specific requirements for a particular show. For further information, see relevant email contacts on website. Actors' CV and Spotlight can be shared via their online form. They encourage actors to introduce themselves with their name, contact details and outline their skills and interests.

Midland Actors Theatre (MAT)
25 Merrishaw Road, Northfield,
Birmingham B31 3SL
tel 0121 608 7144, *mobile* 07946 006511
email david@midlandactorstheatre.com
website www.midlandactorstheatre.com
Facebook /midlandactors
X @MidlandActors
Instagram @midlandactors
Director David Allen, *Associate Director* Gillian Adamson

Production details: Founded in 1999. Produces classics and new work. Specialises in theatre tours, community productions and schools-based projects. Stages one to 2 productions annually with 30–40 performances during the course of the year. Tours on average to 25 different theatres, schools and other venues in the West Midlands, East Midlands and nationally each year. Around 2–5 actors are involved in each production. Offers ITC/Equity-approved contracts and does not subscribe to the Equity Pension Scheme.

Casting procedures: Sometimes holds general auditions. Actors should write requesting inclusion when auditions are advertised; general casting enquiries are most welcome in January and June. Casting breakdowns are publicly available via the Equity Job Information Service. Advises that the company is primarily interested in actors who are Midlands based. Actively encourages applications from disabled actors and promotes the use of inclusive casting.

Mikron Theatre Company
Marsden Mechanics, Peel Street, Marsden,
Huddersfield HD7 6BW
tel (01484) 843701
email admin@mikron.org.uk
website www.mikron.org.uk
Facebook /mikrontheatre
Instagram @mikrontheatre
Artistic Director Marianne McNamara

Production details: Theatre anywhere for everyone, by canal, river and road. Has been touring for over 50 years: "Mighty little Mikron" (*Guardian*). Only works with actor musicians. Tours on Tyseley, the company's historic narrowboat, on the inland waterways of Britain in the summer, and by road in the autumn months.

Casting procedures: Actors are advised to keep an eye on the website. Casting breakdowns are publicly available from the website, via Spotlight. Asks actors to "please bear in mind that this is a hard tour: boating all day and shows and get-ins every night. Do consult the website before applying".

Mimbre
Unit 4, Energy Centre, Bowling Green Walk,
London N1 6AL
tel 020-7613 1068
email info@mimbre.co.uk
website www.mimbre.co.uk
Artistic Directors Lina Johnansson, Silvia Fratelli

A female-led producing company, creating delicate, breathtaking and highly-skilled acrobatic theatre for outdoor and unusual settings, touring nationally and internationally, with a strong digital presence. Collaborate across the Creative Industries, as consultants and creators. Runs a vibrant local youth programme and an Artist Development Programme for physical performers.

Production details: Mimbre use circus and movement innovatively as a physical language to illuminate human connections. They pull down barriers to reach beyond social, financial, and cultural boundaries and facilitate everyone's place within the arts. In all work they aim to challenge gender stereotypes and promote a positive, diverse, and inclusive image of cis and trans women as well as non-binary people. Stages one to 2 main shows and works in collaboration with 50–60 performances in 15–20 arts centres, outdoor and festival venues, and theatres across the UK and Europe. In general 3–6 performers are involved in each production.

Casting procedures: Uses in-house casting directors; holds general auditions only when producing a new show. Welcomes letters (with CVs and showreels) from individual performers previously unknown to the company, sent by email. Accepts performance notices and invitations to view performers' websites. Actively encourages applications from disabled actors and promotes the use of inclusive casting.

New Earth Theatre
The Albany, Douglas Way, Deptford,
London SE8 4AG
tel 020-8694 6631
email admin@newearththeatre.org.uk
website www.newearththeatre.org.uk
Facebook /NewEarthTheatre
X @NewEarthTheatre
Instagram @newearththeatre
Artistic Director Ailin Conant

Production details: Presents and develops work with British East and South East Asian (BESEA) artists that asks key questions of identity, of the world we live in and our place in that world. It produces touring plays and readings across the year, nurtures BESEA talent through their New Earth Academy courses (Performing, Writing, Offstage) and targeted professional development programmes, and engages with communities, museums and schools. New Earth Theatre was established in 1995 and is a member of ITC.

Casting procedures: Casts in-house. Sometimes holds general auditions. Welcomes emails with CVs and photographs from actors with East and South East Asian heritage only. Promotes the use of inclusive casting.

East and South East Asian includes: Brunei, Burma, Cambodia, China, East Timor, Hong Kong, Indonesia, Japan, Laos, Malaysia, Mongolia, North Korea, Philippines, Singapore, South Korea, Taiwan, Thailand, Vietnam and their diasporas.

New Perspectives Theatre Co.
8 Park Lane Business Centre, Park Lane,
Nottingham NG6 0DW
tel 0115 927 2334
email info@newperspectives.co.uk
website www.newperspectives.co.uk
Facebook /newperspectivestheatrecompany
X @NPtheatre
Instagram @nptheatre
Artistic Director Angharad Jones

Production details: Founded in 1973. A leading East Midlands touring theatre company; also tours nationally. On average stages 2 productions each year, touring all over the county including theatres, arts centres and rural venues. Equity-approved contracts as negotiated through ITC.

Casting procedures: Promotes the use of inclusive casting. Casting breakdowns are available through Spotlight Link and from the website.

New Shoes Theatre
email admin@newshoestheatre.org.uk
website www.newshoestheatre.org.uk
Facebook /NewShoesTheatre
X @newshoestheatre
Artistic Director Nicolette Kay

Production details: The company aims to stage one production annually and provides workshops. Currently developing a new play. Up to 8 actors can be involved in each production.

Casting procedures: Uses in-house casting directors. Casting breakdowns can be found on sites such as their website, *The Stage*, Spotlight, Mandy and Arts Jobs, and social media such as Twitter and Facebook.

Northern Broadsides Theatre Company
E Mill, E110, Dean Clough, Halifax HX3 5AX
tel (01422) 369704
email info@northern-broadsides.co.uk
website www.northern-broadsides.co.uk
Facebook /NorthernBroadsides
X @NBroadsides
Instagram @northern_broadsides
Artistic Director Laurie Sansom, *Executive Director* Ruth Cooke

Production details: A theatre company that creates bold, accessible and irreverent productions that speak directly to contemporary audiences. For over 32 years, they have toured widely across the UK and internationally, bringing high-quality theatre to audiences everywhere.

They are known for staging Shakespeare, as well as classic and new plays that reflect the cultural landscape and diverse voices of the North. Their work is characterised by vitality, humour and humanity - connecting past and present through irreverent storytelling.

In addition to producing and touring their own work, they run creative engagement programmes that support emerging talent. Their Life in a Northern Town playwriting scheme, and Park Youth Theatre in Halifax, help young people across the North find their voice. They also run The Writer's Refuge, a poetry and performance group for refugees and people seeking asylum, in partnership with local organisations.

NTC Touring Theatre Company
The Dovecote Centre, Amble,
Northumberland NE65 0DX
tel (01665) 713655

email admin@northumberlandtheatre.co.uk
website www.northumberlandtheatre.co.uk
Facebook /NTCtheatre
Instagram @ntctheatre
Artistic Director Louis Roberts

Production details: Founded in 1978 as Northumberland Theatre Company. Small-scale touring theatre company performing at village halls, small theatres and community venues in predominantly rural areas. Main areas of work are new writing and physical theatre pieces. Stages 2-3 high quality shows annually. Over the last 6 years they have travelled over 42,037 miles in their truck with more than 29,496 people having seen an NTC show.

Casting procedures: Holds audition workshops for locally based actors, usually in the spring. Casting breakdowns are available on the website, Facebook via Equity and Arts Jobs. Welcomes submissions (with CVs and photographs) by email. Also accepts invitations to view individual actors' performances and will always reply to individual actors. Particularly interested in locally based actors or actors with local origins, and will keep details on file for future reference unless requested to do otherwise. Actively promotes the use of inclusive casting.

Open Clasp Theatre Company

The Stephenson Building, 173 Elswick Road, Newcastle-upon-Tyne NE4 6SQ
tel 0191 272 4063
email info@openclasp.org.uk
website www.openclasp.org.uk
Facebook /openclasp
X @OpenClasp
Instagram Instagram @openclasp
Artistic Director Catrina McHugh MBE

Production details: Open Clasp makes truthful, risk-taking and award-winning theatre informed by the lived experiences of working-class women, women disenfranchised in the theatre and society, those from minority communities and women affected by the criminal justice system. They take a special interest in women and young women from the North, shining a light on their experiences. Open Clasp make space for debate, encouraging audiences to walk in the shoes of the most disempowered women in society. Their work is performed in theatres, prisons, village halls, schools, conferences and community centres. It has also performed at the Edinburgh Fringe and off-Broadway to national and international acclaim. It resonates deep into the communities where it is created and outside ensures the under-represented are seen in a new light by women, men and those with the power to make a difference.

On average stages one touring production per year, usually in October and November, first stage developments in March and one-off project commissions. Tours/previews include approx. 30 performances in 20+ arts centres, theatres and educational and community venues in the North East, South East, Yorkshire and London.

Casting procedures: Sometimes holds general auditions; actors requesting inclusion should write in January. Casting breakdowns are available from the website, by postal application with sae, and from online casting services. Welcomes letters (with CVs and photographs) from individual actors previously unknown to the company, sent by post or email, but does not accept showreels. Will consider invitations to view individual actors' websites if accompanied by a full CV. Encourages applications from disabled actors. "It is paramount that our actors share the ethos of the company. Open Clasp ensures that casting is representative of the diverse groups we work with, the issues explored, and the characters they have created."

Original Theatre

Dovedon Hall Office, Chedburgh Road, Whepstead, Bury St Edmunds, Suffolk IP29 4UB
tel (01284) 598025
email info@originaltheatre.com
website https://originaltheatre.com
Facebook /OriginalTheatre
X @OriginalTheatre
Bluesky @originaltheatre.bsky.social
Instagram @originaltheatrecompany
Artistic Director Alastair Whatley

Production details: Operating and touring since 2004, the Original Theatre company has toured extensively all over the UK and in 2020 launched Original Theatre online.

Casting procedures: Uses dedicated Casting Directors who post callouts on their behalf.

Ovation Productions

mobile 07973 502189
email john@ovationproductions.com
website www.ovationuk.com
Directors John Plews, Katie Plews

Main activities: Licensing of Ovation's original plays and musicals. Produces revivals of both plays and musicals.

Paines Plough

Stockroom, 38 Mayton Street, London N7 6QR
tel 020-7240 4533
email office@painesplough.com
website www.painesplough.com
Facebook /painesploughHQ
X @painesplough
Bluesky @painesplough.bsky.social
Instagram @painesplough
Co-Artistic Directors Charlotte Bennett, Katie Posner

Production details: Founded in 1974, the company is dedicated to producing and touring new writing. They discover, develop and empower writers across the country and share their explosive new stories with audiences all over the UK and beyond.

Casting procedures: Holds open auditions throughout the year to meet new actors as a way to broaden their horizons. They travel up and down the UK and also hold open auditions online. Everyones details are kept on file and are looked back on everytime they cast a new show. Open auditions will be announced on their website at **painesplough.com/get-involved/open-auditions** and also through their mailing list and social medias.

Pendle Productions

Bridge Farm, 249 Hawes Side Lane, Blackpool, Lancashire FY4 4AA
tel (01253) 839375
email admin@pendleproductions.co.uk
website www.pendleproductions.co.uk
Director T.S. Lince

Production details: Touring professional theatre company. Stages between 10 and 15 productions each year, with 600 performances nationally in 300 venues of all types.

Casting procedures: Sometimes holds general auditions; actors should write in April–June requesting inclusion. Casting breakdowns are publicly available via the usual channels. Welcomes letters (with CVs and photographs) from individual actors previously unknown to the company sent by post or email. Accepts showreels but prefers not to receive invitations to view individual actors' websites. Actively encourages applications from disabled actors, and promotes the use of inclusive casting.

Pentabus Theatre Company

Ludlow Assembly Rooms, 1 Mill Street, Ludlow, Shropshire SY8 1AZ
email info@pentabus.co.uk
website www.pentabus.co.uk
Facebook /pentabustheatre
Bluesky @pentabustheatre.bsky.social
Instagram @pentabustheatrecompany
Artistic Director Elle While

Production details: The nation's rural theatre company, based in Shropshire. They are the only rural touring company committed to producing new work and performing to communities across the UK and beyond. Their work brings communities and young people together, delivering outstanding contemporary productions with sector-leading creative teams directly to isolated rural areas, while also platforming rural stories in urban settings. Over 5 decades, they've produced over 329 new plays, supported 258 playwrights, and reached more than half a million audience members. They've won awards and created lasting relationships with artists, venues, and audiences across the country, and were the first to live stream from a village hall. Pentabus excels at finding and nurturing new talent and has hosted Writers in Residence since 2014.

These playwrights have gone on to be commissioned by the Birmingham Rep, Bristol Old Vic, Hampstead Theatre, HighTide, Manchester Royal Exchange, Nottingham Playhouse, Royal Court, The Bush, and the National Theatre.

Casting procedures: Occasionally uses freelance casting directors. No CVs or email enquiries. Will attend shows by invitation.

The People's Theatre Co

email ptc@ptc.org.uk
website www.ptc.org.uk
Facebook /peoples.theatre.company
X @the_ptc
Instagram @ptcuk
Director Steven Lee

Production details: Producing interactive, fun-filled musicals that are created for children and grown ups to enjoy together. Stories are told with a mixture of live action, puppetry, animation, illusion, fx, magic and parkour. They tour as widely as possible. Some of their productions are taken into schools as well as their investment to education by creating drama workshops and providing free resources for teachers.

Casting procedures: Casting is done in-house. Holds general auditions. Actors should only write requesting inclusion in response to casting calls. Actors can also follow the company on social media for first alerts to castings. Casting breakdowns are obtainable via the usual array of sources including Spotlight and Mandy.com. Accepts submissions (with CVs with training, experience and skills – signing particularly relevant – listed and photographs) from individual actors previously unknown to the company; submissions sent by email are also accepted. Applications from disabled actors are considered to play disabled characters. New actors and recent graduates welcome.

People Show

Pophub, 41 Whitcomb Road, London WC2H 7DT
tel 07916 027682
email people@peopleshow.co.uk
website www.peopleshow.co.uk
Facebook /peopleshowltd
X @peopleshow
Instagram @peopleshowltd
Company Gareth Brierley, Sadie Cook, Fiona Creese, George Khan, Mark Long

Production details: The longest-running experimental theatre company in the UK, touring nationally and internationally since 1966, creating devised work for arts centres, theatres, and outdoor and site-specific venues. More recently working on film and education/community projects also. Offers Equity-approved contracts as negotiated through ITC.

Casting procedures: People Show is an ensemble company with a core group of 6 artists, and an extended network of 45 plus associate artists. Does not use freelance casting directors or hold general auditions. Welcomes approaches from performers previously unknown to the company.

Pilot Theatre
The Guildhall, St Martins Courtyard, Coney Street, York YO1 9QL
tel (01904) 635755
email info@pilot-theatre.com
website www.pilot-theatre.com
Facebook /pilottheatre
X @pilot_theatre
Instagram @pilot_theatre
Artistic Director Esther Richardson, Executive Producer Amanda Smith

Production details: Pilot Theatre is an international touring theatre company based in York, UK. They devise and develop projects with particular focus on working for and with young audiences. They also work across platforms to produce and distribute work digitally, run training conferences, livestream events and performances, provide a wide range of online educational resources.

Casting procedures: The company regularly posts casting information online. Please email your details to: **casting@pilot-theatre.com**.

A Play, a Pie and A Pint
Òran Mór, Byres Rd, Glasgow G12 8QX
tel 0141 357 6208
email info@playpiepint.com
website https://playpiepint.com/contact-us/
Facebook /playpiepint/?locale=en_GB
Bluesky @playpiepint.bsky.social
Instagram: @PLAYPIEPINT
Artistic Director Brian Logan

This successful lunchtime theatre experience is based at Òran Mór, Glasgow and tours throughout Scotland and beyond. Founded in 2004 by theatre maverick and maker David MacLennan, its core principles have remained the same: a new play at lunchtime every week lasting no more than an hour, accompanied by a pie and a pint. With 30 brand-new plays a year, as well as Summer and Christmas pantomimes, A Play, A Pie and A Pint is a prolific producer of new writing in the UK, working with established playwrights as well as producing and advocating for work from first-time and emerging writers. Their David MacLennan Award, dedicated to their late founder, is a biannual open writing competition with the winner having their play professionally produced.

Prime Cut Productions
Unit 5, The Refinery, 8 Maxwell Street, Belfast BT12 5FB
tel 07879 557341
email info@primecutproductions.co.uk
website www.primecutproductions.co.uk
Facebook /PrimeCutProductions
X @prime_cut
Instagram @primecutproductions
Artistic Director Emma Jordan

Production details: Established in 1992, Prime Cut Productions is an independent theatre producing organisation based in Belfast. They are committed to producing excellent contemporary theatre that is accessible and entertaining for as wide an audience as possible, forging artistic links locally and internationally, and nurturing the development of theatre practice and artists in Northern Ireland. They have produced 60 acclaimed Irish premieres of the best of international theatre as well showcasing the work of Northern Irish theatre artists across Ireland and beyond.

Since 2014 Prime Cut have been the recipients of the BBC Performing Arts Fellowship, 3 Weston Jerwood Creative Fellowships, the Allianz Arts & Business Board Member of the Year Award (2015), Artistic Director Emma Jordan received the Paul Hamlyn Foundation Breakthrough Award and the 2015 Spirit of Festival Award at Belfast International Arts Festival. The 2019 production of Fionnuala Kennedy's *Removed* was selected as the only one of two show from the island of Ireland for IPAY2020 and is the recipient of the Irish Writers Guild Award for Best Theatre Script.

Prime Cut delivers under three main strands: CREATE, INNOVATE and PARTICIPATE.

• CREATE: an artistic programme of two professional productions annually of the best of international drama featuring casts and creative teams of the highest quality.

• INNOVATE: Annual Artistic Development Programme. It drives forward the development of Northern Irish professional theatre through the provision of the finest international training and professional development opportunities for Northern Irish artists.

• PARTICIPATE: Community Engagement Programme providing year-round opportunities for arts access and participation for young people, older people, disadvantaged people and people from minority groupings, through a range of arts including theatre, dance, movement, film, music and visual art.

Proteus Theatre Company
Proteus Creation Space, Council Road, Basingstoke, Hants RG21 3DH
tel (01256) 354541
email info@proteustheatre.com
website www.proteustheatre.com
Facebook /proteustheatrecompany
X @proteustheatre
Artistic Director Mary Swan

Production details: Established in 1981. Touring theatre company operating nationally. Stages 2–3 productions annually touring to 80 venues including arts centres, theatres, outdoor venues, educational and community venues.

Casting procedures: Casting breakdowns available via the website and Equity Job Information Service. Does not welcome unsolicited CVs. Actively encourages applications from disabled actors and promotes the use of inclusive casting. Offers ITC/Equity-approved contracts.

Punchdrunk

One Cartridge Place, Woolwich, London SE18 6ZR
tel 020-8191 0100
email info@punchdrunk.com
website www.punchdrunk.com
Facebook /punchdrunkint
Instagram @punchdrunkint
Artistic Director Felix Barratt

Since 2000, Punchdrunk has pioneered a game-changing form of theatre in which roaming audiences experience epic story-telling inside sensory theatrical worlds. Blending classic texts, physical performance, award-winning design installation and unexpected sites, the company's format rejects the passive obedience ususally expected of audiences. Much of the work has a strong and choreographic focus.

Punchdrunk has developed a reputation for transformative productions that focus as much on the audience and the performance space as on the performers and narrative. Inspired designers occupy deserted buildings and apply a cinematic level of detail to immerse the audience in the world of the show.

This is a unique theatrical experience where the lines between space, performer and spectator are constantly shifting. Audiences are invited to rediscover the childlike excitement and anticipation of exploring the unknown and experience a real sense of adventure. Free to encounter the installed environment in an individual imaginative journey, the choice of what to watch and where to go is theirs alone.

Offers Equity-approved contracts through ITC; does not subscribe to the Equity Pension Scheme.

Punchdrunk Enrichment works with schools, colleges, community groups and partner organisations.

Casting procedures: Apply for auditions when advertised, following the instructions. Advertises on website, social media, arts job- and dance-specific websites. Unable to view productions for casting purposes but encourages aplpications from all.

Pursued by a Bear Productions

Trestle Arts Base, Russet Drive, St Albans AL4 0JQ
website https://pursuedbyabear.co.uk
Artistic Director Rosamunde Hutt

Production details: Theatre and digital film company specialising in new writing commissions. PBAB produces and tours one new (Arts Council funded) theatre production annually and creates large-scale community and educational film (most recently funded by Heritage Lottery).

Casting procedures: Welcomes submissions (with CVs and photographs) sent by post or email. For more information see Contact page on website.

Red Ladder Theatre Company

3 St Peter's Buildings, York Street, Leeds LS9 8AJ
tel 0113 245 5311
email info@redladder.co.uk
website www.redladder.co.uk
Facebook /RedLadderTheatre
Bluesky @redladder.bsky.social
Instagram @redladdertheatrecompany
Artistic Director Cheryl Martin

Production details: Red Ladder's mission is to create theatre based around, and influenced by, human struggle. They aim to create galvanising and life-affirming productions that redefine and reclaim notions of the popular, the political and the radical in a theatre context. The company, founded in 1968 in London, has a colourful history. It spans 50 years, from the radical socialist theatre movement in Britain known as agitprop, to its current position.

The company moved to Leeds in the 70s and is still based in the city. During the 80s it re-defined itself, changing its co-operative structure to a hierarchy. Acknowledged today as one of Britain's leading national touring companies producing high-quality new plays.

Red Rose Chain

Gippeswyk Hall, Gippeswyk Avenue, Ipswich, Suffolk IP2 9AF
tel (01473) 603388
email info@redrosechain.com
website www.redrosechain.com
Facebook /redrosechain
X @red_rose_chain
Instagram @red_rose_chain
Artistic Director Joanna Carrick, Producer David Newborn

Production details: A film and theatre company which spends every summer outdoors with its theatre-in-the-forest event. Runs workshops and develops new writing. "Our diverse work all serves to underpin Red Rose Chain's aim: to use theatre and film to challenge thinking and make connections with those who are normally ignored or avoided by mainstream arts."

Casting procedures: Sometimes holds general auditions; casting breakdowns are available via the website. Welcomes letters (with CVs and photographs) from individual actors previously unknown to the company, sent by post or email. Also welcomes showreels and invitations to view individual actors' websites. Actively encourages applications from disabled actors and promotes the use of inclusive casting.

Riding Lights Theatre Company
Friargate Theatre, Lower Friargate, York YO1 9SL
tel (01904) 655317
email info@rltc.org
website www.ridinglights.org
Facebook /ridinglights
Artistic Director Paul Birch, *Executive Director* Oliver Brown

Production details: Initially a community theatre project founded in York in 1977, today Riding Lights tours at least 4 diverse productions a year throughout the UK. The company is recognised both as a pioneer in reinstating the value of theatre in Christian communication and for significant original and artistic achievement.

Rifco Theatre Company
Watford Palace Theatre, 20 Clarendon Road, Watford WD17 1JZ
tel (01923) 810305
email info@rifcotheatre.com
website www.rifcotheatre.com
Facebook /RifcoTheatre
Instagram @rifcotheatre
Artistic Director Pravesh Kumar MBE

Production details: Rifo Theatre Company develops, produces and tours vibrant, accessible and high-quality theatre locally from its base in Watford. The company develops both new plays and musicals of scale and spectacle, and works alongside a wide range of artistic collaborators. The work is developed to encourage and engage new and diverse audiences, reflecting and celebrating contemporary British South Asian experiences, culture and society.

Offers UK Theatre/Equity-approved contracts.

Casting procedures: Casting opportunities are posted to their website where information about applying is available: **rifcotheatre.com/get-involved/jobs-opportunities.**

Mary Rose Productions
Basement Flat, 42 St Andrews Road, Southsea, Portsmouth PO5 1EU
tel 07907 178448
email maryroseproductions.theatre@gmail.com
website www.maryroseproductions.co.uk
Facebook /MaryRoseProductions
Instagram @mary_rose_productions
Directors April Singley, Joseph Scatley

Production details: Established in 2024. Named after the Mary Rose ship, the Portsmouth based company renovates old theatre traditions by creating a new repertory-style productions for today's theatre-makers. The company looks to help bridge the gap between early career/emerging artists and experienced professionals through collaboration and artistry.

Casting procedures: Their mission is to engage actors, designers, producers and stage managers from within the local community, where possible. However, they also recruit creatives from across the country where particular roles or positions cannot be filled locally. Casting notices are posted via a variety of online platforms.

Shared Experience
26 South Road, Kirkby Stephen CA17 4SD
tel 07887 578143
email admin@sharedexperience.org.uk
website www.sharedexperience.org.uk
Facebook /SharedExperience
X @setheatre
Instagram @sharedexptheatre
Director Conrad Lynch

Production details: An award-winning theatre company founded during the 1970s, Shared Experience tours productions on the small, mid and large scale. On tour to venues across the UK. Acting companies vary from one person shows to larger-scale musicals.

Casting procedures: Uses freelance casting directors. Advises that actors should contact the office by email to enquire about the current casting director. Offers UKT/Equity-approved contracts.

Simple8 Theatre Company
Heath House, Lyneham Road,
Milton-under-Wychwood, Oxon OX7 6LW
mobile 07710 174717
email chris@simple8.co.uk
website www.simple8.co.uk
X @simple8theatre
Directors Chris Doyle, Sebastian Armesto, Emily Pennant-Rea, Dudley Hinton, Hannah Emanuel, Mat Wandless

Production details: Simple8 is a critically-acclaimed and award-winning ensemble based theatre company who specialise in creating innovative, bold new plays using large casts – all performed on a shoestring. Their approach is rooted in 'poor theatre', which focuses on the story and revolves around the ensemble, who create the atmosphere and setting without relying on extravagant lighting, scenery, props or sound. Simple8 have produced 8 productions to date, at Arcola Theatre and Park Theatre. Simple8 is an associate company of Shoreditch Town Hall. Winners of the Peter Brook Award for Best Ensemble 2013 and 2015.

Casting procedures: Uses freelance casting directors, but does not hold general auditions. Instead Simple8 recommend actors submit their details for consideration once they have seen a Simple8 production, attended a workshop, or introduced themselves in person. Welcomes both CVs and letters from actors previously unknown to the company and unsolicited CVs and photographs. These should be sent via email. Also welcomes invitations to view individual actors' websites and attend productions, but does not welcome showreels. Happy to consider disabled actors, though this is dependent on each individual project.

Sky Blue Theatre Company
1 Kelling Gardens, Croydon CR0 2RP
mobile 07941 012293
email info@skybluetheatre.com
website www.skybluetheatre.com
X @SkyBlueTheatre
Director John Mitton

Production details: Founded in 2007. A London-based company touring schools, theatres and community venues with new plays, Shakespeare productions and workshops. Founded the British Theatre Challenge, an international playwriting competition. Offer script appraisals.

Casting procedures: Holds general auditions, for which breakdowns are available via Mandy and the website. Welcomes letters (with CVs and photographs) from individual actors previously unknown to the company, sent by email.

Slung Low
The Warehouse in Holbeck, Crosby Street, Holbeck, Leeds LS11 9RQ
email info@slunglow.org
website www.slunglow.org
X @SlungLow

Production details: Founded in 2000, Slung Low is an award-winning theatre company specialising in making epic productions in non-theatre spaces, often with large community performance companies at their heart. The company's south Leeds venues, theatre equipment and vehicles are shared with other artists and community groups on a Pay-What-You-Decide basis.

Casting procedures: Slung Low's casting depends on the nature of the project. Send your CV to **info@slunglow.org**. Also offers producing and production internships.

Small World Theatre
Theatr Byd Bach, Bath House Road, Cardigan, Ceredigion SA43 1JY
tel (01239) 615952
email info@smallworld.org.uk
website www.smallworld.org.uk
Facebook /SmallWorldTheatre
Instagram @smallworldbydbach
Executive Director Ann Shrosbree, *Administrator* Hélène Cheung, *Artistic Director* Bill Hamblett

Production details: Small World Theatre artists and performers create environmental puppet theatre and giant processions, with core projects supporting community, mental health and wellbeing. Small World Theatre is an arts and sustainability organisation housed in an unique near zero carbon venue in West Wales. It works in a variety of ways including producing original performances and touring theatre, outdoor street theatre and giant puppet/lantern parades. The company presents a year-round programme of events in its venue, as well as delivering its own projects supporting arts, health and wellbeing, theatre in education and training. In addition, it has a thriving aerial circus school and aerial circus facilities.

Casting procedures: Uses in-house casting directors to cast actors as puppeteers and to play speaking roles (delivered in Welsh and English languages). Casts actors with disabilities in inclusive roles, and to play differently able roles. Will consider submissions (letters, CVs and photographs) from actors previously unknown to the company, sent by post or email. No unsolicited showreels.

Sole Purpose Productions
The Playhouse, Artillery Street, Derry BT48 6RG
tel 028 7127 9918
email solepurpose@mac.com
website www.solepurpose.org
Facebook /solepurposeproductions
Instagram @solepurposeproductions
Development Officer Mairead Nic Bhloscaidh

Production details: Sole Purpose Productions is a multi-award winning theatre company founded in 1997. It creates new dynamic theatre on social and public issues. The company has toured extensively throughout Ireland, the UK and the USA.

Each production consists of 2–5 actors and, on average, the company presents 1–2 productions per year, touring to theatres and community venues nationally and internationally.

Casting procedures: Holds general auditions at various times throughout the year and a casting breakdown is available via the Sole Purpose website when a production is coming up. Welcomes both CVs and letters from actors previously unknown to the Company and unsolicited CVs and photographs. Also welcomes invitations to view individual actor's websites and showreels. Sole Purpose promotes inclusive casting and welcomes applications from ethnic minorities, refugees, asylum seekers, LGBTQIA+ and disabled actors.

Spanner in the Works
95 Old Woolwich Road, London SE10 9PP
tel 020-7193 7995
email info@spannerintheworks.org.uk
website www.spannerintheworks.org.uk
Artistic Director Darren Rapier

Production details: Spanner in the Works produce plays and films, as well as running workshops in all media disciplines for a variety of clientele. The company produces films and books in partnership with Tualen Pictures and Tualen Press. Primarily, Spanner in the Works concentrate on stage productions and workshops. They have produced musicals, plays, short films and audio drama, as well as community theatre pieces.

Casting procedures: Uses in-house and freelance casting directors. Casting breakdowns are available, although this is dependent on the project. Will happily consider applications from disabled actors, but their inclusion is dependent on the nature of each individual project.

Sphinx Theatre Company
78 Lyford Road, London SW18 3JW
tel 020-3669 8210
email info@sphinxtheatre.co.uk
website www.sphinxtheatre.co.uk
Artistic Director Sue Parrish

Production details: Established 30 years ago, the company specialises in writing, directing and developing roles for women. Recent work includes: the Sphinx 30 playwright development programme, What Share of the Cake? Research project, and Women Centre Stage.

Casting procedures: Casting breakdowns are available via email (with CVs and photographs)

Ed Stephenson Productions
7 Hawthorn Road, Little Sutton, Cheshire CH66 1PR
tel 0151 339 6145
email roger@edstephensonproductions.co.uk
website www.edstephensonproductions.co.uk
Company Administrator Diane Barker

Production details: Founded in 2004. Film, stage and podcast company. Stages on average one production every 1–2 years.

Casting procedures: Uses in-house casting directors. Sometimes holds auditions. Uses casting agencies for auditioning. Welcomes letters (with CVs and photographs) from individual actors previously unknown to the company, sent by post or email. Accepts showreels and invitations to view individual actors' websites. Will consider applications from disabled actors where appropriate for the role. "Our contracts are heavily based on ITC/Equity contracts."

Tabs Productions
151 Birches Lane, South Wingfield,
Derbyshire DE55 7LZ
email karen@tabsproductions.co.uk
website www.tabsproductions.co.uk
Director Karen Henson

Production details: Founded in 1989, the company stages approximately 6 productions each year totalling around 300 performances. Produces large- to middle-scale tours, including a co-productions with repertory theatre companies and one West End production at The Ambassadors Theatre. Generally tours to about 45 different arts centres, theatres and outdoor venues across the UK annually. The average cast size is 4–8 actors.

Casting procedures: Welcomes applications from actors previously unknown to the company. Actors should only write when a job has been advertised to agents.

Taking Flight Theatre Company
Chapter Arts Centre, Market Road, Canton,
Cardiff CF5 1QE
tel 029-2023 0020
email elsie@takingflighttheatre.co.uk
website www.takingflighttheatre.org.uk
Facebook /Takingflightco
Instagram @takingflighttheatre
Artistic Director Elise Davison

Production details: Established in 2007. Accessible, professional productions with integrated casts/support teams. They make bold, unusual theatre shows with Deaf, disabled, non-disabled and neurodiverse performers. Their work tours Wales and beyond.

Casting procedures: Sometimes holds general auditions and actors may write at any time to request inclusion. Casting breakdowns are publicly available via the website, Equity Job Information Service and Mandy, as well as from the Disability Arts Cymru site. Welcomes letters (with CVs and photographs) from individual actors previously unknown to the company sent by post or email, as well as showreels and invitations to view individual actors' websites. Actively encourages applications from Deaf and disabled actors. "We are very eager to hear from Deaf, disabled and/or sensory impaired actors."

Talawa Theatre Company
Fairfield Halls, Park Lane, Croydon, Surrey CR9 1DG
tel 020-7251 6644
email contact@talawa.com
website www.talawa.com
Artistic Director & Joint Ceo Michael Buffong,
Executive Director & Joint Ceo Carolyn M.L. Forsyth

Production details: Founded in 1986, Talawa is the UK's outstanding Black British Theatre company, whose purpose is to champion Black excellence in theatre, to nurture talent in emerging and established artists of African or Caribbean heritage and to tell inspirational and passionate stories, reflecting Black experiences through art like no other. Talawa's work ranges from local community engagement and national tours to international collaborations. As Talawa approaches its 40 year anniversary, it is more determined than ever to be courageous and creative in their programming, shine a spotlight on Black creative talent, inspire dialogue across a diverse range of audiences and enrich the cultural life of all.

Offers ITC/Equity contracts and has Ethical Management Status.

Casting procedures: Often co-produces work, but when available casting details can be found on the website.

Tamasha Theatre Company

38 Mayton St, London N7 6QR
tel 020-7749 0090
email admin@tamasha.org.uk
website www.tamasha.org.uk
Facebook /tamashatheatre
Instagram @tamashatheatrecompany
Artistic Director Pooja Ghai

Production details: Their vision is to redefine UK theatre with stories that celebrate the world we live in. They are a powerhouse of new writing, talent, development and digital innovation. Developing Artists is their year round programme for emerging and established theatre artists.

Casting procedures: Casting for the main touring productions is done in partnership with the show director and a freelance casting director. Casting calls are usually sent directly to agents. Any open calls will be advertised via social media and their newsletter. Agents must sign up to receive Tamasha's casting calls and can do so via the contact details on their website. Tamasha try their best to attend all shows they are invited to, show invites should be sent via email to **submissions@tamasha.org.uk**.

Tara Theatre

356 Garratt Lane, London SW18 4ES
tel 020-8333 4457
email info@taratheatre.com
website www.taratheatre.com
X @taratheatre
Artistic Director Natasha Kathi-Chandra

Production details: Founded in 1977, Tara Theatre is a 100-seat theatre and producing house in Earlsfield, London. It is a contemporary and democratic space platforming South Asian and global majority storytelling. Tara Theatre creates innovative, political theatre harnessing the power of co-creation. Its work explores the complexities of the world through a South Asian lens, championing South Asian voices and artists, identifying new narratives, new ideas and new forms.

Theatr Genedlaethol Cymru

Y Llwyfan, College Road, Carmarthen SA31 3EQ
tel (01267) 233882
email hello@theatr.com
website www.theatr.com
Facebook /TheatrGenedlaetholCymru
X @TheatrCymru
Instagram @theatr.cymru
Artistic Director Steffan Donnelly

Production details: Founded in 2003, Theatr Genedlaethol Cymru is the Welsh-language national theatre of Wales. Its work includes national tours, community projects and site-specific work. Offers Equity-approved contracts negotiated through UK Theatre.

Casting procedures: Uses a variety of casting tools, directories and agencies, including Spotlight. Performers are welcome to send their details via email to creu@theatr.com. Upcoming productions can be discovered on their website and social medias. Rarely holds open auditions, but will be advertised on social media when they do. Theatr Cymru understand the importance of visibility and representation on stage and are passionate about reflection the diversity of Wales in their work.

Theatre-Rites

Unit 3, Energy Centre, Bowling Green Walk, London N1 6AL
tel 020-7164 6196
email info@theatre-rites.co.uk
website www.theatre-rites.co.uk
Facebook /TheatreRites
X @TheatreRites
Instagram @theatrerites
Artistic Director Sue Buckmaster

Production details: Committed to creating challenging productions which push the boundaries of theatrical form by experimenting to combine different artistic disciplines. Highly imaginative visual experiences for families to share together. Stages 2 productions annually, with around 45 performances in 12 arts centre and theatres across all English regions, in Scotland and internationally. In general 4–8 actors go on tour, playing to audiences of various ages, often 5+. Actors are sometimes expected to lead workshops; singing, musical instrument, dance physical theatre and puppetry skills, depending on the project.

Casting procedures: Casting breakdowns are available via the website and artsjobs. Welcomes letters (with CVs and photographs) from actors previously unknown to the company. Also welcomes showreels and invitations to view individual actors' websites. Offers Equity-approved contracts as negotiated through ITC. Promotes the use of inclusive casting. Multi-disciplined performers are always very welcome.

Theatre Absolute

Shop Front Theatre, 38 City Arcade, Coventry CV1 3HW
tel 07799 292957
email info@theatreabsolute.co.uk
website www.theatreabsolute.co.uk
Facebook /theatreabsolute
Instagram @theatreabsolute
Artistic Director/Writer Chris O'Connell, Artists/Producer Julia Negus

Production details: Founded in 1992, the company commissions, develops and produces new work for theatre. In 2009, Theatre Absolute founded the UK's first professional Shop Front Theatre in Coventry, West Midlands. Work includes performances, script readings, writing workshops, and mentor support for actors, writers, producers and emerging theatre makers.

Casting procedures: Actors should consult the website for details of the next project. "If you are a local actor, do come to a show/event or drop in and introduce yourself in the first instance".

Theatre Alibi
Emmanuel Hall, Emmanuel Road, Exeter EX4 1EJ
tel (01392) 217315
email info@theatrealibi.co.uk
website www.theatrealibi.co.uk
Facebook /TheatreAlibiUK
Instagram @theatrealibi
Producer Elaine Faulkner

Production details: After going through a period of transition, the venue has reinvented itself as a place for children and young people. They host performances, workshops, live music and an immersive pine tree forest. Their mission is to create playful, safe and inclusive spaces where children can explore their creativity. Alibi works closely with schools.

Casting procedures: They have an artist mailing list where artists can sign up to hear about opportunities, availability, offers and more. This can be found at theatrealibi.co.uk/opportunities.

Theatre Lab Company
76 St Dunstan's Avenue, London W3 6QJ
mobile 07541 974613
email theatrelabco@gmail.com
website www.theatrelab.co.uk
X @TheatreLabCo
Instagram @theatrelabcompany
Artistic Director Anastasia Revi

Production details: Established in 1997, Theatre Lab is an international company, known for visual storytelling, mesmerising imagery and physical theatre. Works on classical texts, contemporary Greek writing, new writing and devised experimental theatre. Stages 2–3 productions annually, including 2–3 week runs at theatres in London, and tours in other UK cities and abroad. The average cast size is 8. Contracts vary: some are Equity-approved as negotiated through ITC when funded; some are non-Equity.

Casting procedures Uses in-house casting directors. Holds production-specific auditions and actors may contact the company to request attendance. Casting breakdowns are published on Spotlight and posted on the website and social media. Welcomes applications through Spotlight, emails (with CVs and headshots) and showreels. Encourages applications from disabled actors and promotes the use of inclusive casting.

Théâtre Sans Frontières
2A Tanner's Yard, Hexham,
Northumberland NE46 3NL
tel (01434) 603114
email info@tsf.org.uk
website www.tsf.org.uk
Facebook /theatresansf
X @theatresansf
Artistic Directors Sarah Kemp (CEO), John Cobb

Production details: Founded in 1991. Set up by former students of Philippe Gaulier and Monika Pagneux. Specialises in physical theatre and stages texts in different languages for adults and children using international performers. Stages 2–3 productions annually with 60–100 performances in venues including arts centres, schools and theatres. In general 3–6 actors are involved in each production.

Casting procedures: Sometimes holds general auditions. Actors may write at any time requesting inclusion. Casting breakdowns are available on request. Welcomes submissions (with CVs and photographs) sent by post or email. Invitations to view individual actors' websites are also accepted. "We are usually looking for actors who have languages other than English (especially French, Spanish or German), and who have a clear physical theatre training (i.e. Le Coq, Gaulier, Pagneux or Complicite)."

Theatre Tours International Ltd
The Ivy Cottage, 4 Northaw Road West, Northaw, Herts. EN6 4NR
email theatretoursint@gmail.com
website www.theatretoursinternational.com
Facebook /GuyMastersonTTI
Instagram @GuyMasterson, @theatretours
Artistic Director Guy Masterson

Production details: Olivier Award-winning West End and Broadway producer of small- to mid-scale touring theatre work. Stages 4–10 productions annually. Tours national and international venues, including arts centres, theatres, arts festivals and outdoor, educational and community venues.

Casting procedures: Rarely holds auditions. Mainly works with actors seen previously or by invitation.

Theatre Without Walls
Hillsborough, County Down BT26 6AS
tel 028 928 2125
email hello@theatrewithoutwalls.org
website https://theatrewithoutwalls.org
Directors Jason Maher, Genevieve Swift

Production details: Established in 2002. Award-winning theatre company specialising in forum, education and new writing. Productions represent only one-fifth of its output; also produces television and corporate films. 2 productions are staged annually with 60 performances per year, touring to 20 venues including arts centres, theatres and outdoor venues. Tours cover the UK, Ireland and Europe. 3 actors are involved in each production. Actors are employed under ITC/Equity-approved contracts.

Casting procedures: "We cast mostly through agents and our own knowledge/word of mouth/recommendations. We sometimes post casting information via Equity JIS and other 'freely available resources'. We never use casting services which actors have to pay for, except for Spotlight. Any information obtained via paid-for services has simply been copied from another source. Please don't send us any information (such as photos, CVs, showreels, etc.) unless we have requested it. We regularly hold actors' labs and often cast from them." Theatre Without Walls is a member of ITC and most of its work is undertaken using Equity contracts. Those working with vulnerable adults or children must have a current enhanced Criminal Record Bureau/Police Check and hold full insurance equal or greater than that provided by Equity for its members. Considers applications from disabled actors to play disabled characters.

See also the company's entry under *Role-play companies* on page 308.

Tilted Wig Productions
email katherine@tiltedwigproductions.com
email info@tiltedwigproductions.com
website www.tiltedwigproductions.com
Facebook /tiltedwigproductions
X @tiltedwiguk
Instagram @tiltedwig
Producers Matthew Parish, Katherine Senior

Production details: Tilted Wig Productions was formed in 2017. Has over 17 years' experience producing and touring plays throughout the UK both as Tilted Wig and Creative Cow – a Devon-based theatre company co-founded in 2007. An ensemble of actors, crew and creatives has taken over 20 productions on the road, touring in the depths of the British countryside, setting up shows in pubs and skittle alleys. Shows now tour to some of the biggest theatres in the UK yet that same ethos is still the driving force behind the company.

Casting procedures: Does not hold general auditions; the company works with a pool of performers, but is always interested in meeting new actors – either by personal recommendation or by seeing their work. Casts for some roles via agents through Spotlight. Encourages applications from disabled actors and promotes the use of inclusive casting.

Tin Shed Theatre Co.
Based in Newport, Wales
email connect@tinshedtheatrecompany.com
website www.tinshedtheatrecompany.com
Facebook /TinShedTheatreCo
Instagram @tinshedtheatreco, @theplacenewport, @newportfringefestival
Creative Director George Harris (she/her), Company Manager Naomi Cummings

Production details: A civic arts organisation with over 15 years of experience creating socially engaged, public-specific performance and participatory arts projects. The company is deeply embedded in the cultural life in Wales and is recognised across the UK and internationally for its commitment to inclusive practice, creative placemaking, creatively reimagining public spaces, artist development and high-quality, large-scale artistic production.

The company seeks to connect with creative collaborators in socially engaged arts practice with call-outs regularly shared across their social media accounts. Tin Shed curate the Newport Fringe festival seeking to connect with emerging artists and new work.

Casting procedures: Often workshop led, however the company favour creative collaborations and longer term artist relationships. Welcomes unsolicited approaches by post and email, and accepts showreels and invitations to view individual actors' websites/visit other productions. Encourages applications from disabled actors and promotes the use of inclusive casting.

Tin Shed Theatre Co.
The Place, Newport NP20 4AL
email connect@tinshedtheatrecompany.com
website www.tinshedtheatrecompany.com
Creative Director George Harris (She/Her), Company Manager Naomi Underwood Cummings

Production details: A civic arts organisation with over 15 years of experience creating socially engaged, public-specific performance and participatory arts projects. The company is deeply embedded in the cultural life in Wales and is recognised for its commitment to inclusive practice, creative placemaking, creatively reimagining public spaces, artist development and high-quality, large scale artistic production.

As a civic organisation, TSTC places public good, imaginative storytelling and creative development at the heart of its creative mission. Their work is driven by a desire to reflect and serve the people they engage with through meaningful, collaborative arts experiences. They specialise in site-responsive and outdoor performance, delivering work that transforms everyday spaces (bridges, squares, parks, disused buildings and negative spaces) into platforms for creativity, connection, and shared storytelling. Their approach blends professional artistry with socially engaged practice, often co-creating and elevating the work of everyday people into professionally produced masterpieces.

Casting procedures: TSTC champions emerging creatives of all ages and backgrounds often providing space, support and bespoke programmes of work to ensure that pathways to the creative industries remain open and accessible. The casting process is bespoke and unique to each production; see website for more details.

Middle- and smaller-scale companies 231

Tinderbox Theatre Company
The MAC, 10 Exchange Street West, Belfast, BT1 2NJ
tel 028-9043 9313
email info@tinderbox.org.uk
website www.tinderbox.org.uk
X @tinderboxNI
Instagram @tinderboxtheatreco
Artistic Director Patrick J. O'Reilly, Creative Producer Ciarán Haggerty

Production details: Founded in 1988. Produces, develops and stages new work and provides professional theatre training. Stages 2–3 productions annually.

Casting procedures: Holds open calls for auditions. Offers Equity-approved contracts. Promotes the use of inclusive casting.

Told by an Idiot
c/o Unicorn Theatre, 147 Tooley Street, London SE1 2HZ
tel 020-7407 4123
email info@toldbyanidiot.org
website www.toldbyanidiot.org
Artistic Director Paul Hunter

Production details: Founded in 1993, the company tours to theatres nationally and internationally. A critically acclaimed UK theatre company that explores the human condition through ambitious, experimental and accessible theatre.

Casting procedures: Casting is either in-house or with a freelance casting director, depending on the project. Opportunities can be found on their website. Offers ITC/Equity contracts.

Trestle Theatre Company
Trestle Arts Base, Russet Drive, St Albans AL4 0JQ
tel (01727) 850950
email admin@trestle.org.uk
website www.trestle.org.uk
X @TrestleTheatre
Instagram @trestletheatre
Executive Director Clare Winter, Creative Director Helen Barnett

Production details: Founded in 1981 as a touring theatre company, now also with a home venue (Trestle Arts Base), national and international workshop programme and a global business making and selling handcrafted theatre masks. Performers/facilitators used across all areas of the company. All projects concentrate on new, devised or commissioned work, incorporating mask, text, physical theatre, dance and other movement forms, storytelling, puppetry, music and song. Currently 2 shows touring schools with high quality performances, workshops and resources – national and international tours. In general 2–5 performers are involved in each project. Offers ITC/Equity contracts.

Casting procedures: Rarely holds general auditions. Does not welcome on-spec CVs. Will consider invitations to see actors in shows if the performance style is relevant to the way in which Trestle works. If looking for suggestions, casting breakdowns will be posted on the website. Usually casts actors with strong physical/visual theatre acting training or experience. Actively encourages applications from disabled actors and promotes the use of inclusive casting.

Tribe Arts
Mabgate Mills – Mill 2, Macaulay Street, Leeds LS9 7DZ
email holla@tribearts.co.uk
website www.tribearts.co.uk
Facebook /tribeartsuk
X @tribe_arts
Instagram @tribearts
Artistic Director Tajpal Rathore

Production details: Tribe Arts is a radical-political, actor-led theatre and media production company. Their mission is to amplify the stories and voices of the current black and Asian generation by working across artforms, platforms and disciplines, responding to current trends and political conversations that contribute to contemporary British black and Asian diasporas. Tribe Arts also produces Off/Stage Zine, dedicated to black and Asian theatre and culture.

Casting procedures: Creatives are invited to send their CV and a short covering note to holla@tribearts.co.uk with the subject line CASTING. Specific roles are advertised on the Opportunities page of the website.

TYPE (The Yellowchair Performance Experience)
89 Birchanger Lane, Birchanger, Bishop Stortford, Herts. CM23 5QF
email contacttype@gmail.com
Key contact Hugh Allison

Production details: Aims to give new talent their first break on the UK Fringe (not limited to actors).

Casting procedures: Does not use freelance casting directors or hold general auditions. Actors may write in at any time. Casting breakdowns are usually available at www.mandy.com. Welcomes letters (with CVs and photographs) from individual actors previously unknown to the company, sent by post. May cast disabled actors, depending on the role.

Unrestricted View
109 St Paul's Road, Islington, London N1 2NA
tel 020-7704 2001
email henandchickens@aol.com
website www.unrestrictedview.co.uk
Artistic Directors Felicity Wren, James Wren, Theatre Manager Mark Lyminster

232 Theatre

Production details: Unrestricted View produce new writing and comedy. Run by actors for actors, the company offer a safe, supportive space for creative people to work in. The theatre is also can be a cinema space. Theatre productions are hosted on 1–3 week long runs and comedy shows are hosted on an individual basis, with the theatre in use as a performance space 355 days per year.

The main theatre space has 54 seats, which are end on and raked. Hire-rates vary, please contact the theatre on the email above for details.

Casting Procedures: For in-house productions, uses in-house casting directors and will post about auditiond on Mandy and social media.. Upcoming productions can be seen on the website, Instagram, Twitter and Facebook. Happy to chat to actors about how to stage their own shows. Happy to consider applications from disabled actors.

Vanguard Productions
30 Coombe Rise, Findon Valley, Worthing, West Sussex BN14 0ED
tel 07718 345167
email vanguardproductions573@gmail.com
website www.vanguardproductions.co.uk
Artistic Directors Nelson. E.Ward, Amaryllis Crooke, Rachel Ward, Rachel Madden-Ward

Production details: Founded in 1996, Vanguard takes theatre and entertainment to areas of the community that are socially excluded. This includes residential and nursing homes, day centres, museums and village halls as well as small-scale theatre venues. An outreach programme also exists for schools and colleges. Village hall productions usually employ 3–4 actors and Vanguard presents 4 productions per year. This equates to about 30 performances annually at venues across the south of England.

Casting procedures: Uses an in-house casting system and only holds general auditions periodically. Casting breakdowns are put on Mandy, Spotlight and Equity job information service. Welcomes both CVs and letters from actors previously unknown to the Company and unsolicited CVs and photographs. These should be sent via email.

Volcano Theatre Company
27–29 High Street, Swansea SA1 1LG
tel (01792) 464790
website www.volcanotheatre.wales
Facebook /volcanotheatrecompany
X @volcanouk
Instagram @volcanotheatreuk
Artistic Director Paul Davies

Production details: Original theatrical productions and site-specific events. Small-scale national and international touring company based in Wales. Devised and collaborative work, physical theatre, new writing, adaptations/deconstructions of classics. Also an annual series of solo performances. Venues include arts centres and theatres in the UK, Europe and worldwide. Usually 2–8 performers per production.

Casting procedures: There are no casting breakdowns. Performers are selected through workshops and invited auditions. Unsolicited admissions are read but not held on record.

Walk the Plank
Cobden Works, 37–41 Cobden Street, Salford M6 6WF
tel 0161 736 8964
email info@walktheplank.co.uk
website www.walktheplank.co.uk
Facebook /Walk.the.Plank.arts
Bluesky @walk-the-plank.bsky.social
Instagram @walktheplankarts

Production details: Walk the Plank is one of the UK's leading outdoor arts organisations, creating innovative productions and performances which engage artists and communities in a wide range of outdoor settings. Based in Salford, the company works regionally, nationally and internationally.

Has a track record of making work that engages citizens in public celebration founded on ambitious creativity that connects with ordinary people. From Capital of Culture opening ceremonies to fire gardens and site-responsive installations to parades and podcasts, the company showcases talent from a range of performing artforms.

Starting your own theatre company
Pilar Ortí

The first question you should ask yourself before starting a theatre company is – do you really need to set up a company, or do you just want to put on a show? In order to put on a show you don't need to go through all the hassle of setting up a company. If you *do* want to set up a company – why? In some cases this might be as difficult a question to answer as, "Why do you want to act?", but it's worth having an idea of why you want to invest so much time and energy in setting up and running an organisation rather than looking for acting work. Whatever your answer, be honest with yourself. And the clearer you can be, the better, as your answers will affect the kind of organisation you end up creating.

Of course, many companies emerge after a group of actors produce a show together: at some point, someone decides that, as a company of people, you are worth keeping together. If this is the case, then you are ready to run a company of your own. But there are many ways of making theatre, as you well know, and the range of theatre produced is also vast. What kind of work do you want to do? At this point it is worth bearing in mind your 'artistic policy', and coming up with a couple of sentences that describe the work you do. I know that 'policy' sounds dry, but if you end up constituting yourself as a non-commercial organisation and applying to public funds (or trusts and foundations), you will need to learn a whole new vocabulary which seems to have little to do with your art. You should never lose sight of your artistic dreams and ambitions – but you may need to talk about them in terms of policy, objectives, qualitative evaluation, benefits, management structure, cultural diversity, contingency ... the list goes on and on. This article is meant to inspire you, not send you off to sleep, so don't despair: learn the language and then use it in a creative way that makes sense to you.

Allow yourself to dream
Long-term plans are necessary – so learn to dream. (Okay, give it a try in the first instance by putting on a show. Then, if you enjoy it, carry on!) Plans, of course, can change along the way: I suggest that you have an absolutely ambitious dream plan and a let's-try-and-see-what's-possible-now plan. Opportunities arise when you least expect them, and if you know where you are heading, you can grab them without letting them throw you off-course.

I view running a theatre company rather like directing a show: the more theatre you watch, the stronger the idea you will have of what *you* want the show to be, what is unique about it, and what you can realistically achieve. So if you, like me, trained as an actor or actress and suddenly find yourself running a company, seek advice and look at how others operate. If you consider how other people do things, you will be able to adapt the bits you like and which make sense to you. In a sector such as ours, it is not difficult to find those who are pleased to help – and the freshness of people just starting out reminds us all of how much can be achieved when we don't know our limitations.

Seek help
There is an awful lot of free/cheap advice out there. During the year in which we focused on building the administrative foundations for our company, my colleague and I talked

to as many consultants, local authority officers, venue managers, etc. as we could. Some of these conversations came about through informal meetings; others, by taking part in official programmes. We found out what funders were really looking for, and what other companies were doing in our area; we learnt to draw up business plans with budgets covering three and five years; and we discovered what our strengths and weaknesses were, and what threats and opportunities exist 'out there'.

A word of warning: take *all* advice (including that which I am giving you now) with a pinch of salt, especially from those who hardly know you and your work. Follow your gut instinct. When we were in pre-production for *Antigone*, a business consultant suggested that we invite Funeral Services to advertise in our programme, "seeing as how they all die in the end". Mmm.

The best consultancies are those which have been carefully structured so that the consultant spends time with you, getting to know you and your plans, and then helps you find your own answers by providing their expertise.

Making it 'proper'

Once you have decided on the work you want to do and how you want to go about producing it, you will need to find a legal structure for your company. This shows outsiders that you are serious, and it also makes monetary transactions easier.

Forbidden's first show was produced in Edinburgh: the only 'proper' thing the company had was a bank account (and a name!). We then registered the name and became a limited company, and after our first London show, became a registered charity. This was a good idea as our income mainly comes from trusts and foundations (most of which require you to be a charity in order to receive their grants, for tax purposes); it also allows us to claim Gift Aid when we receive donations from individuals. (Gift Aid is great: the donor claims their donation as tax-deductible, and you receive an extra 23% from the Inland Revenue.)

Setting up a charity still allows you to pursue your own artistic programme: making theatre for the public is considered to 'advance education', which is a charitable objective. So you can still run your company as a business, drawing salaries, etc. and making sure that any annual profits stay within the company.

Just like a limited company, a registered charity is governed by a Board. The main difference between the two set-ups is that those who sit on a charity's Board (the Trustees) do so on a voluntary basis. It therefore would make no sense for *you* to be part of the Board (although there is talk of a possible change in the law to allow Trustees to be remunerated for their work). This means that, in theory at least, you are putting the fate of your company in the hands of other people. So choose your Trustees very carefully, and try to include people who have some knowledge of legal matters and accountancy.

This set-up worked for Forbidden, as we had been extremely lucky: we managed to find experienced individuals with integrity and a passion for what we do. You might prefer a different kind of set-up which gives you more legal control: banks and Business Links offer free advice on the different options. If you want some focused advice and have a bit of cash to spare, you might attend the Independent Theatre Council's (ITC) seminar on 'Starting a Theatre Company'. And when you have a bit more cash, you might want to join the ITC – membership is bound to come in handy when questions on legal matters arise. (Have a look at the website, **www.itc-arts.org**.)

Learn as you go along

Know your strengths and weaknesses. Setting up a theatre company will involve doing ten thousand things you might never have done before; however, a lot of it can be learnt along the way, and much of it is common sense. It won't take you long to discover those things you are useless at, and those that you absolutely hate. You then have two choices: do them anyway, or find someone else to do them for you/with you.

If there are more than two of you running the company, decide who will be in charge of what. Certain things, like fundraising, might be too daunting for one person to do on their own, but you can break it down into more manageable pieces. Someone might have a clearer head for numbers and can prepare the budget, and someone else can write the description of the show and why it will make a huge contribution to theatre in this country.

Let's talk about money

And seeing that I've come to fundraising, I shall dwell on it. You can't escape it. No matter how much your company grows, no matter how successful you are, no matter how large your staff is – if you are in charge, you will worry about it, so learn to enjoy it. I know that this sounds perverse, but fundraising applications are your chance to enthuse someone else about what you do. To tell them about your plans – about what you want to do and why you want to do it. Tell them how you want to make a difference; about *why* you think it's different; about how it will help you, and others, grow. And yes, you will need to learn some new vocabulary, and be able to distinguish between qualitative and quantitative evaluation, but it helps if you see this as a game with which you have to keep up. (At the last ITC annual general meeting, I found out that 'well-being' is a new way of convincing funders that theatre is necessary to people's lives!) What's really important is to convince funders that you really want to do the work, and that you want to do it well. (When I talk about funders, I am referring to anyone who might want to donate to or invest in your company. I have no experience of commercial deals, but I imagine that these work in a similar way: you find out what it is that people want in return for their money, and then convince them that you can provide it – as well as putting on a really good show.)

This is also where having long-term plans comes in handy: funding applications usually take between six weeks and three months to be assessed. Sometimes, even more: our first successful application for an Education Officer took more than one year from the date on which I sent it to the day the letter of acceptance came through. While I'm on the subject of those who will give you money – *nurture your relationships with them*. We have found that those trusts, foundations and individuals who are willing to help us out once, are likely to do so again.

I have also discovered that funding applications help you plan in detail how you are going to realise a production or a project. Good funding applications might come in useful even if you don't get the money – they will probably provide a good description of your plans, which you can then show others interested in your work. (For books and directories on fundraising, check out the Directory of Social Change's website, **www.dsc.org.uk**.)

Final words

I have left the most important thing until last. *Treat those working with you well, especially your actors.* Make working with you an enjoyable experience. If you hold auditions, make them worthwhile for those attending. When you are able to pay your personnel, pay them on time. Treat them like the professionals that they are. And when things go wrong, as they inevitably will, take responsibility for your company and make up for the hassle with a gesture, however small – custard creams work for me!

When I first started running Forbidden, I kept hearing that I should treat it like running a business. What I have discovered is that it is an exercise in people management. Forbidden exists because people believed in our work and were willing to invest their time and money in what we do. Different organisations work in different ways: I hope these words have helped you find one that will work for you.

After running Forbidden Theatre Company as Artistic Director for seven years, Pilar now uses her people management skills to facilitate learning in leaders and in teams. She was director of Unusual Connections, a company which uses theatre-based training to deliver Leadership Programmes and Strategic Team-Away days. She also freelances as a workshop leader and voice-over artist, and can be found at **www.pilarwrites.com**.

Jack of all trades – and then some
Brian Hook and Kate McStraw, producers
Interview by Aileen Gonsalves

Brian Hook is one half of Hartshorn–Hook Productions. They own and manage the Arts Theatre in the West End and have produced well over 150 productions over the last 18 years, including the Olivier-Award-winning Rotterdam *and the Grammy-nominated* Amélie *and is responsible for immersive shows such as* Gatsby, Doctor Who: Time Fracture, Peaky Blinders *and* The Choir of Man, *as well as many other hospitality and theatre-focused companies. He is a proud alumni of Bury College and owes a whole bunch to the kind guidance of those brilliant folks.*

Kate McStraw is a creative producer and access consultant. She is Co-Founder and Executive Producer of Viv Gordon Company; an organisation that uses arts as social justice to promote narrative change for adult survivors of child sexual abuse (CSA). With over a decade working in disabled-led arts, her work focuses on accessible arts practice for both artists and audiences.

I was saying how people used to hurl the phrase 'Jack of all trades, master of none' at me. And I always thought – how limiting! So, I wanted to talk to people like you – people who've done different things, or even the same thing but differently, and discovered brilliance in that diversity. Kate, I know you've worn many different hats in the arts. Brian, I know you've broken moulds left and right with immersive theatre and innovative producing. I thought it would be incredible to hear your voices in conversation. Let's begin at the beginning. What do you both say you do now?

BH: That's a great place to start. The simplest answer is, "I produce theatre." But that's not really true anymore. I used to produce theatre. I started out as an actor, then moved into producing. Now, I'm buying a theatre – so soon I'll be a theatre owner. I still run a producing company, but these days I'm more of a creative director.

I put on plays and musicals, I sell tickets, and alongside that I run a ticketing business, a marketing company, and a hospitality business. So 'producer' doesn't quite cut it, but it's the easiest way to explain what I do.

KM: *I love that, Brian. Because I say the same thing – "I'm a theatre producer" – even though that's not entirely accurate either.*

I actually started in costume design, which is how I met Aileen. Now I run Viv Gordon Company. We're hoping to become a charity soon. We use the arts for social justice and narrative change, especially around CSA survivor-led work.

My work now is more about inclusion, accessibility, and shifting systems than just producing shows. I often feel like a creative facilitator, or even an activist. So yes, I still call myself a producer – but I think we both have stretched that word to fit what we do.

It's fascinating, the way both of you have moved across disciplines. Did either of you know you wanted to be a producer from the start?

KM: *Not even close! I didn't know what a producer was. I just knew I wanted to make creative things happen.*

I was always organising stuff – cabaret nights, charity gigs, Shakespeare in parks. And one day, I was watching a show with a friend and I said, "You could've designed this better." She looked at me and said, "I don't think that's how designers think."

That moment stuck. I realised I was more interested in trying to match the right person to the right task, to make the best show possible. That's producing. I've never needed to be the centre – I just want to move things forward and support brilliant people.

BH: I completely relate. I also didn't know what a producer was. I fell in love with acting at college – it was the first time I ever worked hard at anything. But producing came from necessity. There was an empty space, and we wanted to put on a show. Then I met my now business partner, Louie Hartshorn, in the Palace Theatre bar in Manchester, and we had three pints of beer and set up a production company. We were barely out of uni. I thought we'd make shows for me to act in, but I quickly realised I loved giving other people the spotlight.

I got obsessed with the jigsaw puzzle of it all – how do you shape a show, tell a story, move an audience? That became my life.

That's so brilliant. Was there a moment when you consciously shifted into producing as your identity?

KM: *Yes, there was a moment. In my final year of uni, I chose to produce a show and design the costumes for my self-directed project. No one on my course had done that before.*

Producing felt like a way to make opportunities happen for myself and others. I used to think, "Well, I'll hire myself to design!" But slowly, I fell out of love with design and into love with producing.

I remember Aileen saying, "You can call yourself whatever you like – just do the job." I thought, Great! I started calling myself a creative producer and just ran with it.

BH: I love that. For me, it was also gradual – but there were milestones. One was a tough conversation with my older brother, who said, "You say you're an actor, but what are you *actually* doing to make that true?" At the time, I was selling ice cream in a theatre.

That lit a fire under me. We had this relentless creative push. Producing became my focus, and acting naturally fell away. And I haven't missed it once. That's how I knew I'd found my real path.

Do all these varied experiences help with what you do now? Do you think of yourselves as 'Jack of all trades' types?

BH: I used to, yes. Louie and I can still produce a show top to bottom. But about ten years ago, I started specialising in immersive theatre and nonlinear narratives, like *Gatsby*, *Peaky Blinders* and *Stranger Things: The Experience*. So while I still have those generalist skills, I've carved out a niche. That led us to work with Disney, Warner Bros., and Paramount. Specialising didn't limit me – it helped me grow.

KM: *It's so funny, Brian, because I feel like I've done the exact same thing, just on a totally different path.*

I used to take offence when someone called me a Jack of all trades. But then I looked up the full quote: 'A jack of all trades is a master of none, but oftentimes better than master of one', and realised, actually, that's me.

I used to do everything: drive the van, cook for the artists, fund the show. And I loved that. But now I crave collaboration. I want to work with brilliant people who love marketing, or access, or logistics.

These days, I'm focused on disability arts, systemic change, and accessible job creation. I've narrowed my focus, not because I can't do it all, but because it's now more interesting to me this way.

I love that. Both of you breaking out of boxes – was that met with resistance? Did anyone ever tell you to stay in your lane?

BH: All the time. But honestly, immersive work came from necessity, not rebellion. We couldn't get programmed at traditional venues. So we asked, "Can we take over this old pub and stage Gatsby across three floors?" And they said yes. From there, it just evolved. We never had a board or trustees—we could make bold decisions fast. And that flexibility let us pioneer new ways of storytelling. So yes, people resisted it, but we didn't wait for permission.

KM: *That's so resonant. I've never had anyone say "You can't do this," but I've heard "It's too risky" a thousand times.*

At Viv Gordon Company we make CSA survivor-led work. Programmers sometimes say, "We don't have an audience for this," or "It's too risky," But that's just not true. So we've taken the DIY route and taken over empty shop spaces for pop-up events, which have sold out.

What we know is there are 11 million adult survivors of CSA in the UK. So it's a pretty big audience. It just isn't recognised in the arts at the moment. So yeah, it's really interesting. But yes it's hard, especially with public funding shrinking. But I can't imagine doing anything else.

It's incredibly inspiring. The belief you both have in your work – how do you keep that going?

BH: Experience. We once poured £100k into developing a musical we loved. But when we realised the final budget would be £4.5 million, way beyond us, we walked away.

It was devastating, but the right choice. And that decision led to some of our biggest successes. That taught me to trust my instincts, to walk away if something doesn't feel right.

KM: *I've learned the same thing. Self-belief isn't about being certain; it's about being committed. And having the right collaborators.*

I'm writing a musical now, Off the Scales, *set in a weight loss group. It's the scariest thing I've done, because it's so personal. But I've had an amazing producer (Molly Scarborough) supporting me, and that makes all the difference.*

BH: Kate, that's brilliant. You've got a producer on the inside now!

KM: *Exactly! Though it's hard to not try producing it myself. But writing has opened something new in me. It's terrifying, but thrilling. And I think that's a good sign.*

Thank you both. You're the perfect examples of how creative evolution, risk-taking, and curiosity can shape powerful careers. You haven't just 'done different things' – you've done things differently. And that's what's so inspiring.

Aileen Gonsalves is a theatre director, actor, writer, and creator of the Gonsalves Method – a pioneering approach to actor training taught in drama schools and universities in many countries.

Finding funding for projects
Sinead Mac Manus

Finding funding for projects is an essential part of the subsidised theatre scene. Unless you are working in the commercial sector, most theatre productions do not generate enough income to cover their costs. Fundraising provides the shortfall. The funding landscape in the UK is wide and varied, and can seem to the beginner to be an impossible terrain to navigate. However, as with most things, there are tricks of the trade that you can learn, and the process *does* get easier with practice.

Starting points
There are two good starting publications that I would recommend for fledging arts fundraisers: the first entitled 'Guide to Arts Funding in England', is an excellent overview of arts funding available to download for free from the Department for Culture, Media and Sport (DCMS) website (**www.culture.gov.uk**). Also recommended is Susan Forrester's and David Lloyd's *The Arts Funding Guide* published by the Directory of Social Change in 2002 (**www.dsc.org.uk**), which may be available in your local library. These guides take the user through the areas where you can find funding for projects, such as Government grants including Arts Council funding, Lottery funding, funding from your Local Authority, grants from charitable trusts and foundations, and bursaries.

Research, research, research
Successful fundraising is all about research, and matching available funds to your projects. If you approach fundraising creatively you should be able to adapt projects to available funds while still retaining your artistic integrity. So how do you discover what is out there? Get on the arts mailing lists to find out about new rounds of funds. Research the funding bodies and their criteria. Talk to your local Council about what funds they can offer you and your project. Find out what venues support new work with bursaries, or support in kind such as free space. Find out what trusts and foundations there are and who they give money to. Look up fundraising directories in your local library or one of the resource centres at organisations such as CIDA in east London and the Directory of Social Change (**www.dsc.org.uk**).

The Grant Finder website (**www.grantfinder.co.uk**) features funding resources including a guide full of useful tips, case studies, insights and news. It highlights funding opportunities and offer support services to help you access funding.

It is important to research the funder that you are applying to, in order to find the 'essence' of the funder. This is essential so that you can match your projects to the relevant funder. For example, a Lottery Funding scheme such as the Community Fund (**www.tnlcommunityfund.org.uk**) distributes public money for the benefit of local communities. Therefore any application to them must be for a project that demonstrates clear benefit to an identified community or body of people.

Similarly, the Arts Councils of England, Wales, Scotland and Northern Ireland all distribute public funds and have to be very open and transparent about how their funds are distributed.

Finding funding for projects 241

Arts Council England (ACE) is the development and funding agency for the arts in England. You can apply to ACE as an individual for funding between £1,000 to £100,000. You can apply any time and there are no deadlines. A decision will be forthcoming within six weeks for grants under £5,000 and twelve weeks for grants over £5,000. ACE set aims every three years which form the basis of their grant-making policy, so it is important for applicants to think about how their project will fit into these aims. As with any funding body, building a relationship is paramount. Even before you approach ACE for funding, you should be inviting them to your productions and telling them about your projects. Full details of how to apply, including guidance notes, are on the website (**www.artscouncil.org.uk**).

The Arts Council of Wales (**www.arts.wales**) has a similar funding system and structure to England, but there are regular funding deadlines throughout the year. Creative Scotland (formerly The Scottish Arts Council; **www.creativescotland.com**) has a slightly more complicated funding system with deadlines for different funding streams. The Arts Council of Northern Ireland (**www.artscouncil-ni.org**) has different funding schemes for individuals and organisations, and different closing dates for individual schemes.

In contrast to the Arts Councils in the UK, many charitable trusts and foundations only distribute funds to limited companies, and, in some cases, registered charities. Some can fund individuals, but they are not many. When applying to trusts and foundations, it is important to remember they were usually set up to address an issue or problem. You will need to identify what this is and ensure that your project addresses this.

Find out what you can about the funding body that you are applying to and what their funding priorities are. Make sure you fit into their guidelines and that you are eligible to apply. Remember that all funders have agendas – they do not give money away for nothing. For example, many Local Authority arts funding schemes usually look for local projects that impact on the community and have public benefit. View researching and applying for funding as you would looking for a job. You would not apply to a company if you did not think you were qualified. Similarly, you are wasting your time and theirs if you apply for funding that you are not eligible to get, e.g. your theatre company is not a registered charity, or they only fund work with older people and you work with children.

The proposal

An easy to read guide on writing funding proposals is Tim Cook's *Avoiding the Wastepaper Basket – A practical guide to applying to Grant Making Trusts* (LVSC, 1998). The book is written from the perspective of the funding body, and looks at examples of good and bad funding proposals.

If there is no application form, write a clear and concise (2 x A4 page) proposal. Write in plain English and do not use jargon. Find what the 'grain' of the funding body is. Do their work for them. Show in your funding application exactly how you meet their criteria and fit into their funding policy. Again to use the analogy of applying for a job, use the exact wording of the guidelines in your application when you are talking about your project, much in the way you would use the wording in the Person Specification when you are applying for a job. You can even highlight their criteria in bold or italics to make it stand out.

Follow the guidelines of the fund to the letter – supply all the information that they require but do not add in additional information if it is not requested. If you have something that you think may be of interest to them, mention in your application that this is available on request. Convey your enthusiasm and passion for your project and your belief in yourself and/or your company. Show how the project will be successful. Funders like to back winners.

When you are finished, show your finished application to a non-arts person and ask them to read it for clarity. If you do get a grant, remember to say thank you! Start to build a relationship with the funder and keep them updated on progress with the project. If you are not successful, ask for feedback from the funder on why.

Business sponsorship

Business sponsorship can be a useful way of raising funds for projects if you are not eligible to apply for grant project funding. Business sponsorship is where a company gives your organisation or project cash, or support in kind, in exchange for publicity for their product or service. It is important to remember that businesses will not give you money or support for nothing – they will require something in return. Sponsorship is essentially a commercial deal between yourself and the business, and therefore there should be a clear exchange of benefits, e.g. advertising benefit for the company and monetary benefit for the arts organisation, and there should be a value to the benefit given or received.

Income generation

An important part of finding funding for projects is generating your own income. Income can be earned or generated from a number of different sources: venues can pay you a fee or share the box office receipts of a production. They can also commission or co-produce a work. You can sell merchandise such as programmes, t-shirts or postcards at your events. You can generate income through education work including fees for workshops and residencies. Individuals can give you money for your projects (angels) or they can invest in your work and expect (or not!) a return. You can also raise funds through events ranging from theatre related events such as benefit performances and cabarets to 'fun' events such as sponsored walks to parachute jumps.

Creative thinking

When you are starting out, it can be difficult to see where you can obtain the money for projects. The Arts Council do prefer to fund artists or organisations with a track record, and therefore you may have to find alternative funding initially for your productions or projects. Trusts and foundations tend to only fund limited companies or registered charities, and so again this may not be an area of funding that you can tap into immediately.

Therefore it is important to think of ways of funding your work outside the traditional funding system. In many cases, this may mean that you have to fund your work yourself and hope that you can get a return on it, or at least break even. This is how the majority of companies fund their Edinburgh Festival Fringe run – by investing the money upfront in the hire of the venue, the accommodation and travel and the cost of the production and hoping that the take at the box office will cover these costs and give everyone involved in the production some wages. If you are using your own money to mount a production, you need to be able to assess what level of risk you are willing to accept and think of ways of lessening this risk. Examine your budget and see where you can reduce or cut costs. You could try to get free rehearsal space from a local school in exchange for workshops or use a local printer for your flyers in exchange for advertising in your programme. Consider sharing your venue with another company for a double bill (check that this is acceptable

LAMDA
London Academy of Music & Dramatic Art

Develop and enhance your acting skills through industry-leading postgraduate courses

Expand your professional skillset with short courses for stage, screen and audio actors

Explore Courses >

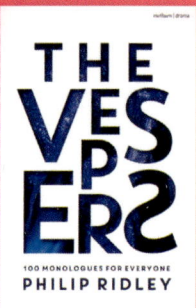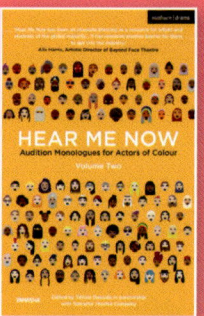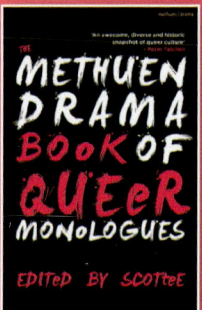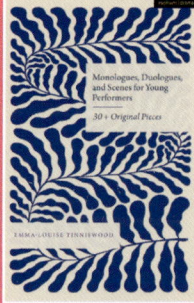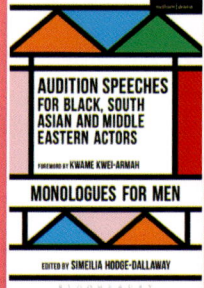

KEEP UP WITH THE DRAMA

From finding out how to email your first agent to understanding the differences between acting on stage and screen, follow our **Actors & Performers blog** for advice articles and career tips, extracts from new books, and Q&As with authors

actorsandperformers.com

methuen | drama

THE BIG HOUSE
HAS A SIMPLE
MISSION:

TO ENABLE
CARE EXPERIENCED
AND AT RISK
YOUNG PEOPLE
TO FULFIL THEIR POTENTIAL.

FOLLOW US @_THEBIGHOUSE_
INFO@THEBIGHOUSE.UK.COM
WWW.THEBIGHOUSE.UK.COM

ALEXANDER & CO
CHARTERED ACCOUNTANTS

Equity Approved Chartered Accountants and Tax Advisors

Assisting clients in the film, TV and theatre industry since 1976.

Strategic planning advice to ensure your business affairs are structured in the most tax efficient way.

We also provide more specialist advice as and when required, including tax advice on other income streams, such as property investments, crypto, shares and pensions.

Frequently used services include Self Assessment tax returns, limited company accounts, Theatre Tax Relief claims and business planning/restructuring.

Please contact us to discuss how we can assist you.

0161 832 4841
info@alexander.co.uk
www.alexander.co.uk

ESSENTIAL BOOKS FOR ACTORS

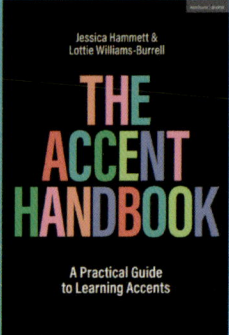
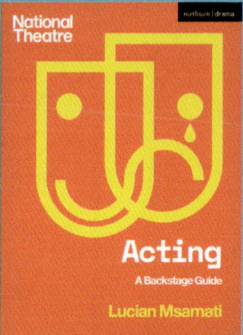
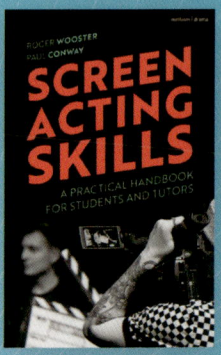
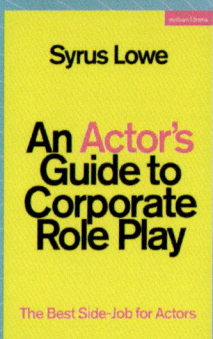
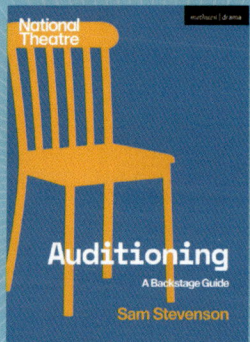
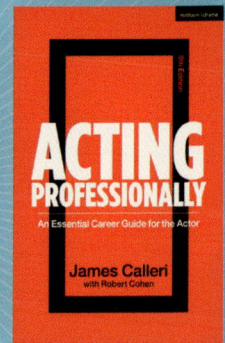
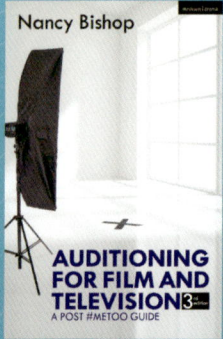
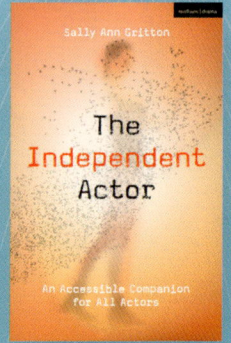

bloomsbury.com/drama methuen | drama

THEATRE RECORD

Chronicling the British Stage since 1981

www.theatrerecord.com

Theatre Record collates theatre critics' reviews for major productions in London and across Britain all in one place, together with production details and cast lists. We also provide listings of current and future productions.

With Theatre Record you can:

- Read the latest theatre reviews for major productions
- Explore and search the full archive of back issues with reviews from more than 55,000 productions spanning over four decades
- Check what's on, where and when, both now and in the future

To discover more or to subscribe

www.theatrerecord.com

James Norton Jack Gleeson

Mark Rylance David Morrissey

SIMON ANNAND
PHOTOGRAPHER
www.simonannand.com
07884 446 776

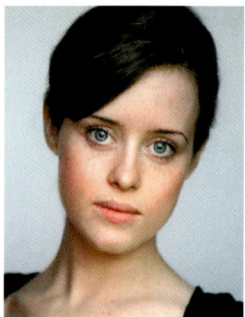

Claire Foy Rosalind Eleazar Vicky McClure

Author of THE HALF, Actors preparing to go on stage
& BACKSTAGE (formerly *Time to Act*)
NT, RSC, Royal Court, Sonia Friedman Productions
40 years experience • £350 full / £310 concession

to the venue in advance) to halve the costs of the hire. Book a venue in your local area that you know so that you can at least invite friends and family to have a guaranteed audience. Ask friends and family to invest small amounts of money in your production. This can be done as a gift or on an investment and return basis e.g. an individual invests £100 and is guaranteed a return of £75 or an amount above £100, depending on how well the show does. Offer credits for purchase in the production as gifts – purchasers get credit in the publicity material, and an invitation to a performance.

There are many examples of artists and companies that have used creative ways to get their projects up and running. One company sold performances in the customer's sitting room on eBay for cash. Another company raised the money for a string of rural performances by doing a sponsored walk from venue to venue. Another company raised the money for a production by offering to do up a local community centre – they got free rehearsal space and a venue as part of the deal.

Remember that you are a creative individual! Use some of that creativity to think outside the box when it comes to finding money for projects.

Sinead Mac Manus has worked for a wide range of arts organisations, including Frantic Assembly, Tall Stories and Mimbre. She is currently a freelance creative business consultant and trainer, and has many years of experience working with and training creative entrepreneurs. She is the author of *eVolve Graduate Handbook: a practical guide to producing performance*. Her activity in developing new business models around the idea of e-learning for creative entrepreneurs using web 2.0 tools and social media led her to be chosen this year as one of the Courvoisier: Future 500 to watch.

Actors and writers: an imperfect creative marriage

Lucian Msamati

I have an ugly, honest confession: I am that annoying actor who believes he *always* has a better version of the dialogue than the meticulously crafted efforts of the writer, even before I have actually bothered to commit a single line to memory. Everyone from Soyinka to Shakespeare, has had the displeasure of my wilful mangling of their worded wizardry. In my defence, and by way of grudging apology, there are three fairly sound reasons for this near sacrilegious compulsion of mine, none of which have anything to do with a spectacularly unself-aware ego, I promise.

Firstly: after acting my next great love is writing. I burn an eternal candle for every playwright and every play I have ever been involved with. I fell in love with playwrighting aged 10 playing the cowardly lion in Avondale Primary School's production of *The Wizard of Oz* in Harare, Zimbabwe, where I grew up. It dawned on me one afternoon during rehearsals that someone made up the characters, words, and songs we were learning and that if *I* were that someone, I could create and perform *anything*. It was quite a eureka moment for my young mind! I am admittedly embellishing things a little under the influence of the warm afterglow of nostalgia and a slightly better vocabulary, but this is precisely why I am in ageless awe of writers and brilliant writing. The ability to capture in words the essence of a moment and have an audience experience it anew again and again is a superpower like no other.

My early efforts to make my own magic included a two-page 'sequel' to *The Wizard of Oz*, consisting mostly of bastardised song lyrics from the original and short scenes I'd later learn were called 'sketches', lovingly plagiarized from my favourite TV shows. I owe back-dated royalty cheques to Lenny Henry, Tracey Ullman, Team Blackadder, Eddie Murphy and the late, great Zimbabwean comedian and band leader Safirio Madzikatire (aka 'Sekuru Mukadota') from the Zimbabwe Broadcasting Corporation's classic *Mukadota Family* sitcom, to name but a few. They were truly my first writing and performing instructors, and I am proud to call myself a glorified living hack-job tribute act to them all. As intellectual curiosity expanded in my teens, I fell under the spell of the greats of neo-colonial African literature such as Wole Soyinka, Charles Mungoshi, Dambudzo Marechera and Ngugi Wa Thiong'o who were soon followed by the likes of Samuel Beckett, Eugene Ionesco, Albert Camus, James Baldwin, and Jean-Paul Sartre to name, yet again, a few! Crucially though, these particular names all had one thing in common: they *loved* and made theatre. It wasn't some smug, intellectual side hustle for them to flex their literary chops but a legitimate, uniquely powerful extension of their creativity. From this moment on, the distinction between 'writer', 'actor', 'director' and 'intellectual' for me dissolved: they were all one and the same thing.

With that in mind, might you then strike a note of empathy on your tiny violin for my second sort of sound reason? As an actor, I am artistically allergic to being treated like a glorified sock-puppet in the rehearsal process. Granted, learning, and delivering lines on repeat for the duration of the gig to the best of your ability is your literal job description. However, the shrill, entitled inner artistic voice in my head screams, 'Hey! Esteemed Playwright, I am not just a voice with great stubby legs, you know! I have *ideas* and *feelings* about those ideas! Sure, *you* spent years in excruciating, creative labour to deliver unto us your wordy treats, but *I* breathed literal oxygen into your scribbling and made them *real*! I'll therefore mangle them however I see fit, *until* they fit!'. All this is really just a cack-handed act of creative self-preservation. The rehearsal process starts off as democratic until the necessary divisions of labour make it a benign despotism. At the point when the discussions have to stop and someone has to get up and physically make the play a real thing, the creative collaborator whose job it is to be most exposed (i.e. the actor), is often the person whose opinion can feel like it matters the least. It is a necessary, quirky irony of an actor's creative responsibility. From the moment you get a script, you have to park your critical faculties in order to find the human and relatable in the play. You can't build empathy out of strong opinions, can you?

Strong – and, increasingly, loud – opinions are only ever an interpretation or a stance on the truth and don't tend to make for interesting stories because they are the antithesis to curiosity. And curiosity is the beginning of empathy. As an actor your opinion therefore has to be secondary to your capacity for empathy. It can be the most dangerous, tenuous but rewarding creative currency to trade in. As the designated 'grown ups' in the rehearsal process (i.e. the director and the writer) work out the bigger picture from a remove, the actor intimately embraces and inhabits all the imperfections of this make-believe world. The necessary cutting, pasting, editing and reworking of the text therefore aren't just practical exercises for an actor. These actions can sometimes feel like major, instantaneous, emergency organ-replacement surgery. With time and experience of course, you can learn as an actor to better manage the emotional and psychological wrench that can occur, but it is and always will be a delicate dance. After all, you're dealing with human beings trying to play human beings (or lions, or trains) that have to feel human enough to connect with a room full of strangers who have parted with good money to be entertained. It's kind of intense! And will invariably get mixed in with ego. That's usually when phrases such as, 'You know, I think my character would do X!' or worse, 'I don't think my character should say Y!' come into being.

It is an exposing, exhilarating exercise because the actor has nowhere to hide in the process: exposure *is* your process. If I had a penny for every time I heard a director say, 'Yeah, I know it's not great, but please can you just do it as it is for tonight?'. And, of course, in the end the actor delivers because, ultimately, it's a creative duty of care to the writing. Sometimes the greatest lesson for a writer is to see and hear their words out loud. An idea may read as glorious on paper and in your head but be a shambolic mess in the flesh and vice versa. This is the great challenge of writing language for performance. It has to start in theory and be continually polished in practice but for the actor it's *all* practice; there is no room really to theorise because for better and for worse, your job is to *be*.

Perhaps it's a crude analogy but an actor ends up becoming something of a creative foster parent to the play. The writer absolutely brings it into the world, but the actor nurtures, raises, and brings it into maturity. It isn't a static thing to picked up and discarded from a shelf. For a time, it is literally a lived, parallel experience for an actor in a way that it isn't for the writer. This is perhaps why certain interpretations of well-known characters in celebrated plays become 'definitive'; so inexorably linked to one actor that to 'see' or 'hear' that role any other way is impossible. How can you as an actor not be a greater authority when it is becomes your identity? Maybe the answer is in the idea of being a 'creative foster parent' or 'Legal Artistic Guardian'. You invest in it knowing that the play eventually returns 'home' to the writer. You invest in it on the understanding that no matter how much you love, care for, understand and maybe even elevate it, it's a beautiful and benign thing. It can never love you the way you love it so you're damned if you do and damned if you don't!

All of which leads to my third unpicked bone: the love-hate relationship between writer and actor. Let me be more specific and say *my* love-hate relationship with writing which kind of then extends to writers. To be fair, 'hate' is actually too strong a sentiment. It's something closer to a conjugal, creative contempt, between my two great loves which might actually be worse! The actor and the writer are connected to each other through the words. It's a beautiful, unspoken intimacy that could be a perfect romantic creative union except for the fact that, in practice, the marriage has to constantly be managed by the necessary interference of the director. It's like having to have the priest conducting events on your wedding night. All three of you are then invested in the child you make together (don't ask) but are convinced that *their* way is the best way to raise it, whilst being fully aware that the other parents have skills and knowledge we can never match! Legendary American playwright Eugene O' Neill, famously, did not trust actors. This might explain why some of his stage directions are so detailed, thorough and read rather brilliantly like screenplays. I think I might have a sprinkle of empathy here because where there are issues of trust, a relationship with vulnerability is not far behind and this actually, is where the beautiful schism really lies between actor and writer.

The writer drills down into themselves to bring up a thing of clarity and beauty. It can be a painstaking, lonely pursuit. The completed play therefore is living proof that the writer has successfully negotiated and largely overcome a very personal and *private* face-off with their vulnerability. A published text is a fait accompli. Whether that work ever gets produced or not, that text is a tangible, relatable and autonomous artistic statement. To hand off your 'art baby' to be brought to life by strangers is terrifying. And yet? Regardless of whether the show is a hit or a dud, the text remains. As an actor though, you have to be vulnerable twice. Firstly, as an individual with a unique lived, professional experience that has to be open to the story, characters, and the play. The actor then has to push past that and for a time become both the conduit and defender of the writer's vulnerability. To serve this properly the written word has to become the authority in the room and in performance; the play must always have the literal and metaphorical final say. Of course it must: that's why we have all gone through those weeks of joyous torture to serve and bring to light! And maybe this the root of my love-contempt: the presumption of intellectual authority over everyone and everything else in the rehearsal room and beyond. What part of this assumed intellect is at play on a rainy Wednesday matinee when that killer line that had the audience rolling in the aisles with laughter on press night, lands like a lead balloon? Same delivery, same timing, same action: tumbleweed. This is the territory that the actor navigates on behalf of the writer. Regardless of the reactions of the crowd or the intentions of the writer, the actor has to become a master of every single permutation of that line and still make the story flow. You cannot intellectualise the unknown. There is an intelligence at play in these moments that is an alchemy unique to the connection between the actor the word and the audience.

When we speak of the 'writing' of play A or show B being good or bad, what do we actually mean? Sometimes I think we are acknowledging the writer's technical ability. Any passionate reader or seasoned theatre goer can hear or spot that. At other times though, the distinction between the technical skill on the page and the interpretation we see on stage can get blurred. Maybe what we're all plugging into is a combination of the two things that look, feel and read as authenticity. We make our greatest art when we trust that those outside of ourselves battle with and value the formless as we do. We diminish the sanctity of that relationship when we try to codify and control it. So many times, those transcendent moments on stage are nothing to do with brilliant writing, acting, direction or even a particularly receptive audience on any given night. It's an alchemy unique to that shared, complicit moment. It is ephemeral. Once the lead becomes gold, that's it. It's gone. What you as an actor is left with is the memory of the sensation of that first time. You can either spend the next however many shows trying to recreate or recapture that fluid alchemy and live with all the frustration that comes with that unholy quest or you start again every night. That's exhausting. And terrifying. And counterintuitive. And all made possible by the bedrock of those beautiful uncontrollable words, words and more words as gifted to us by the writers and as mangled – lovingly at first and then devotedly! – by an epically un-self-aware actor whose delight it is to make you the audience fall in love with these great stories and characters again and again and again; I promise.

Lucian Msamati is an award-winning actor, writer, director and producer on stage and screen.

Acting, writing and making work
Tuyền Đỗ, writer and actor
Interview by Sam Stevenson

Tuyen Do is a British Vietnamese writer and actor working across theatre, TV and film and is one of the recipients of 2020's Channel 4 Playwriting award for her debut play Summer Rolls, *published by Oberon. Her second play was a self-performed one-woman show* Lòng Me (Mother's Soul) *at the Vaults Festival. She has also written for CBBC* Biff & Chip *and has contributed to the* Hear Me Now Monologues, *as well as the publication of* East Side Voices *by Sceptre Books. Acting credits include* The Great Wave *(National Theatre),* Pah La *(Royal Court),* Shadow and Bone *(Netflix), and* The Red King *(Alibi).*

Congratulations on getting *Summer Rolls* published and produced. I think I am right in saying that it's your first published and produced play?
Yes. The seed of the play began seven years before it was staged and underwent many drafts.

It seems to me to be a very personal story.
It is, though I wanted it to reach an audience that was much bigger than my inner circle. The inspiration began when I was part of the Unheard Voices group; I had always wanted to write something from my own experience, drawing on my background and my community. I had so much that I wanted to say, but when you haven't written anything before, you don't yet know how to frame your ideas dramatically. And then I went to see Arnold Wesker's *Chicken Soup with Barley*, which gave me the idea of telling the generational story of this family through jumps in time.

There can be pushback against kitchen-sink dramas because there's an appetite right now for very big political plays, but that's not where my strength lies. In lots of ways, of course, *Summer Rolls* is political; it's a portrait of a family who are affected by all the big decisions made by people in power. It is also the first British-Vietnamese story to be produced for the stage. There are lots of stories set in Vietnam, often about the war, but there was nothing out there that dramatised the personal experiences of growing up in Britain.

Has writing and producing changed how you think about your job as an actor and how you interpret another writer's work?
It has definitely influenced the way that I read scripts and what I might bring to the role that the writer didn't envision. I also respect the writing much more because I know that the writer has probably pored over those lines again and again. Sometimes, as actors, we like to rearrange the dialogue so that it becomes more comfortable to speak, but with experience you learn that, if you really stick to what the writer intended, something more interesting can emerge from your performance.

I think that actors really have to embrace the idea that it's not just about their individual performance; that a change in dialogue can disrupt the rhythm, which in turn is liable to affect the other actors in the scene. It's like playing music, isn't it? A musician wouldn't change the composer's notes or the time signature.
Yes, and even jazz has its rules; you're given a structure in which to work.

When you are training or in the early stages of your acting career, you're still finding your way, so there is a tendency to be quite insular, but it's actually very liberating to realise that it's not just about you and that it is a collaborative process. Theatre and film are extremely collaborative art forms and it can be freeing to surrender to the idea of something bigger than yourself.

Speaking of collaboration, when *Summer Rolls* was in rehearsal, did the actors make choices or contribute ideas that you hadn't thought about while you were writing it?
I had lived with this play for so long, I kind of just let it go when rehearsals started. When Anna [Nguyen] read it, I knew she understood the character. She was brilliant in the role of Mai and was nominated for an Offie for her performance. If I had played it, of course I would have done it differently, but I accepted that that was her vision for the role. And maybe that's the difference – because I am an actor-writer and not a writer-writer, I know that if I give my writing to someone, it's not going to sound exactly as I thought it would in my head. I know that that actor is going to bring something personal to the role.

I was in the rehearsal room if people wanted me to be in there, but I didn't want to micromanage. I wouldn't want that for myself as an actor, so I intentionally stepped away and trusted the director and the process. And it was great; they did a great job.

It's very generous of you, I think, to step away from that process and say, now it's over to you. Have there been any writers that either mentored or influenced you?
Sudha Bhuchar has been a huge influence because she is such an inspiration. There haven't been many female South-Asian actor-writers of her generation and she has managed to both make art as well as being able to make a living through acting, which are difficult things to balance. And for someone to do it with such integrity is just great to see. So, I've tried to model myself on the idea that you can make a living from this industry by embracing all of the creative parts of yourself. You don't have to be just one thing.

What advice, if any, would you give to other actors or artists who are thinking about writing and haven't done so yet?
Play the long game. If you have a story that you really want to tell, have patience and stick with it. It's a process. Share your work with people you trust and ask for help when you need it. Put it in front of an audience, even just your mates, and see what happens. Feedback can be fuel.

Are you writing anything at the moment?
During lockdown I was asked whether I'd be interested in turning *Summer Rolls* into a novel and that's what I've been working on, as well as a couple of plays that I had already started. I'm trying to take my own advice and trust the process because, when you are an actor, things keep coming at you. Self-tapes and auditions require focus, so I prioritise what needs my attention in the moment. I find it very hard to juggle the two, so in order for me not to completely implode, I just do what is in front of me. I do turn down some auditions now, which I never would have done before, because I need to make time for writing. And because writing for me is an expression of myself, I know that I will do it when the time is right.

So, do you say, right, if I only have an hour, this is the hour that I will write? Or is it more fluid than that and you just go with the flow?
Honestly, I tend to go with the flow. I have a vague structure that more often than not gets waylaid and then I forgive myself for it because I know that where your attention goes,

energy flows. I try to make peace with it, otherwise all your energy goes on self-doubt and punishing yourself. You don't want that. In this profession a lot of the process is the journey of self-knowledge and learning to trust your instincts; I think that's the only way that you can sustain yourself. That and going towards people who say 'yes' is very important to help build that faith in yourself that you are enough.

That word, 'enough', comes up a lot. I would put it another way, which is that I think the best performances are where the actor totally owns what they're doing, without the need for approbation. It takes enormous guts to say, 'This is how I want to play the part and if you don't like it, then don't give me the job'.

I'm going to use that one! Halfway house isn't going to work. You need to believe in your own voice and interpretation of the character. To thrive, an actor needs to be open and adaptive to whatever is coming, but also have a core, like a compass, of your own taste and self-beliefs. It's a terrifying profession. I mean, it's a crazy profession.

I can't disagree with you there. It is very scary. I think that actors, performers – all artists really – are asked to share a part of themselves with an audience or with the other creatives in the rehearsal room that can feel exposing. And perhaps people who don't work in the business might not understand what a fragile existence that is.

There are things that you sacrifice for this sort of life and it costs something in quite a profound way. Most actors I meet have a deep need to be seen and heard – I don't mean by being on the cover of Vanity Fair or anything like that – rather, it is a need for a deep connection with humanity and that can only come, I believe, through art.

Get seen as an actor/comedy writer/performer

Chris Head

As an actor, you are often waiting on others. Waiting for someone to write a script, stage a play, produce a movie. You can't show your brilliance until you're given the opportunity to. Until then you have to wait. A well established creative way around this bind is to devise and produce your own theatre work, and there are many examples of actors who have broken through by devising in this way.

Then there is comedy. Stand-up is brilliantly simple to get started at and there are more collaborative paths too like sketch comedy and short film. Writing comedy for yourself makes you proactive, generating your own projects, and it gives you a way to showcase yourself which is not dependent on waiting for others. Then when you do audition you will be a more attractive, match fit proposition; and making your own work can get you that audition in the first place. Here I explore a range of ways that as an actor you can get into comedy.

Stand-up

When Aisling Bea left drama school she found work as a serious actor hard to come by. So she started doing stand-up. Fast forward to 2012 and she wins the So You Think You're Funny stand-up competition at the Edinburgh Fringe and follows that up with an award nomination for her 2013 solo stand-up show *C'est La Bea*. Her comedy career properly launched, Bea went on to write and star in the acclaimed Channel 4 comedy *This Way Up*... and is now an in demand actor.

Of course not everyone will have the stellar trajectory of Aisling Bea, but if you're an actor waiting around for an audition, you could do a lot worse than start doing stand-up. You might shudder at the thought of stand up, but it's the quickest and most direct way to get yourself in front of audiences and with luck and persistence there's a clear progression to paid gigs.

Stand-up courses (ahem, like my own in London) can help ease you into it, and there are many supportive and friendly new act nights especially in cities. Why as an actor might you do stand-up? It shows gumption and bravery, and it means you are getting regular stage time in front of audiences. All far more attractive than "resting" between jobs. It also opens up other avenues such as presenting and compering. And you never know, maybe you will follow in Aisling Bea's footsteps.

The default in stand-up is to appear as a heightened version of yourself. In this case, *you* become a character; you're playing a version of yourself. As part of your act you can also deliver act-outs and dialogue as other characters thereby showcasing your acting and vocal talents. For example, I directed the Hollywood actor and producer Hopwood DePree in a touring festival show *The Manc is a Yank* where he both created a persona for himself and played a range of characters.

Why the title? Researching his ancestry online he discovered that via the long lost British branch of the family he is heir to a crumbling stately home outside Rochdale! Putting his acting on hold he relocated to the UK to pursue this passion project of restoring Hopwood Hall. ("Hopwood" being the original family name.) He didn't want to totally neglect his performing whilst in the UK but at the same time had to juggle the restoration project. So the simple and direct form of stand-up was the perfect vehicle and when he approached me for help it was a no-brainer to develop a festival show with him telling his amazing true story.

In the show, he creates a stand-up version of himself that was a fish-out-of-water, clownish figure (as he says exaggerating the truth just a bit!) and he also gets to play the northern hall caretaker Bob, the local historian Geoff, a bemused hotelier and a shopkeeper and a range of other characters as he tells his stories. In Hopwood's case, an unexpected side effect of telling his story onstage in an hour long show was that it eventually became a book, *Downton Shabby*.

Character comedy

If you don't like the idea of being yourself on stage however, you can also perform as a fictional character in stand-up contexts. I have worked for a number of years with comedic actor-writer-filmmaker Steve Whiteley. On the live stage he has found success performing in character as the spoken word artist Wisebowm. Initially performing short sets in comedy clubs in character, he progressed with me as director to doing full-length festival shows. To make the leap to this broader canvas, we fleshed out the wider world of characters around Wisebowm treating the one-man show in effect like a sitcom. This then made the next step to a BBC Radio 4 sitcom pilot (that I script-edited) a natural one.

Someone else I have worked with as director and coach over a number of years is Katia Kvinge. This Scottish-Norwegian comedian-writer-actor began doing stand-up as herself but felt more at home performing characters. This eventually developed into full-length festival shows where she interacts with the audience as herself *and* showcases a range of character performances. For her this is the best of both worlds. The audience can meet her and hear her story and she gets to perform a range of character pieces too.

This is true too of actor-writer Helen Wood who I have directed in autobiographical one-woman shows on her idiosyncratic passions. Her breakthrough show *The OS Map Fan Club* was seen at Edinburgh, on a national tour and at Ordnance Survey HQ! When she'd previously performed in acting roles she had to hide her glee at playing a role but in these shows her joy at taking on a character is all part of the charm of the piece.

Sketch comedy

A perhaps more sociable way to showcase a range of characters of your own devising is in sketch comedy. Stand-up Janine Harouni also wrote and performed with the sketch group Muriel alongside Meg Salter and Sally O'Leary; all three of whom I have intensively coached in sitcom writing. The discipline of creating characters and sketches is a great grounding for the longer form of sitcom narrative and there are many examples of sitcoms that had their beginnings in sketch work. And what a great opportunity sketch shows present to you, the actor, to show your versatility and range and to try out characters and situations in short form.

Muriel performed live sketch comedy and also made sketches for social media and online consumption, racking up millions of views. This combination, live and online, I feel is the optimum approach giving you invaluable immediate feedback from live audiences alongside a potentially vast online audience. And once you have established an online presence, there are the conventional broadcasters who are commissioning material for their social media channels. The Muriel team produced sketches for BBC3 as has Katia Kvinge who has also made online shorts for Comedy Central and Channel 4.

Short film

Another way to showcase your talents is through the short film. The aforementioned Steve Whiteley took that route with his comedy short *Swiped*, that helped develop and script-edited. It became an official selection at the Palm Springs International Shorts Festival. As well as getting him interest from TV producers as a writer-performer, going over to the festival lead to Steve landing a part as an actor in a sitcom pilot – an acting job he certainly wouldn't have got if he were just waiting for the phone to ring.

I asked Steve if he had any thoughts for someone looking to branching out into the world of comedy writing and performing and I think his insights are the perfect way to end this piece: "Be courageous. Don't be afraid to experiment and try new things. Dying on stage is a rite of passage and every time you die, you are reborn (deep) with a new found knowledge on what you can do differently next time. Be persistent. It takes a long time to develop your act and material, the likelihood of overnight success is slim, but if you have a passion for it and you're half decent then stick with it and good things will eventually happen. Collaborate. The more you workshop your ideas with others the more likely it is that you'll develop your act-material-content quicker and have some thing more rounded. Don't be precious about getting feedback. Finally enjoy it! Otherwise what's the point. You may as well be handsomely paid (or not) and be miserable at a real job."

Chris Head is a comedy coach, consultant and director. He is the author of *A Director's Guide to the Art of Stand-up* and *Creating Comedy Narratives for Stage & Screen*, both published by Methuen. He teaches comedy writing at BBC Writersroom, the British Library, Bath Spa University and online. He also mentors TV screenwriters and directs shows for the stage. See more at **www.chrishead.com**.

An actor's values: establishing principles for success

Paapa Essiedu
Interview by Maggie Norris

Paapa Essiedu is an actor who has worked across the stage and screen. Born and raised in London, he trained at the Guildhall School of Music and Drama. Essiedu started his career acting for the stage, joining the Royal Shakespeare Company in 2012 and performing in a range of productions, including titular roles in both Romeo and Juliet and Hamlet. His acclaimed role in the miniseries I May Destroy You (2020) served as a breakthrough, earning Essiedu wider recognition and multiple award nominations. His further television credits include Gangs of London (2020), The Lazarus Project (2022) and Black Mirror (2023), whist he has appeared in feature films including Murder on the Orient Express (2017), Men (2022) and The Outrun (2024).

It's lovely to chat with you, Paapa. Firstly, having researched and of course seen, some of the wide range of parts that you have played, I am intrigued to know what criteria you use to choose the parts you accept.
There are loads of different things. I was chatting to an actor the other day and she's like, Oscar nominated, whatever. She has three things that she chooses her jobs by and two of them need to be met. And one of them is the script, one of them is the location and one of them is the money. So, she's like, if you can get two out of three of those things, then you're really happy. I'm slightly different. I'm really drawn to things that I feel are meaningful. There's so much bullshit around being an actor and acting and celebrity. There's so much smoke and mirrors and self-inflation. If I lean too much into that, I find it hard to be that proud of what I do.

When I do feel proud of what I do, it's when I see if it makes an impact on the people that engage with it, you know, whatever that impact is. Whether it makes them feel seen or whether it inspires them to think in a different way or whether it provides more opportunities. It's actually making a change in the world. Having a pat on the back is not a sustainable motivation to stay in this industry. For me, it's about how can the work be meaningful, especially in theatre.

So, when I'm doing plays now, there always has to be a component added, it could be in terms of placements. For example, the last couple of plays I did, we bedded into the process that we would have placements for people who hadn't worked in the theatre before. Paid placements for people to join our production and work alongside people on the backstage team, whether that was sound design, lighting, stage management, production, whatever. And then to also feed back into the creative process. And I was talking to someone, who did that on *The Effect*, which I did last year at the National Theatre, and she partnered with us by doing our sound design placement. And now she's just got her first job as an Assistant Sound Designer at the the Donmar Warehouse. So that's tangible confirmation of something that literally wouldn't have happened – well, that may not have happened – had we not expanded the work that we were doing further than just like, let's try and be impressive so that people can tell us that we're good. So there tends to be a political dimension or a challenging dimension to the projects that I choose to engage in.

That's lovely to hear. We are constantly looking for partners in the industry to give placements to our young people at The Big House. When we secure those placements and they turn into a job, it is so rewarding. I am interested in your beginning in the industry. Many people who are reading this will be starting out in their career. How did you get taken on by your agents Curtis Brown?
I went to Guildhall and I had a complicated experience while I was there. Lots of learning. But I definitely wouldn't be an actor now if I hadn't done that course. In your final year, you do maybe six plays across the course of the year that you rehearse properly with a director who's worked in the industry and agents come and see you. But I got cast in really, really small roles in all of the plays, which makes it difficult for you to show what you can do – without making this a "woe is me" kind of story! But then you have this thing called a showcase, which is where each individual in the year does a speech. I did a speech from a play that I'd found and a duologue with my friend in the year, who happened to be Michaela Cole, that she'd written for the two of us. And that's where my agent came and saw that and invited me for a meeting. But even after the meeting, I had to email her and say, "I really think you should take me on. I think I'm really good". I actually found the email a couple of weeks ago. And I think that comes from my upbringing of hustling and trying to make the most out of every opportunity. I had to kind of stick it on her.

Yeah, it's a tough thing promoting yourself, particularly if you value humility. It's difficult because you're selling yourself, as opposed to a hoover or a dishwasher. So, inevitably, you must be able to publicize and promote yourself.
It's hard. I think for me, I'm really fortunate in the fact that I didn't come out of drama school and go straight into a Marvel franchise. I had enough time doing national tours that went to Lancaster and Scarborough to see what that actually looks like. So, I can't really convince myself that I dropped from heaven as a saviour of the industry. I've really seen both sides of it. And, again, I've had it way easier than many people, but it's not just about being on front covers of magazines or premieres, red carpets, all of that. I think, for me, it's really important to remember that and not to detach from that. That is a central tenet of the actor I am today.

    I think I'm lucky that I know a couple of people who are kind of at that level of fame and have seen what it is. And that kind of teaches me. I think some of it is also just a temperament thing. There are certain people that you hope never get famous. People who you're like, please, please, please don't get famous because you'll be insufferable! And I suppose another thing is that I'm actually fortunately still in that place in my career where people look at me and they're like, I feel like I know you, but they're still a bit like, "Do you live near me?", "Were you in Tesco's 20 minutes ago?" type thing. I think the challenge is, how do you attain a level of respect, within the industry that you exist in, without becoming paranoid – still allowing yourself to meet people and see people and believe in people – without detaching from reality, whilst also not being exploited or taken advantage of? Whilst also not disappearing up your own arse! Yeah. It must feel like a tiny violin is being played, but I think it's a real challenge having that level of scrutiny on yourself and that level of inflation. I don't think being famous should ever be the goal. No. It should never be what you're looking for. I think being respected, yeah, for sure.

When I was talking to Michael Wiggs, the agent, I asked him what he was looking for when he interviews or meets an actor. You know, what interests or excites him and what might make him lose interest. He said a red flag would be somebody saying that they want to be a star. He said that when you're working with somebody to create a career, develop their skill set, that's the last thing that you want to hear, because it's divorced from reality.

Yeah. The thing is, when you talk about wanting to be a star, what is that actually connected to? Maybe that's connected to wanting to emulate someone that you've seen on television or that you've read about in the papers. I remember once I went to the Met Gala, which is literally like a vacuum full of the most famous people. I expected to go there and see the most charismatic, the most confident, the most self-actualised people on the planet. But, actually, you're seeing the most nervous, the most stressed, the most anxious. Because they're at an event where their publicists aren't allowed to be, so there's no protection. But also, there is a real confrontation that you must ease into when you're in those kinds of rooms. A confrontation between yourself and your self-consciousness. With people actually thinking about the things that they're *not* good at or how they're *not* beautiful or how they're *not* smart. It's interesting because it comes across in a certain way, but the reality is totally the opposite.

You have a diverse portfolio of work, which is unusual in that you combine some serious heavyweight theatre credits with some major screen credits. Did you find that transition from stage to screen difficult? What training did you have? Or did you make your mistakes in public? Few people do it well...

I find it really hard and, yes, so few people do it well. But I think, again, that's like a situation that's also an issue in our industry because people are so quick to see you as one or the other. I've got quite a juvenile aversion to that. You've talked previously about people at The Big House having issues or frustrations with authority. It's something I've got a huge empathy for. I have a real aversion to anyone telling me that I'm this kind of actor or that kind of actor. Almost to my discredit. Even when I did *Hamlet* at the RSC and then afterwards they were like, "Oh, you're the guy who did *Hamlet*". And I was like, "No, no, I'm not that guy. I can do this". And then I did *I May Destroy You*. And then they were like, "Oh, you're that guy from *I May Destroy You*". And I'm like, "No, I'm not actually, I can do this too". So yeah, I've got a kind of "answering my parents back" type disposition about being pigeonholed.

But in terms of that transition from theatre to screen, it is something that I continue to work on. As I said, I went to Guildhall and I did a BA in Acting, which is a pretty theatre-heavy training, so yeah, you're doing a lot of Shakespeare. And, before that, I didn't really have huge amounts of experience as an actor. I hadn't really done much; even during drama school, I was playing catch-up. So, by the time I got my first television job, which was a Channel 4 series (it was like a two-episode part, playing one of the main character's brother) I literally had no idea what I was doing. I didn't know who the director was because, when you're on the set, there's a director and then there's a first assistant director, second assistant director, third assistant director, who are generally also creative, but more organisational. The first person I met was the third assistant director and I just assumed he was the director. So, I was asking him what I should be doing and he's like, "I ain't got nothing for you". I was in the wilderness and I literally thought the take would start by someone saying, "Lights, camera, action". That's never happened, apart from in the movies. And I was really bad. And by the time it came to the edit, they ended up dubbing over my lines, which I'm trying not to take personally, but it's hard not to take personally. But, you know, it wasn't always easy for me at all. And it still isn't. I'm still learning and I think the beautiful thing about being an actor, if you're given the opportunity, is it should be like a craft that you spend a lifetime working on, becoming more – not more in control of – but having more expression through it. So, I continue to try. But yes, I have failed publicly.

Well, I am still very much developing my craft after 40 years in this industry! How would you like your career to progress over the next 10 years?
I'd love to continue being led by myself and by my instincts and by the things that mean something to me and to others. But, really, for that to provide an openness to opportunity, as opposed to saying that I want to play this kind of part or earn this amount of money or meet this person. I think, for me, it's about creating a body of work that I can look back on and be proud of, so that I can be sat down and talking to you in ten years' time and say, "You know what? I did that because of this and I did this because of that."

I look forward to that conversation! Do you think that will involve you proactively making things happen? Are you interested in directing or producing or writing, for example?
I think being an actor is a huge gift, privilege, honour, but it won't be enough to satisfy my ambition, in terms of my life's work. Partly because of the way the industry is structured and partly because of the reality of life. You can't rely on other people to create the world that you want to see. To an extent, you've got to do that yourself. That requires courage and sacrifice and proactivity. Without a doubt, it's my ambition to produce work and maybe direct work. Actors are always talking about how they'd be better directors than the director or better writers than the writer. I sometimes think though that directors are directors because they're good at directing and writers are writers because they're good at writing. Not exclusively, but I think for me, maybe producing work. I know I'm good at working with people and empowering people to do work and team building. I feel like I have vision and I have the ambition to continue pushing the industry in a direction where there's more equity and power for people that historically haven't been given that. That's definitely a big ambition for me.

Maggie Norris is the founder of The Big House **https://thebighouse.uk.com/**.

Routes to stand-up comedy

Geoff Whiting, stand-up comedian and founder of leading comedy bookers, Mirth Control
Interview by Rob Ostlere

Geoff Whiting has over twenty years' experience as a stand-up comedian and is a successful comedy booker with his company Mirth Control, the UK's largest independent comedy bookers. Geoff is also a manager for new acts and has worked on building the careers of some of the biggest names in the industry. In this interview he explains the pathways into stand-up and what it takes to make it as a comedian.

You've worked with hundreds of comedians, Geoff, but I'd like first to hear about your path into the industry?
I started off in Bath in 1997 as an open-mic spot; in other words, doing five, occasionally ten minutes for various venues. But in 1998 I reached the final of a competition called The *Daily Telegraph* Open Mic Award at the Edinburgh Festival. That was what launched me to a different level. I turned pro within two years and was earning a living within about two-and-a-half from just stand-up.

And this was at the same time as working as a booker and managing other comedians' careers?
That was something I hadn't actually planned. I answered an advertisement in *The Stage* newspaper from a new club in Plymouth. I did fifteen minutes, it went well and after the show the guy said, "Can you come next week?" I explained to him I'm a new comic and that's all I had but I could bring another comedian with me, warm up the audience myself and then introduce them. And that's how I became a booker. In those early years we had lots of notable people: Jason Manford, Jimmy Carr, Russell Howard, John Robins, Jon Richardson. All of them played as an opening act and came back to be the closing act. After that, my career as a booker just snowballed really. At the same time, I was booking for 100 clubs, I was still working four to five nights a week as a comedian. I then eventually opened up a management arm, taking comedians from unknown acts through the levels you go to be a professional.

What are those levels?
The principles haven't changed since I began. You start by doing five minutes for nothing. If that's good then you'll be asked to come and do ten minutes for nothing. If that's good, we'll talk about paying you for ten minutes, then twenty. It could be a few weeks later that you're asked back, it could be a few months; it depends on the club and the demand. After that, you work your way up towards closing a show. That's another hurdle completely because you need to have either a very solid twenty or thirty, or forty minutes for some arts centres. To get to the next level you need forty-five minutes. Then after that you'd get two forty-five minutes together for a tour show.

How long does that take?
It depends but in general, for a brilliant comedian, maybe three to four years. A decent, hard-working comic I'd say we do that journey in five to six years. And a not-inspirational-but-determined comic might make that journey in eight to ten years.

So beyond playing as many gigs as possible, what other routes are there? Comedy courses are becoming more popular aren't they?
I do Q&As on a course in Bath about everything we're talking about; how you go from being an unpaid act to a professional. The actual courses are over several weeks and at the end you'll get in front of an audience of eighty to a hundred people. That's the first time ever for most people on the course and it's crucial; can you get up and do your six or seven minutes without forgetting it, avoiding the pitfalls and without losing the plot. And if somebody has a great show, then they've got a video of it they can promote themselves with.

New act competitions are another way in?
New act competitions are great. They're open access so anybody can enter. The ones like I did with the *Daily Telegraph*, for example the BBC Introducing Radio 4 Comedy Award or So You Think You're Funny, tend to have their finals up in Edinburgh. They're massive platforms with TV, YouTube or radio coverage.

What about Edinburgh more generally?
What's great about Edinburgh is you can do shows that are two, three, or four-handers. You might be an act who's been going for a short while, you've only got fifteen minutes, but it's stuff you've road-tested and you're confident is working. You then find two or three other comedians in the same position. You put together a package and there's four of you to do the marketing, the flyer-ing and the social media for it. Or you do Free Fringe, which has really exploded in the last maybe ten years. Imran Yusuf getting nominated as best new comedian on a Free Fringe show was a breakthrough because suddenly people realised it doesn't mean you're marginalised. All you need to do is pay for the technician, set the room up and make your own flyers and posters. If you get sixty people in and you have a great show they'll put money in the bucket. Four amateurs can get together and, if they're good at promoting it, can breakeven and they've done an Edinburgh run.

How do agents fit into all this?
Some people make it through sheer hard work and go fully from being a new act to a professional without an agent. For others, the breakthrough is getting signed. It depends entirely on your path. I can think of comics who worked for years doing another job at the same time as working their way up. And then there's someone like Joe Lycett, who won the Bath New Act Competition. One of the judges was a TV commissioner, who immediately called a very big agent and told them someone's just stormed it.

It sounds like part of working your way up is trying lots of different things, getting yourself out there?
I learned very early on that a certain percentage is talent and the rest is application. I literally gigged twenty-eight nights out of thirty most months. My contemporaries were doing it as well. Daniel Kitson was famous for only having six nights off an entire year. Russel Howard, when he started, gigged almost every night. It's no coincidence that most of the people who I see on TV now worked night-in night-out all the time as new acts.

That's a lot of dedication!
I appreciate some people might read this interview and say that's all very well but I've got a day job, I work long hours, or I haven't got a car so I can't do gigs all over the place. I

guess it depends on your mindset and how much you want to do it. In my case, once I realised I had the potential – I'd done my first fifteen gigs or so and comics were saying to me you've got something – I had a sort of plan and determination as a comedian. I went into debt to do it and it was three-and-a-half years before I got back to square one. If you're absolutely and utterly determined and focused you can find a way.

What other qualities do you think new comedians need?
You have to be tenacious and prepared to do anything when you start. Jimmy Carr's first ever paid gig was for me. He said to me, "Geoff, anything you got, anywhere, I'll do it, no problem". And I said, "Well, when you say 'anywhere', I've got a gig in Devon on Tuesday. You'll have to drive there and it might only be £80". His answer was, "Fine, I'll be there".

You told me you started out by writing letters to get your first gigs. Nowadays, of course, that's very different
There is way more access to networking, to knowing who books shows and how to reach them, with Facebook groups for the south-east, the south-west and so on, and Edinburgh, new act competitions and more. You can network with other comics and promoters, and posts do go up: "I need some acts tomorrow or next month ... are you free?" Get yourself a Facebook page as a comic, not just your own personal one. Load content on: a decent video, decent pictures and a basic CV with a few bullet points about you. And then go on the forums. You'll get opportunities to do stage-time and you can build from there.

From the thousands of gigs you've done, Geoff, is there one final piece of advice you'd give to someone building their act?
Yes, the audience should be your editor. Record your shows on a phone when you're starting out, even just the audio. Listen to what the audience are laughing at. We all have a favourite joke that doesn't work but you've got to listen to where the audience is laughing and take note of that.

Geoff's booking and management company can be found at www.mirthcontrolcomedy.com.

Pantomime

This section lists some of the major pantomime producers and some of the theatres and arts centres that programme annual pantomimes. The latter largely present touring and amateur productions but some mount their own professional pantomimes. It is worth further research on their websites, or in listings and reviews in *The Stage* each Christmas, or on www.its-behind-you.com which has a comprehensive directory.

Some of these theatres and companies produce shows throughout the year, especially as part of the work of their Education departments. Where possible we have included this information in each entry, but visit the theatre's website for further details.

PANTOMIME PRODUCERS

Chaplins Entertainment Ltd
Chaplins House, The Acorn Centre, Roebuck Road, Hainault, Essex IG6 3TU
tel 020-8501 2121
email fun@chaplinspantos.co.uk
website www.chaplinspantos.co.uk
Directors Mr J Holmes, *Productions Manager* Jessica Djemil

Production details: A touring pantomime and theatre-in-education company which also works in film and television production. Stages 27 productions annually, performing in small theatres, schools, social clubs and community centres.

Casting procedures: Uses freelance casting directors and holds general auditions; actors requesting inclusion are asked to write from July until the end of October only. Casting breakdowns are publicly available from the website, by postal application (with sae), in *The Stage* and via Mandy. During the period specified, the company welcomes letters (with CVs and photographs) from individual actors previously unknown to them, sent by post or email, and will accept showreels and invitations to view individual actors' websites.

Crossroads Pantomimes Ltd
1st Floor, 6 Kean Street, London WC2B 4AS
tel 020-7836 6544
email info@xroadspantomimes.com
website www.pantomime.com
Casting Director/Producer Jonathan Kiley, *Producer/Chief Executive* Michael Harrison

Production details: The largest of the commercial pantomime producers with 23 pantomimes across the UK: His Majesty's, Aberdeen; Grand Opera House, Belfast; Hippodrome Theatre, Birmingham; The Alhambra, Bradford; The Bristol Hippodrome; The Churchill Bromley; New Theatre, Cardiff; Hippodrome, Darlington; Kings Theatre, Edinburgh; Kings Theatre, Glasgow; Hull New Theatre; The London Palladium; The Opera House, Manchester; Milton Keynes Theatre; Theatre Royal, Newcastle upon Tyne; Theatre Royal, Nottingham; Theatre Royal, Plymouth; The Richmond Theatre; Cliffs Pavilion, Southend; Mayflower Theatre, Southampton; The Regent Theatre, Stoke; The New Wimbledon Theatre and New Victoria Theatre, Woking.

Casting procedures: Actors should send CVs and photographs by email to Jonathan Kiley from March (star-casting only in February). Welcomes performance notices by email or by post.

Evolution Productions
Little Statenborough House, Sandwich Road, Eastry, Kent CT13 0DH
tel (01304) 615333
email info@evolution-productions.co.uk
website www.evolution-productions.co.uk
Facebook /evolution.pantomimes
X @EvolutionProdUK
Instagram @evolutionproductionsuk
Producer Emily Wood, *Director* Paul Hendy

Production details: Founded in 2005 and run by husband-and-wife team, Emily Wood and Paul Hendy. Produces pantomimes and large-scale productions. Produced *Mister Maker!* and *The Shapes Live!* (UK tour), *Morcambe* (UK tour), *Dear Santa* (UK and Singapore tour) and *Oliver!* at The Central Theatre, Chatham. Stages 8 pantomimes a year: The Marlowe Theatre, Canterbury; The Hawth Theatre, Crawley; The Grove Theatre, Dunstable; Lichfield Garrick, Lichfield; Lyceum Theatre, Sheffield; Theatre Severn Shrewsbury; Alban Arena, St Albans and the Octogan Theatre, Yeovil. Offers non-Equity, in-house contracts ("Equity equivalent") and does not subscribe to the Equity Pension Scheme.

Casting procedures: Casting process for principal roles begins around March. Actors are requested to send their CV, headshot and Showreel to casting@evolution-productions.co.uk. Ensemble roles casting begins around June and Juvenile assemble auditions are held between June-July. For more information please view their website at www.evolution-productions.co.uk/auditions.

Extravaganza Productions

Old Ferry House, 4 London Road, Boston, Lincs. PE21 8AA
website www.extravaganza-productions.co.uk
Facebook /etravaproductions
Directors David Vickers, Richard Chandler

Production details: Established in 1995. Presenting Pantomimes for The Plaza, Stockport and Middlesborough Theatre. Number of productions staged annually varies.

Casting procedures: Casting is carried out in house; actors can write at any time to request inclusion. Submissions (with CVs and photographs) should be addressed to Richard Chandler, Casting Director. Also accepts invitations to view individual actors' websites, and showreels. Applications from disabled actors are considered to play disabled characters.

Paul Holman Associates

Morritt House, 58 Station Approach, South Ruislip, Middlesex HA4 6SA
tel 020-8845 9408
email enquiries@paulholmanassociates.co.uk
website www.paulholmanassociates.co.uk/home
Facebook /PHApantos
Instagram @phapanto
Managing Director Paul Holman

Production details: Produces Pantomimes, Summer Seasons, Tours and other commercial projects. Stages productions annually across the country. Offers non-Equity (Variety) contracts and does not subscribe to the Equity Pension Scheme.

Casting procedures: Regularly advertises casting requirements on Spotlight, Castweb, Castcall, SBS and through direct contact to agents. Accepts submissions from artists by email or post throughout the year, these are filed and carefully considered when casting decisions are made.

Imagine Theatre Ltd

Trafalgar House, 186 Torrington Avenue, Canley, Coventry CV4 9AJ
tel 024 7630 7001
website www.imaginetheatre.co.uk
Facebook /ImagineTheatre
X @Imagine_Theatre
Instagram @imaginetheatre
Artistic Director Eric Potts, Managing Director Stephen Boden, Business Director Sarah Boden, Head of Casting & Production Louise Redmond

Production details: Imagine Theatre (since 2009; formerly Wish Theatre) produces pantomimes and children's theatre. Offers in-house contracts ("enhanced Equity") and does not subscribe to the Equity Pension Scheme.

Casting procedures: Casts mainly in-house. Professional auditions are by invite only and casting breakdowns are not published except on Spotlight.

Welcomes CVs and photgraphs from actors previously unknown to the company; prefers these to be emailed rather than posted but send only when the casting window is open. See **www.imaginetheatre.co.uk/casting** for current opportunites. Will consider applications from disabled actors to play disabled characters. "Panto isn't a cop-out: it's a serious business. We use actors who can engage with the audience and have fun. It is really useful if actors can indicate their location/home town, which helps with accents and knowing if an individual is local to one of our pantomime venues. Please do not send showreels or invitations to view websites."

New Pantomime Productions

27 Shooters Road, Enfield, Middlesex EN2 8RJ
tel 020-8363 9920
email newpantomime@aol.com
Facebook /newpantomimepro
Instagram @newpantomime
Directors Simon Barry, Paul Graham

Production details: Produces pantomimes at 6 venues: Theatr Colwyn, Colwyn Bay; Brindley Arts Centre, Runcorn; Southport Theatre; Kings Theatre, Southsea; Grand Opera House, York. Offers non-Equity contracts and does not subscribe to the Equity Pension Scheme.

Casting procedures: Casts in house. Holds general auditions; actors should write in July to request inclusion. Casting breakdowns are not publicly available. Welcomes emails only (with CVs and photographs) from actors previously unknown to the company. Does not welcome showreels or invitations to view individual actors' websites. "Make sure you're suitable for the job you're applying for. We have employed disabled actors – and not just to play disabled characters. So long as the actor is good, that's all that matters."

Spillers Pantomimes

Hardup Hall, Lady Lane, Hadleigh, Suffolk, IP7 6AF
tel 07785 327006
email info@spillers-pantomimes.co.uk
website www.spillers-pantomimes.co.uk
Facebook /Spillers-Pantomimes
Production Director Mr Bev Berridge

Production details: Established 1989. Produces pantomimes for Alexandra Theatre in Bognor Regis, Epsom Playhouse and Eastwood Park Theatre. Offers actors non-Equity contracts and does not contribute to the Equity Pension Scheme.

Casting procedures: Casting is done in house. Casting calls and the relevant information can be found via their website at **www.spillers-pantomimes.co.uk/casting-information**.

UK Productions

Brook House, Mint Street, Godalming, Surrey GU7 1HE
tel (01483) 423600

email mail@ukproductions.co.uk
website www.ukproductions.co.uk/pantomimes
Managing Director/Producer Martin Dodd, *Artistic Producer* Damian Sandys

Production details: Established 1995. Produces pantomime, musicals and drama for No. 1 touring, nationally and internationally including West End and Broadway theatres. Also set, costume and production hire. (See entry under *Independent managements/theatre producers* on page 199.) Offers non-Equity contracts.

Casting procedures: Casting is done in house. Does not hold open auditions. Casting breakdowns are distributed via Spotlight. Welcomes performance notices but not any other unsolicited form of correspondence. Will consider applications from disabled actors to play characters with disabilities.

IN-HOUSE PANTOMIMES

Buxton Opera House
Water Street, Buxton, Derbyshire SK17 6XN
tel (01298) 72050
email admin@boh.org.uk
website https://buxtonoperahouse.org.uk
Facebook /BuxtonOpHouse
X @BuxtonOpHouse
Instagram @buxtonoperahouse
Chief Executive Officer Paul Kerryson

Production details: A receiving theatre presenting around 450 performances each year including dance, comedy, children's shows, drama, musical concerts, pantomime and opera as well as Fringe Theatre and Community and Education Programme. Edwardian theatre designed by Frank Matcham, restored in 2001.

Cambridge Arts Theatre
6 St Edwards Passage, Cambridge CB2 3PJ
tel (01223) 578904
email info@cambridgeartstheatre.com
website www.cambridgeartstheatre.com
Interim Co-Chief Executives Victoria Beechey, Rachel Tackley

Production details: Seating capacity 666. A receiving theatre which presents a wide range of work, including children's theatre, music, dance and drama. Produces in-house panto annually.

Casting procedures: The theatre engages a casting director to cast the principal roles for the panto. Submissions should be sent to the casting director, and auditions will take place in London around August/September. The ensemble is cast in-house by the producer and the director, with submissions collated through Spotlight. Actors are welcome to contact the Theatre to register their interest in auditioning, and these will be kept on file for reference by the producer and the director.

The Capitol
North Street, Horsham, West Sussex RH12 1RG
tel (01403) 750220
email contact@thecapitolhorsham.com
website www.thecapitolhorsham.com
Facebook /thecapitolhorsham
X @CapitolHorsham
Instagram @thecapitolhorsham
Venue and Productions Manager Matthew Effemey

Production details: Multi-arts community venue, comprised of a 410 seat Theatre, 2 cinema screens, studio theatre and gallery space. Produces a professional pantomime each year. Offers TMA/Equity-approved contracts.

Casting procedures: Uses in-house casting director. Optimum time to write requesting an audition is in spring/summer. Casting breakdowns are publicly available on the website, or by postal application (with sae). Accepts letters (with CVs and photographs) from individual actors previously unknown to the company, sent by post or email. Also welcomes invitations to view showreels and to attend other productions. Will consider applications from disabled actors to play disabled characters.

The Theatre, Chipping Norton
2 Spring Street, Chipping Norton, Oxon OX7 5NL
tel (01608) 642349
email admin@chippingnortontheatre.com
website www.chippingnortontheatre.com
Facebook /ChippingNortonTheatre
X @ChippyTheatre
Instagram @chippytheare
Director John Terry

Production details: The Theatre is a pivotal part of the artistic life of the area, and takes care to programme as diverse a range of performances – theatre, film, dance, comedy and opera – as possible. Its Community & Education programme takes film and opera out to village halls.

An intimate space, it seats 217 (including 4 wheelchair spaces) in either proscenium (end-on) or in-the-round configurations. While predominantly a receiving house, The Theatre produces 3 shows a year in-house, which includes an annual pantomime which runs for around 80 performances over the Christmas period, as well as occasional smaller ventures. The Theatre offers TMA/Equity-approved contracts and subscribes to the Equity Pension Scheme.

Casting procedures: Does not use casting directors. Casting breakdowns for the pantomime are available March and September via Spotlight Actively encourages applications from disabled actors, and promotes the use of inclusive casting.

City Varieties Music Hall
Swan Street, Leeds LS1 6LW
email frank.burkitt@leedsheritagetheatres.com
website www.leedsheritagetheatres.com
General Manager Ian Sime

Production details: Seating capacity 467. Grade II* listed building, built in 1865. World-famous as the home of BBC TV's *Good Old Days*. Produces a professional rock and roll style pantomime each year, running from the end of November to mid-January. Actors are employed under UKTheatre/Equity-approved contracts and the theatre subscribes to the Equity Pension Scheme.

Casting procedures: Optimum time to write requesting an audition for the pantomime is between January and May. Accepts submissions (with CVs and photographs) from individual actor/musicians previously unknown to the company.

Connaught Theatre
Union Place, Worthing BN11 1LG
tel (01903) 206206
email boxoffice@wtm.uk
website www.wtam.uk
Ceo & Creative Director Amanda O'Reilly

Production details: Part of Wothing Theatres and Museum. Operates as a theatre and cinema. .

The Courtyard
The Courtyard Centre for the Arts, Edgar Street, Hereford HR4 9JR
tel (01432) 346555
email boxoffice@courtyard.org.uk
website www.courtyard.org.uk
Facebook /courtyardhereford
Instagram @courtyard_arts
Chief Executive & Artictic Director Ian Archer

Production details: Seating capacity 436. The Courtyard opened in September 1998 and was the first Lottery-funded theatre to be built in England. It provides "an eclectic programme of work, from produced to received, and offers something for the whole community". Produces a professional pantomime each year, from the end of November to mid-January. Provides actors with Equity-approved contracts as negotiated through UK Theatre.

Casting procedures: Uses in-house casting directors; actors may write in June to request an audition. Casting breakdowns are available from the website, or via CastNet and Castweb. Welcomes letters (with CVs and photographs) from individual actors previously unknown to the company, sent by post or email. Also accepts showreels and invitations to visit other productions. Actively encourages applications from disabled actors and promotes the use of inclusive casting.

The Customs House Trust Ltd
Mill Dam, South Shields, Tyne & Wear NE33 1ES
tel 0191 454 1234
email mail@customshouse.co.uk
website www.customshouse.co.uk
Ceo Kelly Anders, *Deputy Director* Fiona Martin

Production details: Seating capacity 439. Established in 1994 as an arts centre, gallery, cinema and theatre. Produces approximately 9 in-house shows each year, and is a member of the North East Theatre Consortium. Stages a professional pantomime in late November which runs through to the first week in January, as well as new writing and occasional new musicals. Provides actors with Equity-approved contracts.

Casting procedures: Encourages first time applications from people who are new to the industry or haven't heard of The Customs House before. Current opportunities can be found on their website at **www.customshouse.co.uk/get-involved/creatives**. They also share opportunities on their social media, particularly on **Instagram** @tch_productions.

The Everyman Theatre
Regent Street, Cheltenham, Glos. GL50 1HQ
tel (01242) 572573
email admin@everymantheatre.org.uk
website www.everymantheatre.org.uk
Creative Director Paul Milton, *Chief Executive* Mark Goucher

Production details: Seating capacity: main house 668, studio 60. Built in 1891. A receiving theatre which presents a wide range of work, from stand-up comedy to children's theatre and including live music, dance and drama. Also works with many emerging and established theatre companies from Gloucestershire and beyond, creating partnerships and productions that are performed at the Everyman and on tour across the county. Produces in-house plays and pantomime as well as promoting new writing.

Casting procedures: A freelance director is engaged to direct the panto. This director is responsible for the casting process and will choose how and where the casting breakdowns are made available. Actors should write in February to request auditions for the panto, as auditions are held in March and April. Submissions (photos and CVs) are welcomed from actors previously unknown to the company for both panto and new writing projects; these should be marked for the attention of Millie Krstic-Howe (Theatre Secretary). The Everyman also runs an Actor's Lab, providing professional training and opportunities to meet and work with established directors. An equal opportunities employer and gives due consideration to applications from all sectors of the community.

Hackney Empire
291 Mare Street, London E8 1EJ
tel 020-8510 4500
email info@hackneyempire.co.uk
website https://hackneyempire.co.uk
Facebook /hackneyempire
Bluesky @hackneyempire.bsky.social
Instagram @hackneyempire

Production details: Grade II listed Frank Matcham theatre built in 1901. Recently renovated and refurbished. Provides a wide range of productions for the local community and London as a whole. Seating capacity is up to 1,280. Produces an immensely popular and critically acclaimed traditional pantomime, eschewing 'celebrities' in favour of the core elements of traditional pantomime: a well-conceived narrative line, spectacular sets and costumes, magical spectacle, music, dance and slapstick comedy. Offers TMA/Equity-approved contracts.

Casting procedures: Casting breakdowns are not publically available, but actors wishing to audition for the pantomime should make contact by post or email, in August/September. Happy to receive appropriate showreels and invitations to view individual actors' websites. Actively encourages applications from disabled actors and promotes the use of inclusive casting.

Macrobert

University of Stirling, Stirling FK9 4LA
tel (01786) 466666
email boxoffice@macrobertartscentre.org
website www.macrobertartscentre.org
Facebook /macrobertartscentre
X @Macrobert
Instagram @macrobertartscentre

Production details: A busy multi-venue arts centre seating 472, including a studio seating 80. Produces several professional shows per year, in November and December. Offers Equity-approved contracts as negotiated through TMA. Subscribes to the Equity Pension Scheme.

Casting procedures: Welcomes submissions by email. Accepts showreels and invitations to visit other productions. Rarely (or never) has the opportunity to cast disabled actors.

Millfield Theatre

Silver Street, Edmonton, London N18 1PJ
tel 020-8807 6680
email admin@millfieldtheatre.co.uk
website https://millfieldtheatre.co.uk
Facebook /MillfieldTheatre
X @The_Millfield
Instagram @millfieldtheatre

Production details: Produces panto in house and hosts a year-round programme of theatre, comedy, music, dance and variety shows. Home of Platinum Performing Arts Schools.

Casting procedures: Casting is done by liaising with show director and in-house producer. Breakdowns for the panto are sent out to agents via Spotlight Link. Contracts offered are negotiated directly with actors or their agents.

Stafford Gatehouse Theatre

Eastgate Street, Stafford ST16 2LT
tel (01785) 619080
email gatehouse@freedom-leisure.co.uk
website www.gatehousetheatre.co.uk
Facebook /StaffGatehouse
X @Staff_Gatehouse
Instagram @gatehouse_theatre
General Manager Gary Stevens

Production details: Celebrated its 40th anniversary in 2022. A receiving theatre which presents a wide range of work, from stand-up comedy to children's theatre, and including live music, dance and drama. Usually co-produces its own in-house panto, with the occasional co-production. The Gatehouse also stages and produces the annual Stafford Shakespeare production every Summer in the grounds of Stafford Castle.

Includes two performance spaces: the main auditorium seats 545 and the MET Studio seats 140.

Casting procedures: Casting is done either in-house or by freelance casting directors. Breakdowns are available via Spotlight to agents only. Will consider applications from disabled actors to play disabled characters.

Theatre Royal, Bury St Edmunds

Westgate Street, Bury St Edmunds, Suffolk IP33 1QR
tel (01284) 769505
email artistic@theatreroyal.org
website www.theatreroyal.org
Artistic Director & CEO Owen Calvert-Lyons

Built in 1819, the theatre is the only surviving Regency theatre in the country. Produces an annual pantomime at Christmas and 2 other shows a year – a spring drama and a summer community production which includes professional actors working alongside local children and young people. Offers non-Equity contracts.

Casting procedures: Casting breakdowns are published via Spotlight only. Actors wishing to be considered for the pantomime should write to the theatre in April. (The spring and summer shows are cast in January/February and April/May respectively.) Only welcomes letters and emails (with CVs and photographs) from actors previously unknown to the company during these casting periods.

Theatre Royal, Norwich

Theatre Street, Norwich NR2 1RL
tel (01603) 630000
email info@norwichtheatre.org
website https://norwichtheatre.org
Chief Executive & Creative Director Stephen Crocker

Seating capacity 1300. Produces an annual pantomime and growing its producing and co-producing portfolio across its 3 venues. Welcomes emails (with CVs and photographs) from artists and creatives not previously known to the company. Does not welcome showreels or performance notices. Will consider applications from disabled actors on the same basis as for non-disabled actors.

Theatre Royal, Nottingham
Theatre Square, Nottingham NG1 5ND
tel 0115 989 5500
email director@nottinghamcity.gov.uk
website www.trch.co.uk

Production details: Seating capacity 1186. Pantomimes are produced by a national producer; those produced in house are by its education-based Royal Company, which includes members of the community. Offers actors Equity-approved contracts but does not subscribe to the Equity Pension Scheme.

Casting procedures: Actors wishing to request an audition should contact the producers for the 2025/26 season directly (see the website for announcement details).

Theatre Royal, Winchester
21–23 Jewry Street, Winchester, Hants SO23 8SB
tel (01962) 840440
email programmingtrw@playtothecrowd.co.uk
website www.theatreroyalwinchester.co.uk
Facebook /TRWinchester
Instagram @theatreroyalwinch
Chief Executive & Artistic Director Deryck Newland

Production details: Seating capacity 400. A receiving theatre which presents a wide range of work, from stand-up comedy to children's theatre and including music, dance and classic plays. Produces panto in house.

Casting procedures: Casting is done by the director of the show. Artists can express their interest in any of the opportunities listed at **playtothecrowd.co.uk/about-us/opportunities/artists** via email.

English-language European theatre companies

This small section seems to be populated by companies set up by enthusiasts who have kept on going with very little subsidy – and sometimes with none at all. Although living away from home and isolated from auditions, it can be fun working for such companies. It is important to note that the work often involves educational projects and/or touring.

Dear Conjunction Theatre Company
6 Rue Arthur Rozier, 75019 Paris
email dearconjunction@wanadoo.fr
website www.dearconjunction-paris-theatre.com
Artistic Directors Leslie Clack, Patricia Kessler

Production details: Founded in 1991, this bilingual company is composed of professional actors, directors and writers who are resident in Paris and who present productions in both French and English. Past productions include: Pinter's *Ashes to Ashes* and *The Hothouse*; and *Someone Who'll Watch Over Me* by Frank McGuinness.

Casting procedures: Welcomes letters and emails (with CVs and photographs) from actors previously unknown to the company. Contact Leslie Clack for more information.

English Theatre Frankfurt
Gallusanlage 7, 60329 Frankfurt am Main, Germany
tel +49 (0)692 423 1215
email mail@english-theatre.de
website https://english-theatre.de
Facebook /EnglishTheatreFrankfurt
X @TheETF
Instagram @theenglishtheatrefrankfurt
Artistic & Executive Director Daniel John Nicolai

Production details: Founded in 1979. Presents contemporary plays, musicals and classics. 3-5 productions performed in the main house each year.

Casting procedures: Uses London-based freelance casting director Marc Frankum. Send CV and headshot to marc@marcfrankum.com. Auditions held in London.

The English Theatre of Hamburg
Lerchenfeld 14, 22081 Hamburg, Germany
tel +49 40 227 7089
email admin@englishtheatre.de
website www.englishtheatre.de
Facebook /TheEnglishTheatreOfHamburg
Instagram @englishtheatre_hamburg
Contacts Robert Rumpf, Clifford Dean, Paul Glaser

Production details: Founded in 1976 by 2 Americans, Robert Rumpf and Clifford Dean, who originally trained and worked professionally in the USA. Together they published a 336-page book entitled *The English Theatre of Hamburg 1976-2021*. Along with Paul Glaser, they share general management responsibilities, plan the artistic programme and direct most of the productions. Since 1981, the Theatre has occupied its present premises at Mundsburg, 22081 Hamburg. Performs from September through to June. A typical season at the English Theatre includes a classic American or British drama, a comedy and thriller or modern classic.

Gothenburg English Studio Theatre (GEST)
Chapmans Torg 10BV, 414 54 Göteborg, Sweden
tel +46 031-425-065
email info@gest.se
website www.gest.se
Facebook /gesttheatre
Instagram @gest_gbg

Production details: Established in 2005, Gotenburg English Studio Theatre (GEST) is the only professional English language theatre in western Sweden. GEST works with professional actors and directors from Britain and Sweden and aims to produce theatre which is accessible to everyone. As well as performing in Sweden, GEST also performs internationally and collaborates with theatres abroad. They also collaborate with schools, colleges and universities, offering specially reduced student prices, workshops and after-show discussions with actors.

Casting procedures: Opportunities are advertised on the Spotlight casting breakdown service. Actors should be submitted by an agent. GEST do not send casting breakdowns to individual actors and do not accept unsolicited CVs and photographs. Actors without an agent should see the Productions page of the website where new productions are advertised and submit themselves by email.

London Toast Theatre
Vesterbrogade 149 V, bygn 9, 1 sal, 1620 København, Denmark
tel +45 3322 8686
email mail@londontoast.dk
website www.londontoast.dk
Facebook /LondonToast

Instagram @londontoasttheatre
Managing Director Søren Hall, *Artistic Director* Vivienne McKee

Production details: Founded in 1982, London Toast Theatre is the largest English-speaking theatre company in Northern Europe. Presents theatre productions and provides corporate entertainment, stand-up comedy and Murder Mystery shows in Scandinavia and abroad. The company's voice-over bureau, 'Speaker's Corner', provides English and American voices for films and commercials.

Prague Shakespeare Festival

Františka Křížka 362/1, 170 00 Letná, Czechia
email info@pragueshakespeare.org
website www.pragueshakespeare.com
Facebook /pragueshakespearecompany
Instagram @pragueshakes
Artistic Director Guy Roberts

Production details: Founded in 2008. The Festival presents professional theatre productions, workshops, classes, lectures and other theatrical events, of the highest quality, conducted primarily in English by a multinational ensemble of professional theatre artists, with an emphasis on the plays of William Shakespeare. Stages 12–18 productions annually, and holds workshops and classes on an ongoing basis.

Casting procedures: Casts in-house; check the website for annual casting and breakdowns. Welcomes approaches (with CVs and photographs) from actors by post and by email, and accepts showreels and invitations to view individual actors' websites. Actively encourages applications from disabled actors to play characters with disabilities, and promotes the use of inclusive casting.

Simply Theatre

Centre Choiseul, Avenue de Choiseul 23A, 1290 Versoix, Switzerland
tel +41 (0)22 860 0518
email academy@simplytheatre.com
website https://simplytheatre.com
Facebook /simplytheatreacademy
Instagram @simplytheatreacademy

Company details: Founded in 2005. Offers English theatre and courses for young people and families featuring professional actors, and an English-speaking Drama Academy for students. A professional English theatre for Switzerland and Continental Europe; and an English-speaking Drama Academy. Predominantly stages family-orientated theatre and shows for children.

Casting procedures: Casting breakdowns are available exclusively from Spotlight.

Vienna's English Theatre

UK address: VM Theatre Productions Ltd,
c/o Hutchinson Rowntree Ltd,
The Deptford Mission, 1 Creek Road,
London SE8 3BT
tel +43 (0)1 4021260
email office@englishtheatre.at
Theatre address: Josefsgasse 12, A-1080 Vienna
website www.englishtheatre.at/english/home
Facebook /ViennasEnglishTheatre
Instagram @viennasenglishtheatre

Production details: Founded in 1963; the oldest English-language theatre in continental Europe. Stages 5 shows each year in the main house and sends 5 Theatre-in-Education tours around the schools of Austria. The season runs from September to July each year.

Casting procedures: Casting breakdowns are occasionally posted on the website and actors may email the UK address above with their CV and photograph at anytime. UK casting agent is Julia Lintott (**office@vmtheatre.uk**). Showreels are not accepted. "Contracts are especially written for us by Equity."

White Horse Theatre

Boerdenstrasse 17, 59494 Soest, Germany
tel +49 (0)29 2133 9339
email info@white-horse-theatre.eu
website www.white-horse-theatre.eu/index.php/en/
Facebook /WhiteHorseTheatre
Instagram @whitehorsetheatre
Artistic Director Peter Griffith

Production details: Founded in 1978. Tours schools, theatres and art centres in Germany with occasional visits to neighbouring countries and to Japan and China. Has grown to become Europe's largest professional educational touring theatre.

Casting procedures: Does not use freelance casting directors. Holds general auditions; actors should write in April requesting inclusion. Casting breakdowns are available through the website, email application, Equity Job Information Service and Mandy. Welcomes postal and email enquiries from actors previously unknown to the company. Invitations to view individual actors' websites are also accepted. Contracts are approved by GDBA (the German equivalent of Equity). Rarely has the opportunity to cast disabled actors since "all our actors must take part in 3 different plays, and they must also cope with the rigours of touring".

Fringe theatres

The term Fringe theatre dates to 1947 and the inaugural Edinburgh International Festival. Legend has it that eight theatre companies who were disgruntled at not being included in the festival programme went ahead and produced their work anyway on the 'fringes' of the main event. The label quickly caught on as a badge of honour for the burgeoning alternative and experimental scene happening on the fringes of the mainstream in the 1960s. Later the term 'Fringe theatre' was an umbrella for the many – often tiny – theatres, arts centres, rooms above pubs that presented fiercely independent, avant-garde work and provided a vital experimental training ground for generations of artists. Today the Fringe has been diminished by soaring rents and professionalised standards but there is still a thriving Fringe ethos in many spaces, companies and festivals.

Most Fringe shows will be cast directly by the producing company or venue withsubmissions solicited and auditions advertised online. Fringe shows may not use union ormanagement association contracts so make sure you know what you are signing up for.Fringe work is unlikely to be lucrative but if you believe in the show and the company then itcan be a brilliant training ground, a credit for your CV and a chance to invite agents andcasting directors to see you in action. And who knows, perhaps your Fringe show will followin the footsteps of the now famous shows that started small and made it big. *SIX*, *The Play That Goes Wrong* and *Operation Mincemeat* all began life on the Fringe.

The Edinburgh Festival Fringe

The original Fringe is now the largest arts festival in the world. Every actor should experience this magnificent carnival of theatre at least once.

Edinburgh requires huge investments of time, money, energy, enthusiasm, entrepreneurialism and resilience. In return you will find your show, and yourself, in the biggest shop window in theatre. Some shows like Fleabag go on to make their creators mega-stars. Most do not, but that's not the be all and end all. The Edinburgh Fringe is a glorious, messy, melting-pot of talent and being part of it is a rollercoaster ride of meeting new people, making contacts, broadening your artistic horizons and having an indecent amount of fun. Good advice on mounting a production on the Edinburgh Festival Fringe is available from the Festival Office (details below).

The listings that follow are restricted to the more 'established' venues, with performance spaces for hire. Some Fringe theatres only programme in work known to them.

Note: If you are thinking of mounting a Fringe production and/or starting your own theatre company, start researching and planning well in advance. It is well worth consulting the Independent Theatre Council (ITC) – **www.itc-arts.org**.

UMBRELLA ORGANISATIONS

Edinburgh Festival Fringe
The Fringe Office, 180 High Street,
Edinburgh EH1 1QS
tel 0131 226 0026
email admin@edfringe.com
email artists@edfringe.com
website www.edfringe.com
X @edfringe
Instagram @edfringe

The Edinburgh Fringe Festival started in 1947 and the Fringe Society was formed in 1959 to coordinate publicity and ticket sales, and offer a comprehensive information service both to performers and to audiences. It compiles information about venues, press and suppliers, and produces a series of publications designed to answer frequently asked questions. Its brochure contains details for Fringe venues and shows in Edinburgh. The office is open all year round and the staff are available to help by phone, email or personal appointment.

OffWestEnd

email info@offwestend.com
website https://offwestend.com, https://offies.london
X @OffWestEndCom
Instagram @offwestendcom
Managing Director Denholm Spurr

OffWestEnd supports, promotes and celebrates the exciting and innovative work performed in the 100+ independent, alternative and fringe theatres beyond London's West End. Administers the Offies Awards, the first and foremost recognition for independent theatre in the UK.

Society of Independent Theatres (SIT)

mobile 07973 502189
email john@ovationproductions.com
website www.sitgb.org

The Society of Independent Theatres (SIT) is an alliance of small independent theatres (under 300 seats) in the UK. Venue owners, venue managers and artistic directors of independent theatres. Objectives are as follows:

- To raise the profile of small/independent/fringe/pub style venues within the theatre industry and with the general public.
- To encourage the development of the performing arts within independent venues.
- To exchange information on theatre companies and suppliers.
- To exchange ideas and proposals for marketing, promotion and audience development.
- To provide a better understanding of employment laws relevant to our sector of the industry.
- To liaise with Equity and other organisations over issues affecting our industry.

LONDON FRINGE VENUES

The Albany

The Albany: Douglas Way, Deptford, London SE8 4AG
tel 020-8692 4446
Deptford Lounge: 9 Giffin St, London SE8 4RJ
tel 020-8314 7288
email production@thealbany.org.uk
website www.thealbany.org.uk
Facebook /Albany.Deptford
X @theAlbanySE8
Instagram @thealbanyse8
Executive Director Mimi Findlay, *Creative Director* Vicki Amedume

Production details: A multi-use arts centre programming music, spoken word, dance, comedy and family shows. The Albany is an artistic and community resource with a fully equipped theatre space, studio theatre, café and rehearsal and meeting rooms for hire. Has a strong commitment to working collaboratively with the diverse communities of London and encouraging participation, especially by young people and isolated older people and those least likely to engage in the arts. As well as programming performances, the Albany programme and manage two external venues in Lewisham and Southwark. The centre is home to 18 resident organisations and the national Fun Palaces and Family Arts Campaign movements. It is a social hub and facilitator for partnership working. The Albany co-chairs Future Arts Centres with ARC, Stockon, runs a major partnership with Social Housing providor Lewisham Homes and recebtly launched a campaign to provide free theatre tickets to every 5-year-old child in Lewisham.

Seats 300. Performances also take place in the café – capacity 80. All spaces have fully configurable seating; there is also seating on the balcony. Shows usually run from one night to 2 weeks. Hire rates may be subsidised depending on community or charity status – see website for rates of different spaces. There is disabled access.

Casting procedures: Does not produce in-house shows.

artsdepot

5 Nether Street, North Finchley, London N12 0GA
tel 020-8369 5454
email info@artsdepot.co.uk
website www.artsdepot.co.uk
Facebook /artsdepotLDN
X @artsdepot
Instagram @artsdepot_ldn
Chief Executive Monique Deletant

The only professional arts venue in the London Borough of Barnet. Committed to providing a diverse range of high-quality visual and performance arts for everyone. artsdepot has brand new, state-of-the-art facilities in the form of the large Pentland Theatre, smaller Studio Theatre and Education Spaces, for the provision of drama, dance and visual arts, and a gallery, as well as an excellent café and bars.

Barons Court Theatre

Below The Curtain's Up Pub, 28A Comeragh Rd, West Kensington, London W14 9HR
mobile 07833 913760
email info@baronscourttheatre.com
website www.baronscourttheatre.com
Facebook /BaronsCourtTheatre
X @BaronsCourt_W14
Instagram @baronscourtw14
Artistic Director Sharon Willems, *Executive Director* Leo Bacica

Founded 1991. The Barons Court Theatre is a 52-seat theatre in the heart of of West London, between Hammersmith and Chelsea. Situated in the basement of the Curtains Up Pub, close to Queen's Club. Offers a variety of new writing, classical work and magic show.

Battersea Arts Centre
Lavender Hill, London SW11 5TN
tel 020-7223 2223
email boxoffice@bac.org.uk
website https://bac.org.uk
Facebook /batterseaartscentre
Instagram @batterseaartscentre
Artistic Director Tarek Iskander

Battersea Arts Centre's (BAC) mission is to harness the power of art, creativity and collective imagination to create a better future for everyone – a future that is more inclusive, more sustainable and more equitable.

They support artists to develop and present extraordinary work which is deeply rooted in the present moment and responds to the most urgent questions of our time. They are committed to creating welcoming and inclusive spaces where communities, artists and audiences are connected to collaborate and be creative. Ensuring the rich diversity of London is properly represented in the programme is central to their mission and shapes how they programme and develop work.

The best way to start a conversation about developing or presenting work is by inviting BAC to experience the work live or digitally.

Blue Elephant Theatre
59A Bethwin Road, Camberwell, London SE5 0XT
tel 020-7701 0100
email info@blueelephanttheatre.co.uk
website www.blueelephanttheatre.co.uk
Facebook /blueelephanttheatre
X @BETCamberwell
Instagram @betcamberwell
Artistic Director Niamh de Valera

A vibrant arts venue aiming to nurture new and emerging artists across the performing arts. Promotes cross-artform work and all types of theatre, from physical and dance to new writing and classics.

Co-produces all shows and is particularly interested in supporting new and emerging London-based artists across the perfoming arts with work that complements the black-box performance space. Those interested in bringing a project to the Blue Elephant should submit a written proposal with suggested dates and a full background to the Director.

The Bridewell Theatre
Bride Lane, Fleet Street, London EC4Y 8EQ
tel 020-7353 3331
website www.sbf.org.uk

The Bridewell Theatre is a versatile space, which provides both an atmospheric entertainment venue and a unique conference facility in the heart of the City. In addition to a 12x8m performance space, there is a modular tiered seating system that in standard configuration can accommodate a raked audience of 134 people. The theatre also offers dressing rooms with en suite amenities, as well as a box office/reception area and a fully equipped bar. All areas of the theatre are accessible to disabled users via a lift.

The Broadway Studio Theatre
Broadway Theatre, Rushey Green, Catford SE6 4RU
tel 020-8314 9472
email carmel@broadwaytheatre.org.uk
website www.broadwaytheatre.org.uk
X @BroadwayCatford
Theatre Manager Carmel O'Connor

Originally opened in 1932, the venue is Grade II listed by English Heritage as a beautiful example of 1930s art deco architecture. There are 2 venues: the Main Theatre seats 800, and the Studio Theatre seats 100. "The Broadway Studio Theatre has extremely limited availability."

Camden People's Theatre
58–60 Hampstead Road, London NW1 2PY
tel 020-7419 4841
email artists@cptheatre.co.uk
website www.cptheatre.co.uk
Facebook /CamdenPeoplesTheatre
Bluesky @camdenpt.bsky.social
Instagram @CamdenPeoplesTheatre
Artistic Director Rio Matchett

A central London space with a black box theatre and basement performance space, dedicated to supporting early-career artists. In particular, those who create devised and/or unconventional theatre.

Our theatre space is available to hire outside of our regular programming. We offer discounts for emerging artists and community groups. Consult the website or email **hires@cptheatre.co.uk** to find out more.

Canal Café Theatre
Delamere Terrace, Little Venice, London W2 6ND
tel 020-7289 6056 (Box Office), 020-7289 6054
email mail@canalcafetheatre.com
website www.canalcafetheatre.com
Artistic Director Emma Taylor

A cabaret, comedy and new writing 60-seat theatre situated above the Bridge House pub in Little Venice. Home to NewsRevue.

Charing Cross Theatre
(formerly New Players Theatre)
The Arches, Villiers Street, London WC2N 6NG
tel 020-7930 5868
email info@charingcrosstheatre.co.uk
website www.charingcrosstheatre.co.uk

Facebook /charingcrossthr
X @charingcrossthr
Instagram @charingcrossthr

Since 1864 there has been a theatre under the arches at Charing Cross Station. Known by many names over the years, the theatre was rechristened the Charing Cross Theatre in 2011. The venue offers an eclectic mix of drama, musicals, comedy, cabaret and late-night shows, plus periodic Sunday performances of traditional Victorian Music Hall. It is also a distinctive setting for screenings, conferences and corporate hires, complete with on-site bar and kitchen.

Chelsea Theatre

World's End Place, King's Road, London SW10 0DR
tel 020-7352 1967
email admin@chelseatheatre.org.uk
website www.chelseatheatre.org.uk
Facebook /chelseatheatre

A 130-seat theatre or 80 seat cinema. Particularly welcomes emerging artists. Offers a range of other spaces: learning and rehearsal studios, meeting rooms, indoor and outdoor exhibition and performance venues, community café and a terrace bar. Prides themselves on being a flexible space where community, artists and auidences can connect and explore their creativity.

The Cockpit

Gateforth Street, London NW8 8EH
tel 020-7258 2925
email reception@thecockpit.org.uk
website www.thecockpit.org.uk
Facebook /CockpitTheatre
X @cockpittheatre
Instagram @cockpittheatre
Theatre Director Dave Wybrow

Theatre seats 220 (in-the-round) or 170 (in thrust configuration) and should be booked 6 months in advance. Welcomes classics, foreign-language theatre and other niche market work. Also creates own in-house productions.

The Courtyard Theatre

Bowling Green Walk, 40 Pitfield Street,
London N1 6EU
tel 020-7739 6868
email info@thecourtyard.org.uk
website https://thecourtyard.org.uk
Facebook /thecourtyardtheatre
X @CourtyardHoxton
Instagram @thecourtyardtheatre

The Courtyard Theatre is housed within the Grade II listed, former public library in Pitfield Street, Hoxton. It has a 150-seat main house theatre, 80-seat studio theatre, 220 capacity music venue, bar and multiple rehearsal spaces.

Etcetera Theatre

Above the Oxford Arms, 265 Camden High Street,
London NW1 7BU
tel 020-7482 4857
email admin@etceteratheatre.com
website www.etceteratheatrecamden.com
Facebook /etceteratheatre
X @EtceteraTheatre
Instagram @etcetera_theatre_camden

A black-box studio space with 42 raked seats, this intimate theatre is perfect for everything from new writing to comedy and cabaret all the way through to acoustic music. Open 7 days a week with an early and late slot. Available for one-off bookings as well as week runs and any number of shows in between. The Etcetera is also available during the day for rehearsals, auditions and workshops with rates starting from just £30 an hour.

Finborough Theatre

118 Finborough Road, London SW10 9ED
tel 020-7244 7439
email admin@finboroughtheatre.co.uk
website https://finboroughtheatre.co.uk/
Facebook /FinboroughTheatre
X @finborough
Instagram @finboroughtheatre
Artistic Director Neil McPherson

Production details: Founded in 1980, the multi-award-winning Finborough Theatre presents plays and musical theatre, concentrated exclusively on vibrant new writing and unique rediscoveries from the 19th and 20th centuries. The programme is unique – never presenting work that has been seen anywhere in London during the last 25 years.

The main theatre space has flexible seating for 50 in a variety of formats. The normal run of a show is 4 weeks.

Hire rates: Box office profits are split 50/50. The rental is £6,500 per 4 week run.

Many productions transfer to New York and the West End.

Casting procedures: Produces in-house shows but does not hold general auditions. Casting breakdowns are available through the Spotlight Link casting service. Letters (with CVs and photographs) from previously unknown actors are not welcomed, neither are unsolicited CVs or showreels sent by email. Invitations to other productions are welcome. Welcomes applications from disabled performers but there is no wheelchair access to the theatre.

Hackney Empire Studio Theatre

291 Mare Street, London E8 1EJ
tel 020-8510 4500
email hire@hackneyempire.co.uk
website https://hackneyempire.co.uk
Facebook /hackneyempire

Bluesky @hackneyempire.bsky.social
Instagram @hackneyempire
Executive Director Jo Hemmant

Grade II listed building that is one of the largest theatres in London. Has a capacity of almost 1300 seats. Shows include comedy, live music, theatre and opera. They have worked with over 20,000 people through their Creative Futures Programme.

Hen & Chickens Theatre

Above Hen & Chickens Theatre Bar,
109 St Paul's Road, Islington, London N1 2NA
tel 020-7704 2001
website www.unrestrictedview.co.uk/venue
Facebook /TheHenandChickensTheatre
X @TheHenChickens
Co-Artistic Directors Felicity Wren, James Wren

A 54-seat theatre welcoming new writing. Directly opposite Highbury and Islington station. Offers 1–3 week runs for theatre and specific slots on Sundays and Mondays for comedy.

The Hope Theatre

Hope & Anchor Pub, 207 Upper Street, Islington, London N1 1RL
email info@thehopetheatre.com
Artistic Directors Laurel Marks, Toby Hampton

Production details: The multi-award-winning Hope Theatre is a 50-seat pub theatre in the heart of Islington. It nurtures and develops new producing models, working with both emerging and established companies to tell stories that are dramatic, surprising and have something to say about the world we live in. They are committed to nurturing and developing early career creatives with their new writing festival 'Write Club' and their in-house curated scratch performances.

Casting procedures: All in-house productions are cast via Spotlight. Please do not send unsolicited CVs. Invitations to see actors perform at other London venues should be sent via email.

The Jack Studio Theatre

410 Brockley Road, London SE4 2DH
email admin@brockleyjack.co.uk
website www.brockleyjack.co.uk
Facebook /BrocJackTheatre
X @BrocJackTheatre
Artistic Director Kate Bannister, Theatre Producer Karl Swinyard

Production details: A vibrant award winning performance space situated in South East London, offering a diverse theatre programme throughout the year. Home also to Scratch nights, workshops and screenings. End-on performance space with comfortable cinema-style raked seating for 50. The performing space is step-free and wheelchair accessible but the rehearsal room is not. Awards: Off West End Artistic Director Award 2024; London Pub Theatre of the Year 2023; and Best in Creative Sector, Mayor of Lewisham Awards 2023.

Casting procedures: Produces in-house shows; uses both in-house and freelance casting directors. Casting is generally by invitation. Does not welcome unsolicited submissions from actors, but will accept invitations to view individual actors' websites and to visit other productions. Actively encourages applications from disabled actors and promotes the use of inclusive casting.

Jacksons Lane Arts Centre

269A Archway Road, London N6 5AA
tel 020-8340 5226
email admin@jacksonslane.org.uk
website www.jacksonslane.org.uk
Facebook /jacksonslane
Instagram @jacksons_lane
Artistic Director Adrian Berry

Located opposite Highgate underground station, with a foyer and café space open to the public and free to use. A wide range of studios are available for hire on a daily or hourly basis for private functions, rehearsals, filmshoots, meetings and performances. The largest space holds up to 120, with other spaces having capacity for 35 people. The theatre has an audience size of up to 170. The Centre also hosts a programme of contemporary circus, non-verbal theatre and family theatre performances, as well as a thriving community engagement programme.

Jermyn Street Theatre

16B Jermyn Street, London SW1Y 6ST
tel 020-7287 2875
email info@jermynstreettheatre.co.uk
website www.jermynstreettheatre.co.uk
Facebook /Jermynstreettheatre
X @JSTheatre
Instagram @jermynstreettheatre
Artistic Director Stella Powell-Jones

Hire rates: Theatre seats 70. Stage space is 8 metres long x 3.5 metres deep, 2 dressing rooms with fridges, sofas, microwaves, kettles, iron + ironing board. The theatre is air conditioned.

- Main Shows – The theatre is now a fully programmed producing house. However, some weeks can be rented as a receiving house. For enquiries please contact them via email.
- Showcases/Rehearsed Readings/Seminars. Theatre is available on Wednesdays/Thursdays/Fridays between 10am and 4pm (includes technician).
- Sunday Nights (Cabaret Evenings) – can provide technical and sometimes marketing support.

Lion & Unicorn Theatre

42–44 Gaisford Street, Kentish Town, London NW5 2ED
email lionandunicorn@proforca.co.uk
website www.thelionandunicorntheatre.com
Artistic Director David Brady

A 60-seat black box studio theatre based above the Lion & Unicorn pub in Kentish Town. The venue will provides a home for fringe theatre talent and supports new writing, as well as opportunities for associate artists and companies who form part of our diverse artistic programme. Operates a year-round submissions policy for new writing, supported by the in-house theatre company, Proforca (www.proforca.co.uk).

New Diorama Theatre

15–16 Triton Street, Regent's Place, London NW1 3BF
tel 020-7916 5467
email hello@newdiorama.com
website www.newdiorama.com
Instagram @newdiorama
Co-Ceos Jonathan Maydew-Gale (Executive Director), Sophie Wallis (Executive Director)

New Diorama is a multi award-winning 80-seat theatre located in central London, on the corner of Regent's Park. They are dedicated to providing a home for the country's best independent theatre companies and ensembles.

Old Red Lion Theatre Pub

418 St John Street, Islington, London EC1V 4NJ
tel 020-7833 3053
email info@oldredliontheatre.co.uk
email productions.medium.rare@gmail.com
website www.oldredliontheatre.co.uk/theatre.html
X @ORLTheatre
Instagram @weareoldred
Artistic Director Jack Robertson

Founded in 1979, the Old Red Lion Theatre is a 45-seater Fringe Theatre dedicated to high quality productions from ambitious creatives. With seasonal festivals celebrating new writing, horror and classics, there are plenty of exciting opportunities for companies from around the UK and beyond. Production proposals must be sent via email to the Artistic Director; normally programmes 3-6 months ahead.

Omnibus Theatre

1 Clapham Common Northside, London SW4 0QW
tel 020-7622 4105
email enquiries@omnibus-clapham.org
website www.omnibus-clapham.org
Artistic Director Marie McCarthy, Executive Director Bridget Kalloushi

The heart of Omnibus Theatre's ambitious programme lies in classics re-imagined, modern revivals and new writing. Also provides a platform for LGBTQ+ work and aims to give voice to the underrepresented and challenge perceptions.

Since opening in 2013 notable in-house productions include: *Woyzeck* (2013); *Macbeth* (2014); *Colour* (2015); *Mule* (2016); *Spring Offensive* (2017); *Zeraffa Giraffa* (2017); *To Have To Shoot Irishmen* (2018); *Perfect* (2018); *The Little Prince* (2019); *Rice!* (2021); *The Human Connection* (2021); *The Girl Who Was Very Good at Lying* (2021); *Fiji* (2022); *Sad* (2022); *Drum* (2022); *Compositor E* (2023); and *Ice at the End of the World* (2024).

Pentameters

28 Heath Street, Hampstead NW3 6TE
tel 020-7435 3648
email theatre@pentameters.co.uk
website www.pentameters.co.uk
Founder & Producer Léonie Scott-Matthews

Established in 1968. Located in the heart of Hampstead village, among an abundance of cafés, restaurants, bars, pubs and shops and just a minute's walk from Hampstead tube. Aside from the choice of venues to have pre- or post-theatre drinks or dinner, Hampstead is also well-known for its artistic character, offering a supportive, interactive and thriving local community, making it an ideal spot to promote live theatre and creative arts events.

The Playground Theatre

8 Latimer Road, London W10 6RQ
tel 020-8960 0110
email community@theplaygroundtheatre.org.uk
website www.theplaygroundtheatre.org.uk
Artistic Director Peter Tate, Senior Creative Producer Simon Beyer

The Playground Theatre, formerly a bus depot, was set up as a creative space for innovative theatre artists of all disciplines to come and 'play' with their imaginative ideas. One such project, 'Terrific Electric' won the Samuel Beckett Award for Innovative Theatre and was part of the Bite season at the Barbican Theatre. The decision to become a public theatre was born from the desire to bring the exceptional artists work, who 'played' with the company, to full production. Continues to work with both established and emerging artists from the UK and internationally. The ethos is one of cross-fertilisation between different forms and different cultures in search of a universal language that speaks to all. Many international artists were invited to experiment with the Playground Theatre including Poland's Henryk Baranowski, winner of Poland and Russia's top award as best director, Salius Varnus from Lithuania, and Hideki Noda, currently head of Japan's National Theatre. From the UK, the company has worked closely with Marcello Magni, co-founder of Theatre De Complicité, along with his colleague Linda Kerr Scott. Programme includes international plays, classical concerts, dance, and film. The Playground Theatre is located within a very diverse community and its work will reflect this.

Pleasance Theatre Trust

Carpenters Mews, North Road, London N7 9EF
tel 020-7619 6868
email info@pleasance.co.uk
website www.pleasance.co.uk

Facebook /ThePleasance
X @ThePleasance
Instagram @thepleasance
Director Anthony Alderson

Founded in 1985, the Pleasance has 3 versatile spaces: the Mainhouse, seats 199; and the Studio, created to nurture the best in new theatre writing and emerging comedy talent, seats 54.

The standard configuration of the Main House and Studio are end on but the seating is completely flexible in both spaces. Shows are programmed for various lengths of run from one night to 6 weeks. There is no programme of shows in London during August, during which the Pleasance operates multiple sites at the Edinburgh Festival Fringe. Please visit the Pleasance website for hire rates and more information.

RADA Studios

16 Chenies Street, London WC1E 7EX
tel 020-7636 7076
email venuehire@rada.ac.uk
website www.rada.ac.uk/about-us/venue-hire/
Facebook /RoyalAcademyOfDramaticArt
X @RADA_London
Instagram @royalacademyofdramaticart
Venue Manager Ben McMath, *Box Office and Events Supervisor* Benjamin Jones

RADA Studios is a receiving theatre located in Chenies Street at the heart of the West End. The Studio Theatre is a hugely versatile space, and we currently host a large variety of work, including theatre, musicals, dance, opera, radio recordings and screenings.

We also have several studio spaces within the RADA Studios building, perfect for castings, read-throughs, rehearsals or fittings in a vibrant and creative atmosphere that continues to inspire future generations of actors, writers, directors and technicians.

Rich Mix

35–47 Bethnal Green Road, London E1 6LA
tel 020-7613 7495
email events@richmix.org.uk
website https://richmix.org.uk
Facebook /richmixlondon
X @RickMixLondon
Instagram @richmixlondon
Chief Executive Judith Kilvington

A charity connecting diverse audiences to an exciting and ambitious programme of contemporary culture. Their programme boasts every genre imaginable, including: theatre, dance, talks, exhibitions, live music and visual art.

Rosemary Branch Theatre

2 Shepperton Road, London N1 3DT
tel 020-7704 2730
email info@rosemarybranchtheatre.co.uk
website www.rosemarybranch.co.uk
Facebook /RosieBTheatre
X @RosieBTheatre
Instagram @rosiebtheatre

The theatre holds about 55 seats. Presents a diverse programme including opera, classics, new writing, puppetry and just about any genre you care to mention. Affordable rehearsal space available in the Pink Room as well as the theatre during the day. The theatre offers all visiting companies lots of support and goodwill. One-offs, part week and full week rentals all considered.

The Space

269 Westferry Road, London E14 3RS
tel 020-7515 7799
email info@space.org.uk
website https://space.org.uk
Facebook /thespace
X @SpaceArtsCentre
Instagram @thespacetheatre
Artistic Director Matthew Jameson

The Space was founded in 1996 and is managed by the registered charity, St Paul's Arts Trust. In a converted church hall, The Space provides an atmospheric yet flexible Off West End setting. Certainly not a typical 'black box' theatre, a number of staging options are achievable including end-on, in the round, traverse and thrust.

The Space programmes 3 seasons a year. In each season they aim to schedule 3 week runs alongside shorter runs and one-off performances. The Space offers a range of theatre events within each season, including a mixture of classics, new writing, revivals, puppetry, physical theatre, immersive theatre and musicals. It programmes drama and comedy and works with new, emerging and established companies.

The main theatre space seats between 45 and 90 depending on configuration. End on: between 60 (large playing space) and 90 seats (small stage area only, suitable for recitals and solo performances). The end-on configuration can also be reversed, with audience seating on stage. This configuration tends to seat 65 audience members; traverse: between 40–60 seats; thrust: 50–60 seats; in the round: 50–60 seats.

Viewing and speaking with one of their team is recommended before applying. Runs shorter than a week will usually be programmed on a straight hire basis, although this is negotiable.

The main space is used all year round and open submissions are three times a year, announced on the website. Roof Gadren Performance Space is used in the summer only.

Discounts are offered on block bookings for rehearsals.

Hire rates: Rehearsals (10am–6pm) £36/hr including VAT. Performances £300 each (inc. VAT), includes all The Space's marketng, full use of lighting and sound equipment and full box office service.

Premises are accessible to disabled performers.

Theatre at the Tabard
2 Bath Road, Turnham Green, London W4 1LW
tel 020-8995 6035
email info@tabard.org.uk
website https://tabard.org.uk/
Facebook /TheatreAtTabard
X @TheatreAtTabard
Artistic Director Simon Reilly, *Executive Director & Creative Producer* Sarah Reilly

Situated within the Tabard building with own independent entrance, this 96-seat venue is close to Turnham Green tube. Produces its own theatre productions and offers other companies the opportunity to bring their work to the Tabard stage.

Theatre503
Above The Latchmere, 503 Battersea Park Road, London SW11 3BW
tel 020-7978 7040
email info@theatre503.com
website www.theatre503.com
X @theatre503
Instagram @theatre503
Co-Ceos Anthony Simpson-Pike (Artistic Director), Emily Carewe (Executive Director)

Theatre503 is the national landscape for early career playwrights and the artists who bring their work to life. Learning and career development are at the core of what they do, and they play a vital role in the theatre ecology by supporting debut writers and diverse new voices. They programme over 100 new pieces of writing every year ranging from short plays to full runs of superb drama and passionately believe that the most important element in a writer's development is to see their work developed through to a full production on stage, performed to the highest professional standard in front of an audience. They are one of the most prolific theatres and have staged over 1,800 new plays in their 64-seat venue since 2004.

Theatro Technis
26 Crowndale Road, London NW1 1TT
tel 020-7387 6617, *mobile* 07535 801399
email info@theatrotechnis.com
website www.theatrotechnis.com

Theatro Technis has been an independent company and venue for over six decades. Hosting popular events like the Camden Fringe Festival, Shubbak Festival, and showcasing emerging talent from around the world, Theatro Technis remains a vibrant hub for innovative theatre and performance. At its heart, the venue is dedicated to serving its diverse and dynamic community.

120-seat theatre on three sides with a high ceiling, and a licensed front of house/bar. There is one rehearsal room, roughly 5x5m.

Toynbee Studios
28 Commercial Street, London E1 6AB
tel 020-7247 5102
email samuel@artsadmin.co.uk
website www.artsadmin.co.uk/toynbee-studios
Facebook /artsadmin
X @artsadm
Instagram @artsadm
Artistic Director Raidene Carter

Toynbee Studios is run by Artsadmin for the development and presentation of new work. Toynbee Studios comprises a 280-seat theatre, rehearsal spaces, technical facilities, and the Arts Bar & Café, hosting rehearsals, meetings, performances and events throughout the year. Office facilities are also provided for a range of arts organisations.

Toynbee Studios has 6 spaces for hire ranging from the intimate to larger high-spec dance and theatre studios. Requests for public events will be reviewed alongside Artsadmin's artistic policy. Spaces are usually hired daily/weekly Monday-Friday 10am-6pm. Occasional evening and weekend hires are available on request.

Artsadmin was founded in 1979 and has been based at Toynbee Studios since 1995. Artsadmin is a company of creative people working with artists to develop and make performance projects for local, national and international audiences. They offer a range of support for artists and rehearsal studios, workspaces and a programme of public events.

Union Theatre
Old Union Arches, 229 Union Street, London SE1 0LR
tel 020-7261 9876
email info@uniontheatre.biz
website http://uniontheatre.biz
X @TheUnionTheatre
Instagram @theuniontheatre

Primarily a new writing venue, the theatre aims to present a diverse programme featuring the best new talent. Guest performances are supplemented by regular in-house productions.

Upstairs at the Gatehouse
The Gatehouse Pub, North Road, London N6 4BD
tel 020-8340 3488
email gatehouse@chromolume.co.uk
website www.upstairsatthegatehouse.com
Directors Annlouise Butt, Isaac Bernier-Doyle

Founded in 1997. An award-winning, off West End theatre in Highgate Village with an 122-seat Victorian auditorium. Presents a varied programme of musicals, plays, opera and new writing.

White Bear Theatre
138 Kennington Park Road, London SE11 4DJ
tel 07985 500697
email info@whitebeartheatre.com
website www.whitebeartheatre.com
Facebook /WhiteBearTheatre
X @WhiteBearTheatr
Instagram @whitebeartheatre
Founder & Artistic Director Michael Kingsbury

Aims to foster new and established talent and offer a space for creative risk-taking. The studio space has seating for up to 50. Generally prefers new writing but occasionally accepts revivals.

Wimbledon Studio Theatre
93 The Broadway, London SW19 1QG
tel 020-8545 7900 (Admin)
website www.atgtickets.com/venues/studio-at-new-wimbledon-theatre

A black box studio theatre with flexible seating for up to 66. Normally offers one to 2 week runs which are programmed 6 months ahead. The auditorium is wheelchair-accessible.

EDINBURGH FESTIVAL FRINGE VENUES

Many of these venues are only available for hire during the Edinburgh Festival Fringe in August. For a full list of venues, see **www.edfringe.com/venues**.

Assembly Rooms
54 George Street, Edinburgh EH2 2LR
tel 0131 220 4348
email venuehire@edinburgh.gov.uk
website www.assemblyroomsedinburgh.co.uk

The Assembly Rooms have presented more than 1,000 productions featuring most of the major names in British comedy – as well as a huge array of theatre, dance and music events which have been seen by more than 1.5 million people over the last 20 years of the Edinburgh Festival Fringe. Aims to programme a balance of theatre, comedy and new work.

Augustine's
Augustine United Church, 41 George IV Bridge, Edinburgh EH1 1EL
tel 0131 510 0119
website www.paradise-green.co.uk/perform/venues

Part of Augustine United Church. During the Festival it is adapted by Paradise Green to house 3 performance spaces: The Sanctuary seats 110; The Studio seats approx.107; and The Snug seats 30. Programmes theatre, musicals, dance and children's theatre from the UK and elsewhere.

Bedlam Theatre
11B Bristo Place, Edinburgh EH1 1EZ
tel 0131 629 0430
email info@bedlamtheatre.co.uk
email fringe@bedlamtheatre.co.uk
website www.bedlamtheatre.co.uk,
https://bedlamfringe.co.uk/
Facebook /bedlamfringe
Instagram @bedlamfringe

A 90-seat black-box theatre in central Edinburgh housed in a neo-gothic church. The theatre is available for hire when not in use by the Edinburgh University Theatre Company.

C ARTS
tel 0131 581 5500
email info@cvenues.com
website www.cvenues.com
Facebook /cvenues

C ARTS programmes and hosts over 100 productions and events at the Edinburgh Fringe each August at C venues across multiple locations in central Edinburgh, and operates a digitasl arts programme year-round. Buildings include original Fringe venues from the first days of the Fringe and some of the newest venues on the Fringe. Alongside a broad theatre-based programme incorporating drama, new writing, physical theatre, musical theatre and children's theatre, C has developed a speciality programming immersive, interactive and site-specific theatre, and in hosting cabaret, circus theatre, performance art and cross-genre work. C's productions have come from and toured around the world, and have won Fringe First, Total Theatre and other awards. C venues is a founder member of Edinburgh's Associated Independent Venue Producers.

Greyfriars Kirk
Greyfriars Place, Edinburgh EH1 2QQ
tel 0131225 1900
email outreach@greyfriarskirk.com
website https://greyfriarskirk.com

Two performance spaces, one of which is wheelchair accessible. As well as poetry recitals and performances, the acoustics make the space perfect for orchestral and choral concerts and organ recitals.

The Pleasance
The Pleasance Courtyard: 60 The Pleasance, Edinburgh EH8 9TJ; *The Pleasance Dome*: 1 Bristo Square,
Edinburgh EH8 9AL; *The Pleasance at EICC*: 150 Morrison Street,
Edinburgh EH3 8EE; *The Pleasance Administration Office*: Carpenters Mews, North Road, London N7 9EF
tel 020-7619 6868
email info@pleasance.co.uk
website www.pleasance.co.uk
Facebook /ThePleasance

X @ThePleasance
Instagram @thepleasance

The Pleasance presents more than 220 shows across 3 sites and 33 venues during the 4 weeks of the Festival Fringe. With more than 500,000 visitors every year, it remains one of the most popular venues of the Fringe, offering a diverse mix of comedy, theatre, dance, music and everything in-between.

Traverse Theatre
10 Cambridge Street, Edinburgh EH1 2ED
tel 0131 228 1404
email info@traverse.co.uk
website www.traverse.co.uk
Chief Executive & Executive Producer Linda Crooks, *Artistic Director* Gareth Nicholls

Scotland's new writing theatre. All-year-round venue in underground purpose-built theatre with 2 auditoria. Runs 4 seasons across the year: Autumn (Sept–Dec), Spring (Jan–Apr), Summer (May–July) and Festival (throughout August as part of the Edinburgh Festival Fringe).

Underbelly
4th Floor, 36–38 Hatton Garden, London EC1N 8EB
tel 020-7307 8480
email enquiries@underbelly.co.uk
website www.underbelly.co.uk,
https://underbellyedinburgh.co.uk
Underbelly Directors Ed Bartlam, Charlie Wood

Comprises 19 Fringe spaces over 4 sites with multiple bars: George Square, Circus Hub, Cowgate and Bristo Square. Venues cater for audiences of 42–1000 with different seating configurations available. Programmes new writing, theatre, dance, circus and comedy.

OTHER FRINGE LOCATIONS

The Alma Tavern Theatre
18-20 Alma Vale Road, Bristol BS82HY
tel 011-7973 5171
email theatre@almatavernandtheatre.co.uk
website https://www.almatavernandtheatre.co.uk
Facebook AlmaTavernAndTheatre
X @AlmaBristol
Instagram @almataverntheatre
Artistic Director Holly Newton, *Acting Artistic Director* Oliver de Rohan

48 seat black-box theatre above a lovely pub in Clifton, Bristol set up in 1997. They operate mainly as a receiving house with around 150 productions per year. Flat hire rates and box office splits are available. They are always interested to hear from producers and are open to programming a wide range of independent shows including new writing, classics, stand up, improv, magic, clowning and just about anything that will work in a pub theatre!

Komedia
44–47 Gardner Street, Brighton BN1 1UN
tel (01273) 647100
22–23 Westgate Street, Bath BA1 1EP
tel (01225) 489070
email tombrain@komedia.co.uk
website www.komedia.co.uk
Facebook /KomediaBrighton
Instagram @komedia_brighton

Komedia host over 700 performances of comedy, music, cabaret and kids shows and club nights.

Operates two vibrant performance spaces with flexible set-ups and a kitchen serving freshly prepared food at most seated shows.

Komedia's programme features the international and national performers and includes a unique range of Komedia-grown resident shows such as the *Komedia Comedy Club*, *Comic Boom* and *Down the Hatch*.

Lantern Theatre
77 St James Street, Brighton BN2 1PA
tel 01273 818266
email info@lanterntheatrebrighton.co.uk
website www.lanterntheatrebrighton.co.uk
Facebook Lantern Theatre Brighton
X/Twitter @lanterntheatreb
Instagram @lanterntheatrebrighton
Artistic Director/Programmer Janette Eddisford, *Theatre Manager* Daniel Finlay, *Technical Manager* Erin Burbridge

The Lantern is Brighton's premier Fringe Theatre venue, offering 2 fully equipped performance spaces, a licensed café bar and rehearsal studios. It has a capacity of 52 seats; The Grania Dean seats 32. The Lantern has built a reputation for programming bold, innovative theatre with a particular focus on new writing. The Theatre shares premises with the Academy of Creative Training – Brighton's original Drama School which offers professional actor training at low cost. Both groups are run on a non-profit basis and collaborate on offering accessible, affordable classes in theatre, screen and writing for all ages and abilities.

Sevenoaks Stag Theatre
London Road, Sevenoaks, Kent TN13 1ZZ
tel (01732) 450175
email operations@stagsevenoaks.co.uk
website https://stagsevenoaks.co.uk/
Facebook /stag7oaks
X @StagSevenoaks
Instagram @stagsevenoaks
Chief Executive Andrew Eyre

The theatre can seat up to 450 and has provision for wheelchair-users. Companies should book the space up to 6 months in advance. Programmes a wide range of theatre and dance events.

The direction of collaboration

Ned Bennett, theatre director
Interview by Polly Bennett

Ned Bennett is a freelance theatre director. He makes theatre with young people and in prisons, as well as directing professional projects. Most recently he directed Unprecedented for Headlong and BBC Arts, The LeftBehinds and Dick Whittington at the National Theatre, Equus for Theatre Royal Stratford East, the English Touring Theatre and Trafalgar Studios and Baddies with Synergy Theatre. He trained at Manchester University, LAMDA and the Royal Court Theatre.

What common misconceptions do you think there are about what a theatre director does?
I think a common misconception is the term 'director' itself. It implies a top-of-the-pyramid overly hierarchical approach to making work. This may be the case sometimes, but needn't be necessarily. A common misconception is that the director tells everyone what to do, but a large part of the job is facilitating the space for people to find what to do themselves.

Is that something that you're conscious of in your practice?
I'd like to think I am. I'm quite interested in playing and seeing what can come from the room as late as possible, and then going through an editing process. I think it's interesting to drill down into how the 'director tells people what to do' hierarchical approach is dictated by the inherent time and financial structures that force you into a corner. It's specific to an almost one-size-fits-all British theatre way of putting on plays that I imagine has its roots in the rep system.

By which you mean, 'Here's a play. Let's employ a director to do it, director reads it, says "yes please", gets a designer, keeps going through the creative team, lights, sound, maybe movement, maybe dialect if it needs it'. Would you say that's how British theatre is being made?
I think it often is that. Our theatres have to plan so far in advance that productions are fitted into a matrix. I think what I'm trying to do more is work out what the production needs first, before it's gone too far in one direction determined by parameters informed predominantly by previous shows rather than what this particular play and group of people making it require.

And I guess who does this particular play require.
Exactly.

Are you trying to change the system we've become used to then? How do you mitigate this conversation with a theatre?
I think it is starting to happen. It's been expedited over the last few years, with the recognition that artists need to be more embedded in buildings and more involved in decision making. A recurring point of view from freelancers at the beginning of the pandemic was the desire to make less work more slowly.

What might this look like?
It might be about what creatives are in Associate positions or even how planning and programming is made more transparent and collaborative with people who are actually going to be making the shows. But also it could be theatres having a conversation with a potential creative team when looking at what shows to do so that their involvement starts from the get-go.

I'd find that really empowering. That's actually genuinely never happened to me.
Empowering yes. It's a way of preventing anyone being treated as a hired hand and recognising that directing as a job is relatively new in the grand scheme of things, which makes other creative team positions even newer. Which means that the behemoth that is the industry is having to keep up. Sometimes making theatre can feel like you're on a runaway train and the enforced slowing down of things during this period has meant there's been some really constructive, clearer conversations about what people need and how it can be achieved. It feels like organisations are open to re-thinking things from a holistic perspective, considering when is a creative team engaged, what's their input and how early can that be, down to the nuts and bolts of design deadlines and how they relate to a timeline in relation to the building and money stuff.

You used the word 'artists' earlier, which I think lots of people shy away from using in theatre because of the overriding habit to define ourselves by the job role. If you're treating everyone as equal artists, everybody has the capacity to have a voice in the experience more, right?
Yeah, and actually maybe there's something liberating about defining ourselves as artists because perhaps it's the categorisation that is a big part of an inbuilt imposter syndrome. Categorisation implies a definite concrete angle on what your job is, as opposed to how your own sense of creative self can be channelled.

You just made a gesture – like a scooping action from your belly – which perhaps summarises the 'full-bellied', 'on-the-table' way you put on a play and what you want from the people you work with. What does collaboration mean to you?
Ultimately the communal aspect of it, of making a mini-community in a space. I do feel like the more you attempt to bring what you and your team, everyone in the room, are all genuinely actually interested in – whether it's something particular you've seen in a music video or a style of comedy that you've become fixated with on TV, or a political ideology. If you're able to try and bring that into the room, then that's what makes the journey so satisfying and nourishing. There's an unhelpful misnomer about collaboration that it's driven exclusively by a mystical, magical alchemy. Alchemy is certainly a thing, but I also think that collaboration is underpinned by a conscious awareness of how to build a culture between a group of people. I think the freelancing, visiting nature of working somewhere, can sometimes feel like stuff is slightly blocking that. Whether it's an insecurity driven by a lack of experience or whatever it may be, or not knowing where the loo is, not knowing the boundaries of something …

Not feeling welcome in the space …
Not feeling welcome …

Not feeling as able to participate if you are there as ...
...As a visiting guest. And sort of how that affects everything really. So, I think it then becomes a question of how you ringfence time for a creative team to actually hear each other. The Russo Brothers who made *The Avengers* films and the TV show *Community* described the two of them working together not as being double the ideas, but as being an exponential growth of ideas, which I think is such a useful way of looking at collaboration. Which is to say that the more a team can bounce off each other, the more they can go deeper down the rabbit hole in trying to understand what something is and what something can be and where it can go. That's the theory, but in practice, where it gets complicated is the fact that creative teams often feel like their time is crushed by needing to do ten other jobs at once to earn enough money to live, and it sometimes feels impossible to get together in one room for more than half a day before rehearsals.

With these reflections on your own personal practice and how it's developing and changing, what would you say to a theatre director – or artist – coming into the industry?
I am often reminded of Anne Bogart's concept of Learn One, Do One, Teach One. I think she was quoting brain surgeons and how they structure their learning to develop their practice. At first, I was going between different spaces working with community groups, young people and professionals instinctively, I think because I thought I was going to become a teacher. Then a few years ago, I became more consciously aware that *doing* that was actually really vital to my practice. The different spaces become symbiotic to what you learn – you develop how you understand something yourself and you can selfishly experiment with process when there isn't necessarily a result. Doing plays is stressful so it makes for a more manageable, mentally healthy use of time. A director I wrote to a long time ago said to me "passion isn't limitless" and I'm increasingly understanding what he means by that. I think that you find your passion through working with other people and through not having to constantly deliver something. Work becomes more about creativity and collaboration and relationships.

And in terms of the work?
The seeming insularity of the industry can sometimes mean that we end up second-guessing what we think, what should be made or should be said and all of that. I appreciate this is easier said than done but attempt to make what you actually want to see on stage.

To follow Ned's work visit **www.nedbennett.co.uk**

Edinburgh or bust: is it worth it?

Shane Dempsey

The Edinburgh Festival Fringe was established in 1947 and has grown into one of the world's most renowned and diverse arts festivals. From its humble beginnings as an alternative to the Edinburgh International Festival, the Fringe has continued to increase and multiply, and, despite the growing costs to companies and performers alike, it still remains high on the agenda of many. The Fringe can be incredibly daunting and at times even crippling. My aim is not to shatter you, but to ensure that you are armed with as much knowledge as possible before you decide if it's worth it.

In 2025 there were 3352 shows performed in Edinburgh and an estimated 45,182 performances in 265 venues. These figures give you an idea of the level of competition for audiences during the three weeks of August. This is an aggressive and over-saturated market. In the Fringe environment, the efforts of many go unrewarded and often even unnoticed. So, can you break through with your production?

Evaluate your work honestly and realistically

The first thing to do is evaluate the production itself. Ask yourself, "What is the appeal of my particular production? What is it about my show that will make it stand out from the crowd? Do I have permission from the author or their estate to perform the piece? If so, what percentage of my overall income will this take, and what are the possibilities of extending this performance licence post-Edinburgh?"

If the piece is new writing or devised then there are fewer issues with performance rights, but it is crucial to discuss billing and authorship, as these can potentially cause problems later. Circumstances change, so with new work it is essential to secure written agreement over the intellectual copyright of the piece – and this also extends to directorial concepts and vision. Get it down on paper so you always know where you stand and can avoid or deal with any issues that may arise.

As well as fledgling companies taking new work to Edinburgh, the festival is also a testing ground for many established, heavyweight companies and producers. They have years of experience, and they have the economic power to invest large sums in PR and marketing. So ask yourself what will bring an audience to your venue, and why. The reality is that you are in direct competition with these established companies as well as with the other thousands who are newer to the game.

Choose the right venue

There are many venues associated with the Fringe. You need to be clear about the kind of work they are interested in programming; some are very specific as to their requirements, while others have a broader remit. Consider not only the price, but also the reputation and the location of a venue, as they vary considerably.

Your time slot is another point of negotiation: late evenings tend to be dominated by comedy, and a great deal of theatre now plays during the day and late afternoon. A general rule is that the more established venues have the best reputations and tend to charge significantly more for their services than smaller, up-and-coming venues. All venues will require you to sign a contract, and you need to be aware of the small print, as it has been known for companies to skim over this only to discover that they were not aware of all the terms and conditions.

Consider venue costs and other expenses

Many venues offer either a box-office split or ask for a flat fee. Almost all will require a deposit in advance. The average cost of mounting a production in Edinburgh is £17,000–25,000, and deposits will often be required months in advance – so unless you have access to sufficient funds, consider seriously if there is a more cost-effective way of getting your work out there.

And there are other expenses, including music performance rights, public liability insurance and VAT. Accommodation costs soar during the festival, and local landlords take advantage of the influx of artists and tourists, but if you're organised it is possible to secure a deal by booking early. Many companies choose to stay in Glasgow, which is an hour-long commute, but the time and energy required to do this needs to be weighed up against the convenience and cost of staying in Edinburgh.

What do you want from the experience?

Ask yourself early on what you want to achieve out of the experience. Too often this is not given enough thought, so that it is difficult, if not impossible, to achieve any significant outcomes. Remember that Edinburgh is a massive arts market, and that within any market you need to be specific about your audience – be it the general public or producers who can potentially remount your work post-Edinburgh.

If you want a London transfer, regional tour or international tour, target your promotions pack specifically to relevant individuals and always research their programming tastes. Invite them to the show, ensure that they are given complimentary tickets and try to set up a meeting after they have seen your work. Many international producers are seeking work that would be programmed two to three years after the festival, so you have to have a long-term plan for the production and ensure that it has the necessary factors that will support its longevity.

Network!

Many deals in Edinburgh are set up over late-night drinks and midnight meetings, often to fit in with the schedules of producers who are seeing work all day long. They can be fairly informal, but keeping your professional hat on is essential to any success. There are incredible opportunities to meet new people in Edinburgh, and there are numerous events specifically aimed towards networking, including The Producers' Breakfast.

In addition you can take part in a range of informal activities in which you can make connections that may lead to future work and collaborations. This is often triggered by seeing a company's work: the research trip I made to Russia to investigate ensemble practice was greatly aided by contacts I met in Edinburgh. The key to any networking is to find the common links between you and the other practitioner, and then to develop them into a cohesive relationship. Be honest about what you do and why you do it, and people will usually respond positively.

Press officers have essential contacts with the media and could be a valuable asset to your production. They can not guarantee that your work will be reviewed, but having a person working on your behalf can give you a major advantage over the competition.

If, like many companies, you are bringing the show to Edinburgh on a very tight budget, allocate one member of the company to be the designated press officer as this makes life a lot easier for all parties. Again, reputation means a lot in the world of the press and some papers will hold more influence than others. Target the ones that you believe will be interested in your work and be sure to read the reviews every day to get a flavour of what the festival has to offer.

Design, marketing and word-of-mouth

In a market such as the Fringe, the role of good graphic design and web design is often overlooked, but it is essential to ensure that your work is seen – and seen at its best. Ensure that your production pack has strong imagery. The old cliché of a picture painting a thousand words still rings true, especially to overtired editors at the busiest time of their year. The array of flyers that are seen on the streets of Edinburgh is mind-boggling, but eye-catching design can really aid your marketing campaign.

Over and above marketing, however, is word-of-mouth – one of the key influences in persuading people to see your show. Such recommendations are difficult to achieve, and are dependent on your getting healthy, happy audiences early in your run. The majority of companies spend their days marketing their work, sending emails, chasing the press and leafleting: this is the Fringe, and if you're not prepared to do this to the point of exhaustion, stay at home!

For inclusion in the much-coveted Fringe Brochure you will be asked to submit 50 words of copy to describe your production. Keep it simple and clear, and remember that you are going to have to live with this for the life of your show in Edinburgh, so make sure it really sums your work up. It can be useful to have a quote in there from previous work – after all, everybody wants to see a show from a five-star company – but if it's not true, don't claim it to be so! Fabrication rarely, if ever, helps. The Fringe website provides comprehensive guidelines on producing work in Edinburgh: see **www.edfringe.com/take-part**. The information is there if you look for it, so take the time to investigate. It could save you much stress and money.

Dreams can come true ...

The likelihood of your company or show being picked up for a transfer or tour is extremely slim. The financial burden on companies is very high, and you have to weigh this up against the potential exposure and the possibility of gaining other work after the festival. Fragments' production of *The Bay* by Hannah Burke was performed at the Big Red Door, Te-Pooka; we also managed to be seen by representatives of the Traverse, Manchester International Festival, and were transferred into London's prestigious Theatre 503. So yes, dreams can come true … but only after a serious amount of hard graft, and no little luck too.

Shane Dempsey is an Irish Theatre and Movement Director having trained at The National Theatre Studio and E15 Acting School. He ran Stagecraft – one of Ireland's leading youth theatres – from 1998 to 2016. He is also the founding member of Fragments, a dynamic physical ensemble in London working across theatre and film. His productions included *Hamlet* and *Translations* at the National Theatre; *Shining City* at Theatre Royal Stratford East; *rob steal swindle* at Mountview Academy of Theatre Arts; *Continuity* and *The Non-Stop Connolly Show* at the Finborough; *About Last Night* and *Seven Jewish Children* at the Arcola; *The Master and Margarita* at the Bussey Building and Te Pooka, Edinburgh; and *The Bay* at Theatre503, The Space and Te Pooka, Edinburgh.

His movement direction projects include *Hamlet*, National Theatre; *From Out The Land*, Junction Festival Ireland; *Migran-Te* for Plataforma Festival in Sheffield, Halifax and Leeds; *Eating Myself* at Battersea Arts Centre; *The Fight for Stagecraft* at Kickham Barracks, Ireland; *The Good Earth* (R&D) at Wales Millenium Centre); *Ensemble Practise* in New York; and *The Blocks* and *More Shadows Than People* for E15 at Clifftown Theatre. See **shanedempsey.co.uk**.

Open Book: fairer finances for fringe theatre

Piers Beckley

What is 'Open Book Theatre'?

Most fringe theatre productions don't make a profit. And as a large number of fringe productions offer only a profit-share as financial recompense for the actors performing in them, this can be a big problem.

Something that can be especially galling for an actor is to perform in front of a house filled with people, and still not receive any money at the end of the run because the production hasn't made a profit. But if half of those tickets are given away free to fill the house in early shows in order to help word of mouth, then the number of people that you see in the audience may not give an accurate measure of how much money is actually coming in.

If the tickets were priced too low, or the producer failed to get a good deal on the advertising, or any number of other things, it's very easy for a production to make a loss. And without financial transparency throughout the process, there can always be the niggling suspicion that something, somewhere, has gone horribly wrong that need not have.

By its nature, fringe theatre will never have as much money to spend on props, print, advertising, design, or on actors as a fully professional production. But if a company can't provide the cold hard cash which we all desire, the very least that they can provide is transparency in recording what money goes in and comes out, so that everything is fair and above board, and is seen to be so.

Open Book Theatre is a new way of running the financial books for a fringe production, so that every member of the cast and crew can see the business of putting on a show. In an Open Book production, the budget is viewable by anyone involved – from first draft through to final income statements. This means that as well as knowing that they've been treated fairly throughout the entire process, everyone will be able to see how the production is doing – and, if all goes well, exactly how much of the profit-share pot they'll receive when the money comes in from the theatre.

Open Book Management is a set of techniques that have been used by companies across the world over the last 40 years. It's all about giving the people involved a stake in the outcome, and then giving them the tools to affect what that outcome is. In a business environment, the stake is most often shares in the company, while in Open Book Theatre (at least at the fringe level) it usually consists of a portion of the profit from the show.

What does Open Book Management involve?

Free access and exchange

There are three main points at the heart of an Open Book production:
• Free access to all financial information
• Regular updates on changes
• Listening to suggestions and implementing them

So how would you go about bringing this to life?

One of the easiest ways of sharing information is to use budget spreadsheets showing estimated outgoings and income, which are later updated as the real figures come in. These spreadsheets can be placed on a password-protected website, or emailed to the cast and crew every week to show exactly how much money has come in and gone out.

Because the budgets are available for all to see, as well as knowing exactly where the money has gone on advertising, design, print – all of the things that are necessary to a production, but which generally don't cross an actor's desk – then everyone involved can help suggest improvements.

Perhaps someone has a photographer friend who'll be able to take publicity shots in exchange for a credit or a lower fee. Or perhaps they will know a way to get the fabric needed by a costume designer more cheaply. If everyone knows the cost of the things that make up a production, and how those will affect the profits, then they can suggest ways to make things better for all.

As the financial spreadsheets are regularly updated throughout the show, then everyone involved can see the clock ticking towards breakeven – that magical moment when income from sales and advertising rises above what's been spent on the production, and everyone knows that they're going to be taking some money home with them. It's also nice to be able to celebrate when your production reaches a milestone – for example, when half-way to breaking even.

As well as making the budget documents visible to all, an Open Book production will ensure that all of the documents that are legally required are on display: the insurance schedule, health and safety policy, venue contract, and risk assessment documents. Seeing this information proves that you're dealing with a professional company and a professional production – not just one person's vanity project.

Fair profit-share: the 'tronc system'

In a fringe production, the final part of the Open Book story comes with the division of the profit-share pot. After all costs have been paid (and everyone will know what they are, because they can look at the income and expenditure of the show at any point throughout the production), then any gross profits can be divided between those who brought the show to life.

One way of doing this fairly and equitably is to use what's known as a tronc system, based on the tips system used in many bars and restaurants. In a tronc, everyone involved in the production is allocated a certain number of points depending upon their involvement. So the director and writer might have two points each, while each member of the ensemble cast has one point. It's important to be up front about how any profits will be divided – for example, if the star of the show is to receive more points than the other actors.

After the gross profit has been worked out, the value of each point can be derived by simply dividing the profit by the total number of points – and then everyone is paid that amount for each point that they have.

Control and visibility for everyone involved

Taken all together, these practices mean that everyone involved in a show can see exactly where the money flows from and to, and can be assured of the honesty and integrity of everybody involved in the process.

While some producers have been known to say that their books are open if the financial information for the production is published at the end of the show – or even the end of the year – that's not going to help the members of the production get involved. As well as the honesty of the system, Open Book Theatre relies on helping everyone to see the implications of creative decisions, and that means they need to be able to see what's going on throughout the course of production – not just take a look at a spreadsheet at the end.

The Open Book model, especially at the level of fringe theatre, shouldn't be seen as an attempt in any way to replace an Equity contract, which we would always recommend using. What Open Book Theatre should do, though, is provide some protection for actors working in those profit-share productions which currently are not in a position to use Equity contracts.

Running your productions on the Open Book model means more control and visibility for everyone involved, ensuring that you can be confident that things are under control – or, at least, as under control as they get.

Hopefully within ten years the question won't be, 'What is Open Book Theatre?', but rather, 'Why did we ever do things differently?'

Piers Beckley is a writer and producer. He's been a production manager, stage manager, project manager, line manager, extra, actor, web producer, copywriter, interviewer, sub-editor, video editor, and director. Writing credits include *The Treason Show*, *NewsRevue*, *Week Ending*, *Splendid*, *Spooks Interactive*, and acclaimed productions of *A Christmas Carol* and *Oliver Twist* for the Lion and Unicorn Theatre. He produced *The Just So Stories* and *Hans Christian Andersen's Fairy Tales* for Red Table at the Pleasance Theatre. You can generally find out what he's up to at his website **fatpigeons.com**.

Children's, young people's and theatre in education

Paul Harman

Work in this very large sector of employment for actors in the UK varies greatly – both in the style of theatre created and presented, and in the wages and conditions offered by employers. Anyone taking work in the field should always be clear about the aims and status of their prospective employer.

Most producing theatres offer plays for young audiences as part of a season, and Christmas shows and pantomimes are mounted by a large number of receiving theatres and commercial touring companies. Some 200 independent touring companies regularly present original theatre productions, usually in schools, reaching a total audience of at least five million annually. Smaller touring companies may operate for profit, or as profit-share partnerships. Companies which are members of ITC (Independent Theatre Council) offer pay and conditions agreed with the performers' trade union, Equity.

Reality check

There is no official agency that collects reliable statistics or regulates the quality of what is offered. Your work may never be publicly reviewed – and it can be hard and demanding. Casts are often small, and living conditions on the road are sometimes difficult. The work may involve a lot of driving (if you are over 25 and insurable) as well as humping sets in and out of vans. However, the rewards for good-quality work conscientiously presented lie in the warmth of welcome from audiences and bookers alike, and a directness and openness of audience response which is often less evident at more formal, adult-orientated theatre events. In schools, you will perform in daylight, very close to children – so it helps if you like them. They can see every blemish on you, and you can see every reaction on a hundred faces.

You will need physical stamina; the ability to play many parts convincingly; and the facility to hit a peak of performance two or more times in a day, six days a week. You may need skill in playing a musical instrument. In addition, other aptitudes may be called upon. A play may be preceded or followed by workshop activity with young people – from 'hot-seating' in character to involving children in a performance. An understanding of drama education techniques is therefore an advantage, and experience of Youth Theatre useful.

What shows?

For good economic and marketing reasons, most theatre for children presented in larger houses is based on well-known stories by established authors, or on characters from TV shows. Companies may receive financial support from official agencies to present plays on health and social issues. Plays related to the National Curriculum, such as science topics, are in great demand from schools.

Theatre in Education (TIE) is a term commonly used to mean many kinds of theatre in schools. In the strict sense, TIE implies an extended theatre event, combining performance and participatory elements and designed to engage pupils in exploring their own knowledge, feelings and attitudes. This is quite a different process from explaining how magnets work, or presenting an account of an historical event. Very few companies nowadays can afford the time and staffing needed to support real TIE, but there are many opportunities to create and present challenging educational plays on a wide variety of subjects.

Independent touring companies receiving public subsidy from Arts Councils in England, Wales, Scotland and Northern Ireland generally aim to present original, commissioned drama. A small group of writers specialises in this field, addressing personal and social topics, from fear of the dark or the break-up of families to genetics and migration. This group of companies – whose aims are primarily artistic, rather than just to entertain or deliver educational messages – find like-minded companies in 70 countries through ASSITEJ (International Association of Theatre for Children and Young People). Overseas tours and international collaborations are increasing.

Above all, don't look upon this field as an easy step towards something else. Your first experiences may well be tough, but an apprenticeship served with a supportive company will open an area of work that you can return to with growing enjoyment and professional satisfaction.

Paul Harman has worked as an actor and director in professional theatre since 1963. He joined Belgrade Theatre in Education team in 1966, headed Education work at Liverpool Everyman from 1970, and founded Merseyside Young People's Theatre Company in 1978. He was the Artistic Director of CTC Theatre, Darlington (now known as Theatre Hullabaloo) and Chair of TYA (Theatre for Young Audiences) – the UK Centre of ASSITEJ.

Children's, young people's and theatre-in-education companies

Notes:
• Some of the companies listed are members of the Independent Theatre Council (ITC) – www.itc-arts.org.
• The Criminal Records Bureau (CRB) is now called the Disclosure and Barring Service (DBS); CRB checks are now termed DBS checks.

Actionwork Creative Arts
28A High Street, Treharris CF46 6RP
tel (01934) 815163
email actionwork@gmail.com
website www.actionwork.com

Production details: Actionwork is a theatre and film company that seeks to promote empowerment and reduce bullying and violence in schools. They are committed to producing work through a number of different mediums in order to promote understanding of youth conflict and violence.

Each production consists of 3 actors and, on average, the company present 6–10 productions per year to audiences aged between 4 and 17. This equates to over 300 performances at over 150 venues across the UK, ranging from schools to community spaces, art centres and churches. Cast members are sometimes expected to lead workshops and activity sessions and it is advantageous for them to have a driving licence and some singing and dancing ability.

Casting procedures: Uses in-house casting directors and holds general auditions during September. Casting breakdowns are available through PCR and Bristol Online. Welcome CVs, headshots and articles on spec so get in touch to talk about work opportunities.

Aesop's Touring Theatre Company
The Arches, 38 The Riding, Woking, Surrey GU21 5TA
tel (01483) 724633, *mobile* 07836 731872
email info@aesopstheatre.co.uk
website www.aesopstheatre.co.uk
Facebook /aesoptheatre
X @aesoptheatre
Instagram @aesoptheatre
Director Karen Brooks

Production details: Established in 1999, a professional Theatre in Education company specialising in National Curriculum based plays for the nursery and primary age range. Tours extensively on a daily basis performing interactive plays and both associated and bespoke drama workshops. Plays are mostly performed in schools but also embrace theatres, community centres, village halls, arts centres and party venues. On average stages 300 performances each year, in 225 venues across London, in the Home Counties and further afield. 2 actors usually go on tour, plus occasionally a driver or stage manager. Applicants should be fit, versatile, all-round actors and must have their own transport to easily reach bases in Weybridge or Woking, Surrey for very early morning starts. Applicants will be expected to drive the company estate car. A current DBS is essential.

Casting procedures: Auditions are held in May and actors may write in at any time: "We reply to all enquiries."

Arty-Fact Theatre Co.
27 Mount Drive, Nantwich CW5 6JG
tel (01270) 627990
email yvonne@arty-fact.co.uk
website www.arty-fact.co.uk
Artistic Director Yvonne Peacock, *Co-Director* Brian Twiddy

Production details: Has been performing in schools since 1993, running history workshops, original plays and classics. Performs 6–7 projects annually, with an average annual total of 500–600 performances in 200–300 schools across England. In general 2–4 actors go on tour and perform to audiences aged 7–18. Physical theatre skills and a driving licence are required. Actors may be expected to lead workshops.

Casting procedures: Holds general auditions twice a year; actors are advised to write in April and July to request inclusion. Casting breakdowns are available via the website, Equity Job Information Service and Mandy. Welcomes letters (with CVs, self-tapes and photographs) from individual actors previously unknown to the company sent by post or email.

The Big House
151 Englefield Road, London N1 3LH
tel 020-7923 9955
email info@thebighouse.uk.com
website https://thebighouse.uk.com
Facebook /BigHouseTheatre
X @BigHouseTheatre

Children's, young people's and theatre-in-education companies

Instagram @_thebighouse_
Ceo & Artistic Director Maggie Norris, *Associate Directors* Chris Neels, Titash Sen, *Associate Artists* Laura Thompson, Aliaano El-Ali

Works with care leavers and young adults who are at high risk of social exclusion, providing a platform for them to participate in the making of theatre and to have their voices heard. Through the use of performance and long-term wraparound support, The Big House unleashes its members' creative potential and supports them into the next stage of their life. The Big House collaborates with exciting freelance theatre professionals to put on award-winning and critically acclaimed productions. They work to improve access to the creative industry for under-represented groups, and have launched some thriving careers in theatre, film and TV.

Box Clever Theatre Company

c/o Blackfriars Theatre, Spain Lane, Boston, Lincs. PE21 6HP
tel 0333 034 1014
email admin@boxclevertheatre.com
website www.boxclevertheatre.co.uk
Facebook /BoxCleverTheatre
X @CleverTheatre
Instagram @boxclevertheatre
Artistic Director Michael Wicherek

Production details: Founded in 1996, the company produces contemporary theatre for young people, including adaptations of classic text and issue-based, interactive performances, as well as creative workshops. A minimum of 4 major national tours are staged each year with an average annual total of approximately 600 performances in 500 different venues. The company performs to more than 55,000 young people every year. Venues include arts centres, theatres, and educational and community venues nationwide.

Casting procedures: Invites applications from actors with strong physical and movement skills. Actors wishing to audition should submit a self-tape, link to their Spotlight, recent headshot and a short biography. All self-tapes should be uploaded to Youtube or Vimeo and inserted as links into a covering email.

Cahoots NI

Cityside Retail & Leisure Park, 100–150 York Street, Belfast BT15 1WA
email info@cahootsni.com
website www.cahootsni.com
Facebook /CahootsNI
X @CahootsNI
Instagram @cahoots_ni
Artistic Director Paul Bosco Mc Eneaney

Production details: Creates theatrical magic for young audiences. Aims to expand the imagination of children, and to stimulate their artistic creativity through the visual potential of theatre and the age-old popularity of music, magic and illusion. Tours productions to arts centres and theatres both nationally and internationally, as well as schools and healthcare settings. Actors should have singing, musical instrument, physical theatre, circus and magic skills, and are sometimes required to lead workshops.

Casting procedures: Sometimes holds general auditions; actors may write at any time to request inclusion. Welcomes letters (with CVs and photographs) from actors previously unknown to the company sent by post or email, and is happy to receive showreels. Does not welcome invitations to view individual actors' websites. Actively promotes the use of inclusive casting.

C&T

5 Deansway, Worcester WR1 2JG
tel (01905) 349466
email info@candt.org
website www.candt.org
Facebook /appliedtheatre
X @c_and_t
Artistic Director Dr Paul Sutton

Production details: Founded in 1988. A theatre company incorporating performance, learning and digital media. Works in schools, colleges and universities in the UK and across Europe. Normally tours 2–3 projects each year with an average annual total of 50–100 performances. In general 2–3 actors go on tour and play to audiences aged 5–65. Dance/physical theatre skills, proficiency with computers and digital media, and a driving licence are required. Actors are also expected to lead workshops.

Casting procedures: When vacancies arise they will be advertised on their website and via the Arts Council's 'Arts Jobs' service. They are committed to building a rich, diverse team of artists.

Cwmni Theatr Arad Goch

Bath Street, Aberystwyth, Ceredigion SY23 2NN
tel (01970) 617998
email post@aradgoch.org
website https://aradgoch.cymru
Facebook /aradgoch
X @AradGoch
Artistic Director Ffion Wyn Bowen, *Business Director* Nia Wyn Evans

Production details: Founded in 1989. Main focus of work is theatre. Normally tours 5 projects each year with an average annual total of 200 performances and more than 100 different venues. Venues include schools, theatres and community venues across Wales and occasionally abroad. In general 3–6 actors go on tour and play to audiences of all ages. Singing ability, proficiency with a musical instrument, fluency in Welsh and a driving licence are required. Actors may also be expected to lead workshops. Previous productions have included elements of British Sign Language (BSL). The company has also performed works from their repertoire at various venues in Europe, and in Pakistan. Offers ITC/Equity-approved contracts and does not subscribe to the Equity Pension Scheme.

Casting procedures: Holds general auditions every year; actors requesting inclusion should send submissions (CVs and photographs) to the company by post or email. Will also accept showreels and invitations to view individual actors' websites. Will consider applications from disabled actors to play disabled characters.

Fevered Sleep
15A Old Ford Road, London E2 9PJ
mobile 07349 962243
email info@feveredsleep.co.uk
website www.feveredsleep.co.uk
Co-Artistic Directors David Harradine, Samantha Butler

Production details: Established in 1996. All of their work is made in collaboration with people outside the company, and participation is at the heart of everything they do. Their creative process as a kind of research: a way to investigate and reimagine the complex and challenging world in which we live. They invent new kinds of spaces which invite people to come together and share their experiences of things that matter. They have worked with performers, designers, artists, scientists, doctors, teachers, vets, philosophers, social workers, all sorts of other adults and many, many children.

Recent projects have appeared in London, across the UK and internationally. Sometimes they work in theatres and galleries such as The Young Vic, Sadler's Wells, Tate Britain, The Whitworth and Sydney Opera House. Sometimes they turn up in other places where people work, learn and live, most recently at Clifton Green Primary School in York, St George's Shopping Centre in Preston and Sneinton Market in Nottingham.

Casting procedures: Opportunities will be posted on our website, social media pages, and various art jobs websites. We offer Equity-approved contracts as negotiated through ITC and consider applications from disabled actors 'in line with our equal opportunities policy'.

Freshwater Theatre Company
St Margaret's House, 21 Old Ford Road, Bethnal Green, London E2 9PL
tel 020-8983 3601
email enquiry@freshwatertheatre.co.uk
website www.freshwatertheatre.co.uk
Directors Helen Wood, Carol Tagg

Production details: Established in 1996 with the aim of offering high-quality, affordable, innovative drama opportunities to primary school children and teachers, and MFL workshops for secondary schools. Runs workshops and storytelling sessions addressing a range of curriculum areas including history, geography, Shakespeare, citizenship, multicultural studies, maths, science, cross-curricular and modern foreign languages and the needs of early years pupils. Also runs drama CPD courses for teachers. Does not tour, but provides over 200 difference sessions all year round at nurseries, schools, libraries and community venues in Greater London, South West, Essex, the West Midlands conurbation and Greater Manchester. Around 60 freelance facilitators work with audiences aged 3 to 12. Relevant experience is required, and actors are expected to lead workshops.

Casting procedures: Holds general auditions once a year; actors may write in at any time. Welcomes letters (with CVs and photographs) sent by post or email, but only from experienced workshop facilitators. Does not accept showreels or invitations to view individual actors' websites.

Gazebo Theatre in Education Company
2nd Floor, Chancel Court, 2 Wellington Road, Bilston, Wolverhampton WV14 6AA
tel (01902) 296199
email info@gazebotheatre.com
Facebook /Gazebotheatre
Instagram @gazebotheatreuk
Strategic Director Pamela Cole-Hudson

Production details: Has been providing theatre, theatre in education, out of school activities, mentoring, employment, training and community arts for more than 45 years. Delivers high quality productions and programmes for audiences, schools and communities.

Casting procedures: Posts open casting calls on social media and casting platforms. Actors will require an enhanced DBS for certain roles. Submissions should be sent via email with your CV, headshot and link to showreel. They prioritise engagement of actors based in the West Midlands.

Gibber Theatre Ltd
PO Box 236, South Shields NE33 9FW
tel 0191 252 2039
email hello@wearegibber.com
website www.wearegibber.com
Facebook /wearegibber
X @wearegibber
Instagram @wearegibber
Directors Victoria Blackburn (Creative), Tim Watt (Technical)

Production details: Founded in 1999. An educational theatre company specialising in innovative multimedia performances for young people of all ages. The company has built a reputation for making a difference in education, by delivering high-quality, hard-hitting interactive performances that effect positive changes in attitudes and behaviours. On average performs 10 projects each year, with approximately 400 performances in schools across the

Children's, young people's and theatre-in-education companies 293

UK and Australia. In general, 3 actors go on tour, playing to audiences aged 5 to 16. Actors may be required to lead workshops, and should have singing and physical theatre skills as well as a driving licence.

Casting procedures: Sometimes holds general auditions; actors may write at any time. Any specific breakdowns are posted on the company website and social media. Welcomes letters (with CVs and photographs) from actors previously unknown to the company, sent by email. Accepts showreels and invitations to view individual actors' websites. Will consider applications from disabled actors to play characters with disabilities.

Half Moon Theatre
43 White Horse Road, London E1 0ND
tel 020-7709 8900
email hello@halfmoon.org.uk
website www.halfmoon.org.uk
Facebook /halfmoontheatre
X @halfmoontheatre
Instagram @halfmoon_theatre
Joint Ceos Bradley Travis (Artistic Director), Louise Allen (Executive Director)

Production details: Established in 1972, Half Moon is a local organisation with a national remit, based in Tower Hamlets, East London. The company gives young people from birth to 18 (25 for young people with physical, sensory and/or cognitive disabilities) an opportunity to experience the best in young people's theatre, both as a participant and as an audience member. Half Moon tours its own productions nationally, as well as a portfolio of work through its producing arm Half Moon Presents to venues including theatres, libraries, schools, community spaces and festivals. The portfolio covers a range of work from artists and companies drawn from all the genres of theatre, spoken word, new writing and dance, reflecting the UK's contemporary, diverse communities. Half Moon has ethical status with ITC and offers ITC/Equity-approved contracts.

Casting procedures: Casting breakdowns are available through the company's website, circulated to agents and through Spotlight. Actively encourages applications from disabled actors and promotes the use of inclusive casting.

Hopscotch Theatre Company
2nd Floor, 7 Water Row, Glasgow G51 3UW
tel 0141 440 2025
email info@hopscotchtheatre.com
website www.hopscotchtheatre.com
Producer & Co-Manager Thomas McCulloch

Production details: Founded in 1988. A Theatre in Education company touring to primary schools, theatre and community venues across Scotland.

Casting procedures: Accepts CVs, photographs and covering letter from actors previously unknown to the company sent by post or email. Will also accept showreels.

Loudmouth Education & Training
374 Moseley Road, Birmingham B12 9AT
tel 0121 446 4880
email info@loudmouth.co.uk
website www.loudmouth.co.uk
Facebook /loudmoutheducationandtraining
Instagram @loudmouthuk
Company Directors Chris Cowan, Eleanor Vale

Production details: Founded in 1994. Supplies interactive education and training programmes for young people on RSHE (Relationships, Sexual health and Health Education) and accessible training for adults to aid personal and professional development. On average we deliver over 1,000 performances in UK venues each year including schools, colleges, community venues and youth centres. Actors are expected to lead workshops and should have a full UK driving licence. Popular programmes include: *Helping Hands* – primary programme on relationships, online safety and exploitation, *Calling It Out* on sexual harassment, sexual assault and misogyny and *Working for Marcus* – an interactive theatre programme focusing on child sexual exploitation and grooming.

Casting procedures: Holds general auditions. Welcomes letters with CVs and photographs from individual actors previously unknown to the company.

M6 Theatre Company
Studio Theatre, Hamer County Primary School, Albert Royds Street, Rochdale OL16 2SU
tel (01706) 355898
email admin@m6theatre.co.uk
website https://m6theatre.co.uk
Facebook /M6Theatre
Instagram @m6theatre
Artistic Director Gilly Baskeyfield

Production details: M6 Theatre Company specalises in producing and touring high-quality, accessible and emotionally engaging theatre for young audiences. Founded in 1977, the company tours 3–5 productions each year, through approximately 300 performances/workshops. Touring venues include theatres, schools, festivals, prisons and early years settings across the North West and nationally. Cast sizes are generally 2–4; actors may be expected to participate in workshops accompanying productions.

Casting procedures: Casting opportunities are posted on their website, newsletter, and social medias.

Magic Carpet Theatre
18 Church Street, Sutton-on-Hull, East Yorkshire HU7 4TS
tel (01482) 709939
email jon@magiccarpettheatre.com
website www.magiccarpettheatre.com
Facebook /magiccarpettheatre
Artistic Director Jon Marshall

Production details: Professional touring children's theatre company presenting shows and workshops in the UK and abroad. Tours 3–4 productions annually, with around 250 performances in 250 venues including schools, arts and community venues, and festivals. In general 3 actors go on tour, playing to audiences aged 5–11. Actors may be expected to lead workshops.

Casting procedures: Does not hold general auditions; actors may write in the autumn to request inclusion. Advises actors to "ring us rather than sending CVs, etc., to see when we are casting".

Nottingham Playhouse Participation
Nottingham Playhouse, Wellington Circus, Nottingham NG1 5AF
tel 0115 947 4361
email participation@nottinghamplayhouse.co.uk
website www.nottinghamplayhouse.co.uk
Participation Producers Rob Throup, Tia Elvidge, Sarah West (Senior)

Production details: Participation creates 1–2 small-scale productions per year. These are performed mostly in East Midlands schools, with some performances in small theatre venues – including own studio at Nottingham Playhouse. Employs 3–6 actors each year, on contracts usually lasting from 6 to 12 weeks. Actors are usually multi-skilled. Singing and physical theatre are essential for many of the productions, and actors often have workshop skills and/or play a musical instrument as well. A driving licence is helpful. The company has a specialism in creating theatre for young people with profound learning difficulties and autism, and Makaton signing skills are very welcome for these productions.

Oily Cart Company
Smallwood School Annexe, Smallwood Road, London SW17 0TW
tel 020-8102 0112
email oilies@oilycart.org.uk
website https://oilycart.org.uk
Artistic Director Ellie Griffiths

Production details: One of the leading theatre companies in the UK creating highly interactive multi-sensory performances for and with the very young (6 months to 6 years) and young people (aged 3–19) with complex needs and who are on the autistic spectrum. Tours national and international venues like theatres and arts centres with early years shows, and takes its special-needs work to special schools around the UK.

Casting procedures: Casting breakdowns are available on the website and the Arts Jobs website www.artsjobs.org.uk. Offers ITC/Equity-approved contracts. Actively encourages applications from D/deaf or disabled actors and promotes the use of inclusive casting.

Onatti Productions Ltd
8 Greville House, Warwick, CV34 4UJ
tel 07377 410053
email info@onatti.co.uk
website www.onatti.co.uk
X @OnattiProdsLtd
Instagram @onattiproductions

Production details: Produces foreign-language productions performed at Primary and Secondary schools throughout the UK, France and Spain. Plays are produced in French, German, Spanish and English; all are written by the company and used as an exciting way of promoting and enhancing languages in schools. Onatti produces around 5 tours each year. Employs native foreign actors for contracts from 3 to 10 months. Actors are sourced from the UK and Europe.

Pied Piper Theatre Company
1 Lilian Place, Coxcombe Lane, Chiddingfold GU8 4QA
tel (01428) 684022
email info@piedpipertheatre.co.uk
website www.piedpipertheatre.co.uk
Patron Dame Julie Walters, *Artistic Director* Tina Williams, *Associate Director* Nicola Sangster

Production details: Founded in 1984, Pied Piper creates exciting, high quality magical plays for children, babies and toddlers. Tours to schools, theatres, libraries and arts centres in the UK, Europe, the UAE and Asia, specialising in new writing or new adaptations of favourite stories or books. Funded by Arts Council South East. ITC/Equity contracts. Ethical Member and Fair work Approved.

Pilot Theatre
The Guildhall, St Martins Courtyard, Coney Street, York YO1 9QL
tel (01904) 635755
email info@pilot-theatre.com
website www.pilot-theatre.com
Facebook /pilottheatre
X @pilot_theatre
Instagram @pilot_theatre
Artistic Director Esther Richardson, *Executive Producer* Amanda Smith

Production details: A national mid-scale touring company producing a programme of education resources for young people. Stages on average 3–6 projects annually, with 150 performances in 20 arts centres and theatres across the UK. Plays to audiences aged 11–25. Actors are sometimes expected to lead workshops.

Casting procedures: Casting breakdowns are available on the website or via Spotlight. Welcomes unsolicited CVs and photographs if submitted by email. Also accepts showreels and will consider invitations to view individual actors' websites. Offers Equity-approved contracts as negotiated through

TMA/ITC. Actively encourages applications by disabled actors and promotes the use of inclusive casting.

The Play House
2–4 Guild Close, Birmingham B16 8EL
tel 0121 265 4425
email info@theplayhouse.org.uk
website www.theplayhouse.org.uk
Facebook /theplayhouseonline
X @PlayHouseBham
Instagram @theplayhousebham
Artistic Director Jo Sadler-Lovett

Production details: Established in 1986. An educational theatre charity that uses participatory theatre and drama to stimulate and support the language and learning of children and young people. Best known for its *Language Alive!* theatre-in-education tours, which bring the curriculum to life for 3–11 year-olds and a range of issue-based projects as well as INSET and CPD for teachers. Tours an average of 10–15 projects annually, to schools, outdoor and other venues in the West Midlands. In general 1–2 actors go on tour, performing to young audiences aged 3–13. Skills required vary according to the project. Actors may be expected to lead workshops.

Casting procedures: Sometimes holds general auditions; actors should write in when these are advertised.

Playtime Theatre Company
18 Bennell's Avenue, Whitstable, Kent CT5 2HP
tel (01227) 266648
email playtime@dircon.co.uk
website www.playtimetheatre.co.uk
Artistic Director Nickolas Champion

Production details: Established in 1983 with the aim of bringing imaginative and innovative professional theatre and workshops to children and young people. Has grown to become "one of the leading children's theatre companies in the South East", and tours both nationally and internationally. Normally tours 2–4 projects each year with an average annual total of 200 performances and 100 venues. Venues include schools, arts centres, theatres, community venues and festivals. Tours have covered the South East, Yorkshire and various countries in Europe and the Middle East. In general 2–4 actors go on tour and play to targeted audiences of 5–7, 4–11, 7–11, 9–13 and 14+. Actors are expected to offer 1–2 additional skills, e.g. singing, proficiency with a musical instrument, physical theatre, puppetry or mime skills. A full driving licence is useful. Actors may also be expected to lead workshops. Also runs an extensive Drama Workshop programme in Kent. These can be an adjunct to a performance or bespoke.

Casting procedures: Holds general auditions; actors should write in August requesting inclusion. Casting breakdowns are available through the website and Mandy. Applications can be submitted via Mandy, email, post (with sae), or Equity Job Information Service. Welcomes submissions (with CVs and photographs, and a link to a Sptlight profile or Mandy page) from actors previously unknown to the company sent by post or email or via social media. Also accepts showreels and invitations to view individual actors' websites (if actor is shown performing). Advises actors to: "Be truthful. Tell us about the things that make you stand out. Tell us briefly why you want to work in children's theatre and why you like touring. Seriously consider the implications of living away from your base for months on end!" Offers non-Equity contracts. Will consider applications from disabled actors to play characters with disabilities. All actors need proof of DBS.

Polka Theatre
240 The Broadway, Wimbledon, London SW19 1SB
tel 020-8545 8320
email kate@polkatheatre.com
website https://polkatheatre.com
Facebook /polkatheatre
Instagram @polkatheatre
Artistic Director Helen Matravers, *Executive Director* Lynette Shanbury, *Senior Producer* Kate Bradshaw

Production details: Established in 1979. A theatre for children aged 0–12. 3 productions staged annually; the following skills are required from actors: singing, musical instruments, dance, puppetry and physical theatre. Offers TMA/Equity contracts.

Casting procedures: Casting breakdowns sometimes available. Actors are invited for specific shows. Links to showreels and invitations to view individual actors' websites are accepted. Actively encourages applications from disabled actors and is committed to inclusive casting. "Find out in advance what we're doing, come and visit Polka and see the work."

Q20 Events
Q20 Creative Arts Hub, Dockfield Road, Shipley, West Yorkshire BD17 7AD
tel (01274) 221360
email info@q20theatre.co.uk
website www.q20events.co.uk
Facebook /q20eventsuk
Instagram @q20events

Production details: Founded in 1970. Networks and friendships that were born in the theatre and now span over 40 years. Have developed a network of high quality performers as well as over 100 acts designed and created in-house. Supplies street theatre, indoor and outdoor events to national and international audiences.

Casting procedures: Does not hold general auditions – auditions are for specific productions only. Will accept submissions (with CVs and photographs) from actors previously unknown to the company, preferably by email. Will also accept invitations to view individual actors' websites.

Quantum Theatre

The Old Button Factory, 1–11 Bannockburn Road, Plumstead SE18 1ET
tel 020-8317 9000
email office@quantumtheatre.co.uk
website www.quantumtheatre.co.uk
Facebook /quantumtheatreuk
Bluesky @quantum.theatre.bsky.social
Artistic Directors Michael Whitmore, Jessica Selous

Established in 1993. Casting breakdowns available. Holds general auditions. Accepts submissions (with CVs and photographs) from actors previously unknown to the company – email idea. Showreels, voice-reels and invitations to view individual actors' websites are also accepted. Operates own contracts based on TMA Equity terms and conditions.

Replay Theatre Company

East Belfast Network Centre,
55 Templemore Avenue, Belfast BT5 4FP
tel 028-9045 4562
email info@replaytheatre.co.uk
website www.replaytheatre.co.uk
Facebook /replaytheatreco
X @ReplayTheatreCo
Instagram @replaytheatreco

Production details: Started from a spare bedroom in 1988, Replay has grown up to become one of the leading theatre companies in Northern Ireland. Makes innovative, quality work for everyone under the age of 19: from the tiniest babies to the oldest teenagers, for disabled children and young people, for school groups, for families, for festivals. Tours locally, nationally and internationally – from Belfast to Broadway and lots of places in between.

Seeks to ignite imaginations through leading-edge theatre adventures created especially for our audiences. Each show is shaped through creative consultation with their audience.

"We believe that theatre for young audiences has all sorts of benefits – it's fun, it asks questions and starts conversations, it encourages empathy, it creates a climate of aspiration, it speaks to children about their concerns, and it promotes imagination. And we believe that every child has the right to imagine."

Casting procedures: Replay holds open auditions on a bi-annual basis. From these auditions a list of potential actors will be registered and contacted when appropriate work becomes available. All auditioning opportunities are announced on the website and social media.

S4K International Ltd

PO Box 287, Oxted, Surrey RH8 8BX
tel (01883) 723444
email office@s4kinternational.com
website https://shakespeare4kidz.com
X @s4kidz
Instagram @s4k_international

Production details: S4K International tours easy to understand musical adaptations of Shakespeare's plays. They have 6 accessible play rotations. Playpacks have been used in thousands of schools around the world to be used as a school production. They also provide DVD's, workshops and learning resources.

Casting procedures: Holds general auditions throughout the year. Casting breakdowns are available through the website and Spotlight. Accepts submissions (with CVs and photographs) from actors previously unknown to the company sent by post or email. Will also accept showreels and invitations to view individual actors' websites.

Sky Blue Theatre Company

1 Kelling Gardens, Croydon CR0 2RP
mobile 07941 012293
email info@skybluetheatre.com
website www.skybluetheatre.com
Facebook /SkyBlueTheatreCo
X @SkyBlueTheatre
Directors John Mitton, Frances Brownlie

Production details: Founded in 2007. A London-based company touring schools, theatres and community venues with new plays, Shakespeare productions and workshops. Founded the British Theatre Challenge, an international playwriting competition. Offers script appraisals.

Casting procedures: Holds general auditions, for which breakdowns are available via Mandy and the website. Welcomes letters (with CVs and photographs) from individual actors previously unknown to the company, sent by email.

Small World Theatre

Theatr Byd Bach, Bath House Road, Cardigan, Ceredigion SA43 1JY
tel 01239 615952
email info@smallworld.org.uk
website www.smallworld.org.uk
Facebook /SmallWorldTheatre
Instagram @smallworldtheatre
Executive Director Ann Shrosbree, Artistic Director Bill Hamblett

Production details: Small World Theatre are creators giant puppets, environmental theatre, outdoor events, public art and projects. The company works bilingually (Welsh and English) and offers regular training, learning and support programmes for all ages from a near zero carbon venue in West Wales.

Casting procedures: Works with inclusive casting practices to engage freelance artists and theatre makers. It uses in-house casting and will advertise opportunities online and through its marketing channels. Submissions are by emailed CV with links to past and present projects. No unsolicited showreels.

Children's, young people's and theatre-in-education companies

Solomon Theatre Company
Station House, Station Road, Turvey,
Bedford MK43 8DB
tel (01722) 786845
email office@solomontheatre.co.uk
website www.solomontheatre.co.uk
Facebook /solomontheatre
X @SolomonTheatre
Instagram @solomontheatrecompany

Production details: Founded in 2003. Specialises in communicating messages that result in crime reduction, improved community safety and the promotion of healthy schools and healthy lifestyles. Has performed award-winning plays to tens of thousands of people in schools and community locations across the country, as well as producing films and support material for national programmes. Performs around 7 tours annually in more than 300 venues, including schools, theatres and community venues in the South West, South East, Midlands, Wales and Northern Ireland. Likes to hear from actors with a driving licence, this would be great be not essential and may be required to lead workshops.

Casting procedures: Solomon have their own casting agency where they are on the look out for talent to keep on their books. They like to see their talent in appropriate roles when touring with them whilst also searching for new roles that their actors would be perfect for. To enquire about onboarding please visit www.solomontheatre.co.uk/solomon-casting.

Splendid Productions
5 Marischal Road, London SE13 5LE
tel 020-8318 6469
email info@splendidproductions.co.uk
website www.splendidproductions.co.uk
Artistic Director Kerry Frampton

Production details: Founded in 2003. Splendid Productions are theatre makers with 20 years' experience of touring high-impact theatre. They tour creative adaptations of classic texts to schools, colleges and theatres across the UK, and this regular audience of over 15,000 per year has given them a base for establishing a strong theatrical identity creating work that appeals far beyond the education sector. Splendid also provide a range of practical drama-based workshops and teaching resources that are sold across the world. Splendid are also now cited as influential practitioners by WJEC/Eduqas, EdExcel and OCR exam boards at both GCSE and A level. Students across the UK and throughout the world are studying the company, performing its adaptations and creating their own work in the Splendid style.

The company works with schools and colleges in the UK and internationally. They have performed at the Edinburgh Festival Fringe, the National Theatre's "Watch This Space" Festival, and are programmed at numerous theatres including The Pleasance London and The Lowry in Salford. Splendid are double Olivier award-nominated for Best Family Show with *Rough Magic* (2025) and *Midsummer Mechanicals* (2023) their co-productions with The Globe.

Actors require strong physicality, some musical skills, an understanding of clown, must be politically engaged and ideally hold a driving licence.

Casting procedures: Does not hold general auditions. Actors may write during April/June to request inclusion. Welcomes emails from actors previously unknown to the company. Does not accept showreels but is happy to receive links to individual actors' websites. Will consider applications from disabled actors to play characters with disabilities. "We work hard and are very passionate about working with young people. You need to be flexible, approachable and keen to create good theatre in education. Look at our website to see what we do before getting in touch."

Theatre Online
10 Millbank Street, Dalrymple,
East Ayrshire KA6 6FE
tel 0800 158 3840
email office@theatre-online.co.uk
website www.takeawayproductions.com
Producers Lee O'Driscoll, Hazel May MacGregor

Production details: Founded in 2007 as The Take Away Theatre Company. A theatre-in-education company delivering "high-impact and dynamic drama projects in schools and other venues throughout the UK". Tours multiple projects annually with performances at schools, arts centres, theatres and community venues. Actors may be expected to lead workshops and should hold a current driving licence; singing, musical instrument, dance and physical theatre skills are an advantage.

Casting procedures: Sometimes holds general auditions; actors may write at any time to request inclusion. Casting breakdowns are available via the website, by postal application (with sae), and from Mandy and CastNet. Welcomes letters (with CVs and photographs) from individual actors previously unknown to the company, sent by post or email. Also accepts showreels and invitations to view individual actors' websites. Will consider applications from disabled actors to play characters with disabilities.

Tall Stories Theatre Company
Tall Stories Studio, 68 Holloway Road,
London N7 8JL
tel 020-8348 0080
email info@tallstories.org.uk
website www.tallstories.org.uk
Artistic Director Toby Mitchell, Executive Director Tara Wilkinson, Producer Marcus Marsh, Marketing Manager Sophie Coke-Steel, Production Coordinators Finley Adams, Eman Ansari, Creatives Programme Coordinator Fiona Bines, Creative Programmes & Production Administrator Production Administrator

Dela Ruth Hini, *Marketing Coordinator* Rachel Benson, *Marketing Assistant* Shelay Matrix, *Executive Assistant* Jennifer Njie

Production details: Tall Stories brings great stories to life for audiences of all ages. Founded in 1997, Tall Stories is a registered charity which is internationally recognised for its exciting blend of storytelling theatre, original music and comedy. Performers are expected to have good singing and devising abilities, and experience of physical theatre, and the ability to play an instrument is useful. Performers may occasionally be expected to lead workshops, with training given. Each production consists of 3–4 actors and the company undertakes an average of 3 UK tours per year as well as international touring. Venues range from small regional arts centres to West End theatres, and the company currently has a residency at the Lyric Theatre with Nimax.

Casting procedures: Tall Stories holds 3–4 workshop auditions a year for up to 70 actors. Actors can send in a CV and covering letter at any point during the year for consideration. Casting breakdowns are either posted on Spotlight, or the company invites actors that have written to them directly or via agent recommendations. Offers contracts based on ITC, UK Theatre or SOLT guidelines. Welcomes applications from disabled actors and promotes inclusive casting.

Theatr Iolo

c/o Chapter, Market Road, Canton, Cardiff CF5 1QE
tel 029 2061 3782
email hello@theatriolo.com
website www.theatriolo.com
Artistic Director Lee Lyford

Production details: Theatr Iolo has been at the forefront of creating theatre for children in Wales for nearly 40 years. We are passionate about nurturing and igniting the imagination and creativity of young minds, to help children make sense of the world around them and to find their place within it. We work with the best artists, writers and creatives, to create memorable and bold live theatre, workshops and activities in both English and Welsh. Our work for babies, children and teenagers is toured across Wales, the UK and internationally.

Casting procedures: Where possible we hold open call out auditions as well as direct bookings. Accepts submissions with CVs and photographs by email. Offers ITC/Equity approved contracts and rates of pay. We are committed to ensuring our performers are as diverse as our communities, and so we welcome applications from individuals with protected characteristics. We are particularly interested in hearing from Black, Asian, minority ethnic and disabled people to ensure that we better represent communities in Wales. We welcome applications in Welsh, English or BSL. Applicants must be UK-based and have the right to work in the UK.

Theatr na nÓg

Unit 3, Milland Road Industrial Estate, Neath SA11 1NJ
tel (01639) 641771
email drama@theatr-nanog.co.uk
website https://theatr-nanog.co.uk
Facebook /theatrnanog
Instagram @theatrnanog
Artistic Director Geinor Styles

Production details: For over 40 years, Theatr na nÓg has produced original theatre for UK and worldwide audiences from our home in Neath, South Wales. The organisation thrives on bringing to life inspirational stories of Welsh characters who achieve the extraordinary.

Works in both Welsh and English. The theatre embraces the bilingual nature of Wales, celebrating both languages and encouraging and supporting those who are learning Welsh. Our mission is to give people of all ages and backgrounds the opportunity to experience the magic of live theatre.

Casting procedures: Although most casting goes through Spotlight and casting agents, Theatr na nÓg also holds general auditions (depending on the project); actors may write at any time requesting inclusion. Accepts submissions (with CVs and photographs) from actors previously unknown to the company sent by post or email. Will also accept invitations to view individual actors' websites.

Theatre-Rites

Unit 3, Energy Centre, Bowling Green Walk, London N1 6AL
tel 020-7164 6196
email info@theatre-rites.co.uk
website www.theatre-rites.co.uk
Facebook /TheatreRites
X @TheatreRites
Instagram @theatrerites
Artistic Director Sue Buckmaster

Production details: Committed to creating challenging productions which push the boundaries of theatrical form by experimenting to combine different artistic disciplines. Highly imaginative visual experiences for families to share together. Plays for under 5's and improves production standards in theatre for 5-11 year olds. Actors are sometimes expected to lead workshops; singing, musical instrument, dance, physical theatre and puppetry skills may all be advantageous, depending on the project.

Casting procedures: Casting breakdowns are available via the website. Welcomes letters (with CVs and photographs) from actors previously unknown to the company. Also welcomes showreels and invitations to view individual actors' websites. Offers Equity-approved contracts as negotiated through ITC. Promotes the use of inclusive casting. Multi-disciplined performers are always very welcome.

Children's, young people's and theatre-in-education companies

Theatre Centre
1 Town Barn Road, Crawley RH11 7XG
tel (01293) 304377
email admin@theatre-centre.co.uk
website www.theatre-centre.co.uk
Facebook /Theatre_Centre
X @TCLive
Instagram @theatrecentre
Artistic Director Rob Eleanor Manners, *Executive Director* Emma Rees

Production details: Theatre Centre brings world-class theatre straight into the heart of schools. Productions present big ideas and difficult questions that can help young audiences make sense of a complex and changing world. Uses the power of stories, writing and performance to support students and teachers in their learning across a range of subjects to build confidence and aspirations.

"Our vision is that children and young people are empowered in their activism and leadership through theatre, using their voices and ideas to make change in themselves and the world around them."

Offers ITC/Equity and ITC/WGBB contracts. Subscribes to the Equity Pension Scheme.

Casting procedures: Casting breakdowns are available through the website, Spotlight and agents.

Theatre Hullabaloo
The Hullabaloo, Borough Road, Darlington DL1 1SG
tel (01325) 405680
email info@theatrehullabaloo.org.uk
website www.theatrehullabaloo.org.uk
Facebook /TheatreHullabaloo
Instagram @theatrehullabaloo
Artistic Producer Miranda Thain

Production details: Founded in 1979. A specialist producer of theatre for young audiences based in specialist venues for children and families. Tours regionally, nationally and internationally for audiences aged 0 to 16 years, with an emphasis on theatre for early years.

Casting procedures: General auditions are sometimes held and casting opportunities are advertised mainly through social media. Welcomes letters (with CVs and photographs) from individual actors previously unknown to the company but who have a demonstrabletrack record in TYA, sent by post or email. Also accepts showreels and invitations to view individual actors' websites. Offers Equity-approved contracts as negotiated through ITC.

Theatre Porto
(formerly Action Transport Theatre)
Whitby Hall, Stanney Lane, Ellesmere Port, Cheshire CH65 6QY
tel 0151 357 2120
email info@theatreporto.org
website https://theatreporto.org/
Facebook /theatreporto
X @theatreporto
Instagram @theatreporto
Artistic Director Nina Hajiyianni

Production details: Stages 3 projects annually, with around 60 performances in 10 venues including schools, arts centres, theatres and community venues across the UK. Plays to family (5+) and adult audiences. Incoming actors should have singing, musical instrument and physical theatre skills, and may be expected to lead workshops.

Casting procedures: Casting opportunities are posted on their website with a brief of relevant information. Actors are required to submit a CV and headshot via email. ITC/Equity agreements are available. Actively encourages applications from artists from the global majority and also those from underrepresented communities. All artists are DBS checked.

Travelling Light Theatre Company
Wellspring Settlement, 43 Ducie Road, Barton Hill, Bristol BS5 0AX
tel 07305 015081
email info@travellinglighttheatre.org.uk
website www.travellinglighttheatre.org.uk
Facebook /TravellingLightTheatre
X @tl_theatre
Instagram @tl_theatre
Artistic Director Lizzy Stephens, *Ceo* Dienka Hines

Production details: Since 1984 the company has produced work that inspires creativity and imagintion in young audiences using live music, visual and physical performance in its work. Its artistic programme enables thousands of children each year to experience the joy of stories told through theatre, as both creators and audience members. Produces on average one or 2 tours each year. Venues include theatres, arts centres, community venues, local schools and festivals across the UK. Target audiences vary from babies to adult. Casts are usually one to 3 actors.

Singing ability, proficiency with a musical instrument and physical theatre skills are often required; most plays are devised with the cast.

Casting procedures: Castings are listed on the company website, Arts Jobs and Disability Arts Online. Speculative CVs are not accepted.

Unicorn Theatre
147 Tooley Street, London SE1 2HZ
tel 020-7645 0500
email stagedoor@unicorntheatre.com
website www.unicorntheatre.com
Facebook /unicorntheatre
X @Unicorn_Theatre
Instagram @unicorn_theatre

Production details: The Unicorn Theatre was founded by Caryl Jenner as a touring company in 1947, with a commitment to giving children a valuable and often first-ever experience of quality theatre, and a philosophy that "the best of theatre for children should be judged on the same high standards of writing, directing, acting and design as the best of adult theatre".

Today, the Unicorn is the national home of theatre for children and young people. It presents and tours to around 80,000 people every year, with a catalogue of 20 shows. It is an Arts Council National Portfolio Organisation. Offers TMA and ITC/Equity-approved contracts and subscribes to the Equity Pension Scheme.

Casting procedures: Generally by invitation via agent, but will read CVs and photographs from actors previously unknown to the company if sent by email.

Wizard Theatre Ltd
Blenheim Villa, Burr Street, Harwell,
Oxon OX11 0DT
tel 0800 583 2373
email info@wizardtheatre.co.uk
website www.wizardtheatre.co.uk
Facebook /WizardTheatre
X @WizardTheatre
Artistic Director Leon Hamilton, *Associate Producer* Oliver Gray, *Production Manager* Richard Tall

Production details: Established in 2002, received the 2024 and 2025 Prestige Award for TIE Company of the Year. Performs in schools, theatres and conferences across the country. Message-based shows and workshops are commissioned annually. Working with various organisations, and delivering ongoing drama therapy classes in schools with their Power of Drama and Power of Reading programmes. Their winter show tours in theatres.

Stages 10+ projects annually, with more than 800 performances in 400 venues across London, the Home counties and beyond. In general 2–4 actors go on tour, playing to audiences aged 4–18. Actors may be required to lead workshops. Good singing, musical instrument, driving and stage combat skills are useful. They are always looking for excellent facilitators and drama teachers. The Power of Drama Project also always requires goood actor/teachers to join the team.

Casting procedures: Sometimes holds general auditions; actors are welcome to write in at any time. Casting breakdowns are available via Spotlight, Mandy and on the Equity Job Information Service. Welcomes unsolicited approaches by actors/facilitators/teachers by post or email. Also accepts showreels and will consider invitations to view individual actors' websites.

Young Shakespeare Company
213 Fox Lane, Southgate, London N13 4BB
tel 020-8368 4828
email youngshakespeare@mac.com
website https://youngshakespeare.org.uk
X @youngshakeco
Instagram @youngshakeco
Artistic Directors Christopher Geelan, Sarah Gordon

Production details: One of the longest-established and most respected educational theatre companies in the UK. Currently performs Shakespeare to more than 50,000 young people each year, working in schools and theatres across UK and overseas. 4 actors per show perform to audiences aged 6–12 years.

Casting procedures: Casting breakdowns are available via Spotlight link. Also welcomes emails from individual actors previously unknown to the company that includes a CV and a detailed cover letter explaining why you would like to work with the company.

Festivals

These are populated by all kinds of companies listed in previous sections. Some are hired in by a festival's organisers; others hire space in order to participate. The latter predominate at the most famous festival of all – the Edinburgh Festival Fringe. Hiring a space in order to participate in a festival can be a passport to enormous fun, networking opportunities and the chance to see other productions but it is important to budget carefully and sensibly and acknowledge the chances of making a profit or securing a transfer are small.

UMBRELLA ORGANISATIONS

British Arts Festivals Association (BAFA)
mobile 07756 309844
email admin@artsfestivals.co.uk
website www.artsfestivals.co.uk
Facebook /BritArtsFests
X @BritArtsFests

Provides information and a professional network for the festivals movement in the UK, working to promote the profile and status of arts festivals. As well as providing a festival directory on the website, BAFA produces an advance festivals press pack each January and May and is the British hub for the prestigious European Festivals Association. Members have the opportunity to attend BAFA conferences, access to partnership deals and discounts and vital festival resources. Membership is open to all arts festivals in the UK and associate membership to other arts organisations, universities, students and agents.

The European Festivals Association
Saincteletteesquare 17, 1000 Brussels, Belgium
tel +32 (0)2 644 48 00
email info@efa-aef.eu
website www.efa-aef.eu/en/home
Facebook /EuropeanFestivalsAssociation
X @EFAfestivals
Instagram @europeanfestivalsassociation

The European Festivals Association (EFA) is a community dedicated to the arts, artists and audiences. Established in 1952, it is the umbrella organisation for festivals across Europe and beyond. The EFA connects festival-makers, including individuals, organisations and stakeholders, to enrich the festival landscape in Europe and beyond. It provides knowledge and training, and facilitates connections and collaborations.

UK ARTS FESTIVALS

Arundel Festival
Registered Office: Carpenter Box, Dukes Court, Bognor Road, Chichester PO19 8FX
email secretary@arundelfestival.co.uk
website www.arundelfestival.co.uk
Facebook /ArundelFestival
Instagram @arundelfestival

For 10 days each August, the market town of Arundel is host to a multi-arts festival which began in 1977. Street theatre and a festival Fringe are regular features, as are concerts, exhibitions, fireworks and jazz. The festival culminates in an open-air production of a Shakespeare play in the grounds of Arundel Castle. Each production is led by a cast of experienced professional actors, and extended with members of the local community, who work with the professionals throughout the 6-week rehearsal period.

Brighton Festival
email info@brightonfestival.org
website www.brightonfestival.org
Facebook /brightonfestival
X @brightfest
Instagram @brightonfestival

Founded in 1967 and the largest curated annual arts festival in England. For 3 weeks in May, a celebration of music, theatre, dance, circus, art, film, literature, debate, outdoor and community events takes place in familiar and unusual locations across Brighton & Hove and further afield.

Brighton Fringe
tel (01273) 764900
email info@brightonfringe.org
website www.brightonfringe.org
Facebook /brightonfringefestival
Instagram @brightonfringe

Running alongside Brighton Festival, Brighton Fringe has been running for 20 years, and is the biggest in England, showcasing a variety of artforms and activities. The Fringe is open access meaning that anyone can pay the registration fee, find a venue and put on an event. Applicants for the Fringe should first read the 'Participant Info Pack' document available on the website, and then register online.

Canterbury Festival
Festival House, 8 Orange Street, Canterbury, Kent CT1 2JA
tel (01227) 452853

email info@canterburyfestival.co.uk
website https://canterburyfestival.co.uk/
Facebook /CanterburyFest
Instagram @canterburyfest

One of the UKs longest established arts festivals, the Canterbury Festival takes place in the Autumn. Classical concerts in Canterbury Cathedral, world music of all kinds plus circus and cabaret in the beautiful Spiegeltent, the programme also includes theatre, dance, science, talks, walks and exhibitions. Spanning school half-term, there is a wide range of events for families and young people. With over 200 events in the fortnight, the Festival is the highlight of Canterbury's cultural calendar – and a marvellous time to visit the historic city. Festival guests in the past have included Van Morrison, Sir Bryn Terfel and the Tallis Scholars, while the year-round public engagement programme works with more than 2,000 young people annually.

Dumfries and Galloway Arts Festival
tel (01387) 259627
email hello@artsdg.org.uk
website https://dgartsfestival.org.uk
Chief Executive Simon Hart

Established in 1979. Scotland's largest perfoming Arts Festival – runs for 8 days at the end of May. The festival programme includes a diverse programme of world class events covering music, contemporary dance, theatre, comedy and spoken word. Events take place in a wide range of venues throughout the region including arts centres, pubs, theatres and village halls.

Also runs Dumfries and Galloway Arts Live, established in 2016. A network of venues, promoters and performing artists set up to bring quality live events to venues throughout Dumfries and Galloway year-round. Organised by the Dumfries and Galloway Arts Festival team.

Edinburgh Festival Fringe Society
The Fringe Office, 180 High Street,
Edinburgh EH1 1QS
tel 0131 226 0026
email info@edfringe.com
email artists@edfringe.com
website www.edfringe.com
Facebook /edfringe
Bluesky @edfringe.bsky.social
Instagram @edfringe

The Fringe began in 1947, when 8 theatre companies decided to perform uninvited alongside the first Edinburgh International Festival. It now hosts more than 3,000 shows in more than 250 venues across Edinburgh each August. The Fringe remains entirely open-access and anyone who wants to bring a show can do so.

The Fringe Society was formed in 1959 to help artists bring work to the festival, assist audiences to navigate the programme and to celebrate the Fringe and its values all over the world. You can contact the Society year round with general questions and advice on how to take part.

Edinburgh International Festival
The Hub, Castlehill, Edinburgh EH1 2NE
tel 0131 473 2000
email performing@eif.co.uk
website www.eif.co.uk
Facebook /EdintFest
X @edintfest
Instagram @edintfest
Festival Director Nicola Benedetti

Founded in 1947, the Edinburgh International Festival is an annual event held over 3 weeks in August, using venues across the city. With music, opera, classical music and dance, the festival is recognised as one of the world's most important celebrations of the performing arts. Also offers a programme of year-round education and outreach activities. Performance at the Edinburgh International Festival is by invitation only, issued by the Festival Director.

Fierce Festival
103 Argent Centre, 60 Frederick Street,
Birmingham B1 3HS
email contact@wearefierce.org
website https://wearefierce.org/
Artistic Director Clayton Lee

Has an international reputation as one of the UK's most daring contemporary arts festivals. Includes performances of live art in theatres, bars, clubs, galleries and public spaces across Birmingham and the West Midlands. The festival takes place in October with smaller events and artist development opportnuities throughout the year.

Greenwich and Docklands International Festival (GDIF)
10 Munroe Way, Design District,
Greenwich Peninsula SE10 0EJ
tel 020-8305 1818
email admin@festival.org
website https://festival.org/
X @gdifestival
Instagram @gdifestival
Artistic Director Bradley Hemmings MBE

GDIF programmes multi-disciplinary arts events around East London each summer. As well as programming large-scale, visually impressive work, the festival places emphasis on educational projects and participatory arts.

HighTide
24A St John Street, London EC1M 4AY
tel (01473) 459200
email hello@hightide.org.uk
website https://hightide.org.uk
Artistic Director Titilola Dawudu

HighTide Theatre develops productions and programmes that engage diverse communities with new theatre writing in the East of England and beyond. It is renowned for identifying and developing talented new playwrights, showcasing the future of British theatre.

Hotbed: Cambridge New Writing Theatre Festival

Cambridge Junction, Clifton Way, Cambridge CB1 7GX
tel (01223) 403361
email patrick@menagerie.uk.com
website menagerie.uk.com/hotbed-festival
Facebook /MenagerieTheatreCompany
Instagram @menagerietheatreco

Menagerie Theatre Company and Cambridge Junction (www.junction.co.uk) join forces to present Hotbed: Cambridge New Writing Theatre Festival. Events include new full-length plays, short commissions from the Young Writers' Workshop, guest productions and a selection of workshops, talks, masterclasses and seminars also included in the programme.

All opportunities are advertised on the Menagerie website. For further information about the next Hotbed and how to get involved contact Paul Bourne at **paul@menagerie.uk.com**.

Lichfield Festival

Donegal House, Lichfield, Staffs. WS13 6NE
tel (01543) 306271
email info@lichfieldfestival.org
website https://lichfieldfestival.org
Facebook /lichfieldfestival
X @lichfieldfest
Instagram @lichfieldfest
Festival Director Damian Thantrey

Annual 11-day multi-arts festival in July, Literature Festival in March, Chamber Music Festival in October, plus seasonal events that include Christmas concerts.

London International Festival of Theatre (LIFT)

Toynbee Studios, 28 Commercial Street, London E1 6AB
tel 020-7968 6800
email info@liftfestival.com
website www.liftfestival.com
Facebook /liftfestival
X @liftfestival
Instagram @liftfestival
Interim Executive Director Jo Gooding

Started in 1981, LIFT is London's international festival of theatre. Every 2 years, LIFT brings bold and unforgettable performances to London, turning the city into a stage. Alongside their biennial festival,

Festivals 303

LIFT connects international artists to locals. LIFT supports the development of projects and ideas that have the power to transform the industry and drive conversation around important topics. LIFT is known for bringing risky and daring theatre to London, whether that's art that tackles difficult themes, or performances that disrupt our understanding of what theatre is or can be.

Manchester International Festival (MIF)

Aviva Studios, Water Street, Manchester M3 4JQ
tel 0161 817 4500
email info@factoryinternational.org
website https://factoryinternational.org/about/manchester-international-festival/
Facebook /factoryinternational
X @factoryintl
Instagram @factory_international
Artistic Director John McGrath, *Executive Director* Sheena Wrigley

Manchester International Festival (MIF) is a biennial festival of original, new work, created by a wide range of major international artists. The first festival took place in June–July 2007; the next edition will take place in July 2027. Strengthening Manchester's reputation as a leading cultural city, the Festival features work reflecting the spectrum of performing arts, visual arts and popular culture. MIF supports a year-round Creative Engagement programme, bringing opportunities for people from all backgrounds, ages and from all corners of the city. MIF also run Aviva Studios, the world-class cultural space in the heart of Manchester. It commissions, presents and produces a year-round programme, featuring new work from the world's greatest artists and offering a space to make, explore and experiment.

The Minack Theatre

Porthcurno, Penzance, Cornwall TR19 6JU
tel (01736) 810181
email info@minack.com
website www.minack.com

The Minack Theatre stages a full programme of live performances from Easter to October, including music, drama, musicals and opera. The Minack supports Cornish artists but also welcomes national and regional touring companies.

National Student Drama Festival (NSDF)

LCB Depot, 31 Rutland Street, Leicester LE1 1RE
mobile 07539 768087
email info@nsdf.org.uk
website www.nsdf.org.uk
Facebook /NSDFest
X @NSDFest
Instagram @nsdfest
Director Nathan Powell, *Executive Director* Kiki Kollimada, *Producer* Lotty Holder

304 Theatre

For over 60 years, NSDF has been at the heart of the British Theatre. NSDF selects and presents work created by young people and empowers and inspires young talent – providing masterclasses, workshops and year-round practical advice from experienced professionals including a core team of selectors.

The NSDF has a remarkable alumni including Olivia Vinall, Ruth Wilson, Alex Jennings, Lucy Prebble, Simon Russell Beale, Meera Syal, Kate Mellor, Steve Pemberton and many, many more.

For all information, please visit the website. NSDF is an Arts Council England National Portfolio Organisation.

Totally Thames
(Formerly Thames Festival)
tel 020-7928 8998
email contact@thamesfestival.org
website https://thamesfestivaltrust.org/
Facebook /ThamesFestivalTrust
X @thamesfesttrust
Instagram @thamesfestivaltrust
Director Adrian Evans

A free, month-long season of river and river-related events along the whole 43 miles of the River Thames riverfront in London, from Hampton Court Bridge in the west to the Dartford Crossing in the east. Using the river as a powerful unifying symbol for the whole of London, one of the festival's main aims is to enable more collaborations between artists and community groups. Throughout September, it programmes events such as night carnivals, fireworks spectaculars, mass choirs, music stages, a range of participatory activities, and both artist-led and river-orientated events.

Role-play companies

The precarity of the acting profession has long seen actors deploying their skills in other arenas to subsidise their earnings on stage and screen. Increasingly the corporate world has recognised the value actors bring in skills ranging from public speaking to presentation style, body language to voice training. Role-play companies and practitioners use a range of techniques from forum theatre to hot-seating to train corporate employees in a range of settings. An actor might find themselves playing a patient in a training programme for Junior Doctors, or an angry customer in a conflict management exercise for bank managers.

The established companies – mostly created by actors – have built up a great deal of expertise in this world and do not take on new 'role-players' lightly. It is therefore important to research each individual company's modus operandi before contacting them. If you can find a way in, it's a more exciting, developmental and lucrative outlet for your skills than working in a bar or a call centre.

Activation
The Old Coach House, 83 Dennis Road,
East Molesey KT8 9EE
tel 020-8783 9494, *mobile* 07966 299026
email paul@activation.co.uk
website www.activation.co.uk
Director Paul Gilmore

Company's work: A leading provider of bespoke interactive training. Services include forum theatre, role-play, scriptwriting and performance and the design and delivery of training programmes. Incoming actors are trained by the company, according to the requirements of the project. Strong acting and listening skills are required of all the actors. Cients include: the NHS, UK Parliament and Mclaren Mercedes.

Recruitment procedures: Periodically extends its actor-base, often by word-of-mouth but also posting announcements online. Welcomes letters (with CVs and photographs) from actors previously unknown to the company if sent by post, but not by email. Does not welcome showreels, but is happy to receive invitations to view individuals' websites. Will consider applications from disabled actors to play characters with disabilities.

Actors in Industry Ltd (Aii Training)
Trident House, 46–48 Webber Street,
London SE1 8QW
tel 020-4586 3787
email enquiries@actorsinindustry.com
website www.actorsinindustry.com
Director Jeff Heaver

Company's work: Established in 1992. "We are the foremost experiential training company in the UK, using role-play, facilitation and interactive training and coaching to create meaningful skills improvement and behavioural change for individuals and organisations." Requires incoming recruits to possess a good knowledge of business, giving feedback, and the ability to understand the perspective of delegates on training programmes. Provides training for associates in the form of an induction, group workshops and one-to-one sessions. Recent clients include: PWC, Amey, Linklaters, Astellas, Barclays, Lilly, Kraft, Johnson & Johnson, RBS, IBM, Jones Lang Lasalle, Mercer and Ernst & Young.

Recruitment procedures: Interviews twice yearly, and recruits via emailed CVs (business and role playing) and covering letter. Advises recruits to be honest about experience; over-elaboration will be discovered very quickly. When submitting files with an application, please make sure that all file names contain the name of the applicant, e.g. NOT roleplay CV but John Smith roleplay CV.

Adhoc Actors
47 Newton Street, Manchester M1 1FT
tel 0161 2360 618
email info@adhocactors.co.uk
website www.adhocactors.co.uk
Facebook /adhocActors
X @AdhocActors
Instagram @adhoc_actors
Artistic Director Guy Hepworth

Company's work: Founded in 2005, Adhoc Actors have worked mainly in the public and private sector business. They have provided training, writing, drama, entertainment and educational workshops to a number of different organisations. The company requires its actors and performers to have excellent feedback skills and experience of working in corporate role-play, as well as being skilled at improvisation, and comfortable with interactive/immersive performance. However, there is a thorough briefing before any job is undertaken. Clients include: Merseyside Police, Penguin Random House, Macmillan Cancer Support, Next and Arrow Global (Breathe POD).

Recruitment procedures: Uses in-house casting directors but does not hold general auditions. Casting breakdowns can be available from the Equity JIS and Mandy websites. Welcomes letters (with CVs and photographs) from individual actors previously unknown to the company and unsolicited CVs with photographs, sent by email. Will consider invitations to view individual actors' websites and performance notices. Also welcomes showreels. Will consider applications from disabled actors to play characters with disabilities.

AKT Productions
tel 020-7620 0843
email info@aktproductions.co.uk
website www.aktproductions.co.uk
Managing Director Marc Bolton

Company's work: Established in 1996. Provider of theatre-based learning and development resources. Recognised as market leaders who operate globally at the highest and most challenging levels of private and public sector activity, right through to the front line.

Recruitment procedures: Holds regular auditions and will accept submissions (with CVs and photographs) from actors previously unknown to the company. Prefers CVs and photographs sent via email. Invitations to view individual actors' websites are also accepted. Applications from disabled actors are welcomed.

Apropos Productions Ltd
tel 020-7062 9198
email info@aproposltd.net
website www.aproposltd.net
Director Paul DuBois

Company's work: Established in 2004. First feature film completes post-production August 2015, *Dark Signal* (executive producer Neil Marshall). Short films: *The Juror*, *X-Why* and *Cocktail*. Web series: award-winning web series: *A Quick Fortune* and *Le Method* (2016). Script events include *My German Roots are Showing* at the Arcola Theatre, London, starring Miriam Margolyes.

Provides training for local, national and international clients. Key focus is on Organisational Behaviour. Training is provided for incoming actors. Corporate experience is useful but not essential. Actor-base is extended annually through agents, the website and Equity Job Information Service. Clients include: SKANKSA, Sony Computer Entertainment, House of Commons, UBM and the Discovery Network.

Recruitment procedures: Accepts submissions (with CVs and photographs) from actors previously unknown to the company. Disabled actors regularly form part of its teams and are actively encouraged to apply.

Michael Browne Associates Ltd (MBA Roleplay)
The Cloisters, 168c Station Road, Lower Stondon, Beds. SG16 6JQ
tel (01462) 812482
email hello@mba-roleplay.co.uk
website www.mba-roleplay.co.uk
Directors Michael Browne, Angie Smith

Company's work: Established in 1997. Holds an extensive database of more than 750 professional, corporate actors. Works closely with clients to cast, devise, manage and interpret events and assessments to inform, challenge, develop, assess and train. Will provide training for incoming actors on particular clients' material as and when required. Actors should have professional drama training and experience in the corporate world using role-play for assessment, training and development. Clients include IOPC, Met Police, the MoD, KPMG, Nationwide, the NHS, CBRE, Local Government, Barclays, HSBC and the Open University.

Recruitment procedures: Periodically extends its actor-base when required "via interview/workshop after personal application and recommendation". Welcomes letters (with CVs and photographs) from actors previously unknown to the company, sent by email. Accepts showreels and invitations to view individual actors' websites. Will consider applications from disabled actors for specific projects.

CentreStage Partnership
South Hill Park Arts Centre, Ringmead, Bracknell, Berkshire RG12 7PA
tel (01344) 304305
email info@cstage.co.uk
website https://cstage.co.uk
Contacts Pippa Shepherd, Julian Hirst

Company's work: A leading development consultancy specialising in the use of drama to enhance learning.

Recruitment procedures: In the first instance, actors should send a CV outlining their acting and business experience, along with a recent photograph and covering letter, to Pippa Shepherd via info@cstage.co.uk.

Dramanon
Twickenham Studios, The Barons, Twickenham TW1 2AW
tel 020-8607 8977
email melanie@dramanon.co.uk
website https://dramanon.co.uk
Director Steven Brough

Company's work: Dramanon is a leading provider of live training using actors in creative scenarios and storytelling. Works in the training room, conference space and for larger immersive programmes of work. Stories are bespoke and written for each buisness area, opeation or the requirements of the message being shared.

Dramanon uses a blend of forum theatre and role-play bespoke to each client to enable the most productive training experience. Works with mainly blue chip business clients and on high profile projects but also supports smaller enterprises and charities and have a broad range of clients across the UK, Europe and beyond.

Dramanon also designs and produces white-board animatied film, audio podcasts and film for drama, documentary, re-contsruction and marketing purposes.

Instant Wit
mobile 07808 960826
email info@instantwit.co.uk
website www.instantwit.co.uk
Facebook /InstantWit
X @InstantWit
Instagram @instantwitimprov
Directors Chris Grimes, Stephanie Weston

Company's work: "A quick-fire comedy improvisation show packed full of sketches, gags, songs, surreal situations, flying packets of 'Instant Whip' and prizes! The show is completely improvised and shaped around audience suggestions. Because of this, each show is unique and takes the form that you – the audience – want it to take."

Maynard Leigh Associates (MLA)
Impact Hub Euston, 1 Triton Square,
London NW1 3DX
tel 020-7033 2370
email info@maynardleigh.co.uk
website www.maynardleigh.co.uk
Instagram @maynard_leigh

Company's work: Associates are required to be expert workshop leaders with an interest in the psychological aspects of human potential development. Clients include: Aviva, DHL, Hewlett Packard, Ernst & Young, BBC TV, Barclays and Visa.

Recruitment procedures: All new consultants and leaders go through a rigorous and lengthy process, regardless of their professional experience. It can take up to 18 months of participation in Maynard Leigh activities before being allowed to represent the consultancy with clients. There are regular personal development sessions. As Maynard Leigh invests heavily in its existing associates, its pace of growth is limited. Professional actors with a good working knowledge of business and corporate life should submit their details by email.

Role-play companies 307

Pearlcatchers Ltd
c/o 635 Bath Road, Slough Berk. SL1 6AE
tel (01753) 670187
email hello@pearlcatchers.co.uk
website www.pearlcatchers.co.uk
Director Sharon M. Young, *Customer Operations Manager* Lucy Foster

Company's work: A training consultancy empowering people, teams and organisations to change, learn and grow. They offer a fresh approach to learning, developing successful and emotionally intelligent people, relationships, organisations and leaders through bespoke, blended, accelerated learning.

Provides actors with opportunities for role play, forum theatre, hot seating, thought bubble and business scenarios.

Requires business skills/knowledge and prior experience in corporate role play and forum theatre. Clients include: UK Emergency Services, BP, Tesco, London Underground, local councils, BUPA and the RAF.

Recruitment procedures: Extends its actor base every 2 years, recruiting via *The Stage*. Welcomes letters (with CVs and photographs) from individual actors previously unknown to the company email. Also accepts showreels and invitations to view individual actors' websites. Considers applications from all actors, no exclusions.

The Performance Business
78 Oatlands Drive, Weybridge, Surrey KT13 9HT
tel (01932) 888885
email info@theperformance.biz
website https://theperformance.biz/
Directors Michael McNulty, Lucy Windsor

Company's work: Provides incoming actors with personal assessments and one-to-one coaching. Requires excellent feedback skills and experience of working in business. Clients include: organisations in the financial, pharmaceutical, engineering, and manufacturing and public sectors.

Recruitment procedures: Periodically extends its actor-base, recruiting via the website and CastNet. Welcomes letters (with CVs and photographs) from individual actors previously unknown to the company, sent by post or email. Will consider invitations to view individual actors' websites. Actively encourages applications from disabled actors and promotes the use of inclusive casting.

Role-Players NGA Ltd
mobile 07984 471512
email info@role-players.co.uk
website www.role-players.co.uk
Proprietor Nick Gasson

Company's work: Established in 2003. Provider of professional actors as corporate role-players to the industry, in both the private and public sector. Incoming actors are expected to have experience of corporate role-play. Clients include accountancy and law firms, property development companies and management consultancies.

Recruitment procedures: Applications are accepted throughout the year, but mostly through personal recommendation from the company's existing actor list, and through potential actors applying having seen their website. Prefers CVs and photographs sent via email and does accept unsolicitied CVs and photographs via the same method. Invitations to view individual actors' websites are also accepted.

Roleplay UK
tel 0333 121 3003
email actors@roleplayuk.com
website https://roleplayuk.com/
Managing Director James Larter, *Chief Strategy Officer* Felicity Hall

Company's work: Established in 1994. Drama-led communications and training. Provides training for incoming actors in the form of workshops.

Recruitment procedures: Books currently full, but regularly posts jobs for specific projects on mandy.com. Does not welcome unsolicited approaches by individuals unknown to the company, but actively encourages applications from disabled actors and promotes the use of inclusive training.

SimPatiCo UK Ltd
63 Petworth Road, London N12 9HE
mobile 07759 085132
email amandajband@hotmail.com
website www.simpaticouk.net
Managing Director Amanda Band

Company's work: Founded in 2003. Supplies experienced role players specialising in communication skills for training purposes and examinations. Focuses on medical and veterinary role-play. Assists organisations in developing and delivering best practice training through a range of roleplay scenarios, from complex programmes to simple communication skills workshops, enabling individuals to achieve their full potential.

Theatre Without Walls
Hillsborough, County Down BT26 6AS
tel 028-928 2125
email hello@theatrewithoutwalls.org
website www.theatrewithoutwalls.org
Directors Genevieve Swift, Jason Parkes

Company's work: Established in 2002. Award-winning producing theatre company with an active training/corporate wing, working in the public and private sector. Also produces television and corporate films. Clients include: National Trust, Gloucestershire Local Authority, Apollo, BBC and The Prince's Trust. Training is provided for incoming actors in the form of workshops and rehearsals in forum, role-play and interactive drama. Incoming actors must have good improvisational skills.

Recruitment procedures: Actors are recruited through agents and Equity Job Information Service. Disabled actors regularly form part of the team and are actively encouraged to apply. See also the company's entry under *Middle- and smaller-scale companies* on page 229.

Media
Introduction

The last few decades have seen incredibly rapid advancements in recording technology, hardware, digital media and most recently AI. There has been enormous growth in the independent production sector, serving the principal broadcasting companies and streaming platforms; this in turn has led to an increase in the number of independent companies employing actors. (Companies whose output does not include drama have not been included in the listings.)

Most film and television companies use casting directors (mainly freelance), and it's usually a waste of time writing to anyone else unless you have a personal contact. It is worth remembering that many companies do work for businesses – training and promotional films, for instance.

Student films may be a somewhat poor relation to Hollywood blockbusters in terms of pay and exposure but they can provide useful experiences, be a good addition to your CV, and have the potential to lead onto something that is better paid and more prestigious. Extracts from such a film could also be useful for your showreel.

Casting for radio is much more akin to that for theatre, although often without the use of a casting director.

Listings in this section:
- *Independent film, video and TV production companies, page 316*
- *Film schools, page 324*
- *Radio and audiobook companies, page 329*
- *Media festivals, page 332*

Auditioning for camera
Nancy Bishop

'The camera is your friend' is the first lesson I teach in my courses on auditioning for camera. The ironic truth is that many theatre actors who feel perfectly comfortable performing in front of thousands of people become timid in front of a small piece of digital equipment. The antidote to camera fear is to practise on screen as often as possible. Own a camera, use it, grow comfortable with the lens, love it – and it will love you back.

What's the difference between auditioning for film and auditioning for theatre?

In theatre, you are often asked to perform a prepared monologue, while in film, you read from 'sides' (short scenes from the actual screenplay.) In theatre, you can find yourself reading with another actor, while in film you might end up reading with a talentless casting director.

Actors are deluded in thinking that if they were actually on location, with all of the props and sets, it would be easier than acting in an empty casting studio. ("If I had the actual laser gun then I could act it so much better.") But acting in a dull audition room or in front of a green screen in a film studio is not so different from acting during Shakespeare's time. The Globe didn't have elaborate sets, which is why characters say obvious lines such as, "Well, this is the Forest of Arden." There was no forest on stage ... just a wooden O. So the actors had to use their imagination.

It's the same now. When you're doing a horror film, the oozy monster doesn't perform with you. He's created by a computer geek later on. *Actors must use their imagination.* This includes imagining that you have a brilliant scene partner to play off, even when you only have a casting assistant in a bad sweater.

What can I expect at an on-camera audition?
Slating and introduction

Your first audition is likely to be a screening process, or 'pre-read'. Often the director will not be there, so the casting director will need to 'slate' – which means slipping a name card in front of camera and asking you to turn both profiles. Yes, it feels like a prison shot, and every casting director has heard that joke before.

Next the casting director may ask you to introduce yourself, for the benefit of the absent director. For some reason, this trips up a lot of actors. They feel perfectly comfortable playing some one *else*, but when they have to be *themselves* for a few minutes they stumble around. The introduction, however, may be the most interesting part for the casters. We want to see who you *really* are, your personality. It's the alchemy between the actor's unique energy and the screenwriter's written word that creates the character.

It's best to have some kind of pithy introduction semi-rehearsed so that you don't corpse for camera when the casting director asks you to introduce yourself. Remember that it's all about spin. This is your opportunity to sell yourself for the role. Be enthusiastic and be yourself. Here are a few examples of good and poor introductions.

If you already have professional credits:

- Poor spin: "I had a tiny role on *Inglorious Bastards*. I waited on set forever and I think my line didn't make it to the final cut."
- Good spin: "I had a great time working with Quentin Tarantino on my last project."

  If you are new to the business:
- Poor spin: "I haven't really played any big roles before. I'm just out of drama school."
- Good spin: "I'm just out of drama school and can't wait to land my first job. I really like this project. I've always wanted to work on a World War II film."

These are the kind of personal details you might include in an introduction (such things humanise you; it's interesting to us if you're a mother, if you like to travel, etc.):
- "I just celebrated my daughter's third birthday."
- "I just got back from a fascinating trip to India."
- "I work part time in a homeless shelter."

It's better not to include such comments as "I'm working as a temp in an office right now and I hate it." This tells us that you're not really a professional. True, you might have to work a day job to support yourself, but you don't have to emphasise it.

How do I best play to camera?

You should ask the camera operator about frame size. It's a perfectly professional question. What does the camera see? Is it wide, medium or close? If it's a close-up, you're wasting your energy with hand gestures. Be careful not to pop out of frame, and calibrate the performance in your face, where the camera will detect inner monologue.

Calibrating a performance to frame size can be one of the trickiest parts of screen acting. Often the actor's fear is that the camera will amplify their performance so that they will appear to be over-acting. In my screen-acting courses, actors sometimes become discouraged when they watch the play-back and realise that they haven't hit the right level; they see themselves either popping out of the screen, or plagued by the opposite problem which I call *dead face* – when a performance is boring and dead. Nice house but nobody is home.

Theatre actors often fall prey to dead face because great screen actors create the illusion, to the unstudied eye, that they are 'doing nothing'. It's a great misnomer. In a close-up, the actor becomes a talking head, and the only thing that matters is the information communicated by the face. Therefore the performance may have to be even intensified in the eyes and face. The antidote to dead face is an active and ever-changing inner monologue. The camera photographs thought and it loves to watch a character thinking.

This is true of acting in any medium, but in screen acting, listening and reacting become more than half of the performance. One of the most common mistakes in an audition is when an actor reads along with his or her scene partner's lines rather than truly listening and reacting in the moment.

Where do I look? Directly into camera?

The answer is no. Unless specifically asked, you only look directly into camera when you are introducing yourself. There are exceptions, like in the mock-documentary genre. In the US TV series *Modern Family*, for example, the characters speak directly into camera as if questioned by an imaginary interviewer. It's the modern form of Shakespeare's soliloquy; the character speaks his/her thoughts out loud to the audience. That is the exception, not the rule. Most film and TV genres still assume the removal of the fourth-wall type of realism, wherein the characters go about their lives, not knowing that they are being observed.

The best place to focus is somewhere near the lens. This will give the viewer a three-quarter view of your face. You want to be as generous as possible about playing towards the camera. We won't cast you if we can't see you. Placing an off-screen reference on the floor will only bring your eyes down. Hopefully the casting director will help you with this by placing the reader directly next to the lens. But if not, you can focus on a fixed point, rather than on the reader. Know your best side for photography and play accordingly.

How can I prepare for a project when I only have a few pages of text?

You can ask for information. The casting director should provide a summary, but if they don't, then ask for information or ask to read the script. Sometimes it's available and sometimes not, but a question never hurts. If you can't get the script, then you need to make decisions about the pages according to the information you have. If the script wasn't available to you, then it wasn't available to other actors either, and you have an even playing field. Start with the basic Stanislavski questions:

- *Who am I?*
- *Where am I?*
- *Who am I talking to?*
- *What do I want?*

I also encourage actors to add:

- *What are the stakes?* Make the stakes as high as possible, and this will drive the dynamics of the performance.

Answering these questions is one of the basic tenets of acting, yet many actors (even experienced ones) forget to do this for an audition, and they find themselves floating in a sea of too many possibilities. Anchor yourself in the 'W' questions; this will guide your performance.

In order for actors to develop their onscreen skills and comfort level, they must practise. Screen acting is like driving a car. No one gets in a car the first time and just drives. You have to learn how to give the car gas and ease up on the clutch so that the car doesn't jerk. This is why I encourage actors to own a camera, practise with it and take on-camera courses. Smartphones with cameras are these days equally useful for practice and self-filmed auditions.

Last of all, I always advise actors to have fun and enjoy the process. If you're enjoying yourself, then so will we, the casters. Love the camera – it will love you back.

"Good actors are good because of the things they can tell us without talking." Cedric Hardwicke

Nancy Bishop csa, is an award-winning casting director, who works internationally from offices in London, Los Angeles and Prague. She is a founding member, and former President, of the Casting Society of America's (CSA) European branch. With over 100 major feature film and television projects among her credits, Nancy has cast hundreds of actors throughout Europe, the UK and the US. Nancy has been retained as casting director by dozens of major screen producers and directors, including Sacha Baron Cohen on *Borat: Subsequent Moviefilm*, for which she won a CSA Artios Award for best casting of a comedy. Other credits include working with Brad Bird (*Mission Impossible IV*), Bong Joon Ho (*Snowpiercer*), and Matthew Weiner (*The Romanoffs*). She also was nominated for an Emmy Award for her casting work on *Anne Frank: The Whole Story*, ABC/Disney Studios.

Owning the frame: grit, growth and giving back

Zates Atour, actor
Interview by Aileen Gonsalves

Zates Atour is a TV and film actor known for roles in Young Wallander, The Witcher, Den of Thieves 2 *and* The Lord of the Rings: The Rings of Power. *He is founder of Film Club, a screen acting course that demystifies performing for the camera, and founder of Palikuku, a film company he set up over 10 years ago, which created the award-winning spoof horror film* When the Screaming Starts.

So, Zates, I met you back in 2011 during your time at ArtsEd doing your MA in Acting. But I'm curious – how did you even get there?

My journey into acting, or rather into storytelling, began long before that, even if I didn't know it at the time. I went to WAC (Weekend Arts College) in Belsize Park. This little place that turned out to be quite pivotal in my life. That's where I met Che Walker. Che cast me in a production back in 2003. I'd never done anything like it before, but the moment I stepped onto that stage, something clicked. I was all in. Ready to dive headfirst into the world of acting.

At the end of that performance, an agent approached me, said they saw something in me and wanted to sign me. I was buzzing. On the way home, I told my dad, "This is what I want to do. I want to act."

And he said something that would shape the next several years of my life. He said, "Help me build a home back in Morocco first. Once we've done that, you can do whatever you want." He was serious. And I understood it. Family duty came first. So, I did exactly that. I focused on the goal, tossed the agent's number in the bin, and walked away from that world – for a while.

Life moved fast after that. I became an entrepreneur. I built businesses. I chased financial independence. In many ways, business became my second love – second only to storytelling and creativity.

But then something started to stir again. My soul was making noise. You know that voice inside, the one that whispers, *"You know what you're really meant to be doing ..."*? I couldn't ignore it anymore. So I picked up the phone and called Che.

After all that time?

Yep – seven, maybe eight years later. I said, "Che, I want to go for it now." And he just said, "You're too old." And deep down, I had this fear, this internal narrative that said, "People like me don't go to drama school." I grew up in a world that felt miles away from Shakespeare, monologues, and black-box theatres. But the world was starting to change. By 2009, the gates of drama schools were opening up a bit more. Slowly. Imperfectly. But, still, it felt like something was shifting.

Che invited me to see him the next day. We dove straight into the classics – working on monologues, scenes, structure, presence. He told me honestly, "You're not getting into RADA or Bristol Old Vic, but you might have a good shot at LAMDA or ArtsEd."

And he was right. It was like a prophecy. I auditioned for all four. Got offers from two – LAMDA and ArtsEd. I landed at ArtsEd, and everything changed.

I remember you didn't audition with me, but I remember hearing about you – especially your love for Meisner.
Exactly. I was told about the Meisner-based work, and I thought, *"A year of that? That's my kind of training"*. So I jumped in.

I showed up to this beautiful little church space, surrounded by 30 other actors. That group and you became family. I still hold those memories so close. The sweat, the breakthroughs, the breakdowns. That environment cracked me open and let the real work begin.

So, did you always know you wanted to act? Or did that come later?
Here's the truth: I never dreamed of being an actor. That wasn't the fantasy. Where I come from, no one tells you it's even an option. You're a product of your environment. And mine was about one thing: making money. Hustling. Providing. Surviving.

There was this constant energy of pressure. And I thrived under it. My dad was the same. He worked full-time in a hospital but had ten side hustles. That was normal for us – juggling three or four jobs at once, just to keep things moving. I respected that. Still do.

I loved the entrepreneurial grind because it gave me control. Freedom. But deep down, I had something else brewing – imagination. I just didn't know what to do with it. What I really wanted was to tell stories. Acting just happened to be the doorway that opened first.

So storytelling was always the core?
Always. If I'm honest, I think if I'd known what I know now, I might've skipped the whole acting thing and gone straight to writing, directing, producing – just making. But then again, I wouldn't have met you. I wouldn't have had those lessons. *Palikuku, Film Club* …You can't connect the dots looking forward. Only in hindsight.

Absolutely. You mentioned Palikuku. What was that all about?
It started at drama school. I realised the film equipment we were using – camera, mic, lights – wasn't out of reach. My business brain kicked in. I did the research, bought the gear myself, and called Connor, Jared, Stuart – told them to come over.

They walked into my flat and saw boxes everywhere. I said, "This is everything we need to make our own films. I don't know how yet – but we'll figure it out." And we did. We wrote, shot, edited – just made things. That raw creativity, right after graduating from ArtsEd, was magic.

What grounded you in that process?
Your method – *The Gonsalves Method*. "Seeing clearly, responding truthfully," and the Five Conditions. Those ideas shaped everything. Those principles became the foundation for everything we built. Without that clarity, nothing else would've worked. That was pure gold.

Why did it matter so much?
Because it made me feel like a kid again – free to create. My only job was to imagine. That's the heart of everything I do. Acting demands truth and vulnerability. We paired that with craft – filmmaking, writing, collaboration. That's when Palikuku really began.

And now?

Now it's about giving back. *Film Club* is a huge part of my life. I meet people trying to break into the industry and just tell them the truth.

What truth?

That this game isn't for everyone. And that's okay. One of the first things I tell people is: *"Don't do it. Quit now"*. Not because they're not talented. But because talent isn't enough. You need grit. You need obsession. You need a "why" that's bigger than ego or validation.

So I lay it all out – what this path takes, what it costs, mentally, emotionally, spiritually. And if someone hears all that and still says, "Yeah, I'm in," then we're off to the races. If not, that's cool too. Walk your path.

So how do people get good, in your opinion?

Find a master. Someone who really knows their craft. Then go to them, with humility, and say, *"Please teach me"*.

And be prepared to pay for it. Their time, their knowledge – it's valuable. But it will fast-track your growth. Perseverance and discipline will carry you through the rest.

Earlier you said, "People like me don't go to drama school." What did you mean by that?

Where I'm from, everything's a hustle. It's survival mode. My parents weren't born in the UK. English wasn't their first – or even second – language. They couldn't help me navigate a career in the arts. That just wasn't in the blueprint.

They'd say, "Tesco's is a great job," and they meant it. And honestly, it *is* – if that's your calling. But for someone like me, bursting with ideas and imagination, being told to stick to a script like that … it didn't make sense.

So we made our own script. We spoke differently. We thought differently. And we had to teach ourselves how to articulate our value to a world that didn't always understand us. And even now, when I'm with my boys from back in the day, I snap right back to that 90s street energy. That's home.

And what's your perspective now – after all these years?

It's a marathon. No finish line. That realisation changed everything for me. I used to be frantic – chasing, pushing, always chasing the next win. Now, I've slowed down. I'm cruising at a height that feels sustainable. That serves my mind, my soul, my relationships.

There's a peace in knowing this isn't about getting somewhere. It's about being here. Creating. Connecting. Contributing.

That comes with age, doesn't it? You learn to choose your rhythm.

100%. You realise success isn't just about credits and accolades. It's about love. Food. Walks in the park. Laughs with people you care about.

And above all, knowing your *why*. I'm not doing this just for me. If I were, I probably would've stopped years ago. I do it for everyone who's still in the bubble, who hasn't seen another way yet. I want to light that path.

Beautifully said. Thank you.

Thank you. Always.

Aileen Gonsalves is a theatre director, actor, writer and creator of the Gonsalves Method – a pioneering approach to actor training taught in drama schools and universities in many countries.

Independent film, video and TV production companies

Companies in this field start up and close down all the time, and it is very important to have a proper contract if offered work with an independent. If in doubt, check with Equity.

ALL3 Media
Berkshire House, 168–173 High Holborn, London WC1V 7AA
tel 020-7845 4377
email info@all3media.com
website https://all3media.com

The group comprises more than 50 production companies. Specialises in high-quality film and television, including BAFTA award-winning *Gogglebox* and *Call the Midwife*, and Oscar award-winning *1917*.

Baby Cow
1 Television Centre, 101 Wood Lane, London W12 7FA
tel 020-3696 5200
email info@babycow.co.uk
website www.babycow.co.uk
Facebook /BabyCowProductions
X @babycowLtd
Instagram @babycow_productions

Production details: Founded by Steve Coogan and Henry Normal in 1999. Baby Cow have created audience-winning comedies such as *Gavin & Stacey*, *Nighty Night*, *The Mighty Boosh* and *Moone Boy*. Their film output includes *Stan & Ollie*, *Alan Partridge: Alpha Papa* and the Oscar- and Golden Globe- nominated *Philomena*.

Submissions policy: Does not accept any unsolicited material and cannot return any unsolicited material.

Casting procedures: Uses freelance casting directors. Does not welcome unsolicited approaches but may view individual actors' online videos.

Big Red Button Ltd
PO Box 75733, London E17 0TY
email hello@bigredbutton.tv
website www.bigredbutton.tv
Key personnel John Burns, Pier Van Tijn

Production details: Established in 2002. Specialises in short films and music videos. Works in live action, puppetry and animation. Also employs actors in drama, comedy and commercials.

Casting procedures: Holds general auditions and actors can write to request inclusion at anytime. Casting breakdowns are available on the website.

Does not offer Equity-approved contracts. Rarely has the opportunity to cast disabled actors.

Big Talk Productions
26 Nassau Street, London W1W 7QA
tel 020-7255 1131
email info@bigtalkproductions.com
website https://bigtalkproductions.com
Facebook /bigtalk
X @bigtalk
Instagram @bigtalk
CEO (Executive) Kenton Allen, *Head of Production* Caroline Richards

Production details: Big Talk Productions Ltd is a British film and television production company founded by Nira Park in 1994. Big Talk was acquired by ITV Studios in 2013.

Recent films: *The Brothers Grimsby*, *Baby Driver* and *The Kid Who Would Be King*. Recent TV: *Raised by Wolves*, *Houdini and Doyle*, *Mum*, *Cold Feet* and *Defending the Guilty*.

Work experience: As an ITV company, offers work experience placements at Big Talk to enable people to experience what it is like to work in a production company and to learn more about the film and television industry in general. Most placements take place at the office on Nassau Street where participants get involved with development tasks, shadow runners and assist them with their varied task load. Provides the opportunity to learn how things operate, meet people in the industry and work on a variety of projects.

Submissions policy: Does not accept unsolicited material. For administrative reasons, does not respond to individual submissions. **Anything sent to Big Talk Productions will not be read and will be destroyed.**

Blueprint Pictures
4th Floor, 32–36 Great Portland Street, London W1W 8QX
tel 020-7580 6915
email info@blueprintpictures.com
website www.blueprintpictures.com
Chairmen Graham Broadbent, Peter Czernin, *Managing Director* Diarmuid McKeown, *Head of Production* Emma Mager, *Head of Film* Ben Knight

Independent film, video and TV production companies

Production details: Founded in 2005 by producers Graham Broadbent and Pete Czernin, Blueprint Pictures develops and produces film and television drama for international audiences.

Submissions: Does not read unsolicited screenplays unless submitted via a recognised agent.

Known for the film: *In Bruges* (2008). Recent films: *The Banshees of Inisherin* (2022), *Lady Chatterley's Lover* (2022), *All of Us Strangers* (2024), *The Beautiful Game* (2024) and *Wicked Little Letters* (2024). Recent TV: *The Outcast* (2015), *The Last Dragonslayer*(2016), *A Very English Scandal* (2018), *A Very British Scandal* (2021) and *A Very Royal Scandal* (2024).

Cactus TV Ltd
1 St Luke's Avenue, London SW4 7LG
tel 020-7091 4900
email reception.cactus@cactustv.co.uk
website www.cactustv.co.uk
Joint Managing Directors Amanda Ross, Simon Ross

Specalises in broad-based entertainment, features and chat shows. Since its inception in 1994, Cactus has produced more than 40 distinct titles in the UK for 10 different channels.

Calamity Films
16 Carlisle Street, London W1D 3BT
email info@calamityfilms.com
website www.calamityfilms.co.uk
X @calamityfilmsuk
Producer David Livingstone

Production details: Develops and produces feature films and television. David Livingstone was President of Worldwide Marketing and Distribution at both Universal Pictures International and Working Title Films. Emily Bray joined Calamity Films after 4 years at Independent Talent Group in the agency's Literary Department. She started out in the industry freelancing in development and production and worked on various music videos, short films and features. Does not accept unsolicited submissions.

Films and TV include: *Pride* (2014), *Last Christmas* (2019), *Judy* (2019) and *Brassic* (2019–22).

Carnival Film & Television Limited
101 St Martin's Lane, London, WC2N 4AZ
tel 020-3618 6600
email info@carnivalfilms.co.uk
website www.carnivalfilms.co.uk
Executive Chairman Gareth Neame, *Managing Director* Nigel Marchant

Production details: Founded in 1978. Part of Universal International Studios, a division of Universal Studio Group. Works mainly in TV production, creating drama with a popular and international feel and employs actors for drama. Commissioned by UK broadcasters including BBC, ITV, Sky One and Netflix. Has received various prestigious awards/nominations, including Oscars, BAFTAs, Golden Globes and Emmys. Recent credits include: *The Last Kingdom: Seven Kings Must Die* and *Downton Abbey: A New Era*.

Casting procedures: Uses freelance casting directors, does not deal directly with actors. Offers PACT/Equity contracts. Will consider casting disabled actors to play disabled characters.

The Comedy Unit
Unit D, Glasgow North Trading Estate,
24 Craigmont Street, Glasgow G20 9BT
tel 0141 674 8222
email info@comedyunit.co.uk
website www.comedyunit.co.uk
X @ComedyUnit
Managing Director Rab Christie

Produces some of Scotland's best-loved television and radio shows, as well as a range of programmes for transmission across network and satellite channels. Formed in 1996 and since 2016 has been a member of the Banijay Group. Does not accept unsolicited scripts.

Company Pictures
4th Floor, 93 Southwark Street, London SE1 0HX
tel 020-7380 3900
email enquiries@companypictures.co.uk
website www.companypictures.co.uk
X @CoPicsTV
Ceo Michele Buck

Does not accept unsolicited submissions. Proposals should be submitted through agents.

Cowboy Films
48 Russell Square, London WC1B 4JP
tel 020-3962 4421
email info@cowboyfilms.co.uk
website www.cowboyfilms.co.uk
Managing Director Charles Steel

An independent production company making feature films, documentaries and television drama.

Films and TV include: *The Last King of Scotland* (2006, *Marley* (2012), *How I Live Now* (2013), *Bill* (2015) and *Top Boy* (2011–23).

Don Productions (London) Ltd
Studio 116, Netil House, 1 Westgate Street,
London E8 3RL
tel 020-3095 9425
email london@donproductions.com
website www.donproductions.com

Japanese/English bilingual TV and media production company based in London and Dubai. Produces commercials, corporate films and TV documentary programmes. Clients include: Japan Broadcasting Corporation, Nippon Television and Channel 4.

Ecosse Films Ltd

Brigade House, 8 Parsons Green, London SW6 4TN
tel 020-7371 0290
email info@ecossefilms.com
website www.ecossefilms.com
Director Douglas Rae, *Head of Drama* Robert Bernstein

Founded in 1988. Works mainly in TV and feature film production and employs actors in dramas and comedies. Recent credits include: *Royal Night Out* (2015), *Hampstead* (2017) and *The Great Escaper* (2023). Uses freelance casting directors. Welcomes CVs but is unable to respond to every submission due to the high volume. Does not accept unsolicited scripts.

Extra Digit Ltd

Kings House, 101–135 Kings Road, Brentwood, Essex CM14 4DR
website www.extradigit.com
X @extradigit

Production details: Founded in 2002. Works in film and television and employs actors in drama, comedy and documentary. Recent credits include: *Somewhere*, starring Hugh Cornwell, and *Life is a Circus*, starring Steve Ryland.

Casting procedures: Occasionally uses freelance casting directors. Welcomes approaches by actors by post only (please see website for postal contact details), with CVs and photographs. Will accept showreels if these do not require a response. Has no equal opportunities policy: "If you can do the part better than anyone else, you get the job – regardless." Please do NOT contact by phone or email, use current contact details from the 'Recruitment' section on the website.

Eye Film

17–19 St George's Street, Norwich NR3 1AB
tel (01603) 441174
email info@eyefilm.co.uk
website www.eyefilm.co.uk
Managing Director Charlie Gauvain

Independent producers of film and TV drama and documentaries. Also produces corporate, commercial, education and training material. Clients include: BBC, ITV1/Anglia, Channel 4, Five and First Take Films. Recent credits include: *Life on the High Wire* (2021) and *My Life Saving Dog* (2023).

Focus Productions Ltd

4 Leopold Road, Bristol BS6 5BS
tel 0117 230 9726
email info@focusproductions.co.uk
website https://focusproductions.co.uk
Director Martin Weitz

Production details: Established 1993. Specialises in TV features and documentaries. Employs actors in TV, radio and film; also for presentation and voice-overs. Notable credits include: *The Real Rain Man*, *Painting the Mind*, *The Piano Player* and *Vivaldi's Fantasia*.

Casting procedures: Holds general auditions. Actors are advised to apply requesting inclusion at any time. Casting breakdowns are available by telephone. Welcomes letters (with CVs and photograph) from actors previously unknown to the company if sent by post, but not by email. Also accepts invitations to view individual actors' websites. Offers Equity-approved contracts. Rarely has the opportunity to cast disabled actors. Proposals for new formats and ideas should be sent to **info@focusproductions.co.uk**.

Fremantle

1 Stephen Street, London W1T 1AL
tel 020-7691 6000
website https://fremantle.com
Facebook /FremantleHQ
X @FremantleHQ
Instagram @fremantle

Production details: Fremantle is one of the largest creators, producers and distributors of scripted and unscripted content in the world. From *Got Talent* to *My Brilliant Friend*, *Family Feud* to *The Young Pope*, *Idols* to *American Gods* and *The Price is Right* to *Neighbours*. Fremantle has an international network of production teams, companies and labels in 27 territories including UFA (Germany), Wildside (Italy), Abot-Hameiri (Israel), Miso Film (Denmark, Sweden and Norway), Original Productions (USA) and Easy Tiger (Australia).

Fremantle produces in excess of 12,000 hours of original programming, rolls out more than 600 formats and airs 400 programmes a year worldwide. Also distributes over 40,000 hours of content in more than 180 territories.

Handstand Productions

13 Hope Street, Liverpool L1 9BQ
tel 0151 708 7441
website www.handstand-uk.eu
Creative Director & Producer Han Duijvendak, *Producer* Nicholas Stanley, *Director of Photography* Jane Duckworth

Established in 1993. Produces documentary TV series, promotional and informational films, and training films. Also creates film-making programmes for schools and youth centres. Rarely requires actors, so please do not submit anything unless a specific casting requirement has been made available on the website.

Hartswood Films

3A Paradise Road, Richmond, Surrey TW9 1RX
tel 020-3668 3060

email films.tv@hartswoodfilms.co.uk
website www.hartswoodfilms.co.uk
Facebook /HartswoodFilms
X @hartswoodfilms
Instagram @hartswoodfilms

Production details: Founded by former agent and producer Beryl Vertue. It has created hit series such as *Sherlock*, *Men Behaving Badly* and *Coupling*. Steven Moffat is a director of the company.

Casting process: Uses freelance casting directors. Does not welcome unsolicited approaches but may view individual actors' online videos.

Submissions Policy: Cannot accept or respond to unsolicited scripts, programme ideas or similar creative material.

Hat Trick Productions Ltd
33 Oval Road, London NW1 7EA
tel 020-7184 7777
email reception@hattrick.com
website www.hattrick.co.uk
X @HatTrickProd
Instagram @hattrickprod
Managing Director Jimmy Mulville

Founded in 1986, Hat Trick Productions is one of the UK's most successful independent production companies working in situation and drama comedy series and light entertainment shows. Recent credits include: *Derry Girls*; *Have I Got News for You*; and *Mastermind*.

Heavy Entertainment Ltd
4 Goodge Place, London W1T 4SB
tel 020-7494 1000
email info@heavy-entertainment.com
website www.heavy-entertainment.com

Production details: Established in 1992. Audio, video and web producers. Areas of work include drama, corporate, commercials, audiobooks and actor showreels (audio and video). Offers Equity-approved contracts.

Casting procedures: Welcomes showreels and voicereels (via agents only), and invitations to view individual actors' websites.

Hurricane Films Ltd
13 Hope Street, Liverpool L1 9BQ
mobile 07889 437186
website www.hurricanefilms.net
Facebook /HurricaneFilms
X @hurricanefilms

Founded in 2000, Hurricane Films develop feature films, feature documentaries and TV series. Credits include: *Of Time and the City* (dir. Terence Davies), *Sunset Song* (dir. Terence Davies), *A Quiet Passion* (dir. Terence Davies), *Unsung Hero: The Jack Jones Story* (dir. Solon Papadopoulos), *A Prayer Before Dawn* (dir. Jean Stephane Sauvaire) and *My Letter to the World* (dir. Solon Papadopoulos). BAFTA-nominated twice; awarded six Royal Television Awards.

Left Bank Pictures
3rd Floor, Clareville House, 26–27 Oxendon Street, London, SW1Y 4EL
tel 020-7759 4600
email info@leftbankpictures.co.uk
website www.leftbankpictures.co.uk
Chief Executive Andy Harries

An independent television and film production company founded in July 2007 by Andy Harries and Marigo Kehoe, and named Best Independent Production Company at the Broadcast Awards in 2011. "We continue to work with the UK's leading writing, directing and onscreen talent to produce bold, innovative feature films, television dramas and cutting-edge comedy. We also pride ourselves on nurturing and championing exciting new talent set to create the hits of tomorrow."

MARV Films
11 Portland Mews, London W1F 8JL
website www.marv.com
Instagram @marv_films
Executive Matthew Vaughn

Production details: Matthew Vaughn is best known for starting his career working as a producer for the Guy Ritchie films: *Lock, Stock and Two Smoking Barrels*, *Snatch* and *Swept Away*. Notable films include: *Stardust* (2007), *Kingsmen: The Secret Service* (2014), *Eddie the Eagle* (2015,; *Rocketman* (2019), *The King's Man* (2021) and *Argylle* (2024).

Casting procedures: Accepts handwritten enquiries only.

Maya Vision International Ltd
tel 020-7796 4842
email info@mayavisionint.com
website www.mayavisionint.com
Facebook /mayavisionint
X @mayavision
Founder & Managing Director Rebecca, *Company Director & Producer* Sally Thomas Dobbs, *Writer* Michael Wood

Maya Vision International is an independent film and television production company, founded in 1983. Since then it has won many awards, and become renowned for making work of the highest quality.

Specialises in producing original, landmark documentaries, features and drama for film and television; has developed a unique style, making some of history's great stories accessible to a wider public.

Working alongside many broadcasters and funders, including the BBC, ITV, Channel 4, Five, PBS, UK Film Council, BFI and Arts Council England. Maya Vision's acclaimed catalogue has been screened in more than 140 territories worldwide.

Merman (and Mermade)
4 Hop Yard Studios, 72 Borough High Street,
London SE1 1XF
tel 020-7846 0650
email info@hellomerman.com
website https://hellomerman.com/
Facebook /hellomerman
X @HelloHerman
Instagram @hellomerman

Production details: Merman is a globally-renowned production and entertainment company working across the UK and US, with a reputation for scripting and producing award-winning TV and film. Founded in 2014 by award-winning duo Sharon Horgan and Clelia Mountford, Merman Television has won multiple accolades under their leadership, including numerous BAFTAs and Emmys. Mermade is its digitally focused sister company, specialising in the creation of content of all shapes and sizes, funded by and for social and streaming platforms, brands and publishers.

Casting process: Uses freelance casting directors. Does not welcome unsolicited approaches but may view individual actors' online videos.

Submissions policy: Does not accept any unsolicited material and cannot return any unsolicited material.

Met Film Production
22 Golden Square London W1F 9AD
tel 020-8280 9127
email assistant@metfilm.co.uk
website www.metfilmproduction.co.uk
Facebook /MetFilmProductions
X @metfilmprod
Managing Director Jonny Persey, *Director* Jerry Rothwell, *Producers* Stewart le Maréchal, Al Morrow, Anna Mohr-Pietsch

Enterprise dedicated to the development and production of feature films and series for national and international audiences.

Recent credits include: *23 Walks, Swimming with Men, Misha and the Wolves, The Reason I Jump* and *Last Breath*.

Neal Street Productions
26–28 Neal Street, London WC2H 9QQ
tel 020-7240 8890
email post@nealstreetproductions.com
website www.nealstreetproductions.com
Co-Directors Sam Mendes, Pippa Harris, Nicolas Brown, *Executive Producers* Julie Pastor, Harriet Spencer, *Head of Development* Lola Oliyide

Production details: Founded in 2003, Neal Street is one of the UK's most respected production companies, producing film, television and theatre for over 20 years. Neal Street makes distinctive, popular, award winning projects on both sides of the Atlantic and is an All3Media company.

Known for the films *1917* (2019) and *Empire of Light* (2023).

Recent TV includes: *Penny Dreadful* (2016–20), *Britannia* (2017–21), *Informer* (2018), *The Franchise* (2024) and *Call the Midwife* (2012–26).

Submissions: Does not accept unsolicited material and will only accept material via an agent.

NFD Productions Ltd
21 Low Street, South Milford, Leeds LS25 5AR
tel (01997) 681949
email info@nfdproductions.com
website https://nfdproductions.com
Director Alyson Connew

Production details: Production company producing feature films specialising in 3D, children and teenage programmes specialising in 3D, and commercials.

Casting procedures: Please send CVs to alyson@northernfilmanddrrama.com. Requires a minimum of four featured/named roles in either a film or TV series.

Number 9 Films
8–9 Stephen Mews, London W1T 1AF
tel 020-7323 4060
email info@number9films.co.uk
website https://number9films.co.uk
X @number9films
Producers Stephen Woolley, Elizabeth Karlsen

Production details: Number 9 Films is a British independent film production company co-founded in 2002 by producers Elizabeth Karlsen and Stephen Woolley, after a long collaboration at both Palace Pictures and Scala Productions. They are best known for *The Crying Game* (1992); *Interview with the Vampire* (1994); *Michael Collins* (1996); and *Made in Dagenham* (2010). In 2005, the company was awarded one of the much sought-after Slate Development Funding schemes by the UK Film Council. The company has gone on to establish itself as one of the UK's leading independent production companies, forging relationships with a wide range of talent in the UK, across Europe and in the US. The company aims to produce between two and three films a year.

Recent films: *The Limehouse Golem* (2016), *Their Finest* (2016), *On Chesil Beach* (2017), *Colette* (2018), *Mothering Sunday* (2021) and *Living* (2022).

Objective Fiction
89 Southwark Street, London SE1 0HX
tel 020-7202 2300
email info@objectivefiction.com
website www.objectivefiction.com
X @Objective_Fic
Instagram @objective_fiction

Production details: Based in the UK and US, Objective Media Group is home to nine production companies. Objective Fiction specialises in original scripted content with a strong track record in comedy as well as drama. Shows include *Peep Show*, *Feel Good*, *The Gold*, *The Larkins*, *Fresh Meat*, *Toast of London*, *Eric*, *Ernie & Me*, *Year of the Rabbit*, *GameFace* and *Witless*.

Casting process: Uses freelance casting directors. Does not welcome unsolicited approaches but may view individual actors' online videos.

Submissions policy: Does not accept unsolicited scripts, except via an agent.

Park Village Ltd
1 Park Village East, Regents Park, London NW1 7PX
tel 020-7387 8077
email hello@parkvillage.co.uk
website www.parkvillage.co.uk
Managing Director Tom Webb, *Managing Partners* Adam Booth, Jack Webb, *Head of Production* Angelica Riccardi

Established in 1972. Film and photography production company working mainly in commercials, music videos and marketing content. Casting is done by freelance casting directors. Recent credits include commercials for Woolmark, Moneybox, Wise, Cazoo; photography for Channel 4; and music videos for Joel Corry. Actors are employed under Equity-approved contracts. Applications from disabled actors to play disabled characters, and diversity of all kinds, encouraged.

Pinball London Ltd
email smash@pinballonline.co.uk
website https://pinballonline.co.uk
Facebook /pinballonline
X @pinballonline
Instagram @pinball_london
Director Paula Vaccaro

Production details: Founded in 2009. Independent film production company assembled by creative and business entertainment industry professionals with a common goal of producing independent auteur-oriented films. Film is main area of work, but may do music promos, TV and web content. Notable credits include: *A Day in Two Lives* (short), *Margo & Max* (long feature) and *Perempay & Dee* feat. Shola Ama (DJPLAY music video).

Casting procedures: Uses freelance casting directors. Sometimes holds general auditions; actors may write at any time to request inclusion. Only accepts postal submissions, which *must* include CV, professional actor's reel on DVD, and headshot photos. Does not accept unsolicited scripts or ideas.

Redeeming Features
Unit 1 Fairmule House, 27 Waterson Street, London E2 8HT
tel 020-3740 3338
email info@redeemingfeatures.co.uk
website www.redeemingfeatures.co.uk

Award-winning film and television production company led by writers and directors. Main areas of work are feature films and documentaries, TV, shorts, music videos, commercials and emerging platforms.

Sightline
Arena Business Centre, Building B, Watchmoor Park, Camberley, Surrey GU15 3YL
tel (01276) 761329
email keith@sightline.co.uk
website www.sightline.co.uk
X @SightlineVideo
Senior Producer & Director Keith Thomas

Production details: Sightline is operated by The Business Magazine Group. Fully resourced, long-established video and interactive content production company specialising in corporate, training, recruitment and brand videos, media for the Web, animation and 360 video. Employs actors in corporate work.

Casting procedures: Welcomes emails (with CVs and photographs) from actors previously unknown to the company. Invitations to view individual actors' websites are welcome.

Sixteen Films
email emma@sixteenfilms.co.uk
website www.sixteenfilms.co.uk
X @KenLoachSixteen
Director Ken Loach, *Producer* Rebecca O'Brien

Film production company. Welcomes CVs from actors, asking them to be directed to casting director Kahleen Crawford (see page 113).

Speakeasy Productions Ltd
3A Royal Elizabeth Yard, Kirkliston EH29 9EN
tel 0131 557 1288
email info@speak.co.uk
28 St Johns Square, London EC1M 4DN
tel 020 7336 6066
website film.speak.co.uk
Facebook /SpeakeasyProductions Ltd
X @speakeasyuk
Managing Director Jonathan Young, *Creative Director* Jeremy Hewitt

Production details: Corporate media production company and event management company based in London and Edinburgh. Works mainly in video production, employing actors in documentary, corporate and commercials. Occasionally holds general auditions. Recent clients include: Lloyds Banking Group, Food Standards Scotland, Student Loans Council, Scottish Enterprise and the Scottish Government.

Casting procedures: Accepts submissions (with CVs and photographs) from actors previously unknown to the company. Will also accept CVs and photographs sent via email. Invitations to view showreels and individual actors' websites are also accepted. Promotes inclusive casting and applications from disabled actors are considered.

Stagescreen Productions

website www.stagescreenproductions.com
Founder Jeffrey Taylor

Founded in 1986, Stagescreen is a film and TV production company with offices in London and Los Angeles. Credits include: *What's Cooking*, directed by Gurinder Chadha (Lionsgate), *Young Alexander the Great* directed by Jalal Merhi (ProSeiben) and *Jekyll*, directed by Douglas Mackinnon and Matt Lipsey (BBC).

Offers PACT/Equity-approved contracts and does not subscribe to the Equity Pension Scheme. Will consider applications from disabled actors to play disabled characters.

Tiger Aspect Productions

4th Floor, Shepherds Building Central, London W14 0EE
tel 0370 042 0042
email general@tigeraspect.co.uk
website www.tigeraspect.co.uk
Facebook /TigerAspectProductions
X @TigerAspectUK
Managing Director Ben Cavey

Founded in 1993. Produces TV comedy and drama with the aim of investing in and working with the leading writers, performers and programme-makers to produce original, creative and successful programming. Credits include: *Ripper Street* (BBC1), *Teachers* (Channel 4), *Good Karma Hospital* (ITV), *Peaky Blinders* (BBC2), *Bad Education* (BBC3), *Benidorm* (ITV) and *Mount Pleasant* (Sky).

Twenty Twenty Productions Ltd

Level 2, 2 College Square, Bristol BS1 5UE
tel 020-7284 2020
email enquiries@twentytwenty.tv
website www.twentytwenty.tv
X @TwentyTwentyTV
Managing Director Leanne Klein, Creative Director James O'Reilly, Director of Programmes Ruth Kelly

One of the UK's leading television production companies, part of Warner Bros., making award-winning documentaries, hard-hitting current affairs, popular drama, attention-grabbing living history series and engaging children's shows.

Run by creative and enthusiastic programme-makers. Its work has been broadcast by networks around the world including the BBC, CBBC, ITV, Channels 4 and Five in the UK, and ABC, The Discovery Channel, Turner Original Productions, Sundance Channel, CNN, The Arts and Entertainment Channel and WGBH in the USA.

Submissions policy: Always looking to work with freelance talent. Contact the Twenty Twenty talent team at **cvs@wbitvp.com**.

Walsh Bros Ltd

email john@walshbros.co.uk
website www.walshbros.co.uk
Facebook /JohnWalshFilmMaker
X @walshbros
Instagram @johnwalsh_filmmaker

Double BAFTA-nominated film company. Productions range from television series and dramas to feature films. Productions include: *Sofa Surfers*(BBC), *Headhunting the Homeless* (BBC), *Don't Make Me Angry* (Channel 4, *Monarch* and *Toryboy: The Movie*.

Wilder Films

1 Fernsbury Street, London WC1X 0HZ
mobile 07775 652078
email info@wilderfilms.co.uk
website www.wilderfilms.co.uk
Managing Director Richard Batty

Production details: Established in 2003. Works mainly in film and video production, especially corporate, brand short films and commercials.

Casting procedures: Uses in-house and freelance casting directors and holds general auditions, but will look for people if needed. Does not welcome unsolicited approaches but may accept invitations to view individual actors' websites.

Working Title Films

26 Aybrook Street, London W1U 4AN
tel 020-7307 3000
website www.workingtitlefilms.com
Facebook /WorkingTitleFilms
X @working_title
Instagram @workingtitlefilms
Chairmen Tim Bevan, Eric Fellner, President UK Production Debra Hayward

One of the UK's most influential and international production companies, founded in 1982. Working Title has produced more than 70 films and won BAFTAs, Academy Awards, and prizes at Cannes and Berlin.

Recent credits include: *Polite Society* (2023), *What's Love Got To Do With It?* (2023), *Roald Dahl's Matilda: The Musical* (2022), *Catherine Called Birdy* (2022), *Cyrano* (2021) and *Last Night in Soho* (2021).

World Productions Ltd

5th Floor, National House, 60–66 Wardour Street, London W1F 0TA
tel 020-7156 6990
email info@world-productions.com
website www.world-productions.com
X @worldprods

Produces TV drama features, series and serials. Recent credits include: *Fifteen Love* (Amazon Prime), *Vigil* (IT, *Line of Duty* (BBC2), *The Bletchley Circle* (ITV), *The Great Train Robbery* (BBC1) and *The Fear* (Channel 4).

Yellow Door Productions
CPL, 8 Gate Street, London WC2A 3HP
email info@yellowdoorprods.com
website www.yellowdoorprods.com
Facebook /YDProds
X @yellowdoorprods
Managing Director Lucy Lumsden, *Head of Production* John Rushton

Production details: Founded by Lucy Lumsden, former BBC Controller of Comedy Commissioning and Head of Comedy for Sky. Yellow Door specialises in narrative comedy and have produced shows for ITV, UKTV and Sky. Recent credits include: *Ruby Speaking, The Cockfields, Hendrix & Handel, The Mysterious Case of Agatha Christie* and *Super*.

Casting process: Uses freelance casting directors. Does not welcome unsolicited approaches but may view individual actors' online videos.

Submissions policy: Cannot promise to respond to every submission but do their best to review material sent, time and resources allowing.

Film schools

Although the work is minimally paid (if at all), it is well worth contacting film schools for casting consideration. Despite mostly working with potentially inexperience, young talent, the potential of the experience is possibly greater than that of participating in a Fringe theatre production as the end result could contain material worthy of use in a showreel. Some schools keep files of actors' CVs and photographs for students to refer to when casting.

Castings for many low- or non-paid films are advertised on online casting boards such as Mandy (see page 364; **www.mandy.com**) or Shooting people (see page 425; **www.shootingpeople.org**). You could try contacting the film school directly to enquire about casting, or network through social media and events like film festivals.

Below are a selection of prominent film schools which may welcome approaches by actors for inclusion in student films.

Arts University Bournemouth
Wallisdown, Poole, Dorset BG12 5HH
email hello@aub.ac.uk
website https://aub.ac.uk/study-at-aub/bournemouth-film-school
Facebook /inspiredAUB
X @inspiredAUB
Instagram @inspiredaub

Students do not only consider local actors for their short films. Actors are either paid Equity minimum (both MA and BA Film Production Films) or are offered their expenses and a DVD copy. Also needs actors for exercises and workshops. Welcomes enquiries (containing CV, photograph and covering letter) from new actors; actors' details are kept on file.

London College of Communication
Elephant & Castle, London SE1 6SB
website www.arts.ac.uk/colleges/london-college-of-communication
Facebook /londoncollegeofcommunication
X @LCClondon
Instagram @lcclondon

A long-established film and television course with both BA and FdA programmes. Students work on 16mm, video and HD, and cast for projects throughout the year. Letters and CVs are welcome. Expenses only are offered, but a copy of finished work is supplied for showreels.

London Film Academy
The Old Church, 52A Walham Grove, Fulham, London SW6 1QR
tel 020-7386 7711
email info@londonfilmacademy.com
website www.londonfilmacademy.com
Facebook /londonfilmacademy
X @LDNfilmacademy
Instagram @London_film_academy
Joint Principals & Founders Daisy Gili, Anna MacDonald

Specialises in professional, practical full-time training and short, specialised courses across all areas of filmmaking. Students make a series of short graduation films and commercials using both professional and non-professional actors.

Students use agents, casting directors and various Internet websites and paper casting publications to recruit actors. Accepts submissions (with CVs and photographs) from actors previously unknown to them. Actors' details are kept on file for student reference and actors are contacted directly. Payment to actors depends on the individual project budgets. Expenses will usually be paid and the actor will be provided with rushes for their showreel.

The London Film School
24 Shelton Street, London WC2H 9UB
tel 020-7836 9642
email info@lfs.org.uk
website https://lfs.org.uk

Offers a 2-year MA course in the art and technique of filmmaking, with approximately 120–30 student short films being made each year. Students generally recruit actors through Spotlight, Star Now, and Talent Circle. Expenses and a DVD copy of the film are normally offered to actors cast in student films. The school welcomes enquiries from actors (with CVs and photographs), but asks that students use websites such as Spotlight and CastingCall Pro to recruit their actors.

National Film and Television School
Beaconsfield Studios, Station Road, Beaconsfield HP9 1LG

tel (01494) 671234
email info@nfts.co.uk
website https://nfts.co.uk
Facebook www.facebook.com/NFTSFilmTV
Instagram @nftsfilmtv

Offers 2-year MA courses in Cinematography; Composing for Film and Television; Creative Business for Entrepreneurs and Executives; Digital Effects; Directing Animation; Directing Documentary; Directing Fiction; Directing and Producing Science and Natural History; Directing and Producing Television Entertainment; Editing; Film Studies Programming and Curation; Games Design; Marketing, Distribution, Assistant Camera (Focus Pulling and Loading); Assistant Directing and Floor Managing; Cameras, Sound and Vision Mixing for Television Production; Creative Producing for Digital Platforms; Directing Commercials; Factual Development and Production; Graphics and Titles for Television and Film; Model Making for Animation; Production Accounting for Film and Television; Production Management for Film and Television; Sound Development; Sports Production; Writing and Producing Comedy.

Students generally recruit actors through casting directors and Spotlight. Has a formal agreement with Equity. Welcomes enquiries (with CVs and photographs) from new actors. Actors are often used throughout the year for workshops and CVs/photographs are kept for this purpose. Graduation projects are cast by external casting directors.

Screen and Film School
84–86 London Road, Brighton, East Sussex BN1 4JF
tel (01273) 602070
email info@screenfilmschool.ac.uk
website www.screenfilmschool.ac.uk

Film-industry recognised. Provides training in all aspects of motion-picture production: screenwriting; directing; cinematography; editing; and production management. More than 100 student short films are made each year. Students generally recruit actors through their sister college, the Institute for Contemporary Theatre (ICT).

University of the Creative Arts
Farnham campus: Falkner Road, Farnham GU9 7DS
tel (01252) 722441
email enquiries@uca.ac.uk
website www.uca.ac.uk

BA (Hons) Film Production at Farnham is accredited by the BKKSTS, the International Moving Image Society and CILECT. The course offers students the opportunity to work on 16mm film and HD formats on both fiction and documentary. Students can specialise from the second year in directing, producing, screenwriting, cinematography, editing, sound and production design. Over 100 short films are produced every year.

University of Westminster
Harrow campus: Watford Road, Northwick Park, Middlesex HA1 3TP
tel 020-7911 5000
email course-enquiries@westminster.ac.uk
website www.westminster.ac.uk/film-and-television-courses

Westminster Film School: Makes around 40 short films per year, from 3 minutes to 20 minutes in length, on 16mm film and digital. Films regularly win prizes at international and UK film festivals. Expenses are reimbursed and a DVD copy of the film is supplied to actors. Welcomes letters (including CV and photograph) from actors previously unknown to the school.

Actors and video games
Mark Estdale

As the game industry continues to grow, the demand for actors grows too. With thousands of games businesses in the UK, Europe and the US covering all stages of development, the opportunities are myriad.

Games have changed the way we are entertained. As a medium they bring together two strands of human leisure; the active nature of playing and interacting, and the passive engagement of being an audience. The essence of the video game experience is choice and consequence.

Games embrace every genre. And it's no exaggeration to say games are also transforming the way we inform and live our lives. They're in the classroom and they're on your phone, your watch, your car's computer and in your workplace. Games are never far away when you go online and they are at the frontiers of Virtual Reality and Augmented Reality. They are everywhere, they are here to stay, and they are brimming with performances. They require actors of all ages, accents and nationalities.

So how does an actor get started in acting for games?
Games currently present actors with two avenues down which work can be found: performance capture and voice acting.

Performance capture
The UK boasts some of the world's most well-known performance capture studios working with games.

Since the technique was first truly brought to public attention with Andy Serkis's definitive performance as Gollum in Peter Jackson's *Lord of the Rings*, performance capture has grown into a global industry serving hundreds of games and films every year. And as performance-capture technology advances, it becomes more accessible cost-wise and more commonplace. The trend is not going to slow down.

Training resources like The Mocap Vaults (Twitter: **@themocapvaults**) are the perfect place to start a journey into the rapidly expanding world of performance capture. Actors should also look up studios like Audiomotion, Centroid and Andy Serkis's Imaginarium to find out more. The film *Avatar* and the acclaimed *Uncharted* series are great examples of this type of work.

Voice acting
For voice acting, the story is a similar one. Ultimately the demand is high and growing, yet recording for games does have its challenges.

A game script is unlike any other. The mapping needed to create player choice and consequence can make a script huge and complex. A game with hundreds of characters and 30,000 lines of dialogue isn't unusual. Imagine any play, TV or film script as a piece of string with a beginning and an end. Pull the ends and you have a straight line. A game script, by comparison can be a huge knot, like a mussed-up, detailed map of London with no street names.

Now add the fact that your performance is in a virtual environment. There's no set, and no audience, and potentially no other actors around to perform against. The skill for the actor is in being true to the moment however it is presented to you.

Casting

To be cast for a game, the first obvious thing is to be open to taking part in casting and letting your acting and voice agent know you are available and keen to work with games. Some agents still remain blissfully unaware of this US$184.3+ billion global industry. Spotlight and online services like **voices.com** are worth trawling for opportunities.

Second, it is helpful to have a pertinent showreel. The ideal reel is a dramatic character one with real characters and perfect accents. If you approach the reel as if it were a film casting which is to be shot in close up, you'll be in the right space: real and intimate.

Have no other voice on your reel than yours, and don't use music or sound effects. You may be required to keep in character consistently for weeks in the studio, so don't include performances you cannot sustain. The most common submission error is to think of games as 'games' then produce a reel that is cartoony and heightened.

When casting for a game, I think like an intelligence officer selecting an agent to work undercover. If the candidate can be who I want them to be, in an alien environment, and not attract suspicion, they have potential. I look for decisive character choice and flexibility. Good game actors are instinctive. Being true to character whatever is thrown at them is core. Spycraft is a powerful perspective as agents working undercover have no script and there's no scene rehearsal. It is character first.

For an audition you will usually get a short character brief, hopefully with an image and a few lines of text to perform. Make firm decisions and flesh out the character with what you have. After a first run through expect to be asked to interpret the character differently and to be given something to cold read as well. Sight reading is an essential skill as it is rare that you will get a script in advance once hired.

Valuable acting skills that are beneficial to voice acting in most games are strong sight reading, radio drama, ADR and experience. Performance capture that combines movement with voice recording is staged theatrically. It requires precise physical performances where screen, theatre and acrobatic skills come into play.

Pay

An actor adding their voice to a game character is paid well. They normally get more for a few hours in session than they would for a week on the West End. However, being paid well is not quite as simple as it could be as there are no industry pay standards for voice work in video games. It is a buyer's market and as such voice actors are being exploited.

I know of actors being offered credits on IMDb as 'payment' for working on a game. I have also heard of actors being used as pawns in bidding wars between production companies; undercutting their competition by offering to pay significantly less to the cast.

In 2024, Equity, as part of its Game On! campaign, set recommended minimum rates for the payment of video game performers for the first time. According to Equity:

> The recommended minimum rates are intended for use on AAA games – games that are created and released typically by mid-size or major publishers; usually anything that cannot be classified as 'indie'. Recommended rates had not been set by Equity in the past due to prior legislation that prevented the union from publishing them where there is no collectively bargained agreement. As minimum fees, the rates are negotiable between a performer (or their agent) and the engager. They include minimum fees for voiceover per hour, motion and performance capture per day, promotion work per

hour, overtime per 30 mins past wrap time, and more. Equity encourages AAA, indie and low budget productions to contact the union to discuss these rates and other contractual arrangements.

You can find the latest suggested rates for voiceover, motion capture and performance capture, as well rates for usage buy-out, overtime etc. at www.equity.org.uk/media/hazdaxj0/recommended-rates.pdf, along with FAQs as to how these (UK) rates have been arrived at.

If you're still unsure what the games industry can offer you, here are a few statistics. The UK has the largest games-development community in Europe, with the most recent statistics (2025) indicating that over 2,000 games-development companies are based here, with 26,000 people employed directly in the video games industry of whom almost 10,000 are creative staff. Data from the UCAS web portal for undergraduates demonstrates that there are 223 specialist video games degree courses in the UK.

And the audience may surprise you. Fifty per cent of players are women and 25% of over 65s say they play video games (2024 survey figures). The number of gamers trajectory is upwards for all ages, with 85% of 16-25 playing and 41% of those between 55 and 64. Violent crime rates have gone down as game sales have increased. That may or may not be related, but games today are too diverse and established to be the stimulant for aggression that some headlines might have you believe.

According to industry figures, the average gamer age (worldwide) in 2024 was 36 years; in 2004 they were on average aged 29. Another trend worth mentioning is the gradual rise of indie games.According to a survey made by 2024's GDC State of the Game Industry, 32% of developers in 2023 were working for indie studios versus 28% working for AAA and 11% for AA ones.

To embrace the opportunity in games the willing actor jumps in. Games need actors.

Originally an actor, **Mark Estdale** founded **Outsource Media Ltd** (**OMUK**) in 1996. It is the UK's largest independent production company providing voice casting and recording of video games. Mark also coaches actors for working with games. OMUK has produced audio content for hundreds of titles including titles nominated for numerous BAFTA Game Awards.

Radio and audiobook companies

Unlike in the visual media, many radio directors have their roots in theatre and will go to stage productions to inform their future casting. They tend to have a good understanding of actors and acting and be open to casting against obvious physical type.

The BBC has by far and away the biggest radio drama output and also uses actors to read poetry, narrations and stories. Some of this output is made in-house; a good proportion is contracted out to independent companies. This is one area of work that doesn't very often use casting directors. It is a good idea to listen to radio drama in order to become aware of its ways – you won't hear much swearing, for instance. Also see 'Voiceover agents' (page 105) and 'Showreel, voicereel and website services' (page 386); some of the latter have excellent advice on making a voice demo on their websites.

INDEPENDENT RADIO COMPANIES

The Comedy Unit
Unit D, Glasgow North Trading Estate,
24 Craigmont Street, Glasgow G20 9BT
tel 0141 674 8222
email info@comedyunit.co.uk
website www.comedyunit.co.uk
X @ComedyUnit
Managing Director Rab Christie

Production details: Founded in 1996. Works in TV and radio productions. Areas of work include drama, sitcoms, comedy and other light entertainment.

Casting procedures: Sometimes holds general auditions. Actors can write at any time requesting inclusion. Submissions from actors previously unknown to the company are accepted, sent by post or email. Voice demos and invitations to view individual actors' websites are also accepted.

Curtains for Radio
Little Ossington House, Ossington Street,
London W2 4LY
tel 020-8964 0111
email contactus@curtainsforradio.co.uk
website www.curtainsforradio.co.uk
Facebook /CurtainsforRadio
Producers & Directors Andrew McGibbon, Jonathan Ruffle, Nick Romero, Louise Morris, David Quantick

Production details: Established in 2001. Specialises in comedy, comedy drama, drama, factual, music and arts in film, television and audio. The ability to perform in foreign languages, regional dialects and singing are among the skills required by actors. Records/films one production play annually.

Casting procedures: Casting is carried out by freelance casting director Rachel Freck and others. Accepts submissions from actors previously unknown to the company. Voice demos and invitations to view individual actors' websites are also accepted. Voice demos can only be accepted on MP3/wav files. Online links to audio, music or film are accepted. Voice-over artists are employed under Equity-approved contracts. Actively encourages applications from disabled actors and BAME actors, and are committed to diversity both on and off air.

Heavy Entertainment Ltd
4 Goodge Place, London W1T 4SB
tel 020-7494 1000
email info@heavy-entertainment.com
website www.heavy-entertainment.com

Production details: Established in 1992. Audio, video and web producers. Areas of work include drama, corporate, commercials, audiobooks and actor showreels (audio and video). Offers Equity-approved contracts.

Casting procedures: Welcomes showreels and voicereels (via agents only), and invitations to view individual actors' websites.

Loftus Media Ltd
2A Aldine Street, London W12 8AN
tel 020-8740 4666
email office@loftusmedia.co.uk
website www.loftusmedia.co.uk
X @loftusmedia
Instagram @loftusmedia
Directors Richard Berry, Kirsten Lass, Joanne Rowntree

Production details: Award-winning content production company which produces podcasts, documentaries and readings. Requires plain narration and poetry from actors. Titles include *Book of the Week* and *Original Non-fiction* for BBC Radio 4; *What's Up Docs?* with Drs Chris and Xand for BBC Sounds; and their own podcast *Where Are You Going?*

330 Media

Casting procedures: Accepts submissions from individual actors previously unknown to the company. Will also accept submissions sent via email. Straight narration is preferred on voice demos and should be sent as an MP3. Actors are employed under Equity-approved contracts. Applications from disabled actors are welcomed.

Pier Productions
Based in Brighton
tel (01273) 691401
email broadcastassistant@pierproductionsltd.co.uk
website www.pierproductionsltd.co.uk
Facebook /pierproductionsltd
X @PierProdLtd
Managing Director Peter Hoare

Production details: Founded in 1993, an award-winning company and a significant supplier of factual and drama productions to BBC Radio 4. The company employs actors for drama productions and is keen to work with talent located in Brighton and the surrounding area.

Casting procedures: Does not hold general auditions. Not currently accepting unsolicited submissions. It must be emphasised that opportunities in radio drama are limited and that the company does not use the services of voice-over artists.

Whistledown Productions
8A Ayres Street, London SE1 1ES
tel 020-7407 8001
email info@whistledown.net
website https://whistledown.net

Production details: Founded in 1998. One of the largest independent suppliers to BBC Radio, with a background in features and landmark documentaries, as well as programme strands such as Radio 4's *The Reunion*. Also podcast and online audio producers. Custom-built studio available for commercial hire.

The Wireless Theatre Company
email casting@wirelesstheatre.co.uk
website www.wirelesstheatre.co.uk
Facebook /wirelesstheatre
X @wirelesstheatre
Executive Producers Cherry Cookson, David Beck, *Production Manager* Sarah Golding

Production details: Multi-award winning London-based audio production company at the forefront of modern, online audio drama. Provides original audio plays, comedy, stories, sketches and more to be downloaded from the website and produces long form multi-cast audio content for external clients such as BBC Radio 4 and Audible.

The company is very keen to hear from versatile actors with a large range of accents and vocal styles. Experience is not essential, but does prefer some sort of audio sample from actors when applying. Records many new audio plays across the year, often including live recordings in theatres. Recent titles include: *Oliver Twist* (executive produced by Sam Mendes starring Daniel Kalyuua, Brian Cox and Nicola Coughlan), *Hell Cats, Open Air, Rum Runner Sue, Love for Menabilly, The Hound of the Baskervilles, The Jane Austen Collection, Little Women, Black Beauty, Les Liasons Dangereuses, Lance Manley* and *Bog Girl.*

Casting procedures: Casting done in-house. Advertises casting through Mandy and Backstage, but once an actor has worked for WTC they become part of the company and are used frequently. Also casts through Facebook and X. Welcomes submissions of new scripts and voicereels by email at **submissions@wirelesstheatrecompany.co.uk**, and all details are kept on file. Prefers applications with voicereels: simple, definitely without long musical introductions (rarely will listen to more than two minutes of any voicereel) and with one example of natural accent and some other, shorter samples of accents or voices. Welcomes invitations to view individual actors' websites. Roles are paid.

AUDIOBOOKS

HarperAudio
HarperCollins Publishers, 1 London Bridge Street, London SE1 9GP
tel 020-8741 7070
email audiobooks@harpercollins.co.uk
website www.harpercollins.co.uk
Audio Publishing Director Fionnuala Barrett, *Senior Audio Editor* Rebecca Fortuin

Production details: Has produced more than 2,000 titles for both children and adults. Work spans all genres including crime, comedy, literary fiction, mass market fiction, non-fiction and classics. Foreign languages and regional dialect skills are required from actors.

Casting procedures: Does not use freelance casting directors. Advises actors to make contact through an agent or studio.

Isis Audio (a division of Ulverscroft Ltd)
(a division of Ulverscroft Ltd)
Unit 14, Kings Meadow, Ferry Hinksey Road, Oxford OX2 0DP
email studio@ulverscroft.co.uk
Facebook /Isis.Soundings
X @isisaudio
Instagram @isisaudio
Audio Production Manager Catherine Thompson

Production details: Founded in 1975. Records titles for Ulverscroft Ltd, as well as Boldwood and Orenda.

Casting procedures: Does not use freelance casting directors. Accepts submissions by email, but does not welcome telephone enquiries. Actors should have a

range of voices and good sight-reading ability. Offers non-Equity contracts and does not subscribe to the Equity Pension Scheme. Actively encourages applications from disabled actors and promotes the use of inclusive casting.

Macmillan Audio Books

The Smithson, 6 Briset Street, London EC1M 5NR
narrators@macmillan.com
website www.panmacmillan.com/genres/audiobooks

Casting procedures: Casts in-house. Does not accept unsolicited demos. See website for contact form.

Naxos AudioBooks

3rd Floor, Forum House, 41–51 Brighton Road, Redhill, Surrey RH1 6YS
tel (01707) 653326
email info@naxosaudiobooks.com
website www.naxosaudiobooks.com
X @NaxosAudioBooks
Managing Director Anthony Anderson

Production details: Founded in 1994. Produces classic fiction, modern fiction, non-fiction, drama, poetry and children's classics for CD and download. Titles include: *The Decline and Fall of the Roman Empire*, *Remembrance of Things Past*, *Middlemarch* and *Julius Caesar*. Regional dialect skills are required from actors. Accepts voice demos from agents.

Orion Audio Books

Orion Publishing Group, Carmelite House, 50 Victoria Embankment, London EC4Y 0DZ
tel 020-3122 6876
email audio@orionbooks.co.uk
website www.orionbooks.co.uk
Audio Publisher Paul Stark

Production details: Established in 1996, Orion Audio draws mainly on the Orion Group imprints to create their audio list, with notable authors such as Ian Rankin, Candice Carty-Williams, Michael Palin, Michael Connelly, Ben Aaronovitch, Sarah Millican, Adam Rutherford, Joe Abercrombie and Patrick Rothfuss. Orion is now firmly established in the digital download market and produces over 250 unabridged audiobooks a year, across all genres.

Casting procedures: Casts in-house. Useful skills include regional dialects and occasionally singing ability. Welcomes submissions and voice demos from actors previously unknown to the company. Happy to receive submissions from actors from all backgrounds with the right skills for the job.

Penguin Random House Audio

Penguin Studios, One Embassy Gardens, Nine Elms Lane, London SW8 5BL
website www.penguinrandomhouse.co.uk
Head of Audio Content Hannah Cawse, *Executive Producer* Roy McMillan, *Head of Audio Production* Chris Thompson, *Senior Producer* Michael Pender, *Producer* Charlotte Davey

Production details: Created in 1991, the Audio Books division of Random House publishes writers such as James Patterson, Andy McNab, Lee Child, Ian McEwan and Kathy Reichs.

Casting procedures: Uses freelance casting directors. Accepts submissions from actors previously unknown to the company, sent by post. Voice demos and invitations to view individual actors' websites are also accepted. Runs the Narrator Mentorship Program, an initative for actors new to audio to make publishing and casting more inclusive.

Media festivals

These are geared towards showcasing directors, rather than actors. However, they can be useful places to network, learn and (if your film is short-listed) to gain extra exposure.

Belfast Film Festival
23 Donegal Street, Belfast BT1 2FF
email info@belfastfilmfestival.org
website https//:belfastfilmfestival.org
X @BelfastFilmFes1

Brings the best of independent, world, local and classic cinema to screens across Belfast. In addition there are panel discussions, workshops, music events and a series of related club events in venues across the city.

Looking for submissions from Ireland for shorts programme and NI Independents feature film strand. Accept fiction shorts either made on the island of Ireland, north or south – or made by an Irish writer/director. By submitting your short you are entering it into consideration for either the Short Film Competition or the New Cinema: Irish Shorts strands. Submissions and eligibility found on website https://filmfreeway.com/BelfastFilmFestival.

BFI London Film Festival
21 Stephen Street, London W1T 1LN
tel 020-7255 1444
website www.bfi.org.uk/lff

Europe's largest public film event taking place in October each year. Leading figures in the film industry present their work at the festival, and the programme is supported by a number of interviews, industry and public forums, lectures, education events, Gala films and special screenings promoting the best in cinema across the world.

Cambridge Film Festival
Arts Picture House, 38–39 St Andrew's Street, Cambridge CB2 3AR
email info@cambridgefilmfestival.org.uk
website www.cambridgefilmfestival.org.uk
Facebook /CambridgeFilmFestival
X @camfilmfest
Instagram @camfilmfest

Established in 1977, the festival is a celebration of film – past, present and future. It's a chance to relive and enjoy past glories, but also to see wha's happening in film right now, and reveal new talents who will shape the future of cinema. Screens films from around the world, many of which may not be available elsewhere. The Cambridge Film Festival attracts big names but is nonetheless intimate and approachable.

Celtic Media Festival
5th Floor, Trongate 103, Glasgow G1 5HD
tel 0141 406 4570
email info@celticmediafestival.co.uk
website www.celticmediafestival.co.uk
X @CelticMediaFest

Celebrates the cultures and languages of Cornwall, Brittany, Ireland, Scotland and Wales in film and in television broadcasting. Awards include: Short Drama Award, Drama Feature Award and Drama Series Award. The festival is attended by producers, directors, commissioning editors, film executives, media students, distributors and schedulers.

Chichester International Film Festival
Chichester Cinema at New Park, New Park Road, Chichester PO19 7XY
tel (01243) 786650
email info@chichestercinema.org
website https://chichesterfilmfestival.co.uk
Facebook /ChichesterCinema
X @NewParkCinema
Instagram @newparkcinema
Director Walter Francisco

A 21-day festival in August/September presenting more than 70 feature films, Q&As with visiting directors and related talks. More than half the films shown are previews and premieres; the remainder form retrospectives on important contributors to the film world.

Encounters (Short Film and Animation Festival)
Studio 1A, 36 King Street, Bristol BS1 4DZ
email hello@encounters.film
website www.encounters.film
Facebook /EncountersSFF
X @EncountersSFF
Instagram @encounterssff

An international short film and animation festival which runs in Bristol for one week in September. It discovers, supports and develops new talent in filmmaking, providing a platform for emerging and established filmmakers from around the world, and a unique meeting place for the industry. The festival celebrates the creativity, diversity and impact of short film. It enjoys excellent links with the prestigious BAFTAs, Cartoon D'Or and European Film Awards. It is a qualifying festival for the Academy Awards. With screenings of diverse new shorts from around the world, alongside special guests and events, parties, awards, seminars, masterclasses and focus sessions, the festival offers insights and advice from industry professionals about every aspect of film. For advice about submitting your work, visit the website.

BFI Flare

c/o BFI Southbank, Belvedere Road, South Bank, London SE1 8XT
tel 020-7928 3232 (Box Office)
website https://whatson.bfi.org.uk/flare

The London LGBTQ+ Film Festival presents the best of British and international queer cinema in all its forms, from the mainstream to the avant garde. Features and shorts are complemented by discussions, interviews, retrospectives and musical performances.

Foyle Film Festival

5–6 Magazine Street, Derry~Londonderry BT48 6HJ
tel 028-7126 0562
email info@nervecentre.org
website www.foylefilmfestival.org
Facebook /FoyleFilmFest
X @FoyleFilm
Instagram @foylefilm
Festival Programmer Christopher Morrison

Established in 1987, the annual festival is the flagship project of the multi-media Nerve Centre. For 10 days in November, the Foyle Film Festival capitalises on all the technical expertise of the Nerve Centre to produce a unique programme of film, music, digital technologies and education. The festival delivers a programme of art house cinema: international and local premieres, foreign language, documentaries, classic film, industry workshops, presentations, outreach events, as well as a stand-alone education programme which is curriculum focused, and targets all local primary and secondary schools, colleges and universities.

The festival competition has received Oscar and BAFTA recognition for its Light In Motion (LIM) Film Awards. Foyle Film Festival is renowned for attracting top industry professionals to the city, with past guests including high-profile names such as: Brendan Gleeson, Ray Winstone, Richard E. Grant, Jim Sheridan, Danny Boyle, Andrea Arnold, Julie Christie, Neil Jordan, Wim Wenders, Kenneth Branagh, Jenny Agutter, Julien Temple, Christiane Kubrick, Andrew Eaton, Brenda Blethyn, Roddy Doyle, Irvine Welsh, Stephen Frears, Ronan Bennett, Jimmy McGovern, Rob Coleman, Sam Taylor-Wood, Kate Adie, Jonathan Rhys Meyers, Cillian Murphy, Ardal O'Hanlon and Dervla Kirwan.

Leeds International Film Festival

Leeds Town Hall, The Headrow, Leeds LS1 3AD
tel 0113 378 5999
email leeds.film@leeds.gov.uk
website www.leedsfilm.com
Director Chris Fell

Presents an extensive programme of new and unseen cinema from around the world since its inception in 1987, supported by a number of events and workshops for those wanting to get into film and TV. The main areas of LIFF include: Official Selection, for new narrative feature films with a focus on emerging filmmaking talent; Cinema Versa, for new documentary features and short films; Fanomenon, for genre filmmaking including comedy, action, horror and science fiction; and LIFF Shorts, which includes the Academy Award-qualifying Louis le Prince International Short Film Competition, the World Animation Competition and the British Short Film Competition.

LIFF also has 2 sister film festivals: Leeds Young Film Festival for children and families each Easter and the INDIs Film Festival for 16–25 year olds every February.

London Independent Film Festival (LIFF)

email info@liff.org
website www.liff.org
Facebook /LondonIFF
X @londoniff

The premier event for micro-budget and no-budget films in the UK. LIFF offers opportunities for indie filmmakers to showcase their achievements, with spaces reserved for first- and second-time filmmakers and for films that have been overlooked by other events. LIFF presents the best of low-budget filmmaking from around the world and mixes it with relevant industry discussions and targeted social networking events. LIFF's audience is London's sizeable independent filmmaking community; it's an indie film festival for indie filmmakers.

Manchester International Short Film Festival

email info@kinofilm.org.uk
website www.kinofilm.org.uk
X @kinofilm

British New Wave and an International Panorama of film provide the main focus to the festival, with a regional showcase, 'Made up North', aimed at promoting films from local and regional filmmakers. Education and Professional Development events are also hosted by the festival and are presented by external curators and organisations.

Short films on any theme, subject or category and made on any format are eligible, as long as they run no longer than 20 minutes and have been made within the 18 months prior to the festival. The Kinofilm Awards acknowledge outstanding achievements in short film, with awards in many categories. Rules, regulations and application forms are available on the website.

Raindance Film Festival Ltd
10A Craven Street, London WC2N 5PE
tel 020-7930 3412
email info@raindance.co.uk
website https://raindance.org
Executive Director David Martinez

The UK's largest independent film festival, committed to screening the boldest, most innovative and challenging films from the UK and from around the world. Weighted heavily towards new talent, the festival offers more than 100 features (many of which are directorial debuts), 20 shorts programmes and a wide range of events, workshops and parties.

UK Jewish Film Festival
tel 020-3176 0048
email info@ukjewishfilm.org
website https://ukjewishfilm.org
Facebook /ukjewishfilm
X @ukjewishfilm
Instagram @ukjewishfilm

Established in 1997, the festival is committed to showing a wide variety of films which celebrate the diversity of Jewish cultures and identity, and which reach both Jewish and wider audiences. In addition to film screenings there are education projects and talks with directors. The UK Jewish Film Festival Short Film Fund offers 2 grants for the production of a short film or video (drama, animation or factual) of a Jewish theme and with a significance both to Jewish and to general public audiences. The UK Jewish Film Short Doc Fund offers 5 filmmakers a budget of £1,000 to make a short documentary about modern British Jewish life, which is then screened at the festival. For application details, consult the website.

Disabled actors
Introduction

This section brings together a directory of companies and organisations dedicated to the work of disabled actors and practitioners, providing a source of work and accessible professional development and support.

To accompany the directory there are two essays. **Jamie Beddard**, previously of Graeae Theatre Company and now Artistic Director of Diverse City, writes on 'Opportunities for disabled people'. Beddard wrote this a number of years ago and further progress has been achieved since the Equalities Act 2010 provided a legal obligation for drama schools to create reasonable adjustments to make training accessible. As a result more disabled actors are treading the boards and getting roles on television than ever. The piece provides relevant insights into the barriers faced by disabled performers and the fight for representation.

Graeae's *Missing Piece* course with London Metropolitan University mentioned in Beddard's essay no longer runs, but Graeae has a new programme called *Beyond*. Other courses are also available such as Access All Areas Theatre Company's *Performance Making Diploma*, run at the Royal Central School of Speech and Drama.

Amongst Graeae's alumni is Liz Carr, best known for playing forensic examiner Clarissa Mullery on the BBC drama *Silent Witness*. Carr was named Best Actress in a Supporting Role at the 2022 Olivier Awards for her performance as Dr Emma Brookner in *The Normal Heart* at the National Theatre. Responding to the accolade, Carr said, "There are so many fears, risks of employing disabled actors. You know what? I think this proves we can do it. We can project. We can fill a stage."

Bringing industry insights more up to date, **Zak Ford-Williams** writes about his own experiences of getting into acting and the support he has found in that process. There are lots of useful snippets of advice peppered throughout the piece that aspiring actors and performers can draw on as they navigate the progression of their own careers.

Note: The UK Government recognised BSL as an official language in March 2003, and the *Yearbook* acknowledges that many deaf people identify as members of a linguistic and cultural minority – Deaf with a capital 'D' – rather than disabled people. For the sake of simplicity, however, this book uses a broad definition of disability to encompass Deaf people (although an individual entry will retain the distinction if present in the material provided to us by that company).

With thanks to Silvie Fisch and the staff of Graeae Theatre Company and Disability Arts Online for their help in compiling this section.

Listings in this section:
- *Opportunities for disabled actors and practitioners, page 336*
- *Support for disabled actors and practitioners, page 345*
- *Rights, advice and support, page 348*

Opportunities for disabled actors and practitioners

The creative industries have improved awareness and accessibility over the last decade meaning we are more regularly seeing disabled actors and performers taking up space at festivals and in theatres across the country. There is still much more to be done. This directory provides a list of companies that are either led by disabled people or have a disability focus. Many of these companies have been working hard over decades to achieve international recognition and are known across the world for their excellence. Their productions can offer unique opportunities for disabled actors and performers, creating roles that are written or devised from lived experience of disability. Some of these companies also provide training for disabled people wanting to break into theatre. Recognising the lack of access within theatre schools, some of this training has a specific impairment focus.

Abnormally Funny People
email info@abnormallyfunnypeople.com
website https://abnormallyfunnypeople.com
Facebook /AbnormallyFunnyPeople
X @AbnormFunnyPeop
Instagram @abnormallyfunnypeople
Producer Simon Minty

Established in 2005 at the Edinburgh Festival Fringe. Shows usually involve 4–6 disabled comedians and their work includes live comedy events and shows, podcasts and songs.

About Face Theatre Company
15A Church Street, Leominster, Heref. HR6 8NE
tel (01568) 616301
email admin@aboutfacetheatre.org.uk
website www.aboutfacetheatre.co.uk
Facebook /aboutfacetheatreuk
Artistic Director Jess MacKenzie

Established in 1995. Work with actors with learning disabilities by offering 4 different experiences: the Performance Company, Drama for All, Theatre Skills and Theatre Foundation. Participants are placed according to interests, abilities and availablity.

Amici Dance Theatre Company
Turtle Key Arts, Lyric Hammersmith, Lyric Square, King Street, London W6 0QL
tel 020-8964 5060
email amici@turtlekeyarts.org.uk
website www.amicidance.org
Artistic Director Elaine Thomas

Dance theatre company integrating disabled and non-disabled artists and performers.

Anjali Dance Company
mobile 07482 16966
email info@anjali.co.uk
website www.anjali.co.uk
Facebook /anjalidance
X @AnjaliDance
Artistic Director Alex Henwood

Production details: A professional contemporary dance company. All Anjali's dancers have a learning disability. The company produces and tours performances, and undertakes educational and outreach work; it is one of the first of its kind in the world. It aims to show that disability is no barrier to creativity. Stages 1–2 productions a year with up to 10 performances over 6–8 venues around the country, such as the Mill Arts Centre (Banbury), Stratford Circus (London) and the Pegasus Theatre (Oxford).

Casting procedures: Casts in-house, does not issue casting breakdowns, and welcomes letters (but not emails) from individuals previously unknown to the company. Welcomes invitations to view individuals' websites, but not showreels.

Apropos Productions Ltd
tel 020-7062 9198
email info@aproposltd.net
website www.aproposltd.net
Director Paul DuBois

Company's work: Established in 2004. First feature film completes post-production August 2015, *Dark Signal* (executive producer Neil Marshall). Short films: *The Juror*, *X-Why* and *Cocktail*. Web series: award-winning web series: *A Quick Fortune* and *Le Method* (2016). Script events include *My German Roots are Showing* at the Arcola Theatre, London, starring Miriam Margolyes.

Provides training for local, national and international clients. Key focus is on Organisational Behaviour. Training is provided for incoming actors. Corporate experience is useful but not essential. Actor-base is extended annually through agents, the website and

Opportunities for disabled actors and practitioners

Equity Job Information Service. Clients include: SKANKSA, Sony Computer Entertainment, House of Commons, UBM and the Discovery Network.

Recruitment procedures: Accepts submissions (with CVs and photographs) from actors previously unknown to the company. Disabled actors regularly form part of its teams and are actively encouraged to apply.

Birds of Paradise Theatre Company
105 Brunswick Street, Glasgow G1 1TF
tel 0141 552 1725
email all@boptheatre.co.uk
website www.boptheatre.co.uk
Artistic Director Robert Softley Gale

Established in 1993, the company offers career opportunities for disabled people in the arts, making game-changing theatre and undertaking strategic work that has left Scotland more diverse and accessible than it was three decades ago. BOP now exports its knowledge around the world to affect positive change for disabled artists and audiences. They challenge the status quo – confronting the absence and exclusion of disabled people from theatre, culture and many areas of society by making theatre that is about disabled people, by disabled people and for everyone. They are a pioneer of Creatively Embedded Access.

Bloomin' Arts
5A Shawlands Court, Newchapel Road, Lingfield, Surrey RH7 6BL
tel (01342) 836785
email info@bloominarts.org.uk
website https://bloominarts.org.uk
Facebook /bloominarts
Ceo Hayley Bull

A theatre company driven by the voice of disabled adults who are performing and visual artists. Working together to create specialist projects, workshops and performance that tours in theatres, schools and community groups.

Blue Apple Theatre
University of Winchester, Sparkford Road, Winchester SO22 4NR
tel (01962) 827352
email admin@blueappletheatre.com
website https://blueappletheatre.com
X @BlueApplePlays
Artistic Director Richard Conlon

Production details: Established in 2005. A creative company that provides opportunities for learning disabled people to develop performing skills and to present theatre, dance, singing, and film performances to public audiences. Blue Apple producitons have been presented in UK venues and have toured internationally in the US, Czechia, Poland and Italy.

Casting procedure: Complete the registration form found on the website, either online or by hand and send to the Blue Apple team. They will be in contact once the form has been received.

Blue Teapot Theatre
Munster Avenue, Galway H91 FVF8, Republic of Ireland
tel +353 (0) 91 520 977
email info@blueteapot.ie
website https://blueteapot.ie
Facebook /blueteapottheatrecompany

Originally founded in 1996, it has evolved from a community arts project within the Brothers of Charity Services Galway to become an award winning independent theatre company that supports an increasingly rich and diverse practice.

They work to radically transform theatre practices by telling stories through the lens of disability, paving the way for inclusive practices to become the norm. By pushing the boundaries of what is possible, we celebrate creativity and challenge the narrative about intellectual disability.

They run an accredited performing arts school, providing training for people aged 18 and over with intellectual disabilities.

Candoco Dance Company
c/o Mountview, 120 Peckham Hill Street, London SE15 5JT
tel 020-7704 6845
email info@candoco.co.uk
website https://candoco.co.uk
Facebook /candoco
Bluesky @candocodance.bsky.social
Instagram @candocodancecompany
Executive Director Melanie Precious

A world-leading contemporary dance company bridging the mainstream and the experimental, Candoco's bold approach and powerful collaborations create distinctive performances and far-reaching learning experiences. The company celebrates different ways of seeing, of being and of making art, putting it at the forefront of conversations around dance and disability. Candoco regularly commissions artists and choreographers to create dance works that tour nationally and internationally. Runs a variety of training courses, residencies and workshops.

Chickenshed Theatre
Chase Side, Southgate, London N14 4PE
tel 020-8292 9222 (181001 020-8292 9222 Typetalk)
email susanj@chickenshed.org.uk
website www.chickenshed.org.uk
Facebook /chickenshed
X @CHICKENSHED_UK
Instagram @chickenshed_uk
Managing Director Louise Perry, *Director of Education and Training* Paul Morrall, *Senior Creative Producers* Dave Carey, Jonny Morton

Disabled actors

Chickenshed brings together people of all ages and from all backgrounds; it is a theatre for everyone. Through productions, performance training, education courses and our outreach projects, they create wonder out of chaos, and change out of challenge.

Using the power of performing arts Chickenshed helps people reach their full potential and feel accepted. They create a truly inclusive environment where people don't stigmatise, label or disregard, but accept and welcome difference.

Chickenshed's vision is a society that celebrates diversity and enables every individual to flourish.

For more company information see page 211.

In addition the company runs:
- An inclusive theatre education workshop programme for more than 800 members from the ages of 5 upwards
- 3 nationally accredited education courses
- Community Outreach projects in the UK and internationally
- A growing number of satellite 'sheds' nationally and internationally
- Training in inclusive practice through workshops and seminars for a range of professionals from a range of fields including education, social services and health.

Corali
Office 3.02, Carlton Mansions,
387 Coldharbour Lane, Brixton, London SW9 8GL
tel 020-7091 7113
email admin@corali.org.uk
website www.corali.org.uk
Facebook /CoraliDance
Instagram @coralidance
Artistic Director Sarah Archdeacon

A dance company created by artists with learning disabilities. Offers a rich programme of high quality performance work, artist development, weekly classes, and workshops in schools, cultural venues and community settings.

Dance classes are available to individuals with a learning disability and include a youth company (ages 14–25) and an adult community class for those aged 18+. Also runs a Professional Development Class for adult dancers with some experience who want to develop their dance and performance further.

CRIPtic Arts
email contact@cripticarts.org
website https://cripticarts.org
Facebook /CRIPticArts
X @CRIPticArts
Instagram @cripticarts
Artistic Director Jamie Hale, *Lead Producer* Caitlin Richards

They provide active disabled leadership which advances world-class arts work with disabled creatives. From high-quality community activities to showcasing breakthrough performers; their Access Services include access advice, workshops, and bespoke training informed by policy, best practice, and experience.

Cutting Edge Theatre
7 Tower Place, Edinburgh EH6 7BZ
tel 0131 531 5282
email info@cuttingedgetheatre.co.uk
website http://cuttingedgetheatre.co.uk

Established in 1995. Creative organisation working with and for those who share one or more protected characteristics defined by the Equality Act 2010. This includes projects and productions across Scotland and abroad, and the Inspire programme working with, and for, disabled people.

Dark Horse
Lawrence Batley Theatre, Queen's Street, Huddersfield HD1 2SP
tel (01484) 484441
email info@darkhorsetheatre.co.uk
website www.darkhorsetheatre.co.uk
Artistic Director Amy Cunningham

Production details: Established in 2000. Production company developing a range of live, recorded and digital projects led by trained actor/theatre-makers with moderate learning disabilities and promoting inclusive working practices. Typically one national touring production per year featuring 6–9 company actors as well as non-learning disabled actors.

Casting procedures: Occasionally uses freelance casting directors. Does not welcome unsolicited CVs. Actively encourages applications from disabled actors and promotes the use of inclusive casting. Offers Equity-approved contracts.

Deafinitely Theatre
PO Box 1160, Wembley HA9 1LQ
tel 020-7387 3586
email info@deafinitelytheatre.co.uk
website www.deafinitelytheatre.co.uk
Facebook /deafinitelytheatre
X @DeafinitelyT
Instagram @deafinitelytheatre
Artistic Director Paula Garfield MBE

Established in 2002 to create theatre for deaf and hearing audiences, the company continues to be deaf-led with a bilingual focus - in British Sign Language and spoken English - which means the work remains accessible to both deaf and hearing people.
Deafinitely Theatre also runs an extensive education and training programme, which includes a youth theatre, CPD for emerging and established artists and an innovative creative development. In their 20 year history they have reached over 35,000 deaf people

and has produced over 40 shows across the UK. Recent productions include: *The Promise* (Lyric Hammersmith Theatre, Birmingham Rep, Northern Stage and HOME Manchester, 2024), *The Vagina Monologues* (Hackney Empire, 2023), *Everyday* (New Diorama Theatre, Birmingham Rep, York Theatre Royal and Northern Stage, 2022); *4.48 Pyschosis* (New Diorama Theatre and Derby Playhouse, 2018 and 2019), winner of Broadway World UK Award for Best Direction of a New Production of a Play; *Contractions* (ND2, 2017), winner of the Off West End Award for Best Production.

DIY Theatre Company

The Angel Centre, 1 St Philips Place, Chapel Street, Salford, Lancs. M3 6FA
email admin@diytheatre.org.uk
website www.diytheatre.org.uk
Facebook /DIYTheatreco
Instagram @diytheatreco

Established in 1994. A theatre company creating accessible theatre and educational projects for performers with learning disabilities.

Extant

2.06 Carlton Mansions, Brixton House, 385 Coldharbour Lane, London SW9 8GL
tel 020-7820 3737
email info@extant.org.uk
website https://extant.org.uk
Facebook /ExtantTheatre
X @extantltd
Instagram @extantltd
Artistic Director Maria Oshodi

Founded in 1997. A theatre company for visually impaired performers, practitioners and audiences. As well as creating touring productions, Extant leads on innovation in professional career training and accessible performance research.

Extraordinary Bodies

c/o Cirque Bijou Ltd, Epstein Building, Mivart Street, Bristol BS5 6JF
tel 0117 902 9730
email info@extraordinarybodies.org.uk
website www.extraordinarybodies.org.uk
Facebook /ExtraordinaryBodies
X @ex_bodies
Co-Artistic Directors Billy Alwen, Claire Hodgson

"Circus for Every Body". A collection between Cirque Bijou and Diverse City. The company combines the talent of D/deaf, disabled and non-disabled artists to create a magical space where diversity is welcome, boundaries are broken, and inclusivity is celebrated.

Runs the Extraordinary Bodies Young Artists programme for disabled and non-disabled 16- to 30-year-olds performers.

Face Front

52 Market Square, Edmonton Green, London N9 0TZ
tel 020-8350 3461
email hello@facefront.org
website www.facefront.org
Instagram @facefronttheatre
Artistic Director Ray Downing, *Associate Director* Sarah-Jane Wingrove

Founded in 1998. Inclusive and accessible theatre for schools and the public with disabled and diverse performers. Working across London and touring nationally. Offers training for emerging disabled artists which include masterclasses and supported artists schemes.

Fingersmiths

email info@fingersmiths.org.uk
website www.fingersmiths.org.uk
X @fingersmiths1
Instagram @fingersmiths_theatre
Artistic Director Jeni Draper, *Producer* Isobel Hawson

Touring theatre company with Deaf and hearing actors. Uses phyiscal theatre with British Sign Language and spoken English to bring to life 20th Century plays. Shows tour nationally to small- and middle-scale venues.

FlawBored

email info@flawbored.com
website www.flawbored.com
X @FlawBoredInstagram
Instagram @flawbored_
Co-founders Samuel Brewer, Aarian Mehrabani, Chloe Palmer

Disability-led theatre company creating darkly irreverent theatre, which addresses complex and uncomfortable issues surrounding identity. Their shows all feature integrated, creative access throughout and they seek to create an environment where all audiences, regardless of impairments and disabilities, are able to access the same show. Opportunities to work with the company are shared on the website.

formidAbility

tel 07968 436588
email info@formidability.org
website www.formidability.org
Facebook /AbilityFormid
X @AbilityFormid
Instagram @abilityformid
Creative Director Joanne Roughton-Arnold

Opera company that puts accessibility at the centre of their process, working for inclusion on stage and off.

Freewheelers Theatre Company

231 Portsmouth Road, Cobham, KT11 1JR
tel (01372) 650908

340 Disabled actors

email info@freewheelerstheatre.co.uk
website https://freewheelerstheatre.co.uk
Facebook /freewheelerstheatre
X @fwtheatre
Instagram @freewheelerstheatre

An inclusive theatre company that brings disabled and non-disabled performers, tutors and technical staff together with support from the local community. Their aim is to change perceptions of disability, breakdown barriers and change lives, through high-quality, hi-tech, innovative theatre, dance, music, film and visual arts. Runs weekly workshops.

Graeae Theatre Company

Bradbury Studios, 138 Kingsland Road,
London E2 8DY
tel 020-7613 6900
email info@graeae.org
website www.graeae.org
Facebook /graeae
Bluesky @graeaetheatre.bsky.social
Instagram @graeaetheatrecompany
Joint Ceos Jenny Sealey (Artistic Director), Kevin Walsh (Executive Director)

Production details: Founded in 1980, Graeae boldly places D/deaf and disabled actors centre stage.

Graeae's signature aesthetic is the compelling creative integration of sign language, captioning and audio description, which engages with both disabled and non-disabled audiences. Championing accessibility and providing a platform for new generations of artists, Graeae leads the way in pioneering, trail-blazing theatre. Graeae also run an extensive programme of creative learning opportunities throughout the year, training and developing the next generation of D/deaf and disabled artists. These programmes include Write to Play and Ensemble.s

Hijinx

Wales Millennium Centre, Bute Place,
Cardiff CF10 5AL
tel 029-2030 0331
email info@hijinx.org.uk
website www.hijinx.org.uk
Facebook /hijinxtheatre
Instagram @hijinxtheatre
Artistic Director Ben Pettitt-Wade

Production details: An award-winning not-for-profit professional theatre company. Hijinx always casts actors with learning disabilities and Autism in their shows which tour the world.

Offers ITC/Equity-approved contracts and does not subscribe to the Equity Pension Scheme.

Casting procedures: Shows are cast by the Artistic Director. Welcomes letters, CVs and photographs from actors previously unknown to the company. Welcomes applications from disabled and non-disabled actors.

IMPACT Theatre

IMPACT Community Arts Centre,
Ealing Central Sports Ground,
Horsenden Lane South, Perivale UB6 8GP
tel 020-8997 8979
email info@impacttheatre.co
website www.impacttheatre.co
Facebook /impacttheatreuk
Artistic Director Kim Mughan FRSA

IMPACT (IMagine, Perform And Create Together) Theatre was founded in 1999. It was set up by and for adults with learning disabilities. While not a professional company, IMPACT helps to develop skills of performance and self-expression for its actors, musicians and dancers. Some of our artists are undertaking professional work. IMPACT Theatre stages original productions featuring up to 60 performers with learning disabilities. In addition to the disability arts that IMPACT has become known for in West London, it is now embarking on innovative inclusive arts work. Its IMPACT Professionals project is also working to enable people with learning disabilities and autism to access more paid roles in TV, Theatre, and Film, areas where they are under-represented.

Lawnmowers Independent Theatre Company

Shields Road, Pelaw, Gateshead NE10 0QD
mobile 07800 844215
email hello@lawnmowerstheatre.com
website https://lawnmowerstheatre.com
Facebook /LawnmowersITC
X @LawnmowersITC

Producing theatre-arts company company addressing issues of concern for people with learning difficulties, often with an international dimension. Uses theatre and drama as a means for people with learning difficulties to explore and develop ideas, and help plan and take control of their futures.

Little Cog

ARC Stockton, 60 Dovecot Street,
Stockton-On-Tees TS18 1LL
email info@littlecog.co.uk
website www.littlecog.co.uk
Facebook /little.cog
X @littlecog1
Artistic Director Vici Wreford-Sinnott

Founded in 2011. A disabled-led production company that seeks to put the hidden stories and experiences of disabled people centre-stage, whilst challenging entrenched historical and medical perceptions of disability and disabled people. They explore and celebrate an extraordinary social phenomenon with phenomenally talented disabled theatre actors, writers, artists, designers, thinkers and practitioners.

Lung Ha

30B Grindlay Street, Edinburgh EH3 9AX
tel 0131 221 9568
email info@lungha.com
website www.lungha.com
Facebook /lunghas
Bluesky @lunghatheatre.bsky.social
Instagram @lunghatheatre
LinkedIn /lung-ha-theatre-company-ltd
Artistic Director Maria Oller

Established in 1984, Lung Ha is a Scottish theatre company for actors and theatre makers with a learning disability or autism. Since it began, the company has worked with over 300 performers with a learning disability creating over 40 original productions. Auditions for new company members are held annually, usually in the Spring, with details published on the website.

Magpie Dance

Community House, South Street, Bromley BR1 1RH
mobile 07470 449558
email admin@magpiedance.org.uk
website www.magpiedance.org.uk
Facebook /MagpieDance
X @MagpieDance
Instagram @MagpieDance

One of the UK's leading companies for people with learning disabilities starting aged 3 with no upper age limit. Based in Bromley, Magpie can also deliver workshops to any region in the UK and offer access to regular sessions online via Zoom. With an emphasis on ability rather than disability, the company has a national reputation for its exciting approach to inclusive dance.

Make a Scene

tel 07900 223646
email makeascene99@gmail.com
website www.makeascene.org.uk
Facebook /inclusivedrama
X @Inclusivedrama
Founder Andrée Trotter

Founded in 2010. An award-winning theatre company dedicated to providing inclusive drama opportunities for young people and adults with learning disabilities. Admission is open to all with bursaries available to cover some or all of the class fees.

Marlborough Productions

c/o 6 Park Street, Brighton BN2 0BS
email info@marlboroughproductions.org.uk
website https://marlboroughproductions.org.uk
Facebook /marlboroughproductions
X @marlboroughprod
Instagram @marlboroughproductions
Creative Director Tarik Elmoutawakil, *Executive Director* David Sheppeard

Established in 2008. UK producer of queer-led, intersectional performance, parties, heritage and radical community gatherings. Their aim is to advance equality and social justice through producing intersectional queer culture.

Recent projects include: *New Queers on the Block*; *Brownton Abbey*; *Radical Rhizomes*; and *The Coast is Queer*.

Marlborough Productions

c/o The Old Courthouse, 118 Church Street, Brighton BN1 1UD
email info@marlboroughproductions.org.uk
website https://marlboroughproductions.org.uk
Facebook /marlboroughproductions
Bluesky @marlboroughprods.bsky.social
Instagram @marlboroughproductions
Creative Directors Tarik Elmoutawakil, David Sheppeard, *Executive Director* Sofia Santos

A leading UK producer of queer-led, intersectional performances. Commissions new work, supports artists locally and nationally, and reclaims creative spaces for the communities they work with. Opportunities to work with the company are shared on the website.

Mind the Gap

Silk Warehouse, Patent Street, Bradford BD9 4SA
tel (01274) 487390
email arts@mind-the-gap.org.uk
website www.mind-the-gap.org.uk
Facebook /mtgstudios
X @mtgstudios
Creative Director Charli Ward

Production details: Established in 1988. Mind the Gap is one of Europe's leading learning disability-led companies. It believes in equality and inclusion, and its mission is to dismantle barriers to artistic excellence so that learning-disabled and non-learning-disabled performers can collaborate, and more learning-disabled performers are seen on our stages and screens. The company has 3 main areas of activity:

- Performance and touring: Since 2014, Mind the Gap has created and toured contemporary new work, and developed these into major projects involving multiple activities.
- Academy: The company's thriving training and professional development supports learning-disabled artists to gain core skills in theatre, music and dance. It supports around 65 aspiring artists through its main programmes each year, and many more through short courses and workshops.
- MTG Studios: Its premises in Bradford offer exemplary access in 3 spaces equipped for excellence in performing arts. The company occasionally hosts work by visiting companies, and provides support for local artists and organisations through the Open Space programmes.

Disabled actors

Casting procedures: Casts in-house and open recruitment. When seeking to recruit an actor from outside the core company, the company contacts agents, and advertises in specialist arts media. Welcomes letters (with CVs and photographs) as well as showreels and invitations to view individuals' websites. Welcomes approaches from people from diverse backgrounds, particularly those who are currently under-represented in the arts. Our contracts comply with Equity standards.

Oily Cart Company
Smallwood School Annexe, Smallwood Road, London SW17 0TW
tel 020-8102 0112
email oilies@oilycart.org.uk
website https://oilycart.org.uk
Artistic Director Ellie Griffiths

Production details: One of the leading theatre companies in the UK creating highly interactive multi-sensory performances for and with the very young (6 months to 6 years) and young people (aged 3–19) with complex needs and who are on the autistic spectrum. Tours national and international venues like theatres and arts centres with early years shows, and takes its special-needs work to special schools around the UK.

Casting procedures: Casting breakdowns are available on the website and the Arts Jobs website www.artsjobs.org.uk. Offers ITC/Equity-approved contracts. Actively encourages applications from D/deaf or disabled actors and promotes the use of inclusive casting.

104 Films
Picture Palace North, The Workstation, 15 Paternoster Row, Sheffield S1 2BX
email justin@104films.com
website www.104films.com
Instagram @justin104films
Creative Director Justin Edgar

Established in 2004, a BAFTA and Royal Television Society winning production company. They are world leaders in disability and disadvantaged cinema and have a mission statement to create a tectonic shift in the representation of disabled people both in front of and behind the camera. Their funders include British Film Institute, Creative Skillset and Creative England.

Join the mailing list to be notified of upcoming opportunites. Recent projects include: *Reasonable Adjustment* for the Southbank Centre's Unlimited festival and the short film *Verisimilitude* starring Ruth Madeley.

Open Theatre Company
Daimler Powerhouse,
Unit 4 Sandy Lane Business Park, Sandy Lane, Coventry, West Midlands CV1 4DQ
email info@opentheatre.co.uk
website www.opentheatre.co.uk/about-us

Established in 1984, Open Theatre work with young people with learning disabilities to explore their creativity through non-verbal physical theatre, utilising play, props, music and physicality, and focusing also on the development of capability and agency. They create opportunities for young people with disabilities to explore the arts and contribute to the cultural landscapes of their communities, breaking down barriers in the process. They organise public performances, school programmes, conferences and research initiatives. Opportunities to work with the company are shared on the website.

Quiplash
email hello@quiplash.co.uk
website www.quiplash.co.uk
Facebook /quiplasharts
Instagram @quiplasharts

Quiplash is a queer disabled-led, community-interest company that focuses on queer, disabled performers and creative workers. Their work has two strands: performance and art-making that prioritises queer, disabled performers, and embedded access with a specialism in integrated and creative audio description. Quiplash also works as access consultants and trainers in audio description, disability justice and disability awareness.

Ramps on the Moon
website https://rampsonthemoon.co.uk
Director for Change Michèle Taylor MBE, *Project Lead* Sarah Holmes

Collaborative partnership, led by New Wosley Theatre, of 6 theatres (Birmingham Repertory, Theatre Royal Stratford East, Nottingham Playhouse, Leeds Playhouse and Sheffield Theatres) and 2 assocaite partners (Wiltshire Creative and RTYDS). The partnership produces an annual, large-scale touring production, led by one of the partnership theatres that aims to normalise the presence of D/deaf and disabled people on and off stage.

Silent Faces Theatre
email info@silentfaces.uk
website www.silentfaces.uk
Facebook /SilentFacesUK
Instagram @silentfacesuk
Co-Artistic Directors Josie Underwood, Jack Wakely, Cordelia Stevenson

Established in 2015. Makes brave, ridiculous, unique and challenging devised theatre. They are an integrated company of disabled and non-disabled artists who make theatre that pushes the boundaries of clown and pysical theatre in a contemporary political context. As well as original productions and performances, they run performance and wellbeing workshops for organisations and schools.

Solar Bear
The Boardwalk, 105 Brunswick Street, Glasgow G1 1TF
email info@solarbear.org.uk
website https://solarbear.org.uk/
Facebook /solar.bear
X @TheSolarBear
Creative Director Jennifer Bates

Established in 2002. Theatre company working with deaf and hearing actors, theatremakers, artists and young people. Their work includes establishing the BA Performance in BSL and English at Royal Conservatoire of Scotland; setting up deaf theatre clubs and awareness training, producing theatre and showcasing work of deaf and hearing professionals.

Spare Tyre Theatre Company
The Albany, Douglas Way, Deptford, London SE8 4AG
mobile 07598 142058
email info@sparetyre.org
website www.sparetyre.org
Instagram @sparetyretheatre
Artistic Director Rebecca Manson Jones

Production details:
- Work with people with dementia and their carers.
- Work with learning disabled and neurodivergent people.
- Work with women who have experienced violence.
- Work with people with long Covid and other long-term health conditions.

London and nationwide. Skills required from actors include workshop-leading and facilitation skills, experience of working with community groups and a sensitivity to, and understanding of, relevant issues.

Casting procedures: Casting breakdowns are published and on the website. Unsolicited approaches at other times – including CVs, showreels and invitations to view individuals' websites – are discouraged. Offers ITC Ethical Manager/Equity-approved contracts. Actively encourages applications from lived experience actors/facilitators and promotes the use of inclusive casting.

Stopgap Dance Company
Farnham Maltings, Bridge Square, Farnham, Surrey GU9 7QR
tel (01252) 745443
email admin@stopgapdance.com
website www.stopgapdance.com
Facebook /Stopgapdance
Instagram @stopgapdance
Co-Artistic Directors Lucy Bennett, Laura Jones

Driven by a diverse creative team who use dance as a movement for change. Stopgap's work demonstrates the compelling power of diversity and inclusivity. They move together to create a remarkable experience that transforms society's perceptions of difference and dismantle the inequity of privilege, in dance and in all aspects of living, collaborating, and creating together as humans. The company is committed to removing barriers to dance, nurturing the talents of dancers born into any body and any mind.

As a global leader of Disability access in dance, they continuously examine best practice and actively advocate for the industry and the wider world to become more inclusive.

Taking Flight Theatre
Chapter Arts Centre, Market Road, Canton, Cardiff CF5 1QE
tel 029-2023 0020
email admin@takingflighttheatre.co.uk
website www.takingflighttheatre.org.uk
Facebook /TakingFlightco
X @takingflightco
Instagram @takingflighttheatre
Artistic Director Elise Davison, *General Manager* Louise Ralph

Founded in 2008. Produces theatre productions for Deaf, disabled and non-disabled performers. Runs inclusive professional training courses and mentoring schemes for deaf and disabled artists.

Casting procedure: Call outs and audition, along with other opportunities, can be found on the website here: **www.takingflighttheatre.org.uk/about-us/opportunities.**

Touchdown Dance
Waterside Arts Centre, Sale M33 7ZF
tel 0161 912 5760
email info@touchdowndance.co.uk
website https://touchdowndance.co.uk
Facebook /touchdowndance
X @touchdowndance
Director Katy Dymoke

Provides workshops based on contact improvisation for visually impaired people. They tour worldwide as a dance company, working with both disability rights organisations and mainstream dance theatre groups.

VisABLE People Ltd
1 St. Mary's Street, Ross-on-Wye HR9 5HT
tel 020-3488 1998, mobile 07729 738317
email office@visablepeople.com
website www.visablepeople.com
Facebook /visablepeople
X @LouiseVisABLE
Instagram @visablepeople
Agents Louise Dyson MBE, Meg Bradley

Founded in 1994, VisABLE is the world's first agency representing only disabled people for professional engagements. It represents artistes with a wide range of impairments and in every age group, including children. 2 agents represent around 120 artistes in all areas of acting, including presenting.

344 Disabled actors

Does not welcome performance notices. Happy to receive applications from disabled actors via VisABLE website only. Showreels should always be via a link sent by email. Also happy to receive invitations to view individual actors' websites. *Commission*: 10%–17.5% (commercials: 20% agency fee).

Vital Xposure
The Albany, Douglas Way, London SE8 4AG
tel 020-8123 9945, *mobile* 07432 421825
email intouch@vitalxposure.co.uk
website www.vitalxposure.co.uk
Facebook /vitalxposure
X @vitalxposure
Instagram @vitalxposure
Artistic Director Josh Elliott

Founded in 2011. A disabled-led theatre company who create and tour radical, political performance championing hidden stories and marginalised voices. They present inclusive theatre, new work and support artists' creative development while championing the value of disabled perspectives in our sector.

Vital Xposure have collaborated with, and supported over, 290 artists and creatives, created and developed connections with 30 organisations and industry peers, in addition to over 3,500 audiences who came to see our touring productions since 2022.

Cathy Waller Co.
Based in London
email info@cathywaller.com
website www.cathywaller.com
Facebook /cathywallercompanyUK
X @CathyWaller
Instagram @cathywallerco

They have worked and toured extensively in the UK and internationally over the last 10 years, to critical acclaim. They showcase high quality dance by both disabled and non-disabled artists, to bring thought provoking dance work to the sector.

Wolf + Water Arts Company
c/o The Plough Arts Centre, 9–11 Fore Street, Torrington, Devon EX38 8HQ
mobile 07846 935949
email clare@wolfandwater.org
website www.wolfandwater.org

Wolf + Water Arts Company has brought its creative and therapeutic approaches to a wide variety of groups locally, nationally and internationally. These groups have included people with learning difficulties; people with mental health issues; people in conflict situations; offenders; young people at risk; children with life-threatening illnesses and their families; and staff groups working with all the above. The company produces original topical performances for conferences and for tour, and provides a wide range of training courses for those wishing to use drama and arts techniques in special-needs situations. Work has taken the company throughout the UK, the Republic of Ireland, Scandinavia, the Middle East and the Balkans.

Support for disabled actors and practitioners

The organisations listed below were established to address the lack of access or ways into the arts for disabled people. Some of these have been working over many decades to address barriers to access. Many of these organisations have a geographic focus for the work they do for disabled people, the exceptions being Disability Arts Online and Unlimited. These organisations also tend to work across art forms, rather than having a specific performing arts remit. Many of the organisations provide resources, advice and support to disabled people developing a career in the arts.

A Relaxed Company
email arelaxedcompany@gmail.com
website www.arelaxedcompany.com

Advises companies, productions and theatres on how to relax a show and a venue, and make it accessible for audiences with autism, neurodiversity and other sensory needs. They work across multiple industries to deliver training, consultancy and advocacy – including in TV and broadcast, visual and performing arts, cultural venues, and education and transport.

Access Scottish Theatre
email contact@accessscottishtheatre.com
website www.accessscottishtheatre.com

Access Scottish Theatre provides information about accessible performances at theatres across Scotland, for Deaf, deafened, hard of hearing and visually impaired audiences.

Listings can be searched on the website through filtering by type of accessible service: Audio Described, BSL interpreted and Captioned. Searches can also be filtered by geographic area and venue. There is also building access information for partnered venues.

The printed guide is produced twice yearly providing information for the Autumn/Winter and Spring/Summer seasons. Brochures can be picked up in participating venues or a pdf of the current issues can be downloaded from the website. A large print version of the brochure can also be requested. In addition, you can subscribe to the AST monthly e-bulletin on the website which emails out the listings of all the accessible performances being performed in the upcoming two-month period.

Arts & Disability Ireland
Digital Depot at The Digital Hub, Roe Lane,
The Liberties, Dublin 8, Republic of Ireland
tel +353 (0)1 658 8470
email info@adiarts.ie
website https://adiarts.ie
Facebook /ArtsAndDisabilityIreland
X @ADIarts
Executive Director Pádraig Naughton

Founded in 1985. A national development and resource organisation for arts and disability. Their aim is to promote engagement with the arts at all levels – as professional artists, audience members and arts workers – for people of all ages with disabilities of all kinds.

Carousel
Community Base, 113 Queens Road,
Brighton BN1 3XG
tel (01273) 234734
email enquiries@carousel.org.uk
website https://carousel.org.uk
Director Liz Hall

Helps learning-disabled artists develop and manage their creative lives, true to their voice and vision, challenging expectations of what great art is and who can create it.

Carousel believes that learning-disabled artists make a vital contribution to the world we live in. It is an organisation that puts learning-disabled people in control of their art, in film, music, performance and production. Their work is planned, managed and delivered by learning-disabled teams and 50% of the board members have a learning disability.

DaDa
The Bluecoat, School Lane, Liverpool L1 3BX
tel 0151 707 1733
email info@dadafest.co.uk
website www.dadafest.co.uk
Facebook /DaDaFest
X @DaDaFest

DaDa is an innovative and cutting edge disability and Deaf arts organisation based in Liverpool, established in 1984. Its vision is to inspire, develop and celebrate talent and excellence in disability and Deaf arts. The organisation's work covers the whole of the North West of the UK, as well as operating on an international scale. DaDa is an integral part of the campaign for greater equality and access for disabled, Deaf and neurodivergent people in the arts.

Deaf Explorer
website https://deafexplorer.com
Facebook /deafexplorers
X @deafexplorer
Instagram @deafexplorer

Deaf Explorer is a Birmingham-based arts organisation that supports D/deaf creatives and produces their work. Through working with a range of other arts and culture organisations and providers, they connect D/deaf creatives with the wider creative sector and promote access and inclusion. They work across a range of art forms and mediums including theatre, dance, music, visual and digital. They also run workshops and partners with schools.

Disability Arts Cymru
Yr Atom, 18 King Street, Carmarthen, SA31 1BH
tel 029-2000 1293, *mobile* 07726 112784
email post@disabilityarts.cymru
website www.disabilityarts.cymru
Facebook /dacymru
Instagram @dacymru
Executive Director Owain Gwilym

The lead disability arts organisation in Wales, and the only organisation in Wales providing Disability Equality Training (DET) specifically for arts providers. DAC works with the arts sector to create career progression routes for emerging/professional disabled artists across all arts forms and to build a future where there is equality of access and opportunity for disabled people. A number of documents are available from the website, which offer advice on a range of subjects including access issues for touring companies.

DAiSY: Disability Arts in Surrey
Hamilton House, 87–89 Bell Street, Reigate, Surrey RH2 7AN
email admin@daisy-arts.org
website https://daisy-arts.org
Facebook /DisabilityArtsinSurrey
Instagram @daisy_artsuk
Managing and Artistic Director Cara Flowers

DAiSY is an umbrella organisation that promotes and celebrates the work of D/deaf, disbaled and neurodiverse artists and disability arts organisations in Surrey. As an organisation, they strive to develop the South East as the lead region in the UK for disability and D/deaf cultural activity, making Surrey a welcoming and accessible place for all artists to practise. They deliver arts programmes, facilitate networking opportunities and advocate for change.

Disability Arts Online (DAO)
c/o Lighthouse, 28 Kensington Street, Brighton BN1 4AJ
mobile 07751 175389
email admin@disabilityarts.online
website www.disabilityarts.online
Facebook /disabilityarts.online
X @disabilityarts
Instagram @disabilityarts

Disability Arts Online offers a platform for the wider arts sector to engage with disabled artists, writers and performers by sharing opportunities on their listings pages, reading about artists' work on blogs and editorial and with partnerships and training facilitated by DAO's consultancy services.

Diverse City
3 Manwell Drive, Swanage, Dorset BH19 2RB
email info@diversecity.org.uk
website https://diversecity.org.uk
Facebook /DiverseCity1
Instagram @diverse_city

A performing arts company that advocates for, and delivers, diversity and equality of opportunity in culture and learning through making and touring new shows, nurturing fresh creative voices and engaging communities in artistic activism. All their work is audio-described and BSL interpreted.

Prism Arts
5 Market Street, Carlisle CA3 8QJ
tel (01228) 587691
email office@prismarts.org.uk
website https://prismarts.org.uk
Director Catherine Coulthard

Promotes art without barriers through diverse access to creative arts activities in Cumbria. Runs Studio Theatre for learning-disabled performers.

Think Bigger
mobile 07538 194422
email enquiries@thinkbigger.org.uk
website www.thinkbigger.uk.com
Facebook /thinkbigger.uk
X @thinkbigger_org
Instagram @thinkbigger_org
Managing Director Edi Smockum

Training and consultancy designed to build equality and inclusive environments in screen industries. Current courses include Disability Awareness Training. Consultants have both lived experience of disability and advise companies on how to reach disabled talent, be inclusive in their hiring, and as well as providing support for adaptations to production offices and working practices.

TripleC
email triplecmanchester@gmail.com
website https://triplec.org.uk/
Facebook /TripleCUK

X @TripleC_UK
Instagram @triplec.uk
Co-Creative Leads Cherylee Houston, Melissa Johns

A BAFTA award-winning disabled-led organisation wih a mission to drive up the role of deaf, disabled and neurodivergent people in the arts and screen industries, and the role of the arts and screen industries in the lives of deaf, disabled and neurodivergent people.

TripleC runs DANC, the Disabled Arts Networking Community made up of over 2,000 deaf, disabled and neurodivergent people who work in the arts and screen industries at all career levels. Through DANC, TripleC run an extensive professional development programme of events, masterclasses and workshops. They also work closely with the industry, providing training and consultancy around access and inclusion.

University of Atypical for Arts and Disability

109–113 Royal Avenue, Belfast BT1 1FF
tel 028-9023 9450
email administration@universityofatypical.org
website www.universityofatypical.org
Ceo and Artistic Director Edel Murphy

University of Atypical is a disabled-led arts charity, taking an empowerment-based approach towards supporting D/deaf, disabled and neurodivergent peoples involvement in the arts. The organisation specialises in developing and promoting the work of D/deaf, disabled and neurodivergent artists and in reaching D/deaf, disabled and neurodivergent audiences.

Unlimited

WX Wakefield Exchange, Union Street, Wakefield WF1 3AE
mobile 07506 679968
email info@weareunlimited.org.uk
website https://weareunlimited.org.uk
Facebook /weareunltd
X @weareunltd
Instagram @weareunltd
Director Jo Verrent

An arts commissioning body that supports, funds and promotes new work by disabled artists for UK and international audiences.

Rights, advice and support

This section covers practical items and sources of more detailed help and advice on the essentials of the acting trade from good headshots to help with tax returns. Whatever your needs, time taken to formulate your requirements clearly before approaching any of the contacts listed below will be time well spent.

Access All
website www.bbc.co.uk/programmes/p02r6yqw

The BBC's collection of stories shared by people with disabilities about their experiences. Includes disability news and mental health with videos, a podcast and links to resources and support.

Access to Work Guide
tel 0800 121 7479
website https://disabilityarts.online/resources/guides-and-toolkits/access-to-work/atw/

A government-funded resource that provides grants to remove barriers that disabled people face in undertaking paid employment. Disability Arts Online has written a guide to interpret the Access to Work rules and official guidance with specific advice for the arts and cultural sector. Accessible formats available.

All In
website https://allin.online/
X @all_in_online

All In are a disabled-led team who remove barriers to access for D/deaf, disabled and neurodivergent people within the arts and culture sector. They are partnered with Arts Council England, Arts Council of Northern Ireland, Arts Council of Wales and Creative Scotland to improve the experiences of D/deaf, disabled and neurodivergent people across the UK. Their advisory board works with event organisers and venues, including theatres, cinemas, concert halls and museums, to inform their practice and ensure access requirements are met, from ticketing through to attendance.

Creative Diversity Network
35–47 Bethnal Green Road, London E1 6LA
email enquiries@creativediversitynetwork.com
website https://creativediversitynetwork.com/
X @tweetCDN
Executive Director Deborah Williams

Works with the UK broadcasting industry to increase diversity and inspire inclusion. Initiatives include Doubling Disability and Diamond, the online system used by the BBC, BSLBT, Channel 4, ITV, Paramount, Warner Bros., Discover, UKTV and Sky to obtain diversity data on the programme commissioning.

Directgov
website www.gov.uk/browse/disabilities

The government's Public Services portal, with links to information and advice on employment, home and housing options, financial support, health, education and training, rights and obligations, transport, travel and caring for someone.

Disability Rights UK
Plexal, 14 East Bay Lane, Here East,
Queen Elizabeth Olympic Park, London E20 3BS
tel 0330 995 0400
email enquiries@disabilityrightsuk.org
website www.disabilityrightsuk.org
Facebook /disabilityrightsuk
X @DisRightsUK

The UK's leading organisation led by, run by, and working for Disabled people. They work with Disabled People's Organisations and Government across the UK to influence regional and national change for better rights, benefits, quality of life and economic opportunities for Disabled people. They also run the Disabled Students Helpline providing advice to Disabled students, apprentices and trainees in England.

PACT Diversity
3rd Floor, Fitzrovia House,
153–157 Cleveland Street, London W1T 6QW
tel 020-7380 8230
email info@pact.co.uk
website www.pact.co.uk/resource-hub/diversity-equity-inclusion.html
X @PactUK
Head of Inclusion and Diversity Anjani Patel

PACT is the UK trade association (see page 431) that represents and promotes the commercial interests of independent feature film, television, animation and interactive media companies. PACT Diversity hosts a range of information and resources to promote diversity in screen industries.

Quiplash
email hello@quiplash.co.uk
website www.quiplash.co.uk
Facebook /quiplasharts
Instagram @quiplasharts

Quiplash is a queer disabled-led, community-interest company that focuses on queer, disabled performers and creative workers. Their work has two strands: performance and art-making that prioritises queer, disabled performers, and embedded access with a specialism in integrated and creative audio description. Quiplash also works as access consultants and trainers in audio description, disability justice and disability awareness.

Scottish Neurodiverse Performance Network
email neurodiverseperformance@gmail.com
Facebook www.facebook.com/groups/616030068869160

Established in 2019 to address the lack of neurodiverse representation within the arts and performance sectors in Scotland. The network is managed by and for neurodivergent artists to make connections and share projects, practice, politics, advice and support. Information is shared via a Facebook group and monthly meetings take place online.

Opportunities for disabled actors
Jamie Beddard

The plethora of journeys and experiences of disabled performers over the past 30 years has tended to be lonely, demoralising and depressing, and sometimes offensive. The barriers encountered far outreach the regular obstacles preventing non-disabled actors from learning, and plying their trade. Performance attributes of technique, voice, improvisation and movement seem distant concepts when you cannot get through the doors of drama school, producers baulk at the idea of employing disabled performers, and most training and employment opportunities are based around strict notions of 'the classical actor'. This is altogether surprising in the creative industries, which should surely celebrate uniqueness, individuality and diversity. However, where once black actors were denied access to stage and screen, so those with different bodies have fought similar battles for opportunity, acknowledgement and representation. This, against a backdrop in which esteemed, non-disabled actors regularly pick up Oscars for their touching portrayal of characters with disability: Daniel Day Lewis in *My Left Foot*; Jamie Foxx in *Ray*; John Voight in *Coming Home*; Tom Hanks in *Forrest Gump* – there's a long list, and they are one-dimensional replications of impediments, far outweighing any considerations around full and meaningful characterisations. Authenticity has been a label seldom attached to the portrayal of disability in the mainstream.

Personal anecdotes are perhaps best served by exploring the issues faced by disabled performers, as, until ten or so years ago, there were few formal routes of progression into the industry. Those few who have made the periphery have tended to have random and short-lived paths, based around such indeterminates as maverick directors, word of mouth or, as in my particular case, luck. The groundbreaking film *Skalligrigg* (1994) – a road movie in which a rag tag of disabled characters take to the road on a mythical quest – threw my staid career path into chaos, and levered a window (previously boarded up!) into performance. In the absence of disabled actors, many first-timers with no experience were suddenly thrust onto a film set; I thought the sound-boom was a cheap prop! 'Rough diamonds' probably most accurately described those of us fortunate enough to get such a break, and, for me, the film opened up a completely new and exciting world. A mixture of bluff, wide-eyed enthusiasm and no little begging had to suffice in the absence of any formal training.

This 'new and exciting world' was also populated by baffling and disheartening prejudices, and initial enthusiasm soon became tinged with disappointment and anger. A casting director for *Eastenders* once informed me that a disabled character – played by a disabled actor, heaven forbid! – would place the programme in the realm of freak show. So much for diverse communities and gritty realism! This attitude is unfortunately still painfully prevalent, and theatre directors are worried that their audiences will be put off by seeing a disabled person on stage.

I contacted Graeae Theatre Company – a company that had been going since the early 1980s, and was run by, and for, actors with sensory and physical disabilities. Graeae had become accustomed to (and was hardened by) irksome battles against prevalent prejudices and barriers. I found a group of like-minded individuals who were challenging these ridiculous, outdated and offensive attitudes, and were determined to pursue careers considered impractical and unrealistic. They were developing, writing and performing theatre as does any small-scale company; sometimes very good, and sometimes not so good. However, the normal critical faculties brought to bear on other companies seemed strangely absent from assessment of Graeae's work, with emphasis on the 'oh so strange impairments' rather than art. The *Independent*, when reviewing Graeae's 2002 production – *Peeling* – came up with such helpful insights as, "Beaty is four feet tall; Coral has tiny limbs and a torso about the same size as her head." Apart from gross inaccuracies, the obvious offence to the individual actors involved and the banality of such revelations, what relevance has this to the art? Hopefully, the paying public didn't recoil in shock at this assembled collection of bizarre physical specimens!

I always yearned for a bad – rather than ignorant, ill informed and avoiding – review, because this would suggest a considered judgement based on the same criteria as any other performer. Undoubtedly, I have been involved in a few 'turkeys', and they should be recognised as such! However, fascination with individual impediment always seems the central tenet of any assessment of performance. Perhaps it would be interesting to apply such criteria to the wider acting fraternity – solely judging Woody Allen on his glasses, Tom Hanks on his stature, or Kenneth Williams on his nasal inflection.

Over the years, the profile of Graeae, and of disabled performers in general, has grown, and there has been a gradual acceptance that it is no longer acceptable to marginalise their talents, aspirations and contributions. In many ways the Arts have lagged behind society in taking the first steps towards embracing and committing to diversity. Although, there has, in many quarters, been a genuine will to broaden participation, the stick of the Disability Discrimination Act has been instrumental in initiating fundamental appraisal and change. The possibility of legal challenges has shaken many organisations, venues and makers from their comfy inertia. Even tokenism is preferable to apartheid!

Drama schools, in particular, have found the concept of students with disability difficult to grasp, but the introduction of the Dance & Drama Awards (DaDAs) has started the process of drama schools thinking not only about the physical access to their buildings, but also about the attitudinal access, and ways to promote inclusive teaching. This is very exciting, and will no doubt pave the way for young disabled people to go through mainstream training rather than be reliant on Graeae.

While the process of change will take time (especially the attitudinal aspect), Graeae has had to respond to the obvious demand by setting up the training course in conjunction with London Metropolitan University. This course offers all the elements found in drama schools, and provides the skills, disciplines and training that were denied people of my age. Lack of sufficiently trained and experienced disabled actors has long been an excuse for the 'cripping up' of non-disabled actors, while training providers continually stress the unlikelihood of disabled graduates sustaining careers in the industry. A classic chicken-and-egg situation, in which aspirant disabled performers are denied entrance at all levels. However, the percentage of those who have graduated through Missing Piece, and have gone into the industry, compares favourably with other drama schools, and Graeae is frequently approached by casting directors looking for disabled talent. So, young people with disabilities do share the same aspirations as any others; there is an increasing demand for such actors; and the institutions are failing to shoulder responsibility.

Missing Piece is fulfilling this vacuum, and has now been running since 2000. The nine-month (September to May) intensive training allows disabled students to work with a wide range of theatre practitioners – both specialist and mainstream. The course can act as a foundation course to further education or drama school – access and will permitting! – or, as is often the case, a direct gateway into the industry. Academic and practical elements of performance are covered, and opportunities for showcasing and touring afforded. Recent years have culminated in professional touring productions of *Mother Courage* and *George Dandin*, and many relationships have been brokered between Graeae's performers and directors, producers and casting directors. There is a crossover with the Performing Arts degree at London Metropolitan, with disabled performers working alongside, and in collaboration with, tutors and students at the University. As well as the main Missing Piece course, Graeae run a series of taster workshops throughout the year for prospective actors.

So strides are being made by Graeae, and by other companies; the excuses and barriers preventing inclusion are slowly being dismantled. There are viable careers for those with the talent, determination and thick skin when necessary.

BBC has set up a talent fund for disabled actors to try and address dated attitudes, and to encourage writers to write storylines which are not always hospital-based or about the whole 'disability thing'!

However the failure of mainstream films such as *Inside I'm Dancing*, which continue to propagate stereotypes and exclusion – with all the main disabled characters played by non-disabled actors – will hopefully mark a sea-change in attitudes and imaginations among creators. The existing, and perspective, body of talent out there no longer allows for petty excuses or wilful misrepresentation. Disabled people, like any others, can make good, bad or indifferent performers, and should be judged as such. However, we have a right to expect the same opportunities, treatments and prospects as all. Banging the door down has become boring – just let us in. It's not rocket science!

Jamie Beddard is an actor, writer and director. Involved with Graeae since 1991, he was Associate Director of the company for some years. He is currently co-director of Diverse City and Lead Artist of Extraordinary Bodies.

First steps (as it were) as a disabled actor

Zak Ford-Williams

We are living in interesting times – globally, as a country and therefore inevitably as an industry. As a young, disabled actor starting out in 2020, within these interesting times, here are some things I've found useful:

Find your tribe
Feeling you're doing this alone is a weight you don't need to carry. I've entered acting via a traditional route: mainstream education, theatre youth groups, drama school, industry. Although I've been very lucky to do so, my disability means I'm not a traditional figure within this route, and this was at times isolating. When you are growing up in a society created for and by people who are not like you, surrounded by people who are not like you: the sense that you are somehow not enough grows with you, threaded into your bones, your organs, and your dreams. Finding your tribe makes this thread light up, illuminating instead of restricting, as a source of focus, direction and even decoration.

Seek out other disabled actors and discuss everything. Several years ago, when I was exploring pathways into the creative industry, I was fortunate enough to attend the very first DANC networking session. DANC, the Disabled Artists Networking Community, are part of Triple C, and together provide D/deaf and disabled people with access opportunities within the arts and media. Attending sessions in person or remotely, following them on social media and signing up for their email newsletters were my first experience of finding my tribe within the arts. However different the viewpoint and aims of the individuals within it, to be together with other disabled people who work or want to work in the arts was hugely affirming.

Social media, for all its flaws, is at its very best when connecting minority groups. Follow the disability organisations in this yearbook: follow who they link to, read their articles, listen to their podcasts. Let their experience of this challenging field become your normality.

Join Equity. They are our professional safety net. We are their tribe.

You will sometimes, even today, be an ambassador for disabled people. That's okay.
A conversation I had with a good friend in a drama school dressing room stuck with me. They questioned the priorities of actors who, in their view, focus 'too much' on activism instead of focusing on the job of acting. They wondered whether presenting yourself to the world as an activist for social change could have a detrimental effect on an audience's (and casting director)'s ability to view you as someone different when performing.

To be fair to my friend, we were about to enter the industry post-drama school and their focus was very much on increasing their chances. To be allied with any cause that might be contentious to some could be something they wished to avoid at that time. I can see the point they were trying to make. Acting requires people to put aside what they know about you as a person and embrace a carefully constructed character as if it was real. Should you then help them with this by focusing on your job and sidelining activities that may affect people's view of you? Absolutely not. In addition to this viewpoint seeming condescending of an audience's (and casting director's) ability to discriminate, a person has beliefs and passions to live by and express, and the very beauty of our industry is in weaving the curtain between life and art.

For my friend, political activism, campaigning and being an ambassador for causes were worthy but unnecessary add-ons to their primary job as an actor. For me, as for many who visibly belong to minority groups, it is different. To modify something a bloke once said: some are born to a cause, some adopt causes, others have causes thrust upon them. For a visibly disabled person, disability awareness is a cause you are born into; living within our society, disability equality is one you are thrust into; disability activism, or what you want to do with your experiences, is one you can adopt.

Despite the huge developments being made in the field of D/deaf and disabled arts, being a visibly disabled actor at this time you still become an ambassador for disability issues whether you want to or not: it's inevitable. When people see someone like them doing something they would like to do, it gives them permission and encouragement to try. I don't consider myself to be an authority on anything except myself and how my condition affects my place in our world, and this is enough. If an ambassador role means being open about the challenges and successes I encounter, if it means highlighting our society's shortcomings and workarounds within a social model of disability framework, and if – like every person from a minority group – by doing so I provide validation for others to do it too, then do it I can and will, and happily.

It's more than okay that you can't do everything by yourself: it's a creative strength.

In March 2023, I attended the press night of *Village Idiot*, a joyous production from Ramps on the Moon at Nottingham Playhouse, which had D/deaf and disabled and non-disabled cast, creatives and crew. A main plot dynamic of a couple struggling with the fact that, because they couldn't live independently, those around them weren't giving them the autonomy they deserved really rang true. Notably, in a neat example of collaborative working, an actor who did not retain lines was fed them through an earpiece. I only found out about this afterwards; the actor did such a brilliant job that there was no way for the audience to know.

Like many D/deaf, neurodivergent and disabled people educated in mainstream, I had a hangover feeling that being unable to access some things without additional help was a weakness in me, not in the system. The social model of disability calls this out entirely, and I needed to internalise its message that disability is something that is created by society.

By prioritising disability inclusion, organisations tap into unique skills, perspectives and talents of disabled people, building a more diverse, innovative and inclusive environment within our industry. Look at the word 'creative' in creative arts. We are perfectly placed to create environments in which to do our best work. The energy that the presence of disability creates within a production is a resource of creative potential.

In precarious financial times, accessible culture and arts can continue to develop by embedding disability equality as standard practice within our industry's systems, processes and organisational structures. Embedding accessibility within the arts prevents it from being a gracious indulgence of a plentiful time. In trickier times such as now, when the portcullis rattles down on the cultural stronghold, when the rations are strictly controlled, what conversations are had about who is in and who is out?

There will always be a place for a disabled actor to play the tropes and stereotypes of a character there 'to be ill or be killed', but let's continue developing arts where D/deaf, neurodivergent and disabled people are integrated within every aspect, as cast, creative teams and essential backstage and crew roles. Let's have more instances of normalisation, until this integration becomes invisible, expected and accepted and therefore nothing to shout about.

Get a good access rider and don't feel awkward to use it

An effective access rider is a document which lists the reasonable adjustments you require in order to be able to do your job effectively. I've worked with my agent to create an access rider that communicates clearly with each project I'm involved in. Currently, it's an evolving document, as with each job, we discover more about what adjustments work effectively for me.

Be open about what you need in order to do your job the best that it can be done. I was initially hesitant with my access rider as a fresh graduate, somehow convinced that putting everything I needed in order to work on that piece of paper would mean I would be far less likely to be employed. As if I would scare off directors and casting directors simply by asking for wheelchair-accessible rehearsal spaces and a chair to occasionally rest on when performing standing up. These are reasonable adjustments which allow me to do my job. Providing them means the project comes out much better as a result.

Issues will arise if you ask for less than you need, as your well-being and your ability to do your job will be impacted, then nobody wins. Remember at all times the social model of disability: it is not your impairment or condition that disables you; you are disabled by the barriers within society and its unwillingness to adapt to an impairment or condition.

As ambassadors through circumstance, I feel disabled actors help normalise access requirements by fully accepting our own, thereby encouraging it as standard practice. We each deserve an environment in which to do our best work. An access rider in essence could help the working conditions of everyone, not just those who identify as disabled. What of the access rider of the non-disabled people who work with you? What can you provide for them?

Save your spoons where you can

Spoon theory describes energy in terms of spoons. We have sufficient spoons to tackle the expectations of a normal day. Learning how to manage my spoons when working has been a key fundamental thing for me to learn, starting out.

Being disabled takes a lot out of you: for example, navigating a crowded pavement in a wheelchair on the way to the theatre loses spoons I could well do with holding on to for the performance. Training my young tallyho brain to pace itself and rest when it can takes a lot. I've learnt from people who have spent decades in the industry that it is perfectly fine to nap when you can, and to build nap-taking into a hectic schedule of filming or stage performance saves spoons. Mentally, spoons are easily lost through encountering ableist practice; embedding disability equality preserves them.

People are okay. Or they can be

As I write this, social media ripples once again with purposefully inflammatory invective, as a high-profile mainstream presenter asks whether disabled people should be given out-of-work benefits funded by working taxpayers (who are implied non-disabled) in perpetuity. They asked the question to be contentious, to provoke a reaction. However, within this country at this time, we do not have the luxury of casually tossing out ableist rhetoric. To ask the inflammatory question to a country with an artificially constructed cost of living crisis is highly irresponsible and dangerous to a minority who are vulnerable because the society they live in is made for someone other than them.

A view this cynically provocative can only exist in the cracks of people's lived experience, the unknown gaps in our social narrative. Our industry can fill these gaps via its unique access into the front rooms, mobiles, stages, and hearts and understanding of audiences. This is why it is essential for us to embed D/deaf and disabled equality within it.

Early on I experienced shocking ableism from a known name who felt making reasonable adjustments for disability restricted their creative scope. Perhaps instead their creative scope was something they struggled to expand.

There's a peculiar thing about encountering ableism as a visibly disabled person. In my experience there's very rarely genuine malice or bigotry behind it. It's often a lack of exposure, particularly in early life, leading to a distinct lack of understanding and therefore hesitancy or fear. People are often simply scared of getting it wrong. At a time of imposed paucity on our industry, we can make a clear statement that rolling back opportunities and shrinking spaces for marginalised groups is not an option. For those with invisible disabilities or for disabled people with less-visible roles, the statement for change happens within the industry.

As my experience is involved with the normalisation of D/deaf and disabled inclusion, listening to a recent Ramps on the Moon podcast made my brain pop with possibility. They discussed how it felt time to move beyond normalisation, move beyond this thing which seems still to be a goal. Imagine. Amid the cynically provocative ableist mass media narrative, there's a clear voice to not simply continue normalising disability arts, but that it is time to elevate and celebrate it. That's certainly what we experienced with Village Idiot.

I feel amidst the advances being made embedding D/deaf, neurodivergent and disability equality within our industry, a disabled person on a stage or screen is still a political act. The presence of marginalised groups can bring about social and political change: the normalised presence of marginalised groups cements it. The rest is celebration.

Zak Ford-Williams is an actor on both stage and screen. Credits include: *Better, A Christmas Carol: A Ghost Story* and the upcoming production of *The Real and Imagined History of The Elephant Man*. He trained at the Manchester School of Theatre.

Resources
Introduction

This section covers practical items (and sources of more detailed help and advice) that are an absolute necessity to an actor. Some may be irrelevant to you – for instance, you may feel as though you could never have the organisational skills to set up your own company. Others are essential to all actors: good photographs, for example. Whatever your needs, time taken to formulate clearly your requirements before approaching any of the contacts listed below, will be time well spent.

Listings in this section:
- *Equity, page 358*
- *Spotlight, casting directories and information services, page 363*
- *Photographers, page 371*
- *Showreel, voicereel and website services, page 386*
- *Accountants, page 400*
- *Funding bodies, page 418*
- *Publications, libraries, references and booksellers, page 422*
- *Organisations, associations, societies and contacts, page 427*
- *Bibliography, page 435*
- *Webography, page 445*

Equity

Equity is the only trade union to represent performers and people working creatively across the entire spectrum of arts and entertainment, both live and recorded. Made up of 50,000 members, the main function of Equity is to negotiate minimum terms and conditions of employment throughout the whole world of entertainment, and to ensure that these take account of social and economic changes.

Equity pushes for better pay, terms and conditions in the entertainment industry. This includes help with issues such as discrimination and holiday pay; providing legal representation; and providing benefits such as Public Liability Insurance and industry discounts. They also look to the future, negotiating agreements to embrace the new and emerging technologies which affect performers as well as at national level by lobbying government and other bodies on issues of paramount importance to the membership. Recent campaigns include: Break Down Barriers #AbolishAuditionFees; Stop AI Stealing the Show; End wage theft at Cambridge Shakespeare Festival; Scrap the Self-Employment Penalty; and Dignity in Digs.

In addition, they operate at an international level through the Federation of International Artists (which Equity helped to establish) and the International Committee for Artistic Freedom. They also have agreements with sister unions overseas.

As well as these core activities, Equity strives to provide a wide range of services for members so that they are eligible for a whole host of benefits which are continually being revised and developed. These include helplines, job information, insurance cover, members' pension scheme, charities and others. (For more information, visit the Equity website **www.equity.org.uk**. For details of Equity's Job Information Service, see entry under Spotlight, casting directories and information services.)

Equity has 21 networks and 26 branches. Networks focus on specialisms, such as choreographers, drag or puppeteers, while others campaign on issues such as the climate crisis. Branches are regional groups for creatives to find a local community to meet and campaign on issues both locally and nationally.

Further information

Head Office, Guild House, Upper St Martins Lane, London WC2H 9EG
tel 020-7379 6000
email info@equity.org.uk
website www.equity.org.uk
Facebook /EquityUK
X @EquityUK
Instagram @equityuk
President Lynda Rooke, *Vice-Presidents* Jackie Clune, Nick Fletcher
Membership Full membership from £16 a month, based on gross annual income; concession rates available.

Beyond #metoo

Kelly Burke

#metoo

In October 2017, the *The New York Times* published an article accusing Hollywood film mogul Harvey Weinstein of decades of sexual harassment and assault. The entertainment industry's apparent astonishment caused actress Alyssa Milano to tweet, "If all the women who have been sexually harassed or assaulted wrote 'Me too' as a status, we might give people a sense of the magnitude of the problem."

Within 24 hours, 4.7 million people had engaged with #metoo on Facebook alone.[1] Over eighty women came forward with accusations against Weinstein, and a raft of allegations began to surface against other high-profile figures. It became clear that the magnitude of the problem was great indeed.

Since October 2017, conversations have spread through rehearsal rooms and drama schools, agencies, film sets and board rooms, asking the twin questions: How did we get here? and What can we do about it? In the UK, new safeguarding policies have been implemented industry-wide, starting with rigorous guidelines from Equity, the BFI and the Royal Court, geared towards creating safe workplaces, preventing harassment and holding perpetrators accountable. 'Intimacy direction' (in which sex scenes are choreographed by an outside professional, much like stage fights) and ideas around active consent have been gaining traction in creative spaces. Performers are seeking ways to set boundaries and say 'no' without being regarded as difficult or un-creative.

With thousands of people participating in the conversation, there has inevitably been disagreement about where the line between 'harmless' and 'harassment' is drawn, how much banter is too much banter, and how much safeguarding is too much safeguarding. There is anxiety in some corners of the industry that new regulations will compromise artistic freedom, that allegations will turn into witch hunts, and that the logical conclusion of #metoo (in the arts, at least) will be that we're afraid to touch each other, frisson will disappear from our stages and screens, and our work will be condemned to sexless, frightened monotony.

But this puts us in danger of ignoring two important – if subtle – factors:

1. The implementation of codes of conduct, safeguarding, consent negotiations, etc., is not a call for sex to be eliminated from our industry. Instead, it is an insistence that, where sex *does* come into our work, it is negotiated professionally and openly, with input from all involved. Because, of course:

2. The sexual harassment crisis isn't really about sex. It's about power. It's about work.

Power and parity

After all, the women speaking out against Harvey Weinstein weren't sexually assaulted on dates, or by strangers on the street (which would be bad enough). They were assaulted as a condition of their work, in order to get or sustain employment.

To understand why this is so critical, consider:

---

[1]. www.theguardian.com/world/2017/oct/20/women-worldwide-use-hashtag-metoo-against-sexual-harassment

- Men outnumber women 2:1 on screen — and 3:1 in children's programming
- Crowd scenes in film use about 17% women[2]
- Women make up just 7% of film directors[3] and 23% of crews[4]
- 16% of working film writers in the UK are female (this statistic *has remained unchanged for the past 10 years*)[5]
- Only 1 in 5 artistic directors funded by Arts Council England is female; women control just 13% of the ACE theatre funding budget[6]

What does this mean?

Well, to start with it means that women at the beginning of their careers are less likely to work than their male colleagues. This means that a disproportionate number of female film- and theatre-makers are confined to self-producing work on the fringe, often at their own expense. It means that most female performers, writers, directors, stage managers, DoPs, etc., will at some point find themselves working for little – or no – pay. And this is before we consider the repercussions of having children (or being over 40) on a woman's career – or the dire impact of intersectionality, which puts women of African or Asian ethnicities, d/Deaf and disabled women, and queer women at an exponential disadvantage.

Less work overall means a less impressive CV, which leads, again, to less work. It also leads to less opportunity to refine one's craft, so skills start to stagnate and confidence deteriorates. This leads to – less work. In this way, many women's careers can become so precarious that they simply cannot afford to 'speak up', whether to advocate for better pay or to reject unwanted advances.

Even for those women who manage sustainable careers, the work itself can be problematic. Acting jobs overwhelmingly push women into sexually objectified and stereotyped roles, where they are often the victims of violence – and rarely have professional status. (For example, the BFI reports that, although women make up 52% of GPs in the UK, only 15% of on-screen doctors are women. On the other hand, women make up 94% of on-screen prostitutes.[7])

This gives our young people a skewed perception of what to expect from the world, and reinforces the fact that a woman's sexuality ultimately determines her (box office) value. It teaches our aspiring film- and theatre-makers that the stories worth telling are men's stories, which results in more work for men – and the cycle repeats itself.

Encouragingly, there are more and more exceptions to this kind of programming, and every day companies are making commitments towards shifting the paradigm. Indeed, if we truly want to eliminate sexual harassment *as a condition of work*, then the content of our work – and the content-makers – will have to change.

Navigating the grey area

In the meantime, we are suspended between the old industry and a hopeful but as-yet-unrealised one. So, what can we do?

Get involved. Campaigns like ERA 50:50 and Time's Up UK are all doing exciting, proactive work to change the landscape of the industry.

[2.] https://seejane.org/research-informs-empowers
[3.] https://seejane.org/symposiums-on-gender-in-media/gender-bias-without-borders
[4.] https://stephenfollows.com/gender-of-film-crews
[5.] https://writersguild.org.uk/women-shut-out-of-top-screenwriting-jobs-for-over-10-years
[6.] www.thestage.co.uk/opinion/2018/sphinx-theatres-sue-parrish-we-must-break-down-barriers-to-gender-parity
[7.] www.bfi.org.uk/news-opinion/news-bfi/announcements/bfi-filmography-complete-story-uk-film

Be proud and professional. We can often feel so relieved to be employed that we put up with things which are deeply unprofessional. It can be frightening to say 'no', whether in the context of turning down underpaid work or unwelcome advances. But we must remember that we are professionals and expect to be treated professionally, with respect and dignity. This means:

Don't work for free. Unless there's a really good reason (i.e. we've written a solo show for ourselves or are doing our best friend a favour), we should insist on being paid for our work – like professionals in any other industry. It is *illegal* to employ people for less than the minimum wage: we are likely to be much more vulnerable in projects which have already engaged us on dubious terms.

Know your rights. It is essential to understand our contracts so that we know what we are agreeing to – in everything from working hours to nudity. We should also know what can and *cannot* be required of us in an audition.[8] If we have questions about a contract, we can call Equity to talk us through it.

Talk about it. Having a conversation with our colleagues to set down expectations and parameters before starting intimate work can be enormously freeing and reassuring. It allows us to navigate sensitive work by making conscious choices, rather than resorting to unexamined, automatic ones.

Be clear about boundaries. In our industry, where the line between fiction and reality sometimes blurs, there will be inevitable moments of ambiguity, even discomfort. It is important to recognise within ourselves when we are uncomfortable versus when we are *unsafe*, when we are willing to push our boundaries and what consists of a violation of those boundaries.

Know where to go for help. If something untoward does happen, contact Equity immediately (main switchboard: **020-7379 6000**), or, if needed, the police. Anyone you work for has a duty of care, but if you don't feel able to talk to someone in the company, remember that your venue is also responsible for your well-being and approach someone in the building. There are more avenues for support and intervention than we might think.

Don't be a bystander. If you see something inappropriate happening, report it.

Remember, it's up to all of us. Men are also subjected to sexual harassment and assault, and are as straight-jacketed as women by gender stereotypes. Our industry leaves almost no place for our trans and non-binary colleagues. The work towards gender equality is everyone's work, and benefits everyone. But we must be sensitive to each other's experiences along the way, and be compassionate with each other when we fail.

Join Equity. The performing arts union, Equity, is our professional safety net. Not only can they provide support in situations of harassment or bullying (including legal support), they can answer contract questions, protect us on vulnerable jobs, and make sure we're paid correctly. Equity also negotiates the terms of our contracts with the industry's biggest employers and campaigns for equal and diverse representation across the performing arts. The more of us are part of the union, the stronger it is and the better supported we are. It is our industry family.

[8.] For example, the Equality Act states that one should not be asked about age, gender, ethnicity, disability, pregnancy, health or other 'protected characteristics'. Nor should you be asked to undress to any extent without warning and without a mutually agreed third party present. For more information, visit **www.equity.org.uk/getting-involved/campaigns/manifesto-for-casting** or call **020-7379 6000**.

Lastly:

Let's make the work we want to see. We can start changing the industry *by changing the industry*. Write new stories, work with people who excite you, find ways to be nourished by the work you do.

There's no going back from #metoo now. If we insist on parity and respect – and if we make a commitment to looking after one another – we have the chance to turn our industry into something infinitely richer than the one we've inherited.

See you out there.

Kelly Burke is an actor, singer and writer. She trained at RADA and is a former Chair of Equity's Women's Committee and part of the team that drafted the union's Agenda for Change. **www.kellyburke.com**

Spotlight, casting directories and information services

Spotlight is a fundamental and essential part of the fabric of the acting profession. It is the go-to directory of actors and employment opportunities used ubiquitously by theatres, producers, agents and casting directors. Lower-cost alternatives are available but it is important to research thoroughly the value of investing in a presence on one of these. As well as trying to assess whether such an investment will really enhance your visibility to employers, an essential part of that research is to read the small print properly.

Some employers will openly advertise properly paid acting work on Spotlight and other channels. Others will simply contact agents for casting suggestions or rely on the encyclopaedic knowledge of a freelance casting director. This limits the number of submissions and goes some way towards ensuring those suggested for consideration are really suitable for the parts available.

Casting information services – often allied to casting directories – glean their information from all kinds of sources. You should always check the veracity of job opportunities independently. A listing in a directory, no matter how reputable, is not in and of itself a guarantee of legitimacy or quality. That said, many Fringe production and student film roles are directly advertised in this way and offer wages and great opportunities.

ArtsJobs
website www.artsjobs.org.uk
Facebook /artjobs
Details of casting information services: Freely advertises a range of opportunities within the arts sector, including positions that require specialist knowledge and skills, unskilled positions at arts organisations and internships. See website for contact form.

Casting Networks
website www.castingnetworks.com
Facebook /CastingNetworks
Instagram @castingnetworks
Details of casting information services: Offers casting professionals a means to distribute breakdowns and receive submissions, streamlining the subsequent casting process. Includes a range of features such as straightforward actor check-in; integration of audition video-recording into online casting tools; and software for handling the scheduling and arranging of auditions. Actors can upload their photos, reel and CV, search through thousands of projects, and submit their profile for consideration.

Castweb
7 St Luke's Avenue, London SW1 7LG
tel 020-7720 9002
email info@castweb.co.uk
website www.castweb.net
X @castweb

Details of casting information services: Established in 1999. A daily information service is available online, with casting breakdowns circulated to subscribers throughout the day. Castweb has circulated casting opportunities for over 4,000 production companies and casting directors. It is now received by more than 1,000 agents across Europe. Membership from £5 per month.

Dramanic
email info@dramanic.com
website www.dramanic.com
Facebook /people/Dramanic/100064836544597
X @Dramanic
Instagram @dramanic.actor

Details of casting information services: Developed in 2009, this online resource for professional actors, helps you find work opportunities at theatre companies around the UK. "Anyone new to the business will find that keeping tabs on numerous theatre companies is challenging and time-consuming, and marrying that with your normal lives leaves you no time to effectively find acting work. Dramanic takes all the hassle out of that by alerting you when opportunities arise at the hundreds of theatre companies in our system." Features include:

• Casting calendar – know what theatre companies are casting well in advance
• Theatre company profiles giving you information about personnel and actor-relevant news

- Contact details of agents, personal managers and casting directors
- Swap plays/books with other Dramanic users
- Look for casual employment between acting jobs.

IMDb Pro (Internet Movie Database)
website https://pro.imdb.com/

Details of casting information services: Comprehensive database of film and television around the world, that also allows actors to post their photos and CVs ('resumés') for a fee, currently starting at $19.99 per month. Creates an opportunity to network by providing access to a huge international contact database of people and companies, and the facility to track film and television projects from development to post-production.

The Mandy Network
tel 020-7288 7404
email emails@mandy.com
website www.mandy.com
X @TheMandyNetwork

Details of casting information services: Formerly Casting Call Pro and established in 2004, The Mandy Network is the world's leading casting directory, designed with the actor in mind. Featuring over 3.4 million professionals all over the world, the site is updated daily with a wide range of casting breakdowns including film roles, theatre tours, corporate work and commercials. Mandy also provides a wealth of resources for actors, including a directory of photographers, agents and guides. Additional services include a lively forum, news service and free surgeries with top casting directors. All members have an entirely free profile in the online directory, which is used by thousands of employers and casting directors. Additionally, Mandy offers a Premium Service with a wider range of features. The Mandy Network also includes services for dancers, singers, musicians and voice-over artists. To discover more about the benefits of using Mandy as well as current subscription rates and latest updates to the service, please visit the website.

Shooting People
PO Box 51350, London N1 6XS
email contact@shootingpeople.org
website https://shootingpeople.org

Details of casting information services: Allows thousands of people working in independent film to exchange information via a range of daily email bulletins, including a daily UK Casting Bulletin. This allows actors to discuss their craft and receive casting calls from directors, producers and casting directors. Actors can create a public casting profile as well as get significant discounts off key film products and services.

Full membership costs £9.95 per month (reduced to £5.95 for students and low-income earners) and entitles users to a range of other services.

Spotlight
16 Garrick Street, London WC2E 9BA
tel 020-7437 7631
email performers@spotlight.com
website www.spotlight.com
Facebook /spotlightuk
X @spotlightuk

Details of casting information services: Founded in 1927 and has since become a world-famous casting platform. As the industry's leading casting resource, Spotlight is used by TV, film, radio and theatrical companies throughout the UK, and many worldwide. Spotlight connects performers with casting professionals and roles; the industry recognises that the performers are guaranteed to have professional skills and experience. As well as access to exciting acting opportunities, performers benefit from discounts and continued development as a Spotlight member.

Performers can upload showreels, voice-clips and additional photos to enhance their online CVs, which is a far quicker and more cost-effective way of promoting themselves than sending out endless copies to casting directors and agents in the post. Artists are also issued with a pair of unique PIN numbers which allow them to access their CV whenever they wish – keeping credits and skills up-to-date – and to email a link to their Spotlight CV to others. Spotlight is used on a daily basis by production professionals sending out casting briefs to agents, with 99% of UK television work being cast through the Spotlight platform.

Entry is strictly limited to professionally trained and/or professionally experienced performers, and applications are always vetted.

'Point me in the right direction': navigating the casting services

Isabelle Farah

The hardest battle for an actor has and will always be: "Where do I find my next job?" Different services will suit different actors. Some gear themselves more to certain media and some cover all areas with varying degrees of success. My advice, seven years into a career, is to work out what you want from your subscription – is it to make your living exclusively from performing if that includes corporate work, children's parties, etc., or are you looking to expand/improve your show-reel? Do you only want to work in theatre? I hope that this can provide you with some insight as to which might be best for you.

There's no denying that Spotlight is the market leader and has been forever. It's expensive and can feel (particularly if you don't have an agent) like a lot of money with little (or no) payback, but I believe that you cannot be an actor without it. In the US, there is no one market leader and actors are required to pay for several similar services, so while this situation is not ideal, it's definitely not the worst!

It is important to remember that this is your profession, the craft by which you want to make your living. While you may have to accept you have to make money doing something else in between acting jobs and are not going to be employed by Stephen Spielberg straight after drama school, if you are paying for a casting service, you should expect to get work from it. Ideally paid in cold, hard cash, rather than lukewarm exposure.

The best bit of advice about the services is to be astute about them. Keep an eye on what you're spending (particularly in direct debits) and which services are working for you. Is the cost of the service with the time spent going through it as productive as, say, making your own work, writing a carefully considered letter to a casting director or director you wish to work with or doing a workshop once a month? I believe connections made in person are much stronger than any application via a casting service.

It's worth noting that many will advertise that they have had high-profile work cast through them, but these, with some exceptions, will be the ones that require more niche skills (languages, musical skills, etc.) and will likely be on Spotlight as well.

Many of these services have other features included in the cost, but I have looked solely at their capacity as a casting resource.

Backstage www.backstage.com
Cost: £14.99/month; £2.50/month if sign up for annual access
An import from the US, Backstage has been around for a long time and the website is easy to use and navigate. Includes roles for TV, fiilm, theatre, voiceover, commercial and brand influencers.

Casting Networks www.castingnetworks.com
Cost: Free membership or upgrade to a Premium membership for £9.99/monthly or £99.90/ annual
Casting Networks is another import from the US. Some breakdowns appear here from certain casting directors, commercials and short films most often, though generally not exclusive to Casting Networks.

Dramanic www.dramanic.com/uk
Cost: 1 month taster £14.99; 3 months £40.99; 6 months £65.99; 12 months £116.99
Rather than advertising jobs as and when casting directors list them, Dramanic gives you as many details as they have about upcoming theatre projects soon after they have been announced. Dramanic takes out a lot of the research hassle involved in writing letters but, as a letter will almost always be needed, is no quick fix solution to getting a job. Most of the work is in theatre, including some regional touring with small but well-known companies as well as the mainstream West End/Off-West End stuff. All jobs I saw had some payment and many looked like they were offering Equity/ITC rates. If your focus is theatre and you don't have an agent, then this comes highly recommended.

Equity
Cost: included in your Equity subscription
Equity's hook here is that all work is paid and in theory you pay your subscription for more than just the jobs board. The work tends to be teaching rather than performing so worth checking if that's what you're after to see you through a month.

IMDbPro pro.imdb.com
Costs: Individual $19.99/month; $149.99/year
There are breakdowns here, but not many and usually low/no pay; on the flip side, they tend to be very high quality (the film makers are required to be members themselves, and I don't think you'd bother until you're quite serious). It's not one I'd pay for simply for the breakdowns, but if you reach a point where you think it's useful (when I was in a co-op we'd use it for general research and I found it invaluable as an agent) then it can be worth looking through what's available there.

Mandy www.mandy.com
Cost: £20.40/month; £156/year if you want access to paid jobs
Now an amalgamation of the old Mandy and Casting Call Pro, Mandy.com is a stalwart service. The site displays numerous castings. There are some good paid jobs and plenty of unpaid opportunities, including interesting small-scale tours, commercial work, short films and voiceovers. The jobs here are not going to make you a household name, but you can make money from lower-profile jobs and build your CV without an agent using it. Some of the more 'niche' roles in big productions are regularly advertised on here. The premium service includes workshop opportunities, agent and employer directories, and you can upload several photos and reels.

Shooting People shootingpeople.org
Cost: £9.95/month; students and low-income earners £5.95/month
Shooting People is great for independent film work. The site itself is user-friendly and clean with social network type tagging features. Most of the work advertised is still low/no pay films, but the advantage is that these jobs tend to only be listed here and the yearly subscription rate is good value (there are also often discounts floating around the web).

Spotlight www.spotlight.com
Cost: £171.50/year +VAT
Spotlight is where the breakdowns are. I don't think any other service gets as many or from as wide a pool of good casting directors through their sites, let alone exclusive to

'Point me in the right direction': navigating the casting services

their sites. Many features (search functions on the Link board, etc.) are not available to actors. Agents see significantly more than you but don't be fooled into thinking there is nothing there. With some pushing, Spotlight will change things that need to be changed. If you want to be in something, it's probably cast here, and your chance of making your money back is far higher here than anywhere else. Make sure your profile is up to date with your skills as casting directors search on here first.

The Stage jobs.thestage.co.uk
This claims to list the biggest selection of jobs in theatre and the entertainment industry. It's free to sign up to see jobs across the sector.

Work in Europe

These two may be useful for anyone who can, does or wants to work in other markets.

enCAST enCAST.pro
Cost: £7.80/month, £25.90/6 months, £42.90/year
This is relatively new to the market. It covers castings across Europe in all languages so it could well be worth using if you speak another language/s to a high-enough standard. There is a high volume of work advertised but it is spread across all of Europe. France, Belgium, Germany and Italy seem to be the largest players. The jobs are often paid, but it's worth bearing in mind that you are applying as a local, so are unlikely to get travel or accommodation expenses. There is some work in the UK advertised here, but it's likely to be more useful to those who have contacts, bases or interest in building their networks in other countries. You can look at the breakdowns and apply for unpaid work without paying, but must pay to apply for any paid work.

e-TALENTA www.e-talenta.eu
Cost: 57€/year
e-TALENTA is another for Europe-based work. The site looks very shiny and is easy to use, but it does not have a huge volume of work coming through their boards. Its main function is as a platform for CVs with showreels, photos, voicereels, etc. Not-for-profit.

Isabelle Farah is an actor, writer and comedian. She trained as a serious actor at Drama Studio London and after some pratfalls and upstaging, branched into stand up and character comedy. You can find out more about her work by following her @irresponsabelle but preferably not in real life ...

Be prepared for publicity
Jayne Trotman

Congratulations! You get a great job, meet the director, producer, cast members, start work and then someone asks whether you will you do some publicity for the project. What does that really mean and do you have to do it? If you have been asked, then the answer is most probably yes. Publicity plays a vital role in the marketing process of many film, television and theatre projects. Here are some useful tools to help you navigate the publicity process.

What is publicity?

I have worked with many actors and filmmakers during publicity for film campaigns – some seasoned household names and others entirely new to publicity. Whilst publicity is an exciting, vital part of the job, and can mean travelling around the globe for weeks (sometimes longer) on end to promote a film, it is hard work. It's essential that you are well prepared and take good care of yourself.

I am sure many of you will have seen an actor sitting next to a mounted film poster, answering questions about what it was like working with their co-star on a soon-to-be-released blockbuster film. Or you will have watched that co-star on a chatshow sofa recounting tales of pranks that said actor played on set before a clip from the film is shown and the audience applaud. To get back to basics, that is all part of the publicity campaign and another skill that actors should appreciate, practise and perfect.

Granted your first job may not be a Hollywood blockbuster; it may well be a touring show or fringe theatre production where local newspaper coverage, radio interviews and podcasts will be the key. Whatever the job is, you should be publicity-ready as you may well be newsworthy, and you'll make many a producer very happy if you are already well prepared.

How can I prepare?

When you play a role you will have researched and honed that character well. This is no different. It's you on your best day with stories aplenty, open and interested to be meeting new people for a good chat. If there are any things you are uncomfortable talking about, think about them in advance and have answers to those questions prepared.

It's definitely worth seeking out those you admire when they are on the publicity trail. Watch them on TV shows (both here and in the US, if you can), read interviews with them and listen to what they have to say if you hear them on the radio. Sometimes interviews don't go quite so well. Those pieces are worth watching and reading as much as the successful ones. Think what *you* might have done in that situation.

Being interviewed is a skill that needs to be worked on – it's hard work at times and some people are just better at it than others. But if you spend time preparing and practising, you will become more adept. I urge you to do your research as much as you can in advance.

It's also important to think about how you look. You may be able to roll out of bed for an early film or television call, know you will have time to get ready and might even have people to help you – but that's not always the case on the press side. Make sure that you look your best and always ask in advance what the set-up will be and what you are expected to be wearing etc. In my years working for major film studios, we have had actors turn up for press days in old crumpled t-shirts (albeit their favourite one), having to call flatmates to go through wardrobes for extra clothes to be sent across. Or, on one occasion, the person arrived for their first major press conference and photo-call with the world's media in a tracksuit and top. On that occasion we kept thinking they would get changed any minute but they didn't. Luckily, we had a budget, an experienced team on hand to help and just enough time to dash to a shop for an outfit change. They looked great in the end and were quite brilliant, but it did not help their nerves (or ours!) in the run-up.

Your publicity moments should and can be enjoyable. I promise it will help if you have done the work in advance.

What am I publicising?

Essentially, the play, TV show, film, event you are in or have created. Make sure you ask for and come armed with all the key facts about the project. If you have not been directly asked to do press, it is always good to check (usually with the producer, director or creator) that it's OK for you to be talking publicly about the piece and that all the key people involved in the project are aware.

You are also publicising brand 'you'. You are a business, so – as we touched on above – please make sure you are bringing the best version of you to work that day. You should also take a moment to consider what people can find out about you if they were doing their research. You are probably on social media. If so, and even if you have not been active for a while, what would people think about you if they looked at your posts online? Brand 'you' and a career path as an actor or performer may not have been on the cards when you first posted on social media. As you are coming into the public eye, you need to start thinking what you are communicating on each channel. You may well have decided to spend time and money creating a stylish new website to help you get work and to promote you as an actor and performer. This will be useful and you can control and curate everything on there. You now need to be mindful of everything you post on social media, may have posted in the past and what friends and family post about you. Your website may be great, but you don't necessarily want a journalist to see everything that happened on that fun night in Ibiza from a social media post. Always think before you post.

Can anyone help me?

Yes, always ask questions and seek out help and advice. If you are working on a project and have been asked to do publicity, your company manager, director or producer should be happy to advise. If you have one, then ask your agent. It's likely they will have other clients well-versed in the publicity circuit. You can also speak to one of your tutors from drama school as they may well be able to help and advise you. Fellow cast members can be very useful too and often more than happy to share their experiences. There will always be someone who can help. Don't be afraid to talk to people: you will be amazed what you can find out when you open up and start asking questions.

Publicists

A high-profile element of the publicity campaign is what is known as a 'press junket'. This is a series of print and broadcast interviews with the cast and film makers, often in a hotel (watch that scene with Hugh Grant posing as a journalist from *Horse and Hound* in the film *Notting Hill*). Many actors are often accompanied by a publicist – someone hired by the actor or filmmaker to help them navigate publicity requests, promote the film and their role as well as other elements of their careers). You may not need a publicist when you are starting out, unless your first role is on a major high-profile project and, in that case, you may be assigned a publicist to help and advise you. My role as part of a studio's publicity team is to work with the publicist and sometimes directly with the actors, to help and advise them during the publicity campaign. You may well be helped through the process by someone like me if you get cast in a high-profile title.

There are so many additional aspects to the role of being an actor or performer and publicity is often one of the unexpected elements. Please enjoy it, don't be afraid to ask questions, do your research and be prepared. We look forward to seeing the results.

A bit about me: I originally trained as an actor and worked across theatre and television for several years. A colleague I had worked with in a touring theatre company called out of the blue one day and asked if I could help in their London office when their whole team were away covering a film festival. I ended up doing this for many years and, from that and through meeting other people in the industry (and often in between acting jobs), worked for many of the studios before joining Warner Bros as a temp in 1997. I joined the team full time as a publicist, was promoted to Director of Publicity and stepped down as Executive Director of Publicity for Warner Bros UK, having successfully overseen the launch of over 400 films almost 20 years later. I now run my own film and entertainment consultancy.

Photographers

'A picture is worth a thousand words' as the saying goes, and a good photographer is worth their weight in gold. Headshots are an essential part of an actor's professional armoury and they are worth investing in.

Your photograph is a silent, static, two-dimensional representation of vocal, mobile, three-dimensional you. It should be of your head down to your shoulders, reasonably stylish and well-produced without necessarily being too glamorous. It should look natural and have life, energy and personality – especially in the eyes, the most important part of your face.

Crucial to the final result is finding a photographer who understands the world that the end result is intended for and with whom you can work well. In the listings that follow, you'll find a wide range of prices and deals. It is important to research as many of these as possible without making cost your prime consideration. Ask friends, teachers and your agent for recommendations. Browse Spotlight and websites to see samples of work. Read the details under each listing to get a feel for who might produce the goods for you. Once you have a shortlist of possibilities, phone or message each with appropriate questions (what to wear, studio or natural light, and so forth) in order to get a sense of how well you might be able to work with them. Only after you've done all this research should cost be a consideration. Even then, a cheap deal could mean that the photographer will spend much less time and take fewer photographs, than a more expensive one. You might be lucky with the former, but you'll enhance your chances of getting really good results with the latter.

Note: Bear in mind that as the deadline for Spotlight gets nearer, photographers become increasingly busy and it becomes more difficult to book a session.

Copyright

Under the Copyright, Designs & Patents Act 1988, the photographer owns the copyright on any new photograph, even though you've already paid for the original. That means that you have to obtain his/her permission to have new photographs reproduced in Spotlight or anywhere else. Your photographer may be happy to approve such reproduction, but may not be so happy about any cropping or other alterations: you must get permission if you intend to do this. The other important new legal requirement is that your photographer must be credited on any reproduction of the original. Some of the repro companies are now doing this as a matter of course.

*Member of the Association of Professional Headshot Photographers (APHP)

Simon Annand
mobile 07884 446776
email simonannand17@gmail.com
website www.simonannand.com
Services and rates: please see website for details. Session fee £350/£310 concession (full time MA/BA students and the unemployed), which includes at least 500 photos. The whole session is taken away on the day. The actor chooses 6 images and this selection is fully photoshopped in colour and b&w by Simon.

Photos are taken at a home studio with natural light, inside and outside – can travel if required. Home studio is wheelchair-accessible.

Work portfolio: With 45 years' experience, has taken publicity shots for around 5,000 actors. Clients include: Mark Rylance, David Morrissey, Lindsay Lohan, James Norton, Meera Syal, John Hannah, Eddie Redmayne, Claire Foy, Benedict Cumberbatch, Julia Sawalha, Tamla Kari, Dan Stevens, Jane Asher and Vicky McClure. Advises actors: "There is no time-limit for the session and I see one person a day. Please bring 6–8 different tops, to show range. A truly effective headshot, that attracts the attention of experienced casting directors, will pay for itself". Author of *The Half: Photographs of Actors Preparing for the Stage* (Faber & Faber 2010) and *Backstage: Portraits of Actors at Work in the Theatre* (Lannoo/Terra Publishers 2023); has worked for Peter Brook, Sonia Friedman, Ian Rickson, the NT, RSC and the Royal Court amongst many others. Exhibited internationally in Paris, New York, Berlin, Beijing, Moscow (2014) and London (V&A, NT and RSC).

Ric Bacon Photography
1 Augusta Road, Twickenham TW2 5HW
mobile 07970 970799
email ricbacon@gmail.com
website www.ricbacon.co.uk

Services & rates: Headshot photographer, with many years of experience and work in a way that is easy and enjoyable, allowing you to relax and capture images that are both alive and natural. Photo shoot includes photographer's fee, introductory phone call, processing of 4 retouched images (in both b&w and colour) and an online gallery of all images. Session costs £300, with a reduced rate of £250 for students. Shoots in a very relaxed manner, usually outside in natural light or studio.

Work portfolio: Established in 1999. Headshot Photographer with many years of experience who works in a way that is easy and enjoyable, allowing clients to relax and capture images that are both alive and natural.

Tony Blake Photography
2nd Floor, 68 Watergate Street, Chester CH1 2LA
tel 07974 804203
email tony@tonyblakephoto.co.uk
website www.tonyblakephoto.co.uk
X @tonyblakephoto

Services & rates: Established in 2001. Based in the north west of England and shoots natural light headshots in a relaxed studio environment. Offers standard and bespoke packages for actors.

Prices start from £150 depending on shoot length which is normally up to 2 hours. Check the website for full details. Clients receive contact sheets of all edited-down images to select their favourites for re-touching and processing. Digital files only. Photographs are taken in natural light studio. Studio is not wheelchair acccessible.

Work portfolio: A portfolio of images can be viewed on the website.

Nev Brewer Photography
website www.nevbrewerphotography.co.uk
Instagram @nevbrewer

Services & rates: Photographer for actors and performers since 2013. Price £145 which includes 4 retouched images. Additional retouched images cost £30 each.

Shoots in the studio, but if required, outdoors can be accommodated as well. Sessions typically last between 60 and 120 minutes and produce 150–300 images to choose from. This usually gives sufficient time for an informal discussion, the shoot itself – including clothing changes to help develop a range of looks and a review of images both during and at the end of the shoot. "The session time is just a guide; it is important not to feel rushed and so there is no set time limit. The key aims are that you leave having enjoyed the session and happy in the knowledge that you have the images you came for."

Following the session, images (contact sheets) are sent online – usually on the day but always within 24 hours. Once a selection has been made, retouched images are sent for approval before the final files are sent through. Works to a 7-day turn around to cover busy periods this is usually done within 48 hours. Will do everything possible to meet urgent deadlines.

When booking a shoot, full details of how best to prepare and get the most out of the session will be sent.

Sheila Burnett*
tel 023-9273 2187, *mobile* 07974 731391
email sheila@sheilaburnett.com
website www.sheilaburnett-headshots.com
Instagram @sheilaburnettphoto

Services & rates: Multiple packages available (including a discounted student rate). Charges between £250 and £450 for a session. The standard rate includes up to 120 colour proofs plus 6 highly finished hi-res images. Your chosen finished hi-res images are sent to you by email. Sessions take place in Sheila's home studio and locations in nearby Portsmouth Harbour. Sheila works with up to 250 actors a year; clients have included Imelda Staunton, Catherine Tate, David Soul, Paul Freeman, Jon Culshaw, Simon Pegg, Anita Harris, Jackie Clune, Caroline Quentin, Jim Carter and Helen Lederer.

APHP approved.

"Appointments can be made either online or by phone. I always advise on what is good to bring with you on the day. Rail from Waterloo takes 90 minutes to Portsmouth Harbour; easy parking close to premises. My goal is to make sure you have vibrant natural headshots that stand out from the crowd."

Charlie Carter*
mobile 07989 389493
email charlie@charliecarter.com
website http://charliecarter.com
X @charliecphotg

Services & rates: Established in 1998. Digital – colour and b&w. Charges £425 for sessions, tailoring images specifically to you and your casting. Allows plenty of time for many changes of clothing, shaving and reviewing images as the shoot progresses. The shoot includes a web gallery and 4 Spotlight-ready and large file jpegs.

Work portfolio: Examples of work can be viewed on the website and at Spotlight's offices. Clients include: Kenneth Branagh, Simon Russell Beale, Philip Franks, Tom Hollander, Roger Allam, Emily Blunt, Isla Blair, Jemma Redgrave, Jamie Glover, Tom Mison, Cush Jumbo, Chloe Pirrie, Sarah MacRae, Eve Best, Harry Enfield, Eleanor Bron, Martin Shaw, Joanna Van der Ham, Kerry Condon, Jasmine Hyde, Paul McEwan, Serena Evans and Charlie Condou – as well as agents The Artists Partnership, The Richard Stone Partnership, Rebecca Blond Associates, Conway van Gelder Grant, Independent, United, Markham & Froggatt and many others.

"However lovely a photograph is, it has to work. It has to look like you *and* be accurate to your casting – somehow tell the casting directors who to expect will walk through their door. The way I work is totally collaborative – we talk about your casting and what your range is. We look at how you see yourself. We do it together. I suggest you prepare for it as you would for a significant interview by making sure you do what is necessary to look and feel your best."

John Clark Headshot Photography*
82 Heathwood Gardens, London SE7 8ER
mobile 07702 627237
email john@johnclarkphotography.com
website https://johnclarkphotography.com
Instagram @johnclarkphoto

Services & rates: Sessions are £120, last for one hour, includes 3 changes of outfit and one retouched image. Additional images can be purchased for £25 each. See website for latest rates. Book via online calendar; deposit required.

Work portfolio: Established in 1982. Photographs and advice can be found on the website. Recent clients include: actors represented by Roger Carey Associates, Collis Management, Crawfords, Rossmore and Langford Associates.

John Cooper Photography
Unit 2, Kelvin Trading Estate, Eastvale Place, Yorkhill, Glasgow G3 8QG
mobile 07803 929091
email studio@johncooperphotography.com
website www.johncooperphotography.com/index
Facebook /johncooperphotography
X @JohnCooperPhoto
Instagram @jcooper_photo

Services & rates: Sessions fees available on request. Can offer student discount for multiple bookings. Shoots take place at own studio.

Work portfolio: Established in 2005. Has taken publicity photos for hundreds of actors. Recent clients include: Duncan Lacroix (*Outlander*), Grant O'Rourke (*Outlander*), Billy Boyd (*Lord of the Rings Trilogy*), Jordan Young (BBC *River City*), Keira Lucchesi (BBC *River City*), Scottish Opera (emerging artists), Jean-Luc Picard (Assoc. Conductor RSNO),

Greg Esplin (In Your Face Theatre, *Trainspotting*), Mark Cox (BBC's *Chewin' The Fat* and *Still Game*), Katrina Bryan (*Taggart* and Children's BBC), Des Clarke (SMTV Live and Capital Radio), Pamela Byrne (BBC *River City*), Claire Knight (BBC *River City*). Advises actors: "I think a lot of actors' headshots are very intense and serious looking – because it's easy to do. I help my clients produce contemporary publicity images, with energy and personality, which really improves their casting opportunities."

Nicholas Dawkes Photography*
The Space, Reform Road, Maidenhead, Berks. SL6 8BT
mobile 07787 111997
email studio@nicholasdawkesphotography.co.uk
website www.nicholasdawkesphotography.co.uk
Facebook /nicholasdawkesphoto
Instagram @nicholasdawesphotography

Services & rates: Prices start at £325 for headshots (£315 for students and £305 for returning clients). Includes a full consultation, 2.5 hour session in a large fully-equipped studio, shooting in both natural and studio light. Up to 300 pictures taken, with the best 150 included for review. Same-day uploading of images in colour and b&w on private client area, with email links to the client and their agent. Retouching 4 images included in price. Additional images are £15 each.

"The aim of my shoots is to show life and character in your headshots through one-to-one direction and to explore and capture your different casting brackets."

Nick Gregan Photography
Office (not studio): 1A Cowper Rd, London SW19 1AA
tel 07774 421878
website www.nickgregan.com
Facebook /NickGreganHeadshotPhotographer
X @nickgregan
Instagram @nickgregan

Services & rates: Charges £350 for a 2-hour photo shoot, which includes unlimited photos and 4 retouched images (more can be purchased for £25 each). Charges £495 for a 3-hour headshot portfolio session, which includes unlimited photos and 6 retouched images (full or 3/4 length). Students are offered a discount on production of a valid student card. Photos are taken in a studio or outdoor location and both are wheelchair-accessible. Coaching and direction are provided throughout and there is a 24-hour turnaround time for images.

Work portfolio: Established in 1992. Has taken publicity photos for over 20,000 clients, including Graham Norton, Nadia Hussein, Harry Hill, Mariella Frostrup, Ruby Wax and so many more. "My website offers '7 Secrets to an Awesome Headshot" – check it out for loads of useful information. He is also author of *The Headshot Bible - 50 Tips for a Perfect Headshot*.

Claire Grogan Photograpghy*
18 Calverley Grove, Archway, London N19 3LG
mobile 07932 635381
email claire@clairegrogan.co.uk
website www.clairegroganphotography.com
Facebook /Claire-Grogan-Photography-105661542805602
Instagram @clairegroganpix

Services & rates: Actors headshots: shoot price £260 (reduced to £230 for students). Shoot 2 hours in a relaxed environment. Studio lighting and backgrounds no outdoors. Time and facilities for changing clothes/hair/make-up or shaving during shoots. Includes 3 retouched images, with additional images costing £25 each.

Specialises in capturing shots that really reflect the actor's personality and casting potential, also special TLC for those who normally find having their headshots done difficult.

Work portfolio: Established in 1991, with past clients including Denise Welch, Raji James, Martin Freeman, Stephen Tomkinson, Steve McFadden and Heather Peace. Photographs can be viewed on the website, Facebook and Instagram.

Remy Hunter Headshots*
email remy_hunter@hotmail.com
website www.remyhunterphotography.co.uk
Instagram @remyhunterheadshots

Services & rates: Specialist actors headshot photographer since 2001. Natural light studio in North London, N16. Photographs outdoors in the Barbican area of City of London, EC1A. Offers free headshot sessions – only pay for images you love. No deposit required and sessions are either 105 mins or 75 mins (under 16s sessions also available). First image £75, £60, £50 respectively. If ordered and paid for within 2 weeks of session, 20% off first image. Images 2–4 are £50 each for 105 mins and 75 mins sessions. £40 per image for Under 16s. Images 5 onwards are £30 each thereafter. All images ordered include subtle retouching and enhancing & 3 file sizes emailed. Same day online gallery of images – bookings available online.

Matt Jamie Photography
Based in Cumbria and Tyneside
mobile 07976 890643
website www.mattjamie.co.uk

Services & rates: Established in 2000. With over 25 years' experience as an actor, director, filmmaker, and in casting Matt has a wealth of industry insight and understands exactly what makes a standout headshot. Photoshoots cost £145, discounted to £75 for students. A studio fee of £30 applies to all sessions. Group discounts are available when 2 people book for the same date. Each session includes a one-hour shoot and three professionally edited, hi-res images. Additional images can be purchased for £10 each. Sessions are available in-studio (Gateshead) or outdoors at a location of your choice.

Work portfolio: Examples can be viewed online in his portfolio. Matt creates a relaxed, informal atmosphere to help clients feel at ease in front of the camera. "You're welcome to bring a friend along and as many changes of clothes as you'd like; whatever helps you feel confident and comfortable during the shoot. A 100% satisfaction promise is included: if you or your agent are not happy with the final images, no shoot fee will be charged."

JK Photography
12 Worple Road, Epsom, Surrey KT18 5EE
tel (01737) 362043, mobile 07816 825578
email james@jk-photography.net
website https://jk-photography.net

Services & rates: Established in 1997. Sessions in studio and outdoors, which include a minimum of 300–400 images and 4 retouched images, all in hi-res, b&w and colour, delivered the next day. Prices on request.

Work portfolio: Has photographed over 500 actors with 20 years of industry experience. "Our creative team will ensure a relaxed session and images that are a true representation of your casting needs."

Steve Lawton*
9 Arts Lane, Bermondsey, London SE16 3GB
mobile 07973 307487
email info@stevelawton.com
website www.stevelawton.com
Facebook /stevelawtonphotography
X @stevelawtonphotography
Instagram @stevelawtonphotography

Services & rates: Offers 3 different packages from £290, which includes pdf contact sheets; all shots in colour and b&w; and at least 2 touched-up hi-res jpegs. Reduced prices available to students when choosing either the silver or gold package. Additional 10x8in jpegs are priced at £30 each. Advises clients not to bring patterned tops; fitted t-shirts and v-necks in blue, grey or black are most effective.

Work portfolio: Established in 2001. Has taken photographs for more than 3,000 actors and is recommended by Curtis Brown, Independent Talent Group, United Agents, Lou Coulson, Jorg Betts, Shane Collins, International Artists and Bronia Buchanan, amongst others. A full portfolio and price information is available on the website.

L.B. Photography
website www.lisabowerman.com

Services & rates: Working actress and photographer for over 40 years. Charges £280 for a photo shoot (student rate available). No VAT chargeable. Includes 7 hi-res, retouched images in colour and b&w. Based in Reigate (40 mins from London. Trains from both Victoria and London Bridge). If the weather is bad the shoot can be rearranged for a different day. For portfolio and more details, visit website.

Pete Le May
mobile 07703 649246
email pete@petelemay.co.uk
website https://petelemay.co.uk/headshots

Services & rates: Based in Belfast and established in 2002. Typically charges £300 (£250 for students) for a relaxed photography session lasting 2–3 hours, a download link of all low-res, unedited photographs in both colour and black-and-white, and retouching of your favourite 6 images. Photos are made in natural light, both indoors and outdoors. Visit the website for full details and examples of recent work.

MAD Photography*
17 Starling Lane, Cuffley EN6 4JX
mobile 07949 581909
email mad.photo123@gmail.com
email info@mad-photography.co.uk
website www.mad-photography.co.uk

Services & rates: Charges £300 for (£250 for returning clients) Pro Actors photo shoot which includes photographer's fee, studio and location shoot, 200–250 proofs contact sheets emailed same day and 4 high-res digital images. Offers a discounted rate of £225 to students (includes as above, but with 3 digital images); also offers student shared shoots at £150 each (includes as above, but with 100 proofs contact sheets and 2 digital images). Extra digital images are £25. "Hair and make-up should be natural. Bring 4 tops in any colours: one v-neck, one collar, one t-shirt and one jacket. No white!"

Work portfolio: Established in 1997. Photographs can be viewed on the website and in *Contacts* and on Mandy. Has taken publicity shots for over 10,000 actors and student actors. Clients include: Michael Praed, Shane Richie, Michelle Ryan, Susan Penhaligon, Michael Knowles, Jessica Wallace, John Partridge, Tom Law, Belinda Owusu, Janie Dee and Phoebe Thomas.

Kirsten McTernan Photography
Based in Cardiff
mobile 07791 524551
email kirsten@kirstenmcternan.co.uk
website https://kirstenmcternan.co.uk
Instagram @kirstenmcternanphotography

Services & rates: A professional and comfortable, relaxed headshot session in the studio overlooking Chapter Arts Centre in Cardiff. Costing from £100, the session normally lasts around an hour and, as part of the fee, 2 final images (in digital format) are included, with additional images charged at £10 each.

Work portfolio: Established in 2005. Professional theatre and portrait photographer working exclusively within the performing arts industry. Has taken publicity photos for over 400 actors. Recent clients include major casting agents such as: The Artists Partnership, Regan and Rimmer, Emptage Hallett, Boom Talent and David Chance.

John Need
Studio 147, 1 Summerhall, Edinburgh EH9 1QD
mobile 07756 178947
email hello@johnneed.co.uk
website https://johnneed.co.uk

Services & rates: Photoshoot includes 200–250 shots. Prints are optional and charged individually. Only shoots digital. Shoots take place at own studio which is wheelchair accessible.

Work portfolio: Established in 2008. Has taken publicity shots for around 400 actors, a collection of which can be viewed on the website. Advises actors: "I know that getting photos right for media is a high priority for any performer. Whether you're in the biz or trying to get into it, get in touch, as I've shot hundreds of actors, presenters and DJs. First impressions count, so give casting directors what they're after – you!"

Claire Newman-Williams
The Studio, Elfin Cottage, 86 Chittoe, Chippenham SN15 2EL
mobile 07963 967444
email claire@clairenewmanwilliams.com
website www.clairenewmanwilliamsheadshots.com
Instagram @CNWHeadshots

Services & rates: Claire is a fine art and portrait photographer who has 25 years experience working with actors in both the US and the UK. 3-hour+ photoshoots with a session fee of £290. All photographs are digital and each session includes unlimited shots edited down to 150 pictures on contact sheets. Two 10x8in retouched digital images are included as part of the session and further images are available at £25 each. Full details of headshot sessions are available on the website. Studio is easily accessible from London. A make-up artist is available for an extra charge if requested.

Work portfolio: Has photographed around 5,000 actors, among them Stephen Fry, Tom Hiddleston and Dame Penelope Wilton.

North London Headshot Photography
The Studio, 9A Sylvester Road, London N2 8HN
tel 020-8349 3632
email lynnherrick@gmail.com
website www.headshotslondon.co.uk
X @herrickphoto
Instagram @createdbylynn

Services & rates: Charges £150–200 for a photoshoot, which includes 25+ images sent as digital files. Retouching is included in packages. Work takes place in the studio and attached garden. Has taken publicity photos for around 900 actors.

Michael Pollard Photographer*
21 Edenhurst Road, Mile End, Stockport,
Greater Manchester SK2 6BT
tel 0161 456 7470, *mobile* 07800 989457
email photography@michaelpollard.co.uk
website www.michaelpollard.co.uk
Facebook /michaelpollardphotographer
Instagram @michaelpollardphotography

Services & rates: Charges £185 for a 2-hour shoot, includes at least 150 shots on the contact sheets and 5 edited images of your choice. Additional images are charged at £10 each. Session fee reduced for students or actors under 15 years and younger. The shoot is unhurried and relaxed and can be both outdoors in natural light and in a studio environment to give the widest variety of images possible.

"With regards to the shoot, I would suggest bringing a number of tops ranging from darker colours and tones to lighter, brighter tones and colours. Different necklines too, so collar shirts/blouses/tees/polos/jumpers. Casual and formal jackets can work well and if you have any specific looks in mind (classical/period or corporate for example) then bring clothes that might suggest these looks or you can just keep it more open. It's also good to try and push the age range out and so lighter/brighter clothes tend to suggest a younger look whereas darker clothes tend to age an actor up. If the hair is long, then it's good to do some with the hair down but also with it tied up so bring bobbles/grips and if you have facial hair/beard then shots with and without can be useful. I always have a chat with my actors when they arrive so that we can properly plan the shoot out before we start and so that we know the purpose of each look. Ultimately the key is to keep things simple and natural and to be positive and be prepared. Enjoy it and be yourself!"

Work portfolio: Established in 1993. Photographs can be viewed on the website and social media.

David Price Photography
Based in London, Los Angeles and Austin, Texas
mobile 07950 54249
, *tel* +1 323-378-9593
email info@davidpricephotography.com
website www.davidpricephotography.com

Services & rates: Established since 2003. Currently divides his time between Los Angeles and London. Please email for availability. Prices start from £250.

Work portfolio: See website for full details.

Robin Savage Photography*
mobile 07901 927597
email contact@robinsavage.co.uk
website www.robinsavage.co.uk
Facebook /people/Robin-Savage-Photography
X @robinsavagepics
Instagram @robin_savage_headshots

Services & rates: A London-based actors' headshot photographer. Robin has been photographing actors for 18 years, and has worked with actors who have appeared in the West End, the National Theatre, the RSC and theatres all around the world and who have worked in feature films, major TV dramas, soaps, sitcoms, sketch shows and commercials. Sessions start at £160. Visit the website for more information and to get in touch.

Howard Sayer Photography
mobile 07860 559891
email howard@howardsayer.com
website www.howardsayer.com

Services & rates: Casting headshots and portraiture photos, please email for current rates. Fast turnaround and option to shoot on location.

Michael Shelford Photography
Parkhall Business Centre, 40 Martell Rd, Norwood, London SE21 8EN
email shelford.michael@gmail.com
website www.shelfordheadshots.com
Instagram @michaelshelford

Services & rates: Charges from £385 for a standard photoshoot; student discount of rate £300. A portfolio shoot is from £575. Sessions can be booked a month in advance. Additional retouched photos are £24 each.

Work portfolio: Has taken publicity photos for 900-plus actors. Recent clients include: David Adjala (Independent Talent Group), James Norton (Artist Partnership), Alexandra Roach (Gordon and French), Nick Hendrix (Ken McReddie), Daniel Ings (The Rights House), James Rastall (Rebecca Blond), Antonia Thomas (Curtis Brown), Theo James (Markham & Froggatt) and Shazid Latif (Lou Coulson).

Faye Thomas Photography
Based in London
mobile 07813 449219
email booking@fayethomas.co.uk
website www.fayethomas.co.uk
Facebook /fayethomasphotography
X @FayeThomasPhoto
Instagram @fayethomasphoto

Services & rates: Consult website for most up-to-date session rates. Student rate is available. Shoots take place in an outdoor location or studio – neither is wheelchair accessible.

Work portfolio: Established in 2005. Recommended by top London agencies including Hamilton Hodell, Conway Van Gelder Grant, Curtis Brown, United Agents, 42, Independent Talent Group, The Artists' Partnership, Markham Froggatt & Irwin and many more. High-profile clients include: Hayley Atwell, Phoebe Waller-Bridge, Jodie Comer, Emma Corrin, Michelle Dockery, Sam Heughan, Jodie Whittaker,

Maisie Williams, Bradley James, Joseph Morgan, Victoria Hamilton, Evanna Lynch, Emily Beecham, Matt Ryan, Charity Wakefield, Tuppence Middleton, Tom Riley, Lauren Cohan, Marc Warren, Ramin Karimloo, Shaun Evans, Samuel Barnett, Jemima Rooper, Elliot Cowan, Alex Hassell, Sam Spiro, Dervla Kirwan, Freddie Highmore and Phoebe Dynevor. See portfolio, session info and FAQs on website.

Tudor Hart Photography
Based in London SW19
mobile 07958 975950
email info@tudorhartphotography.com
website www.tudorhartphotography.com
Instagram @tudorhartphoto

Services & rates: Natural light indoor studio. Standard Shoot £260 - 4 Retouched Images (student rate £240). Basic Shoot £160 - 2 Retouched Images. Portfolio Shoot £360 - 6 retouched images. Additional retouched images £20 each. For details and more information please see the website.

Work portfolio: Portfolio of images can be viewed on the website.

Steve Ullathorne
Based in London
tel 07961 380969
email steve@steveullathorne.com
website https://ullathorne.photoshelter.com/index
Facebook /SteveUllathornePhotography
X @steveullathorne
Instagram @ullathorne

Services & rates: Fees on request. Will offer a discount to students, negotiable at the time of booking. All clients receive an online contact sheet with a web address that they can pass on to their agent. Prior to the shoot, clothing and locations will be discussed with the client on the telephone. All photos are retouched in Photoshop to remove any blemishes plus any other light retouching required by the actor. Email proofs are sent of each chosen image. Rather than specifying a number of images, prices are dictated by duration of the shoot, which is 2 hours. Actors usually end up with more than 100 shots to choose from.

Work portfolio: Please see website for samples.

Vanessa Valentine Photography
email valentine.photography@hotmail.com
website www.vanessavalentinephotography.com

Services & rates: Headshots. Based in London. Please see the website for more details.

Vincenzo Photography
mobile 07962 338289
email info@vincenzophotography.com
website www.vincenzophotography.com

Services & rates: Actor headshot photographer and self-tapes since 2000. Charges £270 for a 2-hour photoshoot, which includes 8 hi-res digital files, 4 each in b&w and colour. Offers a student rate of £210 per session. Uses a studio with garden for external shots. Pro-actors self-tape service with reader from £50.

Work portfolio: Examples of work can be seen on the website. Has taken photographs for many actors, among them Ken Stott, Hayley Atwell and Jesse Buckley.

Philip Wade
88 Englefield Road, London N1 3LG
mobile 07956 599691
email pix@philipwade.com
website www.philipwade.com
Facebook /PhilipWadeHeadshotPhotography
X @philipwadepix

Services & rates: Provides a variety of packages. Charges £350 for a headshot package which includes pre-shoot consultation, 4 retouched images and 12 images available in hi-res colour and b&w. £225 pro-headshot package includes 6 images. £150 headshot session includes 3 images. £50 Spotlight headshot offer includes one image. Sessions are in the studio and outside with a wide variety of backgrounds. Clients given acces to a personal online gallery to view images.

Work portfolio: Has taken publicity shots for hundreds of actors. Recent clients include: PHM, Abacus, Imperium, Shepherd Management and Sandra Boyce.

Michael Wharley Photography*
mobile 07961 068759
email michaelwharley@michaelwharley.com
website www.michaelwharley.com

Services & rates: Established in 2006. Shoots in digital, featuring studio-lit and outdoor, colour and b&w shooting as standard. Two-hour 'Pro' shoot suitable for all actors. Between 150 and 400 photos taken. Photos supplied in industry-standard web- and print-optimised formats. See website for full details of packages and approach.

Work portfolio: Has taken hundreds of photos for each edition of Spotlight – 'Top Theatre Photographer' (*The Stage*). Works for actors and agencies across the spectrum of the industry. Recent clients have been represented by agencies such as United, Angel & Francis, Curtis Brown and Felix de Wolfe, studied at drama schools like RADA and Central, and worked on high-profile film, theatre and TV projects. Also writes regularly on headshot and digital trends in the acting industry (see www.wharleywords.co.uk).

Getting the most from your photographs

Angus Deuchar

When searching for actors, most casting directors or directors start with a pile of photographs. Their time is limited, so they really only want to see the people who stand a chance of being right for a part – and the picture will be a vital part of their decision-making process. It's important therefore, to ensure that the photographs you use are as good as they can possibly be.

Have a trawl through Spotlight. As well as being compulsive entertainment for any actor, it can be a great way to decide what works and what doesn't. If *you* were the casting director, who would (and wouldn't) you see? Try it for different types of production: a musical, a Shakespeare play, a TV drama. You may be surprised at the assumptions you make based on the photographs.

I'm going to look at what makes a good actor's photograph; help you think through how to choose a photographer; and discuss how you can get the best results from a photo session. Here is a list of, in my opinion, some important qualities to look for in a good headshot. It should be:

- **Honest.** This to me is the key to a good actor's photograph. Decisions at interviews are often largely made in the first few seconds, so it's important that the person who walks through the door is the person they saw in the photograph. If an actor looks different in some way, the interviewer's first reaction may well be disappointment. Which can't be a good start!
- **Well lit.** The face and hair should be well lit. If there are excessively bright areas or shadows on the face, the photo is probably not doing the actor any favours.
- **In focus.**
- **A good connection with the eyes.** These are possibly the most important feature, as these are what we generally look at first. We make a connection with the eyes. They should be well lit, in focus, looking *at* the camera and not squinting. They should also be 'alive' and not glazed over.
- **Well framed.** Ideally just head and shoulders. Not too close up, as it can look a bit overbearing. Likewise, not too far away as the face becomes too small.
- **Nothing 'tricksy'.** No fake hand-gestures, and certainly no props!

Can't I just get my friend to take some pictures in the back garden? Well, you could (in fact, some do). But what kind of image of yourself would that portray? You can always see such pictures on Spotlight – the actor looking awkward, squinting into the sunlight or the picture out of focus. Again, if you were the casting director, would you consider that actor to be serious? There's no point in cutting costs here. Decent photographs can more than pay for themselves.

Finding a photographer

Assuming you've decided to employ a photographer, how do you find the right one? Professional photographers are not all alike. Some who may be fantastic at, say, press or

Getting the most from your photographs

fashion, may not be good at actors' portraits. It's important that the photographer knows the business of Acting. There are countless listings of specialist actors' photographers – in publications like this one; as adverts in *Contacts*; or on posters in The Actors Centre; but the style of photographs, and the ability of the photographers, are as varied as the prices and packages. It is therefore essential to check out their work for yourself. Have a look at their website if they have one, or at least try to see several different examples of their work.

Don't make a choice based solely on price. The amount a photographer charges is not necessarily an indication of how good (or bad) they are. Wherever possible, make your decision about a photographer based mostly on the *work* they produce, rather than how much they charge. It's important ultimately that you get the best possible photographs.

Find out the following:

- **Studio or natural light?** Studio light is easier to standardise and can be used at any time of the day or night and during any weather. It can be made to flatter someone, but won't necessarily show what they will look like in 'real life'. I prefer natural light, as I believe it to be generally more honest. Good natural light can still show someone at their best, but it won't deceive. It can also be more relaxing for the subject to be outside for the session. Casting directors often prefer natural light as it gives a better indication of who is actually going to walk through the door.
- **Film or digital?** Digital technology has moved on to such an extent that the quality of either format is comparable. Digital tends to produce a cleaner, less grainy image *and* you can check the results as you go along. It is essential however, that whoever is preparing the final photograph knows how to convert the image into a good-quality black and white print, with decent contrast and without loss of detail. This takes a reasonable amount of skill and know-how.
- **How much do they charge?** Does that include VAT? If relevant, you may want to ask about concessions for students.
- **How many photos do I get?** Find out how many photos will actually be taken at the session and how many different, finished 8x10 prints you can choose.
- **How will I view my proofs?** Some photographers will put your proofs onto a website enabling you to view them blown up on the screen. You may prefer a paper contact sheet, which, although much smaller to view, is more portable. If you want both, you may need to pay extra – so ask.
- **How long until I see my proofs?** Websites can often be published the same day as the session, while a paper contact will usually need to be produced and posted, so will take a few days. Some photographers will show you pictures on a computer straight away. This can be useful as a guide, but you probably shouldn't try to make final decisions without a bit of time to think.
- **How long will it take until I get my finished prints?** Try to get an indication of how long you should expect to wait after placing your final order. Hopefully, no more than a few days.
- **Do I get a CD?** As well as the prints, a few electronic versions of the final photos are extremely useful. They can be used on a website, to send a submission via email, to send to Spotlight, to print out yourself, or to act as the master-copy for your 'repros'. Find out if the photographer will provide you with a few different versions on a CD, and if it's included in the price.

The session itself

Here are some important things to prepare before – or think about during – your photo session.

- **Your 'look'.** Do you want to appear neutral or as a particular 'type'? For instance, earrings (on men especially) or other piercings, may limit you to modern or even 'alternative' characters. A formal jacket might suggest a business person or MP. Any of these looks may be fine, as they can make you 'ideal' for a particular type of role – but it's likely that that's all you'll ever be seen for while using that photograph! You decide – it really depends upon how you are marketing yourself.
- **Make-up and hair.** Preferably little or no make-up, but certainly no more than you would wear normally, day to day. Some photographers provide a 'hair and make-up' service but I would strongly discourage actors from using this. Don't confuse actors' portraits with having a glamorous photo to stick on top of the piano! If someone else prepares you, you're unlikely to look like the 'normal' you and it may be difficult to recreate that look in the future. Likewise, if you're planning to get a new hairstyle before your session, do so several days in advance to give you a chance to get used to it.
- **What to wear.** Concentrate on the neckline. Wear something you feel comfortable in, but avoid distracting patterns or logos. Most colours are fine, and black often works well. Bright white can affect the exposure so is less helpful. A jacket of some sort for some of the photos can often work well. Jewellery can be distracting so is usually best avoided.
- **Facial expression.** A big smile is often great for musicals or front-of-house pictures, but for other casting purposes it can seem a little over the top. Any kind of 'emoting' can seem over-earnest or, worse, corny. I tend to favour a good neutral expression with 'spark' behind the eyes. A kind of a relaxed, open look with the smallest hint of a smile.

Ultimately, photographs play an important part in helping you get a foot in the door. But once you've been called for the interview, it's over to you.

Angus Deuchar trained as an actor, during which time he subsidised his grant by taking photographs of his fellow students. When he left drama school in 1987 he soon realised that this was an ideal way to make a living between jobs! He pursued both careers for the first seven years, but has continued with just the photography since then.

The changing face of voice overs
Simon Cryer & Marina Caldarone

So, you have a voice, but do you really know how to place it in the voice industry? It is increasingly common for people to call our voice agency and say:

"I've always dreamt of being a voice over, will you sign me?" or
"My friends keep telling me I should be a voice actor, can I be on your books?"
"I've been told I've got a really good voice, can I get into voice over" or even
"How much does it cost for you to represent me?"

Cue the alarm bells … they clearly know little about the industry that they want to be a part of. So, is a call to an agent the appropriate first stage of the process? It isn't.

We always suggest that the potential voice actor should start by getting some training before they step anywhere near a recording studio or indeed before they speak to any other voice agents. Not 'off-the-shelf' online video training that is not tailored to their requirements, but bespoke training to help them focus their personal skillset, to teach them about how the voice works, how to identify delivery styles within the script and for themselves, how to ensure fullest range and connection, how to take direction, how to communicate with the microphone ... all conducted, ideally, with a professional voice coach who works in audio. Professional singers go through years of training to ensure that when they open their mouth, the right sound is produced immediately, not after the third attempt, but instantly – upon demand. The same expectation is at play in the audio industry. Time is money. You'll be re-booked if you work efficiently and creatively within the time constraints. Training supports that.

Think of the voice over like the score to a movie – it should effortlessly, or seemingly effortlessly, guide us to the end result rather than pull focus and fight the content around it. It's an art. You might need professional guidance to get there.

This core skill set is covered for the most part in the standard conventional drama school training.

You would then book an expert to record a voicereel for you to showcase your skill as a voiceover artist. This enables agents and prospective clients to listen to the fullest range within your natural voice, in order to consider you for representation or bookings. So, making the right choice choosing a production company is really important.

There is a cost to making a reel, you are paying for a certain level of expertise, for an industry-standard quality This all helps to ensure that you enter the industry fully 'tooled up'.

How has the industry changed post pandemic?
The voiceover industry has gone through an overhaul during the last few years. This industry moved online during the pandemic and kept going. There are long-standing experts in their fields still thriving (voice agencies), and then there are countless 'pretend' agencies popping up (and closing down) trying to sell 'talent' (industry standard term for 'voice artists') for less than would be their minimum rate.

Home studios (however crudely set up) are then the new norm and this is largely a progressive and positive thing in certain circumstances, however, by taking away the sound engineer and/or director, one loses that extra pair of ears that often helps ensure the client gets a kick ar$e performance rather than a weak or 'safe' performance. Learn to self-scrutinise. Record yourself on your phone, your computer, play back and listen and give yourself notes to improve performance.

There is also an unprecedented volume of unrepresented talent in the market who have completed a 4-week online training course and who then define themselves as 'professional'. Consequently, we sometimes spend time in the studio with clients (the industry standard term for the person/organisation buying the 'product,' or the 'voice') who have tried to cut corners and then find themselves having to re-cast the talent in order to bring their project to life.

The following is a quick guide to some of the terminology of the voiceover world.

A voicereel

This averages 6–10 tracks in length, each track lasting anything from a 20-second commercial to a 90-second piece of documentary or narration. It should be professionally edited to include music and effects where appropriate; it should not be a series of dry recordings of you reading, but rather should play to your strengths. It should not include 'everything' you think should go on – the reel itself needs to be about **diversity within your natural range,** not about you showing every accent you can do. Focus on the different colours and weights and drives within your natural voice. You need not include a drama track/monologue. Voiceover agents won't sell your voice to the audio drama market, but your acting agent might. If in doubt, include one.

The reel needs to include some factual material/documentary commercials and maybe fiction/audio book. This should be delivered to you post-recording as MP3 and wav. files. You must also insist on the voice only files too (the final performance minus the music and effects).

You should also ask for a megamix. This is a 'best of' compilation of excerpts of your full voicereel. Megamixes are (usually) 2 x 1-minute in length (one clip being all commercial excerpts, and the other covering everything else), or 1 x 2-minute maximum compilation of the whole reel.

Voiceover agent as opposed to Acting Agent

A voiceover agent focuses on the unseen performer, and anything that does not require any kind of physical performance. This means they will represent you for all audio-only content (you are promoted for work in radio drama generally by your *acting* agent) Many actors have two separate agents, as the work lies in two very separate spheres.

A **Voiceover Rate Card** specifies what each voice-over artist charges for the work they provide. There is a minimum rate set by Equity; however, the rates aren't always adhered to. And some voiceover agents, in an attempt to get their client the job, will undercut that rate. It's not difficult to see where this leads to – fees spiralling lower for all.

The **Basic Studio Fee** (BSF) is what each voice-over agent will set for their clients. Most rates start at around £275 per hour, sometimes a little less for low-budget games, often much more for larger advertising campaigns.

The **Usage Fee** is a variable based on many other criteria, such as distribution, whether there is web usage, global coverage, amount of airtime, size of the potential audience, passive or paid media, socials, cinema, radio, broadcast TV, VOD – the list goes on. Asking the right questions is crucial before you agree to anything.

When it comes to usage fee, the client will often dictate what they want to pay and try and avoid giving you detailed information on how the content will be used. This should cause concern and clearly they are not versed in industry rates or are trying to save on budget by not paying you the proper rate. Everything placed in the public domain requires a license to do so. This is the usage rights fee and ALL jobs require some level of usage. If you're unsure, ask a friendly voice agent before committing to anything.

Lastly, never sign a contract before you have it checked and NEVER sign away 'All Rights' without having the contract checked by an expert.

The most commonly asked questions – answered

If I make a voicereel, will I get work?
Without a voicereel it is unlikely that you will ever get paid work – potential clients need to hear what you sound like in order to cast you. If you have an agent, they will source work for you, but if you don't, you can join the pay-to-play websites in order to source work. Be careful though, those websites often pay you much less than they should. Know your worth.

So how do I select a company to make my voicereel?
Do your research, check out their credentials and their website. Listen to examples of their work, which should be online. Do they provide a producer/director, or just an engineer, and what is the quality of their edit? Who are their previous clients? Look at testimonials. All companies will recycle, to some extent, the same scripts, but to what extent? They should be able to tell you. If it looks too good to be true, it generally is. Aim for mid-market prices and stay clear of the £99 voicereel – with my agent head on, this will not be suitable. We need content directed by practitioners who are well versed in getting a great performance from you and who are tapped into current market trends in order for the agent to pitch you to clients. Also we need to hear full versions of each track. The £99 package sometimes is *just* the megamix. If you're paying for a service where they just record, edit, deliver and offer little direction, then most agents, if they're interested in you, will ask you to start the process again of making a reel – so shop wisely and choose a specialist rather than a pop-up service.

How do different companies make the voicereels?
Each voice-over production company will have a house style, of sorts, but the first voice we hear on your reel should be the one that is closest to your natural voice; that is undisputed. Some companies, at very little cost, will provide a basic reel, that does not truly tap into nuances of your natural sound, or indeed explore your voice beyond where you naturally use it. This is often not good enough for an agent to source work for you as mentioned earlier. Others will invite you on to their website for you to select your own choice of material from their online archive, adjusting that choice on the recording day if it isn't quite right for you. Some will have a chat with you on the phone, get the measure of your voice and email you relevant material; others will see you for a one-on-one consultation before the recording day, go through scripts and make a selection for you to take away and prep along with direction notes. The latter is by far the most satisfactory for all (although often this is done remotely to save clients travelling to the studio twice).

What should I expect to pay to have a voicereel made?
Anything from £99 to £1,000.

Look for producers in the range of £300–£500 for a full reel and ensure the team that produce are experienced producers and practitioners in the industry and not just suppliers who churn out generic reels at volume to keep the price down.

I have an existing voicereel, but it's a bit tired and old-fashioned. What should I do?
Upgrade it. But check out whether there is anything there you can recycle before getting rid of it all. Send it to the company you are making the reel with; they will listen to it and recommend whether there is anything there you could keep for the new voice-clip and in turn, advise on new material. Note, your voice changes over time, as do script trends, so you should be looking to update your reel every 5+ years.

How do I approach voice-over agents about representation?
Research who they currently have on their books. Your opening gambit, with your voice-clips and CV attached, should be that you note they don't already represent anyone like you. Do not approach anyone who has 'your voice' already. Do not chase for responses, agents are busy and if they're interested, they will be in touch. Follow the guidance on the website to the letter and address your application to a person and not 'Dear Agent'. Some agents will have a submission system and will not accept email requests – so do your homework.

I've got my first voice-over job, what does the employer expect?
For you to be efficient, precise, imaginative, and quick to take and interpret direction and turn it into a performance. To be positive, upbeat, someone who won't let their irritation show when asked to repeat the same sentence 30 times, with the only direction being, 'Can you try something different?' Someone who will be fine about running a little over time. If that really is an issue, take it up with your agent, after the booking; they will know how and whether to act on it. Studio etiquette is paramount, this can't be overstated.

A useful mantra, 'if you're on time, you're late' *always* be early, early, early…

Should I include a Radio Drama track?
Being a strong actor does not mean you will necessarily be a good voice over. The skills are quite different. The pay rates are different, the representation is different, and your 'regular' agent would put you forward for it, not your voiceover agent. As mentioned earlier. So, in spite of some agents saying that there is no need for the actor to have any drama on the voicereel, this can feel like a wasted opportunity. You need to play to your natural casting, as long as it offers an alternative take on your voice. And of course it is the only track on the reel which is *transformative* – every other track is *you* but each track a different version of you.

The Animation and Gaming reel
If the voicereel is all about the fullest range within your *natural* voice, then the animation and gaming clip is about fullest range within the *unnatural* voice. An animation reel needs to include at least 15 extraordinary voices. And the gaming reel needs to play to the gaming archetypes that exist in that world. Do your research. Then create and script your own sentences, to bypass copyright, that respond directly to those industry trends. Show what

you can do. This clip would stand apart from your voicereel. It's a different market. If you want to flag an ability for this market, without making an entire animation clip, then ask whoever is making your reel to find a fantasy story which requires lots of different character voices, characters which ideally aren't 'human', but dragons, elves, giants, witches, animals, monsters …and flaunt your voice acting ability to create totally diverse characters that wow the listener.

Simon Cryer is the CEO of Crying Out Loud and Damn Good Voices and has 25+ years' experience working as a voice-over director. He has been VOD for award-winning international advertising campaigns, corporate content and Documentaries. **Marina Caldarone** is a Voice Director with Crying Out Loud (www.cryingoutloud.co.uk), a company that has been making voice-over reels for actors since 1999. She is a radio drama producer, theatre director and acting coach and is co-author with Maggie Lloyd Williams of the bestselling *Actions – An Actors Thesaurus*. She has been a tutor in actor training since 1984.

Showreel, voicereel and website services

Over the last decade there have been seismic changes in how actors self-promote. With just a mobile phone and an Internet connection, anyone can convincingly and effectively market themselves. There has also been a significant increase in the amount of (sometimes contradictory) advice offered to actors on content, length, format and more.

Voicereels (also known as 'voice demos' and, sometimes confusingly, 'showreels') have been around for several decades and a good one could attract the attention of a voice agent. The world of voice-overs is hard to break into and so a quality-produced 'reel' is very important. Showreels (applied to videoed performances) have become equally crucial, and a good one may just tip the balance in your favour.

Personal websites for actors are becoming more popular but are far from essential if you are listed on Spotlight.

If you intend to put together a professionally produced voicereel or showreel, it's important to check the details (including pricing) of each possible company and the quality of their work. You should also assess whether the financial investment(s) involved could produce sufficient return. Is there a real possibility that one (or more) will enhance your chances of acting work?

Note: It is very important that you have permission from the copyright-holders of any material that you intend to use, and some companies will help with this. It is also important to check the current charges of each company that interests you, as some will change during the lifetime of this edition.

Accent Bank
email info@theaccentbank.com
website https://theaccentbank.com
Founder Sarah Valentine

Voicereel services: A voice-over portal distributed to an international market. Acts as a shop window for experienced voice-over talent specialising in authentic regional and international voices. "Accent Bank provides bespoke one-on-one coaching and workshops for those new to the business. We pride ourselves on a very personal service, using the best coaches and directors, original material and excellent production facilities to bring out the best in your voice. For more information, or to have a chat, contact us byemail."

Actor Showreels
51 The Cut, South Bank, London SE1 8LF
mobile 07766 066870
email post@actorshowreels.co.uk
website www.actorshowreels.co.uk

Showreel services: The actor works with an editor to select the material from pre-existing clips. The edited material is uploaded online, so that the actor's agent can also view the edit. The editing/upload process continues until the actor is totally satisfied with the final edit. The average duration of a showreel is 3.5 minutes. Average cost per showreel is £200. Recent clients have included: Claire Goose (Independent), Sheila Atim (MN Talent), Con O'Neill (The Artists Partnership), Craig Fairbrass (United Agents), Kevin Doyle (United Agents) and Hammed Animashaun (MN Talent).

Actors Apparel
Based in London
email lulu@actorsapparel.com
website www.actorsapparel.com

Showreel services: Established in 2010. Tailor-made showreels; originally written scenes tailored to client's casting type and preference. Charges from £750 for a single scene. HD footage, montage clips, editing and high-quality sound. Online links and hard copies included, as well as online conversion for Spotlight and Mandy. Recent clients include: Max Fowler (Eamonn Bedford Associates), Katie Redford (Red Canyon Management), Verity Hewlitt (Hoxton Street Casting), Nick Lavelle (SCA Management), Cherice

Showreel, voicereel and website services

Mckenzie-Cook (Top Talent Agency), Thea Cantell (Sandra Boyce Management) and Carla Nicholls (Lynda Ronan Personal Management).

Damn Good Voice Studios
218 Chester House, 1–3 Brixton Road, London SW9 6DE
mobile 07809 549887
email simon@damngoodvoicestudios.com
website www.damngoodvoicestudios.com
Key contacts Simon Cryer, Marina Caldarone, Debbie Seymour, Adam Farrell

Voicereel services: Established in 1999. Charges from £395 plus VAT to produce a bespoke voicereel from scratch; this includes a face-to-face consultation with Marina Caldarone or Debbie Seymour to select material, studio time with both producer and director, full editing and production, a copy of the voice-only files, a 2-minute megamix for online services and a 2-year archive.

Clients will record a selection of material consisting of a mixture of commercials, narrative, documentary, corporate, animation, gaming and drama as well as any other content they may wish to add to best suit their strengths.

The team are practitioners in the industry - Simon Cryer (Voice Director and Producer and owner of Damn Good Voices Agency), Marina Caldarone (Director of BBC's *The Archers*) and Adam Farrell (VOD). Limits recording sessions to 20 clients per month - demand is high so book early. Enquire thorugh the website.

Showreel Editing by Anthony Holmes
17 Knole Road, Crayford, London DA1 3JN
mobile 07763 261509
email anthony@showreelediting.com
website www.showreelediting.com
Facebook /showreeleditingservice
X @showreelediting
Instagram @showreelediting
Key contact Anthony Holmes

Services: Showreel, voicereel and sizzle reel editing service. Clients include many award-winning and household names. Works directly with actors, talent management and press agents/publicists (where relevant) to ensure correct branding and career positioning. Charges £95 per hour billed in half-hourly increments (minimum charge one hour). Showreel provided as a digital file for direct upload to Spotlight or other casting websites. Able to record material broadcast on television on request, and to download/record material from streaming services such as Netflix, iPlayer and YouTube (where client has permission to do so). Showreel material archived for easier updates. Those who quote *Actors' and Performers' Yearbook* when booking, will receive a 10% discount. Also offers assistance with selection of material for existing footage if required but does not film showreels. Does not record voicereels, but is able to edit from radio, animation and videogame material and from existing voicereels if required.

The Showreel Ltd
Soho Recording Studios, 22–24 Torrington Place, London WC1E 7HJ
tel 020-7043 8660
website www.theshowreel.com
Facebook /groups/theshowreel
X @theshowreel

Showreel services overview:
- Get started in voice overs with our Intro Workshops (from £175, studio or online)
- Release the voices in your head with our Character Workshops (from £175/day)
- Learn to make money from home with our Home Studio Workshop (from £175)
- One-to-one personal training plans to increase your skills, such as personal voice-over coaching and development (from £85)
- Agents' Demo to get a voice-over agent
- Drama Demo for the BBC
- Character Demo for games and animation
- Audio Book Demo for RNIB, Audible, iTunes and Amazon

For other services, please visit the website.

Silver-Tongued Productions
tel 07468 492935
email stp@mail.co.uk
website www.silver-tongued.co.uk

Voicereel services: Over 25 years of experience recording and producing high-quality voicereels at a competitive price. "We guide you through the whole process of recording your voicereel, from choosing your scripts to directing you during the recording session, making it as simple and as easy as possible. Our voicereels are truly bespoke, so are as individual as you are." Visit the website for full details of services, including singing demos.

Silvertip Films Ltd
Suite 63, Standby Business Centre, Foundry Lane, Horsham, West Sussex RH13 5PX
tel (01403) 221068, *mobile* 07786 331502
email info@silvertipfilms.co.uk
website www.silvertipfilms.co.uk
Facebook /silvertipfilms

Showreel services: Established in 2005.

Offer two types of showreels: editing existing footage or bespoke filmed showreel scene material, edited into a reel with or without any existing material you have.

For the first, edit only production, you can send material remotely via Dropbox or on DVD and give timecodes from which they can edit the reel together or they can watch your material and cut a showreel from content they feel shows you off at your best.

The first draft is sent to you for feedback and a set of amends carried out to create the final draft. This is provided to you as digital files and, if you want it, a DVD copy.

For the bespoke filming option, they will shoot 2–3 scenes with you in a day either: 2 x monologues and a duologue, or 2 x duologues and a monologue. They choose to focus on performance rather than multiple shots and angles because whilst the scenes should look their best, it's about you, not flashy camerawork or editing.

Silvertip's previous clients include: Jessica Jay (cre8 talent), Alexis Peterman (United Artists), Dar Dash (Hobsons), Heather Skermer (Red Hot Entertainment) and Libby Gore (Imperium Management).

SonicPond Studio

70 Mildmay Grove South, Islington, London N1 4PJ
tel 020-7690 8561
email martin@sonicpond.co.uk
website www.sonicpond.co.uk
Key contact Martin Fisher

Showreel services: Editing of existing material only. Charges £250 (£220 for students) to edit a showreel from existing material, uploaded directly to Spotlight for you. The average duration of a showreel is 3–4 minutes. Clients include: Annie Cooper (Felix de Wolfe); Zoe Lister (*Hollyoaks*) and Sid Owen (*EastEnders*). Advises actors: "Don't worry that you may not have enough material; you most likely do. Less is truly more with showreels. Also, don't wait for that copy of the student film you have been waiting to be sent; think of the reel as an organic growing thing which you will add to and change for the whole of your career. Just get it started."

Voicereel services: Supplies scripts for actors to use if desired. Charges £495 to produce a commercial voicereel from scratch; working from existing material the rate is £80 per hour. Broadcast quality MP3 files are included in the package. Nine pieces recorded, commercial and narrative, with a 90-second montage included. Students: £465 for a full voicereel. Game or animation reels £495. Voice clients include: Bob Golding (Hobsons), Bella Ramsey (Bespoke Voices), Kellie Bright (Sue Terry Voices), Sam & Mark (Harvey Voices), Felicity Mantagu (Just Voices) and Milton Jones (Harvey Voices). Advises actors: "Don't worry about the pieces, we will work together to find you the best material. It's much more about finding the tone for each piece, and material that suits you perfectly, rather than the best copy. In the meantime, listen to as much voice over as possible, and think about why any particular voice is used for any piece."

VOICE-REEL.COM

website www.voice-reel.com
Key contact Guy Michaels

Voicereel services: All voiceover demos are recorded and produced remotely. Strict 2 clients a week limit ensures a bespoke service.

Clients receive all full versions of the tracks in addition to the compilation. Full guidance/online client area. Sourcing and choosing material is a collaborative process. Scripts are written and tailor-made for gaming demos. All production elements are copyright free. Voicereels start from £525.

Full voice-over training facility and one-to-one coaching available at **www.voiceoverkickstart.com**.

Showreels: creation and maintenance

Anthony Holmes

What is a showreel, and why does an actor need one?

A showreel, also known as a demo reel or acting reel, is a short video showcase featuring an actor's best clips.

The key objective of a showreel is career development; a reel isn't a compilation of every character an actor has ever played, but a tool with which to help get cast. As such, your primary audience for a showreel should be casting directors, whose job it is to cast or shortlist actors in film and television. Always think of this audience when editing a showreel: *Will it help the casting director cast you?* Have you used your best clips, and are they appropriate for the roles you're applying for? Think like a casting director. Your showreel should represent you as you are now, and reflect your current vital statistics and casting age. A showreel is successful if it fulfils the primary objective; helping the actor get more work. A showreel by itself won't necessarily secure an actor a role (although there have been many cases of actors being cast on the strength of their showreel alone), but it's a crucial part of the mix which leads to casting success.

Many actors have a main general-purpose showreel, and then additional reels to help them target specific roles, e.g. a commercials reel and a comedy reel, ensuring their reel is always relevant to the specific submission.

Once you have your showreel, how is it best used? Spotlight's interactive services have a near monopoly status for professional productions in the UK, although there are a number of other casting websites used, particularly by low budget or no budget productions, which are unlikely to have a casting director on board. Your agent will submit your application through Spotlight for a particular role, and the casting director will view your CV, headshot and showreel on Spotlight, and consider your suitability for the role. You can also send your Spotlight link directly to casting directors, but unless you're responding to a specific open casting call, please check first that the casting director accepts cold submissions. Never send the showreel file itself (or any other large file such as a headshot), but send a link to your Spotlight profile – large files clog up email inboxes and the last thing you want to do is annoy a casting director!

It's also becoming more important to have an active social media following; a large and active fan base will make you more attractive to producers, particularly for high-profile US-produced television shows and major features. Many actors like to promote their showreel on social media, although opinions among agents are mixed; some prefer to keep their clients' reels away from general public view, and prefer to keep them for the eyes of casting directors and other stakeholders only. Shorter clips or 'sizzle' reels are becoming increasingly popular, however, both with actors and agents, and can be used effectively on social media to help promote an actor's appearance in a film or television series, and help the actor to build and maintain a fan-base.

If you're just starting your career, you may not have much in the way of scenes from film and television to include in a showreel. It can be useful to increase the number of your showreel scenes by applying for lower-budget short films and student films. These productions may not have a budget to employ a casting director, and you are likely to be applying directly to the director or producer.

Your headshot will persuade a casting director to look at your CV, and your showreel will persuade them to call you in for an audition. Once you're in the room, your performance and personality can persuade the casting director you're the right person for the job.

You will maximise your opportunities and your chances of being cast if you use the right selection of clips in the right way. A skilled and experienced showreel editor will be able to advise on this.

The general-purpose showreel

Your main showreel should showcase your range, a variety of different roles, and some different looks, but also bear in mind that consistency and suitability for type can be attractive to casting directors.

You may wish to demonstrate your ultimate acting ability by including a range of roles. You should certainly include a good contrast of scenes in your showreel, but bear in mind many casting directors are looking for a type, and you're making their job easier to cast you if you don't try to be all things to all people. This is a difficult balance to strike, especially if you do not wish to be known as a one-trick pony. Theatre casting directors may appreciate a greater contrast of roles than film or television directors, but I do not advise including filmed scenes of theatre work given than the greater part of actor employment is for the screen. If you pride yourself on being a good character actor, you could benefit from a separate reel for each type of character you know you can play, but a more common approach is to edit your general tape for specific submissions, including the most appropriate scenes for that job.

The duration of your main showreel will depend on the experience you have, and the footage you have. Many showreels are around two to three minutes. It's better to have a shorter and tighter showreel featuring the best of the best, rather than padding things out. Casting directors are busy people; if they don't see what they're looking for in the first few seconds, they'll move on – so make the most of your time!

Some actors present an opening montage of moments from the scenes that are to follow. This is generally not recommended. An opening montage to a general reel wastes valuable screen time and a majority of casting directors don't like them. Don't waste time at the start – jump straight into a substantial scene with dialogue. Remember that casting directors want to hear you and see you interact with others, so don't spend long on a moody visual opening shot. Always open with your strongest material. Make it clear who you are, and avoid any confusion; where possible, your showreel should open with a close-up of you rather than a group scene or a close-up of another actor, and be wary of opening your showreel with a scene including another actor of the same gender and age range.

Prioritise your higher profile footage and scenes with better production values. If you have the experience and material, casting directors prefer to see how you handle yourself in the real world, in a fully professional environment; be wary of using 'shot-for-showreel' scenes which often don't reflect a typical working environment, which are likely to have lower production values than even a typical student film, and in which you may be acting with less talented and less experienced actors, dragging down the tone of the showreel and making it less attractive to casting directors. Self-tapes are the way forward for individual castings, but don't belong in your general showreel.

A showreel, like your CV, is an on-going process; keep it up-to-date with your latest footage. If it's not getting you called in for appropriate castings, tweak the edit until it does. Your showreel is all about you. An existing scene can be re-edited to reduce the screen time of other actors, and refocus the scene more on you. Don't forget, though, that casting directors don't just want to see you act, they want to see you react to other actors.

It's important to always focus on your objective; getting cast. Different casting directors and different talent agents often have different preferences, tastes and expectations from a showreel – if you know you're applying for a specific job, and you know what that casting director likes, then tweak your showreel appropriately. Once again, this is where a specialist showreel editor can advise; a good editor will have experience of what is most likely to work best, and will be interacting with a network of agents and casting directors on an ongoing basis.

Specialist showreels

Action reel: this is often more visual, focusing on your physicality. It may be either full action scenes, or a montage of action clips set to music, depending on your skillset and experience.

Comedy reel: this showcases your physical and verbal comic timing and delivery, and may be appropriate if you would like to work in sitcoms and film comedy. Stand-up comedy may be included, but as the skill sets are quite different, with different target audiences, it may be advisable to keep stand-up in a separate reel.

Commercial reel: this includes clips from your commercials, and is crafted specifically to get more work in commercials. A commercials reel is often shorter than your main showreel, with a greater emphasis on visuals rather than dialogue, as would be expected. Creating the right mood both appropriate for and respectful of each brand included in the commercial reel is important, as your audience in this case is not just the casting director but the advertising agency commissioned to represent the brand.

Demo reel: a showreel is known as a demo reel in the US. Quite rapidly, the differences between US demo reels and UK showreels are narrowing, but if you're applying for roles in US-produced drama, your general showreel may benefit from some slight tweaks to make it more attractive to US productions, such as making it a little more 'glam', and emphasising your looks. A demo reel can be important for career development, as it opens you up to higher profile work. Even if you don't want to work in the US, many American productions are shot in the UK.

Dramatic reel: this is often less visually active than the general reel, and focused on character relationships.

Public reel or 'sizzle' reel: unlike your main reel and most other specialist reels, which are aimed primarily at casting directors, your public reel is used on your website or social media channels to help build and maintain a fan base. A sizzle reel can take many forms, but generally has more action than dialogue and is more fast-paced than other reels, often (but not always) well under a minute long. It can feature shortened scenes or short sound-bites (along the lines of a film trailer), or can be a visual montage set to appropriate music. This positive encouragement to consider sizzle reels should not be confused by the disapproval of montages at the beginning of general reels. The general/main reel and the sizzle reel serve very different purposes.

Voiceover reel: actors' use of audio voicereels for their narration/voiceover work is long established, but recently it has become more popular to have a video reel to place their work in context, and to show examples of their work as transmitted, though many casting directors still prefer voicereels. Examples of video voiceover reels include an animation, narration and videogame reels.

Actors can also use visual voiceover reels on their websites and social media to help build and maintain a fan-base. It's also easy to provide an audio-only MP3 file from a video voicereel to provide to casting directors who only want an audio reel; it's not easy to simply add video to an existing voicereel. Starting off with a video voicereel means you have a lot of flexibility for use.

You may prefer to specialise in a specific skillset, or develop latent ability as your career advances necessitating the creation of dance reels, modelling reels or presenting/hosting reels.

All rules are made to be broken! The advice given in this article is applicable to many situations, but there will often be occasions where individual situations require different approaches, particularly as the world of online casting is ever-changing. Your showreel editor will be able to advise on the best approach for your situation. To view some examples of the different styles of showreels and demo reels that are available to actors, visit **www.showreelediting.com**.

Anthony Holmes has nearly twenty years' experience as a specialist editor of showreels, working with actors, agents and casting directors in the UK, US, Canada and Europe. Anthony has edited reels for actors at every stage of their careers; from young actors (under 16s) and recent graduates, all the way to Emmy-Award winners and Oscar nominees. A good showreel editor knows what works, and Anthony has helped to develop the television and film careers of hundreds of actors, from recurring roles on television to major roles in Academy Award-winning films.

Digital wellbeing for actors
Sinead Mac Manus

Getting a web presence
Having a dedicated web presence is increasingly important for any freelance actor. Your personal website can act as a central place on the web for potential employers or collaborators to find you. With free platforms such as WordPress, Posterous or Flavors, it's never been easier to raise your profile online. But, how do you harness the power of the social web without suffering burnout? Read on for some advice.

Your domain name
The first step before choosing a web platform is to register your own domain name. Even if you never use it, for the cost of a few pounds each year it is worth owning your own .com and retaining control of your name online. Use a site such as Netnames to search for your professional name and check that it is available. 123-reg is a company with a good reputation for domain name management in the UK, or you can buy your domain name with your web hosting package (see below).

Now you have your domain name secured, how can you build your web presence?

Building a WordPress site
WordPress's easy-to-use and powerful Content Management System (CMS) makes it perfect for freelance artists wanting to create their own website. The platform is free to install and adapt; the only expenses incurred are registering a domain name and paying for web hosting. The CMS of WordPress is easy to get to grips with: in fact, anyone at ease with Microsoft Word will be able to publish a website using WordPress.

Before you start building your site, have a think about what content you want on it. Suggested pages could be Biography, Photography, Credits, Reviews and Contact Me. With WordPress you can easily add a blog to your website with updates of your work.

For a practical step-by-step guide to using WordPress to build your web presence, do read my two-part series on WordPress written for the London Theatre Blog. Part One covers the basics, and Part Two goes into more detail about design, themes, widgets and plug-ins.

Zen Tip: Use a WordPress-approved web hosting service to install the WordPress software in one click, rather than going through the complicated manual process.

Do I need a blog?
Blogging can be a great way of building your personal brand as an actor. Through text, images, video or sound, you can demonstrate, reflect and comment on your artistic process. Writing a blog is also a powerful learning tool, promoting critical and analytical thinking, as well as being a powerful audience development and marketing tool.

Microblogging platforms such as Posterous and Tumblr are simple and free ways of starting a blog. Easier to set up than a WordPress blog, these platforms really come into their own when blogging on the go; perfect for freelance actors on tour. Both platforms allow you to post snippets of text, photos, quotes, links, dialogues, audio, video and slideshows from the web or direct from your smartphone.

For a look at the multimedia capabilities of Posterous in action, go to my blog *From Apps to Zen*.

Zen Tip: Use the scheduling feature of Posterous or Tumblr to queue your posts for autoposting during busy tour periods.

Other platforms

Flavors is a relative newcomer to the platform scene, but a fantastic way of creating a personal portal for all your online content in minutes. Simply register your Flavors name (or use you own custom domain), design your layout and background, and then add your choice of 30 social websites. You can pull in posts from your X or Bluesky feed, your Wall activity from your Facebook page, videos from YouTube or Vimeo, posts from your Posterous, Tumblr or WordPress blogs, or photos from Flickr or Instagram.

Have a look at some of the wonderfully creative sites on the Flavors' Directory for inspiration.

Zen Tip: Use the Promote tab to add a Search Engine Optimised (SEO) title and description of your page to ensure you are easily found in the search engines.

Using social media

There is a wide range of social media networks and platforms that you can use to communicate and connect with people in the creative industries. Social networks such as Facebook and X, as well as multimedia platforms such as YouTube and Flickr, can help you market yourself, raise your profile and connect with potential employers.

Getting started on social media is relatively easy as the entry barriers are low, both technologically and financially. Social media also harnesses the most highly prized of the marketing methods: word of mouth. It allows you to exponentially expand your marketing potential and reach many more potential audience members or clients than you could using solely an offline approach.

All good so far … But if social media is so effective and easy to use, why isn't every artist jumping on board?

The number one reason why creative people do not get engaged with social media is lack of time, and specifically a fear that if they do engage, it will eat up large chunks of an already busy day. Questions to consider are: do you have the time to plan how you are going to use social media in your work? Do you have the time to set up profiles and start connecting with people? Do you have the time to maintain your online presences and maximise the return from these sites?

I think social media has a bad reputation for being a source of time-wasting. Many of us are guilty of having spent too much time on Facebook or YouTube when we could have been doing something more productive! However, social media does not have to be an unnecessary drain on your time. Rebecca Coleman, a Canadian PR consultant in the performing arts, has written an excellent guide to getting started in social media. She recommends that artists create a Social Networking Marketing Plan, outlining what they want to achieve with social media; what platforms and tools they will focus on; and lastly, how much time they are going to dedicate to being online. Think of social media like email: a brilliant innovation which, when used strategically, can enhance your business and increase opportunity. Of the social media-savvy people I know, many deliberately limit their time online to one or two hours a day for this very reason.

LinkedIn

My first recommendation would be to set up a LinkedIn profile for your professional name. As a popular social networking site for professionals, featuring high in the search engine rankings, you can use LinkedIn as an opportunity to shine.

Setting up a LinkedIn profile is easy. A great profile picture is essential, and an easy one for actors – you can use one of your headshots.

Next, add a juicy-sounding headline that highlights your talents, e.g. 'Freelance Actor, Facilitator & Workshop Leader specialising in Site-Specific Theatre'. Add Current and Past employments, bearing in mind that LinkedIn lists these in order of start date with the latest position appearing at the top. Claim your 'vanity' URL, i.e. http://uk.linkedin.com/in/yourname by clicking on the Edit link beside it.

Spend some time writing a Summary for your profile. Have a search for other actors on LinkedIn for inspiration. Highlight any noteworthy achievements or credits. Use the Specialities section to summarise any particular talents or skills that you have, e.g. workshop facilitating, fluent Spanish speaker, trained ballet dancer, mask skills, etc.

Recommendations on LinkedIn are a powerful example of what's called 'social proof' – proof to your potential clients that others have already gone before and had a positive experience working with you. No one wants to be the guinea pig!

Now you are ready to start connecting. Use the Add Connections button to find people through your email contacts or through LinkedIn's recommendations. I make a point of connecting on LinkedIn with people I meet socially or at networking events to keep them in my network.

LinkedIn can be a great way of getting introductions to a particular person, e.g. a director or agent that you want to connect with. The more you build your network on LinkedIn, the more likely it is that someone in your network might know them and can provide an introduction.

Video sharing

The practical application of being able to upload and share video on the web to someone working in theatre is fairly self-explanatory. With video cameras built into almost everything, it's inexpensive to make high-quality videos to showcase your talents.

There are many different video hosting and sharing sites, but a handful do stand out from the rest. YouTube is the world's most popular video sharing site, and it is easy to see why. The site is free to use and, once you have set up an account, videos are easy to upload either singly or in batches. YouTube videos, now that the company is owned by Google, also rate highly in the Google search engine, and therefore clever tagging of your videos can help potential customers and audiences find your work. Another good video sharing site is Vimeo, which features a lot of content from creative people.

The mobile office

An actor's life is sometimes a nomadic one, and therefore it is essential to be able to access your email and important documents wherever you go. I find a combination of Gmail as my email client and file storing and sharing site Dropbox fulfils all my needs when I am away from the office for any period of time.

Using Gmail on your smartphone can mean that you don't need to travel with a laptop and you can process your emails on the go. Similarly, with Dropbox, you can access all your important documents for reading, forwarding or printing direct from your smartphone.

Final thoughts

The social web can provide many benefits to the jobbing actor. It can provide an online showcase for your work, connect you to potential clients, and be used to manage your work.

With mobile computing so readily available, the social web is not going to go away. The smart actor can use these free tools to promote her/himself above the rest of the bunch.

Sinead Mac Manus is founder of 8fold (**www.eightfold.org**), a digital wellbeing company that helps busy people work better. She writes about mindful 21st-century working at her blog *From Apps to Zen* (**www.fromappstozen.com**) and is the author of *From Apps to Zen: 26+ Ideas for Building a Business with Balance*. Sinead has worked for, consulted and provided training for organisations as diverse as the Independent Street Arts Network, London Metropolitan University, CreativeCapital and the Anne Peaker Centre for Arts in Criminal Justice. Sinead's activity in developing new business models around the idea of e-learning for creative entrepreneurs, using web 2.0 tools and social media, led her to be selected in 2009 as one of the Courvoisier: Future 500 to watch.

Building your personal brand on social media

Daniel Heale, CEO and Chief Strategy Officer, Way To Blue
Interview by Rob Ostlere

Daniel Heale is an award-winning marketer, and the CEO and Chief Strategy Officer of Way To Blue. Way To Blue's campaigns include major films and television series, alongside their work with actors; both established stars and up-and-coming performers. Here, Daniel explains how major projects are marketed and shares tips for performers at all levels of the industry.

Could you first give an overview of the work you do with Way To Blue?
We're an entertainment marketing agency that does the full marketing mix for film, television and talent. Often we're asked to deliver strategy for a TV series or a film; how to position a show in order to give it the best possible opportunity for success, particularly online. Then we look at how to use the marketing campaign to go about achieving those objectives; things like what platforms should they be on? The next level down would be what type of things should you be doing on those platforms? There's also a creative team that does everything from ideation right the way through to the production of content; from the static graphics you get on social to long-form video. For me, it's great that we work right the way through the lifecycle of a project; you build relationships with people on the production team and the talent.

What work do you do with the individual actors in a production?
I'll have a team of people rotating on set, spending hours and hours with the cast, pulling content either during shoot days or indeed when they're having downtime. We also advise the actors on how to develop and curate their own feeds, relevant to them but also to positioning themselves as stars of the show when it comes on air.

Does the size of their following matter?
Some of them could have a million followers, some a few hundred thousand and others much smaller numbers. But if you can do something interesting with that person – seed a piece of content that gets editorial coverage and pickup – it can really help them to grow their profile. Generally, it's not about the volume of followers you've got but the level of engagement with your content. You can have 5,000 followers be really engaged with what you do versus a million who don't have a clue who you are and never see any of your content. So, it's really useful for actors early on in their careers to think about that brand because when it comes to getting the job marketers can use that and that's only going to help the actor.

What are the first steps for performers who want to use social media in a more constructive way?
You can work with a professional and pay them a fee to help you. But you can just follow some basic guidance. Over and above everything, authenticity is the most important thing; remaining true to the values that you have as a person and the things that are interesting to you. Start with a 'landscape analysis' on yourself: what are your hobbies, your interests,

what would your perfect day look like, where would you'd be and what would you be doing, what are your favourite holiday destinations, what quotes inspire you, what do you do outside of work, are their causes that you are passionate about? These sorts of things can help you understand your sense of self, something that is real for you, your thing, your brand.

And that's the basis for content?
Yes, it's then about how that sense of self would be translated into posts and imagery. That could be something broad like what do you want to engage with most, or more specific like what's your colour palette? The idea is for some sense of both visual and copy tone-of-voice around you as an individual. The reason it's so important to get it right at the beginning is that it will become a long-term thing. The brands within the brand will obviously evolve over time but there needs to be threads that run through everything. People should look at your feed and say, "Oh yeah, I get a sense of who that person is and what their interests are."

What are some of the common mistakes you see on social media?
Generally, people can quite quickly sniff out something that isn't authentic. My advice is to be careful about how you position your alignment with something if you haven't been engaged with it or talked about it before. I've seen a lot of missteps happen in that way. People do go back and look, and if you start to grow some profile, it'll be journalists. They might see that one minute you're talking about things that feel very relevant and worthy but a few years ago you posted a photograph or a tweet that wasn't quite saying the same thing. We always advise people to go back, delete or archive things, to clean up their feed. If you are being authentic at all times, then it's likely you will be consistent too. One follows the other.

How do actors balance promoting themselves and their projects with not upsetting their employers?
For emerging actors, I think it is important to follow the rules. Those social media embargoes are in place for good reasons. I would always say as a blanket rule never post any pictures that you take on set unless you've got permission from the producer or from the studio to do to so.

Is there a mindset that perhaps can help actors to use social media more positively?
I think it's about seeing it as a tool that's going to be of benefit to you from a career perspective. Using it as personal brand building is using social for good purpose. It's something that people definitely look at more than ever before, so it needs to tell your story. Think about what that is and then get all of those building blocks in place.

15 key tips from Daniel Heale for building your social media presence
1 Your overall aims are to develop a well-balanced and curated feed, increase the quality and number of posts, and build followers and engagement.
2 Decide which platforms to focus on. For performers the starting point is often Instagram.
3 Think about what you want to portray to followers. Balance showing off your personality with reflecting your acting career.

4 Use your bio to give followers just enough info about yourself while keeping them wanting more.
5 The 'About me' should be short, clever and direct. Add where you're from, plus links to your website or latest project.
6 Acting-related posts that tend to work well are: photos that include you; headshots/publicity photos; behind-the-scenes and cast photos and other project-related posts.
7 Archive any old posts that aren't well shot and/or don't fit in to the rest of the feed.
8 Improve the quality of photos with filters and editing. Planning can help you capture key moments.
9 Write engaging copy: short, sweet, clever and relatable.
10 Use hashtags that will draw followers to your account. Putting hashtags in the comment section will avoid cluttered captions.
11 Insights will show you the best times to post.
12 Stories are there to share the fun activities you're doing that day.
13 Engage with people who comment and like your posts.
14 Follow relevant accounts with large followings.
15 Increase the amount you post. Create an even mix of photoshoots, behind-the-scenes shots, project-promotion, events and everyday life.

And some advanced tips:
• Hire a photographer so you can have an existing bank of photos. Use the same photographer and have different shoots so you have a spread. Other photos can then be sprinkled in between.
• IG Live allows followers to get a real look into your life.
• Add polls to your stories or do a quick Q&A to create even more engagement.

To find out more about Way To Blue, visit **www.waytoblue.com**

Accountants

Alexander & Co

The Harley Building, 77 New Cavendish Street, London W1W 6XB
tel 020-7167 7220
Centurion House, 129 Deansgate, Manchester M3 3WR
tel 0161 832 4841
email info@alexander.co.uk
website www.alexander.co.uk
X @alexandercoMCR
Accountants John McCaffery, Emma Ball

Established in 1976, Alexander & Co is an Equity-approved and recommended firm of chartered accountants and tax advisors who have looked after clients in the film, TV and theatre industry for circa 50 years.

The firm provides strategic planning advice to ensure that you make the most of the opportunities within the current tax system, and your business affairs are structured the most tax efficient way. Alexander & Co also provides more specialist advice as and when required. This includes tax advice on other income streams, such as property investments, crypto, shares and pensions.

Frequently used services include Self-Assessment tax returns, limited company accounts, Theatre Tax Relief claims and business planning/restructuring.

Alexander James & Co.

Upper Deck, Admirals Quarters, Portsmouth Road, Thames Ditton, Surrey KT7 0XA
tel 020-8398 4447
email actors@alexanderjames.co.uk
website www.alexanderjames.co.uk
Accountant Andrew Nicholson

Established in 1991. Fees vary according to complexity and completeness of information supplied. Costs are on average between £500 and £800 per annum. First meeting is free, with ongoing support by phone, Zoom/Teams and email with regular e-newsletter. Entirely UK-based staff accustomed to working with media industry clients. Advisory work during the year is billed on completion. Online accounts support including HMRC's Making Tax Digital (Xero, Quickbooks, Sage etc.) or by spreadsheet (template provided). Around 15% of clientele are actors or other entertainment industry professionals. Home or workplace visits can be arranged.

Angela Mead Ltd

2nd Floor, 5 Cobden Court, Wimpole Close BR2 9JF
tel 020-8467 1167
email info@angelamead.co.uk
website https://angelamead.co.uk

Client support includes face-to-face meetings, telephone and email, as well as fee protection insurance and freepost record envelopes. Also offers accounts support and tax compliance. Supplies clients with MS Excel spreadsheet templates. 50% of the client base comprises actors, and 30% other entertainment industry professionals. Offices are wheelchair accessible.

Breckman & Company

49 South Molton Street, London W1K 5LH
tel 020-7499 2292
email info@breckmanandcompany.co.uk
website www.breckmanandcompany.co.uk
Accountants Graham Berry FCCA, Richard Nelson FCCA

Established for more than 60 years. Costs are dictated by complexity and time spent. Initial meeting is free during which the fee structure will be discussed. Client support includes face-to-face meetings, phone and email.

Services include: audits, independent examinations, Theatre Tax Relief claims, limited company accounts, self-employed accounts, VAT and wages preparation.

P O'N Carden

56–58 High Street, Ewell, Surrey KT17 1RW
tel 020-8394 2957
email info@poncarden.com
website www.poncarden.com
Accountants Mondane Carden, Andrew Fairmaner

Founded in 1977. Charges minimum £498 (inc. VAT) for a complete set of accounts and tax return for sole traders. "Time and complexity increase this.

Tailor-made packages for complex cases and limited companies." Provides face-to-face meetings in-person or via Zoom. "Our actor clients make clear how much support they feel they need, and the programme of work is tailored accordingly." Provides Excel spreadsheets appropriate to the client's needs. Alternatively an app is available to record income and expenditure; a Making Tax Digital for Income Tax ready firm. The offices are not wheelchair accessible, but meetings can be held in wheelchair-accessible locations. Advises actors *not* to "just give your accountant bags of receipts. Provide information about why you are claiming particular expenses. Do be obssessive about keeping payslips and remittance advices".

Jonathan Ford & Co.
Maxwell House, Liverpool Innovation Park,
360 Edge Lane, Liverpool L7 9NJ
tel 0151 426 4512
email info@jonathanford.co.uk
website www.jonathanford.co.uk
Director Alison Brown

Premium services starting from £130/month (+ VAT), depending on the level of bookkeeping the client has done themselves. All fees are agreed in advance. Client service is comprehensive and includes face-to-face meetings, telephone and email support, all included within the fee. Supplies Excel spreadsheet templates, so MS Office is required; the software is suitable for all operating systems. Has clients who are actors and other entertainment industry professionals. Offices are not wheelchair accessible.

Goldwins
75 Maygrove Road, London NW6 2EG
tel 020-7372 6494
email info@goldwins.co.uk
website www.goldwins.co.uk
Accountant Anthony Epton

Established in 1987. Specialises in the entertainment industry, handling the tax and bookkeeping affairs of around 200 actors. Price for preparing an actor's tax return can vary depending on the complexity of the job. Face-to-face meetings, phone and email support included in this price. Does not provide software or spreadsheet templates. The company's offices are wheelchair accessible.

H and S Accountants Ltd
90 Mill Lane, West Hampstead, London NW6 1NL
tel 020-3174 1905
email hstaxplan@gmail.com
website www.hstaxplan.com
Accountants David Summers, Chet Haria

Established in 1982. Charges start from £300 (+ VAT) for preparation of annual self-employed accounts and the self-assessment tax return. A quote is given at the initial meeting, which is free of charge.

The services offered also include preparation of limited company accounts and corporate tax returns, VAT registration, payroll, tax-planning advice, etc. Client support includes face-to-face meetings, phone, email and dealing with day-to-day queries as they may arise (all included in the price). Approximately 10% of clients are actors or members of the entertainment industry.

Hentons
Northgate, 118 North Street, Leeds LS2 7PN
tel 0113 234 0000
email info@hentons.com
website www.hentons.com
Facebook /HentonsAccountants
X @hentonandco
Instagram @hentons_accountants
Managing Partner Nadeem Ahmed, *Head of Operations* Peter Watson, *Partners* Emma Panayi, Chris Howitt, Brett Davis, Chris Maher, David Walker, Fahad Ahmed, Stuart Heaney, Effie Charalambous, Gary Olding

Experienced team of industry specialists and accountants for performers, proving business management and accounting services to a wide spectrum of entertainment businesses including performers, actors, producers and many other individuals connected or associated with the industry.

Hogbens Dunphy Ltd
3rd Floor, 104–108 Oxford Street, London W1D 1LP
tel 020-7016 2450
email anything@hogbensdunphy.co.uk
website www.hogbensdunphy.co.uk
Director Richard Wadhams

Established in 1921. Offers complete support to actors and other theatre professionals in dealing with their business, accounting and taxation needs. Prices are dependent on each individual client's needs.

Lees
Hogarth House, 136 High Holborn,
London WC1V 6PX
tel 020-7242 1134
email mail@leesaccountants.co.uk
website https://leesaccountants.co.uk

Chartered Certified Accountants and Registered Auditors. Established in 1925, Lees specialist Media and Entertainments Team act as enthusiastic and trusted advisors to a multitude of performers playing a variety of roles in TV, Film and Theatre, our aim is to help you keep your tax and financial affairs in great order, to allow you to focus on being creative and doing what you love most, performing.

Services include: bookkeeping and software, VAT returns and compliance, annual accounts preparation, self-assessment tax returns, tax planning and compliance, Payroll, and advice on business structures.

MHA

6th Floor, 2 London Wall Place, Barbican, London EC2Y 5AU
tel 020-7429 4100
website www.mha.co.uk
X @MHAaccountants
Accountants Neil Stern, John Coverdale, Rachel Doyle, Kathryn Edmands

Established in 1880, MHA acts for over 2,000 individuals in the media and entertainment industry, with 23 national offices and extensive overseas support throughout the Baker Tilly International Network.

Offers a full accountancy service from cloud accounting advice to high-end tax solutions. A fee structure is set out at the first complimentary meeting when media and entertainment specialists will discuss tax needs; arrangements can include monthly payments. They are happy to support clients through face-to-face meetings, telephone or email. Offices are wheelchair accessible.

Nyman Libson Paul LLP

124 Finchley Road, London NW3 5JS
tel 020-7433 2400
website www.nlpca.co.uk

Established in 1933, creative industry accountants that have been servicing the entertainment industry for over 90 years.

Performance Accountancy

6 Pankhurst Drive, Bracknell, Berks. RG12 9PS
tel (01344) 669084
email louise@performanceaccountancy.co.uk
website www.performanceaccountancy.co.uk/actors
Accountant Louise Herrington

Established in 2012. Charges from £350 (+ VAT) for early years tax returns based on the client's bookkeeping records; if bookkeeping done by the company then £55 (+ VAT) per hour is charged. If Equity number is quoted, then price starts at £245 (+ VAT) for the return and £40 (+ VAT) per hour for bookkeeping. For more established actors and performers who may have more complex returns, such as overseas income, the charge can go up to £750 (+ VAT). Offers an ebook and support by phone, Zoom, webinars and video. Offers face-to-face meetings when starting out, either in Bracknell or Egham. First 30-minutes consultation is complimentary. Offers monthly services to handle bookkeeping and accounting requirements for the self-employed or those who operate through a company. This will help prepare for quarterly digital accounts starting in April 2026.

Range of services in addition to personal self-assessment return include company accounts and company tax, bookkeeping, payroll, VAT, strategic planning and help with managing your money. Investment advice not offered. Excel workbook can be supplied to actors and performers with typical categories of spend to help with bookkeeping. Software offered works with Windows, but not so well with Mac. Clients are mainly actors, musicians and others in the entertainment inductry. The company is recommended by Equity and is the preferred supplier of tax returns for the Independent Society of Musicians.

Premises not suitable for wheelcahirs but face-to-face meetings can be arranged in a wheelchair-accessible location.

Streets Mark Carr

London office: 60 St Martins Lane, London WC2N 4JS
tel 020-3897 9384
Brighton office: Intergen House, 65–67 Western Road, Hove, East Sussex BN3 2JQ
tel (01273) 778802
email mark.carr@streets.uk
website www.markcarr.co.uk, www.streets.uk

"We are recognised as one of London's and the UK's leading specialist providers of accountancy, financial and tax services to actors, entertainers, agents, singers, musicians and dancers. In fact, anyone in or connected with the entertainment industry and the arts world.
  We are fully aware of the unique set of circumstances that those within the industry live and work in and the challenges of juggling income generating work with the need to ensure their financial affairs are in order."

Theataccounts Ltd

Greek Street, London W1D 4EG
tel (01905) 706050
email info@theataccounts.co.uk
website www.theataccounts.co.uk
X @theataccounts
Accountant Alex Dyer

Specialist entertainment industry accountants established in 1967. Charges are based on a sliding scale according to each client's requirements. Basic package can start from £200. Offers unlimited support to clients through face-to-face meetings, phone, email, Zoom, etc. No particular software is provided unless required. All clients are actors and other entertainment industry professionals.

Simia Wall LLP

Devonshire House, 582 Honeypot Lane, Stanmore, Middlesex HA7 1JS
tel 020-8732 5500
Longcroft House, 2–8 Victoria Avenue, London EC2M 4NS
email nik@simiawall.com
website www.simiawall.com
Partner Nik Fisher FFA FCCA

Established in 2005. Charges between £250 and £750 on average, depending on the amount of work involved. Offers actors face-to-face and email/phone support and aims to teach actors how best to keep their books and records, to save on accountancy fees. Can provide spreadsheet templates in Excel and for VAT analysis, suitable for a range of software platforms. Around 15% of clients are actors, and 25% other professionals in the entertainment industry.

Wyatts Partnership
247 Church Street, London N16 9HP
tel 020-7241 6779
email admin@wyatts.uk.com

Friendly and clear accounting service. Specialists with actors, artists and performers. Reasonable and transparent scaled fees and charges. Client base is 100% arts and entertainment industry professionals. Offices are wheelchair accessible.

Tax and National Insurance for actors

Philippe Carden

Actors are treated as self-employed for income tax purposes, but can benefit from certain advantages not generally available. Many actors choose to instruct an accountant to benefit from those advantages and to avoid the attendant pitfalls.

The income tax advantages include being able to claim a deduction for expenses against income in arriving at taxable net profit (or allowable loss), provided that those expenses are incurred 'wholly and exclusively for the purposes of the trade'. The Equity Tax and National Insurance Guide, available free of charge to its members, provides a very helpful list of usually allowable expenses, with suitable notes to restrain the enthusiasm of actors to stretch definitions to their limits. Self-imposed restraint in claiming for expenses is sensible in minimising the risk of being selected for an enquiry by HM Revenue and Customs (HMRC). Some accountants produce their own list of generally allowable expenses.

It is helpful to assess the types of expense according to the risk of being challenged by the Revenue. Here are some examples:

Low risk or no risk
- Commission paid to agent (including VAT)
- Annual subscription to Equity
- Travel and subsistence on tour
- Photographs and publicity (repros, showreel, Spotlight entry)
- Classes to maintain skills, e.g. voice, movement
- Business stationery and postage
- Fee paid to accountant

Medium risk
- Professional library – scripts, books, CDs
- Publications – *The Stage*, *Empire* magazine
- Travel and subsistence when not on tour
- Visits to theatre and cinema

High risk
- Home as office unless making the standard simplified claim (Google: home as office HMRC)
- Cosmetic dentistry

Very high risk
- Wardrobe – renewal, dry cleaning and repair
- Hairdressing and make-up – before auditions reduces the risk
- Gratuities to dressers and stage door-keepers
- Osteopathy and other treatments – lower risks for circus performers and stunt persons
- Gym membership – for a specific role or if you are ready to make a business case
- Television licence and subscription channels – a 50% business proportion?

As the risk rises, so too must the care taken in deciding which to claim and which to discard. Engaging an accountant to use his or her experience, skill and judgement in carrying out a review of expenditure claims is a source of considerable reassurance to many actors. It is worth noting that entertaining, as in paying a meal for another person (even if a casting director), and gifts are never allowed.

An accountant's review may also be key in calculating the business proportions of motor car expenses, landline and mobile telephone charges (including internet access), television and film hire, including subscriptions to Sky, Netflix etc. An accountant's help in computing capital allowances for expenditure on capital items (computer, motor car, musical instruments) is appreciated by all but the most self-confident.

The emphasis so far has been on the income tax advantages of being self-employed. Whilst many actors are happy to register themselves as self-employed, others enlist the help of an accountant, even at that stage, to help with form-filling and provide a buffer-zone between themselves and HMRC. Once registration is done, a Unique Taxpayer Reference (UTR) will be issued, often still referred to as a Schedule D number except by HMRC. Registration is for both income tax and national insurance (NICs).

If an actor achieves only a very modest net profit from his or her self-employment, less than £6,725, the actor can pay Class 2 NICs voluntarily as it is a cheap way of securing entitlement to certain basic state benefits such as maternity allowance and the state pension. It is charged at a weekly flat rate of £3.45 a week. The Treasury is promising further reform and eventual abolition.

For the sake of completeness, Class 4 NICS are payable by actors if their annual net profit rises above the threshold: currently £12,570. That class of NIC is the earnings-related charge borne by self-employed people. It is currently charged at 6% up to £50,270 and 2% thereafter. It confers no benefits to the payer and is collected by HMRC as part of the self-assessment system.

The complexities of the NI regime encourage co-operation between actor and accountant almost as much as does the application of the criteria for acceptability of expenses for income tax purposes.

Core services provided by an accountant include the following:

- Annual income and expenditure account
- Capital allowances computations
- Completion of the annual Tax Return
- Preparing a tax calculation and checking the Revenue's version
- Applying to reduce income tax payments on account, if appropriate

Additional services would include completing quarterly returns for actors successful enough to be registered for VAT, and advice on the tax and NIC implications of performing abroad. Student loan repayments and tax credit deadlines can also be discussed and planned for. Universal Credit has replaced a whole range of means-tested benefits including tax credits (other examples are income-based jobseeker's allowance, income support, income-related employment support allowance). When applied to the self-employed, the Department of Work and Pensions usually assumes an arbitrary amount of income called the 'Minimum Income Floor'. Equity provides expert advice in this difficult area.

Most accountants charge according to time spent and the seniority and expertise of the persons doing the work. Here is an example of how this might work in practice for a young actor: he would need five hours of a bookkeeper, an hour for a manager's review and tax return and finally half-an-hour of the principal's/partner's time for overall review and quality control. With perhaps a few telephone calls and shortish meeting, the annual fee would typically be £425 plus VAT, i.e. £510. Accordingly, careful sorting of expenses by expense type can save both time and money.

In my experience, as the cost of the initial meeting is rarely charged for, I make a loss in year one of a new client. I break even in year two, and only make a profit in year three and subsequent years. It is not a surprise, therefore, that I see my relationship with a client as a long-term one – one which has time and effort invested in it by both actor and accountant.

To an actor in the early years of her/his/their career, the accountant's annual fee of about £500 represents a significant expense. The decision to instruct an accountant is a personal one. Some actors are much more comfortable and confident than others in dealing with money matters, taxation and National Insurance. Others shy away from such a course of action and choose to have an ally in the form of an accountant.

In general terms, for an actor with gross earnings of less than £25,000 but who still makes a profit, having an accountant is optional. For one with smaller earnings and who makes a loss, having an accountant could be worthwhile to relieve that loss and seek a refund of income tax. For those with gross earnings in excess of £25,000, the choice is compelling. For those with low earnings and perhaps suffering hardship, advice from Tax Aid can be invaluable. Tax Aid is a charity which helps people on low incomes with their tax problems: **http://taxaid.org.uk**. Helpline **0345 120 3779**.

Having made the decision to use an accountant, choose the firm carefully. The most desired method is word of mouth. A personal recommendation from another actor, from your drama school or indeed from the company manager works well. It is important that the accountant selected knows about the taxation and NIC of actors rather than being a general practitioner. It is also important that the accountant be a member of one of the professional bodies of accountants as an indication of quality – and just in case a dispute arises which cannot be resolved amicably. Most of the institutes have a system of arbitration for fee disputes, for example, which can be used as a last resort.

Another factor in the choice of accountant is the size of the firm. The range is huge: from a sole practitioner to a multinational firm employing thousands. The former will be suitable for an actor of modest means, while the latter might be a good match for a performer with very considerable earnings and royalties from several countries around the world. In between those extremes are smaller firms with one to five partners which specialise in the tax affairs of those who work in theatre, television and film, and larger firms which have an entertainment and media department with a similar specialism. The smaller firms are likely to provide a more personal service and lower fees. The larger are likely to have access to a greater breadth of related expertise (such as film finance, production accounting) but fees will be correspondingly higher.

Each accountant will have his or her favoured way for actors to keep records. The most important point is that an actor must co-operate with his or her accountant to save time and maximise the return on effort. Here are some guidelines and handy hints:

- Keep all agent's remittance advices, payslips and invoices.
- Only claim expenses incurred 'wholly and exclusively for the purposes of the trade'.
- Use the Equity list of usually allowable expenses for guidance and perhaps an Excel spreadsheet to record them.
- Keep receipts for all expenses and write explanatory notes on them (for example, 'for audition with X') and consider using an App to help you.
- File carefully details of any other income such as interest or dividends received, P60/P45s from employments (for example, bar work), rental income as well as Gift Aid payments made and any other item which may be needed to complete your tax return.
- Deliver your accounts papers to your accountant *as soon as you can* after the end of the tax year (5th April) – never leave it until close to the 31st January deadline! The sooner your return is submitted, the earlier the warning of any tax liability payable 31st January and of any other payments on account due for the following year.

Watch this space! A glimpse into the future

HMRC introduced Making Tax Digital (MTD) in April 2019 for VAT registered businesses with an annual turnover exceeding the VAT threshold, currently £90,000. MTD involves quarterly reporting to HMRC, a considerable administrative burden. MTD for Income Tax will be introduced for accounting periods commencing 6 April 2026 for the self-employed and landlords, with income over £50,000. This will mean digital record keeping – something to plan for with care.

Philippe Carden is a chartered accountant specialising in the taxation of actors and other individuals working in theatre, film, television and dance, onstage and backstage, artistic and technical. He co-wrote *Investing in West End Theatrical Productions* (Robert Hale, 1992) and has written articles for the *Guardian*, *The Stage* and other publications.

Equity Pension Scheme

Andrew Barker @ First Act

Auto-Enrolment, what is it?

Since October 2012, new legislation has gradually applied to all UK employers to ensure that they provide a suitable pension product for their workers. This legislation includes actors and is calledAuto-Enrolment (AE). If you are aged over 22 and below State pension age there is a probability that any production company that you work for *will* auto-enrol you into their chosen pension scheme. They are legally bound to enrol you. You have no choice on being auto-enrolled, but you can choose to opt out afterwards. The nature of your occupation could result in you ending up with many separate pension pots over the time span of your career.

However, there is an alternative and a way to avoid AE: the Equity Pension Scheme (EPS). The EPS has been in existence since October 1997. Designed and administered by First Act (the preferred insurance advisers to Equity and its members), it has become the pension scheme of choice for actors. If you are engaged on an Equity Agreement, whether it be in theatre, television, film or radio, the production company has an obligation to contribute to the EPS on your behalf and at rates that are higher than those that apply to AE.

The EPS' status as a qualifying workplace pension scheme will ensure that if you are an EPS member, and you inform each company manager of the production companies you work for, they will *not* auto-enrol you into their AE scheme resulting in you having one pension receiving all your contributions.

The EPS provides access to a market-leading pension product for all those working in the creative arts sector (Equity membership is not required). It is the ideal way to start or improve your personal pension arrangements.

Here is how it works

If you are working under an Equity agreed contract you could get your manager to contribute to your EPS.

Current qualifying contracts are issued by: BBC, ITV, PACT & TAC, SOLT, UK Theatre Commercial, UK Theatre Sub Rep, ITC, RSC, RNT, Disney Theatrical, plus a number of in-house arrangements.

Equity Pension Scheme – questions and answers

Q How does the EPS work?

A The funds are managed by AVIVA, one of the UK's largest and most respected pension providers. The EPS has access to over 280 investment funds catering for all attitudes to investment risk, including ethical and sustainable funds.

You have total flexibility. You contribute when you are working, and when you are not, you can take a break. The EPS is penalty-free and currently has a base charge on the core funds of 0.7% cent per annum i.e. £0.70 for every £100 in your personal pot.

Q How do I make payments into the EPS?

A You can make contributions in several ways:

• You can make contributions related to your engagement only; this way you can pay in when you are working but freeze payments when you are not.

Equity Pension Scheme

- You can make additional regular personal payments by direct debit on a monthly basis.
- You can make additional single personal contributions on-line or by cheque.

Q How does the EPS work in theatre?
A As an EPS member you benefit from a contribution paid by your employers, equal to a percentage of your weekly wage. To qualify, you agree to make a contribution from your weekly wage. The employer contribution is added to your wages and then deducted together with your personal contribution. The employer contributions are sent directly by the employer to First Act, for investment on your behalf. Once with Aviva, basic rate tax relief is added.

Q Which theatrical managers contribute to the EPS?
A Most theatrical employers now contribute to the scheme.

West End managers (SOLT), Disney Theatrical and Shakespeare's Globe
Managers will contribute an amount equal to 5% of your weekly rehearsal or performance wage up to a maximum of 5% of 1.75 x the minimum performance wage. Two years' continual employment with the same manager increases this to 7.5%, 10% after 5 years.

You pay a 3% personal contribution, rising to 3.75% and 5%.

Subsidised repertory theatres (UK theatre)
The manager will contribute an amount equal to 5% of your weekly rehearsal or performance wage up to a maximum of 5% of 1.5 x the appropriate middle-range salary level (MRSL).

You pay a 3% personal contribution.

Commercial theatre (UK theatre)
Managers contribute an amount equal to 5% of your weekly rehearsal or performance wage.

You pay a 2.5% personal contribution.

Independent Theatre Council (ITC)
Managers contribute an amount equal to 5% of your weekly rehearsal or performance wage.

You pay a 3% personal contribution.

Royal National Theatre
You have a choice of:
1. RNT pay 5%; you pay 3%
2. RNT pay 5.5%; you pay 4.5%
3. RNT pay 6%; you pay 6%
4. RNT pay 7.5%; you pay 7.5%

Royal Shakespeare Company
The RSC contribute an amount equal to 5% of your weekly rehearsal or performance wage.

You pay a 2.5% personal contribution.

Q How does the EPS work in television?
A Basically, the scheme works in the same way in television as it does in theatre, but your contribution will be based on either your episode fee or weekly fee, whichever basis brings

you the most benefit. It is the responsibility of the artist to notify the producer prior to the engagement that they are a member of the EPS and to provide their pension membership number in the space provided in the form of engagement.

Q Which TV and film managers contribute to the EPS?
A Most TV and film employers will contribute to the scheme.
BBC Television and ITV companies will contribute an amount equal to 5% of your engagement/episode fee or weekly fee.

You pay a 2.5% personal contribution.

PACT and TAC independent TV production companies will contribute an amount equal to 5% subject to a maximum per engagement/weekly/episode fee.

You pay a 2.5% personal contribution.

Film companies will contribute an amount equal to 6% of your fee, subject to a reviewable maximum per production.

You pay a 3% personal contribution.

BBC Radio will contribute an amount equal to 5% of your engagement/weekly/episode fee.

You pay a 2.5% personal contribution.

Details of the current minimum engagement fees/wages for your production company are available from Andrew Barker at First Act 020 8686 5050, by e-mail **eps@firstact.co.uk** or at **firstact.co.uk**.

Q How can I join the EPS
A On-line at firstact.co.uk, by email **eps@firstact.co.uk** or by telephone 0208 686 5050.

Andrew Barker is a Director of Hencilla Canworth Ltd (First Act). Hencilla Canworth is an independent insurance intermediary having facilities with the UK's leading insurers and underwriters. It specialises in insurance products for performing arts companies and groups. He was part of the original team that designed and introduced the EPS in 1997 and has continued to oversee its management to this day.

Physical and mental fitness for actors

Alex Caan

The instrument or tool of the actor is the body. Like a musical instrument, if it is left idle it will become out of tune and lose its ability to function effectively.

Actors need to constantly develop their instrument to get the best out of it. Unlike a musical instrument, we carry our tool with us every day. With good habits and practice we can alleviate many of the problems that need to be fixed before they start. The work required to have a positive ongoing effect is not as great or as demanding as one would expect. Before we look at what we can do to make our bodies outstanding, let's look at what our bodies really are.

In a person of average weight and build, 70 per cent of the mass of the body is muscle and bone. Therefore we can have a large effect on our bodies, by focusing on our muscles and bones. Before we can affect change in our muscles and bones we need to understand how they work and what relationships they have with each other.

The structure of the body is extremely complicated but can be viewed in quite a simplistic manner. Originally we would have walked on all fours, which is why our upper limbs have very similar corresponding joints to our lower limbs. Each hand has five digits, with a dominant thumb; our corresponding lower body part is the opposite foot, with the big toe as the dominant digit. The wrist and ankle are similar multi-directional joints, whereas the elbow and knee are both hinged joints. The shoulder and hip are ball and socket joints.

The upper and lower limbs are also connected by corresponding groups of muscles. The quads, which are in the front of the thigh, are related to the upper body through the triceps, which are in the back of the upper arm. The hamstrings, at the back of the upper leg, are related to the biceps. The gluteus or buttocks are related to the pectorals or chest muscles. So rather than looking at muscular activity in isolation, we must see muscles as groups working together.

When the body moves forward, the opposite arm and leg swing. The combination of muscles working together propels our bodies. Muscles move limbs by shortening.

Muscles work together synergistically, and in a healthy, well-maintained body are balanced. If bad habits occur, this simplicity of movement can lead to long-term health problems by over-use of some muscles, and under-use of others. This constant over-use/under-use will lead to a tired or sore body part in a specific area, often one side of the neck or lower back.

As we move forward, the chain of movements pass through the centre of the body. This passing through the centre is a clue to the focus of long-term fitness and wellbeing for the actor.

The centre of the body is the place where all life stems from. It is here that a baby is connected to its mother through the placenta, that later becomes the belly button. In the centre of the body is the diaphragm, from which, through correct training, all breath should originate.

The movement of our bodies creates heat and energy. Contrary to what some directors believe, we are not beings that live in our head or brain space. We live in our bodies, and movement produces powerful emotional responses. This is encapsulated in the phrase 'Motion creates Emotion'. This is why actors talk about getting the walk of the character, because this allows them to get into the body of the character, which in turn allows them to get into the personality of the character. Some actors do this instinctively, but it is and can be a learned skill.

Actors communicate thoughts in the vast majority by speaking. There are, of course, actors who use mime and dance to communicate, but mainly thoughts are communicated verbally, using speech or song. Words are merely a manipulation of breath using the tongue, mouth and vocal cords. Without breath we have nothing to carry our thoughts over large theatrical space.

Coincidentally, breath or oxygen is the most important nourishment our bodies need. Without food one can live for 40 days or more; without water one can live for 7–10 days; but if you don't breathe for five minutes you will die.

Using this as our guide, the focus of the actors' fitness should be built around the development of a robust powerful tool that can create large amounts of powerful breath. Not just large volumes of breath, but outstanding control of the mechanism that delivers that breath.

The mechanism that delivers the breath is the lungs and diaphragm and their supporting muscles. These muscles need to be strong, but also need to be mobile and have excellent endurance.

Lastly, the value of water cannot be underestimated. A five per cent drop in hydration can lead to mild dehydration, which can lead to a large drop in bodily function, both mental and physical. Even a two per cent drop in hydration can have a very damaging and negative effect on our voice. In temperate climates we lose 2.5 litres of water throughout an average day. If we are performing, rehearsing or undertaking strenuous physical activity we will use much greater amounts of water than this. Therefore we must monitor our bodies and increase water intake when needed. Passing clear urine is a good indicator of hydration – if not first thing in the morning, then definitely throughout the day.

So where does one start in the nitty-gritty of training the actor's body? Actors come in all shapes and sizes. I am not advocating that all actors try to become slim and pert: who would play all the non-slim, non-pert roles? Equally, I am not advocating that all actors develop muscular physiques. We need to be limber in the joints and muscles, but there is no point in the serious actor developing big muscles at the expense of range of movement. I believe that you can be tall, short, slim, rotund, lanky or squat and at the same time be very fit. Olympic shot putters are very large but all can run great distances and move like ballet dancers.

Fitness for actors doesn't require a massive overloading of the body. To reach Olympic-standard fitness we would need to break the body down systematically over a period of time, in order to allow the body to regenerate stronger than before. This regeneration occurs during periods of rest. But this overloading is not really needed for general fitness for actors.

In all of our fitness development we need to place breath control and posture at the forefront. The ideas and concepts of the Alexander Technique are pivotal to this. Its values are based on excellent posture and good use of muscles, rather than overuse and bad postural habits. So when performing any movement, be aware of the alignment of the head, neck and back. Often actors strain their voices because they are tight in another part of their body, which pulls the head and neck out of alignment, resulting in a sore throat or strained voice. For those of you who are not familiar with the Alexander Technique, I would recommend that an awareness of posture and balance is vital to long-term fitness.

A simple starting point for general fitness for actors is walking. Walking is the most underused and undervalued exercise we can do. It involves a good pair of training shoes and a place to go! Between 20 and 60 minutes' continuous walking a day will increase lung capacity and make our heart a great deal stronger. I know many actors say that they walk at least that in a day – going shopping, walking to the bus or train, and so on. I am not discounting that, but I am advocating a steady brisk walk with arms swinging back and forth in time with the opposing leg. By doing this, the whole body is being exercised, and the core muscles through the centre of the body are activated. It is akin to the phase of human development that we know as crawling. The same benefits cannot be achieved through passive day-to-day walking.

Walking has a very effective return for the amount of effort expended, because there is little detrimental impact on the joints of the lower limbs. The swinging of opposing arms and legs also helps reinforce correct neurological pathways. This helps us to move our bodies more effectively and efficiently as a kinetic chain, rather than as disjointed isolated movements.

A walking regime three days a week is a good place to start. You will not only build your lungs and heart, but also the tissues around your joints in the legs, arms and back. These need time to adapt and grow to the new stresses being placed on them. Taking a day off in between will allow the tissues throughout your body to regenerate during the periods of rest.

If you are a fitness novice, then building up to an hour-long walk is an achievable goal. Start with a ten-minute walk that builds systematically over a period of between four and six weeks, rather than blazing into a brisk hour-long walk initially. Increasing your walks by three minutes each walk will let you achieve an hour-long walk from a ten-minute starting point in just six weeks. Three minutes may sound a lot, but since it requires adding just one and a half minutes to your outward journey, it is not an unrealistic amount.

Swimming is also an excellent way to work the heart and lungs without placing any stress on the joints, as it is a non-weight bearing form of exercise. However, it is important to swim using the front crawl and backstroke rather than predominantly using the breast stroke, so that we continue to move opposing upper and lower limbs to work our core muscles. A mixture of all swimming strokes would be best to work the greatest range of muscle groups and minimise the likelihood of housemaid's knee (a common breast stroke-related injury)! Learning to swim with your head partially submerged in the water is vital, in order to maintain correct alignment of the spine.

The same incremental approach to developing fitness through walking, as recommended above, should be applied when undertaking a swimming regime. Rather than using the increment of time, the number of lengths swum is a very simple starting point. Do bear in mind the length of each pool that you may swim in may vary! It is likely that the more often you swim, the quicker you will become. So increasing the number of lengths that you swim each session may require little or no extra time in the pool.

We have exercised the heart and lungs with walking and swimming. We need now to develop our range of movement and strength. Basic yoga movements are also a simple and effective way to increase inner strength and develop range of movement and good posture. I am not looking at the more physical jumping around or sauna types of yoga. I am advocating basic yoga moves.

Yoga has many positive effects, which include large ranges of movement and mobility. By getting into certain yoga positions, we are not only stretching the muscles, but also massaging the internal organs. Yoga also has the benefit of establishing excellent breath control. The breath floods into the centre of the body and has to be released with control and in a sustained manner. This has a very relaxing and meditative effect. This helps us switch off our overactive minds, the value of which cannot be underestimated.

Buying a book or signing up to a YouTube channel on yoga or joining a yoga class is an excellent place to start. If yoga doesn't appeal to you, then pilates is an excellent alternative. Both yoga and pilates are fantastic for developing breath control and posture control techniques.

Let us look at a sample week's exercise programme – for example, walking or swimming on Monday, Thursday and Saturday, with yoga or pilates on Tuesday and Friday. This gives you two days off, on Wednesday and Sunday, which follow either two or three days of activity. Rest is vital to regeneration. We only become fitter and stronger by allowing our bodies to recover and grow.

> **Further information**
>
> For more information about any of the suggested forms of exercise, see the websites listed below:
> Alexander Technique www.alexandertechnique.com
> Walking www.thewalkingsite.com
> Swimming www.britishswimming.org
> Yoga www.bwy.org.uk (British Wheel of Yoga)
> Pilates www.pilatesfoundation.com

These days off give the individual physical downtime, which can then be filled with mental stimulation of some kind, including meditation, vocal and singing practice, reading or other pursuits that aid the actor's development as a whole.

This is a brief overview of the most suitable and simple exercises to cover what is required for the stresses and strains of most acting jobs. All of these suggestions can be carried out from home or on tour. The time and effort required to train in this manner will not be detrimental to the actor's performance. By starting small, and increasing gradually, the actor will feel more invigorated and energised from undertaking an exercise programme.

The actor's body should be viewed as a communication tool. Bodies require stimulation to develop. Without stimulus, the body and mind will deteriorate. Permitting this to happen is an injustice to the craft of acting. We all only have one body, and we need to look after it and maintain it for our specific needs.

Alex Caan was an international athlete before training at RADA for three years. Since graduation, he has worked extensively in theatre, TV and radio. As a consultant Alex teaches business people powerful communication through effective use of the body. As a sports coach Alex has coached Premiership football and rugby players to international level. He has coached sportsmen and women to Olympic and World level in a range of different athletic disciplines. He is currently National Event Coach for High Jump in the UK, and prepared the group of talented high jumpers for the London 2012 Olympics.

Mental health in the performing arts
Claire Cordeaux, Director of the British Association for Performance Arts Medicine
Interview by Rob Ostlere

Claire Cordeaux is the director of the British Association for Performance Arts Medicine (BAPAM), a specialist healthcare charity supporting individuals and organisations in the performing arts. BAPAM provides free clinical services, expert training, essential resources and clinical leadership. In 2020, BAPAM worked in association with Equity to create a new dedicated 24/7 mental health helpline for union members throughout the UK, with individual assessments and up to six counselling sessions available.

Perhaps you could start by giving us an overview of the services BAPAM provides for performers and the industry?
BAPAM was set up about thirty years ago by a group of doctors initially, although we've added lots of different health care professionals since, including psychologists and psychotherapists. We focus on the health needs of performers and other creative practitioners – these can be quite specific because of the context they are working in. We offer free assessments with expert clinicians who are highly qualified, but also used to treating performing arts professionals so they understand where they're coming from and the demands of the job. The aim is very much to help people get back into work and learn strategies to manage conditions in an ongoing way to sustain their careers. Alongside that we also do a lot of health education. At the moment we're running a whole series of webinars on keeping mentally and physically healthy, preventing injuries and also focusing on vocal health. We want people to have the knowledge – hopefully before they've got a problem – on how to look after themselves so that they can prevent it from happening.

Another core part of BAPAM's work is researching mental health in the industry. One of the stats that stood out to me on your website is that nearly 75 per cent of performers report mental or physical health problems.
The national average is about one in four people, so it is significantly higher in the performing arts than the general population. I think one of the key messages to take from that research is everybody in the industry should recognise that it is a normal thing to happen. If you haven't got those health issues yourself, you're likely to be working with somebody who has.

What can performers do to protect themselves and others' mental health?
Just having that knowledge – that it's quite likely that this is something you will come across – is important, particularly if you're starting out in your career. Then, think about ways of managing it; develop a mental health practice that you can draw on so that if a problem does occur, you've got resources and a plan of what to do. Take every opportunity to learn strategies. Learn about good mental health practise just as you would learn about your craft. And then, if there is an issue, get help – use the services available – as soon as you can. Support your friends and colleagues in creative communities by sharing resources and nurturing environments where communication and respect are priorities.

What steps are being taken more widely in the industry to address mental health issues, for example in drama schools and the training sector?
I work with drama schools and I know that mental health is very much at the forefront for educators and institutions. There's a lot more research now into what happens, what's likely to happen and what interventions are useful. It is essential that training teaches future professionals the skills they will need to sustain a very psychologically demanding career. Even if drama schools haven't got it perfectly right yet, what I'm pleased about is that the dialogue seems to be shifting to acknowledging problems and implementing improvements and interventions.

What about steps being taken to address mental health in workplaces; in rehearsal rooms, in theatres and on sets?
It's an ongoing dialogue which is had differently at different levels. The larger organisations often have infrastructure in place; they might have counsellors in or accessible through the theatre, which is fantastic. Obviously for smaller companies it's much harder; there isn't the budget necessarily and they're dealing with how they're going to wash the costumes and get the props from A to B. Where there's a bit more of a looser arrangement and not necessarily a plan in place, it's about trying to get a clearer understanding of what are healthy practices. BAPAM has been putting out information about that: is there a checklist we can look at and what should the organisers of an environment do to support people to keep healthy? Where do we signpost people for additional help? And we have a group that's currently working on trying to get areas of best practice highlighted so that people can see that, actually, it's not that difficult to do. We're trying to get the message out there: here's what you can do on a very low budget and it does make a difference.

And you work with industry organisations directly?
That's right; we currently have a collaboration with the Centre for Performance Science, which itself is a collaboration between Imperial College and the Royal College of Music, though they cover all art forms. We have a PhD student looking at all the risk factors that might cause health problems in a performer. Some of these are things that you can't necessarily do anything about but being aware of them is useful. There are risks that you carry yourself: that you're a certain age, a certain physique or you might have some mental health issues in your family background. Then there's the environmental factors: poor equipment or no breaks, for example. There are problems caused by prejudice or bullying. And then there might be the inciting event, which is the thing that's sort of the straw that breaks the camel's back: the long tour or the new show that is really very challenging. The aim of our work was to help people understand what are the things that actually causes health problems and how we as an arts community can work together to avoid them happening. We want it to be something that is much more of a can-do type of programme, that tries to create better environments by celebrating what's already good.

A problem for most performers is facing periods of unemployment. Is there advice on how to cope with the challenges that creates?
Well, if we use the lockdown as an example, then one of the things we worked on with performers was seeing the time as an opportunity to develop skills by setting goals and creating a routine that they follow every day. That included taking breaks, looking at when

you do physical exercise, when you develop your mental practice, picking up skills that you wouldn't normally have the time to do, and socialising; to be your full human self as opposed to just your performance self. Of course, I'm totally aware that this is easier said than done. When you're not working, and it's not a situation of your choosing, you can feel quite paralysed I think about doing anything. It's quite hard to get motivated to do anything if you don't know what you're working towards. And it's difficult in a situation where you're not sure about your finances. We see lots of people trying to do things and they can't even begin to even think about it because other issues in their life are just so overwhelming. What one of our trainers on mental health was saying at a session the other day is try to think of one thing you can do that's achievable, however small. Then the fact that you do it is brilliant; you've met the goal and you celebrate that thing. That's as opposed to setting unrealistic goals and weighing yourself down with things that you're not going to be able to achieve.

BAPAM have been working with Equity on their new support system for performers. How has that been going?
Equity have a helpline number that you can call which is staffed by counsellors, and they can pick up a whole range of issues. So, if you're an Equity member and you recognise there's a problem, then you can call BAPAM and we will organise a free assessment with a clinician who is experienced working with creative artists. If you would then benefit from some counselling, up to six sessions are provided via Equity funding. If this approach isn't likely to be helpful for you, the clinical assessor will look at what else could be put in place. For many people it has and will be incredibly helpful, and we've got some amazing counsellors working with us on it.

That sounds like a hugely positive step for the industry
We have to try and be positive, to try and look for what can be done better. Not to minimise the problem but to reframe the discussion so that we're moving everything forward.

To learn more about BAPAM and the many resources and services they provide for performers, visit **www.bapam.org.uk**, or contact them at **info@bapam.org.uk, 020 8167 4775.**

Funding bodies

We are fortunate in the UK to have subsidy for arts and culture through the national arts councils. Additionally, numerous foundations, funds and charities are devoted to supporting artistic enterprises. But competition for funds is fierce. Successful funding applications require extensive research and planning, and exemplary presentation of your proposed project.

The listings below include various funding bodies. Check their websites for more detailed information, funding criteria and application guidelines. Many funding bodies are happy to advise on form-filling, what kind of projects stand a chance and what could constitute a realistic amount to ask for.

You can also seek advice, instruction and experience online and social media where you will find various guides to applying for funding or even one-on-one sessions to help guide your specific application. It is also well worth going on one of the Independent Theatre Council's (ITC; see page 430) courses for assistance in the complex world of funding applications.

Bodies that offer individual funding should be approached with similar care and attention.

NATIONAL ARTS COUNCILS

Arts Council England
47 Lever Street, Manchester M1 1FN
tel 0161 934 4317
email enquiries@artscouncil.org.uk
website www.artscouncil.org.uk
Facebook /artscouncilofengland
X @ace_national

Arts Council England champions, develops and invests in artistic and cultural experiences that enrich people's lives. It supports a range of activities across the arts, museums and libraries, from theatre to digital art, reading to dance, music to literature, and crafts to collections. "Great art and culture inspires us, brings us together and teaches about ourselves and the world around us. In short it makes us better."

Between 2018 and 2022, they invested £1.45 billion of public money from government and £860 million from the National Lottery to help create these experiences for as many people as possible across the country. For 2023–26, they aim to invest £446 million each year in 990 organisations, including music venues, galleries, museums, arts centres, libraries and more.

Application forms, guidance notes and information sheets can be downloaded from the website. A wide range of resources, publications, links and information about other funding sources is also accessible on the website.

Arts Council of Northern Ireland
The MAC, 10 Exchange Street West, Belfast BT1 2NJ
tel 028 9262 3555
email info@artscouncil-ni.org
website www.artscouncil-ni.org

The prime distributor of public support for the arts, the Arts Council of Northern Ireland is committed to increasing opportunities for artists to develop challenging and innovative work. In addition to funding schemes for organisations and community groups, the council has developed a special programme of schemes to extend support for the individual artist. This programme includes the General Arts Award, which provides funding for specific projects, specialised research and personal artistic development; and the Major Individual Award, which supports established artists in the development of ambitious work.

Arts Council of Wales
Bute Place, Cardiff CF10 5AL
tel 0330 124 2733
website https://arts.wales

Responsible for funding and developing the arts in Wales, using money from Welsh Government and the National Lottery. Provides arts organisations and individuals in Wales with the opportunity to apply for funding towards clearly defined arts-related projects. Scheme guidelines for the funding programmes are available on the website.

Funding bodies

Creative Scotland
Edinburgh office: Waverley Gate, 2–4 Waterloo Gate, Edinburgh EH1 3EG
email enquiries@creativescotland.com
Glasgow office: The Lighthouse, Mitchell Lane, Glasgow G1 3NU
website www.creativescotland.com
Facebook /CreativeScotland
X @CreativeScots
Instagram @creativescots

The public body that supports the arts, screen and creative industries across all parts of Scotland. Through distributing funding from the Scottish Government and the National Lottery, Creative Scotland enables people and organisations to work in and experience the arts, screen and creative industries in Scotland by helping others to develop great ideas and bring them to life. Creative Scotland supports film and theatre professionals based in Scotland through a range of funds and initiatives.

It helps "Scotland's creativity shine at home and abroad ... We invest in talented people and exciting ideas. We develop the creative industries and champion everything that is good about Scottish creativity."

REGIONAL ARTS COUNCIL OFFICES

Arts Council England, London
21 Stephen Street, London W1T 1LN
website www.artscouncil.org.uk/your-area/london

Area covered: Greater London.

Arts Council England, Midlands
Nottingham office: Rooms 005 & 005A, Arkwright Building, Nottingham Trent University, Burton Street, Nottingham NG1 4BU
Birmingham office: The Foundry, 82 Granville Street, Birmingham B1 2LH
website www.artscouncil.org.uk/your-area/midlands

Area covered: Nottingham office: Derbyshire, Leicestershire, Lincolnshire (excluding North and North East Lincolnshire), Northamptonshire, Nottinghamshire, Rutland. Birmingham office: Birmingham, Coventry, Dudley, Herefordshire, Sandwell, Shropshire, Solihull, Staffordshire, Stoke-on-Trent, Telford & Wrekin, Walsall, Warwickshire, Wolverhampton and Worcestershire.

Arts Council England, North
Newcastle office: 5th Floor, St James' Gate, Newcastle Upon Tyne, NE1 4BE
Leeds office: 1st Floor South, Marshall's Mill, Marshall Street, Leeds LS11 9YJ
Manchester office: 47 Lever Street, Manchester M1 1FN
website www.artscouncil.org.uk/your-area/north

Area covered: Newcastle office: Darlington, Durham, Gateshead, Hartlepool, Middlesbrough, Newcastle upon Tyne, North Tyneside, Northumberland, Redcar & Cleveland, South Tyneside, Stockton-on-Tees and Sunderland; Leeds office: Barnsley, Bradford, Calderdale, Doncaster, East Riding of Yorkshire, Kingston upon Hull, Kirklees, Leeds, North East Lincolnshire, North Lincolnshire, North Yorkshire, Rotherham, Sheffield, Wakefield and York. Manchester office: Blacburn with Darwen, Blackpool, Bolton, Bury, Cheshire, Cumbria, Halton, Knowsley, Lancashire, Liverpool, Manchester, Oldham, Rochdale, Salford, Sefton, St Helens, Stockport, Tameside, Trafford, Warrington, Wigan and Wirral.

Arts Council England, South East
Brighton office: Unit A, Level 4, New England House, New England Street, Brighton BN1 4GH
Cambridge office: Brooklands, 24 Brooklands Avenue, Cambridge CB2 8BU
website www.artscouncil.org.uk/your-area/south-east

Area covered: Brighton office: Bracknell Forest, Brighton and Hove, Buckinghamshire, East Sussex, Kent, Medway and Milton Keynes ; Cambridge office: Bedfordshire, Cambridgeshire, Essex, Hertfordshire, Luton, Norfolk, Peterborough, Southend-on-Sea, Suffolk and Thurrock.

Arts Council England, South West
4th Floor, 66 Queen Square, Bristol BS1 4JP
website www.artscouncil.org.uk/your-area/south-west

Area covered: Bath & North East Somerset, Bournemouth, Bristol, Cornwall, Devon, Dorset, Gloucestershire, Hampshire, Isles of Scilly, Isle of Wight, North Somerset, Plymouth, Poole, Portsmouth, Southampton, Somerset, South Gloucestershire, Swindon, Torbay and Wiltshire.

NATIONAL FILM AGENCIES

Northern Ireland Screen
3rd Floor, 21 Alfred House, Belfast BT2 8ED
tel 028 9023 2444
email info@northernirelandscreen.co.uk
website www.northernirelandscreen.co.uk
Facebook /northernirelandscreen
X @NIScreen
Instagram @northernirelandscreen

Northern Ireland Screen is the national screen agency for Northern Ireland. Its aim is to accelerate the development of a dynamic and sustainable screen industry and culture in Northern Ireland.

REGIONAL FILM AGENCIES

Film London
The Arts Building, Morris Place, London N4 3JG
tel 020-7613 7676

email info@filmlondon.org.uk
website https://filmlondon.org.uk

Film London is the capital's public agency for feature film, television, commercials and other interactive content, including games. "Our aim is simple: to ensure that London has a thriving film sector that enriches the capital's businesses and its people." The government has charged Film London with developing and managing a national strategy to generate inward investment through film production via a public-private partnership with key industry bodies.

North East Screen
The BIS, 13–17 Whitby Street, Hartlepool TS24 7AD
tel 0191 823 8233
email hello@northeastscreen.org
website https://northeastscreen.org
Facebook /northeastscreen
X @nescreen_
Instagram @northeastscreen

North East Screen is the screen agency for the North East of England. "Our vision is to create a strong commercial creative economy in the North East, by investing in talent and ideas."

Screen South
Digital Hub, The Glassworks, Mill Bay, Folkestone, Kent CT20 1JG
tel (01303) 259777
email info@screensouth.org
website www.screensouth.org

A cultural development organisation, specialising in Creative Tech and Film. Their aim is to be a resource that helps people get their ideas off the ground, providing them with bespoke support and advice from industry experts at any stage of their project. They promote talent, support innovative creation, diversity in the cultural sector and find ways of presenting exciting projects to new audiences. Screen South is an Arts Council National Portfolio Organisation.

Screen Yorkshire
Studio 30, 46 The Calls, Leeds LS2 7EY
tel 0113 236 8228
email info@screenyorkshire.co.uk
website www.screenyorkshire.co.uk
X @screenyorkshire

Screen Yorkshire champions the film, TV, games and digital industries in Yorkshire and the Humber. Screen Yorkshire offers production financing through its Yorkshire Content Fund. Since it launched in February 2012, Screen Yorkshire has invested in 50 film and TV projects including: *Peaky Blinders, The Duke, Ali & Ava, Official Secrets, Bonus Track, All Creatures Great and Small, Ackley Bridge, Sky Peals, The Confessions of Frannie Langton, A Bunch of Amateurs, Dark River, Yardie, Ghost Stories, Dad's Army, '71, National Treasure* and *The Great Train Robbery*.

OTHER SOURCES OF FUNDING

Unless explicitly mentioned, most of the organisations listed below do not provide assistance with drama school fees or maintenance.

Actors' Benevolent Fund
6 Adam Street, London WC2N 6AD
tel 020-7836 6378
email office@abf.org.uk
website www.actorsbenevolentfund.co.uk

Since 1882 the Actors' Benevolent Fund has provided support to professional actors, actresses and stage managers unable to work due to poor health, an accident or old age.

Jerwood Foundation
PO Box 186, Ludlow, Shropshire SY8 9DX
tel (01584) 823413
email info@jerwood.org
website www.jerwood.org

Established in 1997 for John Jerwood MC (1918–91) by Alan Grieve CBE (1928–2025), the Jerwood Foundation supports (through grant funding of organisations) excellence and emerging talent in the arts in the UK. To date they have donated over £113 million. In 2023 the Foundation merged with the Jerwood Charity (Jerwood Arts) to create a single future-facing foundation.

Please note that Jerwood Foundation does not award grants to individuals

Evelyn Norris Trust
Plouviez House, 19–20 Hatton Place, London EC1N 8RU
tel 020-7831 1926
email info@equitycharitabletrust.org.uk
website www.equitycharitabletrust.org.uk/other-grants/evelyn-norris-trust/
Facebook /people/Equity-Charitable-Trust/100069876914775/
X @ECT_performer

A charity that accepts applications for grants from members of the concert and theatrical professions. The Trust aims to help with the cost of convalesence or a recuperative holiday following illness, injury or surgery.

The Oxford Samuel Beckett Theatre Trust Award
PO Box 2637, Ascot, Berks. SL5 8ZN
email OSBTTA@barbican.org.uk
website www.osbttrust.com
website www.barbican.org.uk/our-story/our-programme/theatre-dance/the-oxford-samuel-beckett-theatre-trust-award

This bi-annual award is designed for innovative theatre/performance artists who are at the stage in their career where they can demonstrably benefit from moving on to a fully resourced and funded production. Artists from all disciplines are encouraged to apply. Due to be awarded again in 2026.

The award is for a company or individual to create a show for the Barbican's studio theatre, The Pit. The winning show will be part of the Barbican Theatre season.

The Royal Theatrical Fund
11 Garrick Street, London WC2E 9AR
tel 020-7836 3322
email admin@trtf.com
website www.trtf.com
Facebook /theRTF1839
Instagram @royaltheatrefund

The Royal Theatrical Fund helps people from *all* areas of the entertainment industry. The Fund makes grants which will alleviate the suffering, assist the recovery, or reduce the need, hardship or distress of those in the entertainment industry or their families/dependants. To be eligible to receive a grant, a person must be unable to work due to illness, injury or infirmity, and to have professionally worked in the theatrical arts (on stage, radio, film or television) for a minimum of 7 years.

Publications, libraries, references and booksellers

This section lists the major sources for scripts and sheet music – and routes to finding that elusive script or score. While the Internet can be extremely useful in such a quest, it sometimes requires some lateral thinking to find what you want. It is possible to find out-of-print plays via libraries or book-finding services, and by combing second-hand bookshops. Some publishers (even a few playwrights' agencies) will organise a reading copy – for a fee.

Also, the British Library (in theory) has a copy of every play ever performed in this country, but there can be complications in actually getting hold of a copy. Start with your local library if you're determined to find a specific play; if they don't have it, they may well be able to get it from another library (via the inter-library loan system), but be prepared for it to take a long time. Another route is to try to find a theatre at which the play has been performed: they may be able to help.

AbeBooks.com
website www.abebooks.com

Excellent website which will search the catalogues of hundreds of second-hand booksellers in this country and around the world.

Actors & Performers
website https://actorsandperformers.com/

Actors & Performers is a professional online resource to help you manage your career in the performing arts, brought to you by the team at Methuen Drama. Our blog posts offer a diverse mix of specially edited and curated articles about working in the performing arts. From finding out how to email your first agent to understanding the differences between acting on stage and screen, to reading exclusive extracts from Methuen Drama's practice and performance books written by industry professionals, each article will help you to further your career.

Amazon.co.uk & Amazon.com
website www.amazon.co.uk, www.amazon.com

Lists plays and scores that are currently in print. Also provides links to second-hand retailers who sell out-of-print plays or scores.

Barbican Library
Barbican Centre, London EC2Y 8DS
tel 020-7638 0569
email barbicanlib@cityoflondon.gov.uk
website www.barbican.org.uk/your-visit/during-your-visit/library
website www.cityoflondon.gov.uk/services/libraries

Situated on level 2 of the Barbican Centre, this is the largest public lending library in the City of London. In addition to the general library, the strong arts and music sections reflect the Barbican Centre's emphasis on the arts. The library is fully accessible to wheelchair users. *Opening hours*: Monday, Wednesday and Fridays: 9.30am–5.30pm; Tuesday and Thursday: 9.30am–7.30pm; Saturday: 9.30am–4pm.

The British Library
St Pancras Building, 96 Euston Road, London NW1 2DB
Legal Deposit Office: The British Library, Boston Spa, Wetherby, West Yorkshire LS23 7BQ
email legal-deposit-books@bl.uk
website www.bl.uk
Facebook www.facebook.com/britishlibrary
X @BritishLibrary
Instagram @britishlibrary

The British Library is the national library of the United Kingdom and contains a substantial collection of plays and manuscripts from the UK and Ireland, as well as from other parts of the world. The sound archive also includes just about everything from the sound of Amazonian tree frogs to classic recordings of Shakespeare's plays. Users need a Reader's Pass (details on how to acquire same are on the website) to access and read particular publications. The library will, for a fee, allow photocopying – subject to copyright legislation.

Contacts
See the entry for Spotlight under *Spotlight, casting directories and information services* on page 364.

Doollee.com

website www.doollee.com

An online guide to modern playwrights and theatre plays which have been written, or translated, into English since the production of *Look Back in Anger* in 1956. It contains information on 56,653 playwrights and 193,348 of their plays.

Dress Circle

Unit 8D Shakespeare Industrial Estate,
Watford WD24 5RR
tel 020-7096 3144
email sales@dresscircle.london
website www.dresscircle.london

Formerly had a shop in London's Covent Garden; it now operates online only. It aims to supply the widest selection of musical theatre and cabaret-related products from around the world – CDs, DVDs, posters, cards, mugs, collectibles and more. "If we can't get it – no one can!"

Fourthwall

(incorporating The Drama Student)
3rd Floor, 207 Regent Street, London W1B 3HH
tel 020-3371 0995
email editor@fourthwallmagazine.co.uk
website www.fourthwallmagazine.co.uk
Editorial Director Phil Matthews, *Editor* Josh Boyd-Rochford

Covers the whole journey, from auditioning for drama school through to graduation and beyond. Believes that to succeed in this industry, it is important that we constantly challenge ourselves, and often that means the training never leaves us. *Fourthwall* is at the forefront of that passion, delivering a magazine that is informative, amusing, intelligent, thought provoking, accessible and challenging. "Above all, we're a publication that is passionate about careers in the performing arts."

Nick Hern Books

The Glasshouse, 49A Goldhawk Road,
London W12 8QP
tel 020-8749 4953
email info@nickhernbooks.co.uk
website www.nickhernbooks.co.uk
Facebook www.facebook.com/NickHernBooks
X @NickHernBooks
Instagram @nickhernbooks
Editor Publisher & Ceo Matt Applewhite

Nick Hern Books (NHB) is the UK's leading specialist independent theatre publisher with over 2,000 plays by writers including Jez Butterworth, Caryl Churchill, debbie tucker green, Lucy Kirkwood, Lynn Nottage, Conor McPherson, Winsome Pinnock and Jack Thorne. Also publishes practical books by renowned practitioners such as Mike Alfreds, Peter Brook, Declan Donnellan, Richard Eyre and Harriet Walter.

Offers online discounts and special promotions via their website, plus downloadable extracts, exclusive signed editions and more. Enquiries for performing licences to their plays can also made online. The online Play Finder allows searches by genre, cast size, length and more.

Useful series for actors include *The Good Audition Guides*, which offer classical, Shakespeare and contemporary monologues and duologues as well as guidance on how to perform them; the *Compact Guides* covering a range of skills including accents, line learning, getting into drama school and getting an agent; and the *So You Want To...?* career guides, giving advice on a range of careers in the performing arts, written by practitioners with a wealth of knowledge and expertise in their field.

Nick Hern Books publishes plays in the English language alongside major professional productions on stage in the UK or Ireland. Submissions can be emailed to the Commissioning Editor at **submissions@nickhernbooks.co.uk**.

Internet Movie Database (IMDb)

website www.imdb.com

A comprehensive database and news round-up of film and television around the world.

The Knowledge

Standard House, 12–13 Essex Street,
London WC2R 3AA
tel 020-8102 0900
website www.theknowledgeonline.com
X @TheKnowledgeUK

Covering all aspects of production, The Knowledge Online contains contacts and services for the UK film, television, video and commercial production industry. The website features around 14,500 contacts, is free to use and does not require registration. Its subscription service Production Intelligence features contact details for casting directors and line producers for forthcoming productions.

London Arrangements

tel 020-7096 1801
email enquiries@londonarrangements.com
website www.londonarrangements.com
Facebook /londonarrangements
Director Stephen Robinson

London Arrangements specialise in the production of professional backing tracks ranging from stage and screen, swing and jazz, to classical and easy listening genres. Samples of all tracks can be listened to online, and the majority may be ordered in any key at no extra charge. Also produce bespoke backing tracks, piano rehearsal tracks and piano/vocal sheet music.

London Theatre
tel 020-4538 6967
website www.londontheatre.co.uk
X @londontheatre
Instagram @london_theatre

A website containing news, reviews, events, booking information and seating plans for London's theatre scene.

Methuen Drama
50 Bedford Square, London WC1B 3DP
tel 020-7631 5600
website www.bloomsbury.com/uk/academic/drama-performance-studies
X @MethuenDrama

As the largest performing arts imprint and part of Bloomsbury Publishing Plc, Methuen Drama's output spans the performing arts, including contemporary plays, critical editions of plays, play anthologies, books for practitioners, and books within the field of Shakespeare, performance and theatre studies. It also is the publisher of the successful digital platform Drama Online. Methuen Drama are happy to consider proposals for books on their list.

For submission details go to the website **www.bloomsbury.com/uk/connect/contact-us/writing-for-bloomsbury/**.

Music Theatre International
12–14 Mortimer Street, London W1T 3JJ
tel 020-7580 2827
website www.mtishows.com

Theatrical licensing agency. A great resource for researching songs – some of which can be partially listened to and read about on the website.

Musicroom
130 Shaftesbury Avenue, London W1D 5EU
tel (01284) 725725
email info@musicroom.com
website www.musicroom.com

The world's largest online retailer of sheet music, tutor methods, instructional DVDs and videos, music software and instruments and accessories.

National Theatre Bookshop
National Theatre, South Bank, London SE1 9PX
tel 020-7452 3456
email bookshop@nationaltheatre.org.uk
website https://shop.nationaltheatre.org.uk/
Instagram @ntbookshop

Britain's leading specialist theatre bookshop. An inspiring selection of books, plays and design-led gifts. *Opening Hours*: Monday to Saturday: 10am–10.30pm (this varies on certain public holidays).

PlayDatabase.com
website www.playdatabase.com

US site that helps theatre-lovers find monologues and plays for production.

Project Gutenberg
website www.gutenberg.org

An online library of more than 70,000 ebooks – and many classic plays – which have gone out of copyright in the USA. Also a growing collection of music recordings and scores.

Royal Court Library
Sloane Square, London SW1W 8AS
tel 020-7565 5050
email info@royalcourttheatre.com
website https://royalcourttheatre.com/your-visit/royal-court-library
Facebook /ConcordUKShows
X @ConcordUKShows

Previously the Samuel French bookshop, the converted space is set across 3 floors, the theatre reference library houses 5000 scripts and theatre books (and counting) donated by Concord Theatricals. Available to browse and read in our building entirely for free.

Screen Daily
Standard House, 12–13 Essex Street, London WC2R 3AA
tel 020-8102 0900
website www.screendaily.com

International news and features on the film business. Subscriptions cost from £239 per annum for:

• Screen Daily – 12 monthly issues delivered to digitally and/or in print
• ScreenDaily.com – instant access to the latest news, reviews and industry moves available online
• Global box office data available online – structured by territories, films and distributors
• Screenbase – the new online, interactive database providing vital production and financing information for the top five European territories

Script Websites
Although subject to rules on copyright, a number of websites make the scripts for films and television shows and suggestions for audition speeches available online. These sites tend to come and go, but here are some that are current at the time of going to press:
• www.sfy.ru
• www.imsdb.com
• www.playscripts.com
• www.simplyscripts.com
• www.whysanity.net/monos
• www.singlelane.com
• www.filmsite.org/bestspeeches.html
• https://escript.ws

The Sheetmusic Warehouse
email pianoman@sheetmusicwarehouse.co.uk
website www.sheetmusicwarehouse.co.uk

Specialists supplying old music, rare music, music from the shows, musicals and operetta, popular music, wartime music, jazz music, Deep South American music, music hall music, classical music, modern music ... "You name it, we've probably got it. Music to play, music to sing to or music to frame and hang on your wall!"

Shooting People
PO Box 51350, London N1 6XS
email contact@shootingpeople.org
website https://shootingpeople.org

A network of thousands of independent filmmakers, who cast and crew around 200 films each week using SP services. SP supports and spotlights all creatives working in film by offering a range of resources. Specific SP resources for performers and actors includes:

• Daily castings for independent films and open casting calls for major feature films and TV shows.
• Curated news about agents seeking actors to represent, performance showcase opportunities, competitions and grants.
• Live masterclass events. Past actor speakers include Alex Lawther (*End of the F***ing World*), Will Sharpe (*White Lotus*), Erin Doherty (*The Crown*), Alice Lowe (*Prevenge, Sightseers*) and the Sundance Grand Jury Prize winner Desiree Akhavan (*The Miseducation of Cameron Post, Appropriate Behaviour*).
• The New Shoots Awards, presented by Shooting People, is an annual award programme that celebrates creatives working in film. The New Shoots: Actors award winner receives mentorship from world-renowned casting director, Des Hamilton, Spotlight membership, self-tape equipment and a cash prize. 11 other actors receive other prizes and support.

Membership costs £9.95 per month (concessions available). Shooting People also organises a number of parties, screenings, workshops and other events for which full members receive advanced notice.

Skoob Books
66 The Brunswick, Marchmont Street, London WC1N 1AE
tel 020-7278 8760
website www.skoob.com

An excellent resource for the peforming arts. Large collection of second-hand plays, including many translated works and as-new titles at half RRP. Strong theatre, film, music and TV sections in a very large basement bookshop. All academic areas covered, and masses of paperback fiction. Lift access and knowledgeable, friendly staff. More/different books are available to buy online via the website. Skoob is the leading UK supplier of books to TV, film and theatre productions; please contact our Didcot office for hire enquries at **skoobhire@psychobabel.co.uk**.

The Stage Media Company Ltd
47 Bermondsey Street, London SE1 3XT
tel 020-7403 1818
email reception@thestage.co.uk
website www.thestage.co.uk

Online and weekly print publication for the entertainment industry. Established in 1880. Advice, news, reviews, features and recruitment for theatre, entertainment, opera, dance, TV, radio, backstage and technical, management, education and training. *The Stage* is also available on iPad, Android, Kindle and other tablet devices.

Theatre Record
(The continuing chronicle of the British Stage)
4 Waverley Road, Weymouth, Dorset DT3 5EB
email editor@theatrerecord.com
website www.theatrerecord.com

Established in 1981 as *London Theatre Record*, the website collates the complete, unabridged reviews of all new shows in the UK covered by national press, leading magazines and the internet. As well as reviews, each show is represented by a full listing of cast, technical credits and production photographs. Updated daily, the search feature enables in-depth research on all archive productions to 1981.

Theatrevoice
website www.theatrevoice.com
X @theatrevoices

The leading site for audio content about British theatre, featuring journalists from across the UK press, and practitioners from across the theatre industry. It was set up in 2003 to see if theatre could be talked about in a new way – critics to be more expansive than what the usual space constraints of the print media allowed; to enable actors, writers, directors and designers to be heard talking in detail and at length about their work; and to help members of the public interact more directly with theatre-makers and commentators. The Theatre Museum, now V&A Theatre Collections, which provided technical assistance and a place for recording from the site's inception, assumed management responsibilities for the site in the summer of 2005, to ensure that Theatrevoice's growing archive of material would be preserved for posterity. In April 2008, V&A Theatre Collections and Rose Bruford College agreed to support the site in partnership. Theatrevoice acknowledges with gratitude all the input that has been and still is freely given.

TheatreVoice is managed by the Department of Theatre & Performance at the V&A.

Theatricalia
email principal@theatricalia.com
website https://theatricalia.com
X @theatricalia

Theatricalia is aiming to become "the repository of theatre productions on the Internet". In doing so, it will enable people to discover theatre that is going on around them, follow actors they have seen in previous productions and record memorable events of productions they have seen.

UK Theatre Network
Admiralty Way, Teddington TW11 0NL
tel 020-3652 7453
email editor@uktheatre.net
website www.uktheatrenetwork.com
Facebook /uktheatrenet
X @UKTheatreNet

Established 2001. A theatre community with a UK-wide team of reviewers who attend the best of regional theatre and share their experience and ticket information. New members can join by visiting the website and subscribing.

Westminster Reference Library
35 St Martin's Street, London WC2H 7HP
tel 020-7641 6200
email referencelibrarywc2@westminster.gov.uk
website www.westminster.gov.uk/leisure-libraries-and-community/library-opening-times-and-contact-details/westminster-reference-library

A West End public library with an art and design and music collection of national significance, along with a performing arts collection, Access to these collection is free and open to all. There are regular talks, workshops, performances in support of the collections, with the library open to suggestion for future events. Opening Hours: Monday to Friday: 10.00am–8.00pm; Saturday: 10.00am–5.00pm.

Organisations, associations, societies and contacts

This section contains details of all kinds of ways (not listed elsewhere in this *Yearbook*) of getting involved, sourcing useful information, learning, finding interesting lectures, networking, and simply keeping in touch with what's going on. It is important for the 'jobbing' actor to keep up to date with developments within the industry, and getting involved in related activities can pay dividends in the future.

The Actors' Guild of Great Britain
The Actors' Guild Hub at Spotlight,
16 Garrick Street, London WC2E 9BA
email mail@actorsguild.co.uk
website www.actorsguild.co.uk
X @ActorsGuildGB

The Actors' Guild is a community of professional actors who meet with leading acting tutors, casting directors, directors, artistic directors, producers and agents to develop their craft, maximise their career development and benefit from the professional networking opportunities that membership brings.

The Guild was formed as an antidote to the increasing number of enterprises that seemed to be taking advantage of actors. Providing a haven, a support network and the opportunity to work with the very people you meet in the audition room.

"Our unique set-up means we are able to swing the pendulum of power firmly back to the actor. Our programme is dictated purely by feedback from our membership; we never ask you to book casting director workshops in 'blocks', and believe quality does not have to cost the earth and are run both in person and on Zoom. We also offer an exclusive range of industry discounts for our members."

American Actors UK (AAUK)
email admin@americanactorsuk.com
website americanactorsuk.com
Chair Amelia Sciandra (she/they)

American Actors UK is an association of North American actors with legal right to work both in the UK and their home country. We are a database and resource for casting directors looking for genuine American accents. As a member-led organisation we look to create opportunities to connect with each other and practice our craft as well as meet casting directors.

Membership is open to genuine North American professional actors who can legally work on both sides of the Atlantic, have proof of professional contracts and are on Spotlight UK. We are not an agency but provide contacts to agents and CDs.

ASSITEJ International
16 Via Matteotti, Bologna, 40129, Italy
email sg@assitej-international.org
website https://assitej-international.org

ASSITEJ International (Association Internationale du Théâtre et Arts Vivants pour l'Enfance et la Jeunesse) states: "Since the theatrical art is a universal expression of mankind, and possesses the influence and power to link large groups of the world's people in the service of peace, and considering the role theatre can play in the education of younger generations, an autonomous international organisation has been formed which bears the name of the International Association of Theatre for Children and Young People." Also see Theatre for Young Audiences (TYA), below.

ASSITEJ UK
(International Association of Theatre for Children and Young People)
c/o the egg, Theatre Royal Bath, Sawclose,
Bath BA1 1ET
email info@tya-uk.org
website www.tya-uk.org
X @ASSITEJ

ASSITEJ UK – The Gateway for Scotland, Wales, Northern Ireland and England to ASSITEJ International. A network for makers and promoters of professional theatre for young audiences, aiming to raise greater awareness of the value of theatre.

AudioUK
c/o Unit 2, Olympic Court, Boardmans Way,
Whitehills Business Park, Blackpool FY4 5GU
email admin@audiouk.org.uk
website www.audiouk.org.uk
X @WeAreAudioUK

AudioUK is the trade association for UK audio production companies, with over 120 members across the UK, making high-quality award-winning podcasts, radio and audiobooks. Offers business affairs support for members and negotiates terms of trade with the BBC as well as liaising with talent unions. Also runs the Audiotrain skills programme and organises the annual Audio Production Awards.

BAFTA
195 Piccadilly, London W1J 9LN
tel 020-7734 0022
email reception@bafta.org
website www.bafta.org
Chief Executive Officer Jane Millichip

Founded in 1947, BAFTA is the UK's pre-eminent independent charity bringing the very best work in film, games and television to public attention, and supporting the growth of creative talent in the UK and internationally. BAFTA does this by identifying and celebrating excellence, discovering, inspiring and nurturing new talent, and enabling learning and creative collaboration. BAFTA's awards are awarded annually by its members to their peers in recognition of their skills and expertise. In addition, BAFTA's year-round learning programme offers unique access to some of the world's most inspiring talent through workshops, masterclasses, lectures and mentoring schemes, connecting with audiences of all ages and backgrounds across the UK, USA and Asia.

British Association for Performing Arts Medicine (BAPAM)
63 Mansell Street, London E1 8AN
tel 020-8167 4775
email info@bapam.org.uk
website www.bapam.org.uk

The British Association for Performing Arts Medicine is a unique medical charity helping performing arts professionals and students with work-related health problems, both physical and psychological.

BAPAM provides:

• Free confidential clinical advice from medical practitioners who have specialist understanding of industry professionals' needs
• Directory of Performing Arts Medicine Practitioners – a list of clinical specialists and practitioners in many branches of healthcare who have an interest in treating performing arts professionals
• Health-information resources enabling you to understand what you can do to keep in peak condition throughout a demanding career
• Healthy Performance talks and training for a wide range of audiences, including introductory sessions for student groups and educational institutions. Bespoke sessions for clients including performers, teachers, clinicians and employers.

British Council
Bridgewater House, 58 Whitworth Street, Manchester M1 6BB
tel 0161 957 7755
email arts@britishcouncil.org
website www.britishcouncil.org/arts
Facebook /Arts.BritishCouncil
X @BritishArts

The British Council is the UK's public diplomacy and cultural organisation, and works in 100 countries, in arts, education, governance and science. The Arts Group supports around 2,000 arts events every year, encouraging international collaborations, performances and exchanges with some of the top UK artists. In addition they support arts-based workshops, seminars and online events.

The form of support which is offered varies according to the project. In most cases the Council acts as an advisory body, and brokers partnerships with overseas contacts such as artistic programmers and producers, venues, choreographers and festival directors. Although most work is geared towards young people aged 16–35, this isn't an exclusive emphasis, and classic or traditional work is supported, especially if it has a modern slant.

Resources available on the website include an annual directory of UK drama, dance, live art and street art companies that have work suitable for overseas touring; specialist information about drama/performing arts education in the UK; and *Britfilms* https://film.britishcouncil.org – a portal site for the UK film industry with information about international film festivals, UK film directors and films, making a film in the UK, training and careers advice.

Not open to the public except by appointment. Write, phone or email to establish contact, or get in touch with an artform specialist.

British Film Institute (BFI)
21 Stephen Street, London W1T 1LN
tel 020-7255 1444
BFI Southbank, Belvedere Road, South Bank, Waterloo, London SE1 8XT
tel 020-7928 3535
website www.bfi.org.uk

Established in 1933, the BFI strives to increase the level of understanding, appreciation and access to film and television culture. In addition to the BFI Reuben Library, which provides access to the largest collection of written material on film, television and the moving image in the word, the organisation runs the BFI National Archive, BFI Southbank (formerly the National Film Theatre), BFI Flare: London LGBTQ+ Film Festival and the London Film Festival (see entry under Media festivals). It also publishes books, releases films in cinemas, on DVD and via its VOD platform BFI Player, runs educational programmes, and has one of the largest collections of film stills and film posters in the world. The BFI also awards Lottery funding to film production, distribution, education, audience development and market intelligence and research.

British Music Hall Society
email contact@britishmusichallsociety.com
website www.britishmusichallsociety.com
Facebook /BritishMusicHallSociety
Bluesky @musichallsociety.bsky.social

Founded in 1963, the society aims to preserve the history of music hall and variety, to recall the artistes who created it and to support entertainers working today. Members receive copies of the society's quarterly magazine *The Call-Boy* containing news, views and information about the sector; they also have the opportunity to attend evening 'In the Limelight' talks. Arranges live Music Hall and Variety shows. Organises #MusicHallVarietyDay on the 16th of May each year.

Campaign for the Arts
8 Lee Street, London E8 4DY
tel 020-7187 6707
email hello@campaignforthearts.org
website www.campaignforthearts.org
Facebook /campaignforthearts
X @_CFTA
Instagram @campaignforthearts
Director Jack Gamble

The Campaign for the Arts is the UK-wide alliance for the arts. An independent charity, its mission is to champion, defend and expand access to the arts and culture, for and with the public. It does this through a mixture of research, advocacy and public engagement.

Casting Directors Guild of Great Britain and Ireland
website www.thecdg.co.uk
X @CDGNews
Instagram @cdgnews

A professional organisation which represents casting directors working in film, television, theatre and commercials. The Casting Directors Guild aims to standardise professional working practice and to enable the exchange of information and ideas between members.

Election to the Guild is at the discretion of the Committee. Full members must have worked in one or more areas of the industry for at least 5 years, and are entitled to use the initials CDG after their name. Probationary members must have worked as an assistant to a casting director for 2 years.

Members are listed on the website with information about their areas of work and recent credits.

Chortle
tel 020-8281 5204
email steve@chortle.co.uk
website www.chortle.co.uk

Established in 2000 with the aim of being the most comprehensive, critical and up-to-date guide to all aspects of comedy in Britain. Today, the site is the premier source of comedy news, reviews and listings and attracts around 180,000 unique visitors every month.

Co-operative Personal Management Association (CPMA)
email cpmauk@yahoo.co.uk
website www.cpma.coop

Founded in 2002, the CPMA works to further and promote the interests of its members, who are acting agencies located across the UK. Backed by Equity, it seeks to raise the profile of co-ops with both employers and actors, and to represent the interests of co-ops with external bodies. Also works with members to identify and assist in solving the unique problems of a co-operative, to enourage good practice, to develop training skills and opportunities, and to act as an advocate for co-operative working.

Directors UK
4th Floor, 22 Stukeley Street, London WC2B 5LR
tel 020-7240 0009
email info@directors.uk.com
website www.directors.uk.com
Facebook /DirectorsUKcmo
Instagram @Directors_UK
LinkedIn @directors-uk

Directors UK is the professional association of UK screen directors. It is a membership organisation representing the creative, economic and contractual interests of over 8,500 members - the majority of working TV and film directors in the UK. Directors UK negotiates rights deals and collects and distributes royalties to its members. It also campaigns and lobbies on its members' behalf and provides a range of services including legal advice, events, training and career development. Directors UK works closely with fellow organisations around the world to represent directors' rights and concerns, promotes excellence in the craft of direction and champions change to the current landscape to create an equal opportunity industry for all.

Drama Association of Wales
c/o 10 Brachdy Close, Rumney, Cardiff CF3 3AU
email chair@dramawales.org.uk
website www.dramawales.com
Facebook /DramaAssociationOfWales
X @DramaWales
Chair Teri McCarthy

Founded in 1934 and a registered charity since 1973, the Drama Association of Wales aims to increase opportunities for people in the community to be creatively involved in high-quality drama. Its main activities include training courses in all aspects of theatre, including a 5-day residential summer school.

Also runs a playwriting competition and workshops. Organises the Wales National Drama Festival from March to June, culminating in the Wales Final Festival of One Act Plays at the beginning of June.

UK membership costs £15 per year for individuals and £25 for groups, both professional and amateur.

Dramaturgs' Network
c/o Old Coghurst Farm, Rock Lane,
Hastings TN35 4NX
email info@dramaturgy.co.uk
website www.dramaturgy.co.uk
Facebook /dramaturgsnetwork
X @dramaturgs_net

Founded in 2001, the Dramaturgs' Network is an organisation for UK theatre practitioners committed to developing dramaturgy and supporting practitioners' development in the field. A volunteer arts organisation, it was created to share ideas, knowledge, resources and skills in current dramaturgical practices. The network aims to provide support for theatre makers functioning in the role of dramaturg and/or literary manager and educational professionals involved in dramaturgical practice.

The Entertainment Agents' Association Ltd
71-75 Shelton Street London Covent Garden WC2H 9JQ
tel 020 3051 6392
email admin@teaa.uk
website www.teaa.uk
X @TEAAUK
Administrator Carol Richards

Membership Organisation for Entertainment Agents established in 1927.

Federation of Scottish Theatre
c/o Royal Lyceum Theatre, 30ʙ Grindlay Street, Edinburgh EH3 9AX
email info@scottishtheatre.org
website www.scottishtheatre.org
Facebook /FederationofScottishTheatre

Membership and development body for professional dance, opera and theatre in Scotland, bringing the sector together to speak with a collective voice, to share resources and expertise, and to promote collaborative working.

Independent Theatre Council (ITC)
c/o The Albany, Douglas Way, London SE8 4AG
tel 020-7403 1727
email admin@itc-arts.org
website www.itc-arts.org

Founded in 1974, the Independent Theatre Council (ITC) is the management association and political voice of around 450 performing arts professionals and organisations. ITC provides its members with legal and management advice, training and professional development, networking, regular newsletters and a comprehensive web resource.

Working across a variety of art forms, including drama, dance, opera, music theatre, puppetry, mixed media, mime, physical theatre and circus, ITC members usually operate on the middle- and small-scale, and are dedicated to producing innovative work, often in unconventional performance spaces.

ITC has commissioned a wide range of publications which offer guidance on potentially difficult aspects of working in the performing arts, advice on good practice and further sources of information. For more than 20 years the Independent Theatre Council has been organising training for managers and staff across the performing arts.

International Casting Directors Association (ICDA)
website https://the-icda.com
Facebook /theicdn
X @the_icda
President Lana Veenker

The idea for an informal international network was floated during a meeting of casting directors during European Film Promotion's Shooting Stars event at the Berlinale. Until then, casting directors had only been organised in national associations, but ICDN offers them the opportunity to network, connect, share information and raise the profile of the profession. Members include the most influential and high-profile casting directors in film and television.

International Federation of Actors (FIA)
Rue Joseph II 40, Box 4, B-1000 Brussels, Belgium
tel +32 (0)2 235 08 65
email office@fia-actors.com
website https://fia-actors.com

The FIA currently represents 80 performers' unions and guilds in over 60 countries around the world. Membership is limited to unions, guilds and professional associations – individual actors may not join. FIA works internationally to represent and co-ordinate the interests of performing artists and their professional organisations.

Services: Lobbying at European and international level on behalf of performers; defence of artists' freedom; trade union development; information exchange through confrences and meetings; networking.

Objectives: To promote a better understanding of performers' concerns and challenges around the world; to ensure that all main decision-making processes take due consideration of the specific needs of performers; to contribute to improve the social and professional conditions of performers worldwide; to facilitate the sharing of knowledge and experience on all issues of common interest between member organisations.

Irish Theatre Institute
17 Eustace Street, Temple Bar, Dublin 2, D02 F293, Republic of Ireland
tel +353 (0)1 670 4906

email info@irishtheatreinstitute.ie
website www.irishtheatreinstitute.ie

Irish Theatre Institute is a resource organisation that nurtures, promotes and drives the ambition of Irish theatre makers and Irish theatre, from its grassroot beginnings to its presentation on the world stage.

Mirth Control
tel 07974 674133
email geoff@mirthcontrol.org.uk
website www.mirthcontrolcomedy.com
X @MirthControl

Established in 1998, Mirth Control is the UK's largest independent comedy bookers. Books for over 100 comedy clubs in the UK and Europe and holds a database of over 1,500 comedians. Also manages clients.

National Rural Touring Forum (NRTF)
Good Life Hub, Orchard Barn, Manor Farm Barns, Newbury Hill, Hampstead Norreys RG18 0TR
email admin@nrtf.org.uk
website www.ruraltouring.org

The NRTF is the organisation that represents a number of mainly rural touring schemes and rural arts development agencies across the UK. "Our touring scheme members work with local communities to promote high-quality arts events and experiences in local venues."

Pact (Producers Alliance for Cinema and Television)
3rd Floor, Fitzrovia House,
153–157 Cleveland Street, London W1T 6QW
tel 020-7380 8230
website www.pact.co.uk
X @PactUK
Chief Executive John McVay

The UK trade association that represents and promotes the commercial interests of independent feature film, television, animation and interactive media companies. Headquartered in London, it has regional representation throughout the UK in order to support its members, including an office in Leeds. An effective lobbying organisation, it has regular dialogues with government, regulators, public agencies and opinion-formers on all issues affecting its members, and contributes to key public policy debates on the media industry. It negotiates terms of trade with all public service broadcasters in the UK and supports members in their business dealings with cable and satellite channels and streaming services. It also lobbies for a properly structured and funded UK film industry and maintains close contact with other relevant film organisations and government departments.

Personal Managers' Association (PMA)
email info@thepma.com
website www.thepma.com

Established in 1950, the PMA is a membership organisation for agents who represent actors, writers and directors working in film, television and theatre. It aims to empower agents to uphold industry standards and to encourage good agent practice.

Royal Television Society (RTS)
3 Dorset Rise, London EC4Y 8EN
tel 020-7822 2810
email info@rts.org.uk
website https://rts.org.uk

Provides the leading forum for discussion and debate on all aspects of the television industry, with opportunities for networking and professional development for people at all levels and across every sector. The RTS has 14 national and regional centres in the UK, which draw up an annual programme to suit the needs of their members.

Events organised by the RTS include dinners, lectures, conventions, conferences and awards ceremonies. In addition it produces a monthly magazine, *Television*, outlining key industry debates and developments.

Scene & Heard
128A Chalton Street, London NW1 1RX
tel 020-7388 9009
email mail@sceneandheard.org
website www.sceneandheard.org
Instagram @sceneandhearduk

A unique mentoring project that partners the inner-city children of Somers Town, London, with volunteer theatre professionals. Scene & Heard gives children an experience of quality one-to-one adult attention enabling them to write plays to be performed by professional actors. The fundamental purpose of the project is to boost the self-esteem and raise the aspirations of the children by giving them a public platform for their voice and providing a personal experience of success.

Only accepts enquiries from professional actors, directors and writers. The best way to get in touch is to see a performance.

Society of London Theatre (SOLT)
32 Rose Street, London WC2E 9ET
tel 020-7557 6700
email members@soltukt.co.uk
website https://solt.co.uk

Founded in 1908 by Sir Charles Wyndham, the Society of London Theatre is the trade association which represents the producers, theatre owners and managers of the major commercial and grant-aided theatres in central London.

Today the Society combines its long-standing roles in such areas as industrial relations and legal advice for members, with a campaigning role for the industry, together with a wide range of audience-development programmes to promote theatre-going.

The Society of Teachers of the Alexander Technique (STAT)
PO Box 78503, London N14 9GB
tel 020-8885 6524
email stat@alexandertechnique.co.uk
website https://alexandertechnique.co.uk
Facebook /alexander.technique.1
X @AlexanderTechUK

The Alexander Technique has been taught for more than 100 years. In 1958, the Society of Teachers of the Alexander Technique (STAT) was founded in the UK by teachers who were trained by FM Alexander. STAT's first aim is to ensure the highest standards of teacher training and professional practice.

Teaching members of STAT are registered (MSTAT) to teach the Technique after completing a 3-year, full-time training course approved by the Society or one of the Affiliated Societies overseas; they are also required to adhere to the Society's published *Code of Professional Conduct and Competence* and are covered by the professional indemnity insurance.

There are currently more than 2,500 teaching members of STAT and its affiliated societies worldwide. Graduates of STAT training courses are assessed by a system of external moderation; the Society also runs a postgraduate programme of Continuing Professional Development. STAT's further aims are to promote public awareness and understanding of the Alexander Technique, and to encourage research. The Society publishes a regular newsletter, *STATNews*, and *The Alexander Journal*.

The Stephen Sondheim Society
44 Little Lane, Kimberley, Nottingham NG16 2PE
email sondheimsociety@sondheim.org
website www.sondheimsociety.com
X @sondheimsociety
Chairman Craig Glenday, *Administrator* Nina Douglas-Bain

The Stephen Sondheim Society is a registered charity promoting the works of the composer and lyricist Stephen Sondheim. Keeps track of all productions (professional and amateur) of Sondheim's musicals, publishes a newsletter, arranges theatre visits, runs an annual student competition and has an extensive archive housed at Kingston University.

At the time of writing, UK membership is £27 (single), £22 (concession) or £32 (joint), £17 (student/Equity/MU/ISM) and £40 (for international membership) but please consult the website for the latest rates.

Stage Directors UK
7 Bell Yard, London WC2A 2JR
tel 020-7112 8881
email info@stagedirectorsuk.com
website www.stagedirectorsuk.com
Facebook /StageDirectorsUK
X @StageDirectors
Instagram @stagedirectors

A trade union for stage directors, choreographers, movement directors, fight directors and intimacy coordinators across the UK. SDUK represents the interests of stage directors, campaigning and lobbying for better rights and working conditions. SDUK provides a sense of community and a unifying network for its members, and offers support, training and professional development, directing culture towards a greater spirit of collaboration and mutual support.

Summerhall Arts
Summerhall Arts, 1 Summerhall, EH9 1PL
email info@summerhallarts.co.uk
website www.summerhallarts.co.uk
Instagram @summerhallarts
Sam Gough, Tom Forster

Summerhall Arts is built on the important work of the visual and performative arts that has taking place at Summerhall in Edinburgh since 2012, the needs and challenges of a changing sector, the evolution and limitations of the venue and the knowledge and experience of those who have developed an idea that provides a solution to deliver real and vital support and opportunities to local and national creative practitioners.

Summerhall Arts was established to create a stable vehicle for the arts, protecting the fragile artistic community, safeguarding a creative professional development programme and maintaining a safe and inclusive space to showcase new writing and early career practitioners in Edinburgh and Scotland.

They identify, create, support, and deliver a wide and diverse range of opportunities for emerging and established local and national creative practitioners within an established safe space. The size, breadth and diversity of the planned programme is comprehensive and designed to support and galvanise a fragile sector through cross sector collaboration to be stronger by working together.

Summerhall Arts is a Lifeboat – they provide space, opportunity and mentorship to those who have creative ideas but no means or facilities to begin that creative process. Space is so limited to experiment and play within the city that it is often reserved for established creatives – they provide a safe, welcoming, and inclusive space and environment for the process to take shape.

Theatre Chaplaincy UK

St Paul's Church, Bedford Street, London WC2E 9ED
mobile 07501 829491
email info@theatrechaplaincyuk.com
website https://theatrechaplaincyuk.com
Facebook /TCUKchaplains
X @TCUKchaplains
Ceo Holly McBride

A registered charity serving the UK performing arts sector through provisions of chaplaincy services to support the mental health and wellbeing of all performing arts professionals, of all faiths and none.

Theatres Trust

22 Charing Cross Road, London WC2H OQL
tel 020-7836 8591
email info@theatrestrust.org.uk
website www.theatrestrust.org.uk
X @TheatresTrust

National Advisory Public Body for theatres operating as a statutory consultee on theatres in the planning system and as a charity. Champions the future of live performance by protecting and supporting excellent theatre buildings which meet the needs of their communities. They do this by providing advice on the design, planning, development and sustainability of theatres, campaigning on behalf of theatres old and new, and offering financial assistance through grants.

They promote the quality and design of existing and new theatres and protect important historic theatres so that they can be used as theatres in the future. The Trust also advises to ensure theatre buildings meet the current needs and demands of the theatre industry and the audiences they serve.

UK Theatre

32 Rose Street, London WC2E 9ET
tel 020-7557 6700
email members@soltukt.co.uk
website www.uktheatre.org
Facebook /uk_theatre
Co-Chief Executives Claire Walker, Hannah Essex

A membership organisation representing approximately 255 theatre producers, managers, owners and operators across the UK. Also operates as a professional association, supporting over 1,400 individuals working professionally in theatre and the performing arts in the UK. Members benefit from access to a range of services, high-quality training and events, resources and initiatives, and networking opportunities. As well as running the only awards scheme to recognise excellence in theatre throughout the UK, UK Theatre promotes excellence, professional development and campaigns to improve resilience and increase audiences across the sector.

University of Bristol Theatre Collection

Library Services, Vandyck Building, Cantocks Close, Bristol BS8 1UP
tel 0117 331 5045
email theatre-collection@bristol.ac.uk
website www.bristol.ac.uk/theatre-collection

The University of Bristol Theatre Collection is one of the world's largest and most significant collections relating to the history of British theatre. It is an Arts Council England Designated Collection, an Accredited Museum and an Accredited Archive Service. It is a research facility that is open to the public. Its collections cover all aspects of theatre from the seventeenth century up to the present day and includes original documents, photographs, artwork and artefacts.

V&A Theatre & Performance Collections

V&A East Storehouse, Parkes Street,
Queen Elizabeth Olympic Park, Hackney Wick,
London E20 3AX
email theatreandperformance@vam.ac.uk
website www.vam.ac.uk/collections/theatre-performance

The V&A's Theatre and Performance Collections comprise over 80,000 objects and 600 archives exploring the practice, process and history of performance in the UK since Shakespeare's day, covering theatre, dance, popular entertainment, music and film. In 2009, permanent Theatre & Performance Galleries opened at the V&A, replacing the Theatre Museum in Covent Garden which closed in 2007. From 2026, the Theatre & Performance Collections will be available to access at V&A Storehouse, the museum's new Collections and Research Centre opening in Stratford, East London.

Women in Film and Television (UK) (WFTV)

Exchange, Somerset House, Strand,
London WC2R 1LA
tel 020-7287 1400
email admin@wftv.org.uk
website www.wftv.org.uk

The leading membership organisation for women working in creative media in the UK and part of an international network of over 12,000 women. Members come from a broad range of professions spanning the entire film and television industry. WFTV hosts a variety of online and in person events throughout the year, presents a prestigious awards ceremony every December and runs a 4 nations mid-career mentoring programme for women. WFTV also collaborates with industry bodies on research projects, runs bursary initiatives and lobbies for women's interests.

WGGB (Writers' Guild of Great Britain)
1st Floor, 134 Tooley Street, London SE1 2TU
tel 020-7833 0777
email admin@writersguild.org.uk
website www.writersguild.org.uk
Facebook www.facebook.com/thewritersguild
X @TheWritersGuild
Bluesky @writersguildgb.bsky.social
Instagram @writersguildgb
LinkedIn /the-writers-guild-of-great-britain
General Secretary Ellie Peers

WGGB is a trade union for professional and aspiring writers in TV, audio, film, theatre, books, poetry, comedy, animation and video games. WGGB negotiates collective minimum terms agreements with the main broadcasters, streaming services and trade bodies for film, TV, audio and theatre – these cover fees, advances, royalties, residuals, pension contributions, rights, credits and other matters. The union also campaigns and lobbies on issues that affect writers in the UK. WGGB members have access to free contract vetting, free and discounted training, and a pension scheme; the Writers' Guild Welfare Fund gives emergency assistance toFull Members in financial trouble. Members receive a weekly email bulletin containing news and work opportunities, and Full Members are eligible to be listed in the online Find a Writer directory. Founded 1959.

Bibliography

For young, aspiring and student actors

Ben Crystal, *Shakespeare on Toast: Getting a Tasre for the Bard* (Icon Books, 2015). One of the best introductions to the life and works of Shakespeare.

Paul Elsam, *Acting Characters* (Methuen Drama, 2011). Fundamentally practical, this introductory handbook for the aspiring actor helps them create, present and sustain a believable character using different voice and body language.

Helen Freeman, *So You Want To Go To Drama School?* (Nick Hern Books, 2012). A clear and honest guide, written by a teacher and audition panellist with a lifetime's experience of the audition process.

Alison Hodge (ed.), *Twentieth Century Actor Training* (Routledge, 2000). A valuable introduction to the lives, principles, and practices of fourteen of the most important figures in twentieth-century actor training.

Kelly Hunter, *Cracking Shakespeare* (Methuen Drama, 2015). A book that demystifies the process of speaking Shakespeare's language, offering hands-on techniques for drama students, young actors and directors who are intimidated by rehearsing, performing and directing Shakespeare's plays.

Andy Johnson, *The Excellent Audition Guide* (Nick Hern Books, 2013). An engaging, upbeat guide for any student thinking of applying to drama school, this book demystifies the often scary-looking process, leading you through every step with reassurance and encouragement.

Ellis Jones, *Teach Yourself Acting* (Hodder & Stoughton Ltd, 1998). A good overview of acting and the profession.

Samantha Marsden, *100 Acting Exercises for 8–18 Year Olds* (Methuen Drama, 2019). Offers acting exercises to be used with young people in the classroom or by individuals, many based on the teachings of Meisner, Stanislavski and Brecht.

John Matthews, *Training for Performance* (Methuen Drama, 2011). An innovative introduction to the concept of 'askeology' – a field of study that dissolves divisions between disciplines and their exercises – and identifies four meta-disciplinary categories in the process of training that are common to all institutional contexts: vocation; obedience; formation and automatisation.

Jennifer Reischel, *So You Want to Tread the Boards: The Everything-you-need-to-know, Insider's Guide to a Career in the Performing Arts* (JR Books Ltd, 2007).

Anna Scher, *Desperate to Act* (Lions, 1988). Brilliant, basic advice for those so 'desperate', from a lady who should know.

Auditions, auditioning and casting

Margo Annett, *Actor's Guide to Auditions and Interviews* (Methuen Drama, 2004). Now in its third edition, this useful guide outlines the techniques needed to achieve success in the challenging process of getting work, covering all aspects of casting, including gaining a place on a drama course, landing a part in film, TV, commercials or theatre, and becoming a radio or TV presenter.

Nancy Bishop, *Secrets from the Casting Couch* (Methuen Drama, 2009). A practical workbook written from the point of view of a very experienced casting director.

Simon Dunmore, *Alternative Shakespeare Auditions for Men* (A & C Black, 1997). A collection of 50 less-well-known speeches for men.

Simon Dunmore, *Alternative Shakespeare Auditions for Women* (A & C Black, 1997). A collection of 50 less-well-known speeches for women.

Simon Dunmore, *MORE Alternative Shakespeare Auditions for Men* (A & C Black, 2002). Another collection of 50 less-well-known speeches for men.

Simon Dunmore, *MORE Alternative Shakespeare Auditions for Women* (A & C Black, 1999). Another collection of 50 less-well-known speeches for women.

Ed Hooks, *The Audition Book* (3rd edition, Back Stage Books, 2000). Excellent reading if you're thinking of trying your hand in the USA. It's also worth looking at Ed's website for his excellent 'Craft Notes' (www.edhooks.com).

Michael Shurtleff, *Audition* (Walker & Company, 1984). An American book which should be read. It contains brilliant insights and thoughts to help any actor.

Donna Soto-Morettini, *Mastering the Audition* (Methuen Drama, 2012) and *Mastering the Shakespeare Audition* (Methuen Drama, 2016). These thorough handbooks coach the actor to master the audition experience for contemporary and classical speeches, allowing them to master their fear and gain a deeper understanding of the ideas and skills involved.

Acting techniques

Mike Alfreds, *Different Every Night* (Nick Hern Books, 2007). A top ranking director sets out his rehearsal techniques in this vital masterclass.

Mike Alfreds, *Then What Happens?* (Nick Hern Books, 2013). The author makes the case for putting story and storytelling back at the heart of theatre, exploring the whole process of adapting for the stage, and investigating the particular techniques – many of them highly sophisticated – that actors require when performing 'story-theatre'.

Mike Alfreds, *What Actors Do* (Nick Hern Books, 2023). Explores the wellspring of the actor's craft, tracing a pathway to creative freedom through the thickets of competing methodologies and confusing paradoxes that actors will face throughout their training and career.

Brian Bates, *The Way of the Actor* (Century Hutchinson, 1986). Very interesting insights into the inner workings of the actor's psyche.

Augusto Boal, *Theatre Of The Oppressed* (Pluto Press, 1979). Seminal introduction to 'Forum Theatre', Boal's radical approach to community theatre as a forum for social change.

Isaac Butler, *The Method* (Bloomsbury, 2022). Critic and theatre director Issac Butler chronicles the history of the Method in a narrative that transports readers from the Moscow to New York to Los Angeles, from *The Seagull* to *A Streetcar Named Desire*.

Marina Caldarone and Maggie Lloyd-Williams, *Actions: The Actor's Thesaurus* (Nick Hern Books, 2004). A vital companion for actors in rehearsal – a thesaurus of action-words to revitalise performance.

Dee Cannon, *In-Depth Acting* (Oberon Books, 2012). An essential guide to mastering the Stanislavski technique, filtering its complexities and offering a dynamic, hands-on approach.

Alex Clifton, *The Actor's Workbook* (Methuen Drama, 2016). Essential and clear, this workbook for actors, actors in training and teachers of acting and drama provides a step-by-step guide to learning techniques in acting through a system of exercises which will develop core acting skills and offer techniques for developing an authored role and models for devising new work.

Declan Donnellan, *The Actor and the Target* (Nick Hern Books, 2005) A fresh approach to the actor's art from the artistic director of Cheek by Jowl.

Declan Donnellan, *The Actor and the Space* (Nick Hern Books, 2024). An extension of the ideas first presented in *The Actor and the Target*; Donellan offers a universal set of keys to unlock the mysteries of performance.

Vanessa Ewan with Kate Sagovsky, *Laban's Efforts in Action* (Methuen Drama, 2018). An accessible textbook for students and teachers looking for new ways to facilitate the creation of embodied and physically ambitious performance.

William Esper and Damon DiMarco, *The Actor's Art and Craft: William Esper Teaches the Meisner Technique* (Anchor Books, 2008). A clear, concrete, step-by-step approch to becoming a truly creative actor through the study and application of the Meisner's Technique.

Niki Flacks, *Acting with Passion* (Methuen Drama, 2015). A revolutionary new approach to the age-old problems of the actor: dealing with nerves, engaging the body, quieting the inner critic, auditioning, creating a character, and even playing comedy.

John Gillett, *Acting Stanislavski* (Methuen Drama, 2014). Offering a clear, accessible and comprehensive account of the Stanislavski approach, this book demsytifies the practitioner's key words and concepts from the actor's training to final performance.

Uta Hagen, *A Challenge for the Actor* (Macmillan, 1991). One of the best books on acting ever written.

Uta Hagen with Haskel Frankel, *Respect for Acting: Expanded Edition* (Jossey-Bass, 2023). Full of specific and detailed exercises, Hagan guides actors to find truth in the creative process.

Jacques Lecoq, *The Moving Body (Le Corps Poétique)* (Metheun Drama, 2020). Lecoq shares with us first-hand his unique philosophy of performance, improvisation, masks, movement and gesture, which together form one of the greatest influences on contemporary theatre.

Sanford Meisner and Dennis Longwell, *Sanford Meisner On Acting* (Vintage Books, 1987). Meisner is observed in his acting classes and discusses how actors can achieve 'living truthfully under imaginary circumstances'.

Bella Merlin, *Facing the Fear* (Nick Hern Books, 2016). An insightful, empowering and reassuring guide to stage fright: why it happens, how it manifests itself, and how to overcome it.

Nick Moseley, *Actioning and How to Do It* (Nick Hern Books, 2016). Actioning is one of the most widely used rehearsal techniques for actors.

Yoshi Oida and Lorna Marshall, *The Invisible Actor* (Methuen Drama, 2002). A first-hand insight into Oida's work and methods as an actor and director, which blend control and depths of emotion.

Sinéad Rushe, *Michael Chekhov's Acting Technique* (Methuen Drama, 2019). Provides a complete overview of Michael Chekhov's method, offering clear explanations of the principles, practical exercises and application of the exercises to dramatic texts.

Constantin Stanislavski, *An Actor Prepares* (Bloomsbury, 2013). There may be other books that explain and explore Stanislavski's system more clearly, but this is the original. 'Given Circumstances', 'Units and Objectives', 'Emotion Memory', 'Action' – this is where it all started.

Victoria Worsley, *Feldenkrais for Actors* (Nick Hern Books, 2016). A fascinating guide to the Feldenkrais Method, and how it can help actors with presence and posture, emotion, voice and breath, avoiding injury and more.

Voice, speech and audio

Cicely Berry, *Voice and the Actor* (Virgin Books, 2000). Written by 'Cis', the RSC's Head of Voice, this is arguably the most influential book about the actor's voice ever written.

Cicely Berry, *The Actor and the Text* (Virgin Books, 2000). Packed with practical suggestions for working on the speaking of the text.

David Carey and Rebecca Clark Carey, *The Dramatic Text Workbook and Video* (Methuen Drama, 2019). A new edition of The Verbal Arts Workbook, now featuring detailed online supplementary video.

Bernard Graham Shaw, *Voice-Overs, A Practical Guide* (A & C Black, 2000). A useful guide which explains and teaches the skills of voicing radio and television commercials.

Stephen Kemble and David Hodge, *The Voice Over Book: Don't Eat Toast (The Actor's Toolkit)* (Metheun Drama, 2022). A concise handbook outlining the skills, the know-how and the business of voiceovers.

Michael McCallion, *The Voice Book* (Faber & Faber, 1988). A book to help you discover how to use your voice freely, powerfully and with pleasure. The 'practice paragraphs' are a hoot!

Jeannette Nelson, *The Voice Exercise Book* (National Theatre Publishing, 2015). The Head of Voice at the National Theatre shares the voice exercises she uses with many of Britain's leading actors to help to keep their voices in shape.

Patsy Rodenberg, *The Actor Speaks* (Methuen Drama, 2019). A brand new edition of legendary voice coach's work on voice for actors with excellent advice and exercises to develop the performer's voice.

Edda Sharpe and Jan Haydn Rowles, *How to Do Any Accent: The Essential Handbook for Every Actor* (Oberon Books, 2007).

Julia Bianco Schoeffling, *The Art and Business of Acting for Video Games* (Nibi Press, 2022). An oustanding book covering all aspects of working in video games including auditions and casting, video recording, and performance capture.

Movement and the actor's body

Vanessa Ewan, *Actor Movement* (Methuen Drama, 2014). A textbook and video resource for the working actor, this book inspires confidence in the actor to make fully owned physical choices and develop a love for movement.

Lorna Marshall, *The Body Speaks: Performance and Expression* (Methuen Drama, 2001). Lorna Marshall enables actors and performers to recognise and lose unwanted physical habits and discover new possibilities for the body.

Dick McCaw, *Training the Actor's Body* (Methuen Drama, 2018). A practical book that draws on recent research into neurophysiology to illuminate key principles in the movement training of actors.

Kelly McEvenue, *The Alexander Technique for Actors* (Methuen Drama, 2001). The Alexander Technique is a method of physical relaxation that reduces tension and strain throughout the body. F.M. Alexander (1869-1955) was an actor who developed this technique to conquer his habit of straining his voice. This book's exercises are linked to accurate anatomical drawings, showing where stress is most pronounced in the body.

Litz Pisk, with introduction by Ashe Taskiran, *The Actor and His Body* (Methuen Drama, 2017). In this seminal book, Pisk quests to find expression for the inner impulse that motivated actors to move and subsequently offer insight on the specific craft of the actor and the relationship between movement and imagination.

Classical theatre

Giles Block, *Speaking the Speech* (Nick Hern Books, 2014). An authoritative, comprehensive book on understanding and performing Shakespeare's language, by the 'Master of Words' at Shakespeare's Globe. Foreword by Mark Rylance.

David Carey and Rebecca Clark Carey, *The Shakespeare Workbook* (Methuen Drama, 2015). A unifying approach to acting Shakespeare that is immediately applicable in the rehearsal room or classroom.

Ben Crystal and David Crystal, *Shakespeare's Words: A Glossary and Language Companion* (Penguin, 2004). This huge book is a must-have when working on any of Shakespeare's play.

Aileen Gonsalves and Tracy Irish, *Shakespeare and the Meisner: A Practical Guide for Actors, Directors, Student and Teachers* (The Arden Shakespeare, 2021). A super introduction to Meisner in itself, this book explores how Meisner's technique can be used to unlock Shakespeare's words – no mean feat given that Meisner regarded text as an actor's 'greatest enemy'. An engaging and accessible read.

Peter Hall, *Shakespeare's Advice to the Players (The Actor's Toolkit)* (Metheun, 2022). Taking his cue from Hamlet himself, Peter Hall helps actors to uncover the hidden 'stage directions' in Shakespeare's text.

Kirstin Linklater, *Freeing Shakespeare's Voice: The Actor's Guide to Talking the Text* (Nck Hern Books, 2010). From the author of Freeing the Natural Voice this book is packed with useful exercises and guidance to help actors explore the words of William Shakespeare.

William Shakespeare, edited by Jonathan Bate and Eric Rasmussen, *The RSC Shakespeare: Complete Works, 2nd edition* (Bloomsbury, 2022). The best 'Complete Works' for actors. A gigantic and reasonably priced book which should last a lifetime.

Improvisation, devising theatre, comedy and theatre games

Clive Barker, *Theatre Games* (Methuen Drama, 2010). A guidebook to improvisational games for actors, and a comprehensive exploration of acting techniques.

Anne Bogart and Tina Landau, *The Viewpoints Book* (Nick Hern Books, 2014). The Viewpoints are an improvisation technique: a set of names given to certain principles of movement through time and space – they constitute a language for talking about what happens on stage.

Augusto Boal, *Games for Actors and Non-Actors* (Routledge, second edition 2002). A classic book by the founder of Theatre of the Oppressed, it sends out the principles of Boal's revolutionary method.

Chris Head, *A Director's Guide to the Art of Stand-up* (Methuen Drama, 2018). An exploration of the creative process, comic persona, writing stand-up, structuring material and delivering a performance.

Sidney Hoffman and Brian Rhinehart, *Comedy Acting for Theatre* (Methuen Drama, 2018). A textbook for actors and acting students seeking to learn how to be funny on stage.

Keith Johnstone, *Impro: Improvisation and the Theatre* (Faber & Faber, 1979); and *Impro for Storytellers* (Faber & Faber, 1999). Keith Johnstone suggests a hundred practical techniques for encouraging spontaneity and originality by catching the subconscious unawares.

Theresa Robbins Dudeck, *Keith Johnstone: A Critical Biography* (Methuen Drama, 2013). A fascinating account of Keith Johnstone's early years at the Royal Court Theatre and teaching at RADA, and a good assessment of his approach and contributions to theatre and improvisation.

John Wright, *Why Is That So Funny?* (Nick Hern Books, 2006). Along with interrogating what causes us to laugh, the book includes games and exercises devised to demonstrate and investigate the whole range of comic possibilities open to a performer.

Acting for Camera

Bill Britten, *From Stage to Screen* (Methuen Drama, 2014). A handbook for the professional actor packed with advice on how to make the transition from theatre and fully prepare for a film role.

Tom Cantrell and Christopher Hogg (eds.), *Exploring Television Acting* (Methuen Drama, 2018). A collection of eleven essays from internationally distinguished researchers, actor trainers and early-career advisers bring together scholarly and practical perspectives on acting for television for the first time.

Mel Churcher, *Acting for Film: Truth 24 Times a Second* (Virgin Books, 2003). Invaluable insights into the specific techniques involved.

Mel Churcher, *A Screen Acting Workshop* (Nick Hern Books, 2011). An excellent and comprehensive training course in screen acting which includes a DVD showing the work in action.

Daniel Dresner, *A Life-coaching Approach to Screen Acting* (Methuen Drama, 2018). This handbook combines effective life-coaching techniques with screen acting tools to enable actors to approach their characters and their work with self-confidence.

Malcolm Taylor, *The Actor and the Camera* (A & C Black, 1994). Explores ths differences between working on stage and in front of the camera,

Singing and acting in musical theatre

Glenn Seven Allen, *The Singer Acts, The Actor Sings* (Methuen Drama, 2019). An essential handbook for actors and singers looking to combine great acting with great singing technique.

Martin Constantine, *The Opera Singer's Acting Toolkit* (Methuen Drama, 2019). A step-by-step guide detailing how to create character, from auditions through to rehearsal and performance and formulate a successful career.

Louise Dearman and Mark Evans, *Secrets of Stage Success* (Nick Hern Books, 2015). Two of the biggest musical-theatre stars working today offer advice on training, auditions, finding an agent, building your career, staying healthy and more.

Paul Harvard, *Acting Through Song* (Nick Hern Books, 2013). Takes the techniques of modern actor training – including the theories of Stanislavsky, Brecht, Meisner and Laban, amongst others – and applies them to the fundamental component of musical theatre: singing.

Chris Palmer, *Voice and Speech for Musical Theatre* (Methuen Drama, 2019). A workbook with online video resources, which combines traditional voice training for actors and musical training, allowing performers to train their spoken voice specifically for musicals.

Neil Rutherford, *Musical Theatre Auditions and Casting* (Methuen Drama, 2012). A performer's guide viewed from both sides of the audition table.

Jane Streeton and Phillip Raymond, *Singing on Stage: An Actor's Guide* (Methuen Drama, 2014). Singing should be an essential part of every actor's toolkit. This book encourages each actor to explore their own authentic voice as opposed to offering a 'one-size-fits-all' or 'quick fix' approach.

Actor-musicianship

Jeremy Harrison, *Actor Musicianship* (Metheun Drama, 2016). An informative practical guide drawing together expertise from a range of disciplines.

The acting business

James Calleri and Robert Cohen, *Acting Professionally* (9th edition, Methuen Drama, 2024). The first edition was published in 1972, and is now regarded as godfather of this genre in the USA.

Paul Clayton, *The Working Actor* (Nick Hern Books, 2016). A guide to putting yourself in the best possible position to get work, to keep getting it, and to make a living from it. Written by the Chairman of the Actors Centre, with over forty years' experience as an actor himself.

Jane Drake Brody, *Actor's Business Plan* (Methuen Drama, 2015). A smart approach that offers a method for the achievement of dreams through a five-year life and career plan giving positive steps to develop a happy life as an actor and as a person.

Simon Dunmore, *An Actor's Guide to Getting Work* (5th edition, Methuen Drama, 2012). Honest, humorous and thorough, this practical, comprehensive guide draws on the author's rich experience in the field and offers invaluable information and advice to enable actors to succeed in the business.

Felicity Jackson and Lianne Robertson, *Surviving Actors Manual* (Nick Hern Books, 2015). A no-nonsense breakdown of the day-to-day essentials you need to succeed in the industry – including establishing a personal brand and business plan, dealing with agents and casting directors, networking and managing your money – from the team behind the internationally successful Surviving Actors conventions.

Peter Messaline and Miriam Newhouse, *The Actor's Survival Kit* (3rd edition, Simon & Pierre, 1999). Well worth reading if you're thinking of trying your hand in Canada.

Andy Nyman, *The Golden Rules of Acting* (Nick Hern Books, 2012). An honest, witty and direct treasure trove of advice, support and encouragement that no performer should be without.

Robert Ostlere, *The Actor's Career Bible* (Methuen Drama, 2019). A career guide for the modern actor filled with wisdom and inside knowledge from industry experts: key organisations, casting directors, agents, producers, directors and most importantly, actors, at different stages in their careers. Backed by online resources.

Jon S. Robbins, *The Actor's Survival Guide* (Methuen Drama, 2019). Completely revised and updated, this new edition is the perfect business handbook and guide to living and working in Hollywood.

Directors, writers and theatre makers

Peter M. Boenisch, Thomas Ostermeier, *The Theatre of Thomas Ostermeier* (Routledge, 2016). The German director presents his advanced contemporary directorial approach to staging texts, for the first time.

Bertolt Brecht, *Brecht and the Writer's Workshop: Fatzer and Other Dramatic Projects* edited by Tom Kuhn and Charlotte Ryland (Methuen Drama, 2019). A collection of previously uncollected texts from major unfinished dramatic projects dating from all periods of Brecht's creative life.

Peter Brook, *The Empty Space* (Penguin, 1990). Written in the 1960s, but still essential reading.

Peter Brook, *The Shifting Point* (Bloomsbury, 2019). Brook accesses the lessons of his pioneering work.

Richard Eyre and Nicholas Wright, *Changing Stages* (Bloomsbury, 2000). Described by the authors as a "partial, personal and unscholarly view of the century's theatre", told from the point of view of two of theatre's most experienced practitioners.

David Edgar, *How Plays Work* (Nick Hern Books, 2009). The distinguished playwright examines the mechanisms and techniques, which dramatists throughout the ages have employed to structure their plays and to express their meaning.

Gabriella Giannachi and Mary Luckhurst, *On Directing* (Faber & Faber, 1999). Twenty-one directors with very different styles, all working in the UK are interviewed to ascertain how they begin work on a play or performance, what methods they use in rehearsal and answer the question: 'is the modern director an enabler, collaborator or dictator?'

Nicholas Hytner, *Balancing Acts* (Jonathan Cape, 2017). An entertaining behind-the-scenes account of Sir Nick's tenure as Artistic Director of The National Theatre, including many actor anecdotes.

Stephen Jeffreys, *Playwriting: Structure, Character, How and What to Write* (Nick Hern Books, 2019). For over two decades, Stephen Jeffreys's remarkable series of workshops attracted writers from all over the world and shaped the ideas of many of today's leading playwrights and theatre-makers. Now, with this inspiring, highly practical book, you too can learn from these acclaimed Masterclasses.

David Mamet, *True and False* (Faber & Faber, 1998). This book cuts through much of the mythology that surrounds acting.

Katie Mitchell, *The Director's Craft: A Handbook for the Theatre* (Routledge, 2009). Providing detailed assistance with each aspect of the varied challenges facing all theatre directors.

Simon Stephens, *Simon Stephens: A Working Diary* (Methuen Drama, 2016). A fascinating insight into the life and work of one of our greatest contemporary playwrights, including advive on how actors should approach his work.

Kae Tempest, *On Connection* (Faber & Faber, 2020). Not about acting per se, but a powerful, insightful analysis of performance and what it means to connect with an audience.

Actors on acting

Laura Barnett, *Advice from the Players* (Nick Hern Books, 2014). A host of tips and guidance on every aspect of the actor's craft, direct from some of the best-known stars of stage and screen, including Zawe Ashton, Jo Brand, David Harewood, Mark Gatiss, Lenny Henry, Lesley Manville, Simon Russell Beale and Julie Walters.

Simon Callow, *Being an Actor* (Penguin, 1995). Autobiographical books by famous actors are generally useless in terms of practical career advice. However, this one – part autobiography and part advice – has a great deal of down-to-earth common sense. His famous 'manifesto' on directors' theatre is spot on.

Julie Hesmondhalgh, *A Working Diary* (Methuen Drama, 2019). Reveals the numerous projects and preoccupations of a year in the life of one of Britain's best-loved actors.

Julie Hesmondhalgh, *An Actor's Alphabet: An A to Z of Some Stuff I've Learnt and Some Stuff I'm Still Learning* (Nick Hern Books, 2022). Lifting the lid on the realities of life in today's industry.

Paterson Joseph, *Julius Caesar and Me: Exploring Shakespeare's African Play* (Methuen Drama, 2018). A casebook of the RSC's African production of *Julius Caesar*, with audience reactions and a detailed evaluation of the position of ethnic minority actors in Shakespeare productions in general.

Patrick O'Kane (ed.), *Actors' Voices: The People Behind the Performances* (Oberon Books, 2012). Twelve experienced actors share their process, comment on their experiences and consider their role as theatre artists in the broader spectrum of Art and Culture.

William Redfield, *Letters from An Actor* (Viking, 1967). Scabrous insider account of Gielgud & Burton's *Hamlet*, which inspired the hit play The Motive and the Cue and has subsequently been republished and found a legion of fans amongst contemporary actors.

Anthony Sher, *Year of the King* (Nick Hern Books, 2004). A detailed and deeply personal account of how Sher created his astonishing performance of Shakespeare's Richard III. An accomplished artist, Sher's drawings that accompany the text offer additional insights into his remarkable creative process.

Harriet Walter, *Other People's Shoes: Thoughts on Acting* (Nick Hern Books, 2023). A practical guide and personal reflection on the processes involved in performance.

Miscellaneous

Stephen Bourne, *Deep Are the Roots: Trailblazers Who Changed Black British Theatre* (The History Press, 2001). Celebrating the pioneers of Black British theatre.

Adrian Cairns, *The Making of the Professional Actor* (Peter Owen Publishers, 1996). A fascinating study of the history, and possible future, of the art of acting.

Richard Eyre, Nicholas Wright, *Changing Stages: A View of British Theatre in the 20th Century* (Bloomsbury, 2000). Described by the authors as a "partial, personal and unscholarly view of the century's theatre", told from the point of view of two of theatre's most experienced practitioners.

Angela V. John, *The Actors' Crucible: Port Talbot and the Making of Burton, Hopkins, Sheen and all the Others* (Parthian Books, 2015). Dr John presents the emergence of these famous actors as part of a rich culture and commitment to drama long embedded in the town's history.

John Matthews, *The Life of Training* (Methuen Drama, 2019). In this follow-up to *Anatomy of Performance Training* (2014) John Matthews makes a compelling argument that training not only takes time, but also makes time. Employing the mature philosophy of Hannah Arendt.

Ros Merkin (compiler), *The Liverpool Everyman Theatre: Liverpool's Third Cathedral* (Liverpool and Merseyside Theatres Trust Limited, 2004). This book offers brief encounters with some of the people, the plays, the on-and-off stage dramas of the Everyman's first 40 highly eventful years.

Ros Merkin (ed.), *Liverpool Playhouse: A Theatre and its City* (Liverpool University Press, 2011). From its opening in 1911, Liverpool Playhouse has reflected the history of Liverpool – and at times the city itself has appeared on stage as a key character.

Jami Rogers, *British Black and Asian Shakespeareans: Integrating Shakespeare, 1966–2018* (The Arden Shakespeare, 2022). Chronicling ground-breaking castings of Black and Asian actors in substantial Shakespearean roles from the 1960's to the 21st century.

Michael Sanderson, *From Irving to Olivier – A Social History of the Acting Profession* (Athlone Press, 1984). A very expensive, but nevertheless fascinating, study of the actor's world over the last century.

Spotlight, *Contacts* (Spotlight, annually in October). Contact details for everything you can think of (and more) that relates to actors and performers.

Steve Waters, *The Secret Life of Plays* (Nick Hern Books, 2010). Covers the key elements of dramatic writing – scenes, acts, space, time, characters, language and images – to show how a play is more than the sum of its parts.

Webography

What follows is a selected collection of the most important websites for aspirants and professionals, and some others which the editors have found extremely useful, but don't quite fit elsewhere in this book.

Important websites for aspirants and professionals

www.artsjobs.org.uk/jobs/search – extensive number of jobs in the arts posted
www.bbc.co.uk – BBC homepage
www.bbc.co.uk/programmes/p01xddtr – Soundstart – advice on how to get work in radio drama
www.thecdg.co.uk – Casting Directors Guild
http://cpma.coop/ – The Co-operative Personal Management Association
www.ucas.com/conservatoires – Conservatoires UK Admissions Service (CUKAS) provides the facilities to research and apply for practice-based music, dance and drama courses at some UK conservatoires
www.edfringe.com – Edinburgh Festival Fringe
www.eif.co.uk – Edinburgh International Festival
www.equity.org.uk – Equity – the performing arts and entertainment trade union
www.federationofdramaschools.co.uk – Federation of Drama Schools
www.imdb.com – Internet Movie Database; catalogues all sorts of information on more than 250,000 films and the 900,000 people who helped to make them
www.itc-arts.org – Independent Theatre Council homepage with links to member companies' websites
www.mandy.com – The Mandy Network (see page 364)
https://thepma.com/ – Personal Managers' Association
https://shootingpeople.org/ – Shotting People (see page 364)
www.spotlight.com – Spotlight publishes the most important actors' directories
www.thestage.co.uk – *The Stage*, contains news, information and job advertisements which are updated each Thursday
www.ucas.ac.uk – UCAS, the central organisation that processes applications for full-time undergraduate courses at UK universities and colleges

Other useful websites

http://accent.gmu.edu – the speech accent archive uniformly presents a large set of speech samples from a variety of language backgrounds
www.acx.com – create a profile and audition to narrate audiobooks. Some useful resources on audio performance and recording are available.
www.gov.uk/government/organisations/companies-house – Companies House: useful for checking background details (like date of foundation) of individual companies
www.dialectsarchive.com – the International Dialects of English Archive (IDEA) is a useful collection of English-language dialects and English spoken in the accents of other languages

www.dramaonlinelibrary.com – an award-winning digital library from Bloomsbury, the world's leading drama publisher. Their exclusive imprints, Methuen Drama and The Arden Shakespeare, are joined by playtext and streaming content from world-renowned partners.

https://edhooks.com – contains some interesting articles on acting for animators

https://film.britishcouncil.org – lots of articles, reviews and links about British theatre

www.its-behind-you.com – a comprehensive list of pantomimes and their producers

https://officiallondontheatre.com – Society of London Theatre (SOLT) website with news, reviews and booking information. SOLT is a not-for-profit organisation representing the theatre industry. SOLT also runs the Olivier Awards, West End LIVE, TKTS, Theatre Tokens, Kids Week and The Offical London Theatre Sale.

www.shakespeare-online.com – electronic copies of the plays and poems, along with other related material of interest. These copies of the texts should be checked against published editions before use in audition or performance, in order to gain the benefit of modern scholarship

www.shakespeareswords.com – an excellent resource for understanding Shakespeare from David and Ben Crystal

https://shootingpeople.org/ – hooking up filmmakers and actors

www.theatredigsbooker.com – a site aimed solely at touring professionals within the UK entertainment industry

www.stagemilk.com – a site for actors created by Australian actor, Andrew Hearle

www.uktw.co.uk – UK Theatre Web, with information, events and tickets for theatre in the UK

www.usefee.tv – a site which lets performers, their representatives and employers quickly calculate the appropriate use fee for featured players in TV commercials based on the established, industry-endorsed method approved by the Personal Managers' Association, the Association of Model Agents and Equity

https://vocalist.org.uk – a site for singers, vocalists, singing teachers and students of voice of all ages, standards and styles. The site contains useful information on aspects of singing, performance, plus free online singing lessons and articles for vocalists related to singing and getting into the music industry

www.voiceovers.co.uk – a forum for voice-over artists to advertise themselves

www.whatsonstage.com – a UK theatre listing service with search facilities, a ticket ordering service, reviews, news and debate

Index

Index

The index includes the organisations, companies, individuals and associations that have listings entries in this *Yearbook*

A

A Relaxed Company 345
A&J Artists 70
Abbey Theatre Amharclann na Mainistreach 160
AbeBooks.com 422
Abnormally Funny People 336
About Face Theatre Company 336
Academy of Creative Training 49
Academy of Performance Combat (APC) 49
Accent Bank 386
Access All 348
Access All Areas 207
Access Artiste Management Ltd 71
Access Scottish Theatre 345
Access to Work Guide 348
Accidental Theatre 208
accountants 405, 407
Ackie, Naomi 154
Acting Coach Scotland 57
Actionwork Creative Arts 290
Activation 305
Actor Showreels 386
Actors of Dionysus (aod) 208
Actors Alliance 93
Actors & Performers 422
Actors Apparel 386
Actors' Benevolent Fund 420
Actors Centre 379
Actors' Creative Team 94
Actors File, The 94
Actors' Group, The 94
Actors' Guild of Great Britain, The 427
Actors in Industry Ltd (Aii Training) 305
Actors International Ltd 71
Actors Network Agency 94
Actors Touring Company (ATC) 208
Actorum Ltd 94
ActUpNorth 49
Ad Voice 105
Adhoc Actors 305
ADR 327
Aesop's Touring Theatre Company 290
Agency | Dublin, The 71

agent 382
agents 69–70, 134, 407
  rates of commission 70
  voice-over work 105
AHA Talent Ltd 71
Pippa Ailion and Natalie Gallacher Casting 110
AKT Productions 306
Albany, The 270
Alexander & Co 400
Alexander James & Co. 400
All In 348
All Talent Agency Ltd 71
ALL3 Media 316
Almeida Theatre 160
Alpha Actors 94
Alphabetti Theatre 160
Alphabetti Theatre, Newcastle 46
Anita Alraun Representation 71
Amazon.co.uk & Amazon.com 422
Ambassador Theatre Group (ATG) 194
Amber Personal Management Ltd 72
American Agency, The 72
American Actors UK (AAUK) 427
Amici Dance Theatre Company 336
Angel & Francis Ltd 72
Angela Mead Ltd 400
Anjali Dance Company 336
Simon Annand 371
Christopher Antony Associates 72
APM Associates 72
Apropos Productions Ltd 306, 336
ARC Theatre Ensemble 209
Arcola Theatre 161
Arena Personal Management Ltd 95
ARG (Artists Rights Group Ltd) 72
Yvonne Arnaud Theatre 161
Artists Partnership, The 72
Arts & Disability Ireland 345
Arts Council England 418
Arts Council England, London 419
Arts Council England, Midlands 419
Arts Council England, North 419
Arts Council England, South East 419
Arts Council England, South West 419

450 Index

Arts Council of Northern Ireland 418
Arts Council of Wales 418
Arts Councils 289
Arts Emergency 6
Arts University Bournemouth 324
artsdepot 270
ArtsEd 13, 50
ArtsJobs 363
Arty-Fact Theatre Co. 290
Jonathan Arun Group (JAG) 73
Arundel Festival 301
Assembly Rooms 277
ASSITEJ (International Association of Theatre for Children and Young People) 289, 427
ASSITEJ UK 427
Associated International Management (AIM) 73
Attic Theatre Company 209
AudioUK 427
audition 327
Audition Doctor 57
auditions 134, 181, 235
augmented reality 326
Augustine's 277
Auto-Enrolment (AE) 408
Avatar 326
AXM (Actors Exchange Management Ltd) 95

B

Baby Cow 316
Backstage 365
Ric Bacon Photography 372
Badapple Theatre Company 209
Shaheen Baig Casting 111
BAM Associates (UK) Ltd 73
Barbican 161
Barbican Library 422
Barker, Andrew 408
Gavin Barker Associates Ltd 73
Barons Court Theatre 270
Becca Barr Management 108
BBM 73
Battersea Arts Centre 271
BBC Studios Drama Productions Casting 111
Lesley Beastall Casting 111
Beckley, Piers 285

Rowland Beckley 111
Beddard, Jamie 350
Bedlam Theatre 277
Belfast Film Festival 332
Belfield & Wards 73
Belgrade Theatre 161
Olivia Bell Management 74
Bennett, Ned 279
Leila Bertrand Casting CDG 111
Bespoke Voice Agency 105
Jorg Betts Associates 74
Lucy Bevan CDG 111
Beyond Face 209
BFI London Film Festival 332
Big House, The 290
Big Red Button Ltd 316
Big Talk Productions 316
Big Telly Theatre Company 209
Birds of Paradise Theatre Company 337
Hannah Birkett Casting 111
Birmingham Repertory Theatre 161
Birmingham Stage Company (BSC) 162
Bishop, Nancy 310
black actors 350
Blacktress UK 151
Tony Blake Photography 372
Nicky Bligh CDG 111
Bloomfields Welch Management 74
Bloomin' Arts 337
Bloomsbury Alexander Centre, The 50
Blue Apple Theatre 337
Blue Elephant Theatre 271
Blue Teapot Theatre 337
Blueprint Pictures 316
Boden Studios 3
Bold Management Ltd 108
Border Crossings 209
Boundless Theatre 210
Box Clever Theatre Company 291
Michelle Braidman Associates Ltd 74
Breckman & Company 400
Nev Brewer Photography 372
Bridewell Theatre, The 271
Bridge Theatre Training Company, The 13, 162
Bridges: The Actors' Agency Ltd 95
Andy Brierley CDG 111
Brighton Festival 301
Brighton Fringe 301

Index

Brill Talent Agency 74
Bristol Improv Theatre 13
Bristol Old Vic 162
Bristol Old Vic Theatre School 13
British Academy of Dramatic Combat 50
BAFTA 428
British Academy of Stage & Screen Combat, The 50
British Arts Festivals Association (BAFA) 301
British Association for Performing Arts Medicine (BAPAM) 428
British Council 428
British Film Institute (BFI) 428
British Library, The 422
British Music Hall Society 428
British Talent Agency® 74
British Youth Music Theatre 3
Broadway Studio Theatre, The 271
BROOD 74
Michael Browne Associates Ltd (MBA Roleplay) 306
Bruiser Theatre Company 210
Burke, Kelly 359
Sheila Burnett 372
Burton, Harry 62
Bush Theatre 162
Buxton Opera House 263
BWH Agency Ltd, The 75
Aisha Bywaters Casting 112

C

C ARTS 277
Caan, Alex 411
Cactus TV Ltd 317
Cahoots NI 291
Cahoots Theatre Company 210
Calamity Films 317
Caldarone, Marina 381
Calypso Voices 105
CAM (Creative Artists Management) 75
Cambridge Arts Theatre 263
Cambridge Film Festival 332
Cambridge Shakespeare Festival 210
Camden People's Theatre 271
Campaign for the Arts 429
Ross Campbell 57
Canal Café Theatre 271
Candid Casting 112

Candoco Dance Company 337
Cannon, Dudley & Associates 112
John Cannon CDG 112, 131
Canterbury Festival 301
Capitol, The 263
Cardboard Citizens 210
P O'N Carden 400, 404
Carey Dodd Associates 75
Jessica Carney Associates 75
Carnival Film & Television Limited 317
Carousel 345
Anji Carroll CDG 112
Charlie Carter 372
Castaway Actors Agency 95
casting 324, 327, 329
 breakdown 134
 for musical theatre 134
casting directors 70, 309, 329, 378–9
Casting Directors Guild (CDG) 110
Casting Directors Guild of Great Britain and Ireland 429
Casting Networks 363, 365
Castle Players, The 210
Castweb 363
Suzy Catliff CDG 112
CBL Management 75
CCM Actors Agency Ltd 95
CDA Ltd 75
CDM Ltd 75
CDs 379
Celeb Agents 108
Celtic Media Festival 332
Centre Stage Agency 76
Central Line 96
CentreStage Partnership 306
Chain Reaction Theatre Company 211
Urvashi Chand CDG 112
Chaplins Entertainment Ltd 261
Charing Cross Theatre 271
charities, registered 234
Esta Charkham Associates Ltd 76
Cheek by Jowl 211
Chelsea Theatre 272
Chichester International Film Festival 332
Chichester Festival Theatre 162
Chickenshed Theatre 211, 337
children and young people, theatre for 288
Theatre, Chipping Norton, The 263
Chortle 429

Christmas shows 288
Mel Churcher 57
Circuit Personal Management Ltd 96
Citizens Theatre 162
City Actors Personal Management 76
City Lit 13, 51
City Varieties Music Hall 263
Andrea Clark Casting 113
John Clark Headshot Photography 373
Sharry Clark Artists 76
Sam Claypole 113
Clean Break 211
Clic Agency 76
Clod Ensemble 212
co-operative agencies 69
Co-operative Personal Management Association (CPMA) 103
Cockpit, The 272
Ben Cogan 113
M.J. Coldiron 58
Cole Kitchenn Personal Management Ltd 76
Shane Collins Associates 76
Colman, Geoffrey 27
Comedy Unit, The 317
Comedy School, The 51
Comedy Unit, The 329
Company Pictures 317
Complicité 212
Concordance 212
Confident Voice, The 58
Connaught Theatre 264
consultants 234
Contact Theatre 163
Contacts 379, 422
Contemporary Stage Company 194
contracts 70, 316
Conway Van Gelder Grant 76
Alastair Coomer 113
Anna Cooper 113
John Cooper Photography 373
Cooper Searle Personal Management Ltd 77
Co-operative Personal Management Association (CPMA) 429
copyright 386
  on photographs 371
Corali 338
Lou Coulson Associates Ltd 77

Coulter Hamilton Rae (CHR) 77
Court Theatre Training Company 14
Courtyard, The 264
Courtyard Theatre, The 272
Cowboy Films 317
Crampsie Linge Casting CDG 113
Kahleen Crawford Casting 113
Creation Theatre Company 212
Creative Diversity Network 348
Creative Scotland 419
Creative Screen Management 77
Crescent Management 96
CRIPtic Arts 338
Crocodile Casting 113
Crossroads Pantomimes Ltd 261
Sarah Crowe Casting CDG 114
Gilly Poole CDG 114
Cryer, Simon 381
C&T 291
Cumbernauld Theatre at Lanternhouse 213
Curious Monkey, Newcastle 47
Curtains for Radio 329
Curtis Brown Group Ltd 77
Curve 163
Customs House Trust Ltd, The 264
Cutting Edge Theatre 338
CVs 134
Cwmni Theatr Arad Goch 291

D
DaDa 345
David Daly Associates 78
Damn Good Talent 78
Damn Good Voice Studios 387
Damn Good Voices 105
dance 134
Dance and Drama Awards (DaDAs) 12, 351
Dark Horse 213, 338
Gary Davy CDG 114
Nicholas Dawkes Photography 373
Bridget de Courcy 58
Deaf Explorer 346
Deafinitely Theatre 338
Dear Conjunction Theatre Company 267
Dempsey, Shane 282
Denmark Street Management 96
Denton Brierley 78
Derby Theatre 163

Deuchar, Angus   378
Diamond Management   78
Direct Personal Management   96
Directgov   348
directors   70
  radio   329
Directors UK   429
Directory of Social Change   235
disabilities, actors with   335
  opportunities for   350
Disability Arts Cymru   346
DAiSY: Disability Arts in Surrey   346
Disability Arts Online (DAO)   346
Disability Discrimination Act   351
Disability Rights UK   348
Diverse City   346
DIY Theatre Company   339
Do, Tuyen   248
Antonia Doggett   58
Don Productions (London) Ltd   317
Donmar Warehouse   163
Doollee.com   423
Dorset School of Acting, The   14, 51
Kate Dowd Casting CDG   114
DQ Management   78
Drama Association of Wales   429
drama schools   351
Drama Studio London (DSL)   14, 51
Dramanic   363, 366
Dramanon   306
Dramaturgs' Network   430
Dress Circle   423
Carol Dudley CDG, CSA   114
Maureen Duff CDG   114
Jenny Duffy CDG   114
Dukes, The   164
Dumfries and Galloway Arts Festival   302
Dundee Rep and Scottish Dance Theatre Limited   164
Dunmore, Simon   181

E

e-TALENTA   367
earnings, annual   406
East 15 Acting School   14
East Riding Theatre   164
Eastern Angles Theatre Company   213
EBA   78
École Internationale de Théâtre Jacques Lecoq   51   15

Ecosse Films Ltd   318
Edge Theatre, The   213
Edinburgh Festival   301
Edinburgh Festival Fringe   269, 282
Edinburgh Festival Fringe Society   302
Edinburgh International Festival   302
Daniel Edwards CDG   114
Embodiment with Rebecca Reaney   58
Emptage Hallett   78
enCAST   367
Encounters (Short Film and Animation Festival)   332
English Theatre Frankfurt   267
English Theatre of Hamburg, The   267
Equity   103, 316, 358, 366, 407
Equity Pensions Scheme (EPS)   408
Equity Tax and National Insurance Guide, The   404
Essiedu, Paapa   254
Estdale, Mark   326
ET Casting Ltd.   114
Etcetera Theatre   272
ETT (English Touring Theatre)   213
European Festivals Association, The   301
Richard Evans CDG   114
Everyman Theatre, The   264
Evolution Productions   261
Extant   339
Extra Digit Ltd   318
Extraordinary Bodies   339
Extravaganza Productions   262
Eye Film   318

F

Face Front   339
Faction, The   214
Farah, Isabelle   365
Paola Farino   79
Feast Management Ltd   79
Federation of Drama Schools   12, 15
Federation of Drama Schools (FDS)   27
Federation of International Artists   358
Federation of Scottish Theatre   430
festivals   301
Fevered Sleep   292
Fierce Festival   302
Fiery Angel   194
Film London   419
film schools   324

Finborough Theatre   272
Fingersmiths   339
Fiorentini Mosson Talent Agency   79
fitness, physical and mental   411
BFI Flare   333
FlawBored   339
Focus Productions Ltd   318
Kerry Foley Management Ltd   79
Forbidden Theatre Company   234
Forced Entertainment   214
Jonathan Ford & Co.   401
Ford-Williams, Zak   353
Forest Forge Theatre Co.   214
formidAbility   339
42   70
James Foster Ltd   79
Fourth Monkey   15, 51
Fourthwall   423
Robert Fox Ltd   194
Foyle Film Festival   333
Frantic Assembly   203, 214
Frantic Theatre Company   215
Rachel Freck CDG   115
Free Association, London, The   52
Freewheelers Theatre Company   339
Fremantle   318
Freshwater Theatre Company   292
Sonia Friedman Productions   195
Fringe theatre   269, 324
Frontline Actors' Agency   96
funding   234, 240
  bodies   418
fundraising   235

G

Hilary Gagan Associates   79
game industry   326
Gardner Herrity   79
Gate Theatre   164
Gazebo Theatre in Education Company   292
Gibber Theatre Ltd   292
Martin Gibbons Casting   115
Gift Aid   234
Gilbert & Payne Personal Management   80
Giles Foreman Centre for Acting, The   52
Prue Gillett Actor Training   58
Tracey Gillham CDG   115
Global Artists   80
Nina Gold CDG   115
Goldwins   401
Gonsalves, Aileen   9
Gordon & French   80
Gothenburg English Studio Theatre (GEST)   267
Graeae Theatre Company   215, 340, 350
  Missing Piece   351
David Graham Entertainment Ltd   195
Graham, Scott   203
Michael Grandage Company (MGC)   195
Grantham-Hazeldine Ltd   80
John Grayson   59
Green Ginger   215
Jill Green CDG   115
Greenwich and Docklands International Festival (GDIF)   302
Greenwich Theatre   164
Nick Gregan Photography   373
Greyfriars Kirk   277
Grid Iron Theatre Company   215
David Grindrod CDG   115
Grindrod, David   134
Claire Grogan Photograpghy   374
GSA, Guildford School of Acting   16, 52
Guildhall School of Music & Drama   16, 52

H

H and S Accountants Ltd   401
Hackney Empire   264
Hackney Empire Studio Theatre   272
Half Moon Theatre   293
Hall, Lee   144
Hamilton Hodell Ltd   80
Hammond Cox Casting   116
Louis Hammond CDG   116
Hampstead Theatre   165
Hancock, Gemma   131
Gemma Hancock CDG   116
Handstand Productions   318
Harkin & Toth Casting   116
Harman, Paul   288
HarperAudio   330
Martin Harris   59
Harrogate Theatre   165
Hartshorn-Hook Productions   195
Hartswood Films   318
Hat Trick Productions Ltd   319
HATCH Talent Ltd   80

Index

Head, Chris 251
Headlong Theatre 215
Heale, Daniel 397
Heavy Entertainment Ltd 319, 329
Hen & Chickens Theatre 273
Hentons 401
Nick Hern Books 423
Hesmondhalgh, Julie 6
hhush (Hamilton Hodell Universal Soundhouse) 105
Highly Sprung Performance 216
HighTide 302
Hijinx 216, 340
Serena Hill 116
Lotte Hines CDG 116
Historia Theatre Company 216
HM Revenue and Customs (HMRC) 404
Hogbens Dunphy Ltd 401
Holder, Hazel 200
Jane Hollowood Associates Ltd 80
Paul Holman Associates 195, 262
Holmes, Anthony 389
HOME 165
Jennifer Jane Hooker 59
Hoopla, London 53
Hope Theatre, The 273
Hopscotch Theatre Company 293
Julia Horan CDG 117
Horse + Bamboo 216
Juliet Horsley CDG 117
hot-seating 288
Hotbed: Cambridge New Writing Theatre Festival 303
Amy Hubbard CDG 117
Dan Hubbard CDG 117
Mark Hudson 59
Nancy Hudson Associates 81
Charlie Hughes-D'Aeth 59
Hull Truck Theatre 165
Hulsmeier, Adelle 45
Remy Hunter Headshots 374
Hunwick Associates 81
Hurricane Films Ltd 319

I

Icarus Theatre Collective 216
Icon Actors Management 81
iD Agency Limited 81
Identity Agency Group (IAG) 81
Imagine Theatre Ltd 262
IMDb 327, 366
IMDb Pro (Internet Movie Database) 364
IML 97
IMPACT Theatre 340
Imperial Personal Management Ltd 81
improvisation 327
Impulse Company, The 53
Inclusive Talent 81
Independent Talent Group Ltd 81
Independent Theatre Council (ITC) 207, 234, 288, 418, 430
Colin Ingram Ltd 195
Inspiration Management 97
Instant Wit 307
International Actors London and Irish Actors London (IAL) 82
International Casting Directors Association (ICDA) 430
International College of Musical Theatre (ICMT), The 16
International Committee for Artistic Freedom 358
International Federation of Actors (FIA) 430
International School of Screen Acting 16, 53
Internet Movie Database (IMDb) 423
InterTalent 82
Irish Theatre Institute 430
Isabella Odoffin Casting 117
Isis Audio (a division of Ulverscroft Ltd) 330
Italia Conti 17

J

Jack Studio Theatre, The 273
Jacksons Lane Arts Centre 273
Janis Jaffa Casting 117
Jam Theatre Company 217
Matt Jamie Photography 374
Jina Jay CDG 117
Jeffrey & White Management Ltd 82
Lucy Jenkins CDG (Jenkins McShane Casting) 117
Victor Jenkins Casting 117
Jeremy Hicks Associates Ltd 108
Mark Jermin Management 82
Jermyn Street Theatre 273

456 Index

Jerwood Foundation 420
Jikiemi, Pamela 31
JK Photography 374
John Noel Management 108
Gareth Johnson Ltd 196
Jonathan Church Theatre Productions 196
Sam Jones CDG 117
Richard Jordan Productions Ltd 196
Joseph, Paterson 157
JPA Management 82
JWL (Jewell Wright Ltd) 82

K

Kabosh 217
Kali Theatre Company 217
Gavin Kalin Productions 196
Kastwork 118
Kate and Lou Casting Ltd 118
Keddie Scott Associates 82
Robert C. Kelly 196
Steve Kenis & Co 83
Kennedy Casting 118
Bill Kenwright Ltd 196
Beverley Keogh CDG 118
Kew Personal Management 83
Key Theatre 166
Kharmel Cochrane Casting 118
Kiln Theatre 166
Belinda King Creative Productions 118
Knight Ayton Management 108
Knowledge, The 423
Komedia 278
Suzy Korel CDG CDA 118

L

Laine Management 83
Lambert Jackson 197
LAMDA (London Academy of Music & Dramatic Art) 17, 53
Langford Associates Ltd 83
Lantern Theatre 278
Lawnmowers Independent Theatre Company 340
Steve Lawton 374
L.B. Photography 374
Pete Le May 375
Nina Lee Management 83
Leeds International Film Festival 333
Leeds Playhouse 166

Lees 401
Left Bank Pictures 319
Library Theatre, The 166
Lichfield Festival 303
Lime Actors Agency & Management Ltd 83
Limelight Productions Ltd 197
Karen Lindsay-Stewart CDG 118
Lion & Unicorn Theatre 273
Lip Service 105
LipService 217
Little Cog 340
Live Theatre 166
Live Theatre, Newcastle 45
Liverpool Everyman & Playhouse Theatres 167
Liverpool Institute for Performing Arts (LIPA), The 18
Liverpool Theatre School 18
Eleanor Lloyd Productions 197
Loftus Media Ltd 329
London Independent Film Festival (LIFF) 333
London Arrangements 423
London Bubble Theatre Co. 218
London College of Communication 324
London Film Academy 324
London Film School, The 324
London International Festival of Theatre (LIFT) 303
London Metropolitan University 351
London School of Dramatic Art 18, 54
London School of Musical Theatre 19
London Studio Centre (LSC) 19
London Theatre 424
London Toast Theatre 267
Eva Long 83
Gina Long (Longrun Artistes) 84
Lord of the Rings 326
Loudmouth Education & Training 293
Lovett Logan Associates 84
Lung Ha 341
Lurking Truth 218
Lyric Hammersmith Theatre 167
Lyric Theatre 167

M

M6 Theatre Company 293
Mac Manus, Sinead 240
MacFarlane Chard Associates 84

MacFarlane Doyle Associates 84
Cameron Mackintosh Ltd 197
Macmillan Audio Books 331
Macrobert 265
MAD Photography 375
Magic Carpet Theatre 293
Magnetic North Theatre Productions 218
Magpie Dance 341
Make a Scene 341
MANACTCO 218
Management 2000 84
Manchester International Festival (MIF) 303
Manchester International Short Film Festival 333
Manchester School of Acting 54
Manchester School of Theatre at MMU 19
M&C Saatchi Talent 108
Mandy 366
Mandy Network, The 364
Manor Pavilion Theatre 167
Marcus & McCrimmon 84
marketing 181
Markham, Froggatt & Irwin 84
Marlborough Productions 341
Scott Marshall Partners 84
MARV Films 319
Maya Vision International Ltd 319
Maynard Leigh Associates (MLA) 307
McAvoy, Gemma 124
McEwan & Penford 85
Martin McKellan 59
McLean-Williams Ltd 85
Carolyn McLeod Casting 119
McMahon Management 85
Sooki McShane CDG (Jenkins McShane Casting) 119
Kirsten McTernan Photography 375
Alison Mead 59
Meeting Ground Theatre Co. 218
Menier Chocolate Factory 167
Mercury Theatre 168
Merman (and Mermade) 320
Met Film Production 320
Method Acting London 54
Methuen Drama 424
#metoo 359
Thea Meulenberg Casting 119
MHA 402

Michael Chekhov Studio London 54
Middle Child 219
Middle Ground Theatre Co. 197
Middleweek Newton Talent Management 85
Midland Actors Theatre (MAT) 219
Mikron Theatre Company 219
Milburn Browning Associates (MMB Creative) 85
Mill at Sonning Theatre, The 168
Robin Miller 60
Millfield Theatre 265
Mimbre 219
Mime the Gap 60
Minack Theatre, The 303
Mind the Gap 341
Mirth Control 258, 431
Mischief Theatre 197
Mocap Vaults, The 326
Money Management UK 108
Francesca Moody Productions (FMP) 197
Stephen Moore CDG 119
Morello Cherry Ltd 85
Lee Morgan Management 85
Morley College 54
Mountview 19, 54
MR Management 85
Mrs Jordan Associates 86
Msamati, Lucian 244
MSFT Management 86
Mumeni, David 9
Elaine Murphy Associates 86
Music Theatre International 424
musical supervisor 135
musical theatre, casting for 134
Musicroom 424

N

National Association of Youth Theatres (NAYT) 4
National Curriculum 288
National Film and Television School 324
National Rural Touring Forum (NRTF) 431
National Student Drama Festival (NSDF) 303
National Theatre Casting Department 119, 168
National Theatre Bookshop 424

458 Index

National Theatre of Scotland (NTS)   168
National Youth Arts Wales (NYAW)   4
National Youth Music Theatre (NYMT)   4
National Youth Theatre of Great Britain (NYT)   4
Naxos AudioBooks   331
Neal Street Productions   198, 320
John Need   375
Nelson Browne Management Ltd   86
New Diorama Theatre   274
New Earth Theatre   220
New Frame Productions   198
New Pantomime Productions   262
New Perspectives Theatre Co.   220
New Shoes Theatre   220
New Vic Theatre   169
New Wolsey Theatre, The   169
Claire Newman-Williams   375
NFD Productions Ltd   320
1984 Personal Management Ltd   93
Evelyn Norris Trust   420
North East Screen   420
North London Headshot Photography   375
Northern Broadsides Theatre Company   220
Northern Ireland Screen   419
Northern Lights Management   86
Northern Stage   169
Northern Stage, Newcastle   46
NorthOne Management   97
Norwell Lapley Productions Ltd   198
Nottingham Playhouse   169
Nottingham Playhouse Participation   294
NTC Touring Theatre Company   220
Number 9 Films   320
Nyland Management   86
Nyman Libson Paul LLP   402

O

Objective Fiction   320
Octagon Theatre   169
OffWestEnd   270
Oily Cart Company   294, 342
Old Joint Stock Theatre   170
Old Red Lion Theatre Pub   274
Old Vic, The   170
Omnibus Theatre   274
OMUK   328
Onatti Productions Ltd   294

104 Films   342
Open Air Theatre   170
Open Book Theatre   285
Open Clasp Theatre Company   221
Open Door   9
Open Theatre Company   342
Orange Tree Theatre   170
Oren Actors Management   97
Original Theatre   221
Orion Audio Books   331
Orti, Pilar   233
Outsource Media Ltd (OMUK)   328
Ovation Productions   221
Oxford Samuel Beckett Theatre Trust Award, The   420
Oxford School of Drama   20, 55

P

PACT Diversity   348
Pact (Producers Alliance for Cinema and Television)   431
Paines Plough   221
Paling and Jenkins   86
Helena Palmer   119
pantomime   288
Park Theatre   170
Theo Park Casting   119
Park Village Ltd   321
Frances Parkes   60
Susie Parriss Casting   119
pay   327
Pearlcatchers Ltd   307
Pemberton Associates Ltd   87
Pendle Productions   222
Penguin Random House Audio   331
Pentabus Theatre Company   222
Pentameters   274
People's Theatre Co, The   222
People Show   222
Pereira Hind & Dawson Casting CDG   120
Perfect Match Presenters   108
Performance Accountancy   402
Performance Actors Agency   97
Performance Business, The   307
performance capture   326
Personal Managers' Association (PMA)   431
Perth Theatre   171
Frances Phillips   87

photographers 371, 378
photographs 134, 378
Piccadilly Management 87
Pied Piper Theatre Company 294
Pier Productions 330
Pilot Theatre 223, 294
Pinball London Ltd 321
Pineapple Dance Studios 55
Piper, Andrew 190
Pitlochry Festival Theatre 171
Kate Plantin CDG 120
Janet Plater Management Ltd 87
A Play, a Pie and A Pint 223
Play House, The 295
PlayDatabase.com 424
Playful Productions 198
Playground Theatre, The 274
Playtime Theatre Company 295
Pleasance, The 277
Pleasance Theatre Trust 274
policy, artistic 233
Polka Theatre 295
Michael Pollard Photographer 376
Prague Shakespeare Festival 268
Morwenna Preston Management 87
David Price Photography 376
Price Gardner Management 87
Prime Cut Productions 223
Prism Arts 346
Carl Proctor CDG 120
producers, independent 194
Project A, Newcastle Theatre Royal, Newcastle 46
Project Gutenberg 424
Proteus Theatre Company 223
Andy Pryor CDG 120
publicists 369
publicity 368
publicity interviews 368
Punchdrunk 224
Pursued by a Bear Productions 224
PW Productions Ltd 198

Q
Q20 Events 295
Quantum Theatre 296
Queen's Theatre Hornchurch 171
Questors Theatre Ealing, The 55
Quiplash 342, 348

R
Royal Academy of Dramatic Art (RADA) 20, 275
radio companies 329
radio drama 327, 329
Raindance Film Festival Ltd 334
Ramps on the Moon 342
RbA Management Ltd 97
RBM Actors 87
Really Useful Group Ltd, The 198
recording studio 381
Red Ladder Theatre Company 224
Red Rose Chain 224
Redeeming Features 321
Redroofs Associates 87
Leigh-Ann Regan Casting (LARCA) Ltd 120
Regan Talent Group, The 88
Nadine Rennie CDG 120
Replay Theatre Company 296
Kate Rhodes-James CDG 120
Rhubarb Voices 105
Rich Mix 275
Lisa Richards Agency 88
Vicky Richardson CDG 120
Richmond Drama School 55
Riding Lights Theatre Company 225
Rifco Theatre Company 225
Rogues & Vagabonds Management 98
role-play companies 305
Role-Players NGA Ltd 307
Roleplay UK 308
Rom Com Entertainment 109
Jessica Ronane 120
Rose Bruford College 20
Mary Rose Productions 225
Rose Theatre Kingston 171
Rosebery Management Ltd 98
Rosemary Branch Theatre 275
Ross-Williams, Tom 178
Rossmore Management 88
Annie Rowe CDG 121
Royal Academy of Dramatic Art (RADA) 55
Royal Academy of Music 21
Royal & Derngate Theatres 171
Royal Birmingham Conservatoire 21
Royal Central School of Speech and Drama, The 21, 56

460 Index

Royal Conservatoire of Scotland   21
Royal Court Library   424
Royal Court Theatre   172
Royal Exchange Theatre   172
Royal Lyceum Edinburgh   172
Royal Shakespeare Company   172
Royal Television Society (RTS)   431
Royal Theatrical Fund, The   421
Royal Welsh College of Music & Drama   22
Royce Management   88
ROYO   198
Neil Rutherford Casting   121
Richard Ryder Dialect Coach   60

S

S4K International Ltd   296
Robin Savage Photography   376
Savages Personal Management Ltd   88
Howard Sayer Photography   376
Scene & Heard   431
Scottish Neurodiverse Performance Network   349
Scottish Youth Theatre   5
Scream Management   89
Screen and Film School   325
Screen Daily   424
Screen South   420
Screen Yorkshire   420
Script Websites   424
SDM (Simon Drake Management)   89
Second Half Productions   198
Dawn Sedgwick Management   89
Nadira Seecoomar CDG   121
Select Casting Ltd   121
Select Management   89
self-employment   405
Rebecca Semark   60
Sevenoaks Stag Theatre   278
Shakespeare's Globe   172
Shared Experience   225
Sharkey & Co. Ltd   89
Phil Shaw   121
Sheetmusic Warehouse, The   425
Sheffield Theatres   173
Michael Shelford Photography   376
Sheringham Little Theatre   173
Sherman Theatre   173
Shining Management Ltd   106
Shooting People   364, 366, 425

showreel   327
Showreel Editing by Anthony Holmes   387
Showreel Ltd, The   387
showreels   70, 324, 329, 389
  companies   386
sight reading   327
Sightline   321
Silent Faces Theatre   342
Silver-Tongued Productions   387
Silvertip Films Ltd   387
Ros Simmons   60
SimPatiCo UK Ltd   308
Simple8 Theatre Company   225
Simply Theatre   268
Rebecca Singer Management   89
Sandra Singer Associates   89, 109
Sixteen Films   321
1623 Theatre Company   207
Skeete, Cherrelle   151
Skoob Books   425
Sky Blue Theatre Company   226, 296
Slung Low   226
Small World Theatre   226, 296
Smart Management   90
Michelle Smith Casting Ltd   121
Suzanne Smith CDG   121
Society for the Teachers of the Alexander Technique, The   60
Society of London Theatre (SOLT)   431
Society of Independent Theatres (SIT)   270
Society of Teachers of the Alexander Technique (STAT), The   431
Soho Theatre   173
Solar Bear   343
Sole Purpose Productions   226
Solomon Theatre Company   297
Stephen Sondheim Society, The   432
SonicPond Studio   388
Southwark Playhouse   173
Space, The   275
Spanner in the Works   226
Spare Tyre Theatre Company   343
Speakeasy Productions Ltd   321
Sphinx Theatre Company   227
Spillers Pantomimes   262
Splendid Productions   297
Spotlight   134, 327, 363–6, 371, 378
Emma Stafford   122
Stafford Gatehouse Theatre   265

Helen Stafford   122
Stage, The   367
Stage Centre Management Ltd   98
Stage Directors UK   432
Stage Entertainment   199
Stage Media Company Ltd, The   425
Stagescreen Productions   322
Stand-up   251
Stanton Davidson Associates   90
Stanton, Sophie   140
Harvey Stein Associates Ltd   90
Stephen Joseph Theatre   174
Ed Stephenson Productions   227
Robert Sterne CDG   122
Gail Stevens & Rebecca Farhall Casting   122
Sam Stevenson CDG   122
Stevenson Withers Associates   90
Stirling Management Actors Agency   90
Katherine Stonehouse Management   90
Stopgap Dance Company   343
Storyhouse   174
Streets Mark Carr   402
Summerhall Arts   432
Sunderland Culture, Sunderland   45
Lucinda Syson Casting   122

T

Amanda Tabak CDG   122
Tabs Productions   227
Theatre Online   297
Taking Flight Theatre Company   227
Taking Flight Theatre   343
Talawa Theatre Company   227
Talent Agency Ltd, The   90
Tall Stories Theatre Company   297
Tamasha Theatre Company   228
Tara Theatre   228
Tarquin Casting   122
Tarquin Talent Agency Ltd   98
Tavistock Wood   90
tax   234, 404
    expenses   404
TCG Artist Management Ltd   91
Sue Terry Voices Ltd   106
Alma Tavern Theatre, The   278
Entertainment Agents' Association Ltd, The   432
Jamie Lloyd Company, The   199
Theataccounts Ltd   402
Theatr Clwyd   174
Theatr Genedlaethol Cymru   228
Theatr Iolo   298
Theatr na nÓg   298
theatre   143
Theatre Absolute   228
Theatre Alibi   229
Theatre at the Tabard   276
Theatre by the Lake   174
Theatre Centre   299
Theatre Chaplaincy UK   433
theatre companies/managements, starting your own   233
Theatre Hullabaloo   299
Theatre in Education   288
Theatre Lab Company   229
Theatre Porto   299
Theatre Record   425
Theatre Royal Bath   174
Theatre Royal, Bury St Edmunds   175, 265
Theatre Royal Haymarket Masterclass Trust   56
Theatre Royal, Norwich   265
Theatre Royal, Nottingham   266
Theatre Royal Plymouth   175
Theatre Royal Stratford East   175
Theatre Royal, Winchester   266
Theatre Royal Windsor   175
Théâtre Sans Frontières   229
Theatre Tours International Ltd   229
Theatre Without Walls   229, 308
Theatre Workout Ltd   56
Theatre-Rites   228, 298
Theatre503   276
theatres, producing   160
Theatres Trust   433
Theatrevoice   425
Theatricalia   426
Theatro Technis   276
Think Bigger   346
Faye Thomas Photography   376
Katie Threlfall Associates   91
Tiger Aspect Productions   322
Tildsley France   91
Tilted Wig Productions   230
Tin Shed Theatre Co.   230
Tinderbox Theatre Company   231
TMG London   91
Tobacco Factory Theatres   175

462 Index

Told by an Idiot 231
Tongue & Groove 106
Nicci Topping Casting 122
Torch Theatre 175
Totally Thames 304
Touchdown Dance 343
Toynbee Studios 276
Trafalgar Entertainment 199
Travelling Light Theatre Company 299
Traverse Theatre 176, 278
Trestle Theatre Company 231
Jill Trevellick CDG 123
Tribe Arts 231
Tricycle Theatre 176
Triple A Media 109
TripleC 346
Tristan Bates Theatre 276
Tron Theatre 176
Trotman, Jayne 368
TTA (Top Talent Agency) 91
Tudor Hart Photography 377
20 Stories High 207
21st Century Actors Management 93
Twenty Twenty Productions Ltd 322
TYPE (The Yellowchair Performance Experience) 231

U

UCAS 12, 328
UK Jewish Film Festival 334
UK Productions 199, 262
UK Theatre 433
UK Theatre Network 426
Steve Ullathorne 377
Uncharted 326
Underbelly 278
understudying 190
Unicorn Theatre 299
Union Theatre 276
Unique Taxpayer Reference (UTR) 405
United Agents 91
University of Atypical for Arts and Disability 347
University of Bristol Theatre Collection 433
University of the Creative Arts 325
University of Westminster 325
Unlimited 347
Unrestricted View 231

Unseen Acting School 56
Upstairs at the Gatehouse 276
Urban Talent 91

V

Roxane Vacca Management 92
Sarah Valentine 60
Vanessa Valentine Photography 377
V&A Theatre & Performance Collections 433
Vanguard Productions 232
Vienna's English Theatre 268
Vincenzo Photography 377
virtual reality 326
VisABLE People Ltd 92, 343
Vital Xposure 344
Vocal Point 106
voice acting 326
voice actors 327
VoiceBank Ltd 106
voice coach 381
voice demos 105, 329
 companies 386
Voice Shop 106
Voice Squad 106
voice work 327
voice-over, agents 329, 381
VOICE-REEL.COM 388
Voicebank, The Irish Voice-Over Agency 106
voiceover 381
Voiceover Gallery, The 107
voicereel 382
voices.com 327
Volcano Theatre Company 232
Anne Vosser Casting 123
VSA Ltd 92
VSI (Voice & Script International) 107

W

Philip Wade 377
Suzann Wade MGMT 92
Walk the Plank 232
Simia Wall LLP 402
Cathy Waller Co. 344
Walsh Bros Ltd 322
Jo Wander Management 109
Waring & McKenna Ltd 92
Watermill Theatre 176

Watford Palace Theatre   176
Way To Blue   397
Weinman, Mark   37
Wessex Grove   199
West End International   199
West End productions   194
Matt Western   123
Westminster Reference Library   426
WGM Atlantic Talent & Literary Group   92
Michael Wharley Photography   377
Whistledown Productions   330
White Bear Theatre   277
White Horse Theatre   268
Whiting, Geoff   258
Wiggs, Michael   99
Wilder Films   322
Williamson & Holmes   93
Jamie Wilson Productions   199
Wiltshire Creative   177
Wimbledon Studio Theatre   277
Winterson's   93
Wireless Theatre Company, The   330
Spoken States   61
Wizard Theatre Ltd   300

Wolf + Water Arts Company   344
Felix de Wolfe   93
Women in Film and Television (UK) (WFTV)   433
Wendy Woolfson Talent and PR   109
Worcester Repertory Company   177
Working Title Films   322
World Productions Ltd   322
WGGB (Writers' Guild of Great Britain)   434
Wyatts Partnership   403
Edward Wyman Agency   93

Y

Yakety Yak All Mouth Ltd   107
Yellow Door Productions   323
York Theatre Royal   177
Young Shakespeare Company   300
Young Vic   177
Youth Theatre   288
Youth Theatre Ireland   5

Z

Jeremy Zimmermann Casting   123

For your own notes

For your own notes

Writers & Artists

A FREE WRITING PLATFORM TO CALL YOUR OWN

- Exclusive discounts
- Regular writing competitions
- Free writing advice articles
- Publishing guidance
- Save margin notes
- Share your writings
- Bursary opportunities

REGISTER NOW

WWW.WRITERSANDARTISTS.CO.UK